ADULT TIME

Other Baby Blues® Books from Andrews McMeel Publishing

Guess Who Didn't Take a Nap?
I Thought Labor Ended When the Baby Was Born
We Are Experiencing Parental Difficulties . . . Please Stand By
Night of the Living Dad
I Saw Elvis in My Ultrasound
One More and We're Outnumbered!
Check, Please . . .
threats, bribes & videotape
If I'm a Stay-at-Home Mom, Why Am I Always in the Car?
Lift and Separate
I Shouldn't Have to Scream More Than Once!
Motherhood Is Not for Wimps
Baby Blues®: Unplugged
Dad to the Bone
Never a Dry Moment
Two Plus One Is Enough
Playdate: Category 5
Our Server Is Down
Something Chocolate This Way Comes
Briefcase Full of Baby Blues®
Night Shift
The Day Phonics Kicked In
My Space
The Natural Disorder of Things

We Were Here First
Ambushed! In the Family Room
Cut!
Eat, Cry, Poop
Scribbles at an Exhibition
Bedlam
Wetter, Louder, Stickier
No Yelling!
Gross!
Binge Parenting

Treasuries

The Super-Absorbent Biodegradable Family-Size Baby Blues®
Baby Blues®: Ten Years and Still in Diapers
Butt-Naked Baby Blues®
Wall-to-Wall Baby Blues®
Driving Under the Influence of Children
Framed!
X-Treme Parenting
BBXX: Baby Blues: Decades 1 and 2

Gift Books

It's a Boy
It's a Girl

ADULT TIME

rick kirkman
jerry scott

Scrapbook

NO.
35

Andrews McMeel
PUBLISHING®

For Dorothy O'Brien

—Rick & Jerry

BABY BLUES®
Rick Kirkman & Jerry Scott
ZZZZZ

COOKIE?
NOPE. THE HOLIDAYS ARE OVER. TIME FOR ME TO START EATING HEALTHY AGAIN.
LEAFY GREENS, FRESH TOMATOES, CRUNCHY CELERY, AND A WEDGE OF LEMON.
IMPRESSIVE.
YOU ARE AN INSPIRATION...
...AND YOUR CROUTONS ARE LITTLE CUBES OF CHRISTMAS FUDGE!
HEY, I'M AN INSPIRATION, NOT A SAINT... REMEMBER?
©2017, BABY BLUES PARTNERSHIP DIST. BY KING FEATURES SYNDICATE
KIRKMAN & SCOTT 1-1

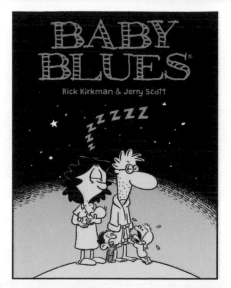

Rick: Well, that's something I'm going to have to try. Maybe. Eww. Okay, just a little. Nah . . . all right. One bite.

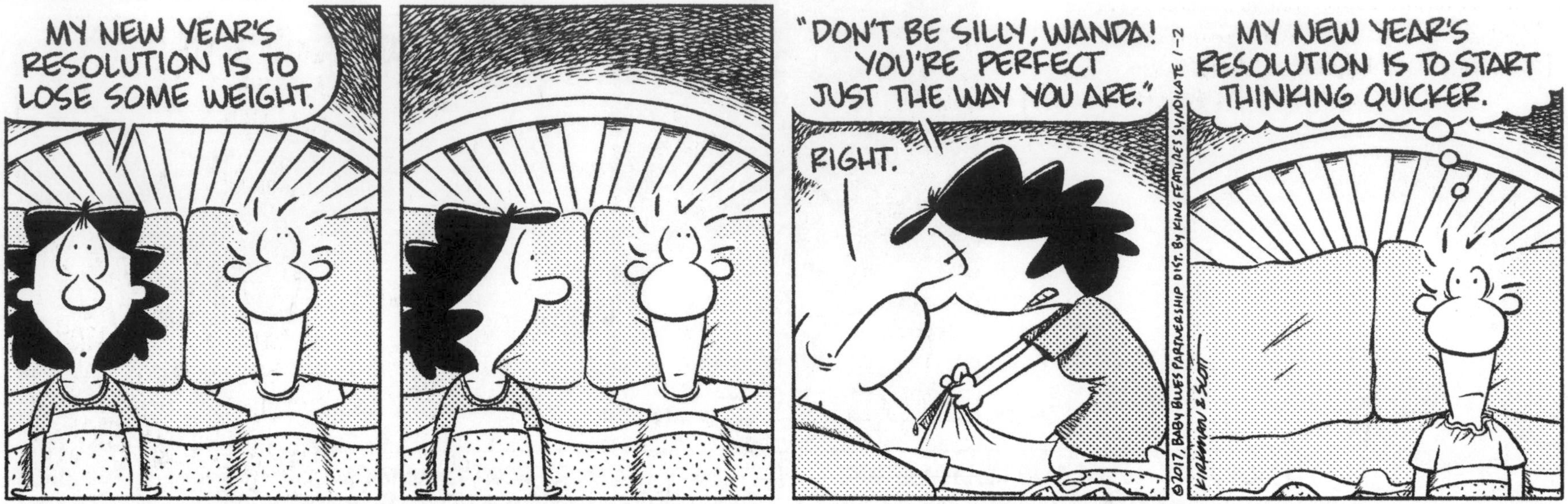
MY NEW YEAR'S RESOLUTION IS TO LOSE SOME WEIGHT.
"DON'T BE SILLY, WANDA! YOU'RE PERFECT JUST THE WAY YOU ARE."
RIGHT.
MY NEW YEAR'S RESOLUTION IS TO START THINKING QUICKER.
©2017, BABY BLUES PARTNERSHIP DIST. BY KING FEATURES SYNDICATE 1-2
KIRKMAN & SCOTT

Rick: Darryl's reflexes are slipping. Ten years ago he would have—on second thought, no he wouldn't.

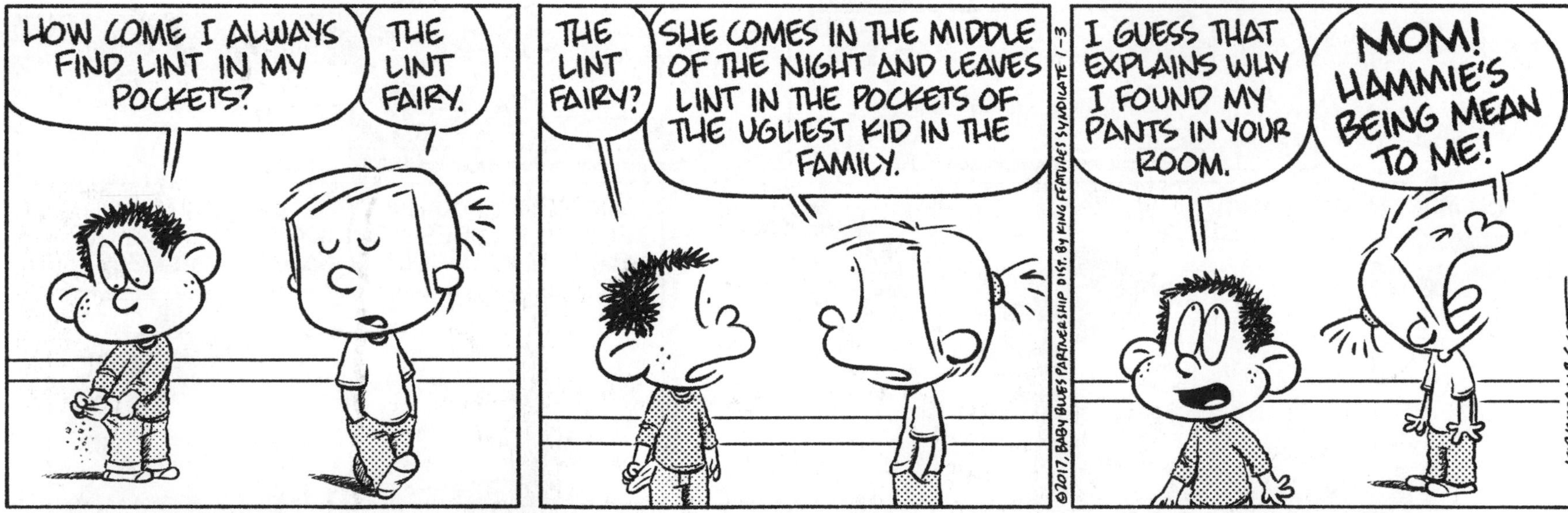
HOW COME I ALWAYS FIND LINT IN MY POCKETS?
THE LINT FAIRY.
THE LINT FAIRY?
SHE COMES IN THE MIDDLE OF THE NIGHT AND LEAVES LINT IN THE POCKETS OF THE UGLIEST KID IN THE FAMILY.
I GUESS THAT EXPLAINS WHY I FOUND MY PANTS IN YOUR ROOM.
MOM! HAMMIE'S BEING MEAN TO ME!
©2017, BABY BLUES PARTNERSHIP DIST. BY KING FEATURES SYNDICATE 1-3
KIRKMAN & SCOTT

Rick: Hammie, on the other hand, does not suffer from slow reflexes. Booyah!

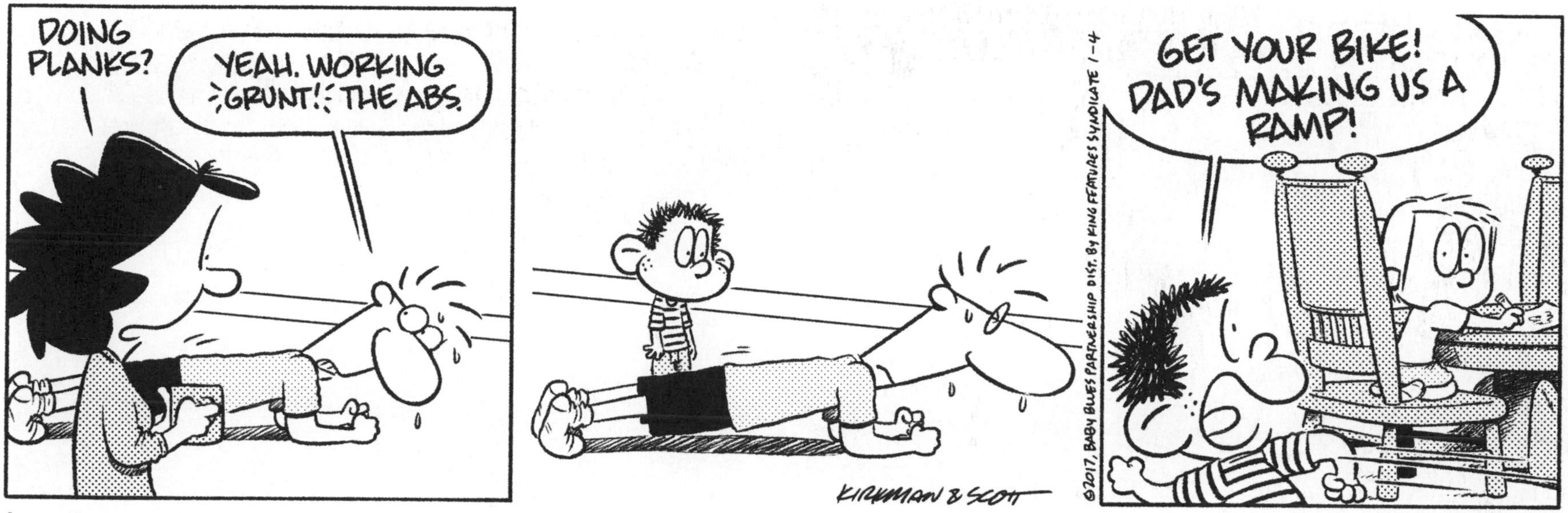
DOING PLANKS?
YEAH. WORKING GRUNT! THE ABS.
GET YOUR BIKE! DAD'S MAKING US A RAMP!
KIRKMAN & SCOTT
©2017, BABY BLUES PARTNERSHIP DIST. BY KING FEATURES SYNDICATE 1-4

Jerry: One man's suffering is another kid's opportunity.

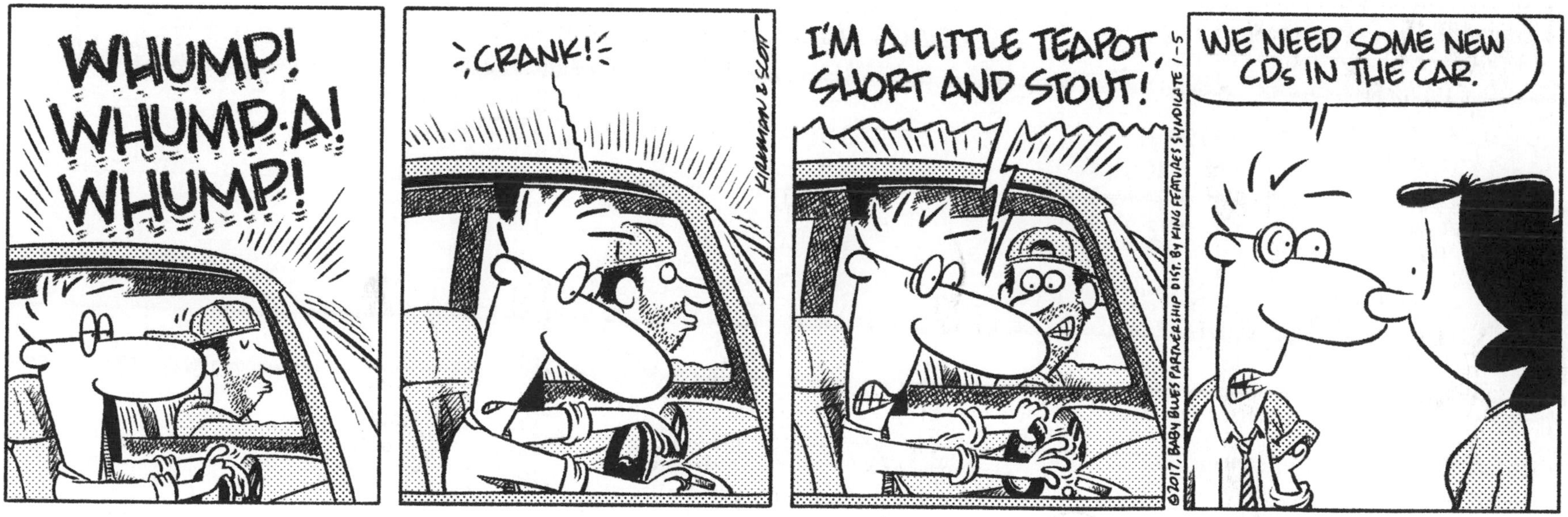
WHUMP! WHUMP-A! WHUMP!
CRANK!
KIRKMAN & SCOTT
I'M A LITTLE TEAPOT, SHORT AND STOUT!
©2017, BABY BLUES PARTNERSHIP DIST. BY KING FEATURES SYNDICATE 1-5
WE NEED SOME NEW CDs IN THE CAR.

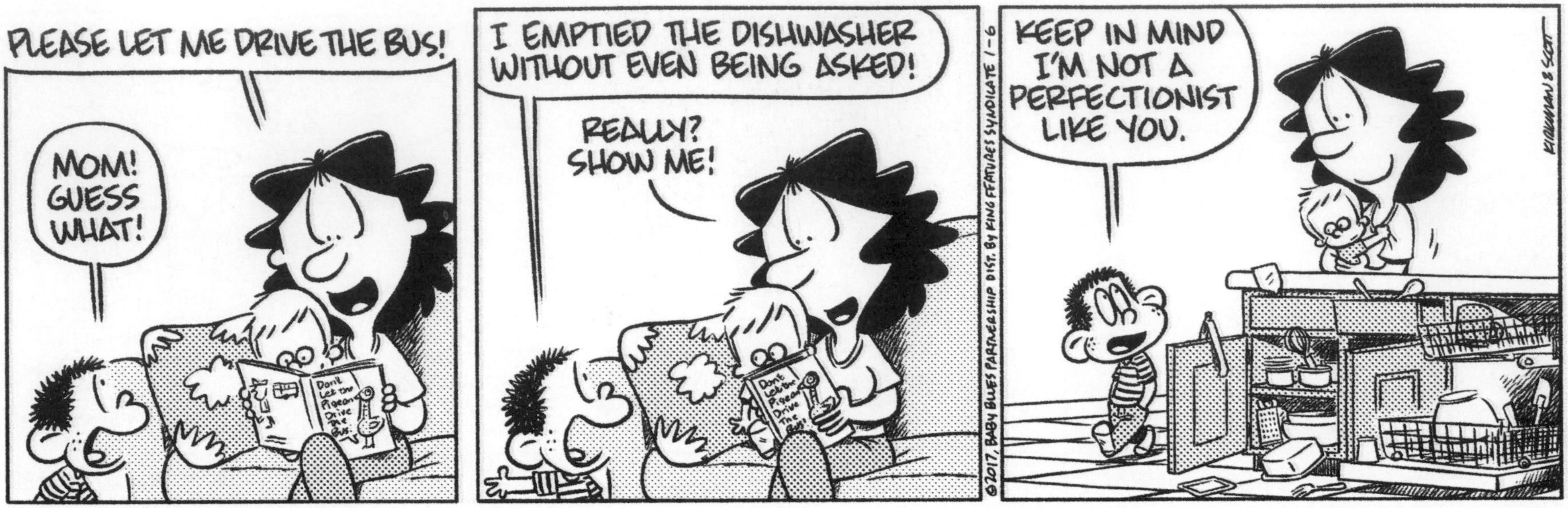
MOM! GUESS WHAT!
PLEASE LET ME DRIVE THE BUS!
Don't Let the Pigeon Drive the Bus!
I EMPTIED THE DISHWASHER WITHOUT EVEN BEING ASKED!
REALLY? SHOW ME!
©2017, BABY BLUES PARTNERSHIP DIST. BY KING FEATURES SYNDICATE 1-6
KEEP IN MIND I'M NOT A PERFECTIONIST LIKE YOU.
KIRKMAN & SCOTT

Rick: Sneaking in a bit of Mo Willems.

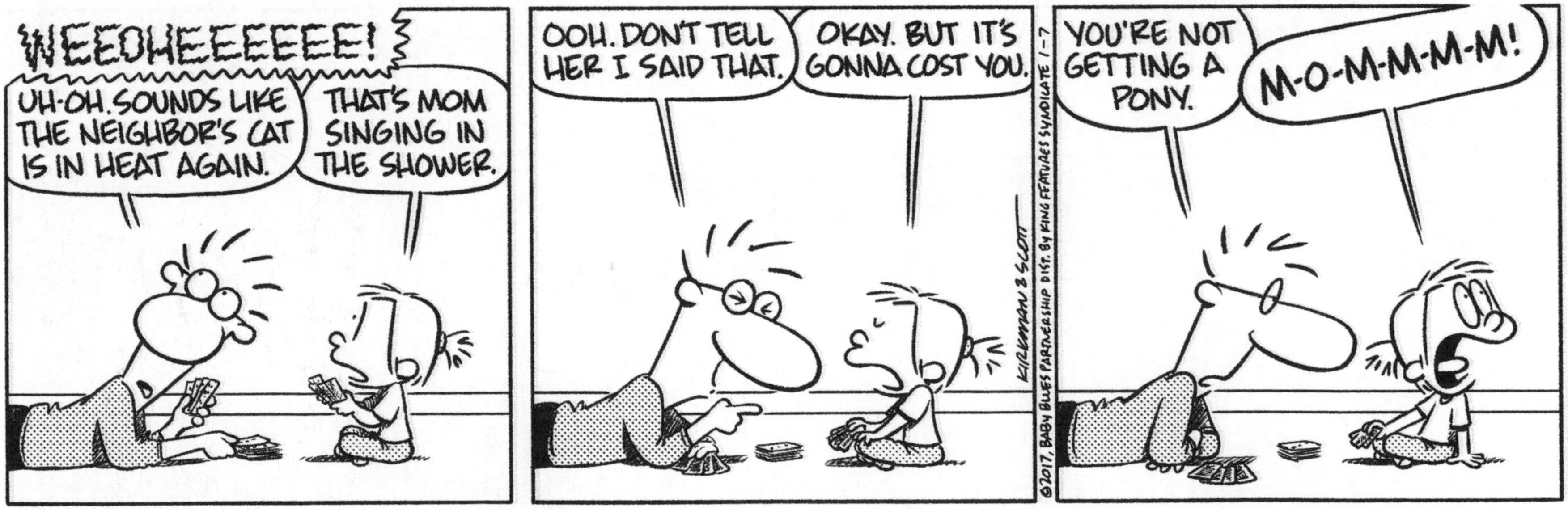
WEEOHEEEEEEE!
UH-OH. SOUNDS LIKE THE NEIGHBOR'S CAT IS IN HEAT AGAIN.
THAT'S MOM SINGING IN THE SHOWER.
OOH. DON'T TELL HER I SAID THAT.
OKAY. BUT IT'S GONNA COST YOU.
KIRKMAN & SCOTT
©2017, BABY BLUES PARTNERSHIP DIST. BY KING FEATURES SYNDICATE 1-7
YOU'RE NOT GETTING A PONY.
M-O-M-M-M-M!

Rick: Little Miss Extortion

BABY BLUES
Rick Kirkman & Jerry Scott
ZZZZZZ

SIGH
SOMETHING WRONG?
I'M JUST BORED. I HATE WINTER.
©2017, BABY BLUES PARTNERSHIP DIST. BY KING FEATURES SYNDICATE
I WANT IT TO BE WARM! I WANT TO PLAY OUTSIDE! I WANT TO COMMUNICATE WITH NATURE!
MAYBE YOU CAN START WITH THAT BIG, UGLY SPIDER CRAWLING UP YOUR BACK.
DID YOU JUST HEAR A SCREAM?
KIRKMAN & SCOTT 1-8

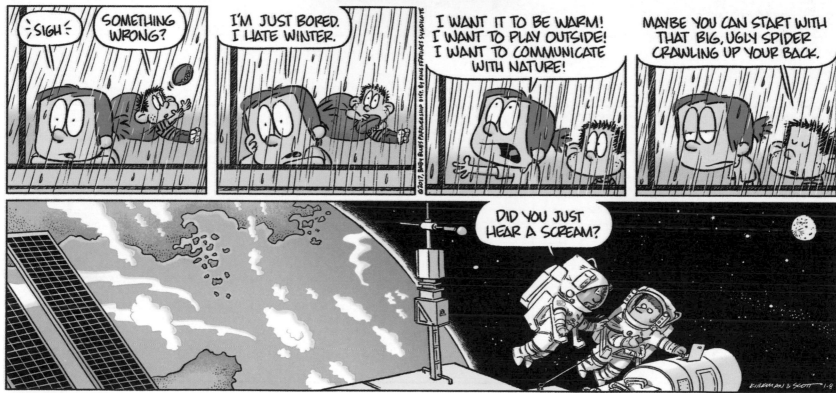

Rick: I guess *Alien* was wrong. Fun to do a view from space, though.

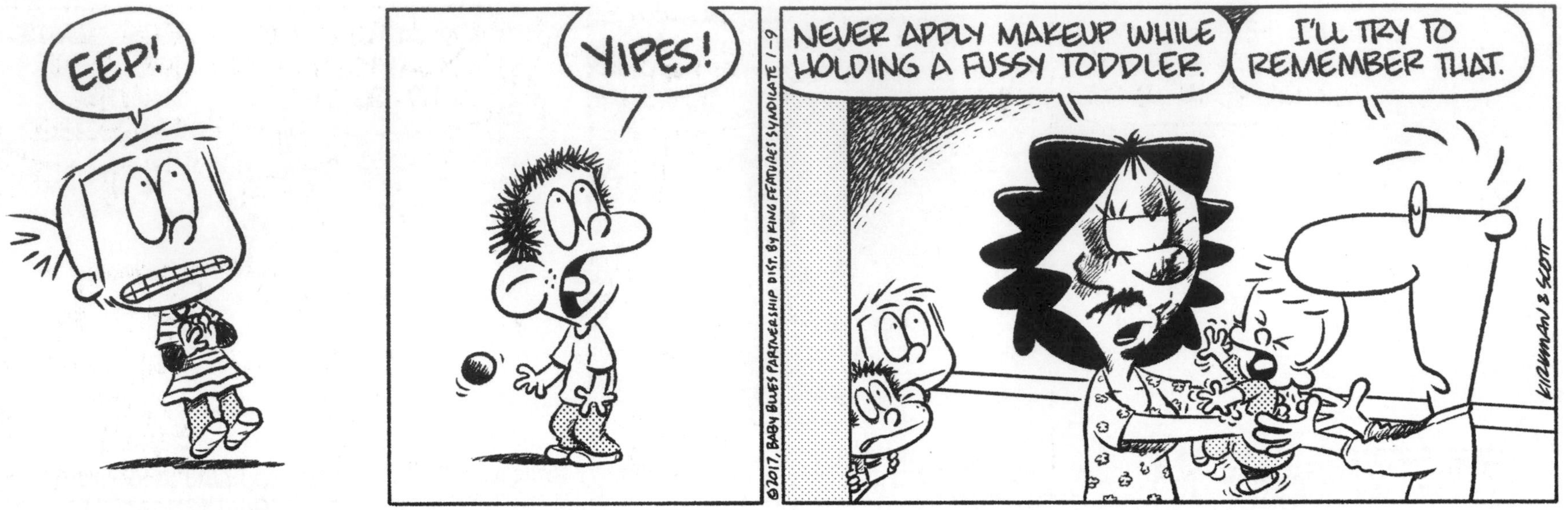
EEP!
YIPES!
©2017, BABY BLUES PARTNERSHIP DIST. BY KING FEATURES SYNDICATE 1-9
NEVER APPLY MAKEUP WHILE HOLDING A FUSSY TODDLER.
I'LL TRY TO REMEMBER THAT.
KIRKMAN & SCOTT

Jerry: Also, razor blade sorting and fire eating.

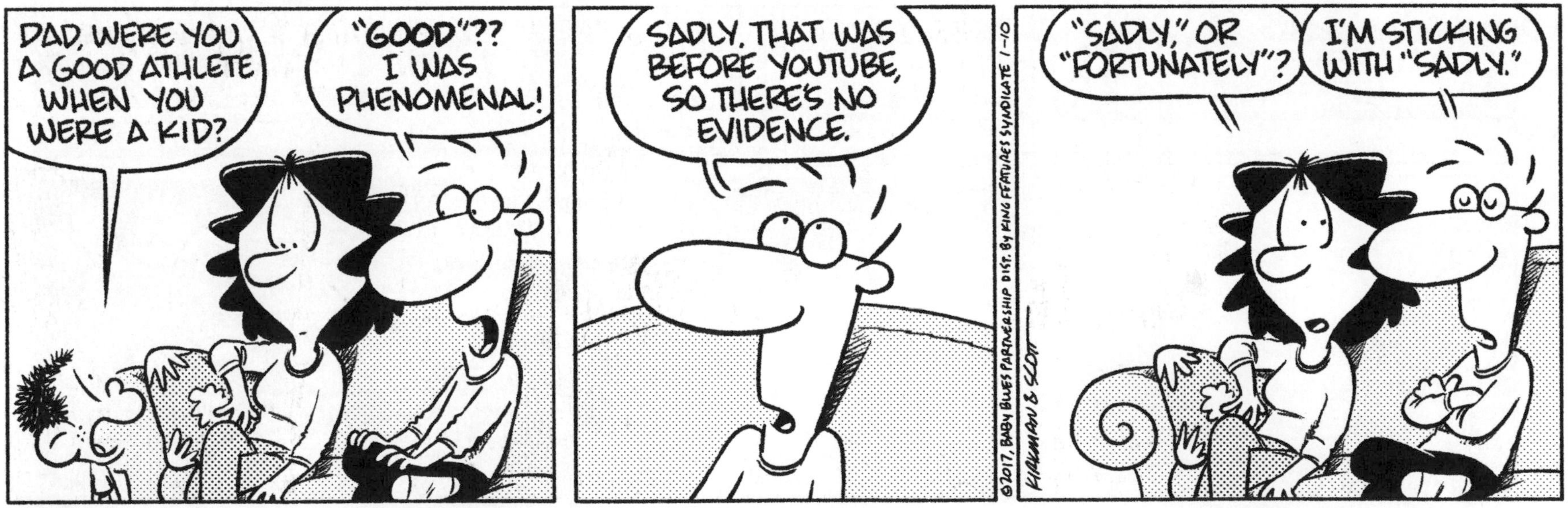
DAD, WERE YOU A GOOD ATHLETE WHEN YOU WERE A KID?
"GOOD"?? I WAS PHENOMENAL!
SADLY, THAT WAS BEFORE YOUTUBE, SO THERE'S NO EVIDENCE.
©2017, BABY BLUES PARTNERSHIP DIST. BY KING FEATURES SYNDICATE 1-10
KIRKMAN & SCOTT
"SADLY," OR "FORTUNATELY"?
I'M STICKING WITH "SADLY."

Rick: Revisionist history is a parent's prerogative.

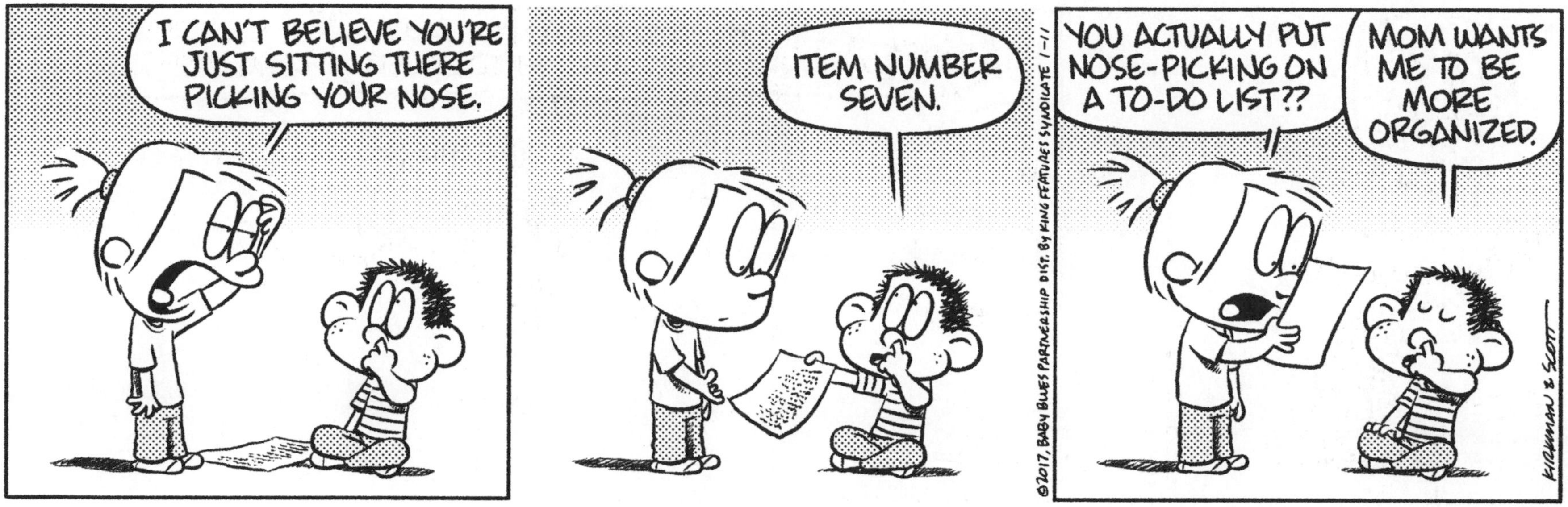
I CAN'T BELIEVE YOU'RE JUST SITTING THERE PICKING YOUR NOSE.
ITEM NUMBER SEVEN.
YOU ACTUALLY PUT NOSE-PICKING ON A TO-DO LIST??
MOM WANTS ME TO BE MORE ORGANIZED.
©2017, BABY BLUES PARTNERSHIP DIST. BY KING FEATURES SYNDICATE 1-11
KIRKMAN & SCOTT

Jerry: Boy, I hope nobody is having breakfast when they read this one.

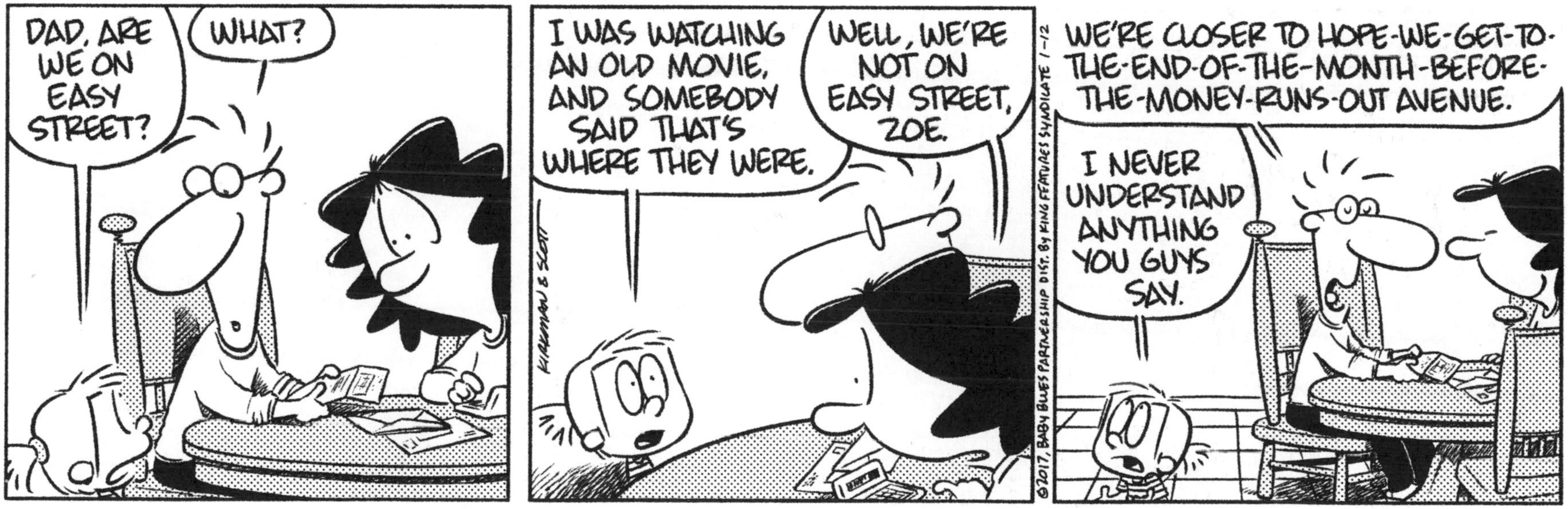
DAD, ARE WE ON EASY STREET?
WHAT?
KIRKMAN & SCOTT
I WAS WATCHING AN OLD MOVIE, AND SOMEBODY SAID THAT'S WHERE THEY WERE.
WELL, WE'RE NOT ON EASY STREET, ZOE.
©2017, BABY BLUES PARTNERSHIP DIST. BY KING FEATURES SYNDICATE 1-12
WE'RE CLOSER TO HOPE-WE-GET-TO-THE-END-OF-THE-MONTH-BEFORE-THE-MONEY-RUNS-OUT AVENUE.
I NEVER UNDERSTAND ANYTHING YOU GUYS SAY.

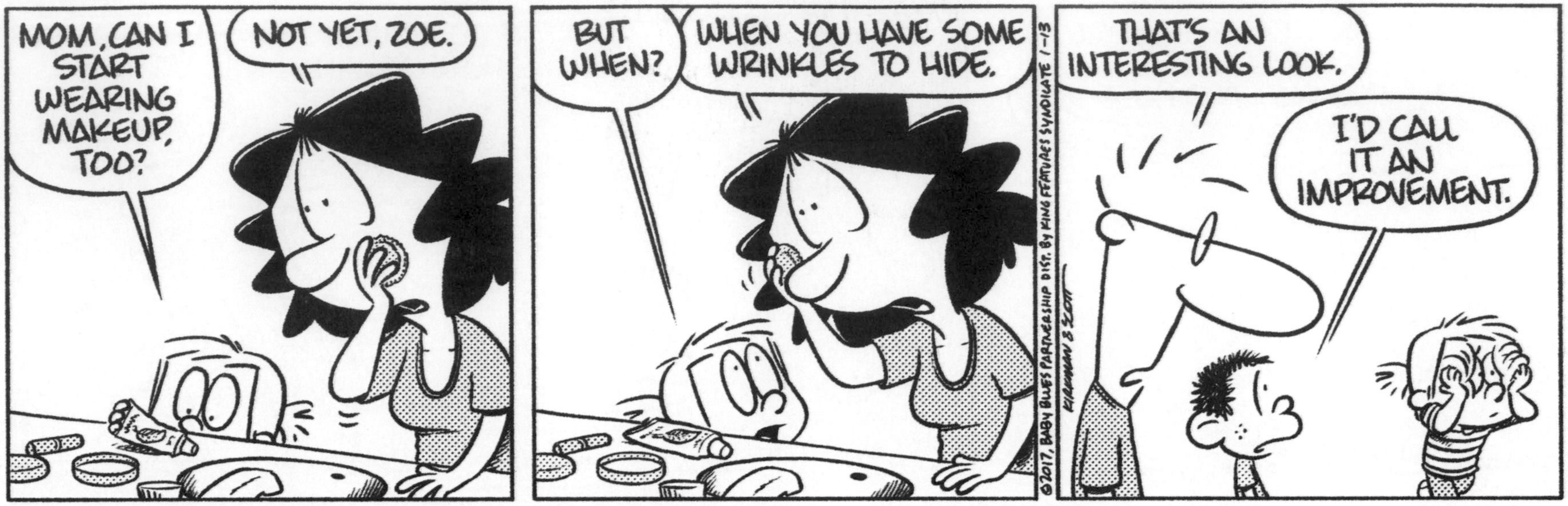
MOM, CAN I START WEARING MAKEUP, TOO?
NOT YET, ZOE.
BUT WHEN?
WHEN YOU HAVE SOME WRINKLES TO HIDE.
©2017, BABY BLUES PARTNERSHIP DIST. BY KING FEATURES SYNDICATE 1-13
KIRKMAN & SCOTT
THAT'S AN INTERESTING LOOK.
I'D CALL IT AN IMPROVEMENT.

Jerry: Okay, I know that's not the only reason people wear makeup, but this is a comic strip, not a Sephora.

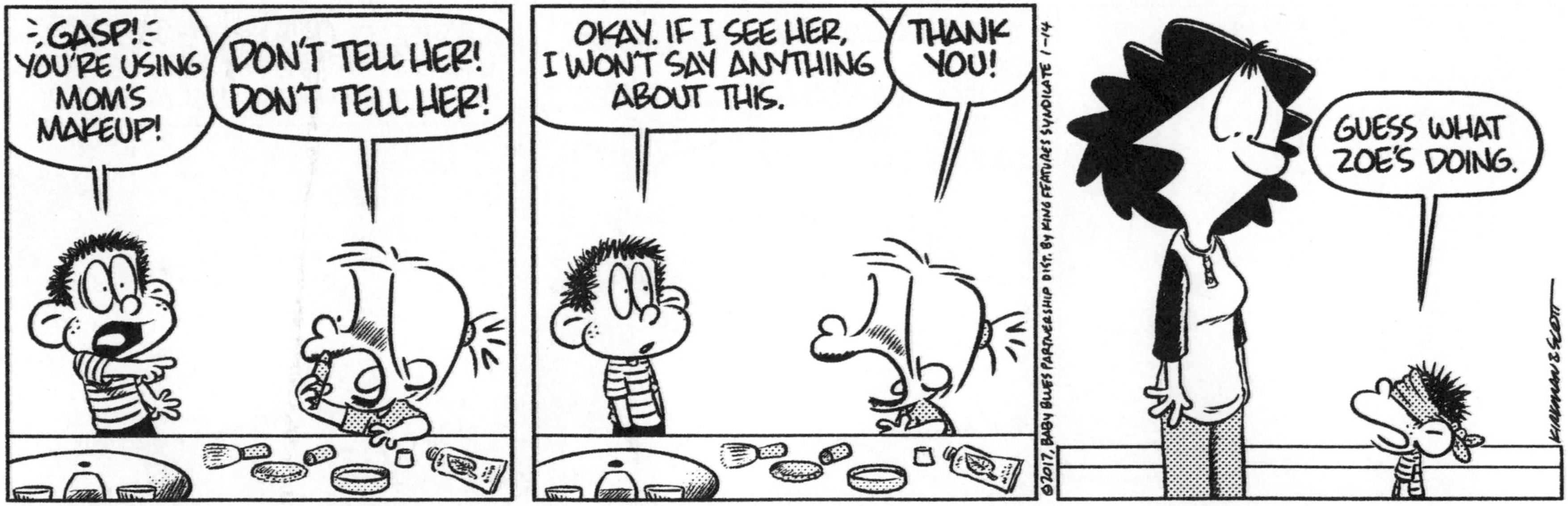
GASP! YOU'RE USING MOM'S MAKEUP!
DON'T TELL HER! DON'T TELL HER!
OKAY. IF I SEE HER, I WON'T SAY ANYTHING ABOUT THIS.
THANK YOU!
©2017, BABY BLUES PARTNERSHIP DIST. BY KING FEATURES SYNDICATE 1-14
GUESS WHAT ZOE'S DOING.
KIRKMAN & SCOTT

BABY BLUES
Rick Kirkman & Jerry Scott
ZZZZZZ

WE'RE ACTUALLY GOING OUT DANCING!
IT FEELS JUST LIKE THE OLD DAYS!
I DON'T THINK WE'VE BEEN IN A CLUB SINCE ZOE WAS A BABY.
YOU'RE RIGHT.
©2017, BABY BLUES PARTNERSHIP DIST. BY KING FEATURES SYNDICATE
I WONDER IF ANYTHING HAS CHANGED IN THERE.
MUSIC...DANCING... WHAT COULD BE DIFFERENT?
CLUB RADISH
CR
CR
1-15
US?
TURN THAT INFERNAL MUSIC DOWN! I CAN'T HEAR MYSELF THINK!

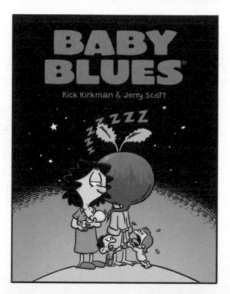

Rick: With deadmau5 in mind, I tried to come up with some ridiculous headgear, and I decided on a radish. This was the most challenging Sunday in a long while, from a technical standpoint. I think I stressed out my computer with layers on this, trying to get the various beams of light and depth inside Club Radish.

MOM, IF YOU HAD IT TO DO ALL OVER AGAIN, WOULD YOU MARRY DAD?
OF COURSE!
HE'S MY KNIGHT IN SHINING...
...SWEATPANTS.
THAT'S THE GLITTER GLUE I SAT IN LAST WEEK.
©2017, BABY BLUES PARTNERSHIP DIST. BY KING FEATURES SYNDICATE 1-16
KIRKMAN & SCOTT

HOW DO YOU GET SO MUCH SAND IN YOUR CLOTHES??
UM... I ROLL AROUND IN A LOT OF SAND PILES.
WHY DIDN'T I THINK OF THAT?
THAT'S LIKE HAMMIE 101, MOM.
©2017, BABY BLUES PARTNERSHIP DIST. BY KING FEATURES SYNDICATE 1-17
KIRKMAN & SCOTT

Jerry: "AP Hammie" would be much more challenging.

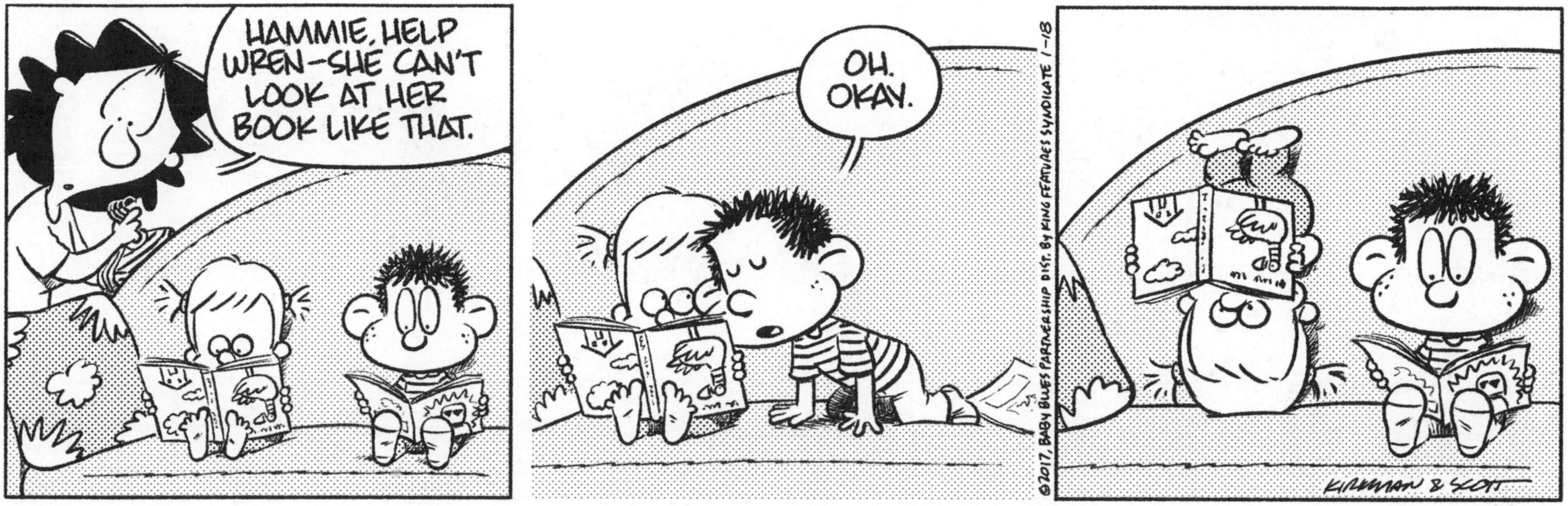
HAMMIE, HELP WREN—SHE CAN'T LOOK AT HER BOOK LIKE THAT.
OH. OKAY.
©2017, BABY BLUES PARTNERSHIP DIST. BY KING FEATURES SYNDICATE 1-18
KIRKMAN & SCOTT

Jerry: Some days just call for silly drawings.

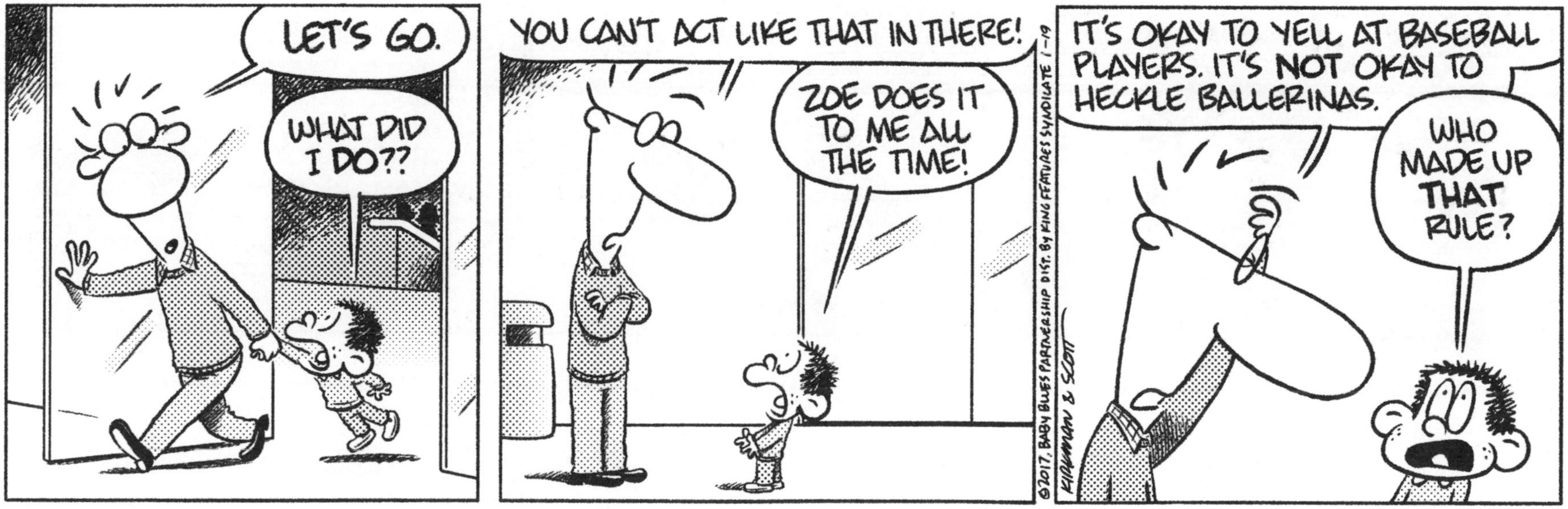
LET'S GO.
WHAT DID I DO??
YOU CAN'T ACT LIKE THAT IN THERE!
ZOE DOES IT TO ME ALL THE TIME!
©2017, BABY BLUES PARTNERSHIP DIST. BY KING FEATURES SYNDICATE 1-19
KIRKMAN & SCOTT
IT'S OKAY TO YELL AT BASEBALL PLAYERS. IT'S NOT OKAY TO HECKLE BALLERINAS.
WHO MADE UP THAT RULE?

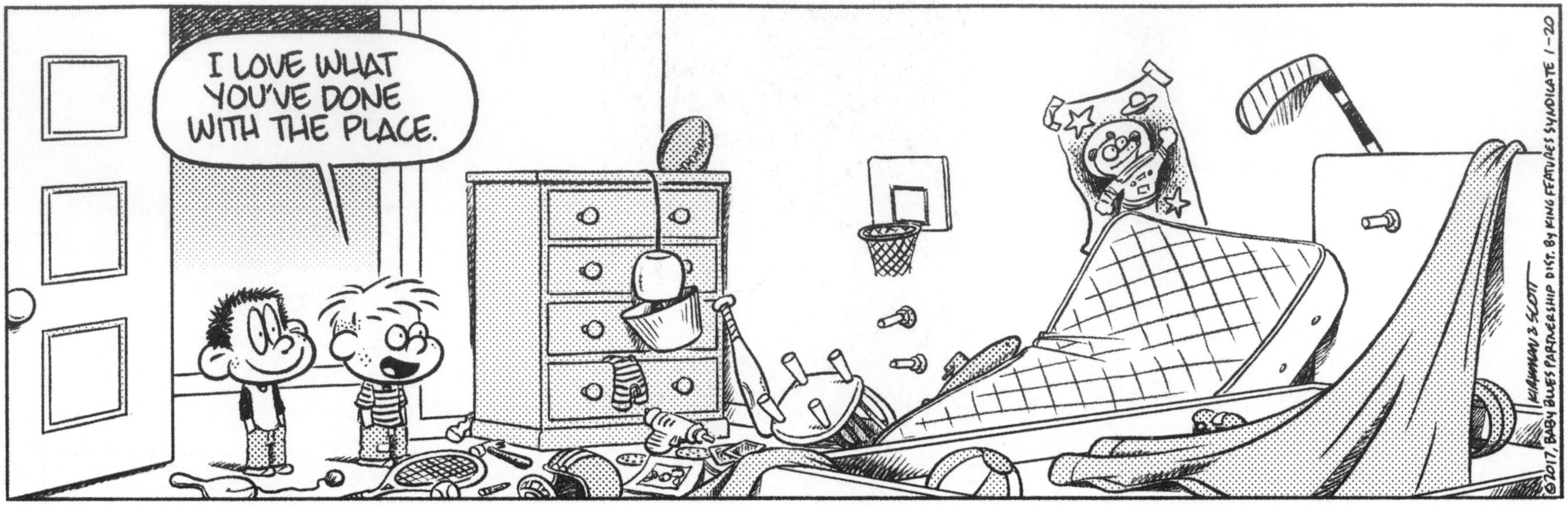
I LOVE WHAT YOU'VE DONE WITH THE PLACE.
KIRKMAN & SCOTT
©2017, BABY BLUES PARTNERSHIP DIST. BY KING FEATURES SYNDICATE 1-20

Rick: I'm kind of interested in that space dog in the poster.
If he were on the moon, he could be a lunar Rover. Heh! Heh!

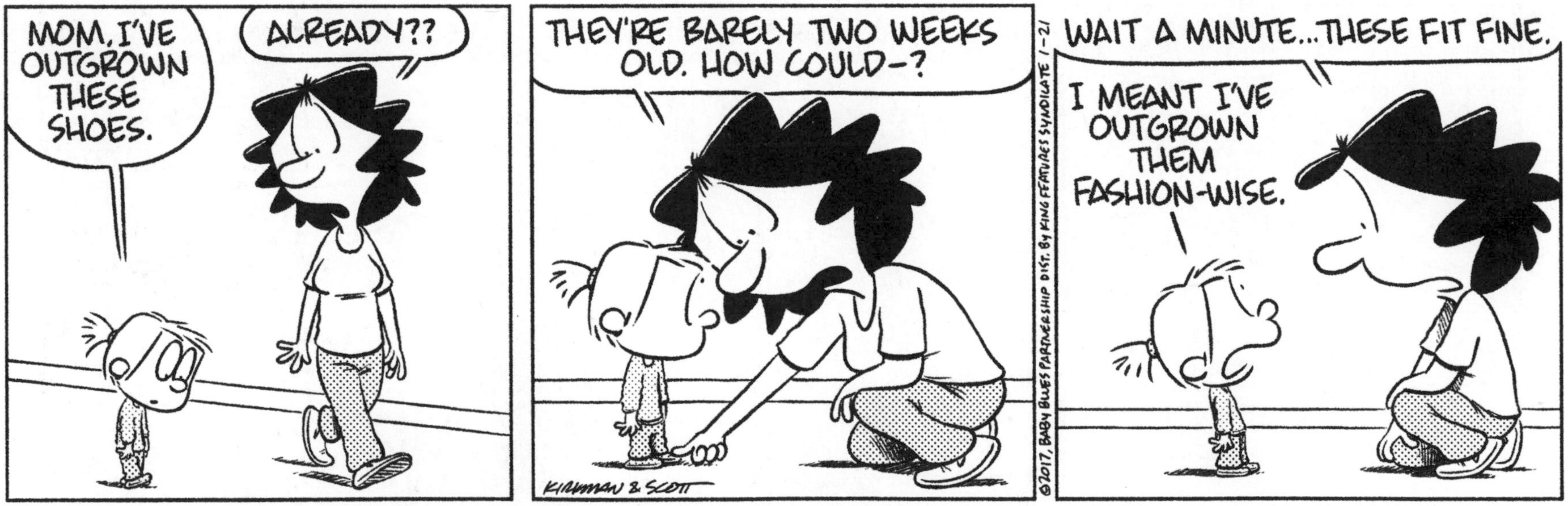
MOM, I'VE OUTGROWN THESE SHOES.
ALREADY??
THEY'RE BARELY TWO WEEKS OLD. HOW COULD-?
KIRKMAN & SCOTT
©2017, BABY BLUES PARTNERSHIP DIST. BY KING FEATURES SYNDICATE 1-21
WAIT A MINUTE...THESE FIT FINE.
I MEANT I'VE OUTGROWN THEM FASHION-WISE.

BABY BLUES
Rick Kirkman & Jerry Scott
ZZZZZ

GASP!
HAMMIE, I WANT YOU TO GO CLEAN UP YOUR BEDROOM!
OKAY.
©2017, BABY BLUES PARTNERSHIP DIST. BY KING FEATURES SYNDICATE
KIRKMAN & SCOTT 1-22
WELL, WHAT ARE YOU WAITING FOR?
TERMS AND CONDITIONS APPLY.

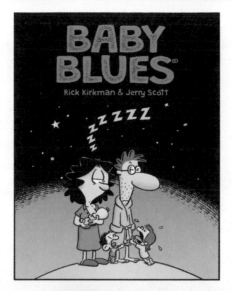

Rick: " . . . aghast at the incredible mess within," the gag said. Translation: wall-to-wall toys and junk. My look in panel 2.

Jerry: And beautifully done, too. The cordless drill on the pillow was a nice touch!

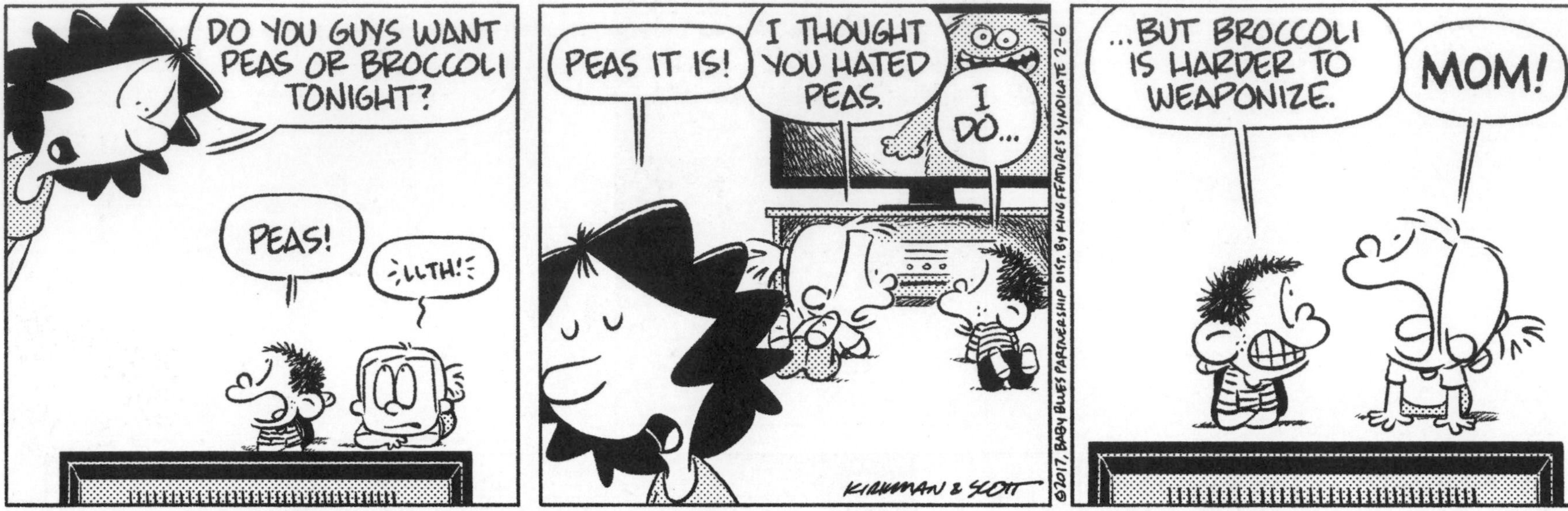
DO YOU GUYS WANT PEAS OR BROCCOLI TONIGHT?
PEAS!
LLTH!
PEAS IT IS!
I THOUGHT YOU HATED PEAS.
I DO...
KIRKMAN & SCOTT
©2017, BABY BLUES PARTNERSHIP DIST. BY KING FEATURES SYNDICATE 2-6
...BUT BROCCOLI IS HARDER TO WEAPONIZE.
MOM!

Jerry: So true. Science needs to genetically engineer "flingable" broccoli.

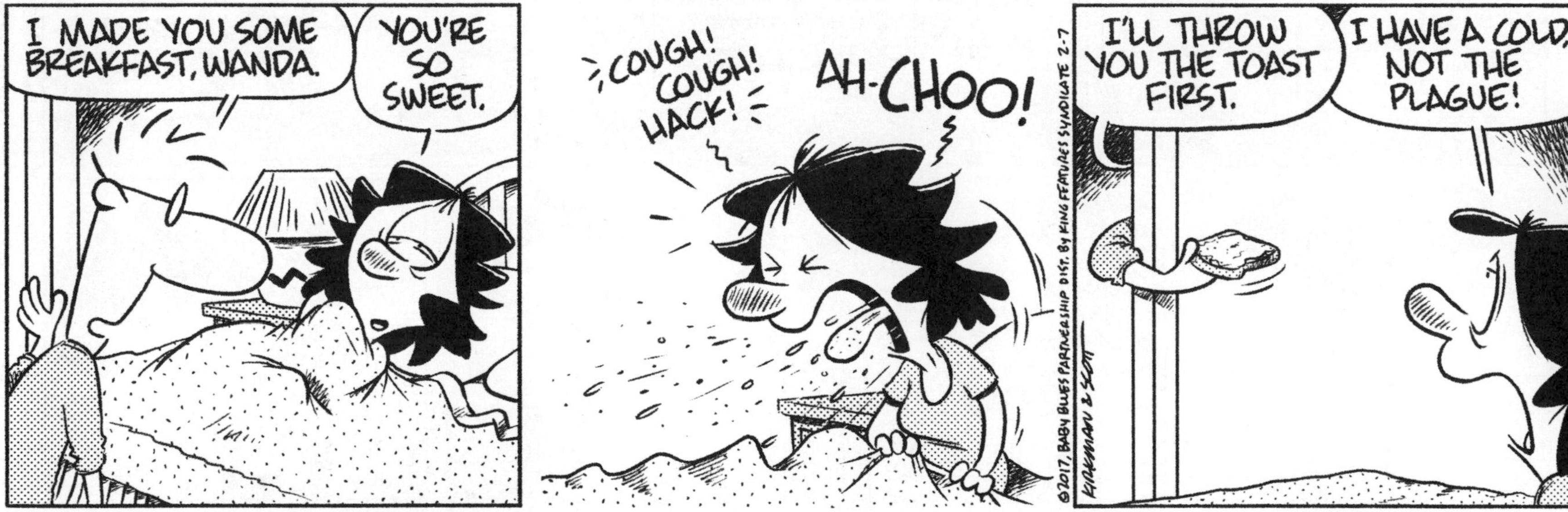
I MADE YOU SOME BREAKFAST, WANDA.
YOU'RE SO SWEET.
COUGH! COUGH! HACK!
AH-CHOO!
©2017, BABY BLUES PARTNERSHIP DIST. BY KING FEATURES SYNDICATE 2-7
KIRKMAN & SCOTT
I'LL THROW YOU THE TOAST FIRST.
I HAVE A COLD, NOT THE PLAGUE!

Jerry: I'm with Darryl. No sense in taking chances.

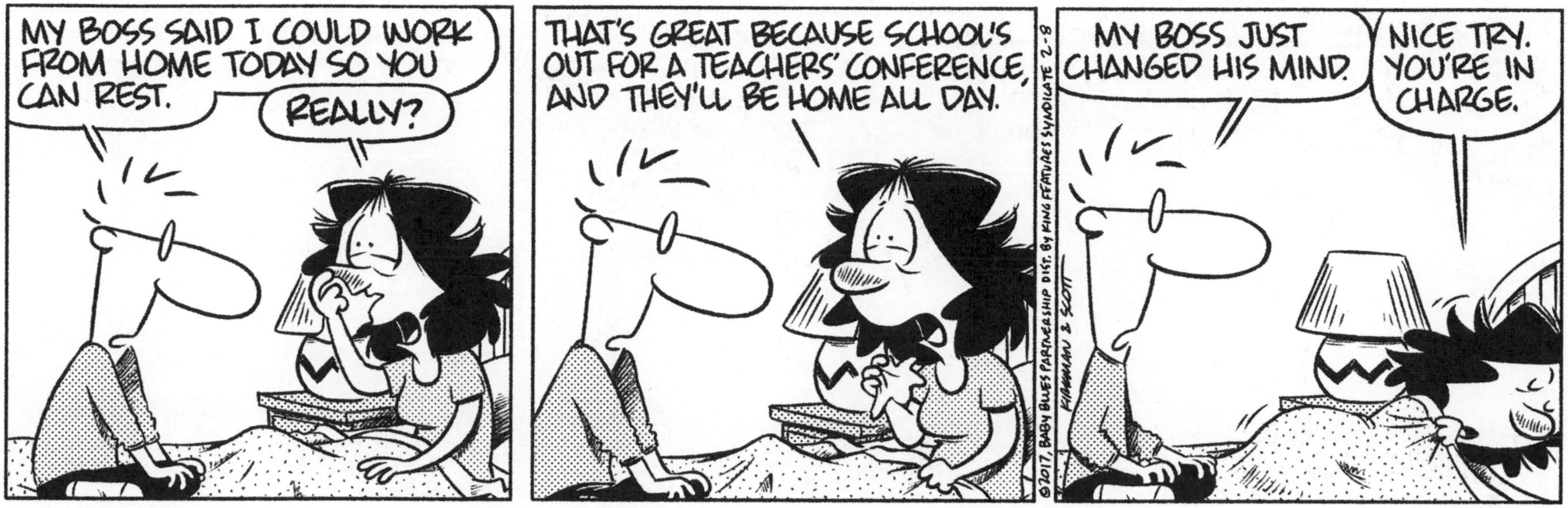
MY BOSS SAID I COULD WORK FROM HOME TODAY SO YOU CAN REST.
REALLY?
THAT'S GREAT BECAUSE SCHOOL'S OUT FOR A TEACHERS' CONFERENCE, AND THEY'LL BE HOME ALL DAY.
MY BOSS JUST CHANGED HIS MIND.
NICE TRY. YOU'RE IN CHARGE.
©2017, BABY BLUES PARTNERSHIP DIST. BY KING FEATURES SYNDICATE 2-8
KIRKMAN & SCOTT

Jerry: I have thirty-five years of experience as a work-at-home dad. I can confirm that it is not for wimps.

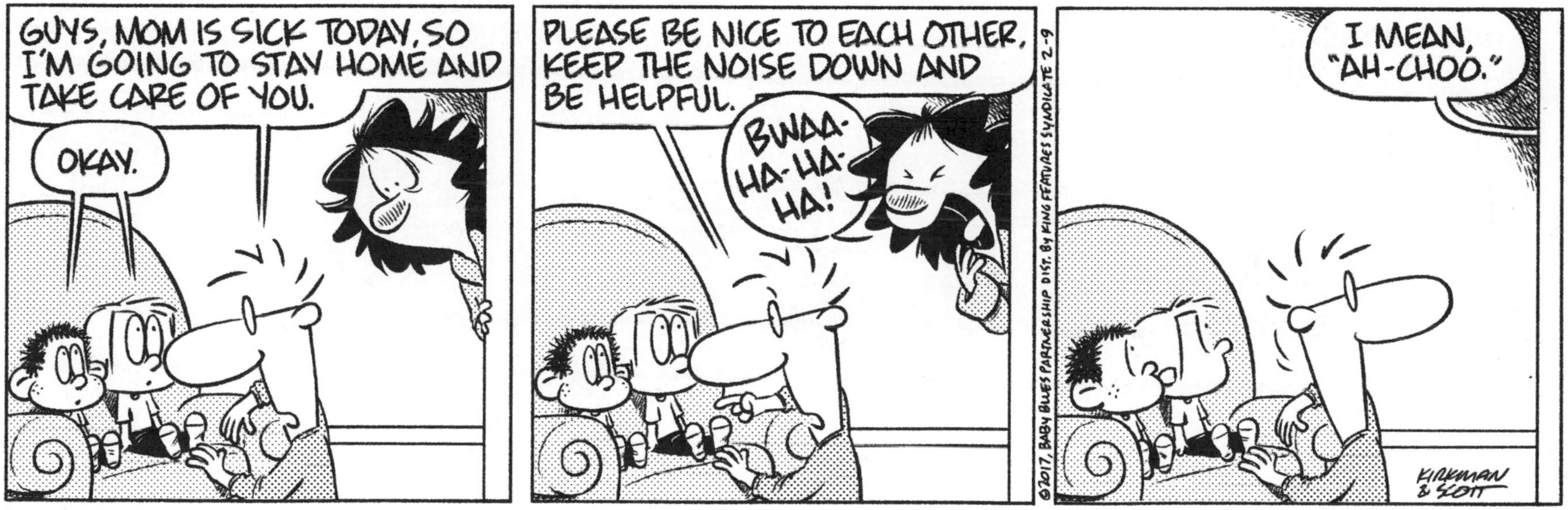
GUYS, MOM IS SICK TODAY, SO I'M GOING TO STAY HOME AND TAKE CARE OF YOU.
OKAY.
PLEASE BE NICE TO EACH OTHER, KEEP THE NOISE DOWN AND BE HELPFUL.
BWAA-HA-HA-HA!
I MEAN, "AH-CHOO."
©2017, BABY BLUES PARTNERSHIP DIST. BY KING FEATURES SYNDICATE 2-9
KIRKMAN & SCOTT

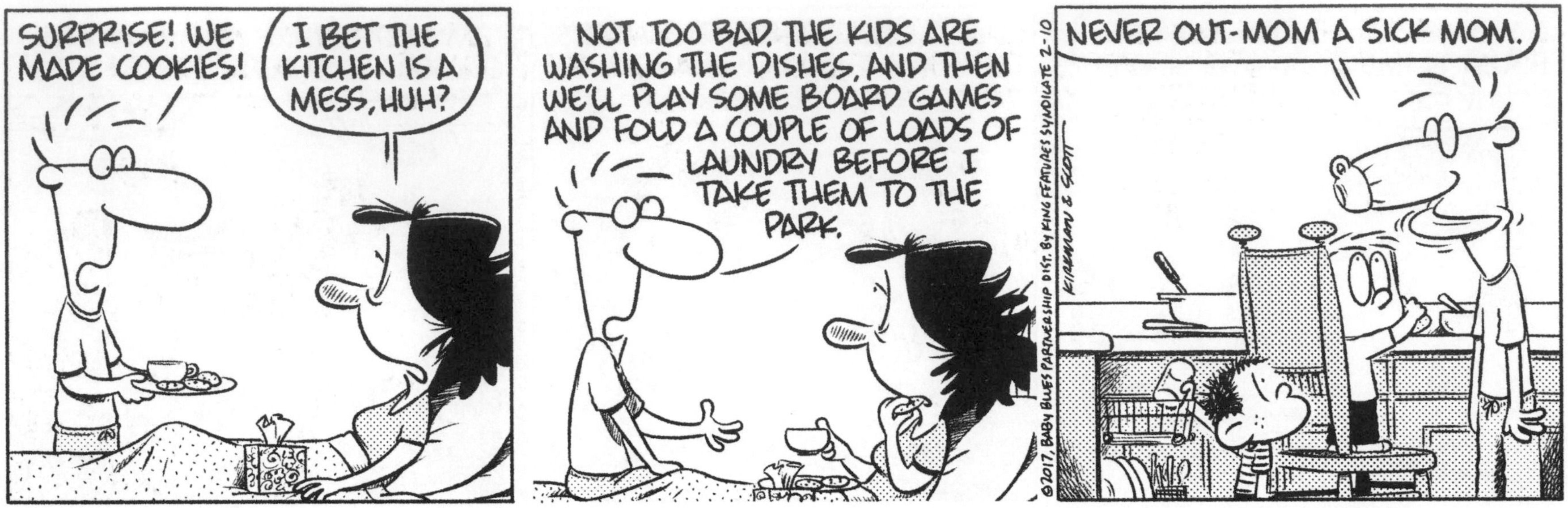

SURPRISE! WE MADE COOKIES!
I BET THE KITCHEN IS A MESS, HUH?
NOT TOO BAD. THE KIDS ARE WASHING THE DISHES, AND THEN WE'LL PLAY SOME BOARD GAMES AND FOLD A COUPLE OF LOADS OF LAUNDRY BEFORE I TAKE THEM TO THE PARK.
©2017, BABY BLUES PARTNERSHIP DIST. BY KING FEATURES SYNDICATE 2-10
KIRKMAN & SCOTT
NEVER OUT-MOM A SICK MOM.

Jerry: Right. Right. Right.

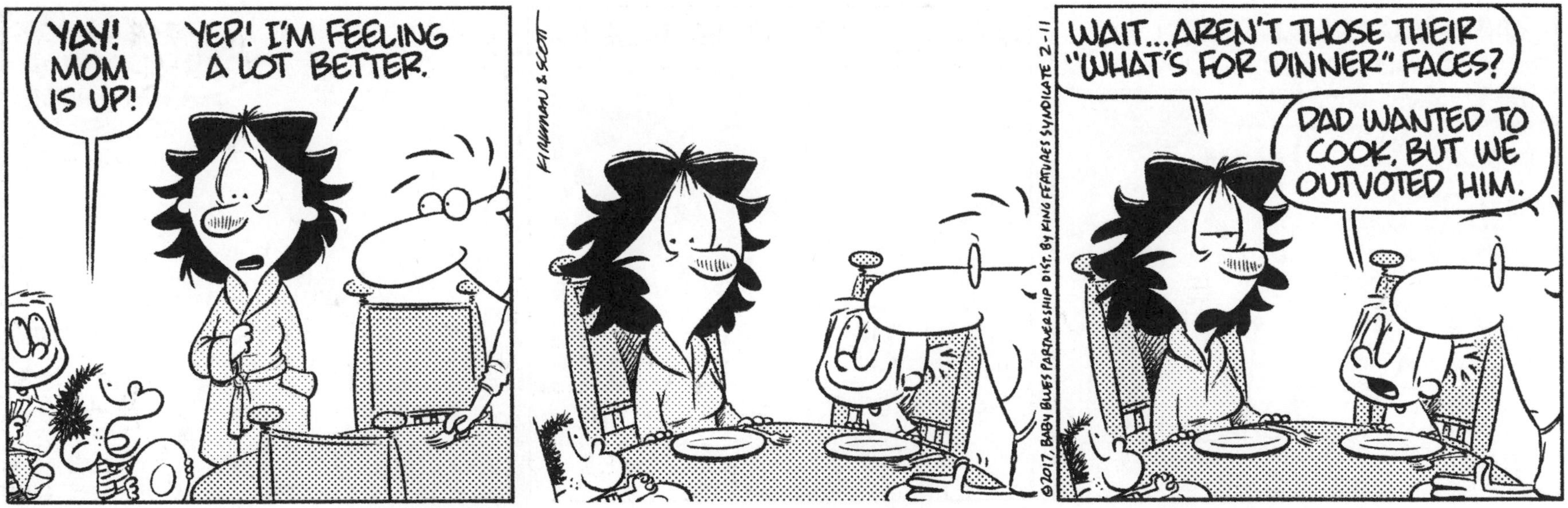

YAY! MOM IS UP!
YEP! I'M FEELING A LOT BETTER.
KIRKMAN & SCOTT
©2017, BABY BLUES PARTNERSHIP DIST. BY KING FEATURES SYNDICATE 2-11
WAIT...AREN'T THOSE THEIR "WHAT'S FOR DINNER" FACES?
DAD WANTED TO COOK, BUT WE OUTVOTED HIM.

Rick: Then, takeout it is.

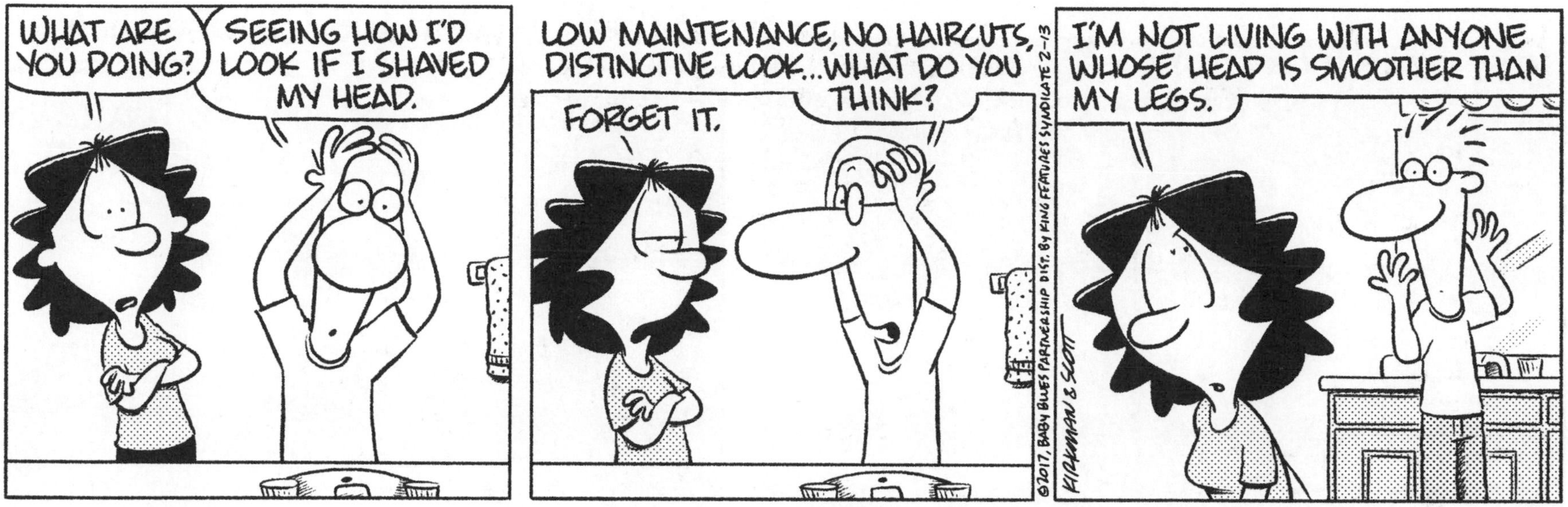
WHAT ARE YOU DOING?
SEEING HOW I'D LOOK IF I SHAVED MY HEAD.
LOW MAINTENANCE, NO HAIRCUTS, DISTINCTIVE LOOK...WHAT DO YOU THINK?
FORGET IT.
I'M NOT LIVING WITH ANYONE WHOSE HEAD IS SMOOTHER THAN MY LEGS.
©2017, BABY BLUES PARTNERSHIP DIST. BY KING FEATURES SYNDICATE 2-13
KIRKMAN & SCOTT

Jerry: I do that imagine-myself-bald thing sometimes, but now I can do it with one hand.

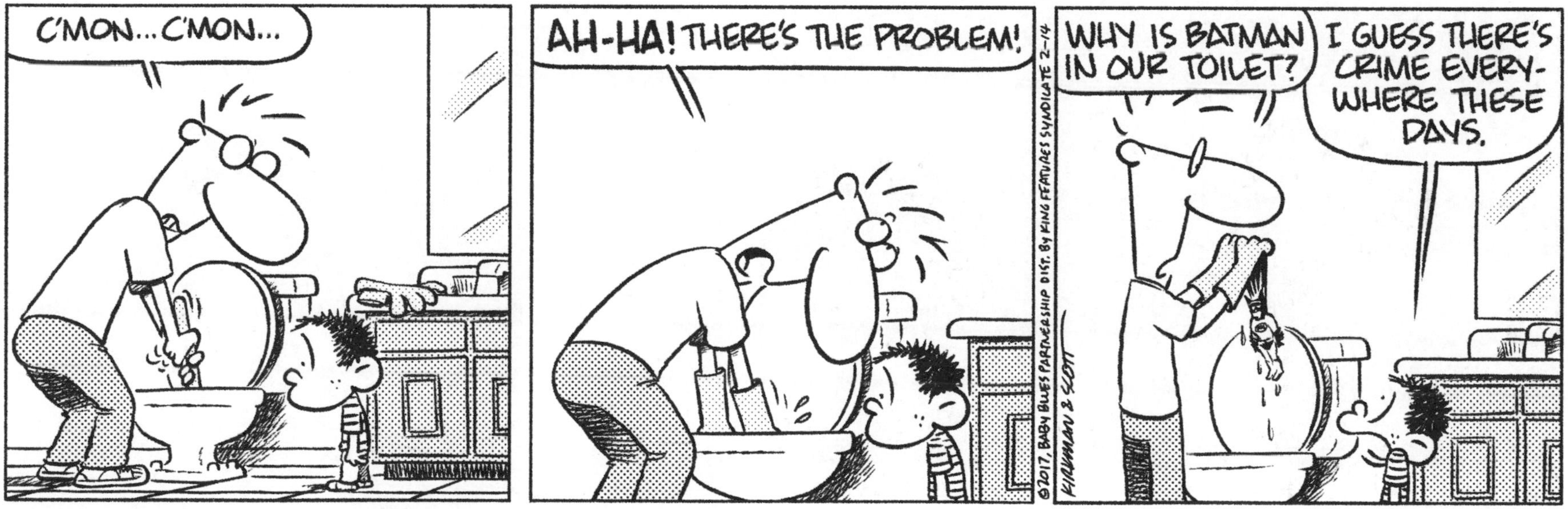
C'MON...C'MON...
AH-HA! THERE'S THE PROBLEM!
WHY IS BATMAN IN OUR TOILET?
I GUESS THERE'S CRIME EVERY-WHERE THESE DAYS.
©2017, BABY BLUES PARTNERSHIP DIST. BY KING FEATURES SYNDICATE 2-14
KIRKMAN & SCOTT

Rick: I'd just let that explanation slide. Don't know if I'd want to hear the real one.

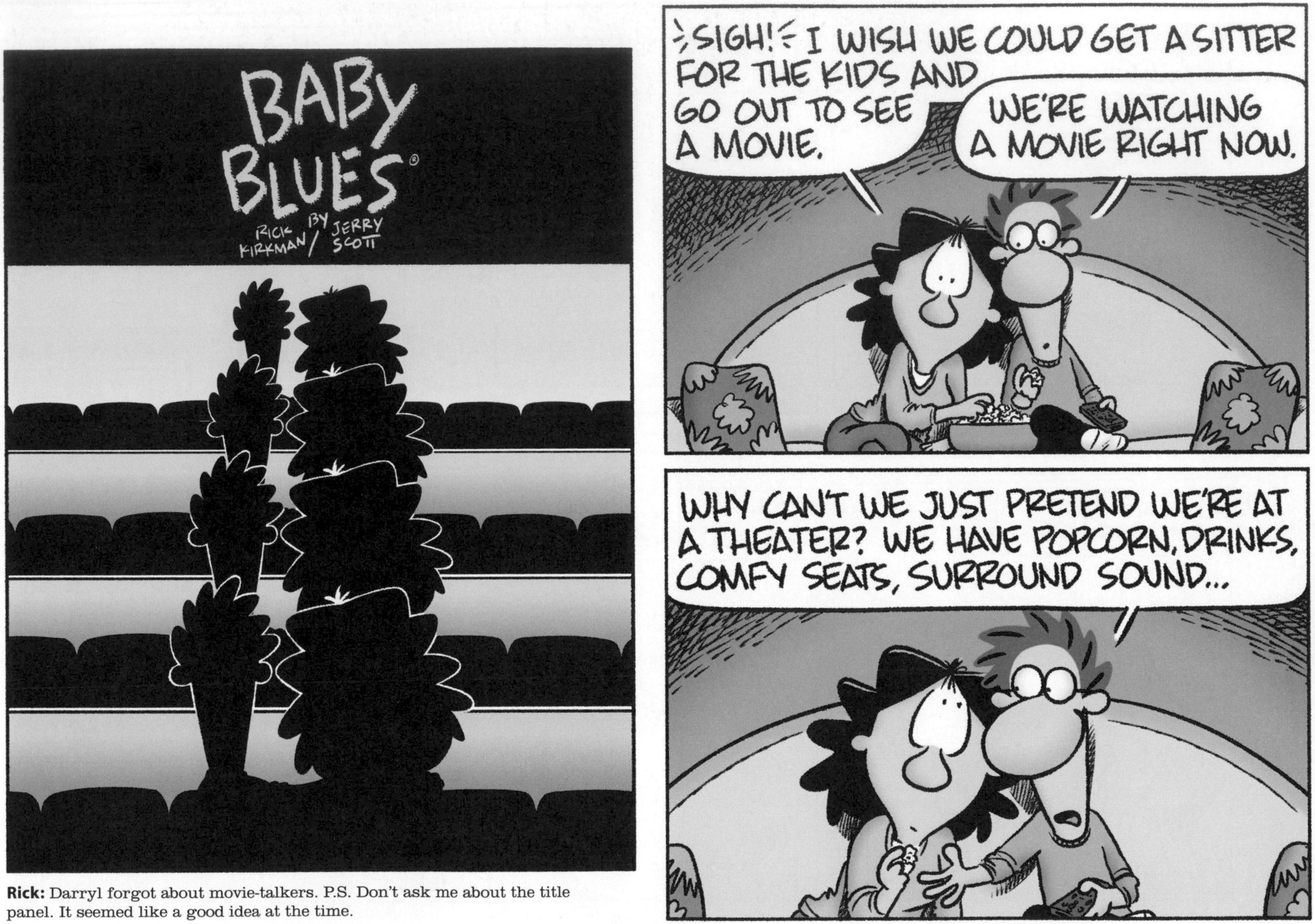
BABY BLUES®
BY RICK KIRKMAN / JERRY SCOTT
SIGH! I WISH WE COULD GET A SITTER FOR THE KIDS AND GO OUT TO SEE A MOVIE.
WE'RE WATCHING A MOVIE RIGHT NOW.
WHY CAN'T WE JUST PRETEND WE'RE AT A THEATER? WE HAVE POPCORN, DRINKS, COMFY SEATS, SURROUND SOUND...

Rick: Darryl forgot about movie-talkers. P.S. Don't ask me about the title panel. It seemed like a good idea at the time.

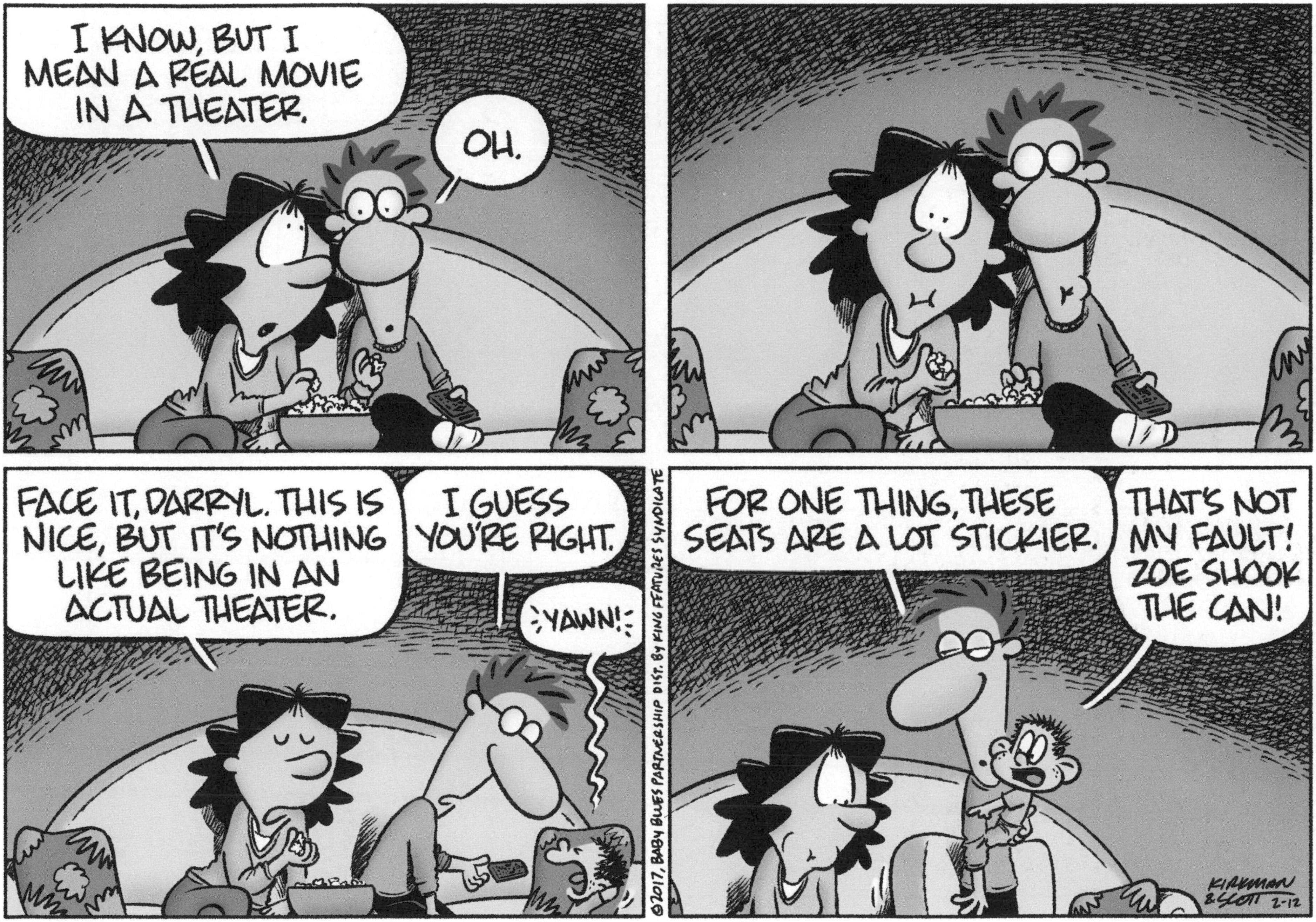
I KNOW, BUT I MEAN A REAL MOVIE IN A THEATER.
OH.
FACE IT, DARRYL. THIS IS NICE, BUT IT'S NOTHING LIKE BEING IN AN ACTUAL THEATER.
I GUESS YOU'RE RIGHT.
YAWN!
FOR ONE THING, THESE SEATS ARE A LOT STICKIER.
THAT'S NOT MY FAULT! ZOE SHOOK THE CAN!
©2017, BABY BLUES PARTNERSHIP DIST. BY KING FEATURES SYNDICATE
KIRKMAN & SCOTT 2-12

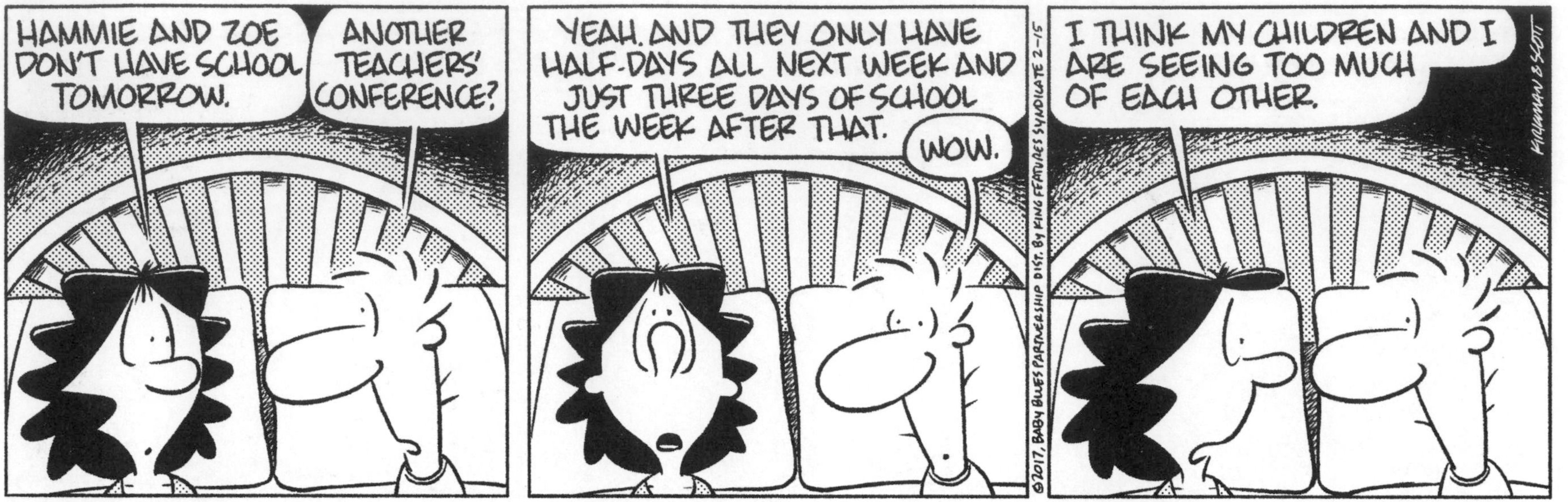
HAMMIE AND ZOE DON'T HAVE SCHOOL TOMORROW.
ANOTHER TEACHERS' CONFERENCE?
YEAH. AND THEY ONLY HAVE HALF-DAYS ALL NEXT WEEK AND JUST THREE DAYS OF SCHOOL THE WEEK AFTER THAT.
WOW.
I THINK MY CHILDREN AND I ARE SEEING TOO MUCH OF EACH OTHER.
©2017, BABY BLUES PARTNERSHIP DIST. BY KING FEATURES SYNDICATE 2-15
KIRKMAN & SCOTT

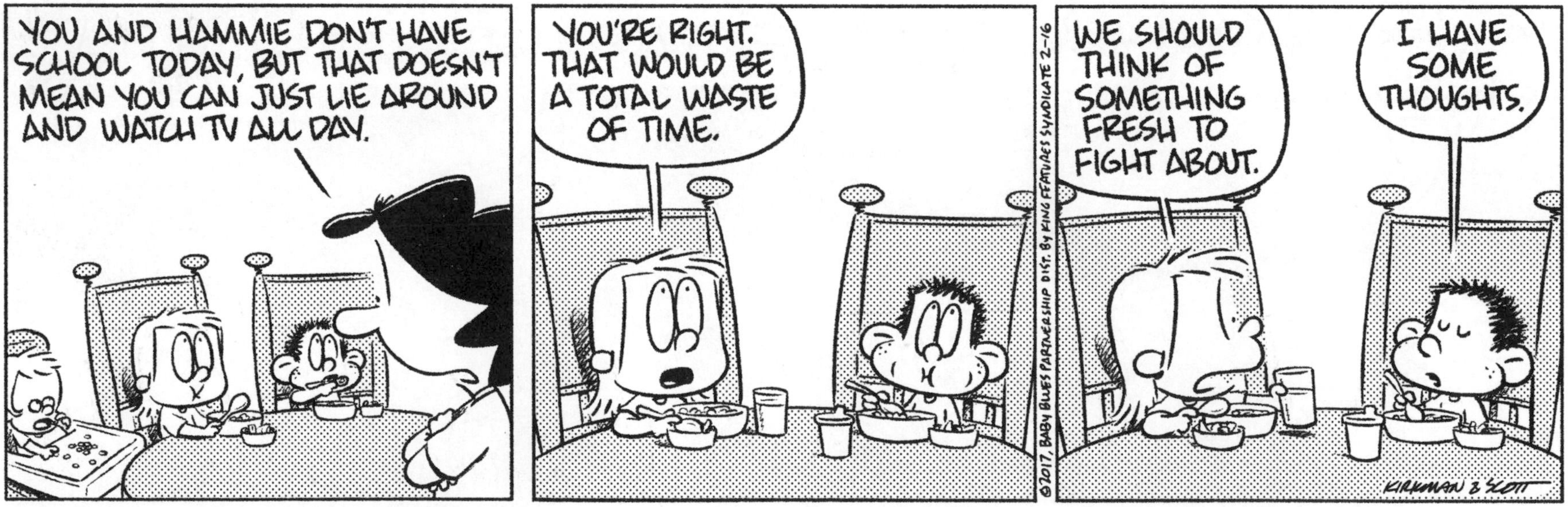
YOU AND HAMMIE DON'T HAVE SCHOOL TODAY, BUT THAT DOESN'T MEAN YOU CAN JUST LIE AROUND AND WATCH TV ALL DAY.
YOU'RE RIGHT. THAT WOULD BE A TOTAL WASTE OF TIME.
WE SHOULD THINK OF SOMETHING FRESH TO FIGHT ABOUT.
I HAVE SOME THOUGHTS.
©2017, BABY BLUES PARTNERSHIP DIST. BY KING FEATURES SYNDICATE 2-16
KIRKMAN & SCOTT

Jerry: The possibilities are endless.

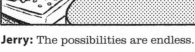

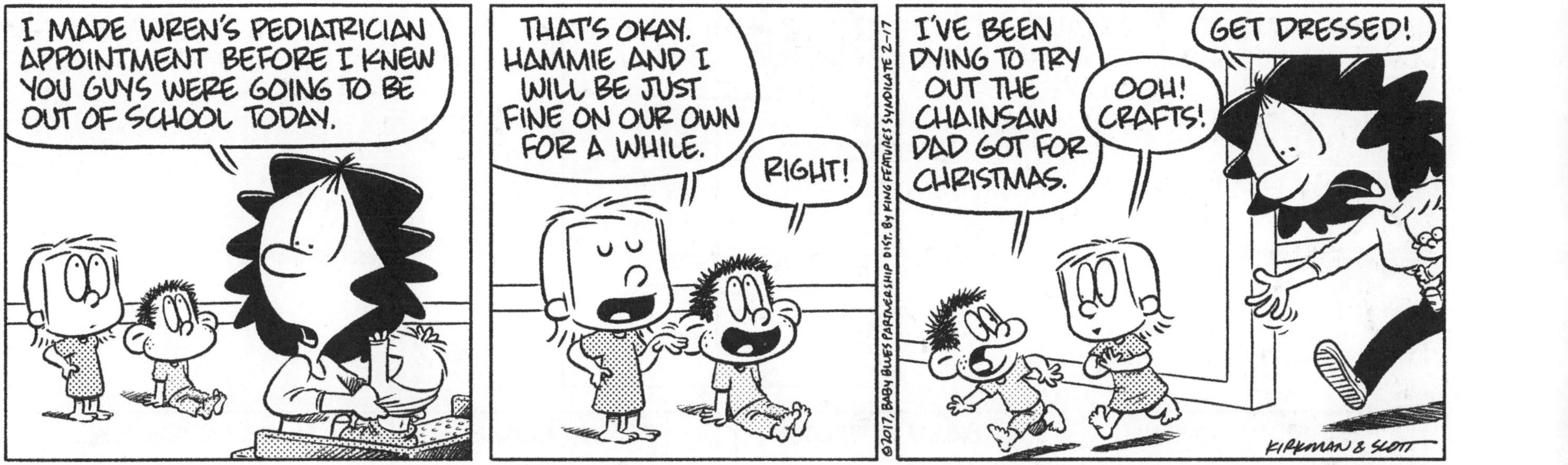
I MADE WREN'S PEDIATRICIAN APPOINTMENT BEFORE I KNEW YOU GUYS WERE GOING TO BE OUT OF SCHOOL TODAY.
THAT'S OKAY. HAMMIE AND I WILL BE JUST FINE ON OUR OWN FOR A WHILE.
RIGHT!
©2017, BABY BLUES PARTNERSHIP DIST. BY KING FEATURES SYNDICATE 2-17
I'VE BEEN DYING TO TRY OUT THE CHAINSAW DAD GOT FOR CHRISTMAS.
OOH! CRAFTS!
GET DRESSED!
KIRKMAN & SCOTT

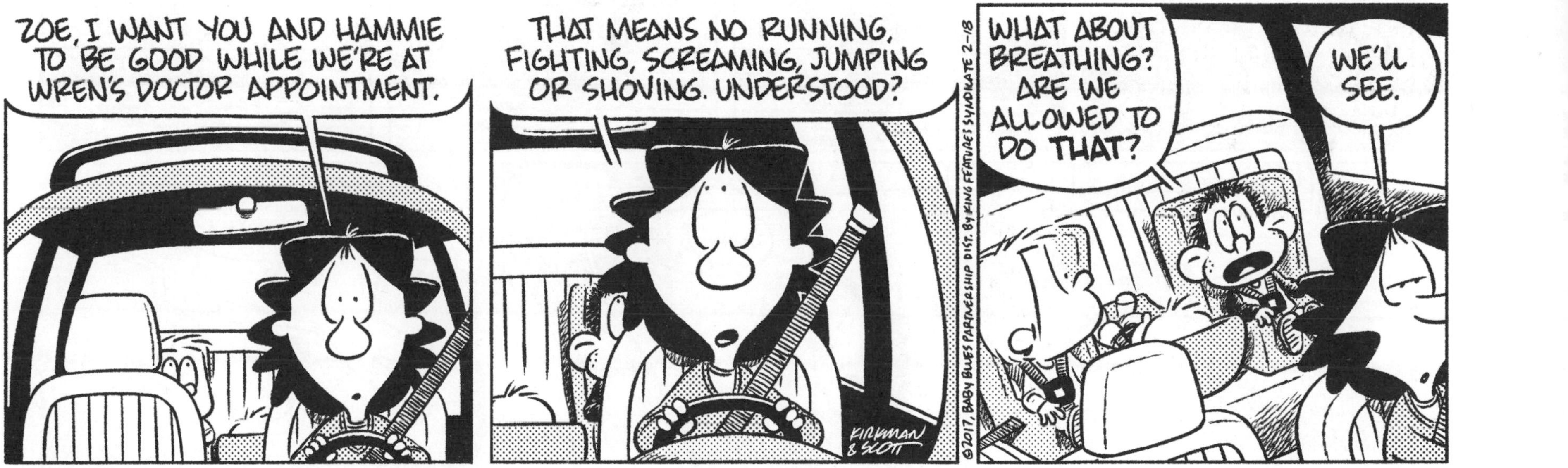
ZOE, I WANT YOU AND HAMMIE TO BE GOOD WHILE WE'RE AT WREN'S DOCTOR APPOINTMENT.
THAT MEANS NO RUNNING, FIGHTING, SCREAMING, JUMPING OR SHOVING. UNDERSTOOD?
KIRKMAN & SCOTT
©2017, BABY BLUES PARTNERSHIP DIST. BY KING FEATURES SYNDICATE 2-18
WHAT ABOUT BREATHING? ARE WE ALLOWED TO DO THAT?
WE'LL SEE.

Jerry: Supervised Breathing: Sometimes it's necessary.

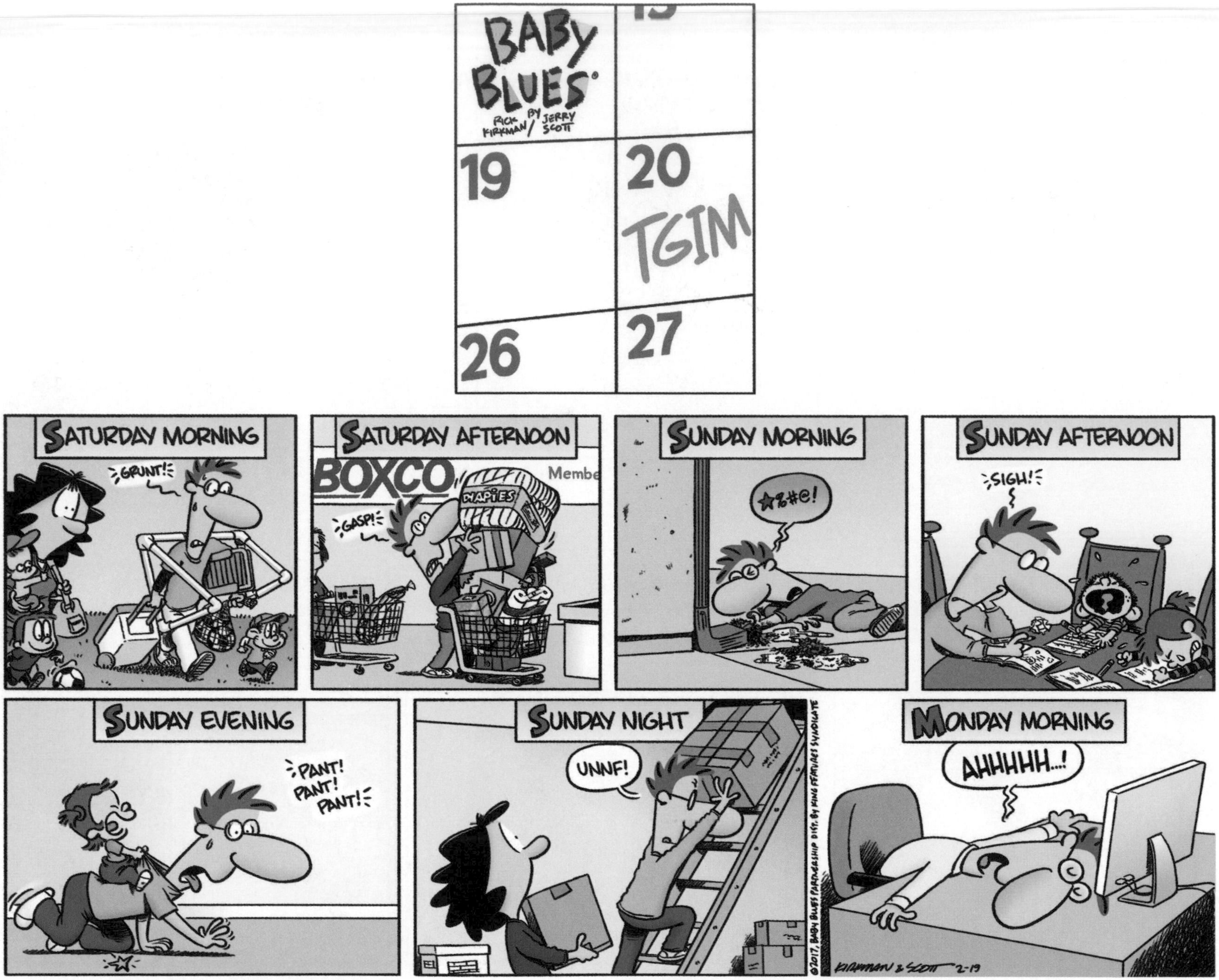
BABY BLUES
RICK KIRKMAN / BY JERRY SCOTT
19
20
TGIM
26
27
SATURDAY MORNING
GRUNT!
SATURDAY AFTERNOON
BOXCO
GASP!
SUNDAY MORNING
★%#@!
SUNDAY AFTERNOON
SIGH!
SUNDAY EVENING
PANT! PANT! PANT!
SUNDAY NIGHT
UNNF!
MONDAY MORNING
AHHHHH...!
©2017, BABY BLUES PARTNERSHIP DIST. BY KING FEATURES SYNDICATE
KIRKMAN & SCOTT 2-19

Rick: I'm exhausted just looking at that.

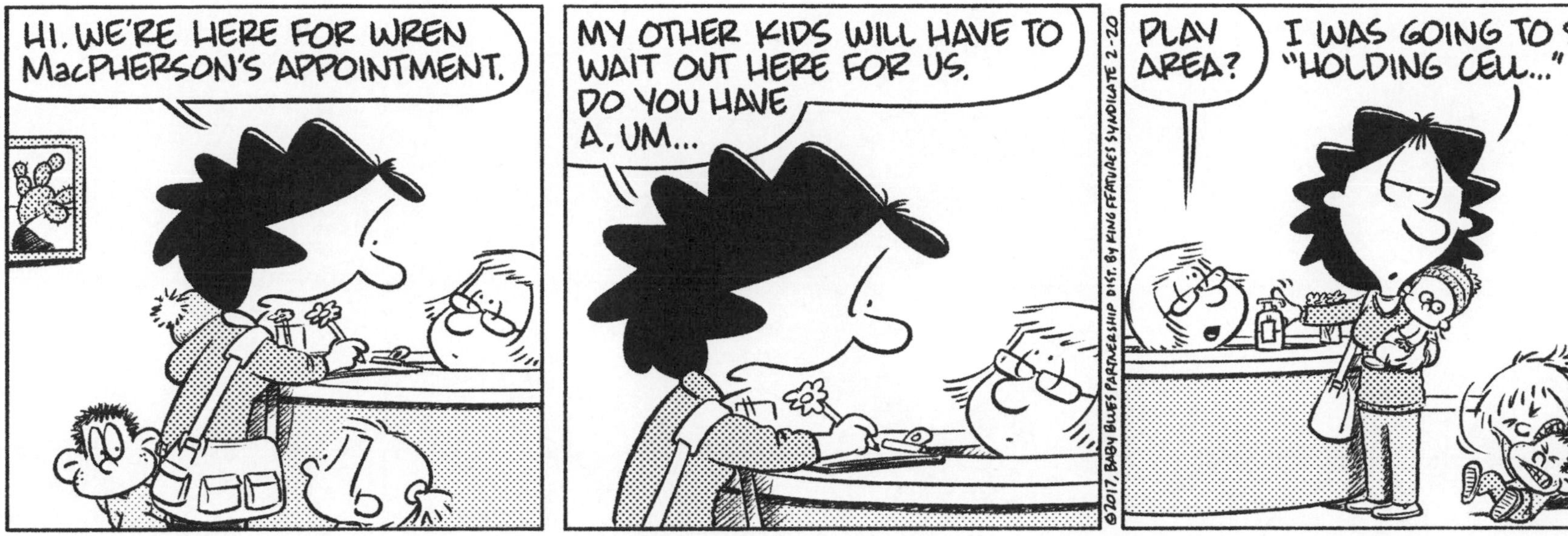
HI. WE'RE HERE FOR WREN MacPHERSON'S APPOINTMENT.
MY OTHER KIDS WILL HAVE TO WAIT OUT HERE FOR US. DO YOU HAVE A, UM...
©2017, BABY BLUES PARTNERSHIP DIST. BY KING FEATURES SYNDICATE 2-20
PLAY AREA?
I WAS GOING TO SAY "HOLDING CELL..."
KIRKMAN & SCOTT

Rick: Is it just me? The receptionist reminds me of Mrs. Landingham from *The West Wing* (the late Kathryn Joosten). She was so great . . .

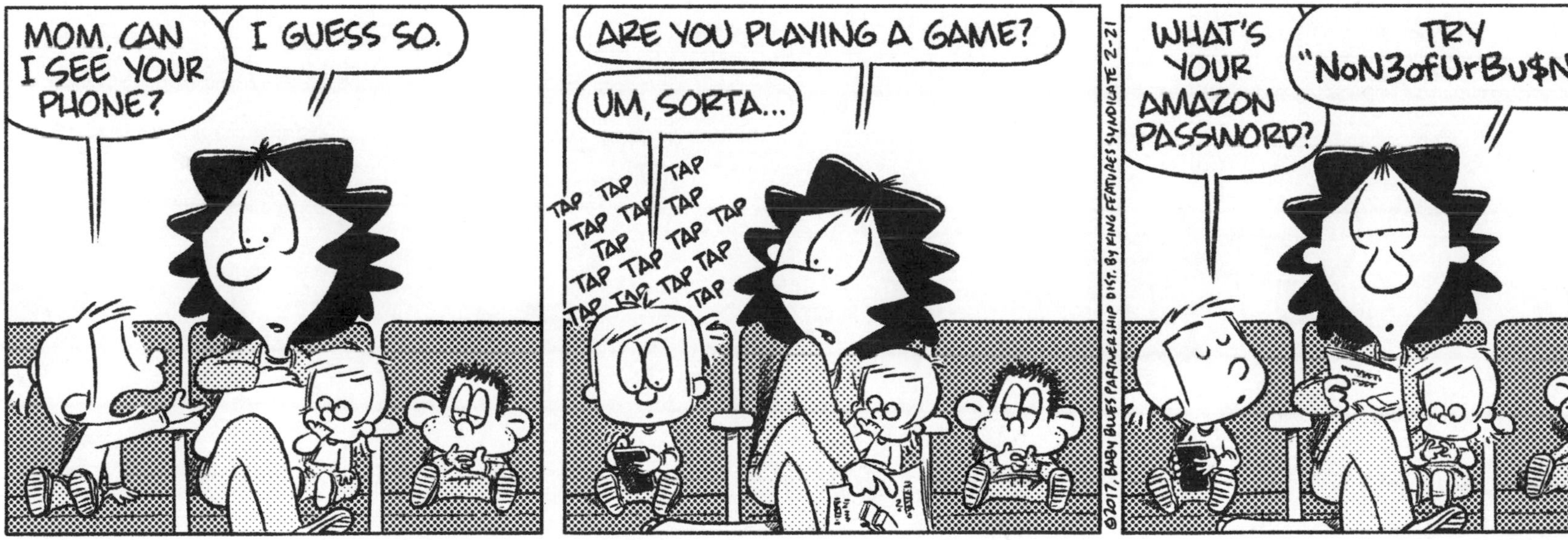
MOM, CAN I SEE YOUR PHONE?
I GUESS SO.
ARE YOU PLAYING A GAME?
UM, SORTA...
TAP TAP TAP TAP TAP TAP TAP TAP TAP TAP TAP TAP TAP TAP TAP TAP TAP
©2017, BABY BLUES PARTNERSHIP DIST. BY KING FEATURES SYNDICATE 2-21
WHAT'S YOUR AMAZON PASSWORD?
TRY "NoN3ofUrBu$Ne$$"
KIRKMAN & SCOTT

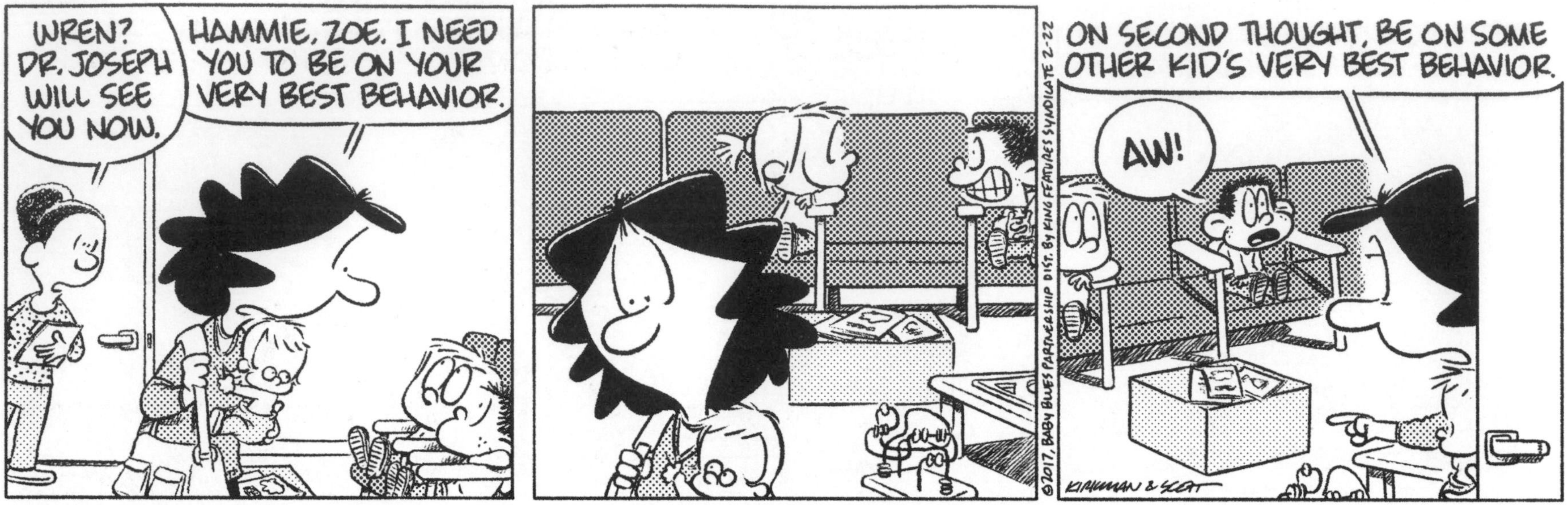
WREN? DR. JOSEPH WILL SEE YOU NOW.
HAMMIE, ZOE. I NEED YOU TO BE ON YOUR VERY BEST BEHAVIOR.
ON SECOND THOUGHT, BE ON SOME OTHER KID'S VERY BEST BEHAVIOR.
AW!
©2017, BABY BLUES PARTNERSHIP DIST. BY KING FEATURES SYNDICATE 2-22
KIRKMAN & SCOTT

Jerry: She almost left a loophole there.

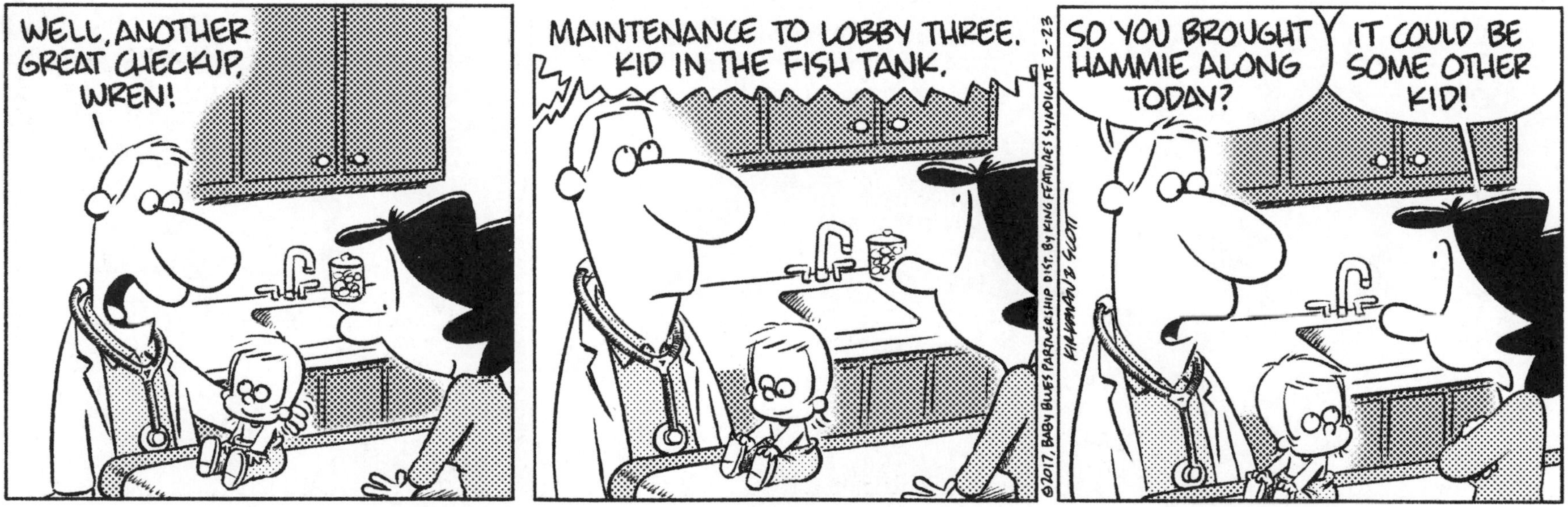
WELL, ANOTHER GREAT CHECKUP, WREN!
MAINTENANCE TO LOBBY THREE. KID IN THE FISH TANK.
SO YOU BROUGHT HAMMIE ALONG TODAY?
IT COULD BE SOME OTHER KID!
©2017, BABY BLUES PARTNERSHIP DIST. BY KING FEATURES SYNDICATE 2-23
KIRKMAN & SCOTT

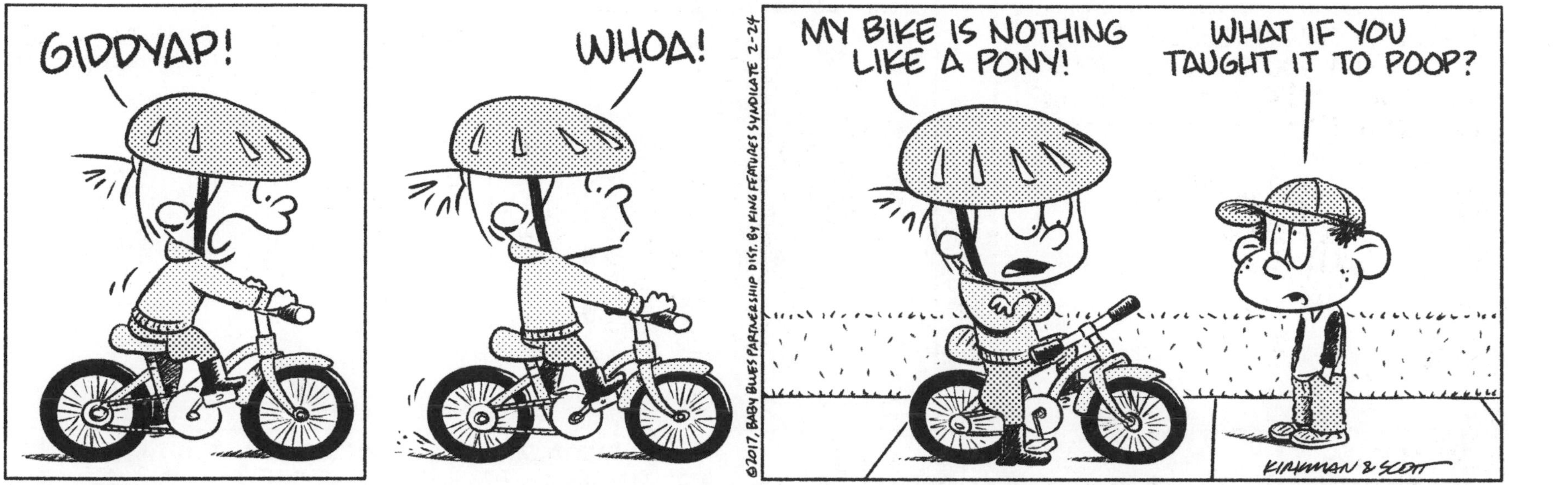
GIDDYAP!
WHOA!
MY BIKE IS NOTHING LIKE A PONY!
WHAT IF YOU TAUGHT IT TO POOP?
©2017, BABY BLUES PARTNERSHIP DIST. BY KING FEATURES SYNDICATE 2-24
KIRKMAN & SCOTT

Jerry: And teach it to pay its own vet bills while you're at it.

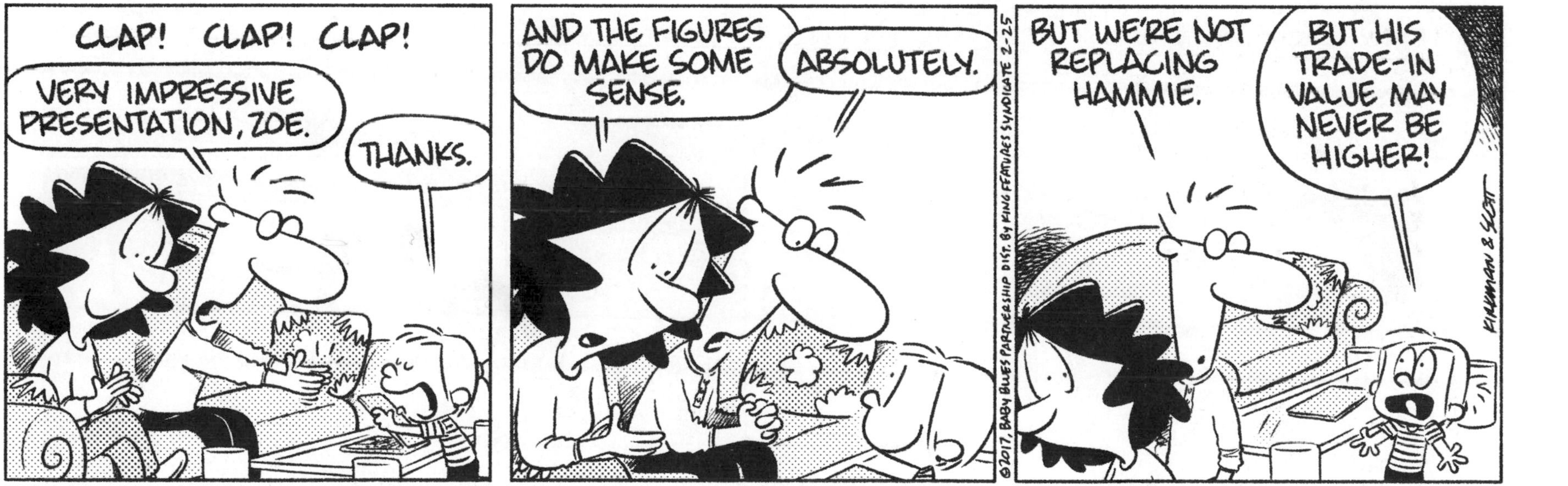
CLAP! CLAP! CLAP!
VERY IMPRESSIVE PRESENTATION, ZOE.
THANKS.
AND THE FIGURES DO MAKE SOME SENSE.
ABSOLUTELY.
BUT WE'RE NOT REPLACING HAMMIE.
BUT HIS TRADE-IN VALUE MAY NEVER BE HIGHER!
©2017, BABY BLUES PARTNERSHIP DIST. BY KING FEATURES SYNDICATE 2-25
KIRKMAN & SCOTT

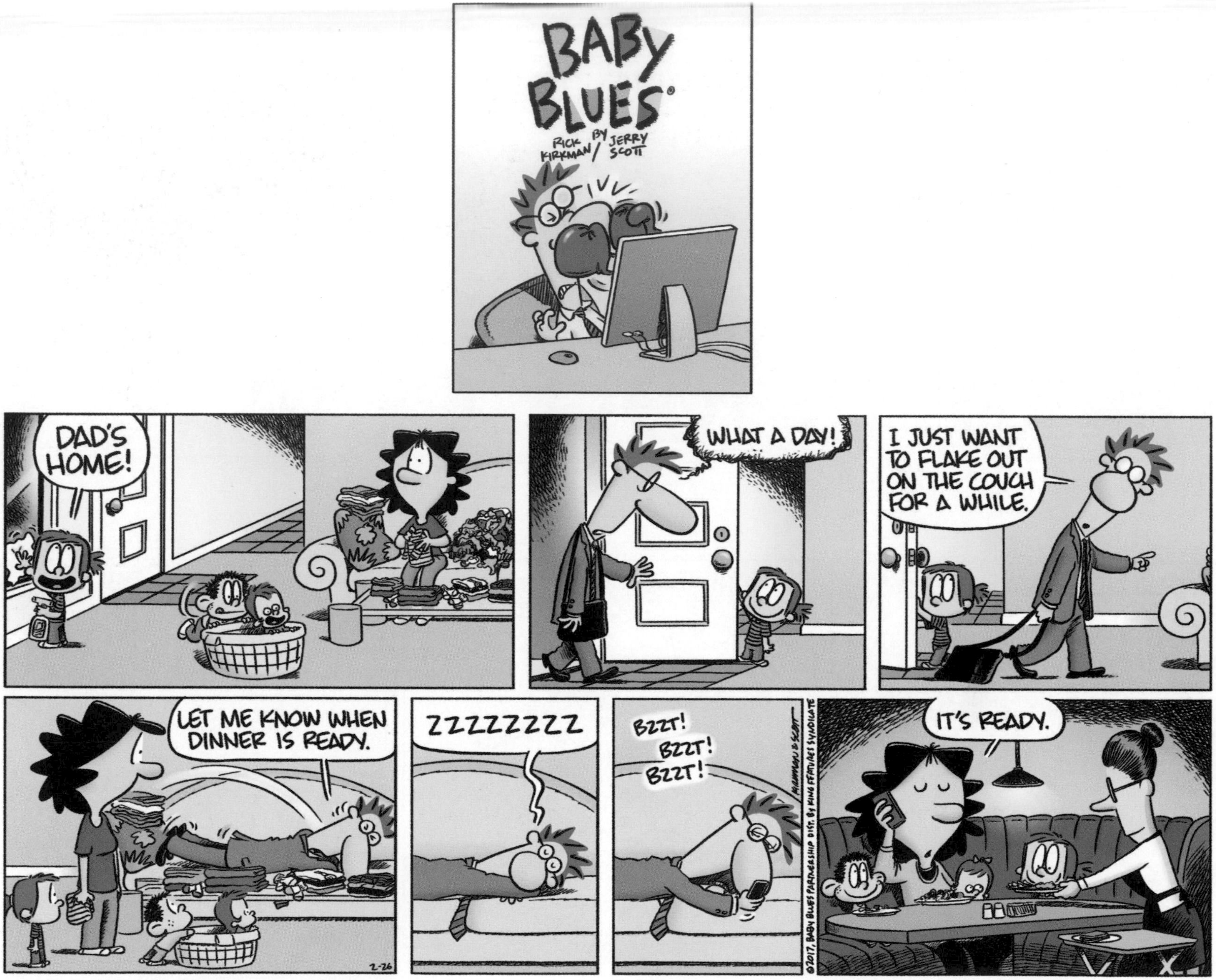
BABY BLUES®
BY RICK KIRKMAN / JERRY SCOTT
DAD'S HOME!
WHAT A DAY!
I JUST WANT TO FLAKE OUT ON THE COUCH FOR A WHILE.
LET ME KNOW WHEN DINNER IS READY.
2-26
ZZZZZZZZ
BZZT! BZZT! BZZT!
©2017, BABY BLUES PARTNERSHIP DIST. BY KING FEATURES SYNDICATE
IT'S READY.

Rick: Revenge is best served in a restaurant.

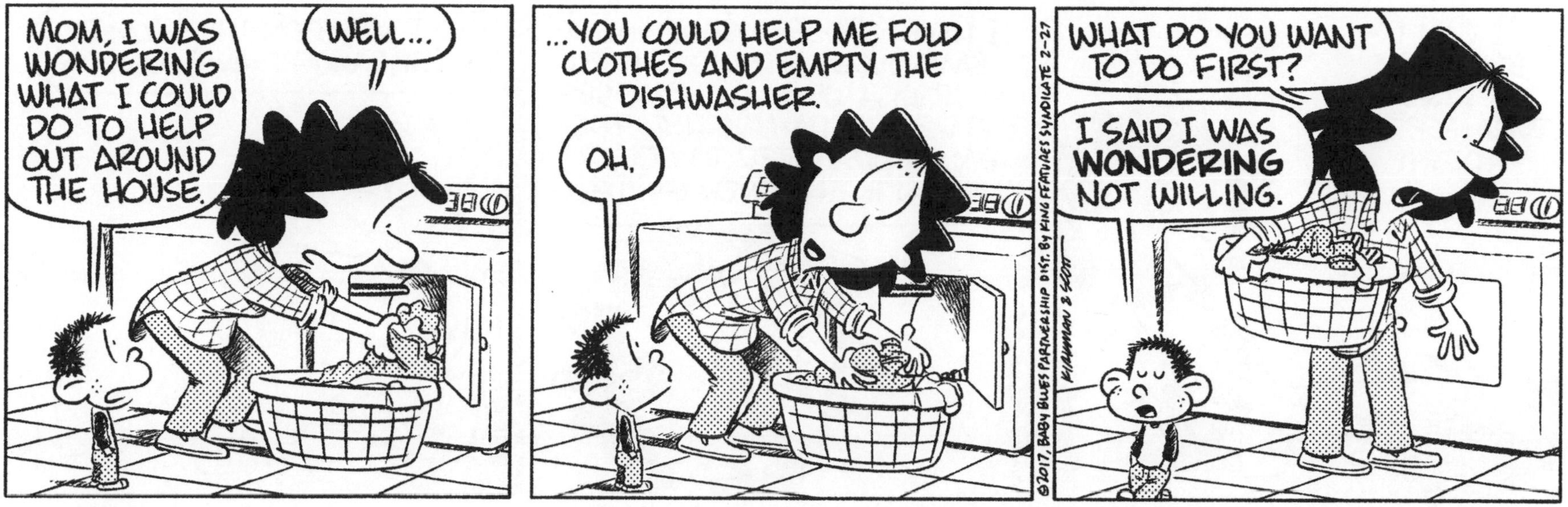
MOM, I WAS WONDERING WHAT I COULD DO TO HELP OUT AROUND THE HOUSE.
WELL...
...YOU COULD HELP ME FOLD CLOTHES AND EMPTY THE DISHWASHER.
OH.
WHAT DO YOU WANT TO DO FIRST?
I SAID I WAS **WONDERING** NOT WILLING.
©2017, BABY BLUES PARTNERSHIP DIST. BY KING FEATURES SYNDICATE 2-27
KIRKMAN & SCOTT

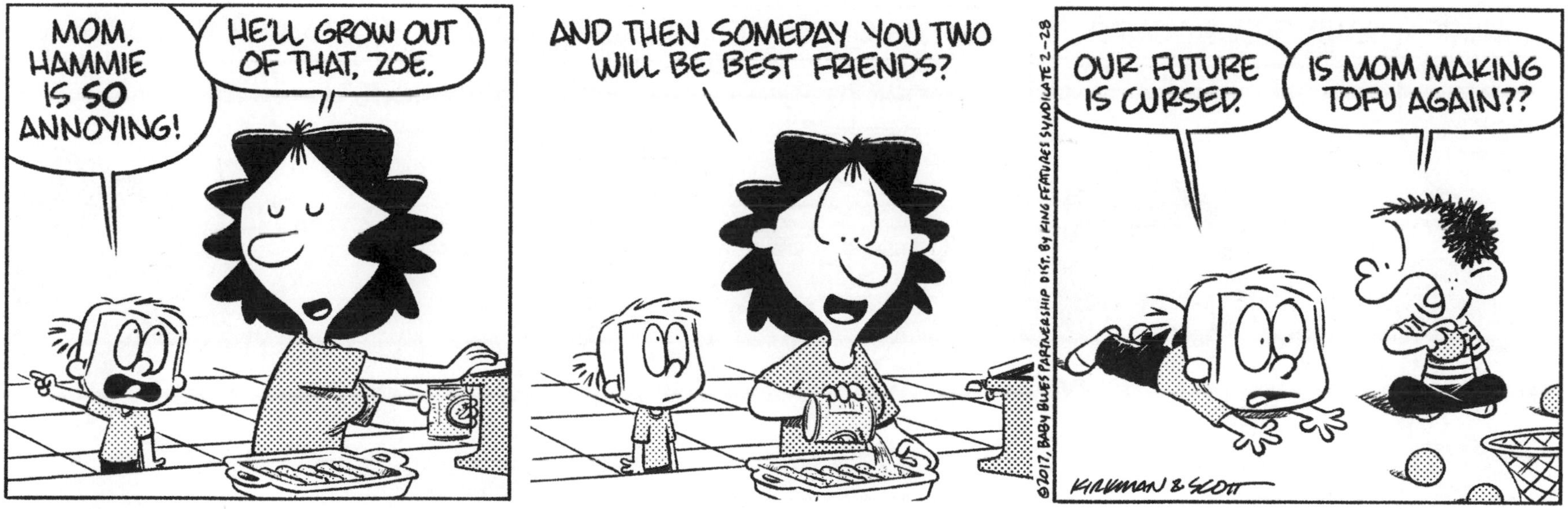
MOM, HAMMIE IS **SO** ANNOYING!
HE'LL GROW OUT OF THAT, ZOE.
AND THEN SOMEDAY YOU TWO WILL BE BEST FRIENDS?
OUR FUTURE IS CURSED.
IS MOM MAKING TOFU AGAIN??
©2017, BABY BLUES PARTNERSHIP DIST. BY KING FEATURES SYNDICATE 2-28
KIRKMAN & SCOTT

Jerry: My mom used to say that my sisters and I would be best friends someday, and she was right. Glad she never made tofu, though.

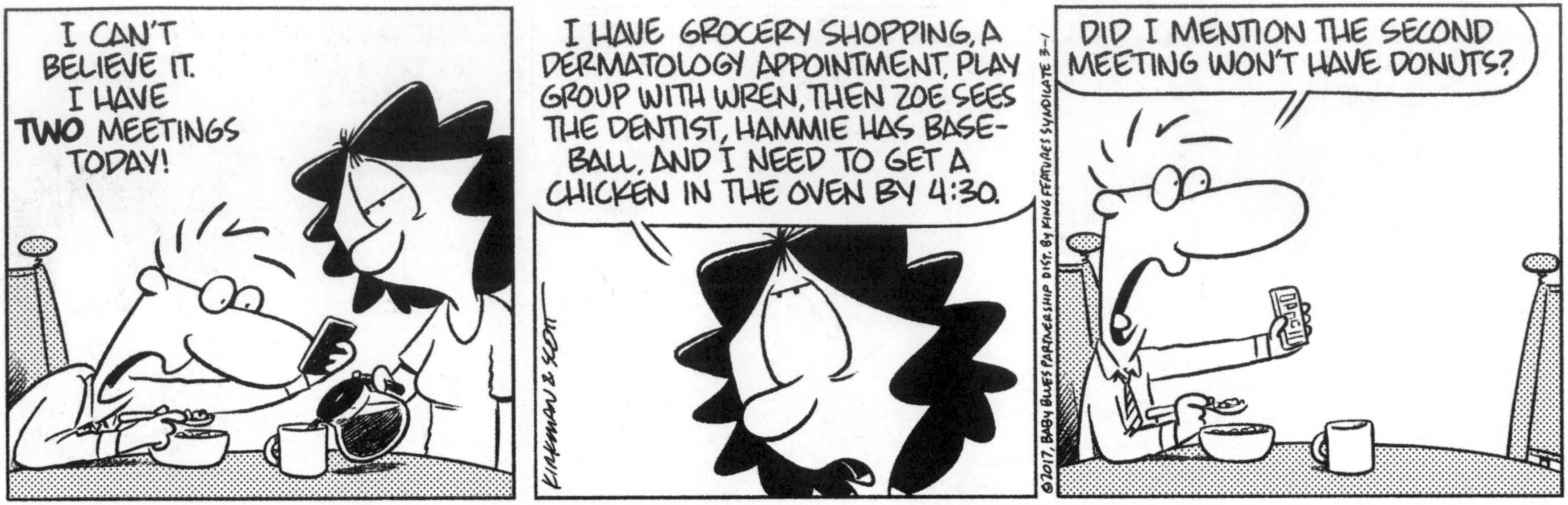
I CAN'T BELIEVE IT. I HAVE **TWO** MEETINGS TODAY!
I HAVE GROCERY SHOPPING, A DERMATOLOGY APPOINTMENT, PLAY GROUP WITH WREN, THEN ZOE SEES THE DENTIST, HAMMIE HAS BASE-BALL, AND I NEED TO GET A CHICKEN IN THE OVEN BY 4:30.
KIRKMAN & SCOTT
©2017, BABY BLUES PARTNERSHIP DIST. BY KING FEATURES SYNDICATE 3-1
DID I MENTION THE SECOND MEETING WON'T HAVE DONUTS?

Jerry: Looking for calendar sympathy from a mom of three is a losing game.

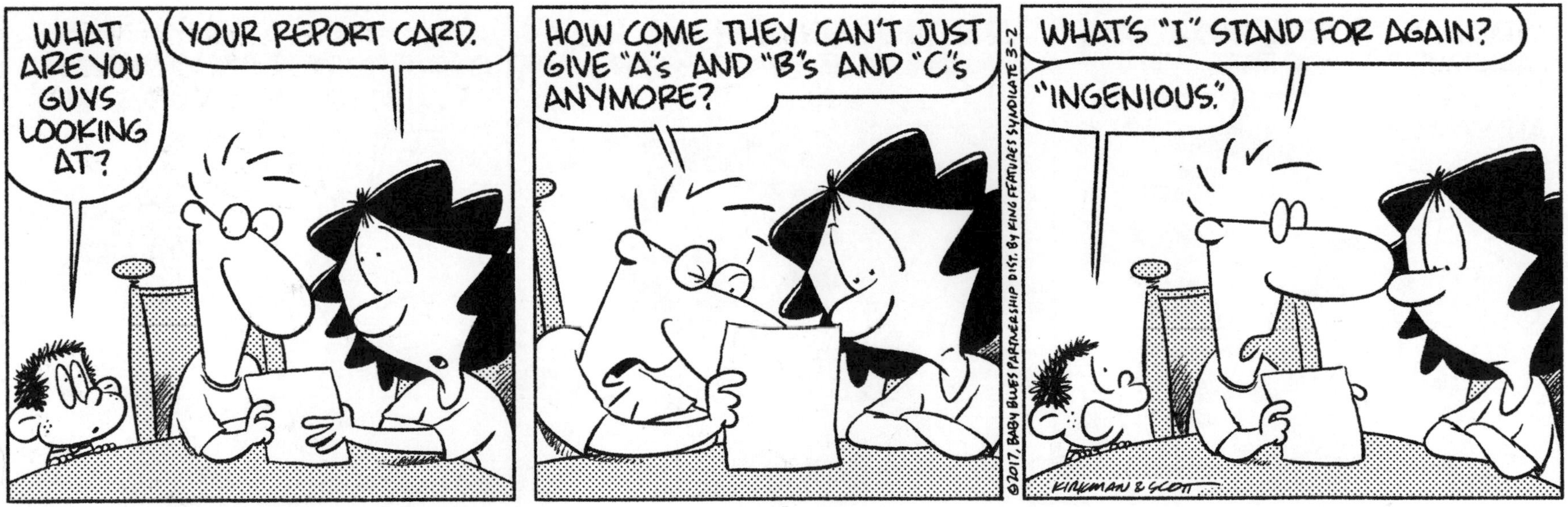
WHAT ARE YOU GUYS LOOKING AT?
YOUR REPORT CARD.
HOW COME THEY CAN'T JUST GIVE "A"s AND "B"s AND "C"s ANYMORE?
©2017, BABY BLUES PARTNERSHIP DIST. BY KING FEATURES SYNDICATE 3-2
WHAT'S "I" STAND FOR AGAIN?
"INGENIOUS."
KIRKMAN & SCOTT

Rick: Or it could stand for "Iquit."

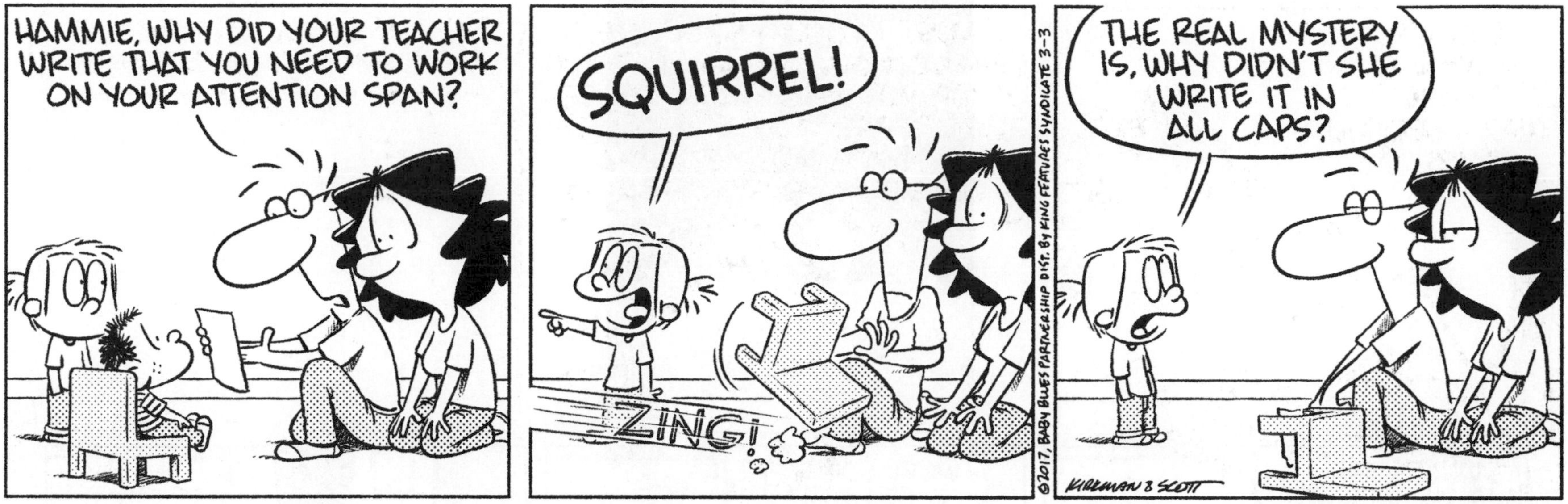
HAMMIE, WHY DID YOUR TEACHER WRITE THAT YOU NEED TO WORK ON YOUR ATTENTION SPAN?
SQUIRREL!
ZING!
THE REAL MYSTERY IS, WHY DIDN'T SHE WRITE IT IN ALL CAPS?
©2017, BABY BLUES PARTNERSHIP DIST. BY KING FEATURES SYNDICATE 3-3
KIRKMAN & SCOTT

Rick: A reader alerted us that I lettered Darryl's first line, " . . . attention spain." Don't know where my head was at when I did that—maybe Spain. Even though it was caught afterward, we didn't fix it until now. It remains that way online. Note to self: Call our editor.

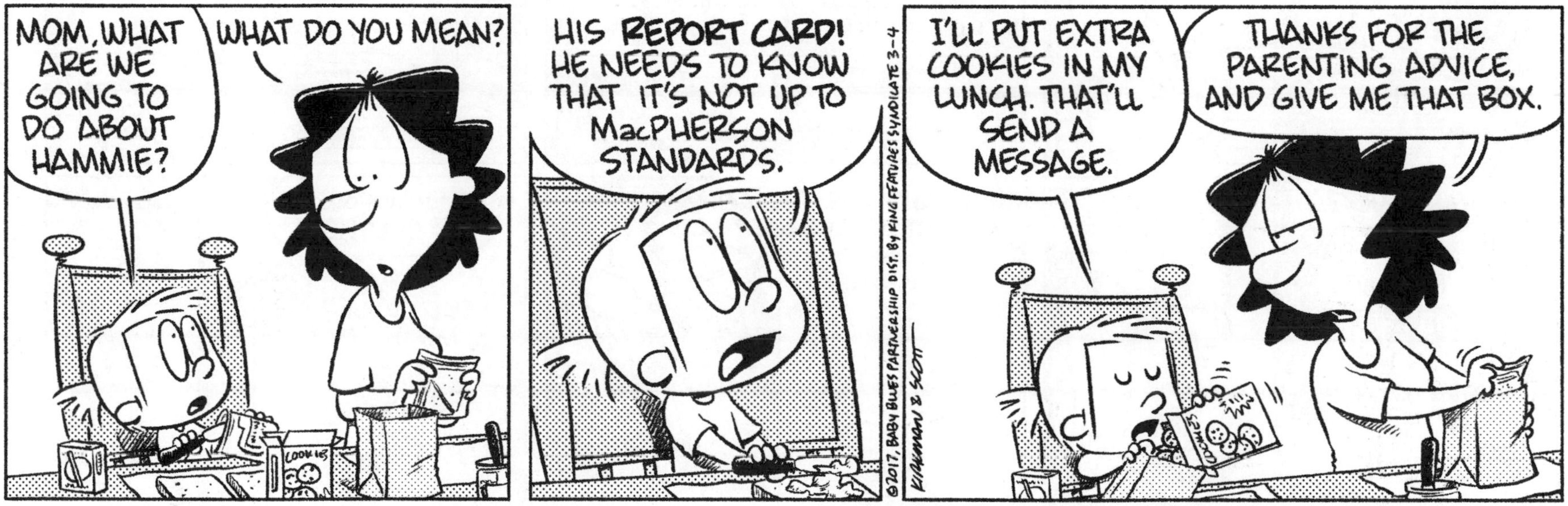
MOM, WHAT ARE WE GOING TO DO ABOUT HAMMIE?
WHAT DO YOU MEAN?
HIS **REPORT CARD!** HE NEEDS TO KNOW THAT IT'S NOT UP TO MacPHERSON STANDARDS.
I'LL PUT EXTRA COOKIES IN MY LUNCH. THAT'LL SEND A MESSAGE.
THANKS FOR THE PARENTING ADVICE, AND GIVE ME THAT BOX.
©2017, BABY BLUES PARTNERSHIP DIST. BY KING FEATURES SYNDICATE 3-4
KIRKMAN & SCOTT

BABY BLUES
Rick Kirkman & Jerry Scott
ZZZZZZ

WHAT'S THE HOLDUP IN THERE?
ZOE CAN'T FIND A HAIRBAND.
WE'RE GOING TO BE LATE!
I'LL TELL HER!
GRRR...
DRUM DRUM
ANY LUCK?
NOT YET!
WHY CAN'T SHE JUST GO WITHOUT A HAIRBAND?
I'LL ASK HER!
KIRKMAN & SCOTT 3-5
©2017, BABY BLUES PARTNERSHIP DIST. BY KING FEATURES SYNDICATE
I WITHDRAW THE QUESTION.
MOM! DAD CALLED ME UGLY!

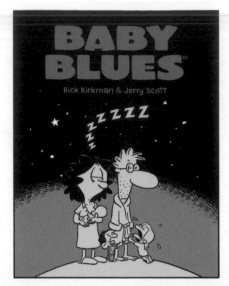

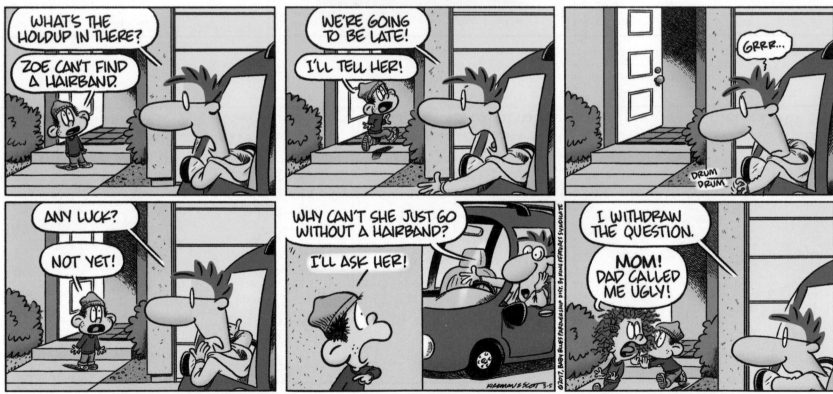

Jerry: This is a nod to my daughter's hair, which has become like a third child in the house, maintenance-wise.

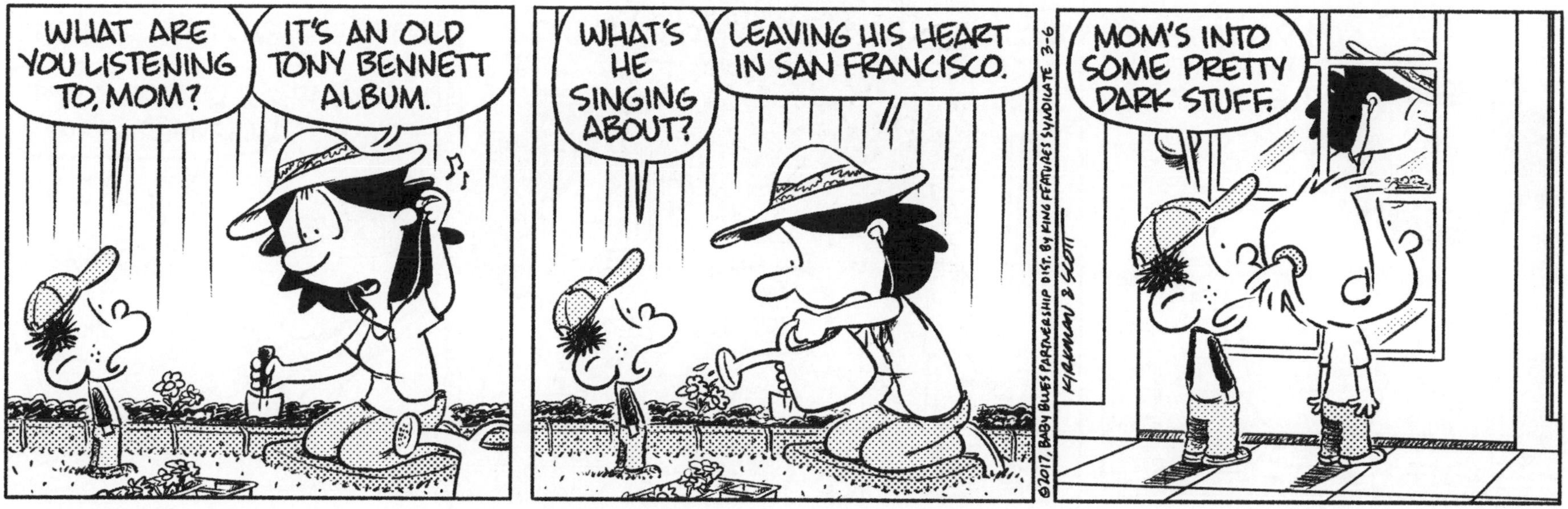
WHAT ARE YOU LISTENING TO, MOM?
IT'S AN OLD TONY BENNETT ALBUM.
WHAT'S HE SINGING ABOUT?
LEAVING HIS HEART IN SAN FRANCISCO.
©2017, BABY BLUES PARTNERSHIP DIST. BY KING FEATURES SYNDICATE 3-6
KIRKMAN & SCOTT
MOM'S INTO SOME PRETTY DARK STUFF.

Rick: Wait till Hammie finds out what she's *really* planting in that flower bed . . . Cue scary music.

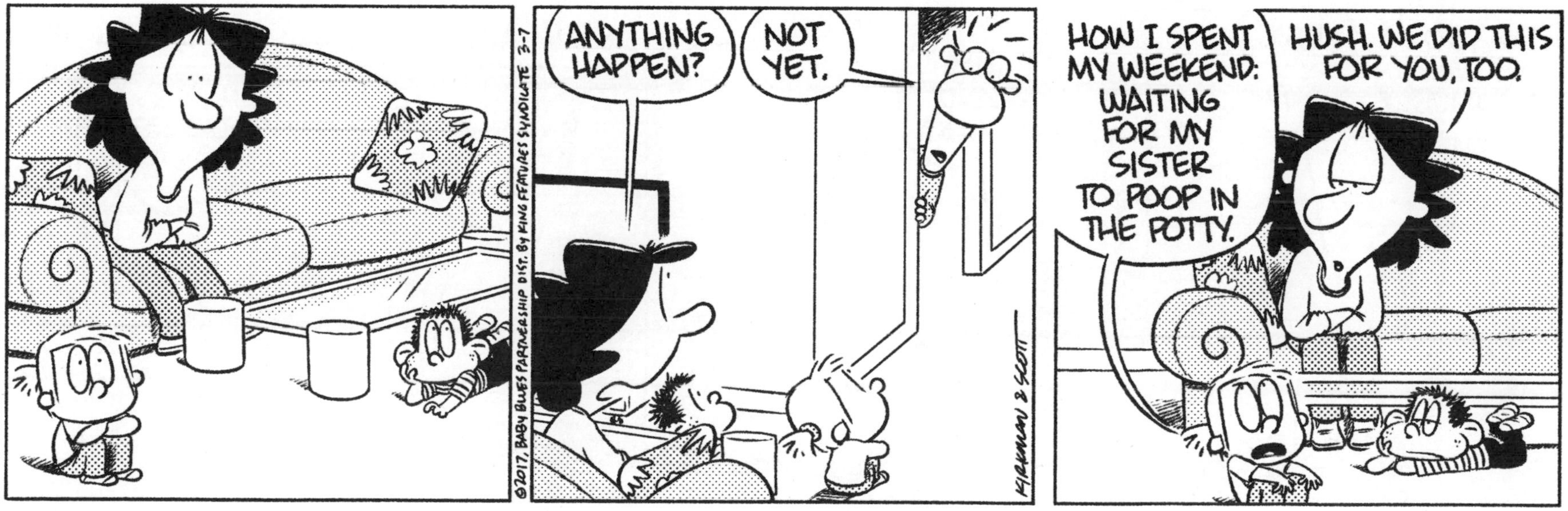
©2017, BABY BLUES PARTNERSHIP DIST. BY KING FEATURES SYNDICATE 3-7
ANYTHING HAPPEN?
NOT YET.
KIRKMAN & SCOTT
HOW I SPENT MY WEEKEND: WAITING FOR MY SISTER TO POOP IN THE POTTY.
HUSH. WE DID THIS FOR YOU, TOO.

Jerry: When I tell people that I'm a writer, I don't always tell them that I write about stuff like this.

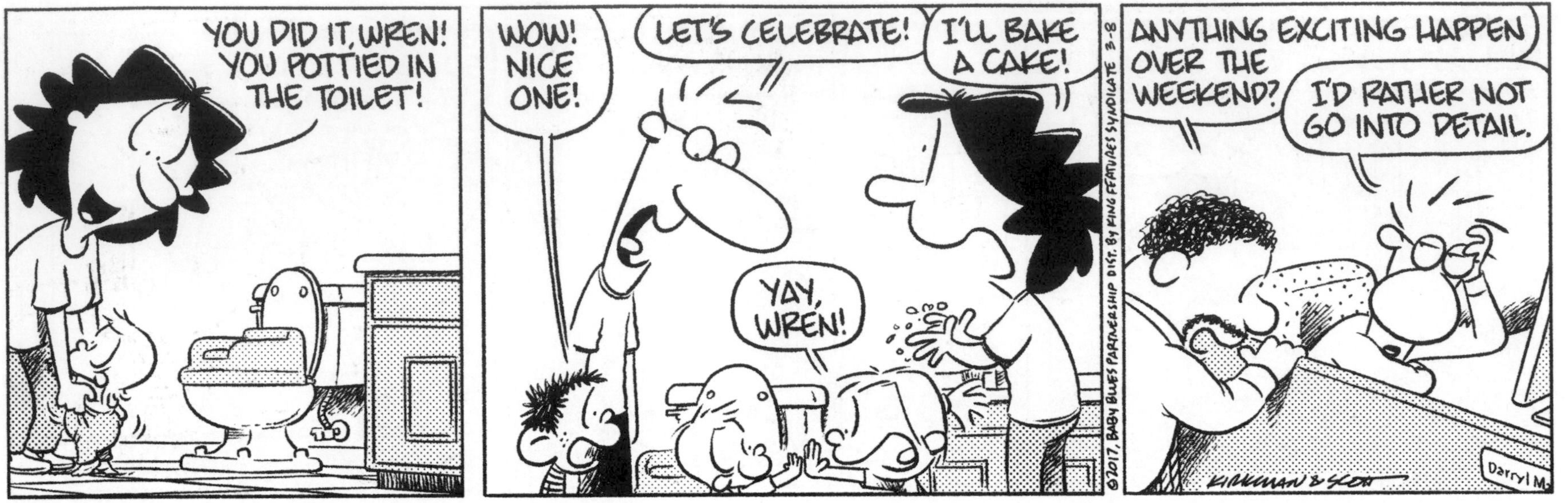
YOU DID IT, WREN! YOU POTTIED IN THE TOILET!
WOW! NICE ONE!
LET'S CELEBRATE!
I'LL BAKE A CAKE!
YAY, WREN!
©2017, BABY BLUES PARTNERSHIP DIST. BY KING FEATURES SYNDICATE 3-8
ANYTHING EXCITING HAPPEN OVER THE WEEKEND?
I'D RATHER NOT GO INTO DETAIL.
Darryl M.
KIRKMAN & SCOTT

Jerry: See why?

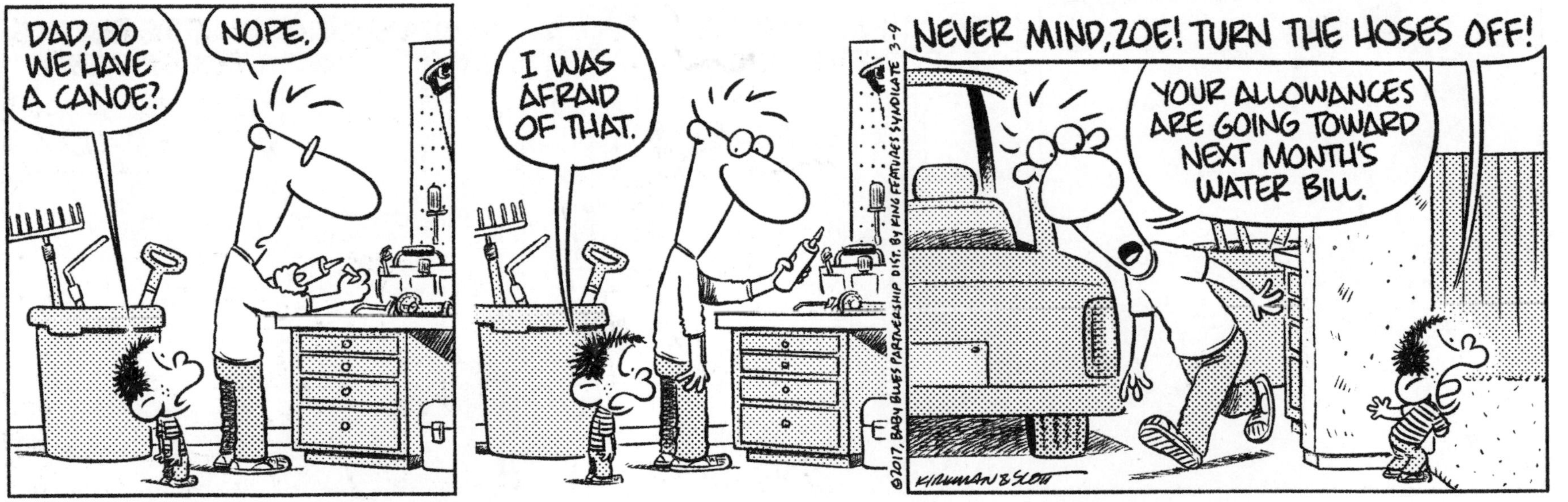
DAD, DO WE HAVE A CANOE?
NOPE.
I WAS AFRAID OF THAT.
©2017, BABY BLUES PARTNERSHIP DIST. BY KING FEATURES SYNDICATE 3-9
NEVER MIND, ZOE! TURN THE HOSES OFF!
YOUR ALLOWANCES ARE GOING TOWARD NEXT MONTH'S WATER BILL.
KIRKMAN & SCOTT

Rick: Parenting Lesson #473: Always question the question.

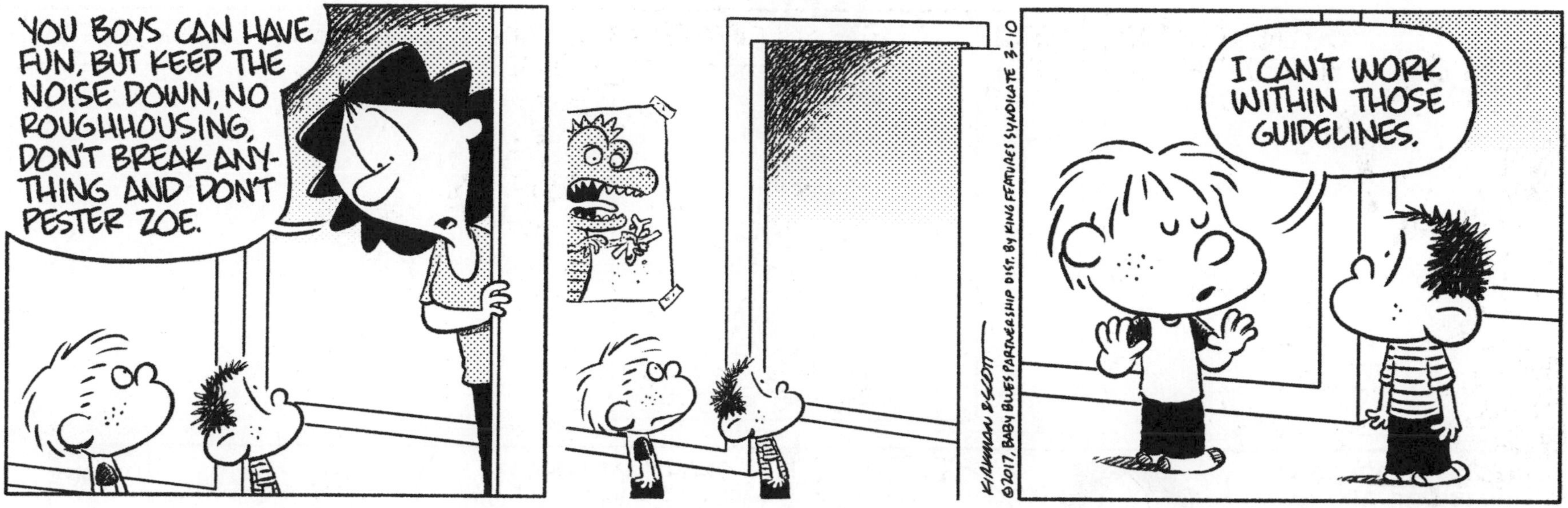
YOU BOYS CAN HAVE FUN, BUT KEEP THE NOISE DOWN, NO ROUGHHOUSING, DON'T BREAK ANYTHING AND DON'T PESTER ZOE.
KIRKMAN & SCOTT
©2017, BABY BLUES PARTNERSHIP DIST. BY KING FEATURES SYNDICATE 3-10
I CAN'T WORK WITHIN THOSE GUIDELINES.

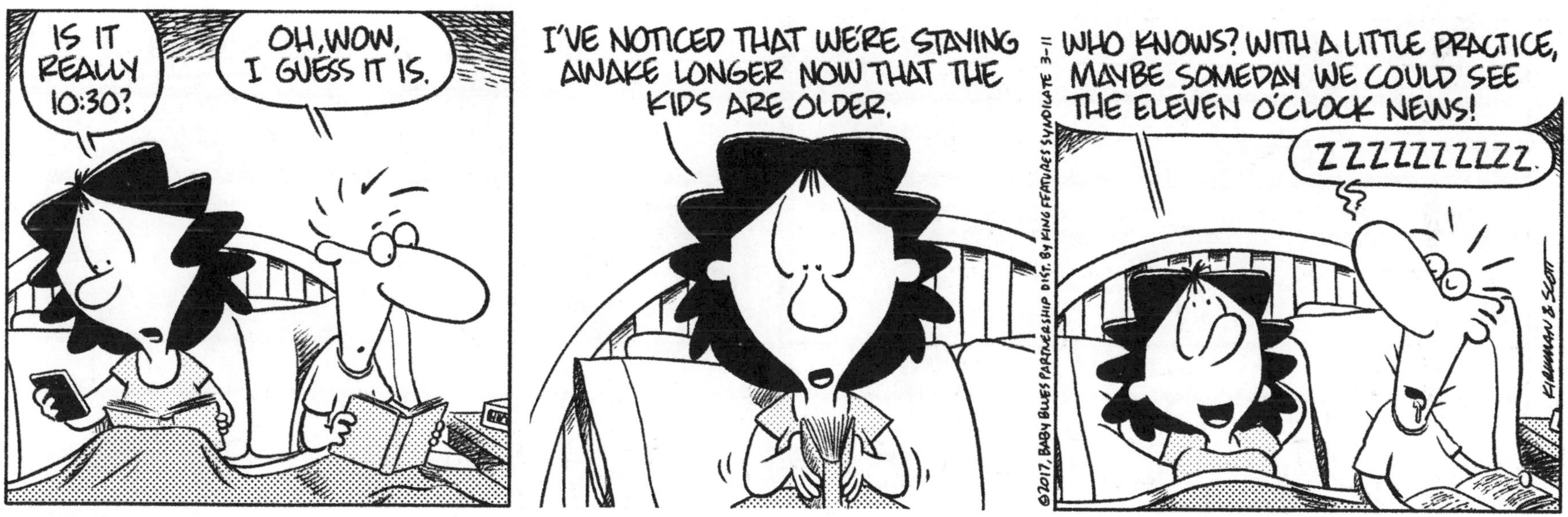
IS IT REALLY 10:30?
OH, WOW, I GUESS IT IS.
I'VE NOTICED THAT WE'RE STAYING AWAKE LONGER NOW THAT THE KIDS ARE OLDER.
©2017, BABY BLUES PARTNERSHIP DIST. BY KING FEATURES SYNDICATE 3-11
WHO KNOWS? WITH A LITTLE PRACTICE, MAYBE SOMEDAY WE COULD SEE THE ELEVEN O'CLOCK NEWS!
ZZZZZZZZZZ.
KIRKMAN & SCOTT

Jerry: A gal's gotta dream.

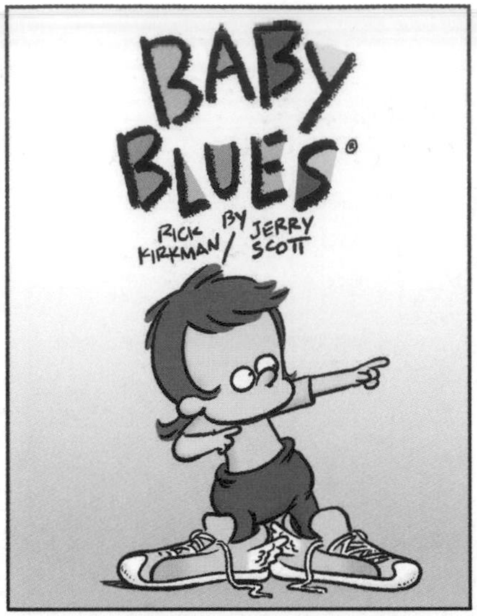
BABY BLUES®
BY
RICK KIRKMAN / JERRY SCOTT

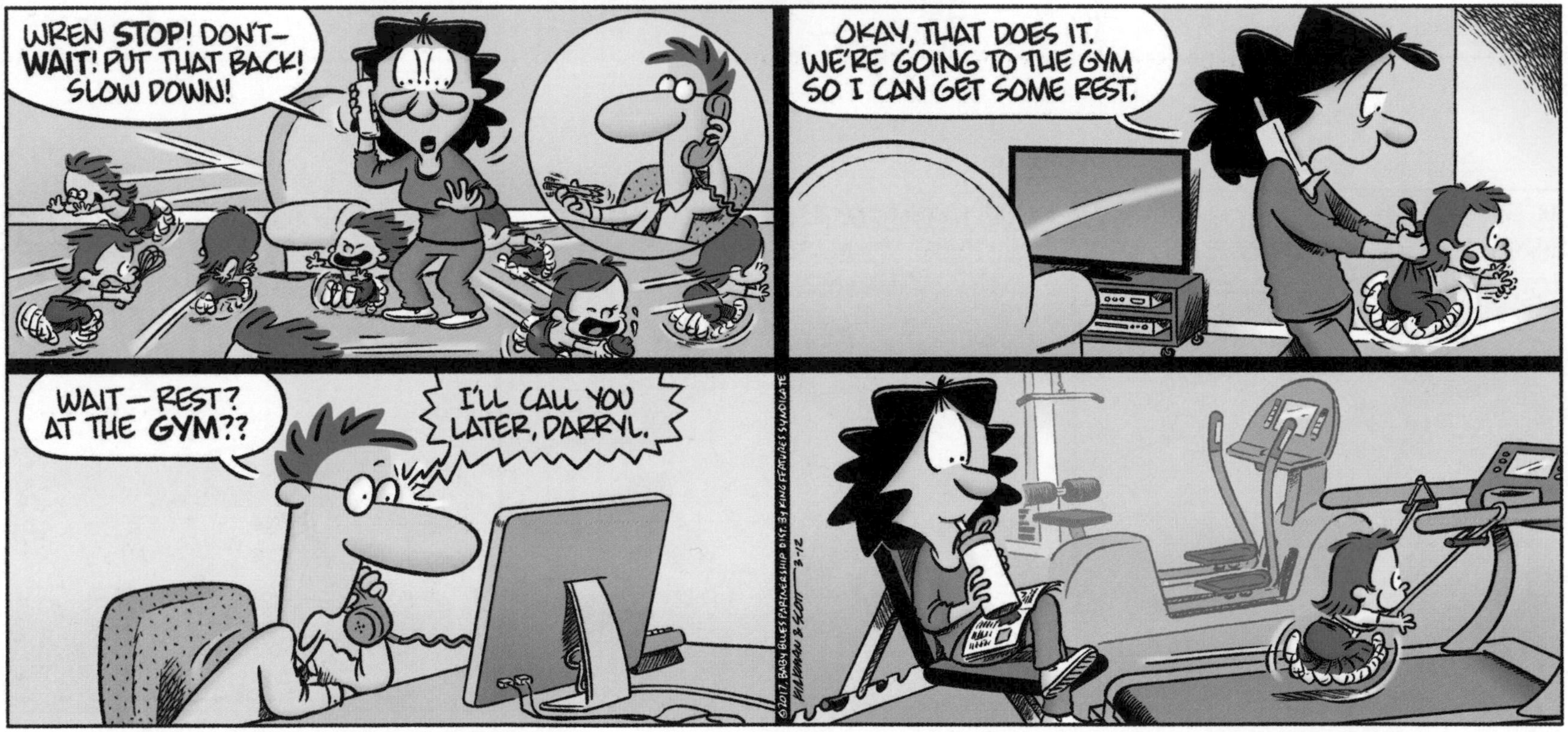
WREN STOP! DON'T— WAIT! PUT THAT BACK! SLOW DOWN!
OKAY, THAT DOES IT. WE'RE GOING TO THE GYM SO I CAN GET SOME REST.
WAIT— REST? AT THE GYM??
I'LL CALL YOU LATER, DARRYL.
©2017, BABY BLUES PARTNERSHIP DIST. BY KING FEATURES SYNDICATE
KIRKMAN & SCOTT 3-12

Rick: Business opportunity?

WHY ARE YOU RUBBING MOM'S BACK?
BECAUSE SHE LIKES IT.
MMM-HMMM...
BACK RUBS ARE JUST SOMETHING I DO FOR MOM.
KIRKMAN & SCOTT
©2017, BABY BLUES PARTNERSHIP DIST. BY KING FEATURES SYNDICATE 3-13
ESPECIALLY WHEN I LIE ON THE REMOTE AND REFUSE TO GET OFF UNTIL I GET ONE.
IT'S BASICALLY A HOSTAGE SITUATION.

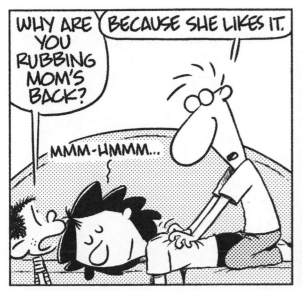

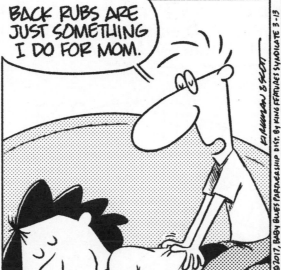

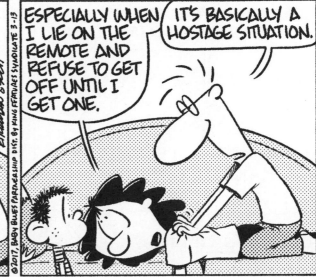

Jerry: Sometimes it's better to just pay the ransom.

OUR FINANCIAL ADVISOR SENT US THIS STATEMENT TODAY.
WHAT'S IT SAY?
IT LOOKS LIKE OUR RETIREMENT ACCOUNT IS MOVING IN THE RIGHT DIRECTION.
WELL, THAT'S GOOD NEWS!
©2017, BABY BLUES PARTNERSHIP DIST. BY KING FEATURES SYNDICATE 3-14
GLACIERS MOVE, TOO, DARRYL.
HEY, WHO WANTS TO RETIRE BEFORE AGE NINETY, ANYWAY?
KIRKMAN & SCOTT

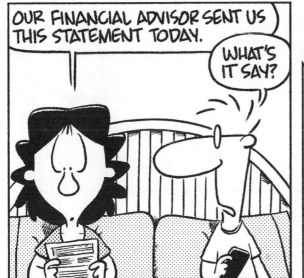

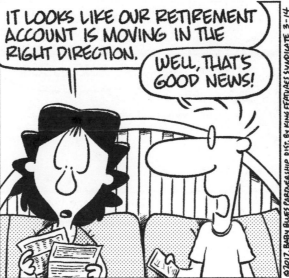

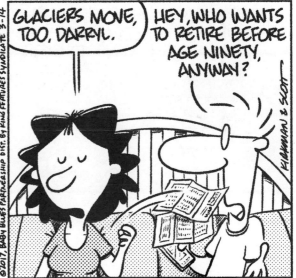

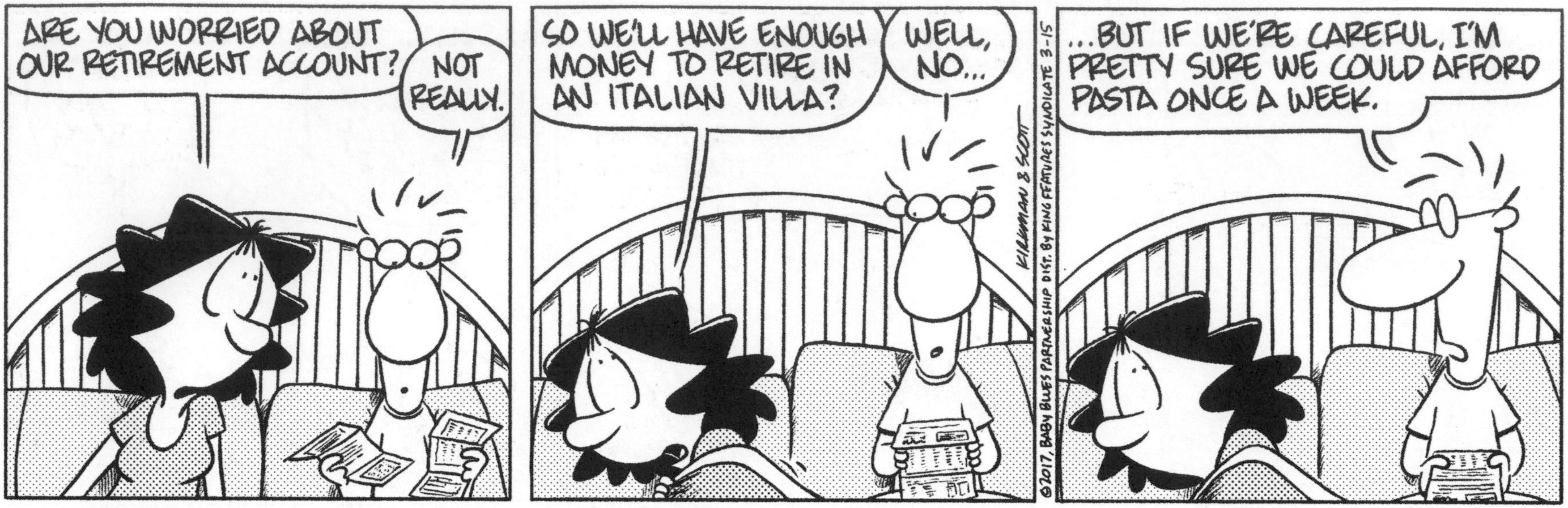
ARE YOU WORRIED ABOUT OUR RETIREMENT ACCOUNT?
NOT REALLY.
SO WE'LL HAVE ENOUGH MONEY TO RETIRE IN AN ITALIAN VILLA?
WELL, NO...
KIRKMAN & SCOTT
©2017, BABY BLUES PARTNERSHIP DIST. BY KING FEATURES SYNDICATE 3-15
...BUT IF WE'RE CAREFUL, I'M PRETTY SURE WE COULD AFFORD PASTA ONCE A WEEK.

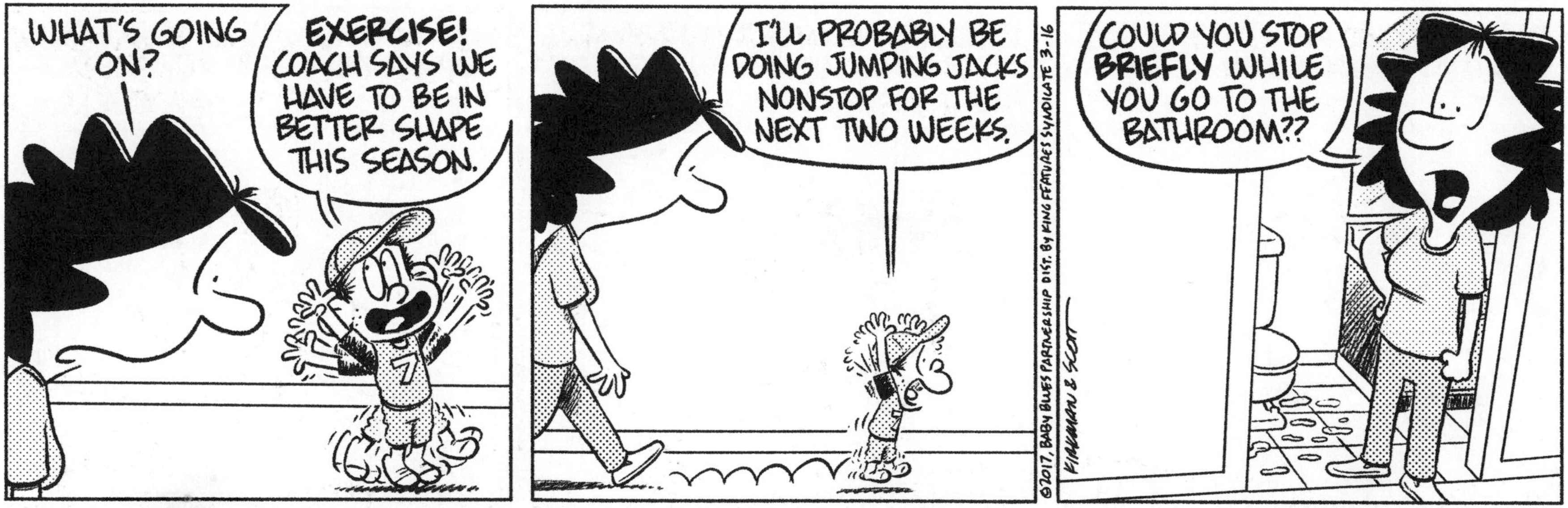
WHAT'S GOING ON?
EXERCISE! COACH SAYS WE HAVE TO BE IN BETTER SHAPE THIS SEASON.
I'LL PROBABLY BE DOING JUMPING JACKS NONSTOP FOR THE NEXT TWO WEEKS.
©2017, BABY BLUES PARTNERSHIP DIST. BY KING FEATURES SYNDICATE 3-16
KIRKMAN & SCOTT
COULD YOU STOP BRIEFLY WHILE YOU GO TO THE BATHROOM??

Rick: Did the editors know what's on that floor? In the color version, the colorist obviously knew.

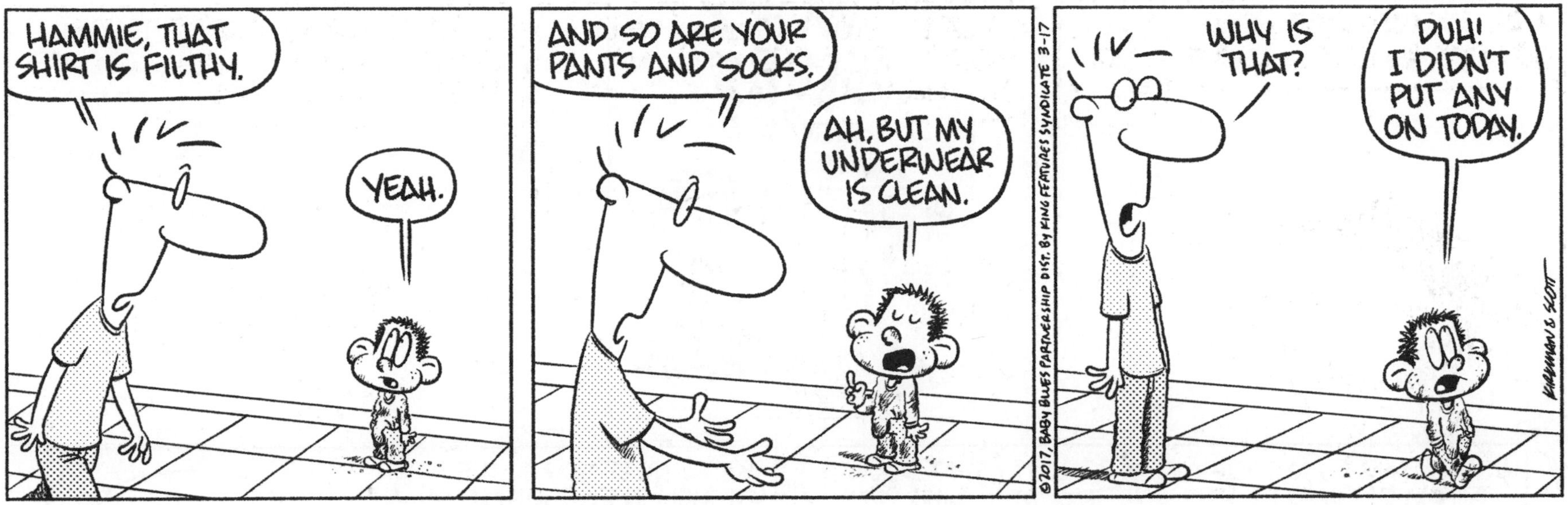
HAMMIE, THAT SHIRT IS FILTHY.
YEAH.
AND SO ARE YOUR PANTS AND SOCKS.
AH, BUT MY UNDERWEAR IS CLEAN.
©2017, BABY BLUES PARTNERSHIP DIST. BY KING FEATURES SYNDICATE 3-17
WHY IS THAT?
DUH! I DIDN'T PUT ANY ON TODAY.
KIRKMAN & SCOTT

Jerry: Hammie offers a glimpse into my childhood. Yeah, I'm glad that's over, too.

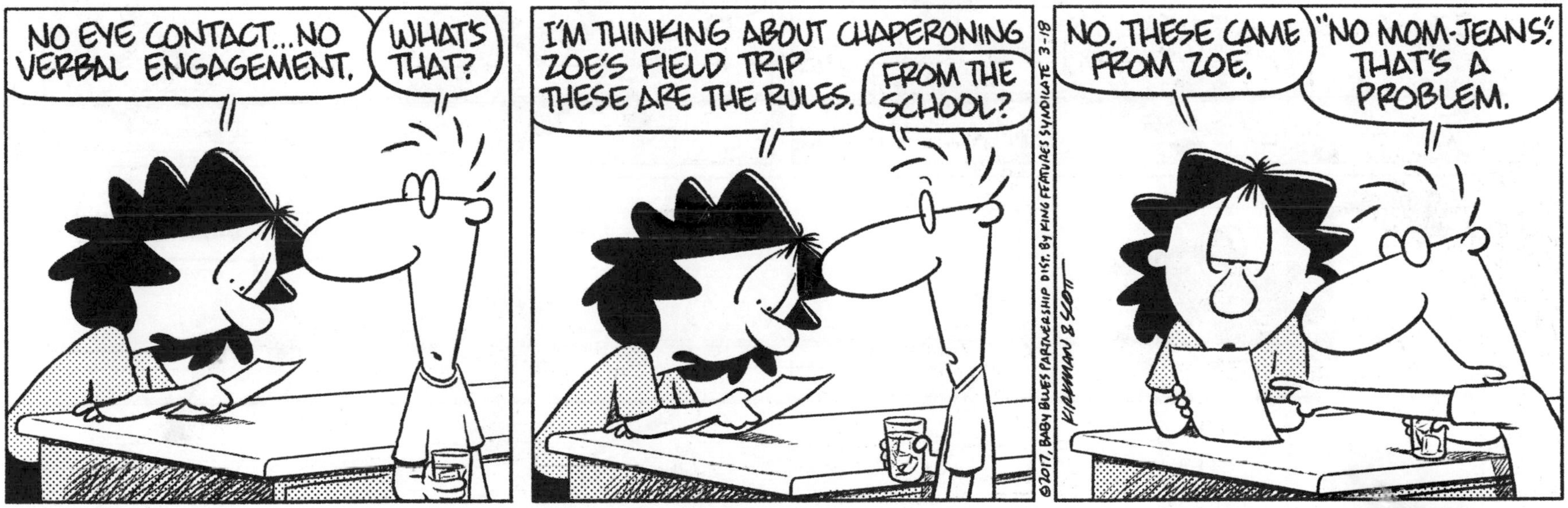
NO EYE CONTACT...NO VERBAL ENGAGEMENT.
WHAT'S THAT?
I'M THINKING ABOUT CHAPERONING ZOE'S FIELD TRIP THESE ARE THE RULES.
FROM THE SCHOOL?
©2017, BABY BLUES PARTNERSHIP DIST. BY KING FEATURES SYNDICATE 3-18
KIRKMAN & SCOTT
NO. THESE CAME FROM ZOE.
"NO MOM-JEANS." THAT'S A PROBLEM.

Jerry: Parent-chaperoned field trips can involve some pretty hard-nosed negotiations.

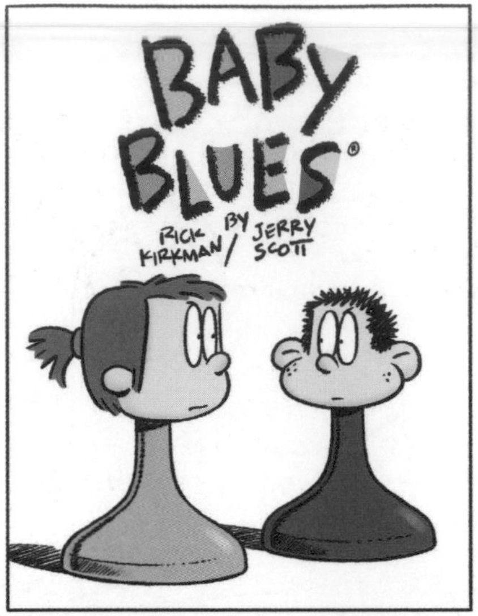
BABY BLUES®
BY RICK KIRKMAN / JERRY SCOTT

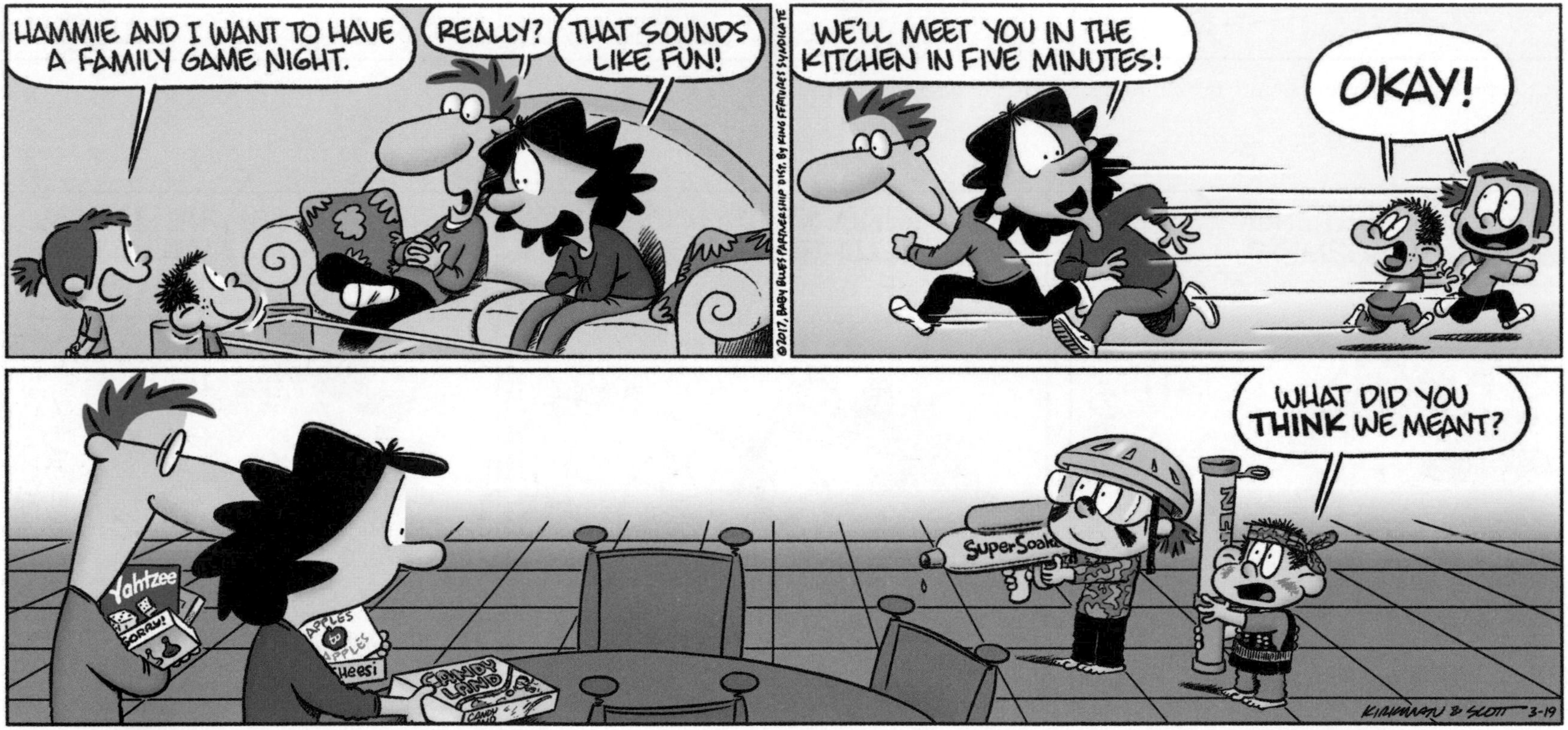
HAMMIE AND I WANT TO HAVE A FAMILY GAME NIGHT.
REALLY?
THAT SOUNDS LIKE FUN!
©2017, BABY BLUES PARTNERSHIP DIST. BY KING FEATURES SYNDICATE
WE'LL MEET YOU IN THE KITCHEN IN FIVE MINUTES!
OKAY!
Yahtzee
SORRY!
APPLES to APPLES
CANDY LAND
Super Soaker
WHAT DID YOU THINK WE MEANT?
KIRKMAN & SCOTT 3-19

Rick: I'm with the kids.

HOW'S IT GOING AT HOME TODAY?
PRETTY GOOD. JUST THINKING ABOUT DINNER AND—
MOM! MOM! MOM! MOM! MOM!
©2017, BABY BLUES PARTNERSHIP DIST. BY KING FEATURES SYNDICATE 3-20
DO YOU HAVE TO GO?
YEAH. THE FIVE-MOMMERS ARE USUALLY SERIOUS.
KIRKMAN & SCOTT

WHATCHA' DOING THERE?
I'M THINKING ABOUT WRITING A CHILDREN'S BOOK, BUT I DON'T HAVE ANY IDEAS.
WELL, THEY SAY "WRITE WHAT YOU KNOW."
©2017, BABY BLUES PARTNERSHIP DIST. BY KING FEATURES SYNDICATE 3-21
KIRKMAN & SCOTT
WHAT RHYMES WITH "WHINING"?

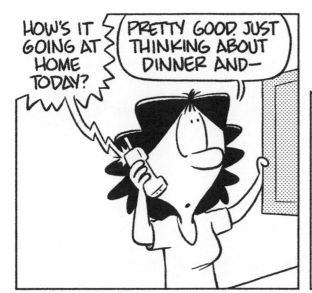

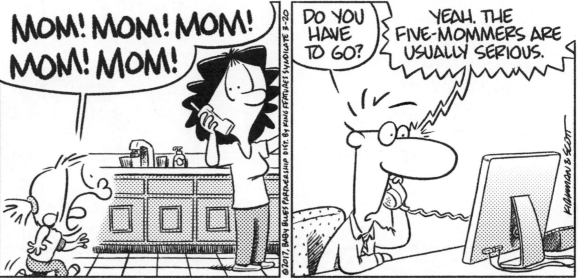

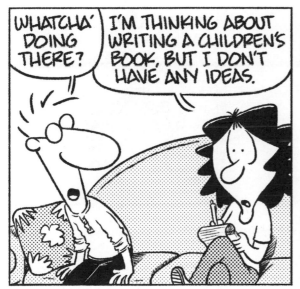

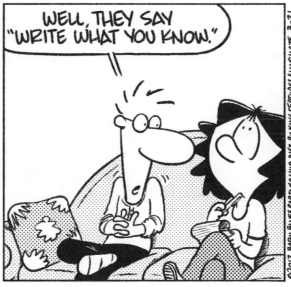

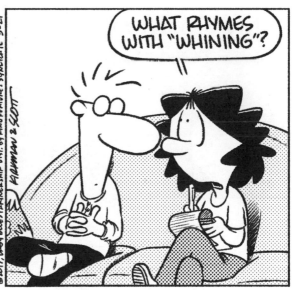

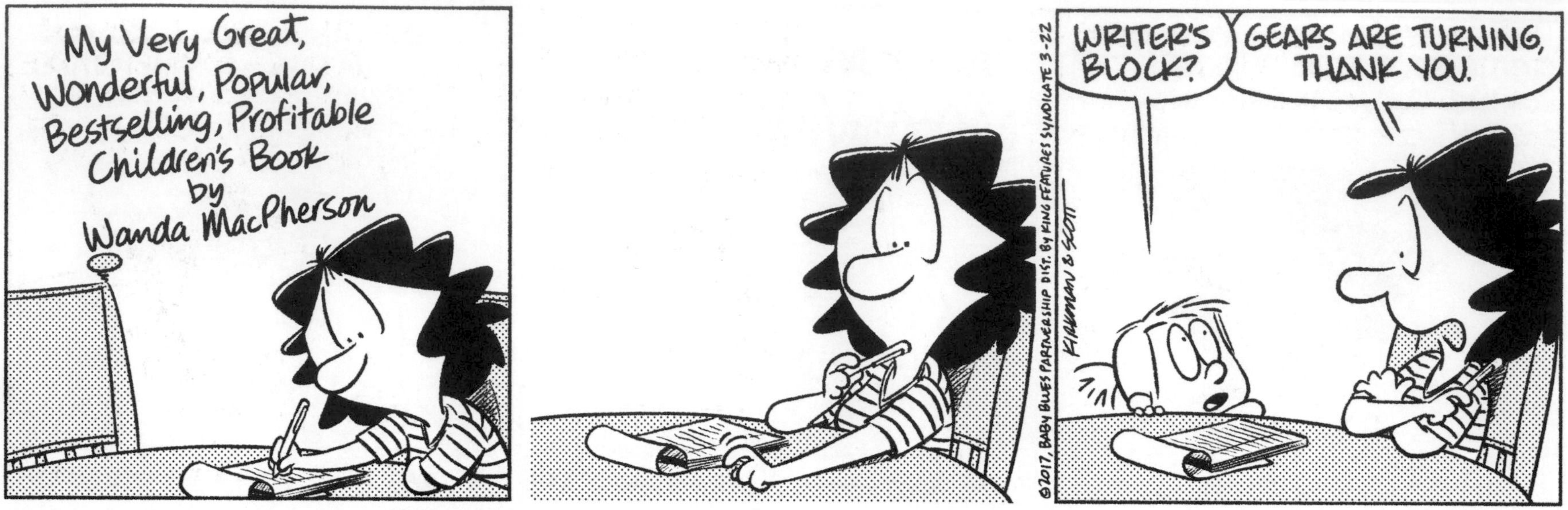
My Very Great, Wonderful, Popular, Bestselling, Profitable Children's Book by Wanda MacPherson
©2017, BABY BLUES PARTNERSHIP DIST. BY KING FEATURES SYNDICATE 3-22
KIRKMAN & SCOTT
WRITER'S BLOCK?
GEARS ARE TURNING, THANK YOU.

Jerry: Could somebody really write a book with that title? Asking for a friend.

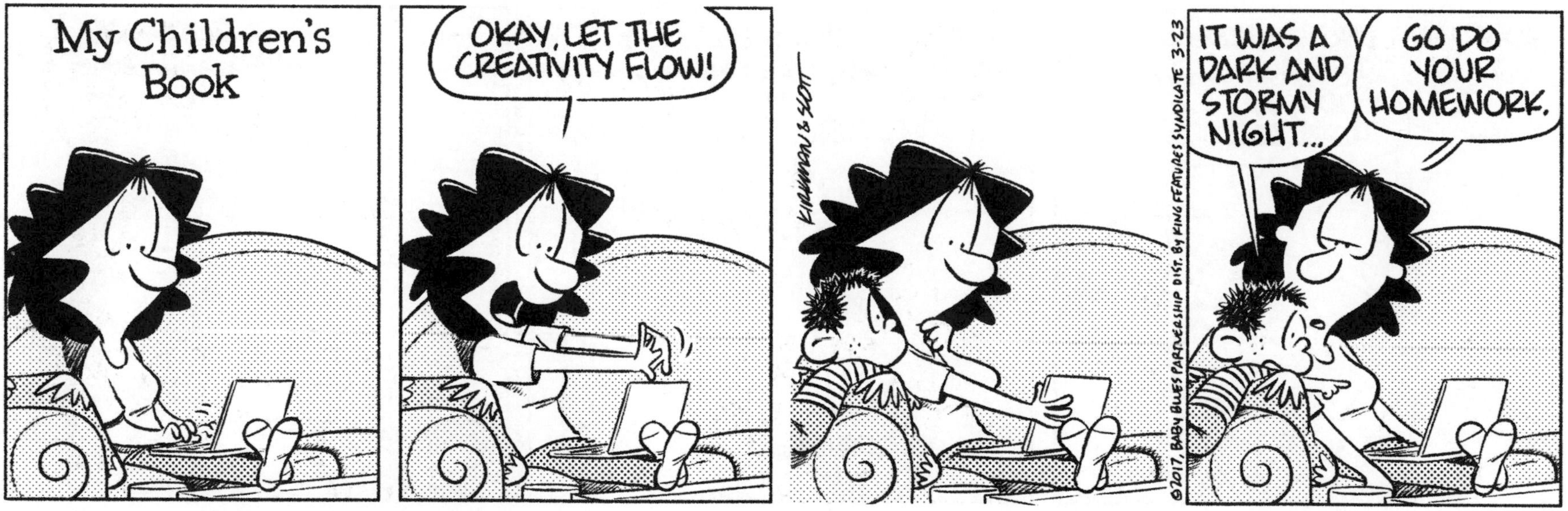
My Children's Book
OKAY, LET THE CREATIVITY FLOW!
KIRKMAN & SCOTT
©2017, BABY BLUES PARTNERSHIP DIST. BY KING FEATURES SYNDICATE 3-23
IT WAS A DARK AND STORMY NIGHT...
GO DO YOUR HOMEWORK.

Rick: Maybe Wanda needs to sit on top of a doghouse to get the ideas flowing.

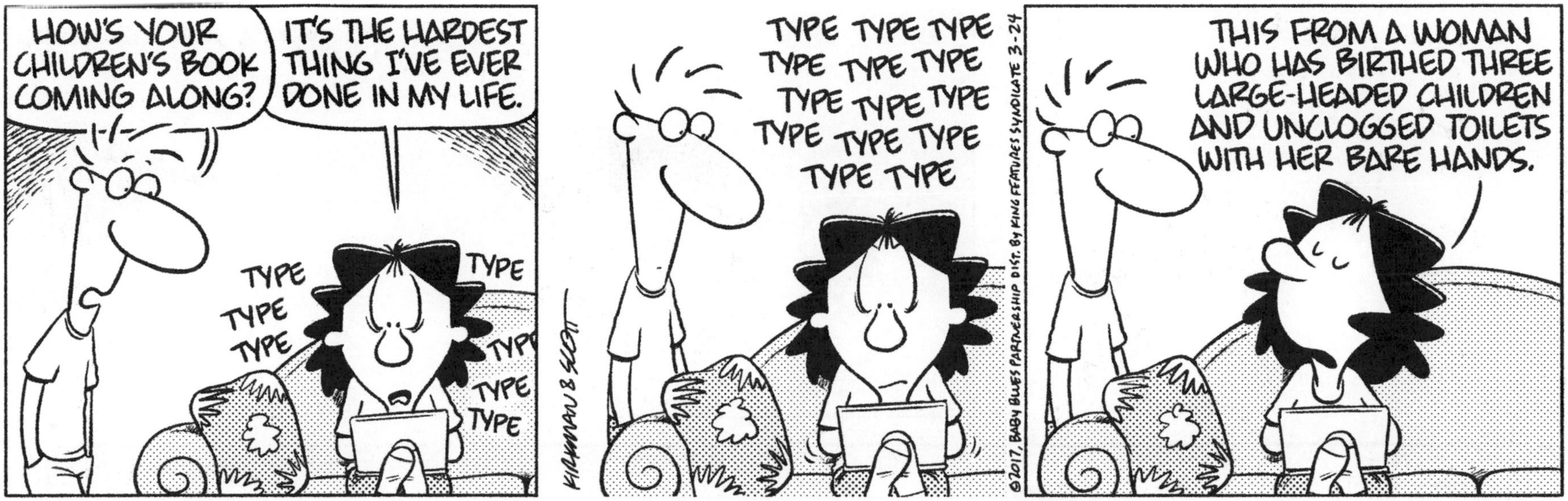
HOW'S YOUR CHILDREN'S BOOK COMING ALONG?
IT'S THE HARDEST THING I'VE EVER DONE IN MY LIFE.
TYPE TYPE TYPE
TYPE TYPE TYPE TYPE
KIRKMAN & SCOTT
TYPE TYPE TYPE TYPE TYPE TYPE TYPE TYPE TYPE TYPE TYPE
©2017, BABY BLUES PARTNERSHIP DIST. BY KING FEATURES SYNDICATE 3-24
THIS FROM A WOMAN WHO HAS BIRTHED THREE LARGE-HEADED CHILDREN AND UNCLOGGED TOILETS WITH HER BARE HANDS.

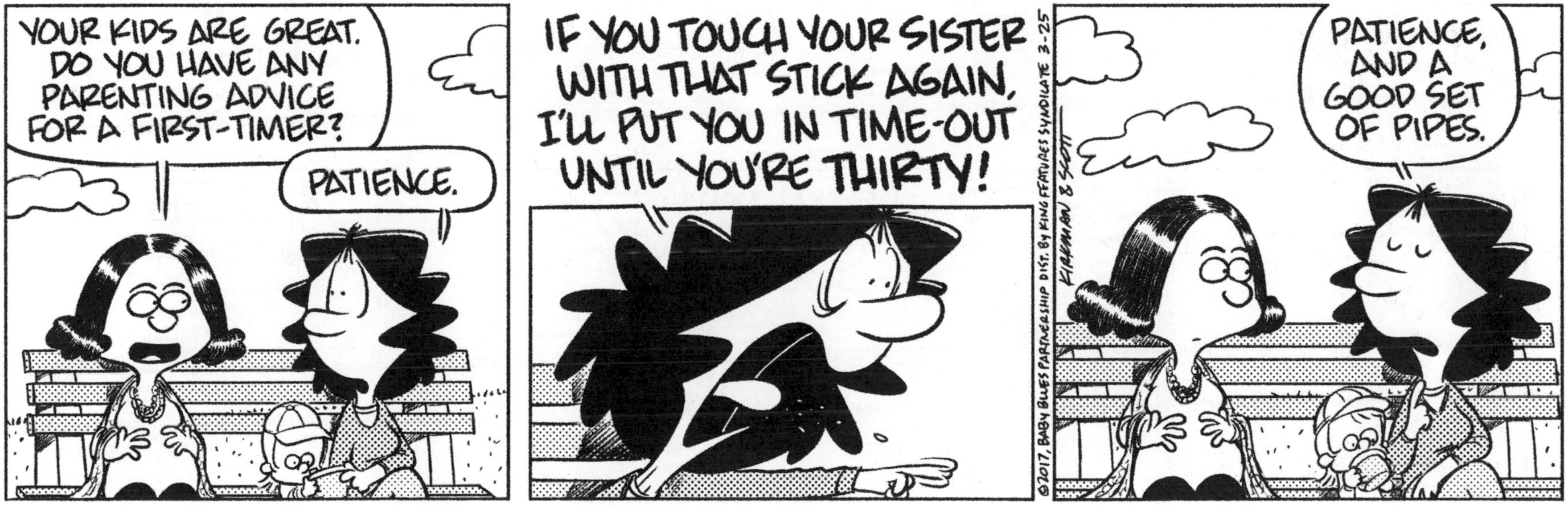
YOUR KIDS ARE GREAT. DO YOU HAVE ANY PARENTING ADVICE FOR A FIRST-TIMER?
PATIENCE.
IF YOU TOUCH YOUR SISTER WITH THAT STICK AGAIN, I'LL PUT YOU IN TIME-OUT UNTIL YOU'RE THIRTY!
©2017, BABY BLUES PARTNERSHIP DIST. BY KING FEATURES SYNDICATE 3-25
KIRKMAN & SCOTT
PATIENCE, AND A GOOD SET OF PIPES.

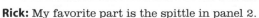

Rick: My favorite part is the spittle in panel 2.

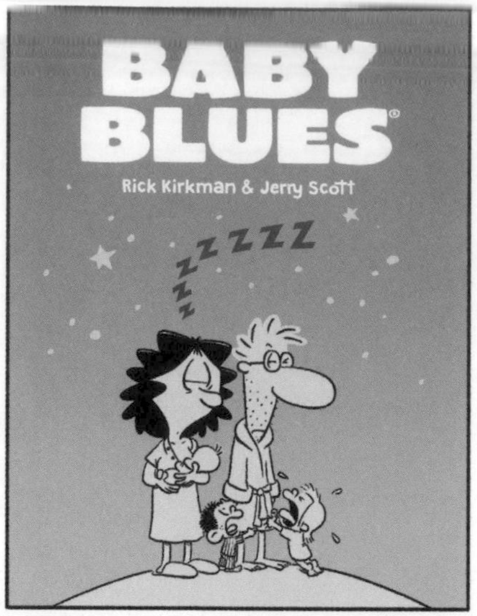
BABY BLUES®
Rick Kirkman & Jerry Scott
ZZZZZZZ

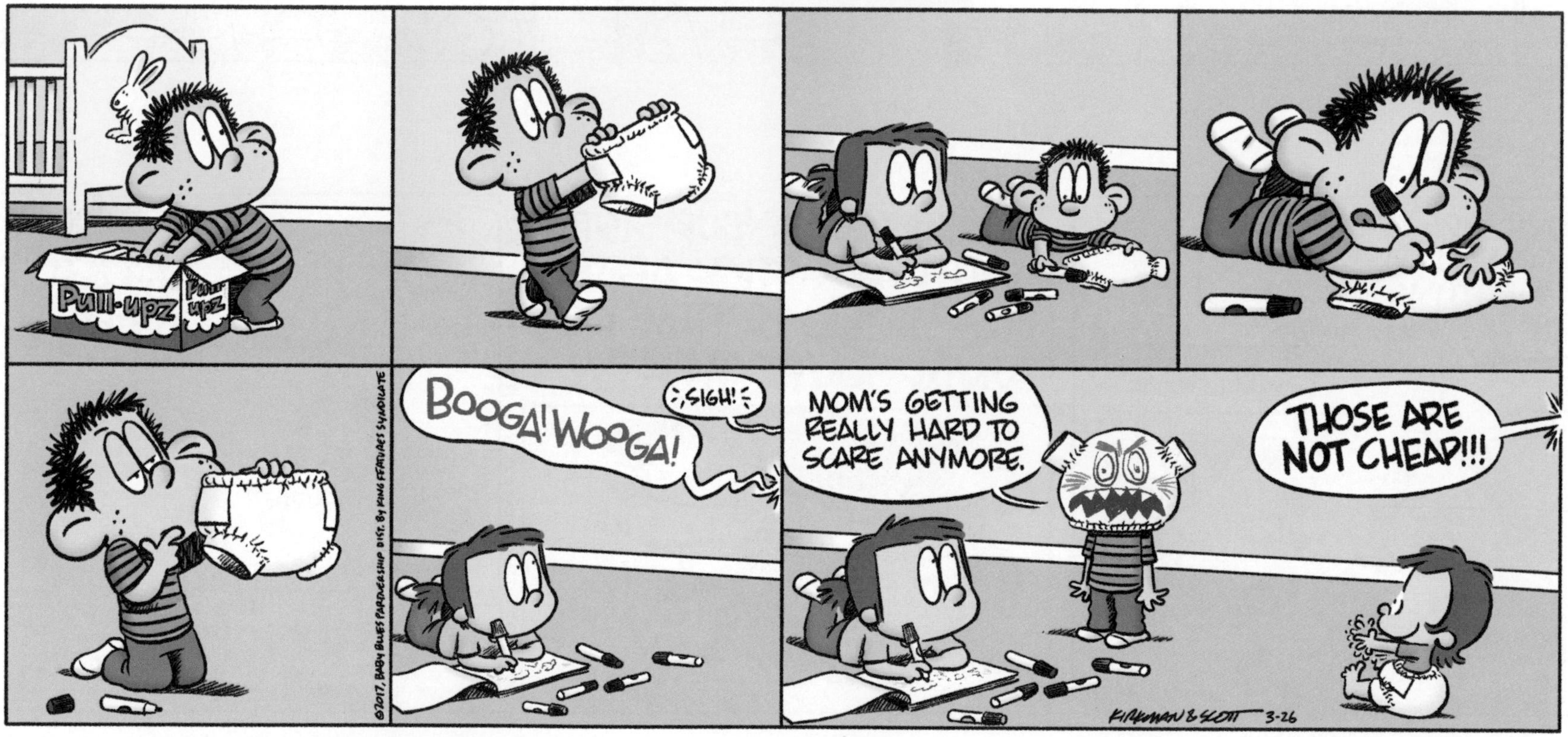
Pull-upz
BOOGA! WOOGA!
SIGH!
MOM'S GETTING REALLY HARD TO SCARE ANYMORE.
THOSE ARE NOT CHEAP!!!
©2017, BABY BLUES PARTNERSHIP DIST. BY KING FEATURES SYNDICATE
KIRKMAN & SCOTT 3-26

Rick: This is the story Hammie will tell in his Oscar acceptance speech for Best Makeup.

MOM, GUESS WHAT HAMMIE DID.
ZOE, DON'T TATTLE ON YOUR BROTHER.
HE SPILLED PAINT IN THE GARAGE.
©2017, BABY BLUES PARTNERSHIP DIST. BY KING FEATURES SYNDICATE 3-27
ZOE!
WHAT? I WAS JUST THINKING OUT LOUD!
KIRKMAN & SCOTT

Jerry: Zoe wins on a technicality.

HURRY! WE'LL BE LATE FOR SCHOOL!
SLAM!
SCREECH
©2017, BABY BLUES PARTNERSHIP DIST. BY KING FEATURES SYNDICATE 3-28
HOW LONG BEFORE SHE NOTICES OUR ESCAPE?
LONG ENOUGH TO TOAST SOME WAFFLES, I HOPE.
KIRKMAN & SCOTT

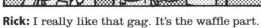

Rick: I really like that gag. It's the waffle part.

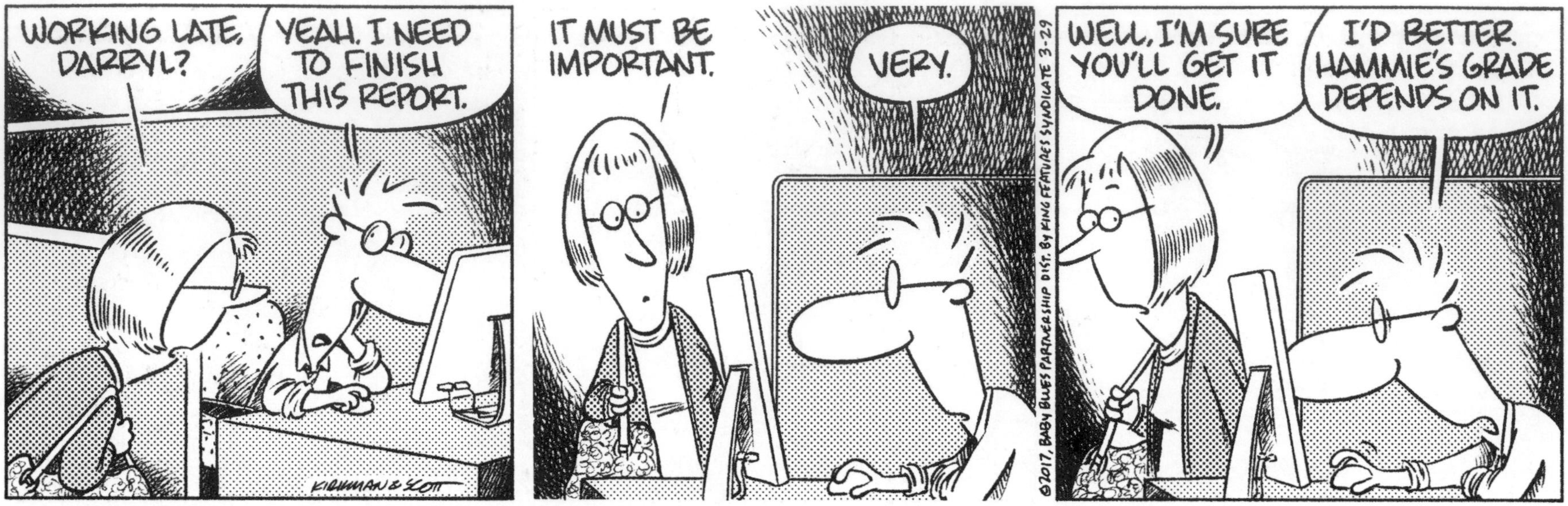
WORKING LATE, DARRYL?
YEAH. I NEED TO FINISH THIS REPORT.
IT MUST BE IMPORTANT.
VERY.
WELL, I'M SURE YOU'LL GET IT DONE.
I'D BETTER. HAMMIE'S GRADE DEPENDS ON IT.
KIRKMAN & SCOTT
©2017, BABY BLUES PARTNERSHIP DIST. BY KING FEATURES SYNDICATE 3-29

Jerry: Elementary school is harder the second time around.

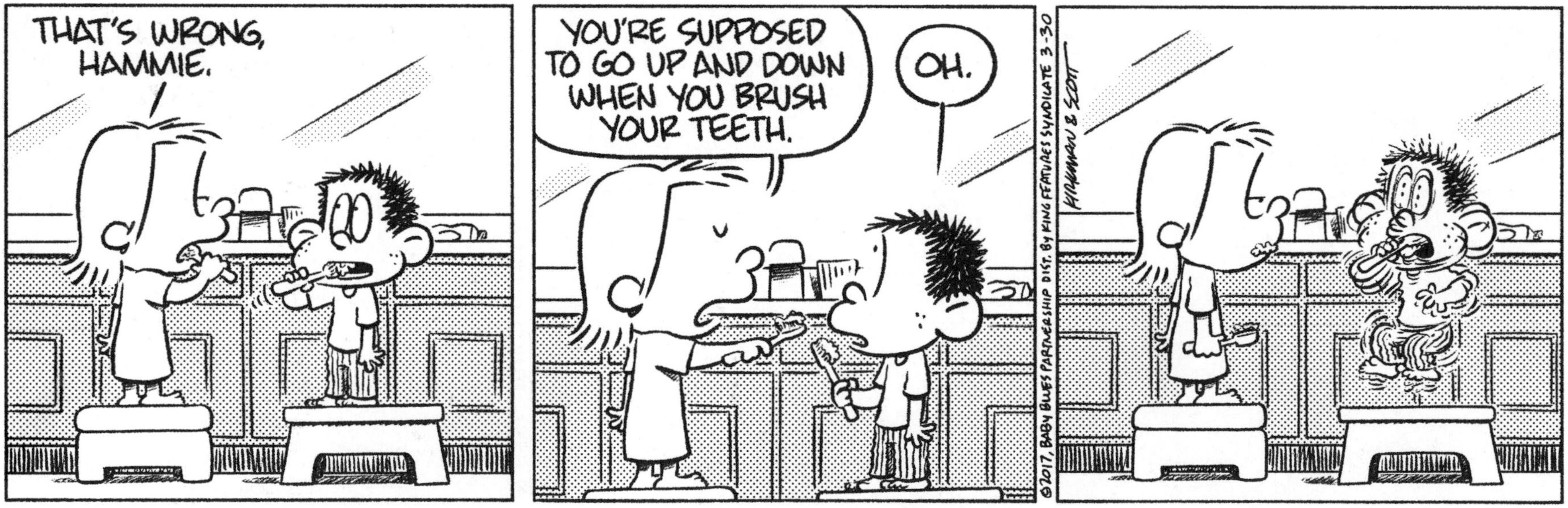
THAT'S WRONG, HAMMIE.
YOU'RE SUPPOSED TO GO UP AND DOWN WHEN YOU BRUSH YOUR TEETH.
OH.
©2017, BABY BLUES PARTNERSHIP DIST. BY KING FEATURES SYNDICATE 3-30
KIRKMAN & SCOTT

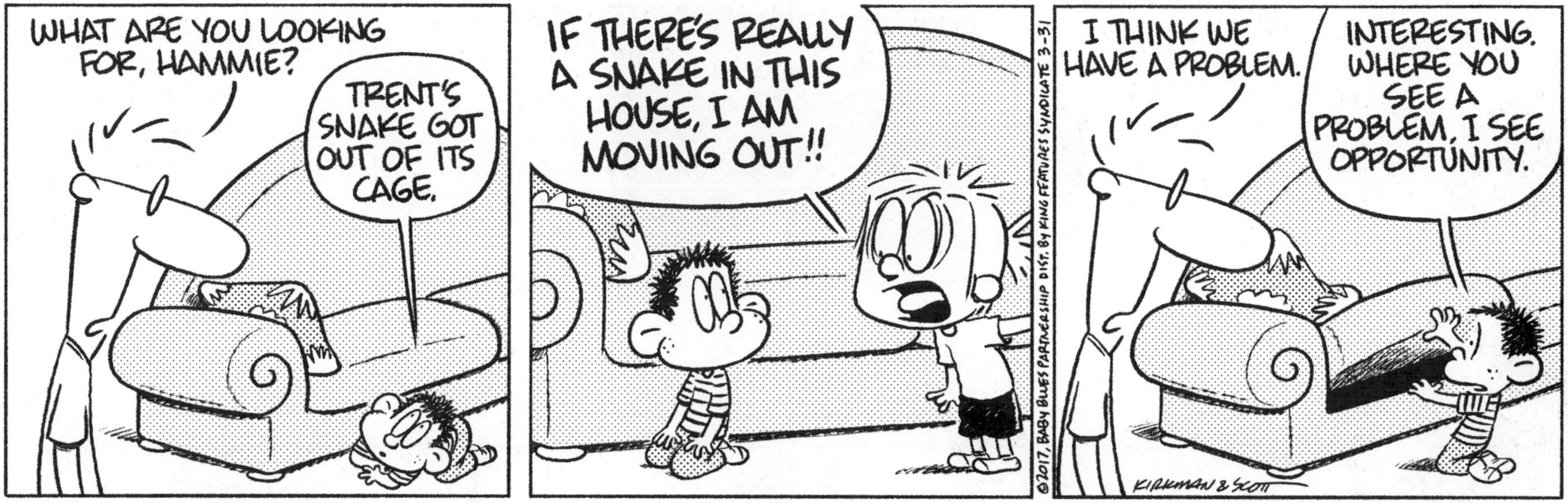
WHAT ARE YOU LOOKING FOR, HAMMIE?
TRENT'S SNAKE GOT OUT OF ITS CAGE.
IF THERE'S REALLY A SNAKE IN THIS HOUSE, I AM MOVING OUT!!
©2017, BABY BLUES PARTNERSHIP DIST. BY KING FEATURES SYNDICATE 3-31
I THINK WE HAVE A PROBLEM.
INTERESTING. WHERE YOU SEE A PROBLEM, I SEE OPPORTUNITY.
KIRKMAN & SCOTT

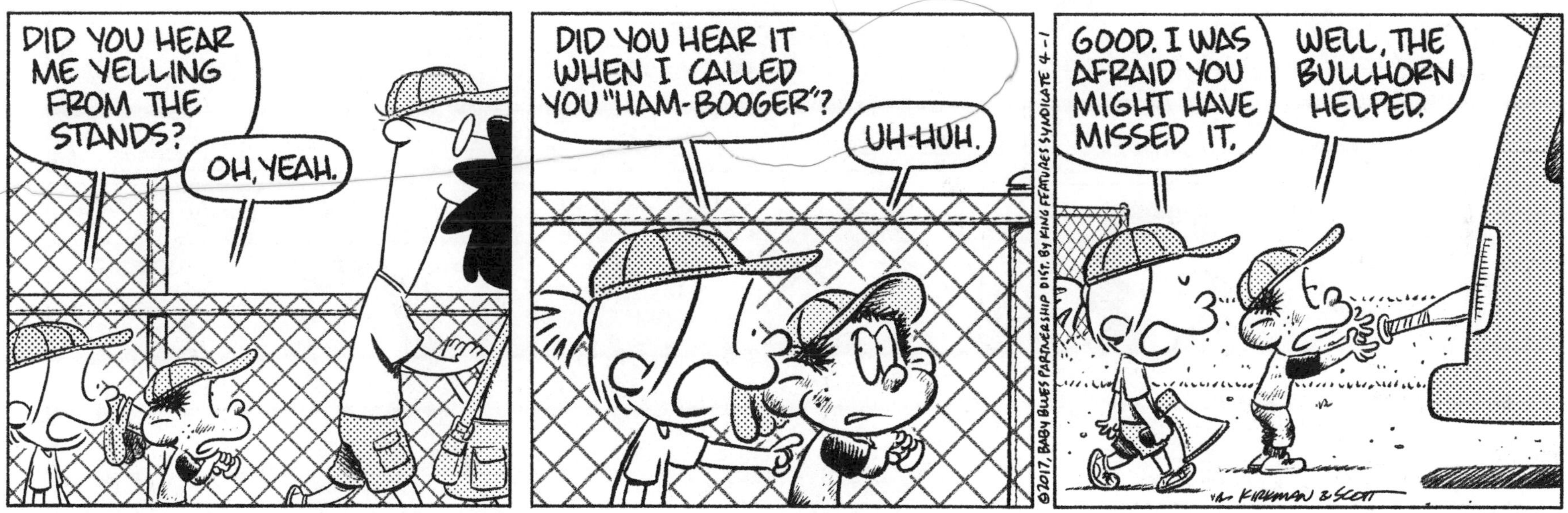
DID YOU HEAR ME YELLING FROM THE STANDS?
OH, YEAH.
DID YOU HEAR IT WHEN I CALLED YOU "HAM-BOOGER"?
UH-HUH.
©2017, BABY BLUES PARTNERSHIP DIST. BY KING FEATURES SYNDICATE 4-1
GOOD. I WAS AFRAID YOU MIGHT HAVE MISSED IT.
WELL, THE BULLHORN HELPED.
KIRKMAN & SCOTT

Jerry: A good heckler doesn't take chances.

BABY BLUES
Rick Kirkman & Jerry Scott
ZZZZZZZZ

SMOOCH!
©2017, BABY BLUES PARTNERSHIP DIST. BY KING FEATURES SYNDICATE
SORRY. I NEEDED A NON-MOM MOMENT.
GLAD TO BE OF ASSISTANCE!
KIRKMAN & SCOTT
4-2

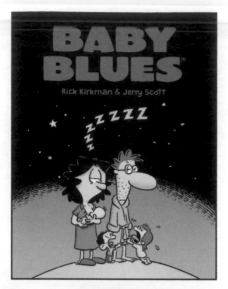

Jerry: Sometimes you just gotta take a break from parenting to do a little adulting.

MOM, HAMMIE IS DELIBERATELY ANNOYING ME!
OH? HOW?
Goldie
HE COPIES EVERYTHING I DO!
HM.
Goldie
©2017, BABY BLUES PARTNERSHIP DIST. BY KING FEATURES SYNDICATE 4-3
HOW CAN I GET HIM TO STOP??
HAVE YOU TRIED WIPING YOUR NOSE OR CLEANING YOUR ROOM?
Goldie
KIRKMAN & SCOTT

WORKING ON TAXES, HUH?
YES.
ANYTHING I CAN DO TO HELP?
JUST GIVE ME SOME PEACE AND QUIET.
©2017, BABY BLUES PARTNERSHIP DIST. BY KING FEATURES SYNDICATE 4-4
ZOE!
IT WAS DAD'S IDEA.
KIRKMAN & SCOTT

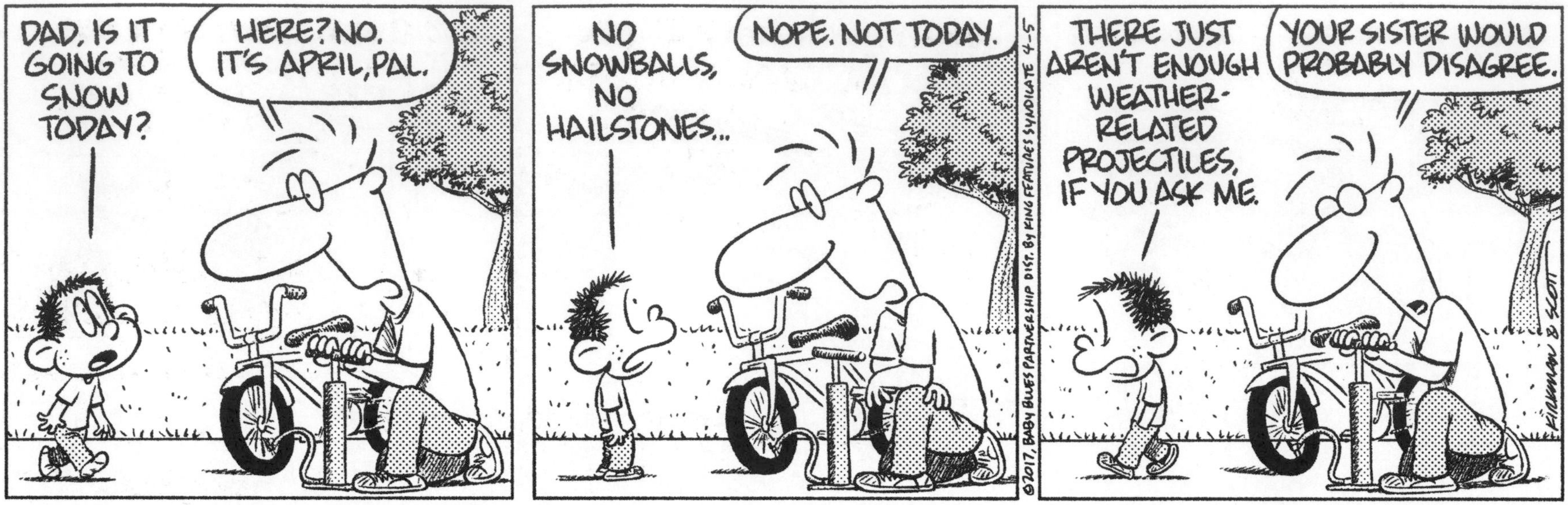
DAD, IS IT GOING TO SNOW TODAY?
HERE? NO. IT'S APRIL, PAL.
NO SNOWBALLS, NO HAILSTONES...
NOPE. NOT TODAY.
©2017, BABY BLUES PARTNERSHIP DIST. BY KING FEATURES SYNDICATE 4-5
THERE JUST AREN'T ENOUGH WEATHER-RELATED PROJECTILES, IF YOU ASK ME.
YOUR SISTER WOULD PROBABLY DISAGREE.
KIRKMAN & SCOTT

Jerry: That's the trouble with nice weather—nothing to throw.

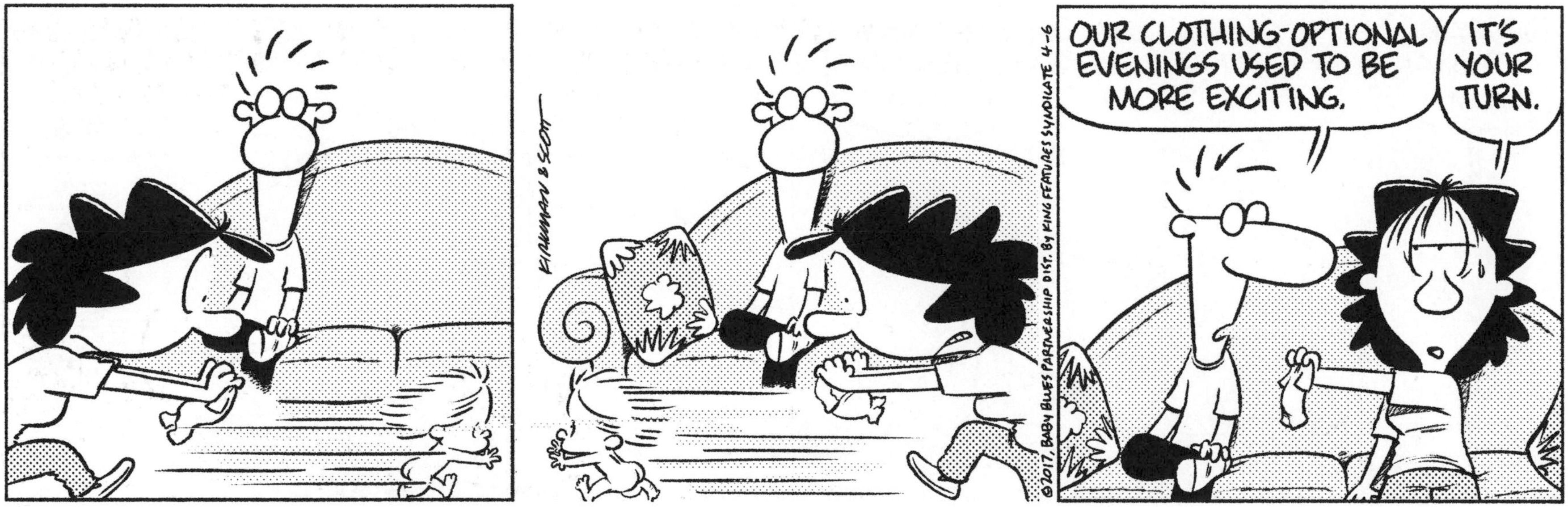
KIRKMAN & SCOTT
©2017, BABY BLUES PARTNERSHIP DIST. BY KING FEATURES SYNDICATE 4-6
OUR CLOTHING-OPTIONAL EVENINGS USED TO BE MORE EXCITING.
IT'S YOUR TURN.

Rick: Nicely put.

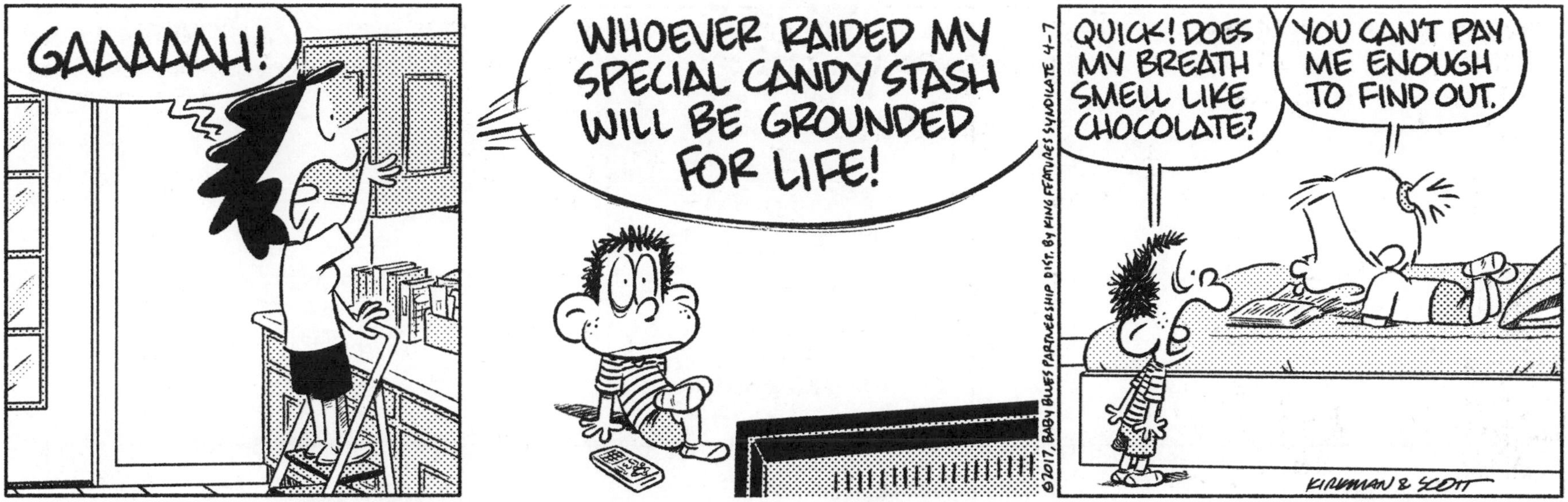
GAAAAAH!
WHOEVER RAIDED MY SPECIAL CANDY STASH WILL BE GROUNDED FOR LIFE!
QUICK! DOES MY BREATH SMELL LIKE CHOCOLATE?
YOU CAN'T PAY ME ENOUGH TO FIND OUT.
©2017, BABY BLUES PARTNERSHIP DIST. BY KING FEATURES SYNDICATE 4-7
KIRKMAN & SCOTT

Rick: There's something I find very satisfying about Jerry telling only the middle of the story here.

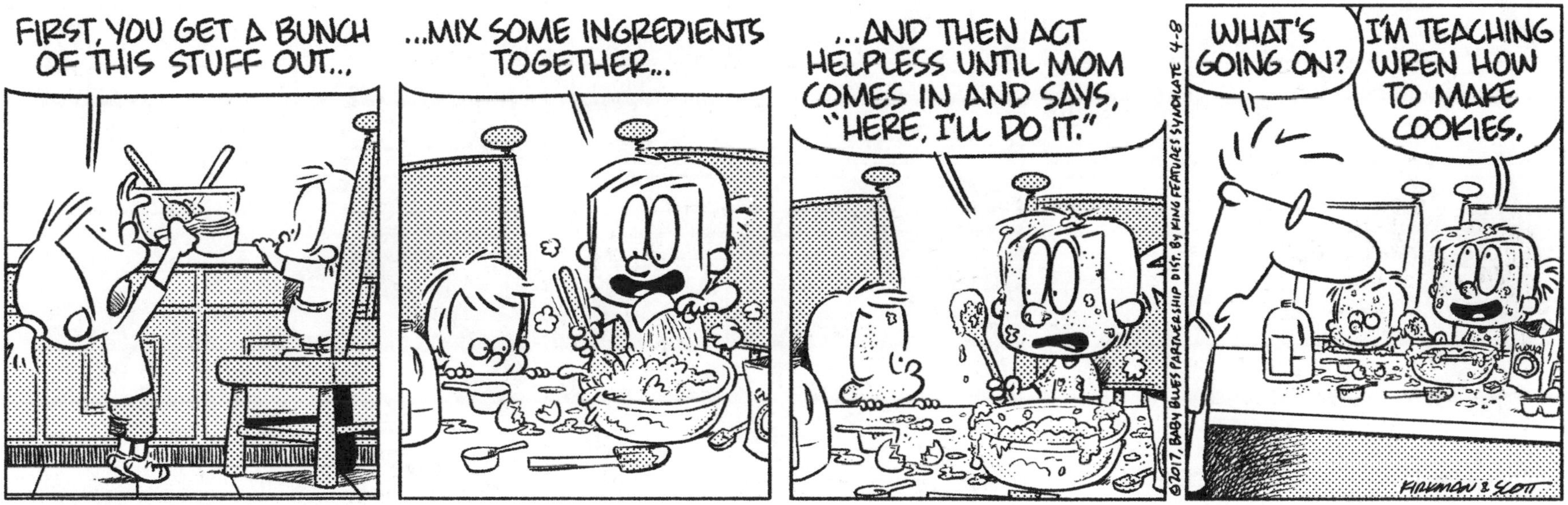
FIRST, YOU GET A BUNCH OF THIS STUFF OUT...
...MIX SOME INGREDIENTS TOGETHER...
...AND THEN ACT HELPLESS UNTIL MOM COMES IN AND SAYS, "HERE, I'LL DO IT."
WHAT'S GOING ON?
I'M TEACHING WREN HOW TO MAKE COOKIES.
©2017, BABY BLUES PARTNERSHIP DIST. BY KING FEATURES SYNDICATE 4-8
KIRKMAN & SCOTT

Rick: Zoe knows too much.

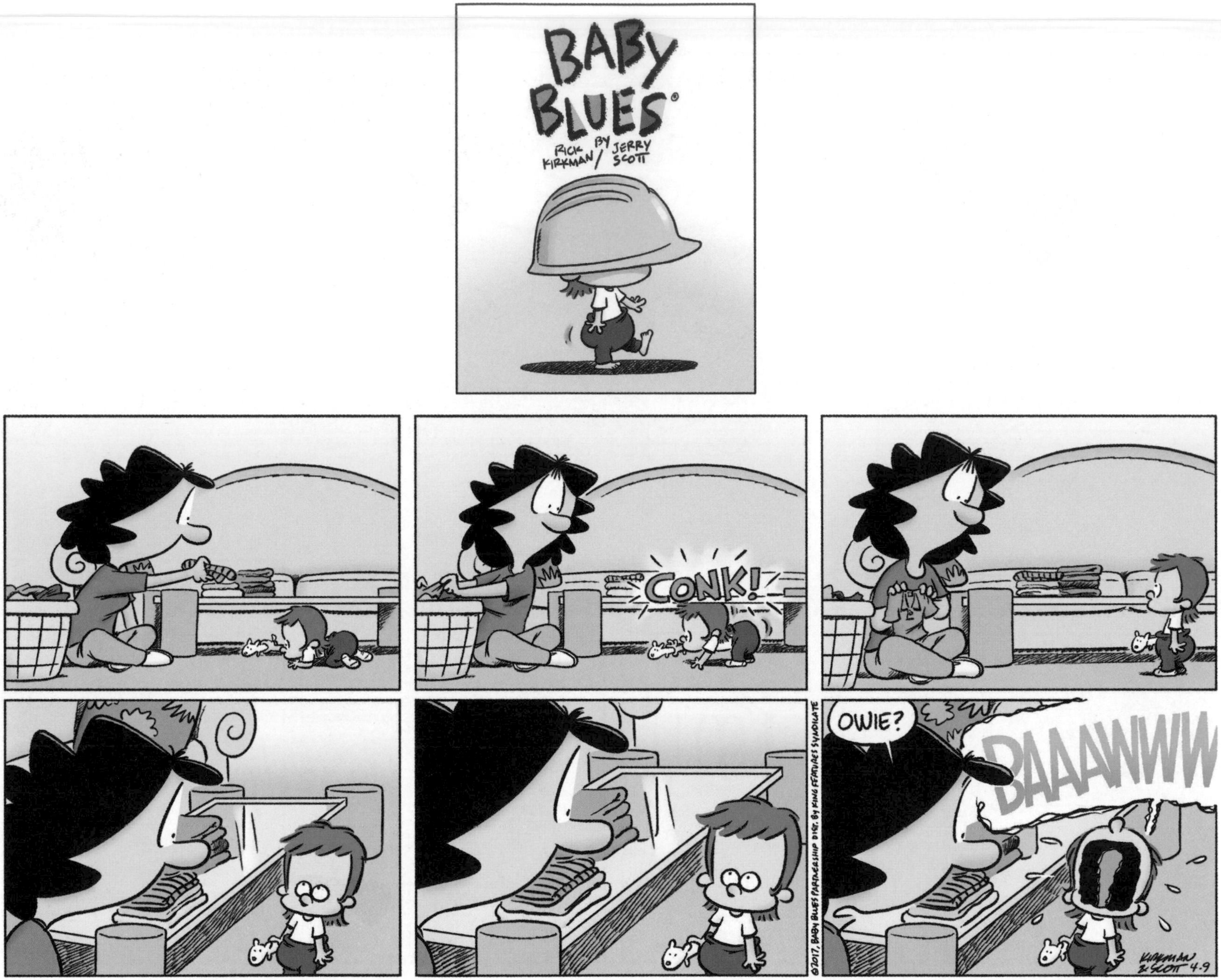
BABY BLUES®
BY RICK KIRKMAN / JERRY SCOTT
CONK!
©2017, BABY BLUES PARTNERSHIP DIST. BY KING FEATURES SYNDICATE
OWIE?
BAAAWWW
KIRKMAN & SCOTT 4-9

Jerry: The delayed cries are the worst. Maybe they take longer to stop because they take longer to start.

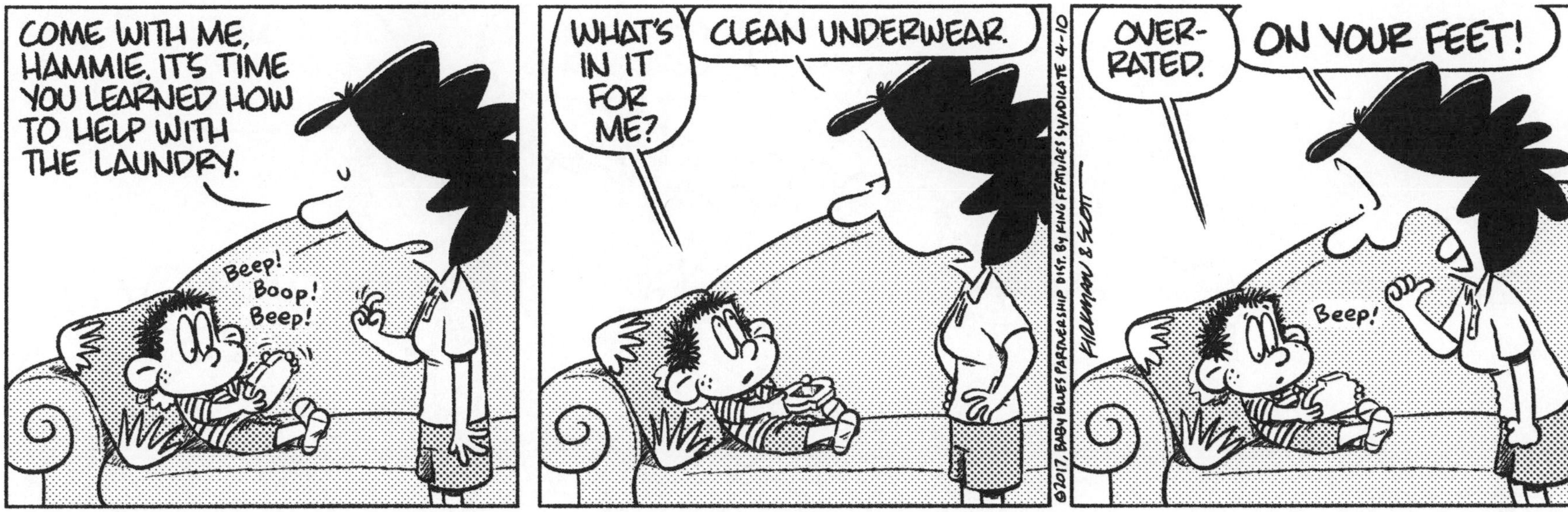
COME WITH ME, HAMMIE. IT'S TIME YOU LEARNED HOW TO HELP WITH THE LAUNDRY.
Beep! Boop! Beep!
WHAT'S IN IT FOR ME?
CLEAN UNDERWEAR.
©2017, BABY BLUES PARTNERSHIP DIST. BY KING FEATURES SYNDICATE 4-10
KIRKMAN & SCOTT
OVER-RATED.
ON YOUR FEET!
Beep!

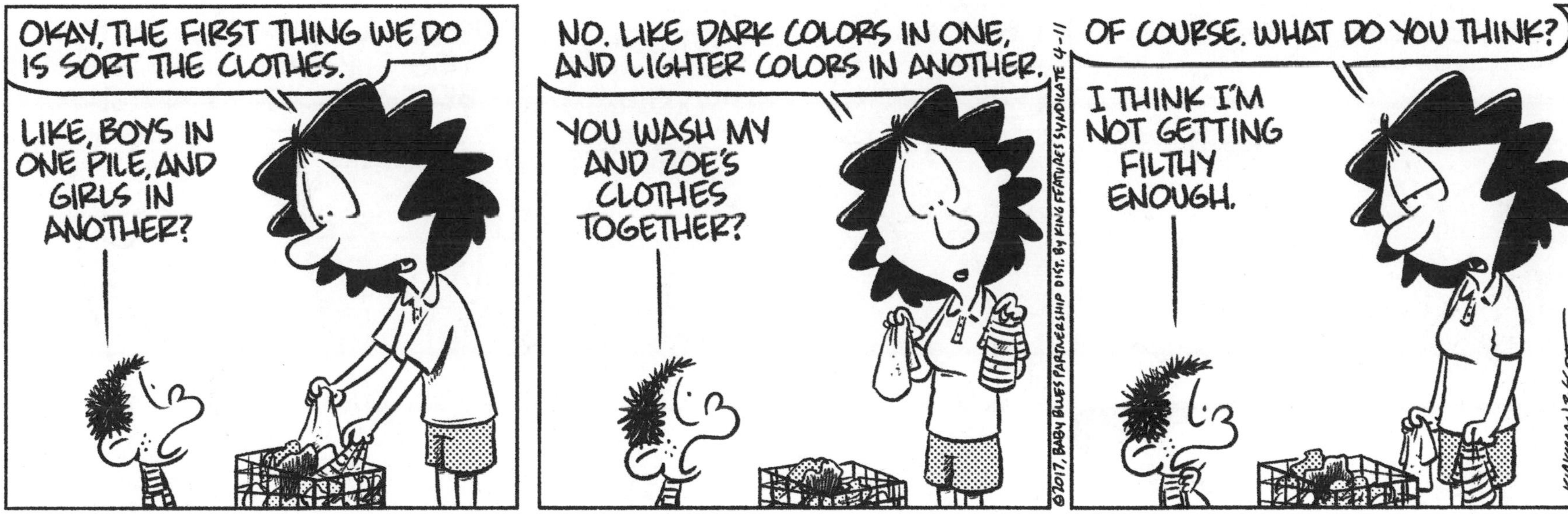
OKAY, THE FIRST THING WE DO IS SORT THE CLOTHES.
LIKE, BOYS IN ONE PILE, AND GIRLS IN ANOTHER?
NO. LIKE DARK COLORS IN ONE, AND LIGHTER COLORS IN ANOTHER.
YOU WASH MY AND ZOE'S CLOTHES TOGETHER?
©2017, BABY BLUES PARTNERSHIP DIST. BY KING FEATURES SYNDICATE 4-11
OF COURSE. WHAT DO YOU THINK?
I THINK I'M NOT GETTING FILTHY ENOUGH.
KIRKMAN & SCOTT

Rick: I love it when the kids have these revelations.

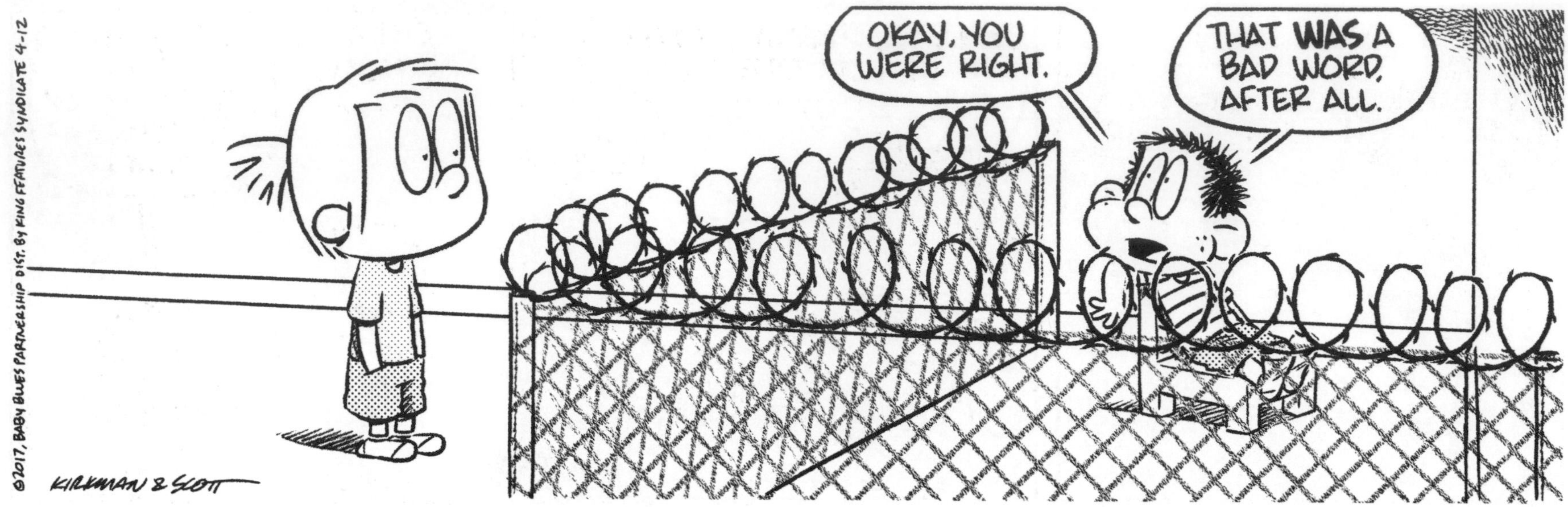
OKAY, YOU WERE RIGHT.
THAT WAS A BAD WORD AFTER ALL.
©2017, BABY BLUES PARTNERSHIP DIST. BY KING FEATURES SYNDICATE 4-12
KIRKMAN & SCOTT

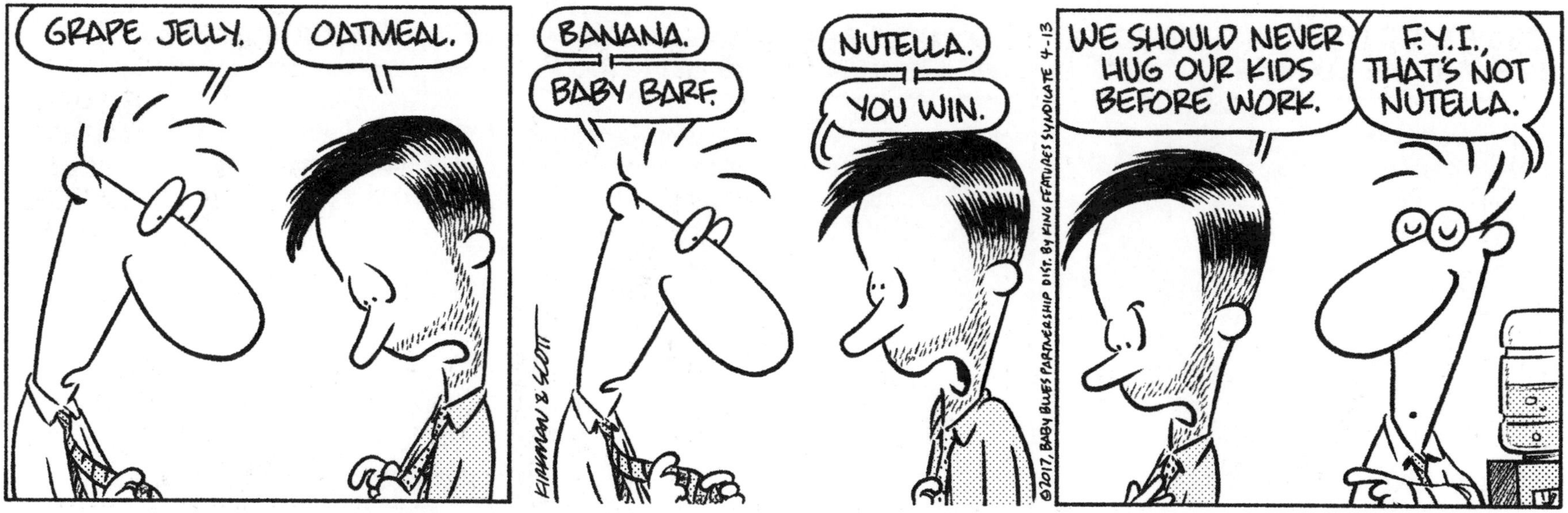
GRAPE JELLY.
OATMEAL.
BANANA.
BABY BARF.
NUTELLA.
YOU WIN.
WE SHOULD NEVER HUG OUR KIDS BEFORE WORK.
F.Y.I., THAT'S NOT NUTELLA.
KIRKMAN & SCOTT
©2017, BABY BLUES PARTNERSHIP DIST. BY KING FEATURES SYNDICATE 4-13

Rick: Eww. And extra points for noticing.

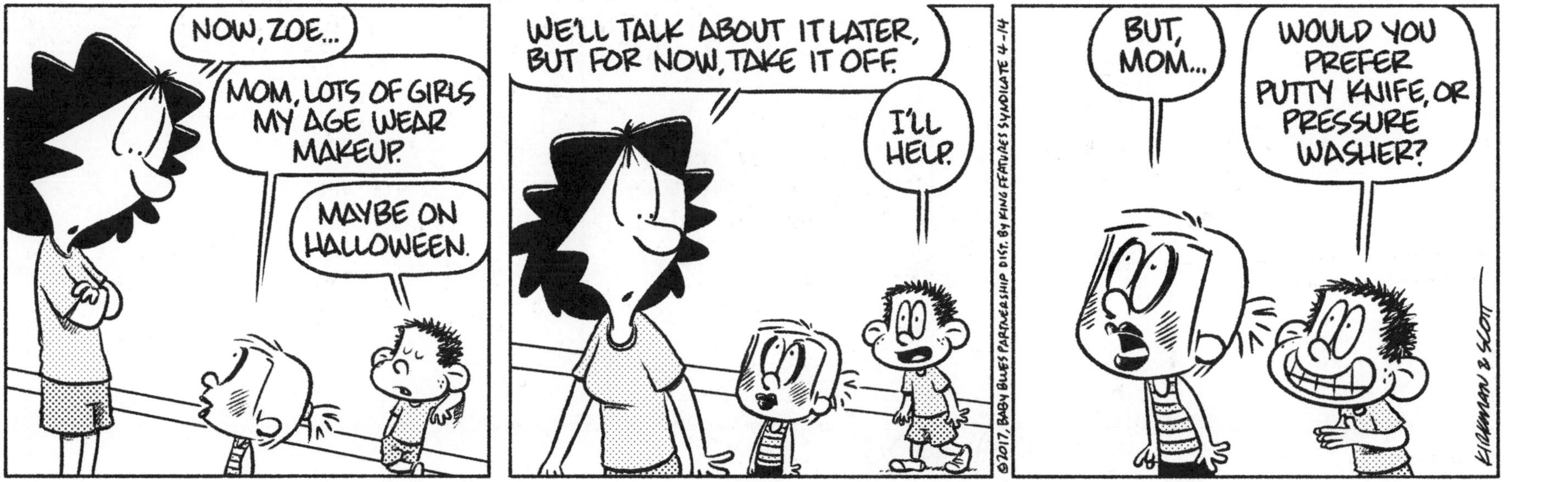
NOW, ZOE...
MOM, LOTS OF GIRLS MY AGE WEAR MAKEUP.
MAYBE ON HALLOWEEN.
WE'LL TALK ABOUT IT LATER, BUT FOR NOW, TAKE IT OFF.
I'LL HELP.
©2017, BABY BLUES PARTNERSHIP DIST. BY KING FEATURES SYNDICATE 4-14
BUT, MOM...
WOULD YOU PREFER PUTTY KNIFE, OR PRESSURE WASHER?
KIRKMAN & SCOTT

Jerry: I like Hammie's "Joe Cool" attitude in the first panel.

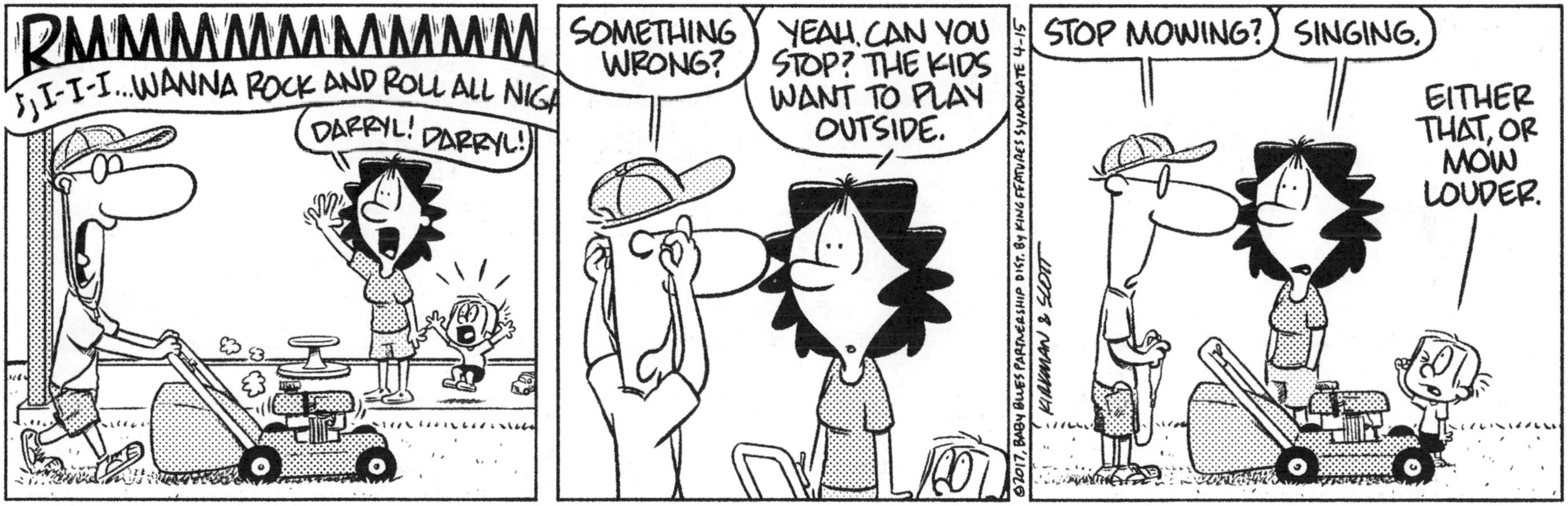
RMMMMMMMMMMM
I-I-I...WANNA ROCK AND ROLL ALL NIG
DARRYL! DARRYL!
SOMETHING WRONG?
YEAH. CAN YOU STOP? THE KIDS WANT TO PLAY OUTSIDE.
©2017, BABY BLUES PARTNERSHIP DIST. BY KING FEATURES SYNDICATE 4-15
KIRKMAN & SCOTT
STOP MOWING?
SINGING.
EITHER THAT, OR MOW LOUDER.

Rick: Think of the children and their sensitive ears.

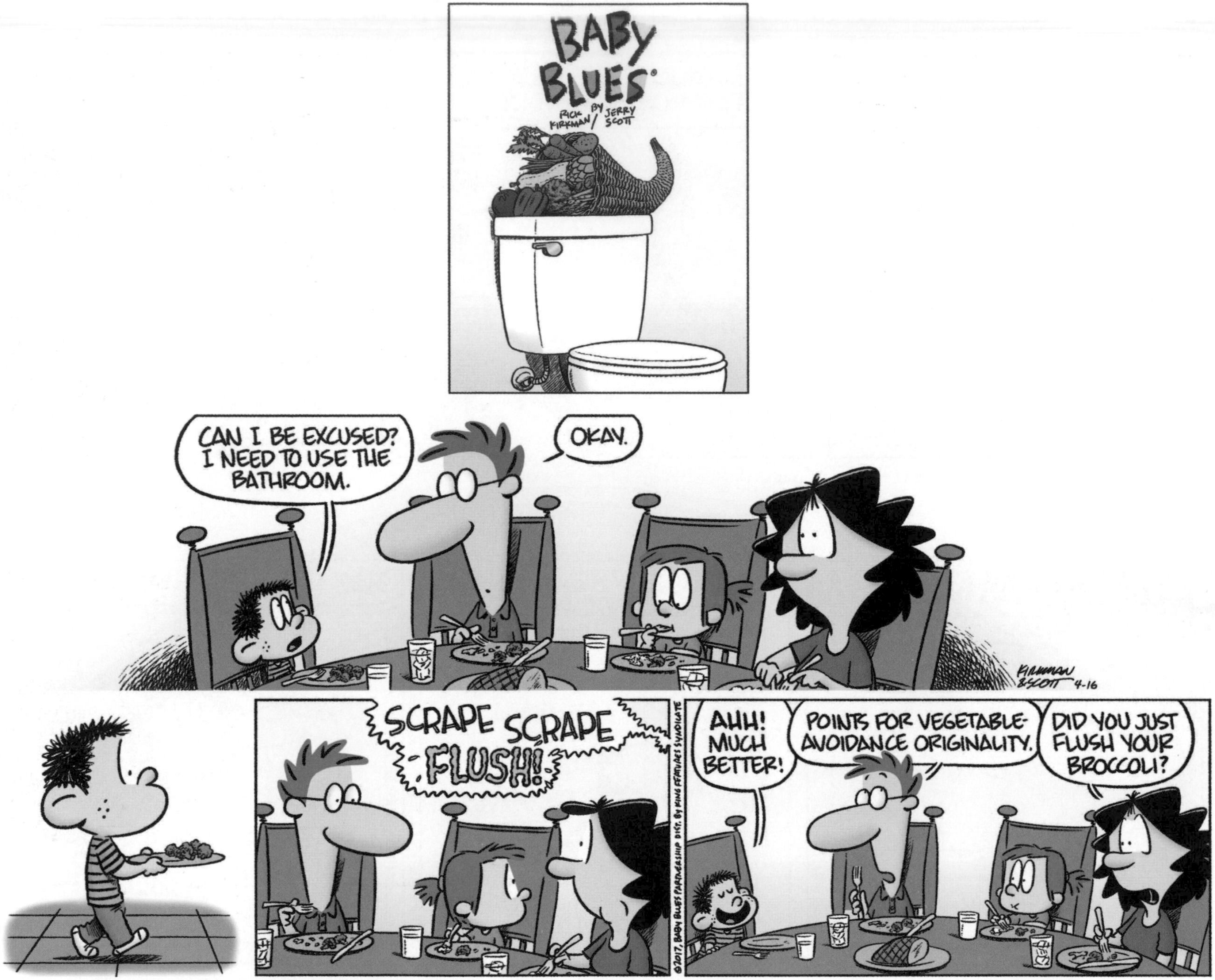
BABY BLUES®
BY RICK KIRKMAN / JERRY SCOTT
CAN I BE EXCUSED? I NEED TO USE THE BATHROOM.
OKAY.
KIRKMAN & SCOTT 4-16
SCRAPE SCRAPE FLUSH!
©2017, BABY BLUES PARTNERSHIP DIST. BY KING FEATURES SYNDICATE
AHH! MUCH BETTER!
POINTS FOR VEGETABLE-AVOIDANCE ORIGINALITY.
DID YOU JUST FLUSH YOUR BROCCOLI?

Jerry: The title panel on a Sunday strip should be a visual joke that doesn't necessarily stand on its own but is related to the punchline. They often don't make sense until after you've read the whole strip. Cartoon class dismissed.

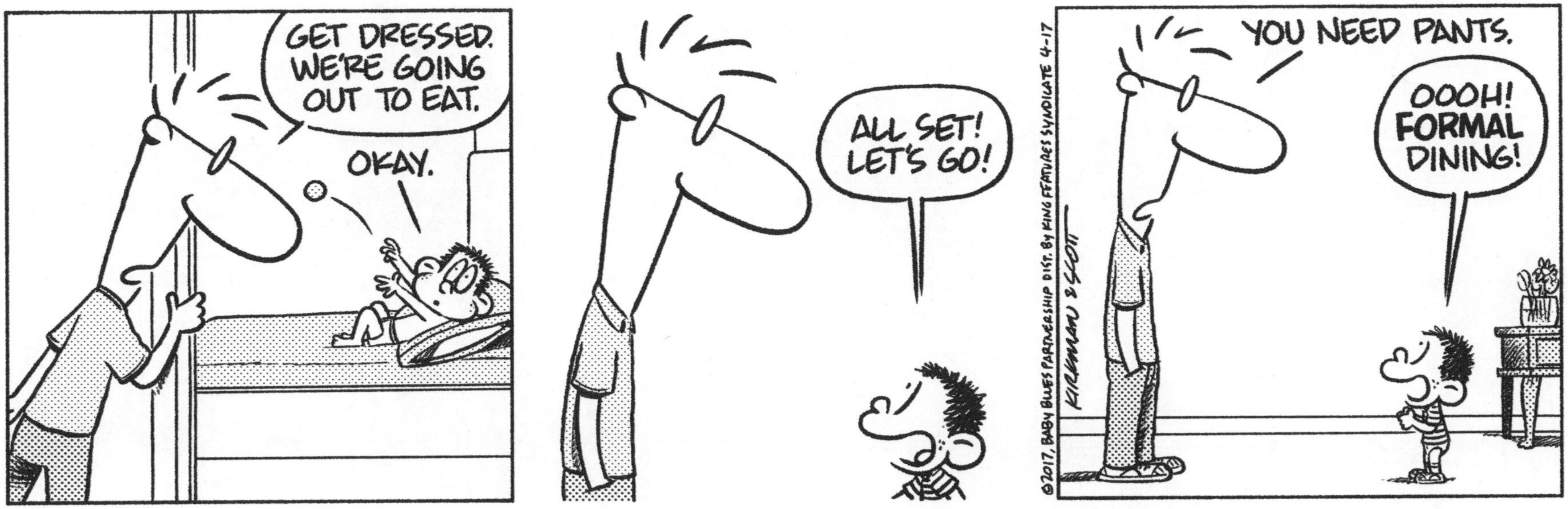
GET DRESSED. WE'RE GOING OUT TO EAT.
OKAY.
ALL SET! LET'S GO!
©2017, BABY BLUES PARTNERSHIP DIST. BY KING FEATURES SYNDICATE 4-17
KIRKMAN & SCOTT
YOU NEED PANTS.
OOOH! FORMAL DINING!

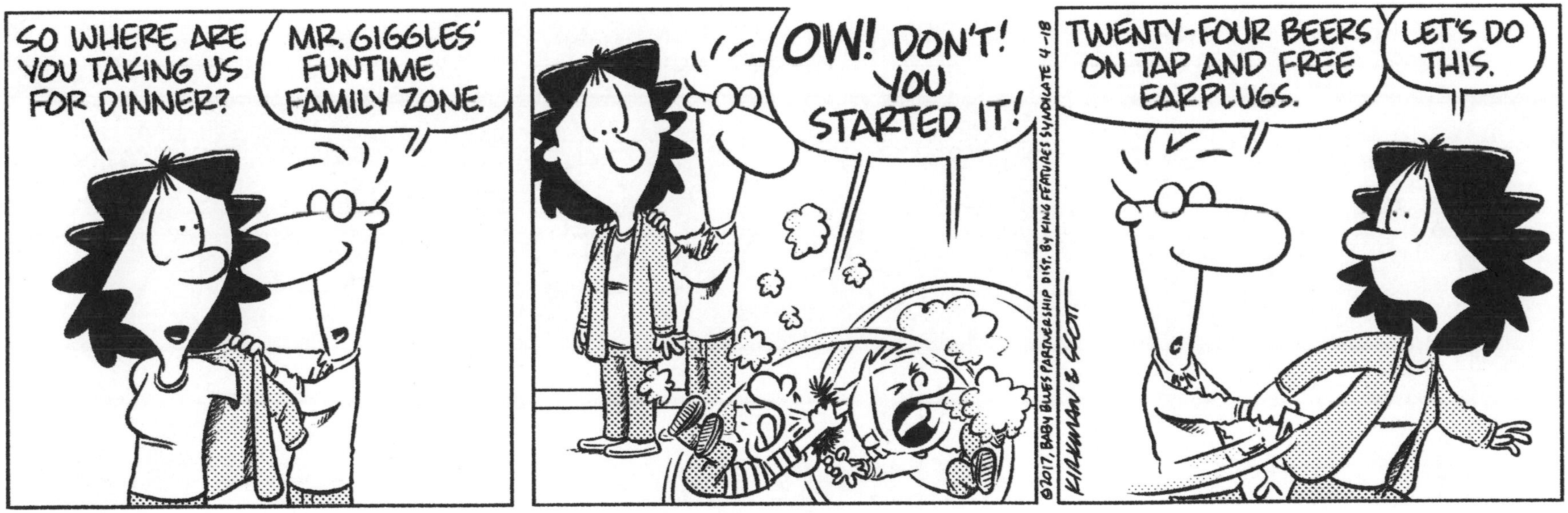
SO WHERE ARE YOU TAKING US FOR DINNER?
MR. GIGGLES' FUNTIME FAMILY ZONE.
OW! DON'T! YOU STARTED IT!
©2017, BABY BLUES PARTNERSHIP DIST. BY KING FEATURES SYNDICATE 4-18
KIRKMAN & SCOTT
TWENTY-FOUR BEERS ON TAP AND FREE EARPLUGS.
LET'S DO THIS.

Jerry: If I had a game token for every hour I've spent at one of these restaurants, I could buy the big pink teddy bear.

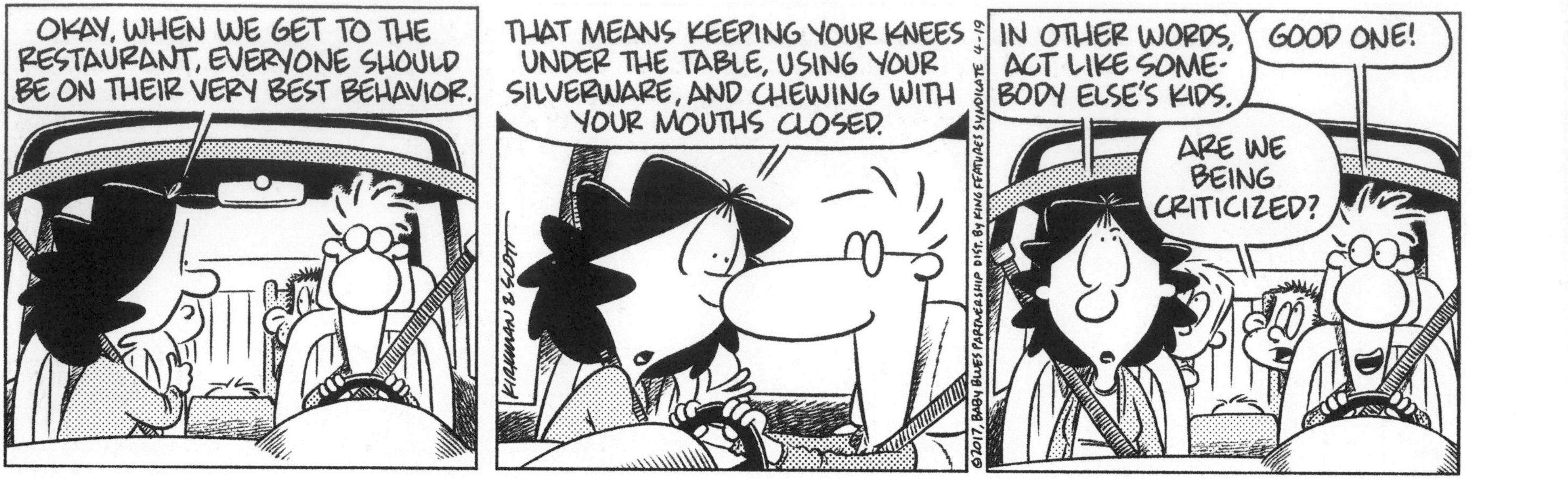
OKAY, WHEN WE GET TO THE RESTAURANT, EVERYONE SHOULD BE ON THEIR VERY BEST BEHAVIOR.
THAT MEANS KEEPING YOUR KNEES UNDER THE TABLE, USING YOUR SILVERWARE, AND CHEWING WITH YOUR MOUTHS CLOSED.
KIRKMAN & SCOTT
4-19
©2017, BABY BLUES PARTNERSHIP DIST. BY KING FEATURES SYNDICATE
IN OTHER WORDS, ACT LIKE SOMEBODY ELSE'S KIDS.
GOOD ONE!
ARE WE BEING CRITICIZED?

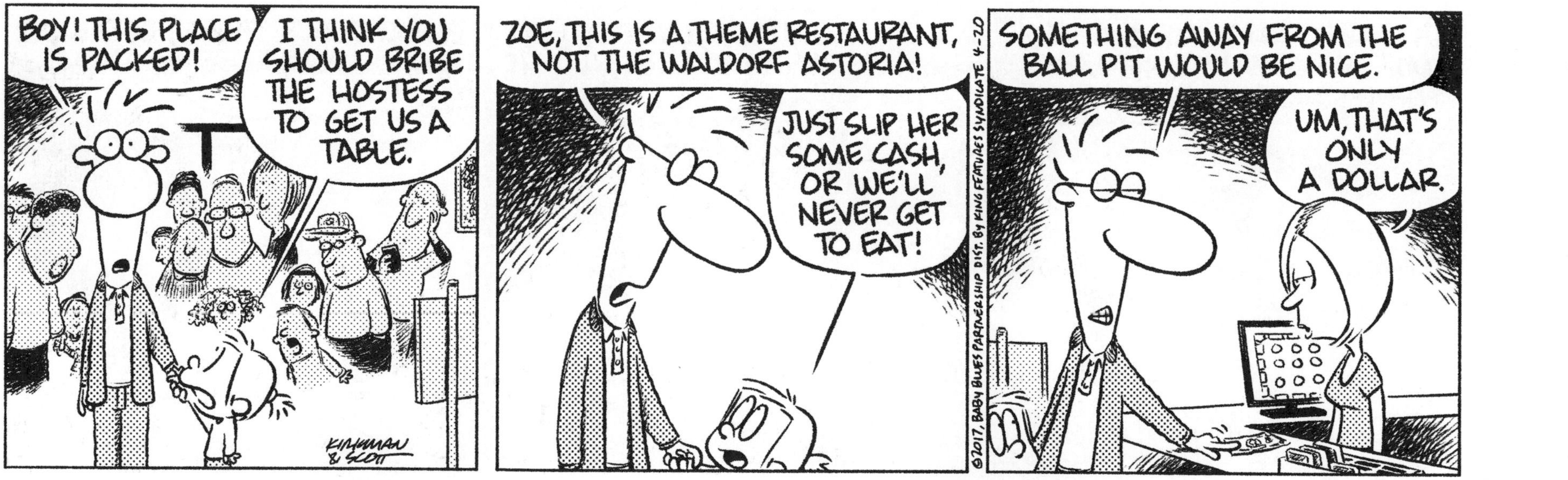
BOY! THIS PLACE IS PACKED!
I THINK YOU SHOULD BRIBE THE HOSTESS TO GET US A TABLE.
KIRKMAN & SCOTT
ZOE, THIS IS A THEME RESTAURANT, NOT THE WALDORF ASTORIA!
JUST SLIP HER SOME CASH, OR WE'LL NEVER GET TO EAT!
4-20
©2017, BABY BLUES PARTNERSHIP DIST. BY KING FEATURES SYNDICATE
SOMETHING AWAY FROM THE BALL PIT WOULD BE NICE.
UM, THAT'S ONLY A DOLLAR.

WELL, THE KIDS SEEM TO BE HAVING FUN.
YEAH. AND FOR A FAMILY RESTAURANT, IT'S PRETTY CLASSY.
HOW'S THE WINE LIST?
THEIR CHOICES ARE "CLEAR" AND "PURPLE."
Wine
©2017, BABY BLUES PARTNERSHIP DIST. BY KING FEATURES SYNDICATE 4-21
KIRKMAN & SCOTT

WHAT DO YOU THINK OF THIS PLACE?
IT'S GOOD.
IT HAS EVERYTHING I LOOK FOR IN A FAMILY NIGHT OUT: DECENT FOOD, CLEAN RESTROOMS...
...AND THREE EXHAUSTED KIDS.
Z
Z
Z
©2017, BABY BLUES PARTNERSHIP DIST. BY KING FEATURES SYNDICATE 4-22
KIRKMAN & SCOTT

Rick: Four stars: One for each kid, and one for the free earplugs.

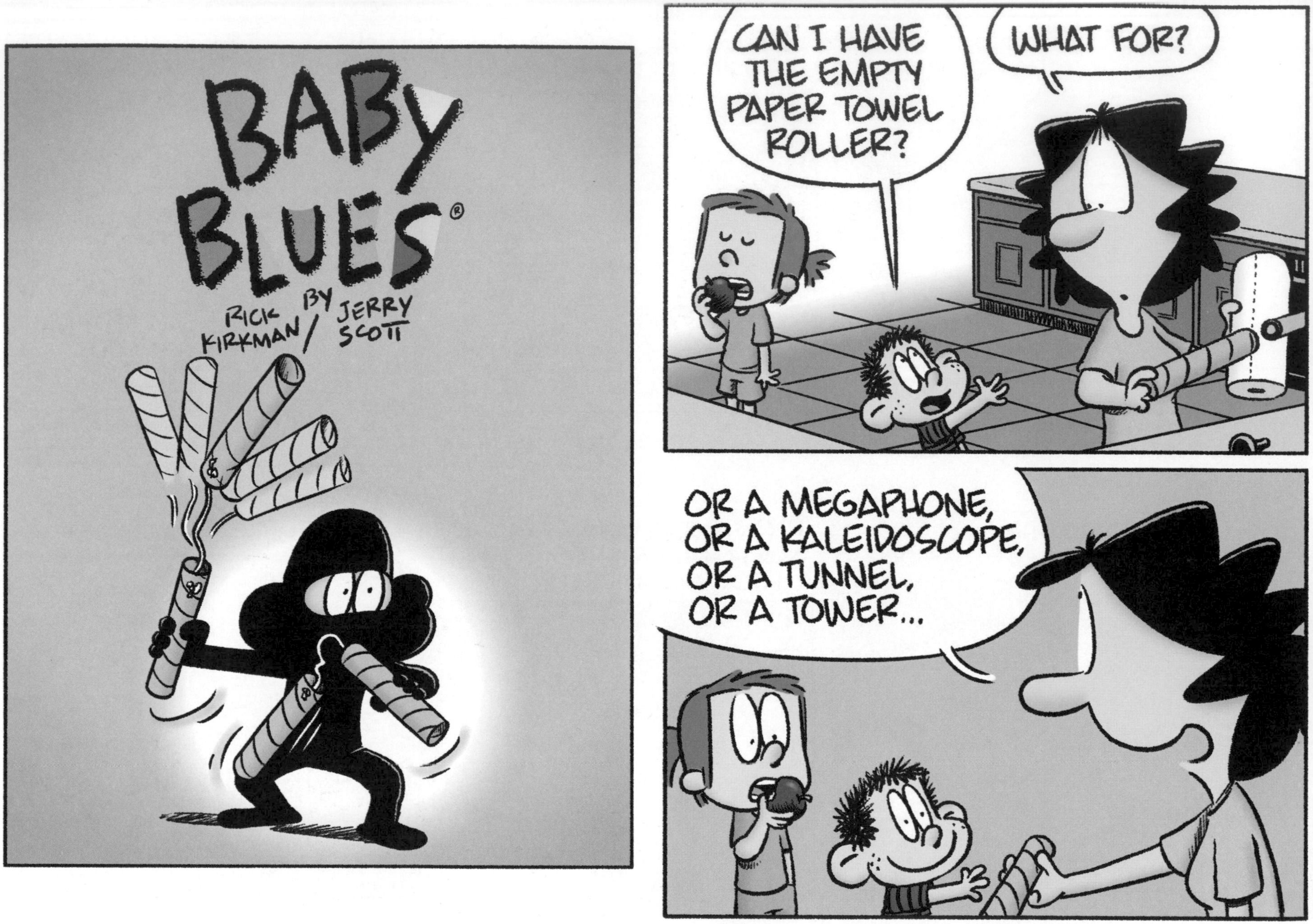
BABY BLUES®
BY RICK KIRKMAN / JERRY SCOTT
CAN I HAVE THE EMPTY PAPER TOWEL ROLLER?
WHAT FOR?
OR A MEGAPHONE, OR A KALEIDOSCOPE, OR A TUNNEL, OR A TOWER...

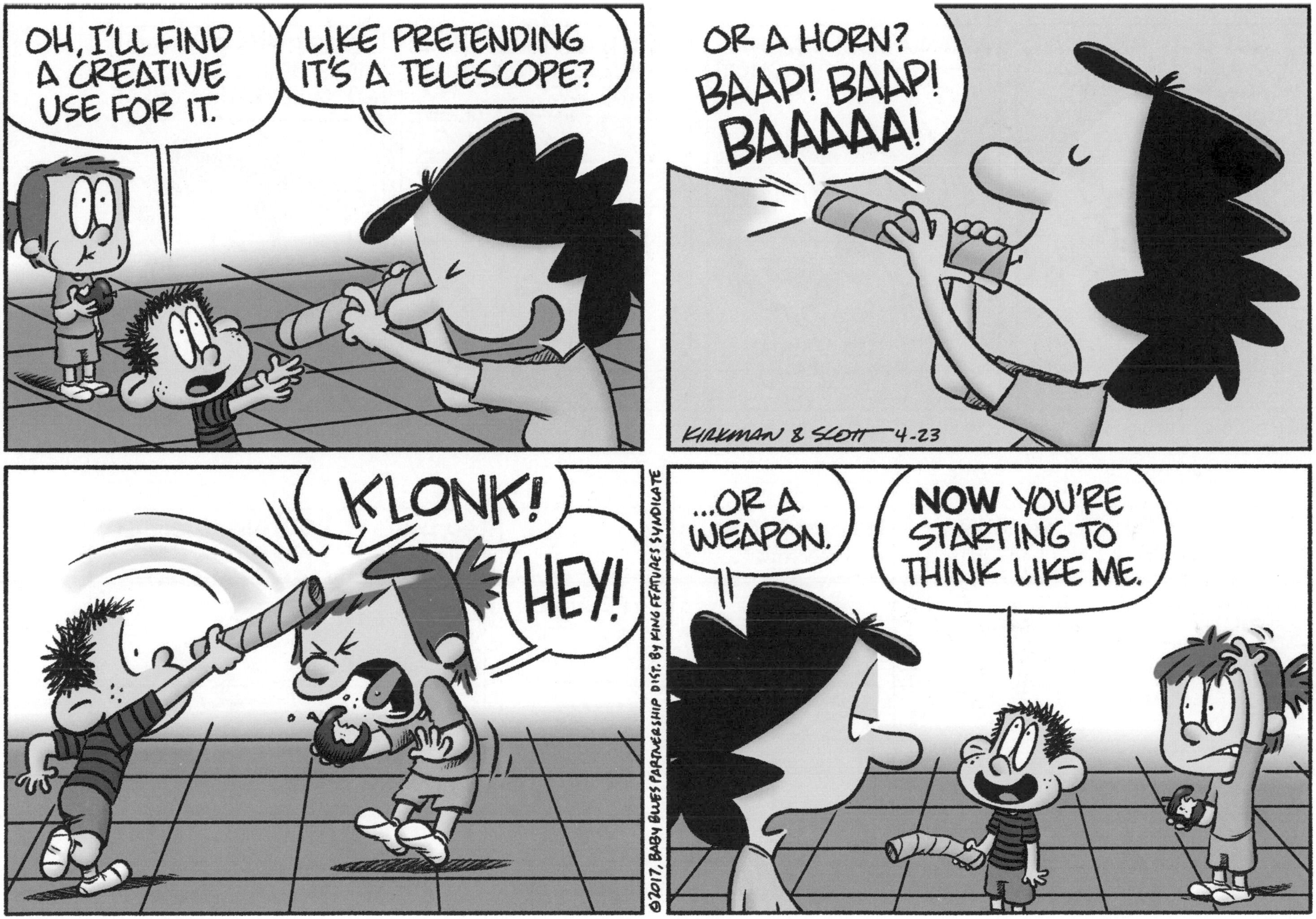
OH, I'LL FIND A CREATIVE USE FOR IT.
LIKE PRETENDING IT'S A TELESCOPE?
OR A HORN? BAAP! BAAP! BAAAAA!
KIRKMAN & SCOTT 4-23
KLONK!
HEY!
©2017, BABY BLUES PARTNERSHIP DIST. BY KING FEATURES SYNDICATE
...OR A WEAPON.
NOW YOU'RE STARTING TO THINK LIKE ME.

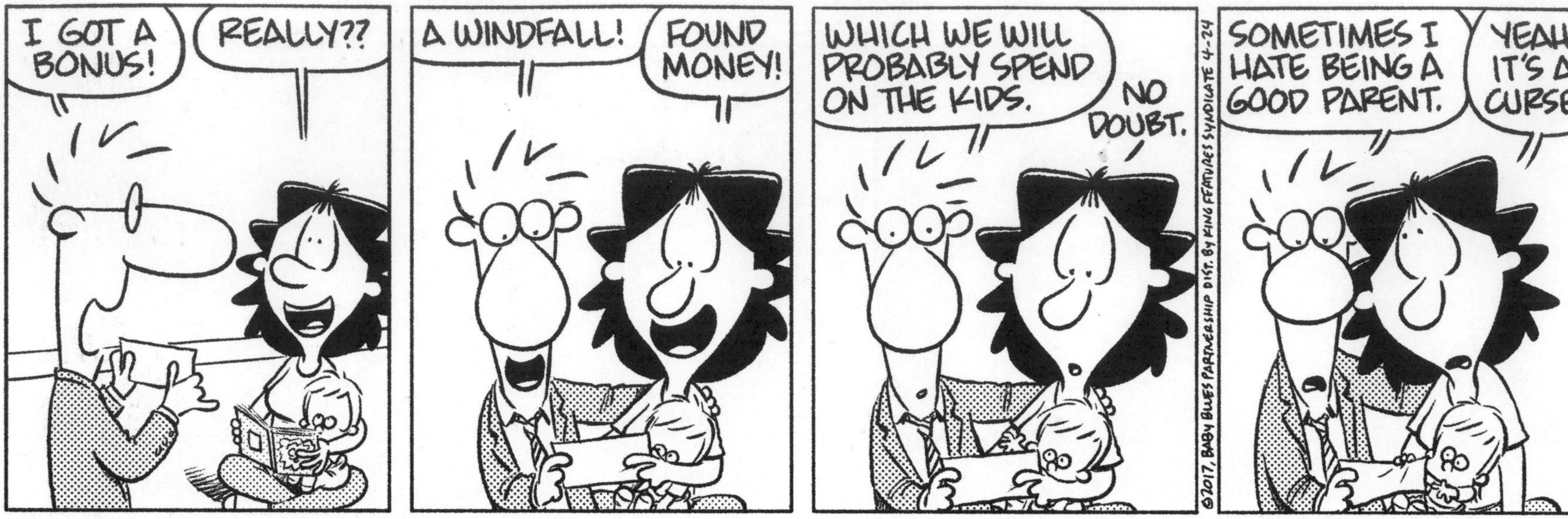
I GOT A BONUS!
REALLY??
A WINDFALL!
FOUND MONEY!
WHICH WE WILL PROBABLY SPEND ON THE KIDS.
NO DOUBT.
SOMETIMES I HATE BEING A GOOD PARENT.
YEAH. IT'S A CURSE.
©2017, BABY BLUES PARTNERSHIP DIST. BY KING FEATURES SYNDICATE 4-24
KIRKMAN & SCOTT

Rick: Darryl and Wanda still have dibs on whatever is under the couch cushions.

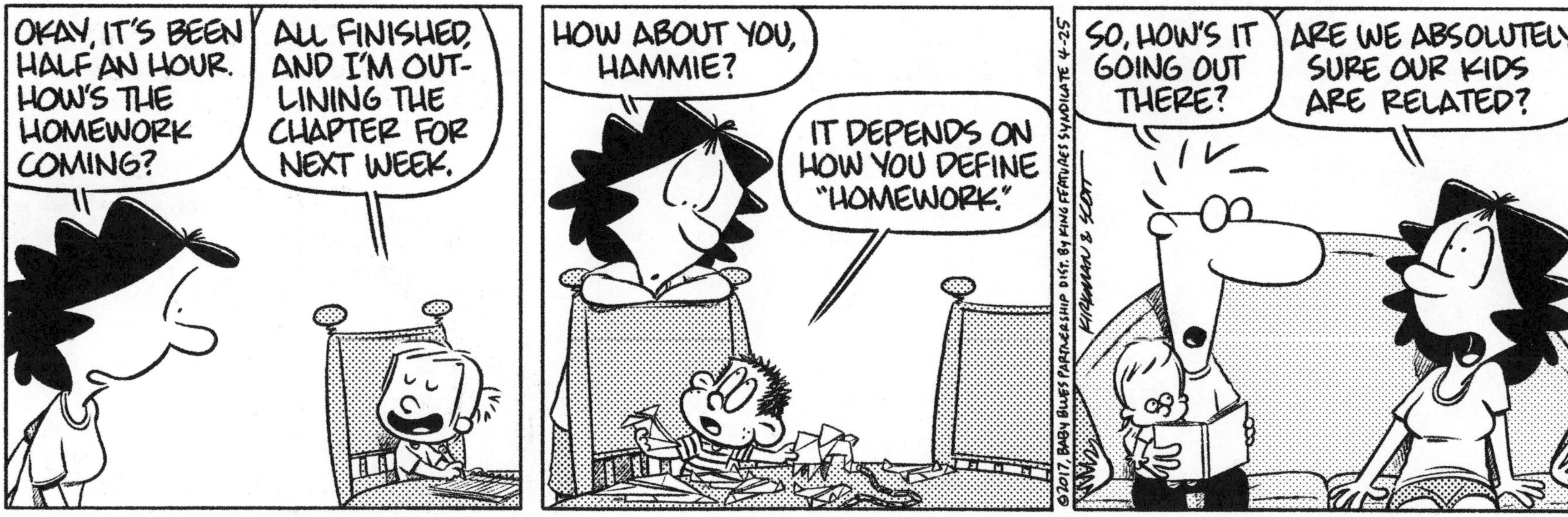
OKAY, IT'S BEEN HALF AN HOUR. HOW'S THE HOMEWORK COMING?
ALL FINISHED, AND I'M OUT-LINING THE CHAPTER FOR NEXT WEEK.
HOW ABOUT YOU, HAMMIE?
IT DEPENDS ON HOW YOU DEFINE "HOMEWORK."
©2017, BABY BLUES PARTNERSHIP DIST. BY KING FEATURES SYNDICATE 4-25
KIRKMAN & SCOTT
SO, HOW'S IT GOING OUT THERE?
ARE WE ABSOLUTELY SURE OUR KIDS ARE RELATED?

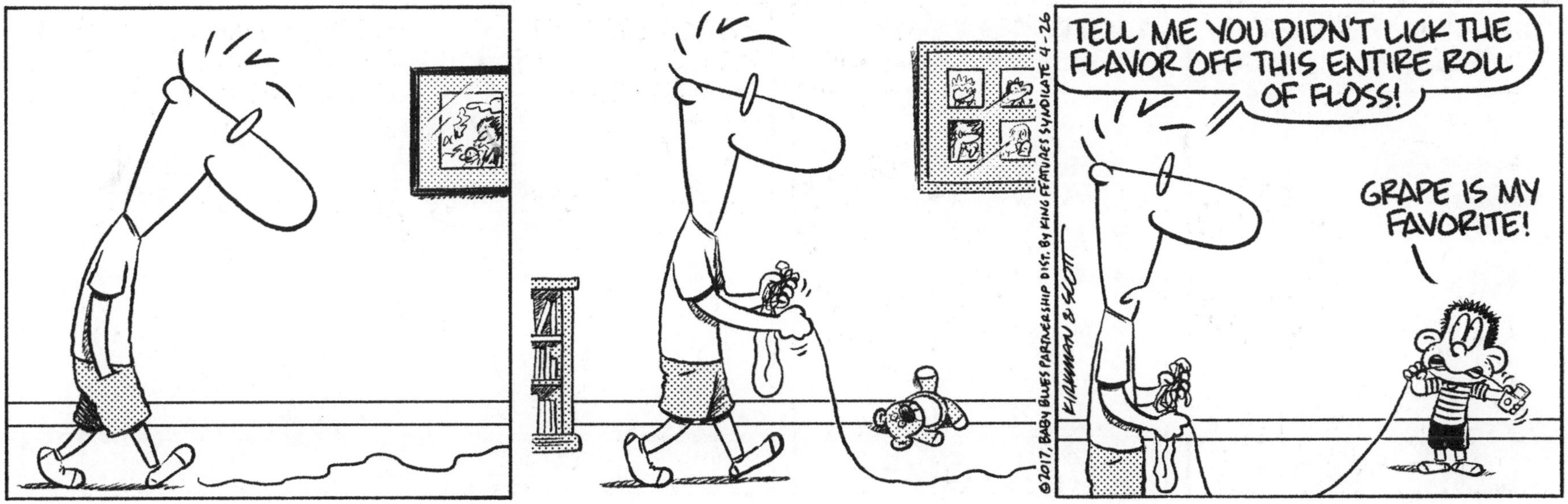

©2017, BABY BLUES PARTNERSHIP DIST. BY KING FEATURES SYNDICATE 4-26
KIRKMAN & SCOTT
TELL ME YOU DIDN'T LICK THE FLAVOR OFF THIS ENTIRE ROLL OF FLOSS!
GRAPE IS MY FAVORITE!

Jerry: Always check to make sure the floss hasn't been rewound.

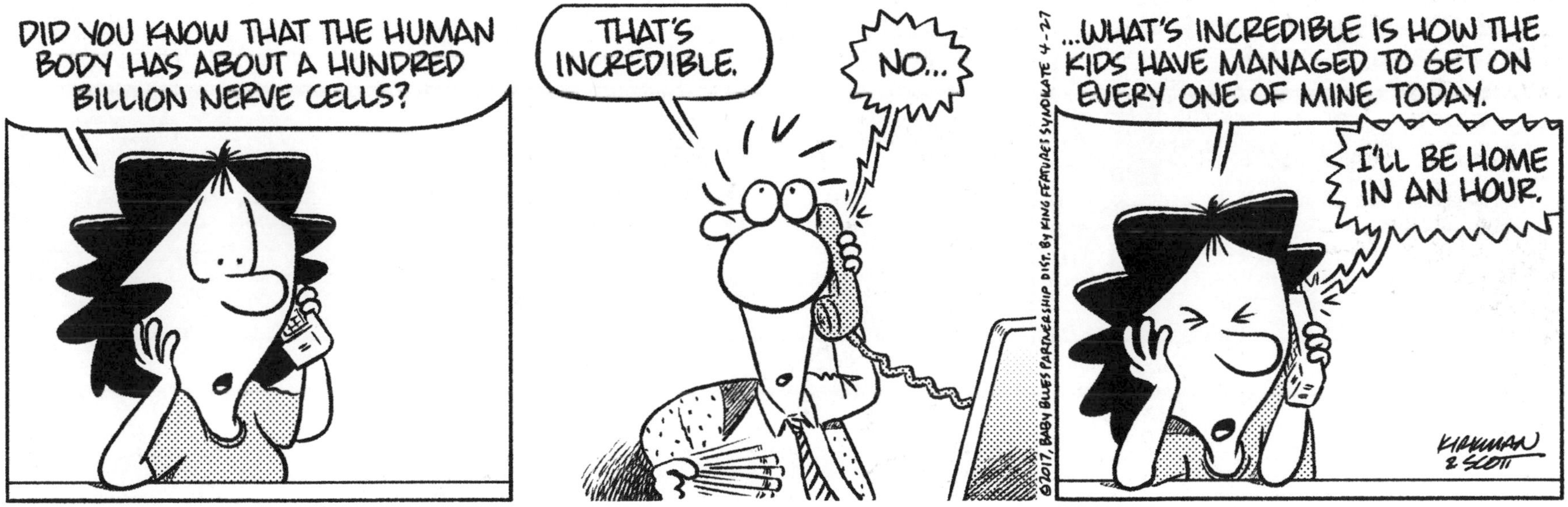

DID YOU KNOW THAT THE HUMAN BODY HAS ABOUT A HUNDRED BILLION NERVE CELLS?
THAT'S INCREDIBLE.
NO...
©2017, BABY BLUES PARTNERSHIP DIST. BY KING FEATURES SYNDICATE 4-27
...WHAT'S INCREDIBLE IS HOW THE KIDS HAVE MANAGED TO GET ON EVERY ONE OF MINE TODAY.
I'LL BE HOME IN AN HOUR.
KIRKMAN & SCOTT

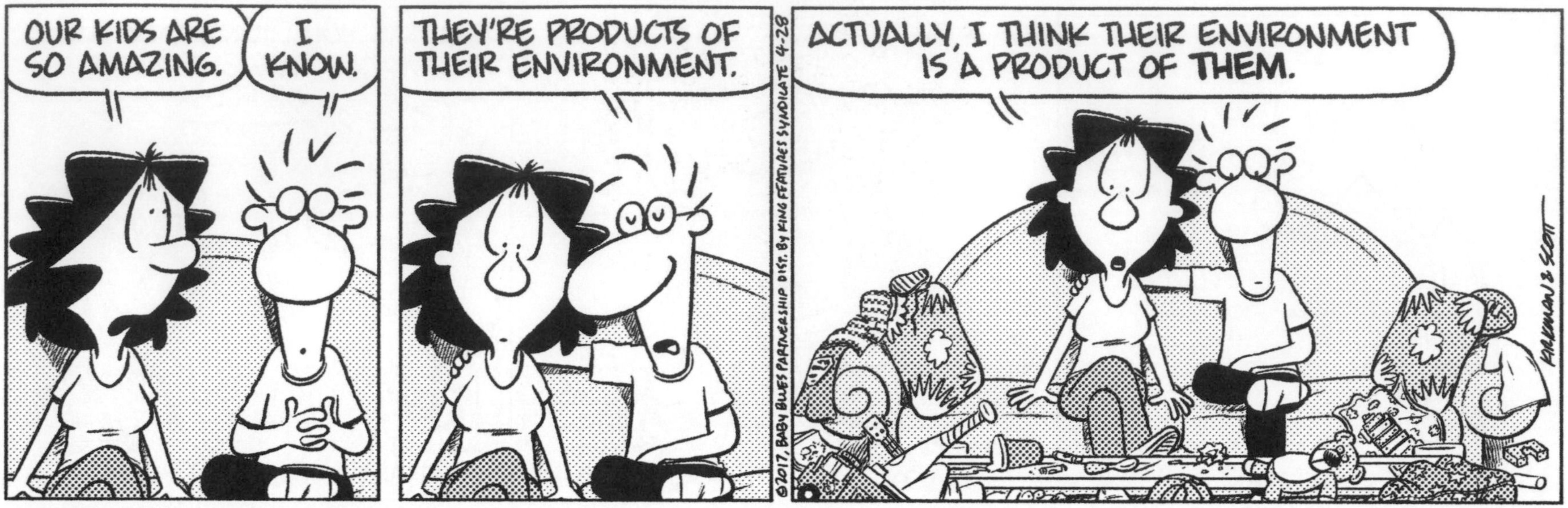
OUR KIDS ARE SO AMAZING.
I KNOW.
THEY'RE PRODUCTS OF THEIR ENVIRONMENT.
©2017, BABY BLUES PARTNERSHIP DIST. BY KING FEATURES SYNDICATE 4-28
ACTUALLY, I THINK THEIR ENVIRONMENT IS A PRODUCT OF THEM.
KIRKMAN & SCOTT

Rick: Can you say "Superfund site"?

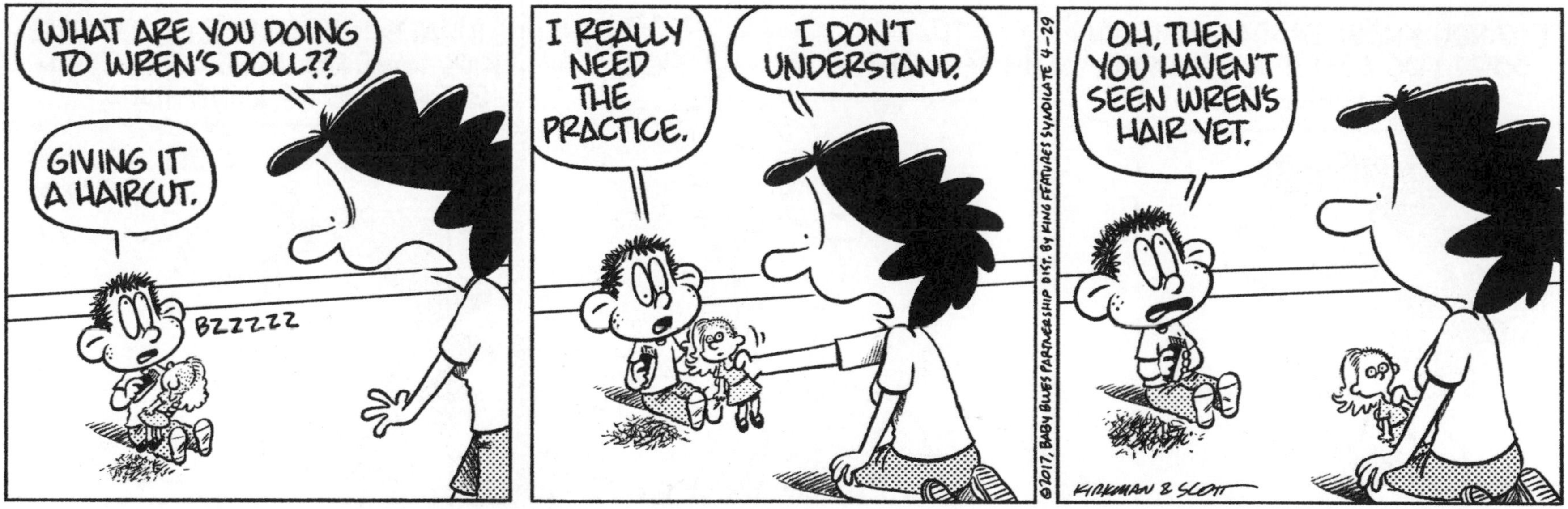
WHAT ARE YOU DOING TO WREN'S DOLL??
GIVING IT A HAIRCUT.
BZZZZZ
I REALLY NEED THE PRACTICE.
I DON'T UNDERSTAND.
©2017, BABY BLUES PARTNERSHIP DIST. BY KING FEATURES SYNDICATE 4-29
OH, THEN YOU HAVEN'T SEEN WREN'S HAIR YET.
KIRKMAN & SCOTT

Jerry: Sometimes it's fun to write a strip with a story that ends before the end. It's almost more interesting to imagine what Wren's hair looks like than to actually see it.

BABY BLUES
Rick Kirkman & Jerry Scott
ZZZZZZZ

AAAAUGH!
WHAT'S WRONG, MOM?
THERE'S CRAFT PAINT ALL OVER THE CARPET!
DO YOU KNOW HOW THIS GOT HERE?
I HAVE A GUESS.
WREN PROBABLY GOT THIS JAR OF PURPLE PAINT OUT OF MY ART SUPPLY BOX, TRIPPED, AND ACCIDENTALLY SPILLED IT RIGHT HERE.
NUH-UH.
©2017, BABY BLUES PARTNERSHIP DIST. BY KING FEATURES SYNDICATE
WREN CAN DEFEND HERSELF!
THE FREE RIDE IS OVER!
KIRKMAN & SCOTT 4-30

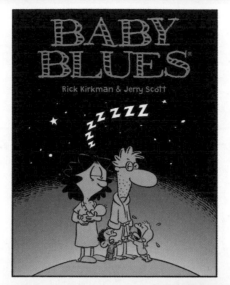

Rick: I love that Wren has now become a force to be dealt with. She doesn't know it yet, but she may be in the catbird seat.

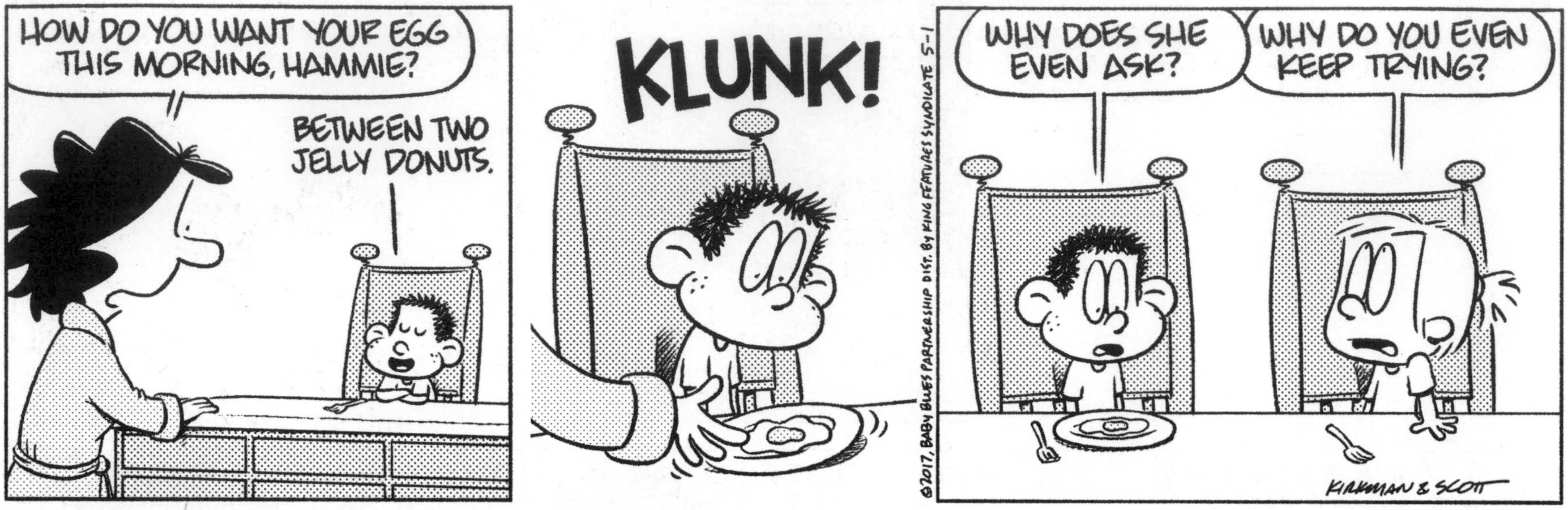
HOW DO YOU WANT YOUR EGG THIS MORNING, HAMMIE?
BETWEEN TWO JELLY DONUTS.
KLUNK!
WHY DOES SHE EVEN ASK?
WHY DO YOU EVEN KEEP TRYING?
©2017, BABY BLUES PARTNERSHIP DIST. BY KING FEATURES SYNDICATE 5-1
KIRKMAN & SCOTT

Rick: Because someday she might slip up.

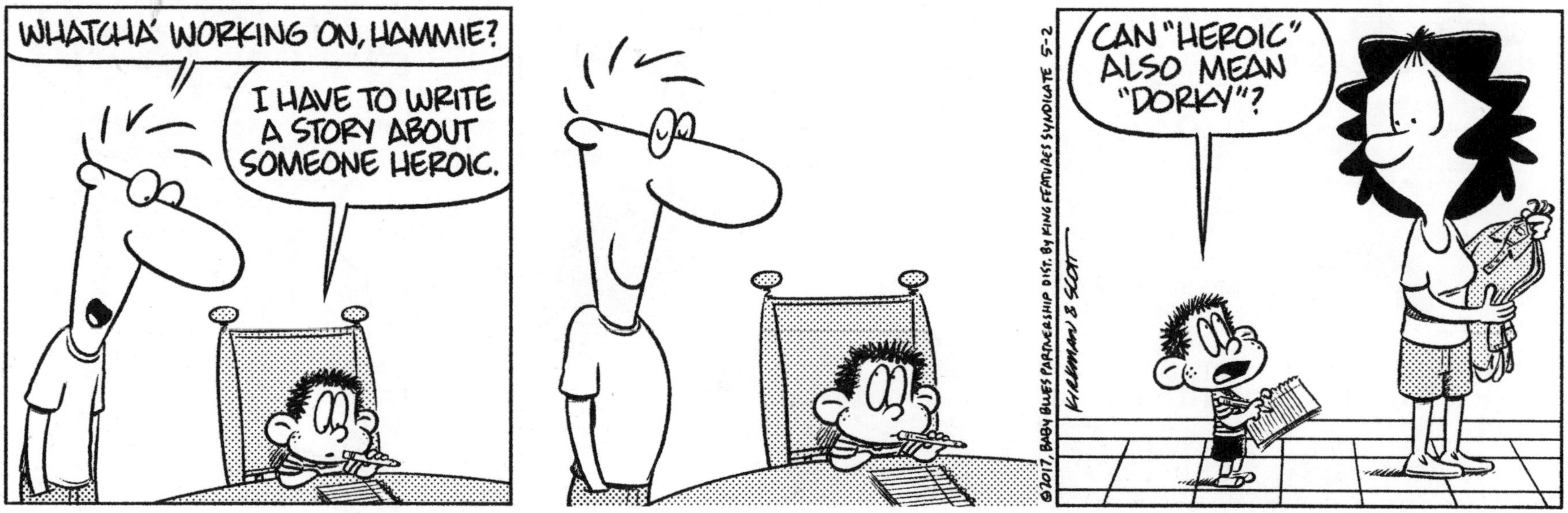
WHATCHA' WORKING ON, HAMMIE?
I HAVE TO WRITE A STORY ABOUT SOMEONE HEROIC.
CAN "HEROIC" ALSO MEAN "DORKY"?
©2017, BABY BLUES PARTNERSHIP DIST. BY KING FEATURES SYNDICATE 5-2
KIRKMAN & SCOTT

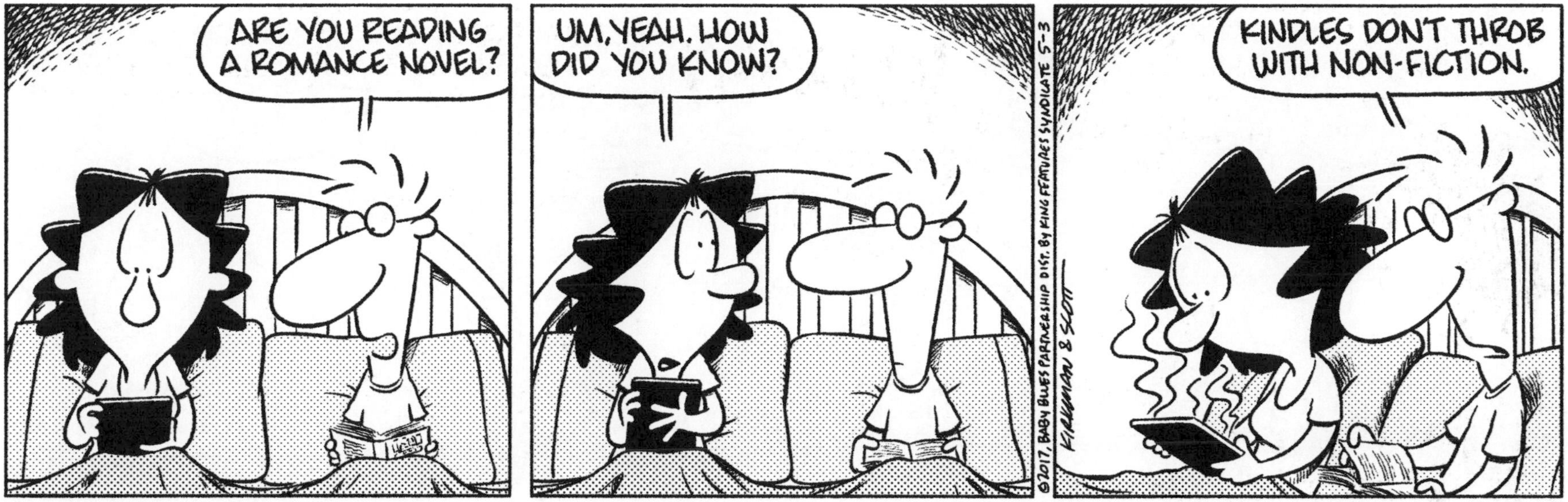
ARE YOU READING A ROMANCE NOVEL?
UM, YEAH. HOW DID YOU KNOW?
©2017, BABY BLUES PARTNERSHIP DIST. BY KING FEATURES SYNDICATE 5-3
KIRKMAN & SCOTT
KINDLES DON'T THROB WITH NON-FICTION.

Jerry: Can you say "throb" in the funnies?

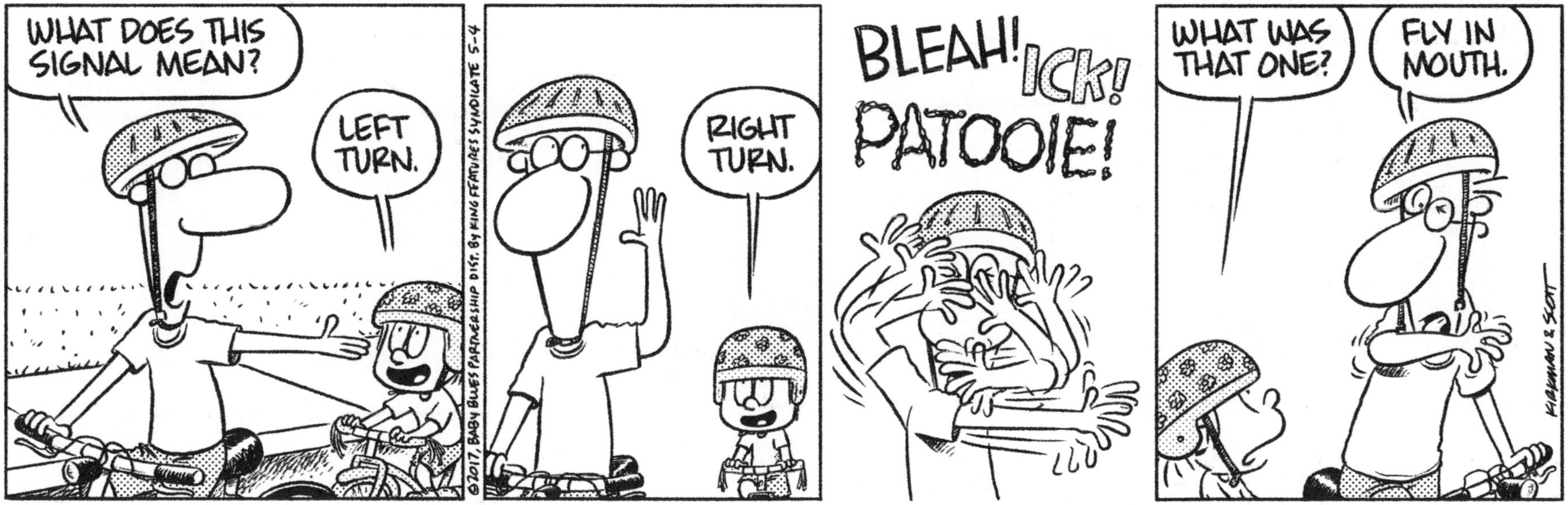
WHAT DOES THIS SIGNAL MEAN?
LEFT TURN.
©2017, BABY BLUES PARTNERSHIP DIST. BY KING FEATURES SYNDICATE 5-4
RIGHT TURN.
BLEAH! ICK! PATOOIE!
WHAT WAS THAT ONE?
FLY IN MOUTH.
KIRKMAN & SCOTT

Rick: I get a kick out of this one for some reason.

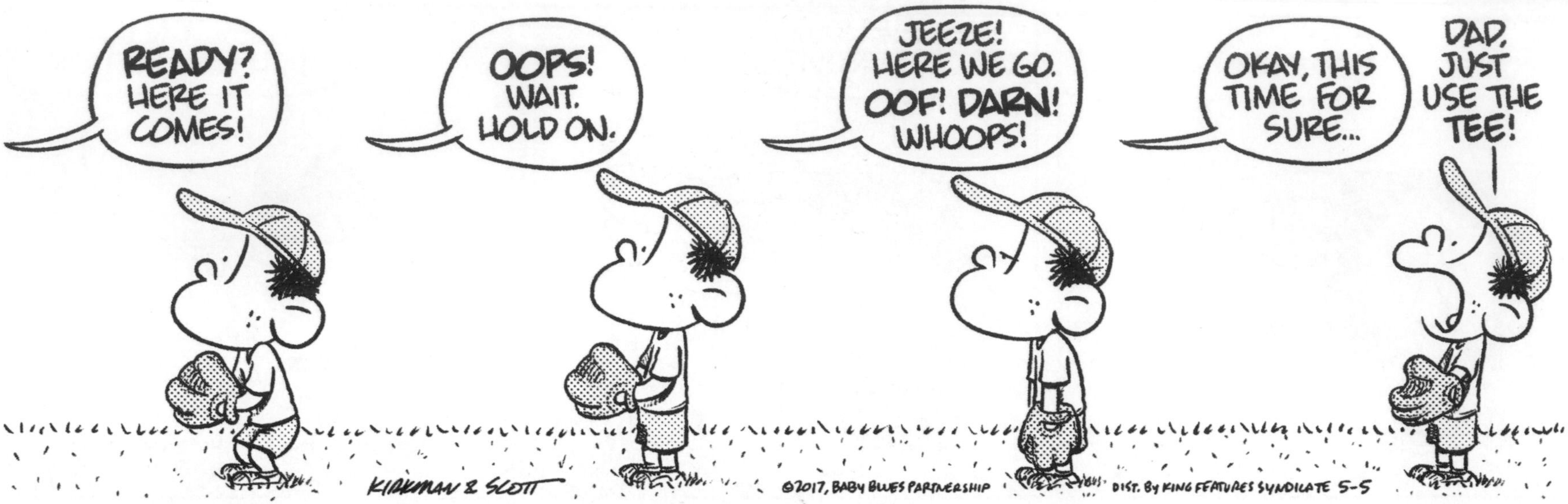
READY? HERE IT COMES!
OOPS! WAIT. HOLD ON.
JEEZE! HERE WE GO. OOF! DARN! WHOOPS!
OKAY, THIS TIME FOR SURE...
DAD, JUST USE THE TEE!
KIRKMAN & SCOTT
©2017, BABY BLUES PARTNERSHIP
DIST. BY KING FEATURES SYNDICATE 5-5

Rick: Really? Why are we piling on Darryl? **Jerry:** Darryl gets his baseball skills from me.

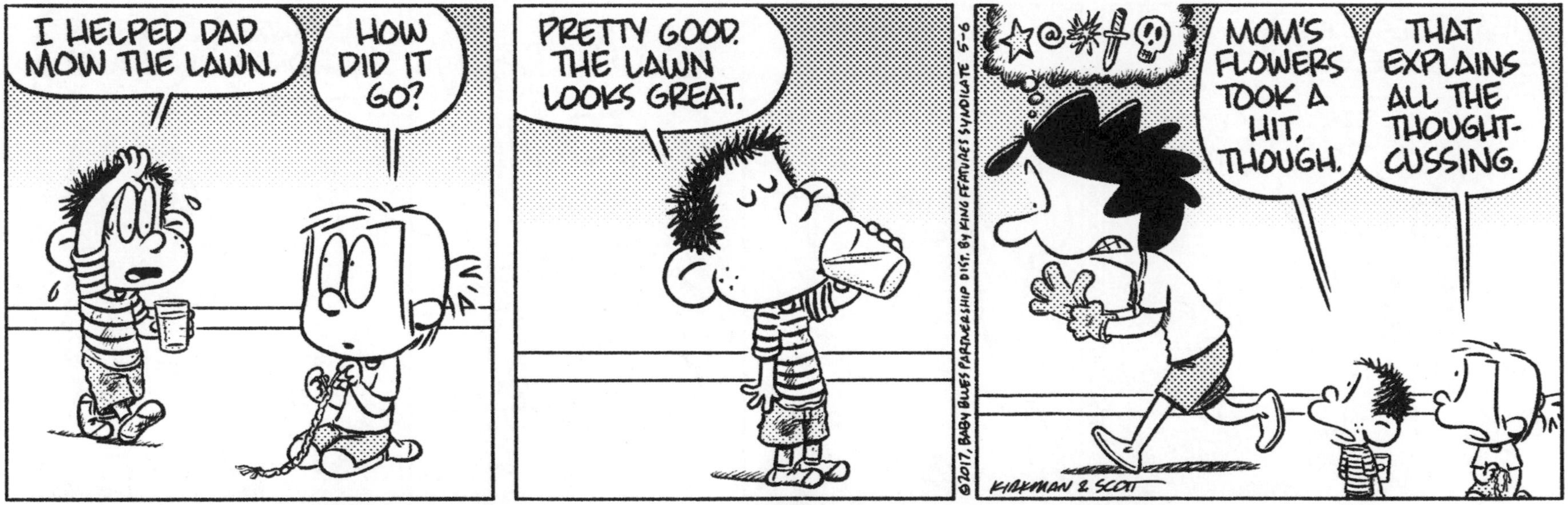
I HELPED DAD MOW THE LAWN.
HOW DID IT GO?
PRETTY GOOD. THE LAWN LOOKS GREAT.
©2017, BABY BLUES PARTNERSHIP DIST. BY KING FEATURES SYNDICATE 5-6
MOM'S FLOWERS TOOK A HIT, THOUGH.
THAT EXPLAINS ALL THE THOUGHT-CUSSING.
KIRKMAN & SCOTT

Rick: Now that I look at this, I think I should've drawn it so Wanda's looking at Hammie from the corner of her eye.

Jerry: Comic strip cussing is totally left up to the reader to interpret. If it seems profane, that's on you. All we did was draw some symbols.

BABY BLUES
Rick Kirkman & Jerry Scott
ZZZZZZ

WHAT ARE YOU DOING?
TRYING TO FIND THE PARKING STUB I JUST DROPPED.
PLEASE HAVE STUB READY
DO YOU FEEL ANYTHING?
YEAH...MAYBE THIS IS IT...
©2017, BABY BLUES PARTNERSHIP DIST. BY KING FEATURES SYNDICATE
NOPE. JUST A BUNCH OF PIZZA COUPONS AND RANDOM RECEIPTS.
I'LL KEEP LOOKING.
NOT THIS...NOT THAT... NOT THIS...NO... ...EWW...NO...
AH-HA! FOUND IT!
KIRKMAN & SCOTT 5-7
LUCKY, HUH?
MFBL.

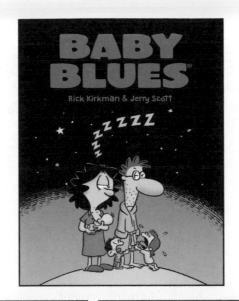

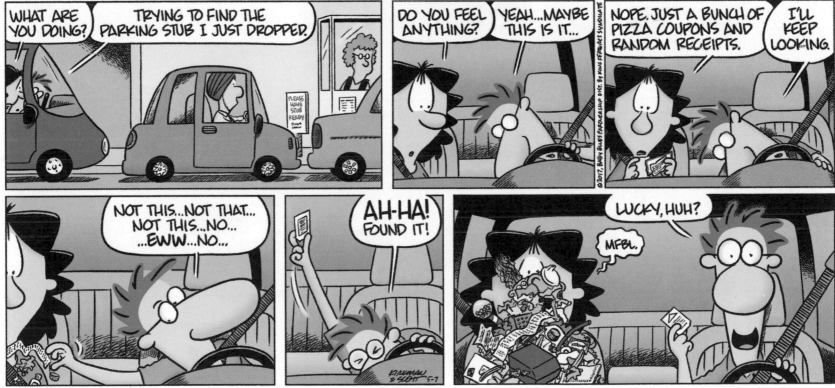

Rick: This one hits a little too close to home.

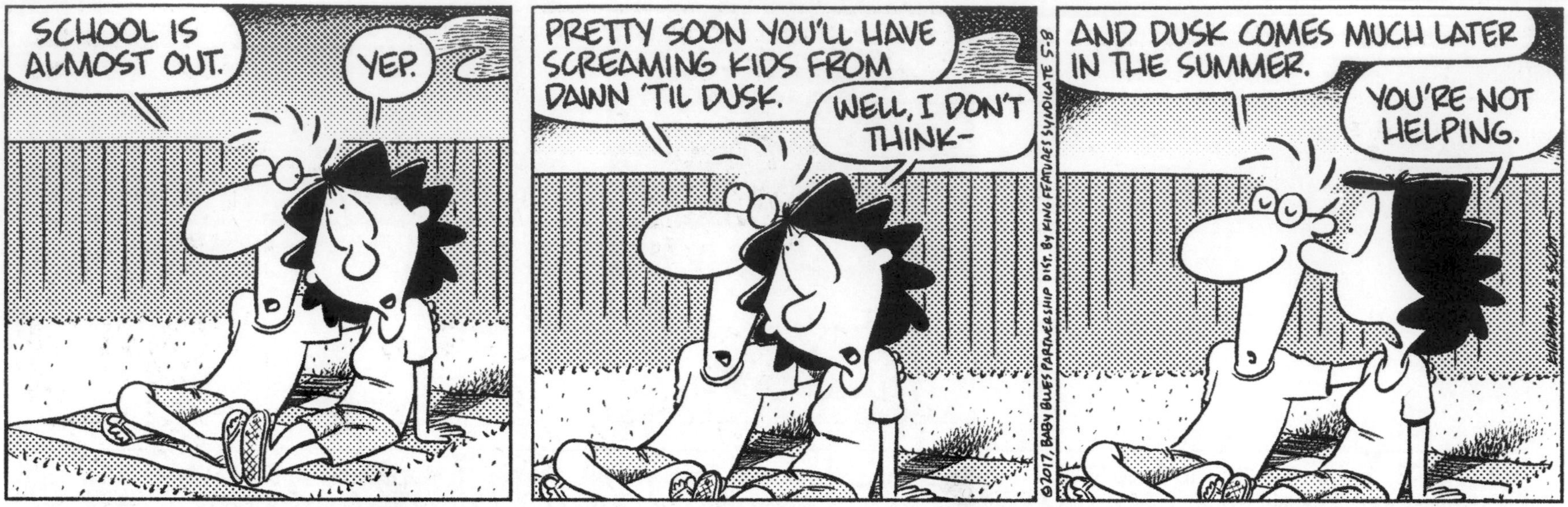
SCHOOL IS ALMOST OUT.
YEP.
PRETTY SOON YOU'LL HAVE SCREAMING KIDS FROM DAWN 'TIL DUSK.
WELL, I DON'T THINK-
©2017, BABY BLUES PARTNERSHIP DIST. BY KING FEATURES SYNDICATE 5-8
AND DUSK COMES MUCH LATER IN THE SUMMER.
YOU'RE NOT HELPING.

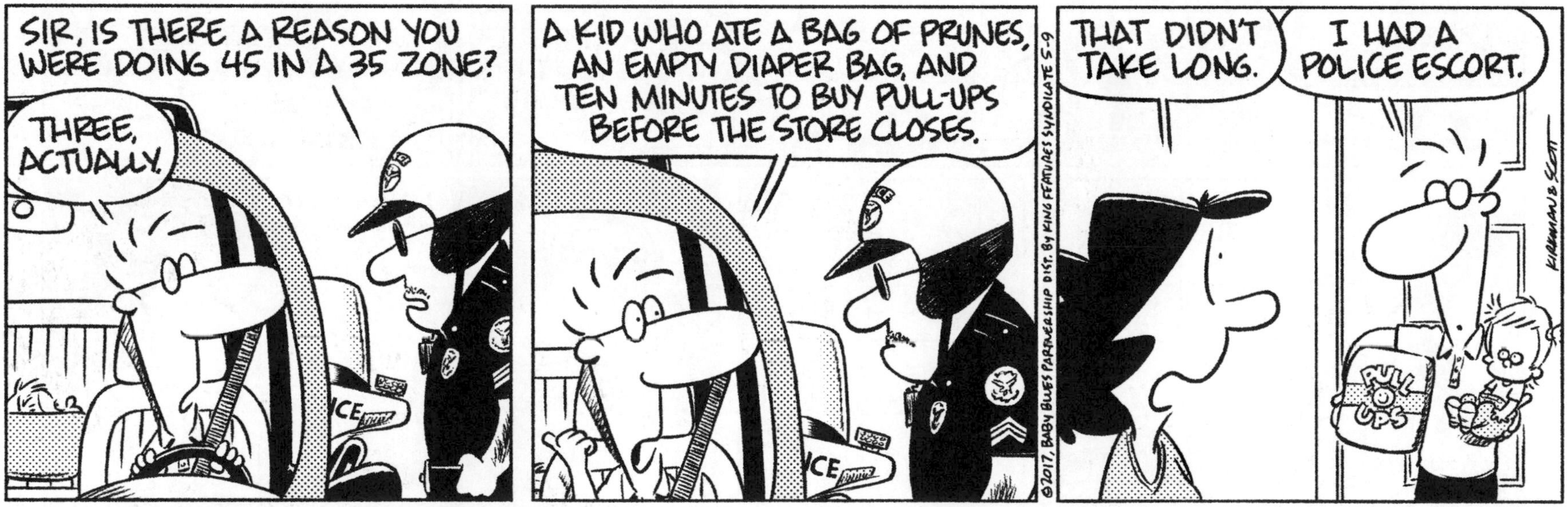
SIR, IS THERE A REASON YOU WERE DOING 45 IN A 35 ZONE?
THREE, ACTUALLY.
A KID WHO ATE A BAG OF PRUNES, AN EMPTY DIAPER BAG, AND TEN MINUTES TO BUY PULL-UPS BEFORE THE STORE CLOSES.
©2017, BABY BLUES PARTNERSHIP DIST. BY KING FEATURES SYNDICATE 5-9
THAT DIDN'T TAKE LONG.
I HAD A POLICE ESCORT.
KIRKMAN & SCOTT
PULL-UPS

Rick: One of my favorite gags of the year.

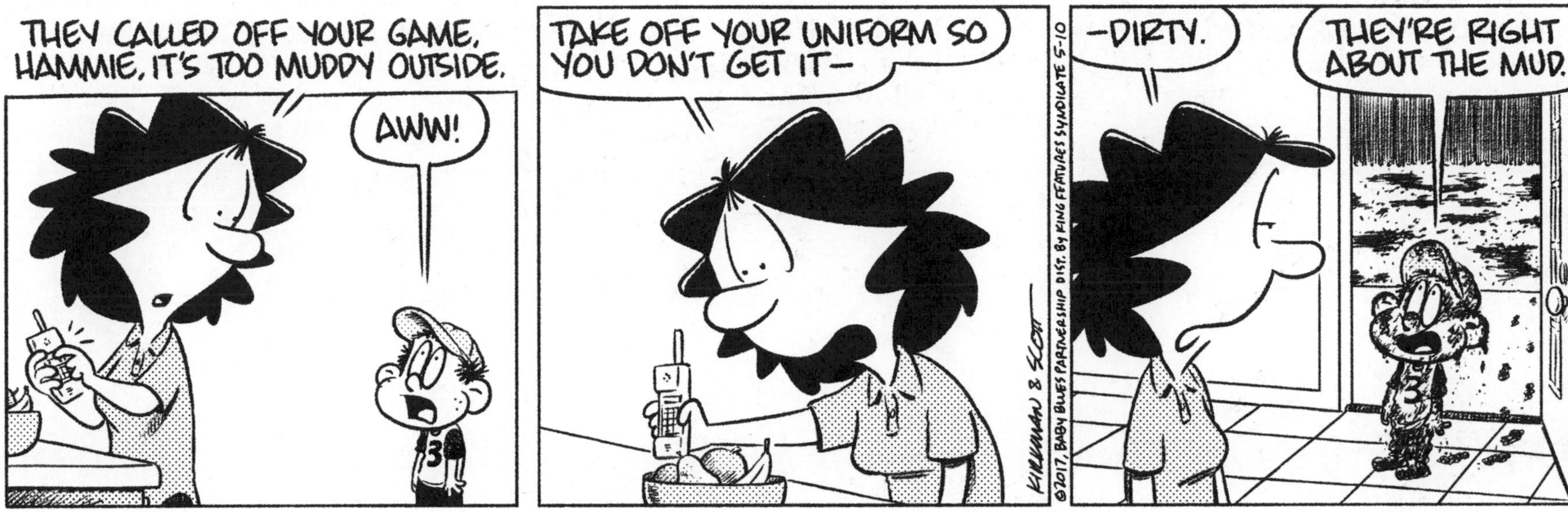
THEY CALLED OFF YOUR GAME, HAMMIE. IT'S TOO MUDDY OUTSIDE.
AWW!
TAKE OFF YOUR UNIFORM SO YOU DON'T GET IT—
—DIRTY.
THEY'RE RIGHT ABOUT THE MUD.
KIRKMAN & SCOTT
©2017, BABY BLUES PARTNERSHIP DIST. BY KING FEATURES SYNDICATE 5-10

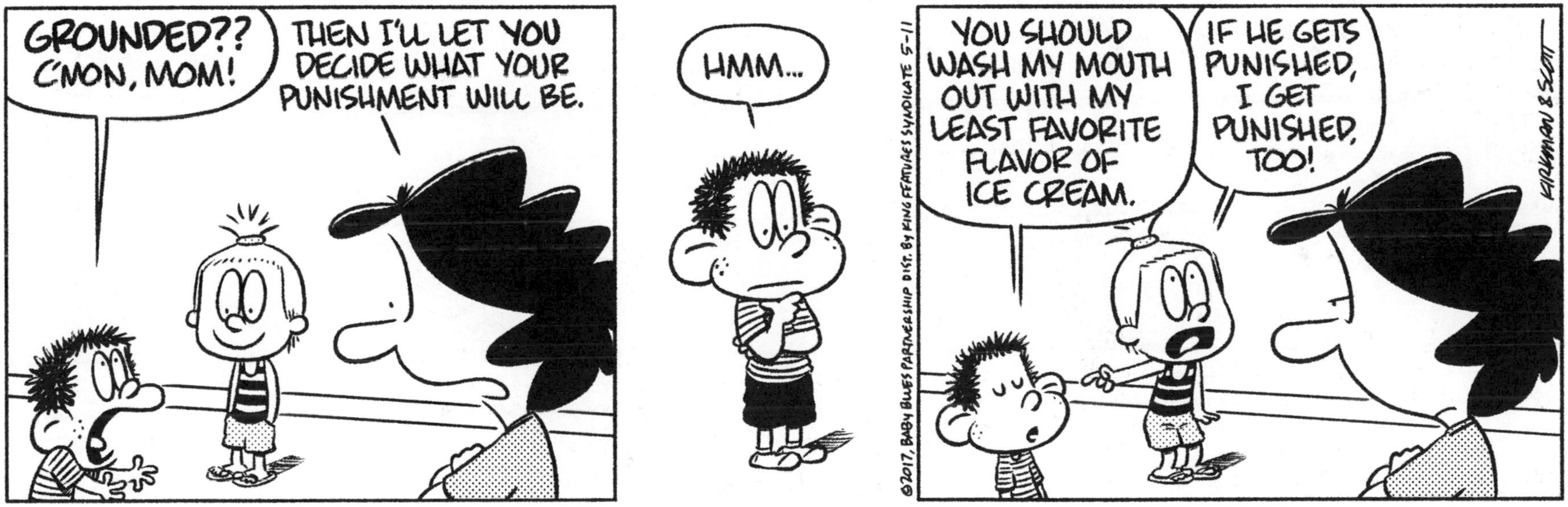
GROUNDED?? C'MON, MOM!
THEN I'LL LET YOU DECIDE WHAT YOUR PUNISHMENT WILL BE.
HMM...
YOU SHOULD WASH MY MOUTH OUT WITH MY LEAST FAVORITE FLAVOR OF ICE CREAM.
IF HE GETS PUNISHED, I GET PUNISHED, TOO!
KIRKMAN & SCOTT
©2017, BABY BLUES PARTNERSHIP DIST. BY KING FEATURES SYNDICATE 5-11

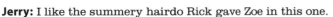

Jerry: I like the summery hairdo Rick gave Zoe in this one.

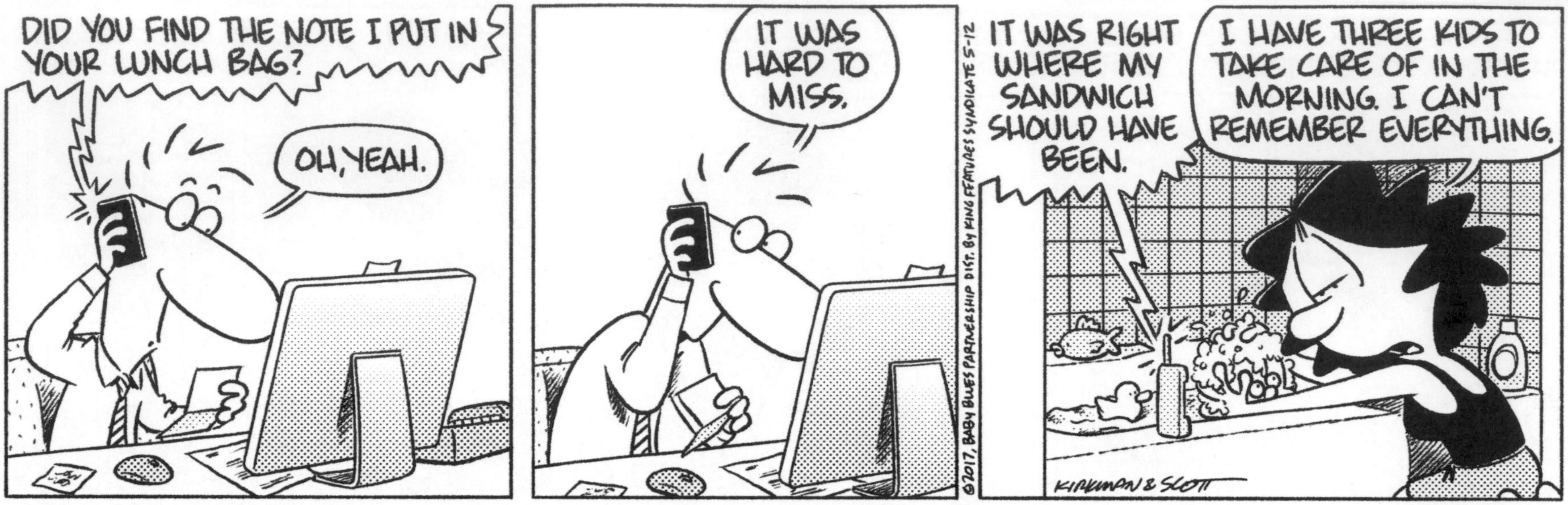
DID YOU FIND THE NOTE I PUT IN YOUR LUNCH BAG?
OH, YEAH.
IT WAS HARD TO MISS.
©2017, BABY BLUES PARTNERSHIP DIST. BY KING FEATURES SYNDICATE 5-12
IT WAS RIGHT WHERE MY SANDWICH SHOULD HAVE BEEN.
I HAVE THREE KIDS TO TAKE CARE OF IN THE MORNING. I CAN'T REMEMBER EVERYTHING.
KIRKMAN & SCOTT

Rick: I love the unexpected payoff in the last panel. I think Darryl needs to start making his own lunch.

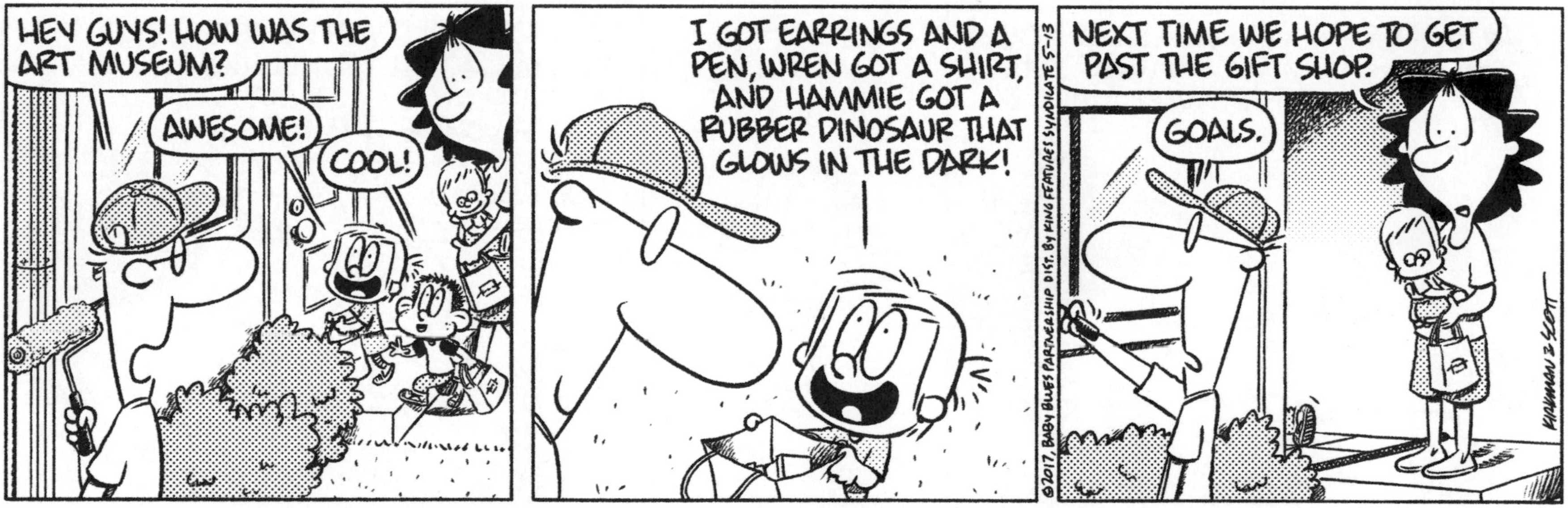
HEY GUYS! HOW WAS THE ART MUSEUM?
AWESOME!
COOL!
I GOT EARRINGS AND A PEN, WREN GOT A SHIRT, AND HAMMIE GOT A RUBBER DINOSAUR THAT GLOWS IN THE DARK!
©2017, BABY BLUES PARTNERSHIP DIST. BY KING FEATURES SYNDICATE 5-13
NEXT TIME WE HOPE TO GET PAST THE GIFT SHOP.
GOALS.
KIRKMAN & SCOTT

Jerry: How many dinosaur-shaped erasers and Van Gogh refrigerator magnets are in YOUR junk drawer?

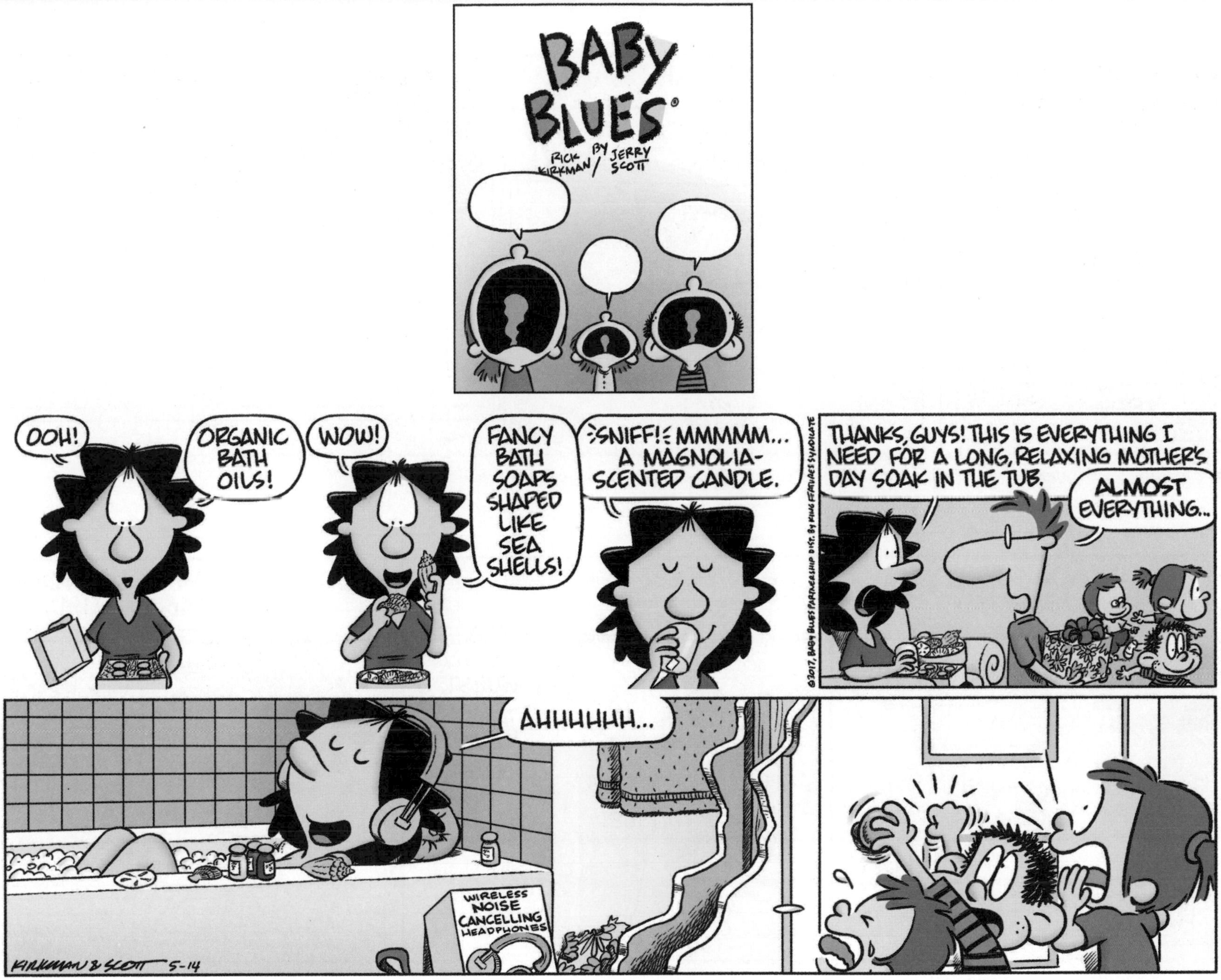
BABY BLUES®
BY RICK KIRKMAN / JERRY SCOTT
OOH!
ORGANIC BATH OILS!
WOW!
FANCY BATH SOAPS SHAPED LIKE SEA SHELLS!
SNIFF! MMMMM... A MAGNOLIA-SCENTED CANDLE.
THANKS, GUYS! THIS IS EVERYTHING I NEED FOR A LONG, RELAXING MOTHER'S DAY SOAK IN THE TUB.
ALMOST EVERYTHING...
©2017, BABY BLUES PARTNERSHIP DIST. BY KING FEATURES SYNDICATE
AHHHHHH...
WIRELESS NOISE CANCELLING HEADPHONES
KIRKMAN & SCOTT 5-14

Rick: Hmm. Challenging last panel solved with a cutaway of the wall.

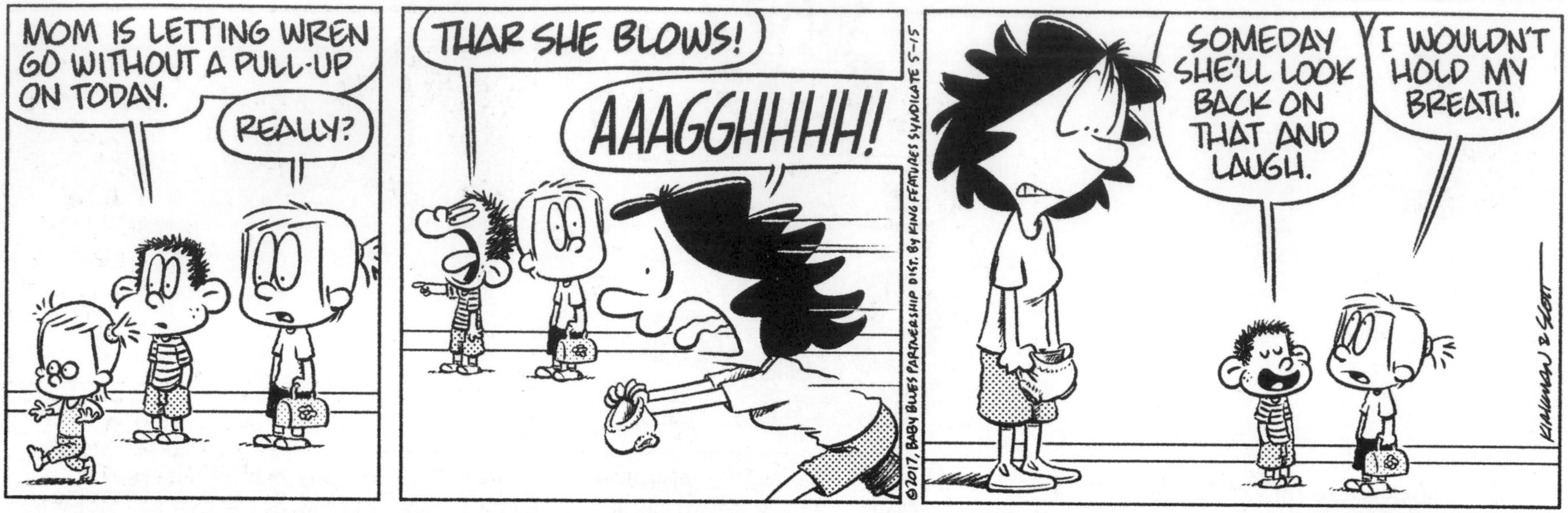
MOM IS LETTING WREN GO WITHOUT A PULL-UP ON TODAY.
REALLY?
THAR SHE BLOWS!
AAAGGHHHH!
©2017, BABY BLUES PARTNERSHIP DIST. BY KING FEATURES SYNDICATE 5-15
SOMEDAY SHE'LL LOOK BACK ON THAT AND LAUGH.
I WOULDN'T HOLD MY BREATH.
KIRKMAN & SCOTT

Rick: That one is definitely better left unseen.

Jerry: There's almost nothing that can't be made more difficult by just adding siblings.

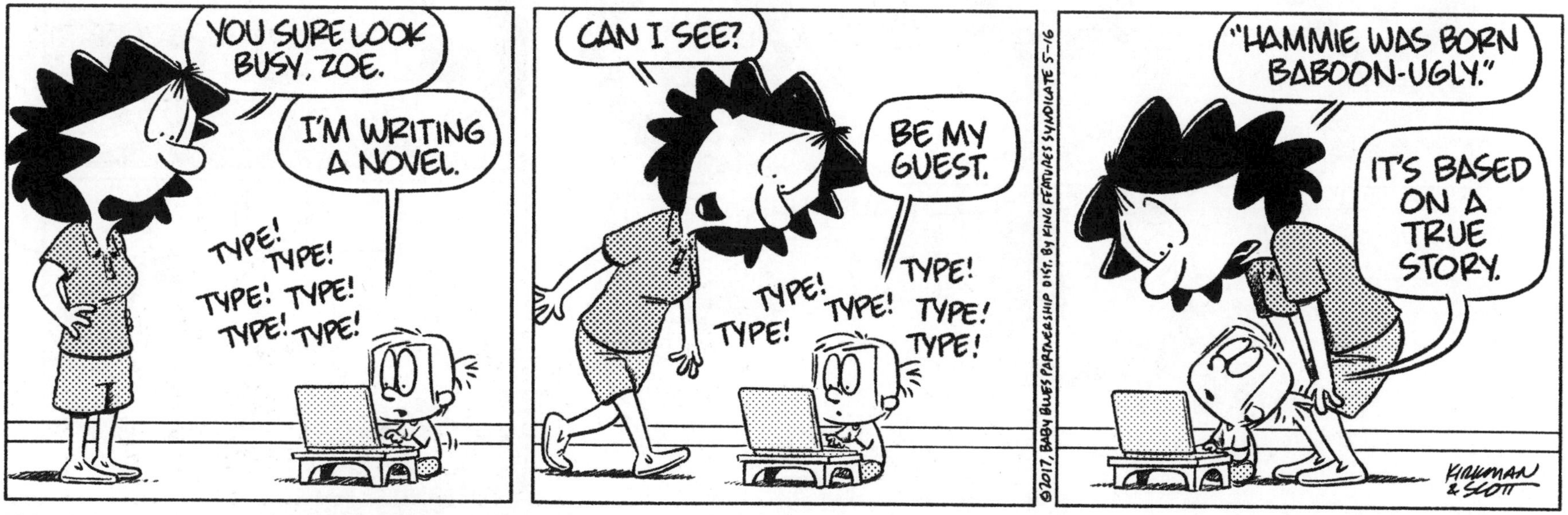
YOU SURE LOOK BUSY, ZOE.
I'M WRITING A NOVEL.
TYPE! TYPE! TYPE! TYPE! TYPE! TYPE!
CAN I SEE?
BE MY GUEST.
TYPE! TYPE! TYPE! TYPE! TYPE! TYPE!
©2017, BABY BLUES PARTNERSHIP DIST. BY KING FEATURES SYNDICATE 5-16
"HAMMIE WAS BORN BABOON-UGLY."
IT'S BASED ON A TRUE STORY.
KIRKMAN & SCOTT

Rick: "Baboon-ugly" is a great description. Unless you're a baboon.

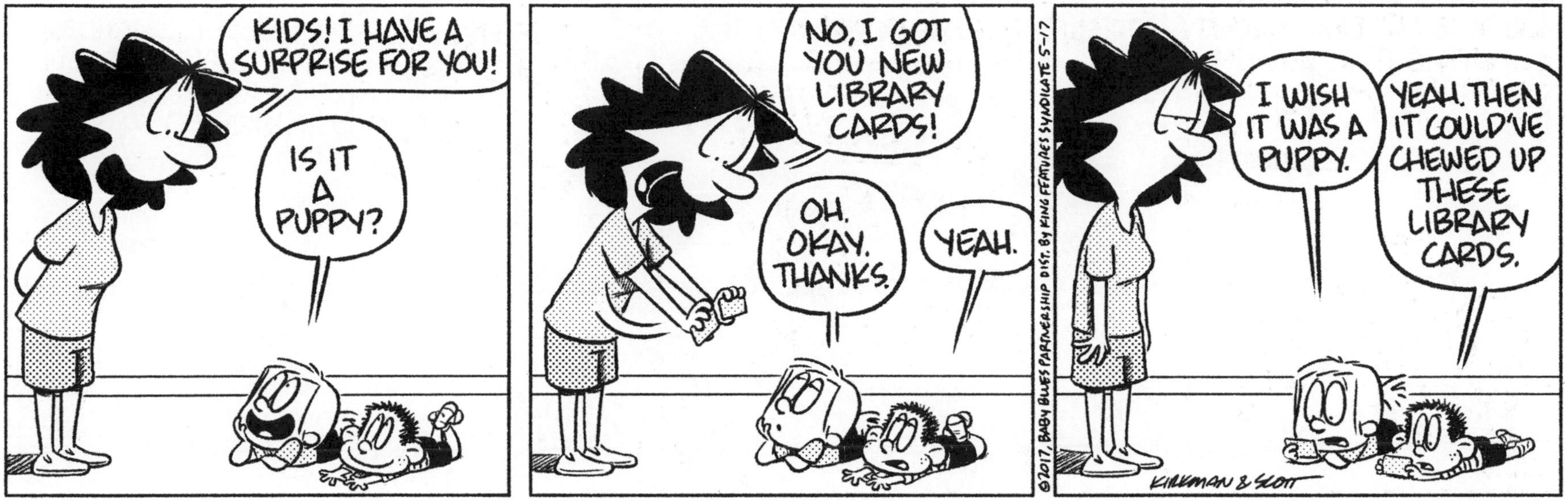
KIDS! I HAVE A SURPRISE FOR YOU!
IS IT A PUPPY?
NO, I GOT YOU NEW LIBRARY CARDS!
OH. OKAY. THANKS.
YEAH.
©2017, BABY BLUES PARTNERSHIP DIST. BY KING FEATURES SYNDICATE 5-17
I WISH IT WAS A PUPPY.
YEAH. THEN IT COULD'VE CHEWED UP THESE LIBRARY CARDS.
KIRKMAN & SCOTT

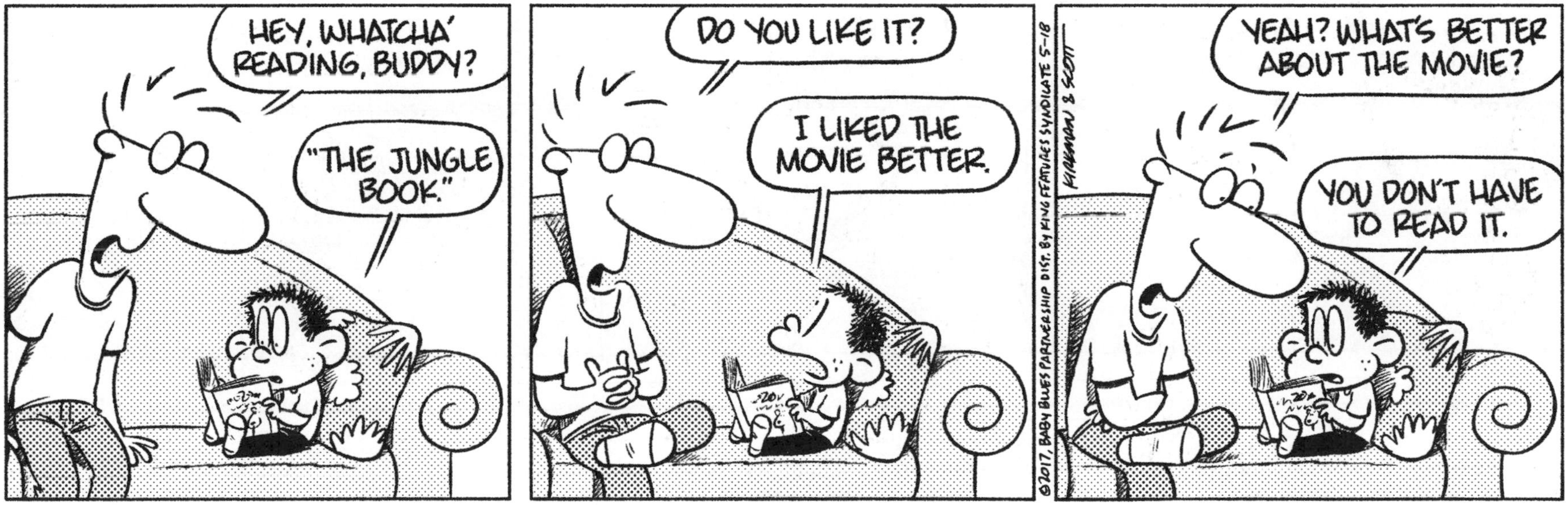
HEY, WHATCHA' READING, BUDDY?
"THE JUNGLE BOOK."
DO YOU LIKE IT?
I LIKED THE MOVIE BETTER.
©2017, BABY BLUES PARTNERSHIP DIST. BY KING FEATURES SYNDICATE 5-18
KIRKMAN & SCOTT
YEAH? WHAT'S BETTER ABOUT THE MOVIE?
YOU DON'T HAVE TO READ IT.

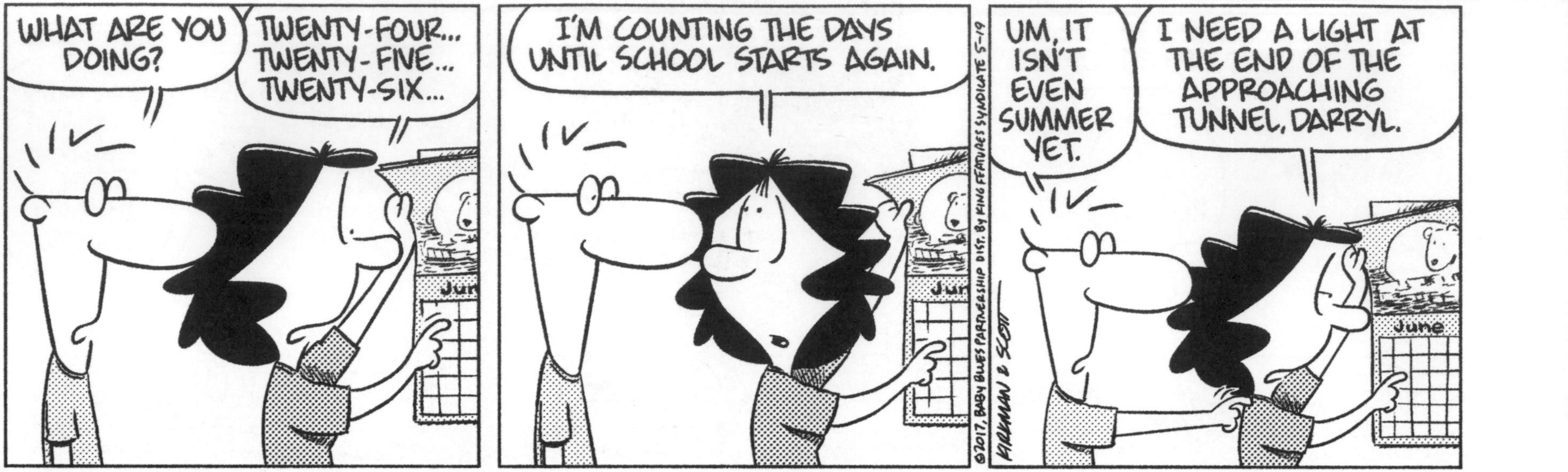
WHAT ARE YOU DOING?
TWENTY-FOUR... TWENTY-FIVE... TWENTY-SIX...
I'M COUNTING THE DAYS UNTIL SCHOOL STARTS AGAIN.
©2017, BABY BLUES PARTNERSHIP DIST. BY KING FEATURES SYNDICATE 5-19
KIRKMAN & SCOTT
UM, IT ISN'T EVEN SUMMER YET.
I NEED A LIGHT AT THE END OF THE APPROACHING TUNNEL, DARRYL.

Rick: I'm trying to figure out why I drew a polar bear on an ice floe on the calendar for June.

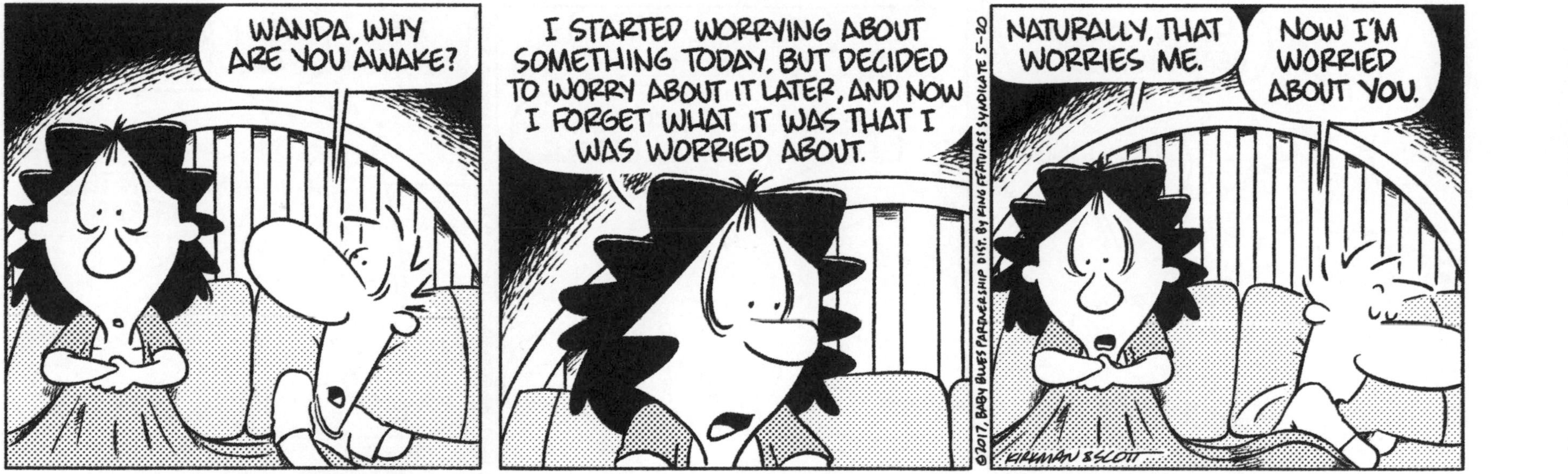
WANDA, WHY ARE YOU AWAKE?
I STARTED WORRYING ABOUT SOMETHING TODAY, BUT DECIDED TO WORRY ABOUT IT LATER, AND NOW I FORGET WHAT IT WAS THAT I WAS WORRIED ABOUT.
©2017, BABY BLUES PARTNERSHIP DIST. BY KING FEATURES SYNDICATE 5-20
NATURALLY, THAT WORRIES ME.
NOW I'M WORRIED ABOUT YOU.
KIRKMAN & SCOTT

Rick: You'd think Jerry was getting paid by the "worry." Well done.

Baby Blues
Rick Kirkman & Jerry Scott
ZZZZZZ

DID YOU FINALLY GET WREN TO BED?
I THINK SO.
©2017, BABY BLUES PARTNERSHIP DIST. BY KING FEATURES SYNDICATE
YOU THINK SO??
KIRKMAN & SCOTT
I SORT OF LOST HER IN THE CROWD.
5-21

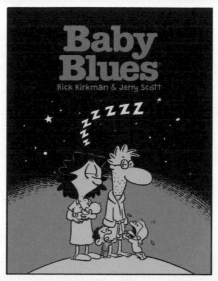

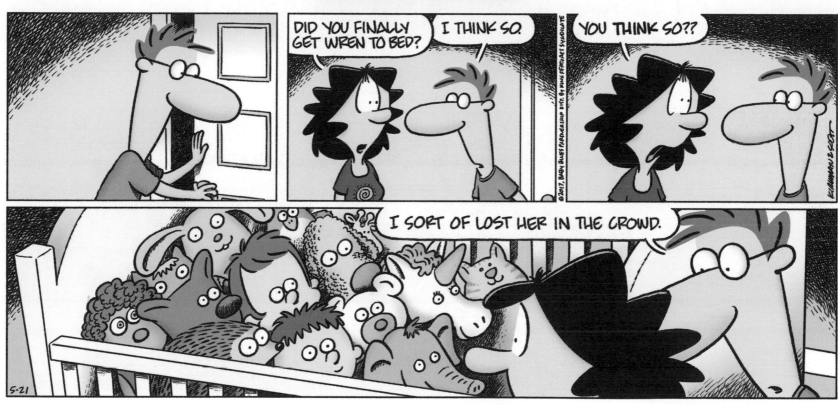

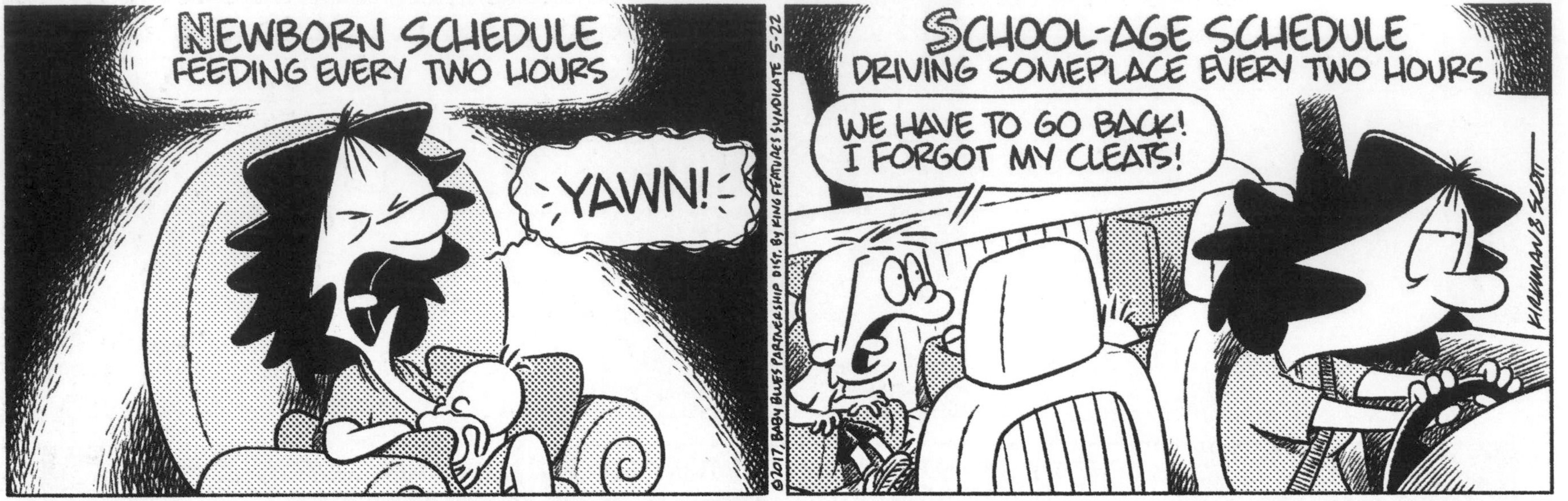
NEWBORN SCHEDULE
FEEDING EVERY TWO HOURS
YAWN!
©2017, BABY BLUES PARTNERSHIP DIST. BY KING FEATURES SYNDICATE 5-22
SCHOOL-AGE SCHEDULE
DRIVING SOMEPLACE EVERY TWO HOURS
WE HAVE TO GO BACK! I FORGOT MY CLEATS!
KIRKMAN & SCOTT

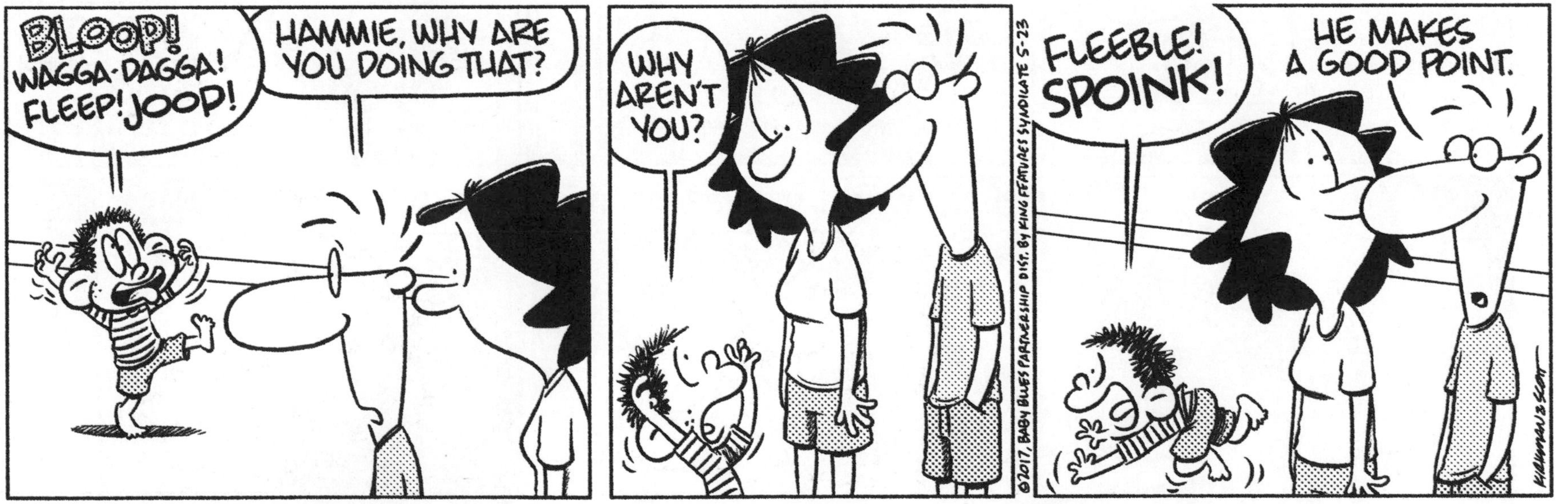
BLOOP! WAGGA-DAGGA! FLEEP! JOOP!
HAMMIE, WHY ARE YOU DOING THAT?
WHY AREN'T YOU?
©2017, BABY BLUES PARTNERSHIP DIST. BY KING FEATURES SYNDICATE 5-23
FLEEBLE! SPOINK!
HE MAKES A GOOD POINT.
KIRKMAN & SCOTT

Rick: Really good point. Spleeka doop feep!

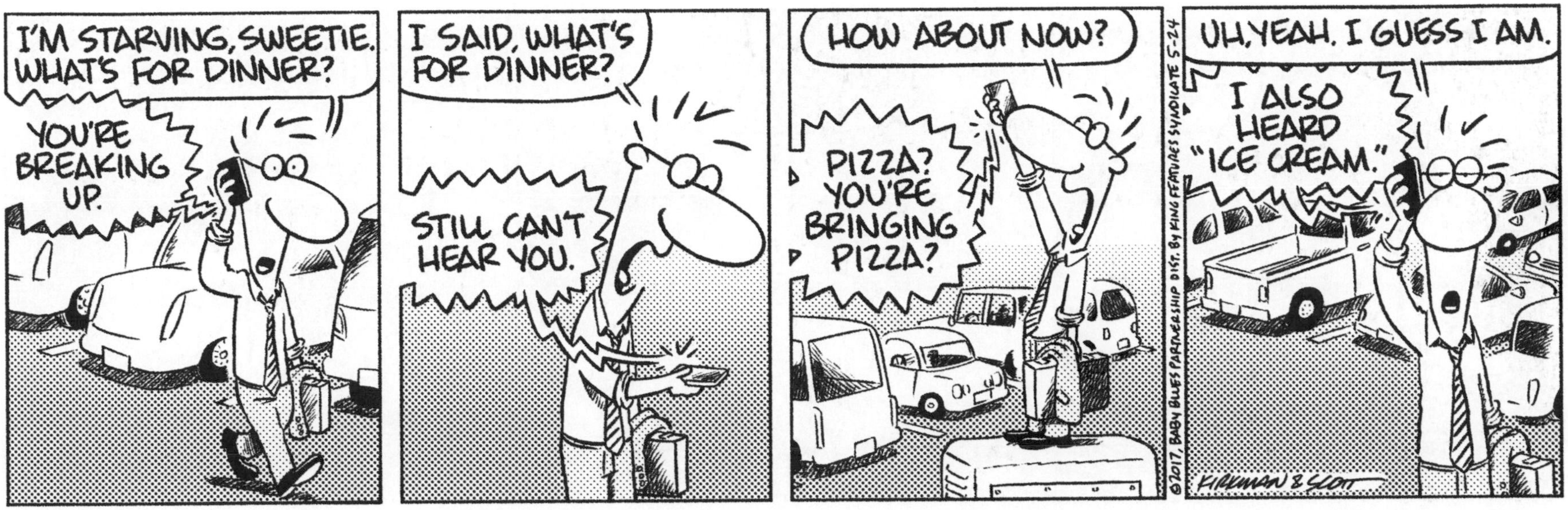
I'M STARVING, SWEETIE. WHAT'S FOR DINNER?
YOU'RE BREAKING UP.
I SAID, WHAT'S FOR DINNER?
STILL CAN'T HEAR YOU.
HOW ABOUT NOW?
PIZZA? YOU'RE BRINGING PIZZA?
©2017, BABY BLUES PARTNERSHIP DIST. BY KING FEATURES SYNDICATE 5-24
UH, YEAH. I GUESS I AM.
I ALSO HEARD "ICE CREAM."
KIRKMAN & SCOTT

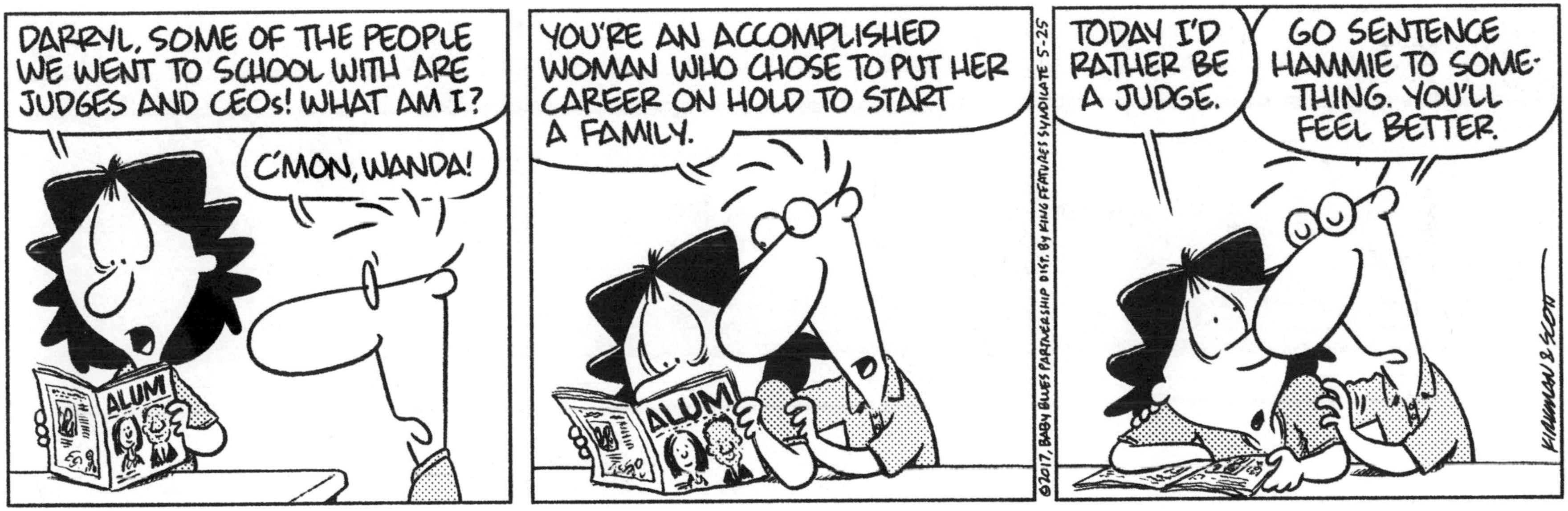
DARRYL, SOME OF THE PEOPLE WE WENT TO SCHOOL WITH ARE JUDGES AND CEOs! WHAT AM I?
C'MON, WANDA!
ALUM
YOU'RE AN ACCOMPLISHED WOMAN WHO CHOSE TO PUT HER CAREER ON HOLD TO START A FAMILY.
ALUM
©2017, BABY BLUES PARTNERSHIP DIST. BY KING FEATURES SYNDICATE 5-25
TODAY I'D RATHER BE A JUDGE.
GO SENTENCE HAMMIE TO SOMETHING. YOU'LL FEEL BETTER.
KIRKMAN & SCOTT

Jerry: Strong, supportive, and sarcastic. Two out of three ain't bad, Darryl.

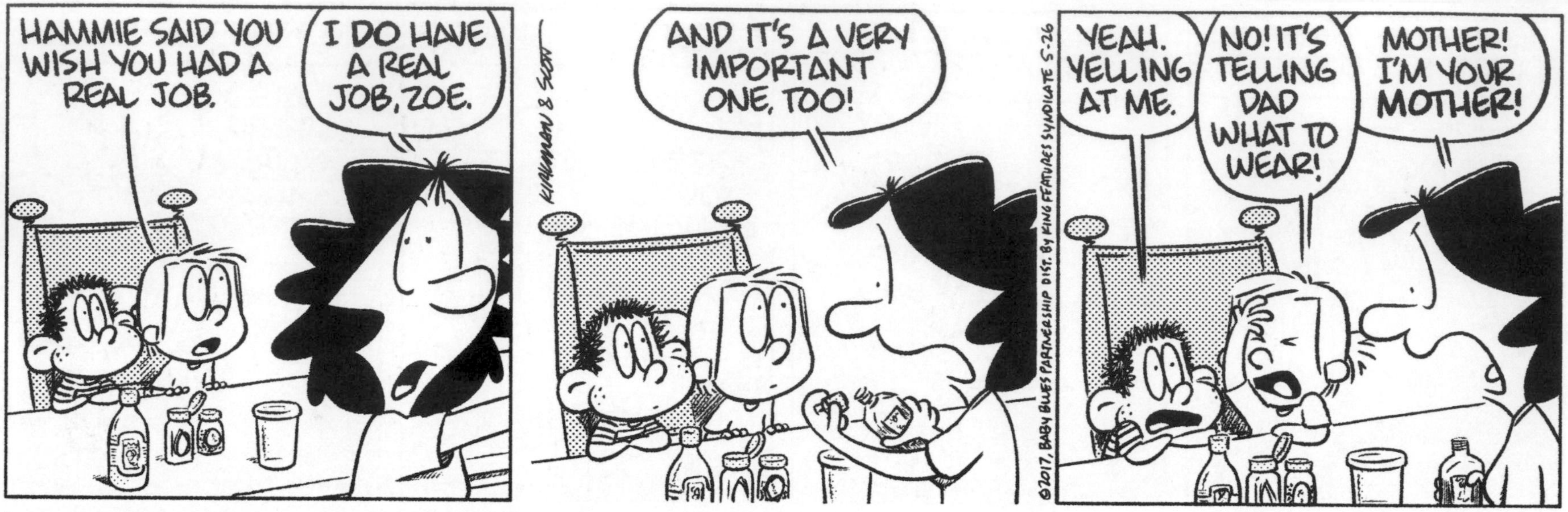
HAMMIE SAID YOU WISH YOU HAD A REAL JOB.
I DO HAVE A REAL JOB, ZOE.
KIRKMAN & SCOTT
AND IT'S A VERY IMPORTANT ONE, TOO!
©2017, BABY BLUES PARTNERSHIP DIST. BY KING FEATURES SYNDICATE 5-26
YEAH. YELLING AT ME.
NO! IT'S TELLING DAD WHAT TO WEAR!
MOTHER! I'M YOUR MOTHER!

Jerry: It's hard to summarize a mom's job description.

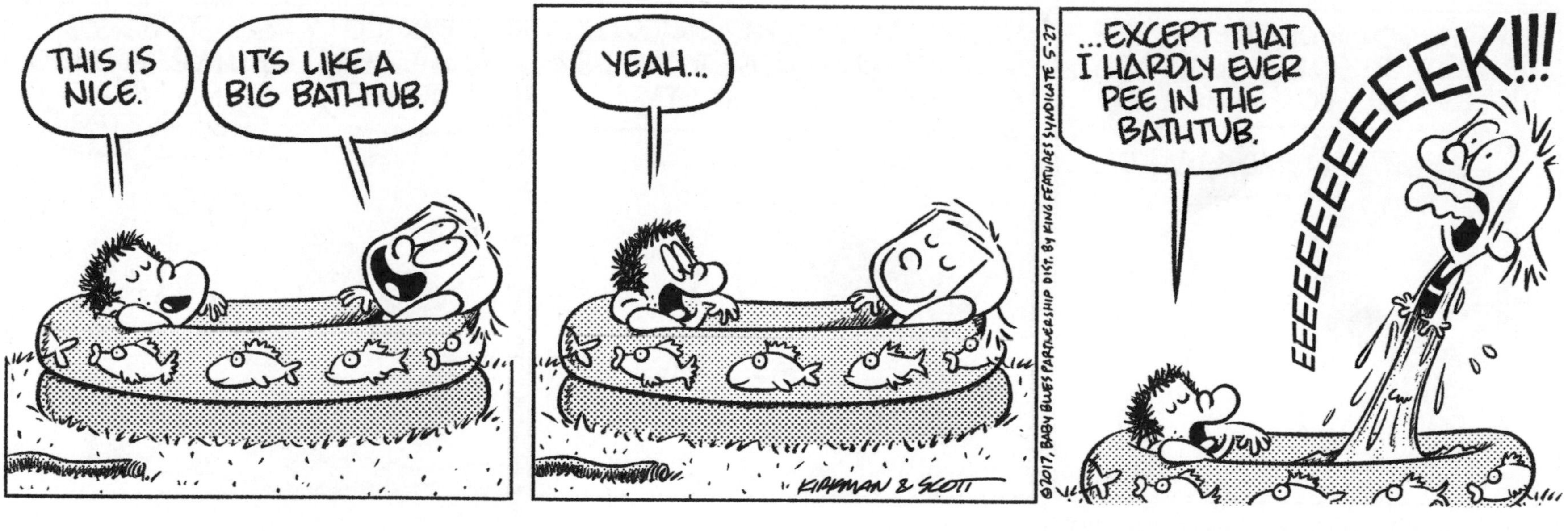
THIS IS NICE.
IT'S LIKE A BIG BATHTUB.
YEAH...
KIRKMAN & SCOTT
©2017, BABY BLUES PARTNERSHIP DIST. BY KING FEATURES SYNDICATE 5-27
...EXCEPT THAT I HARDLY EVER PEE IN THE BATHTUB.
EEEEEEEEEEEEK!!!

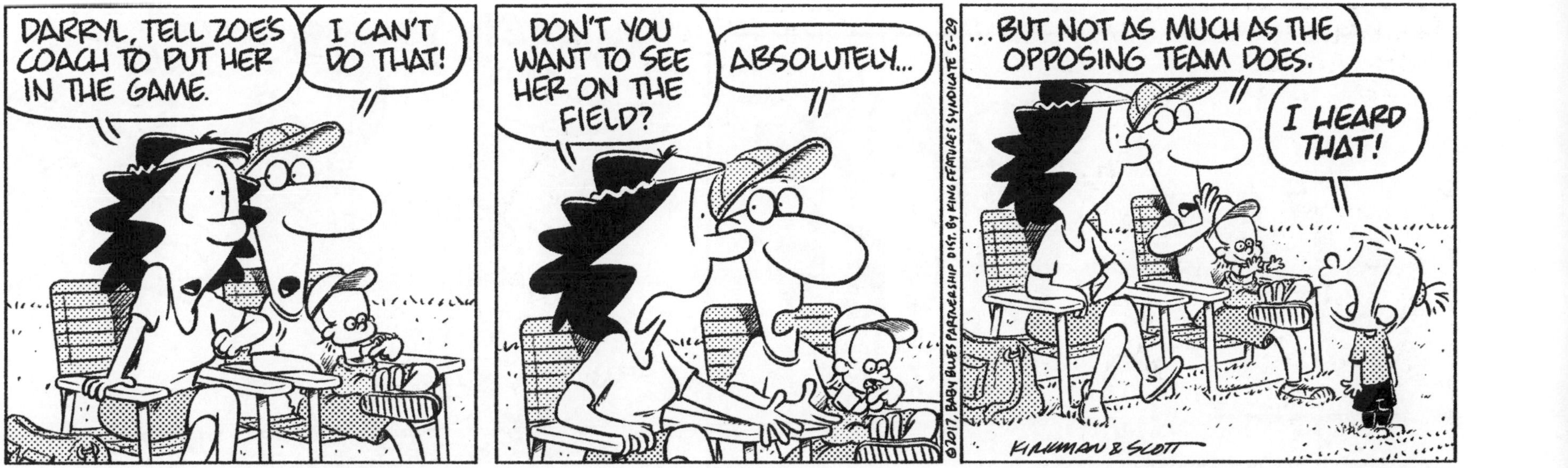
DARRYL, TELL ZOE'S COACH TO PUT HER IN THE GAME.
I CAN'T DO THAT!
DON'T YOU WANT TO SEE HER ON THE FIELD?
ABSOLUTELY...
©2017, BABY BLUES PARTNERSHIP DIST. BY KING FEATURES SYNDICATE 5-29
...BUT NOT AS MUCH AS THE OPPOSING TEAM DOES.
I HEARD THAT!
KIRKMAN & SCOTT

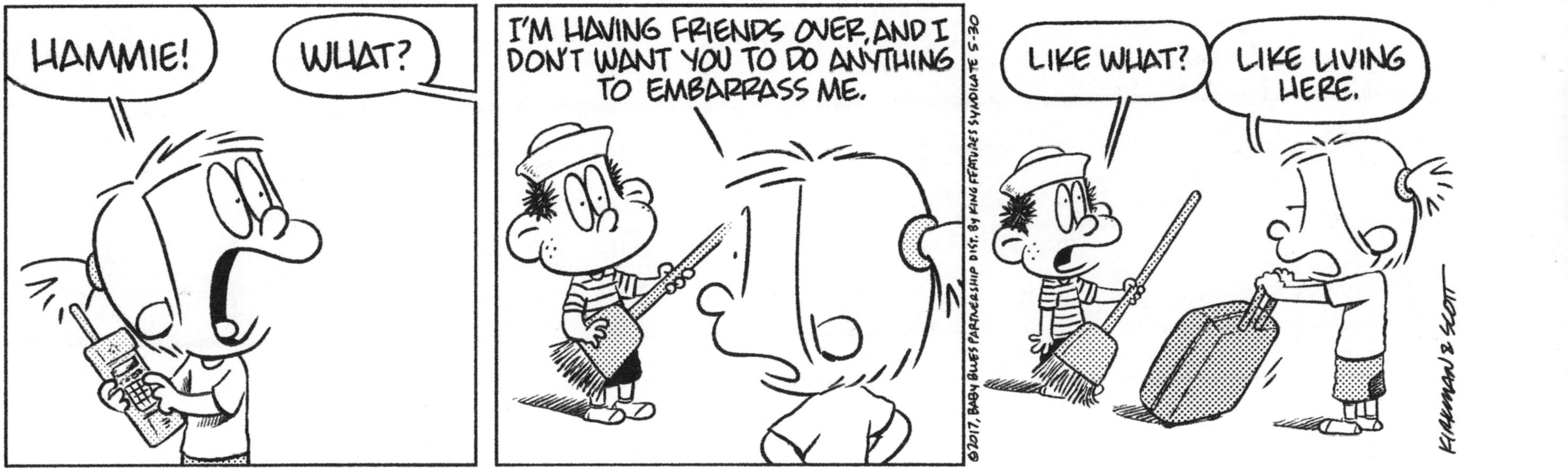
HAMMIE!
WHAT?
I'M HAVING FRIENDS OVER, AND I DON'T WANT YOU TO DO ANYTHING TO EMBARRASS ME.
©2017, BABY BLUES PARTNERSHIP DIST. BY KING FEATURES SYNDICATE 5-30
LIKE WHAT?
LIKE LIVING HERE.
KIRKMAN & SCOTT

Jerry: Well, that would certainly address the problem.

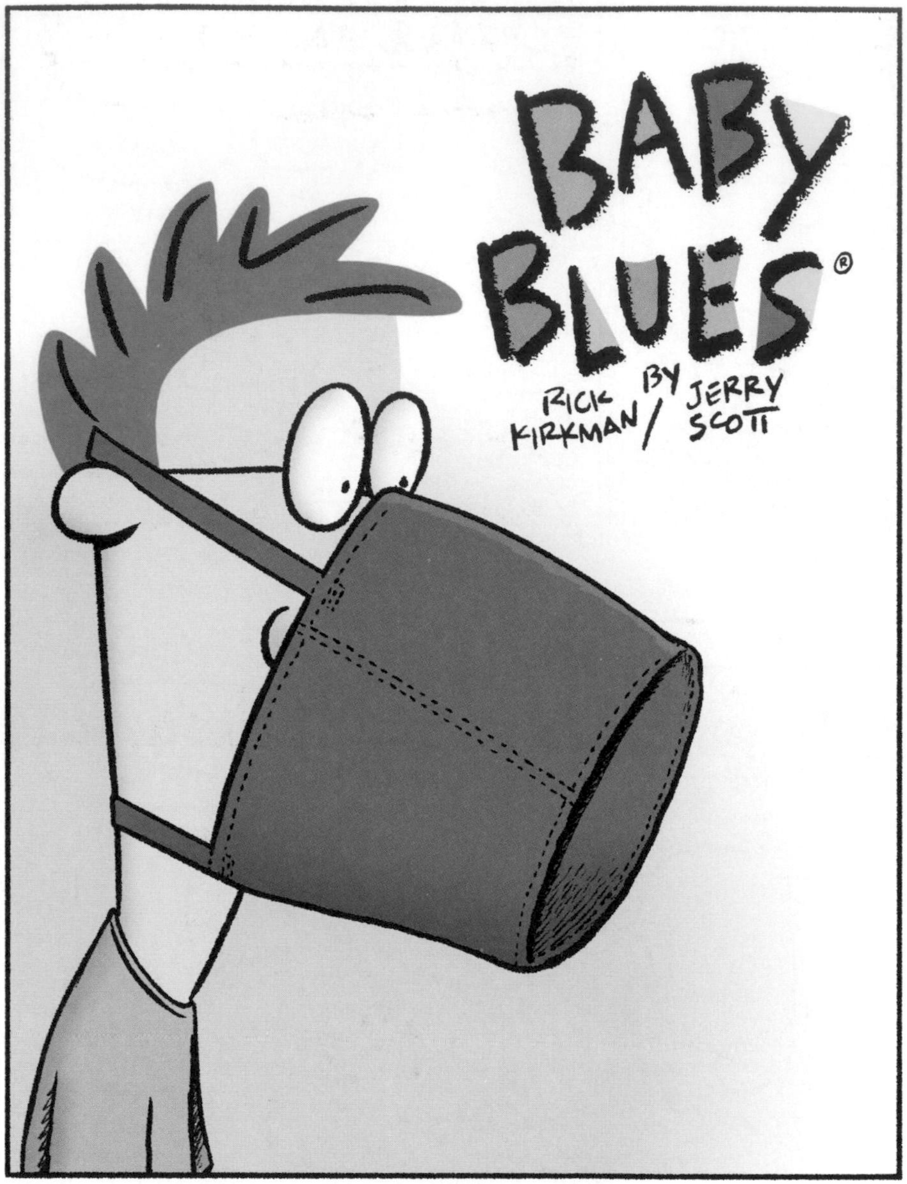
BABY BLUES®
BY RICK KIRKMAN / JERRY SCOTT

Jerry: The comics page is a contest for readers' attention, and I think we won this day. Love these drawings of Darryl and Wren, Rick!

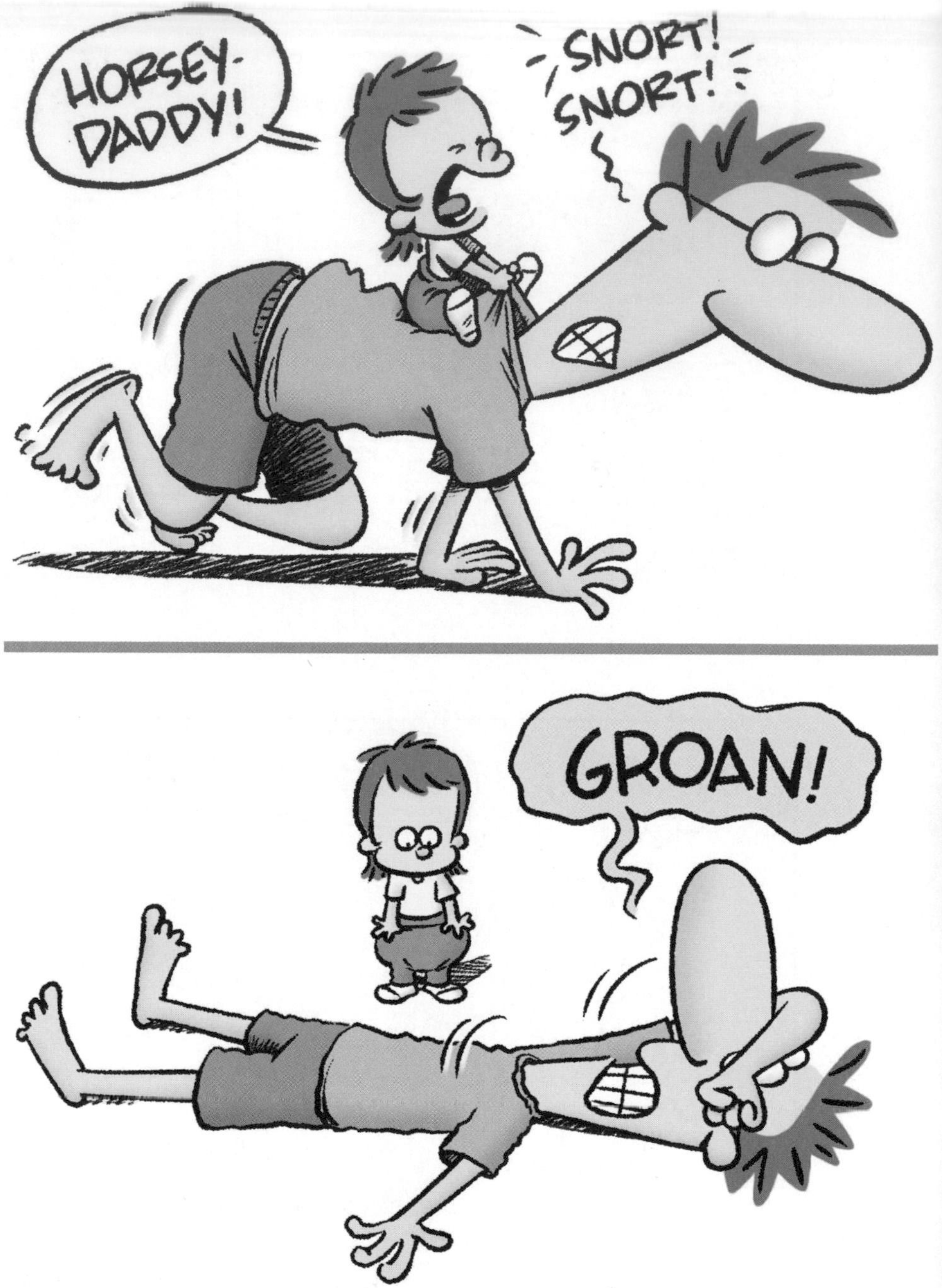
HORSEY-DADDY!
SNORT! SNORT!
GROAN!

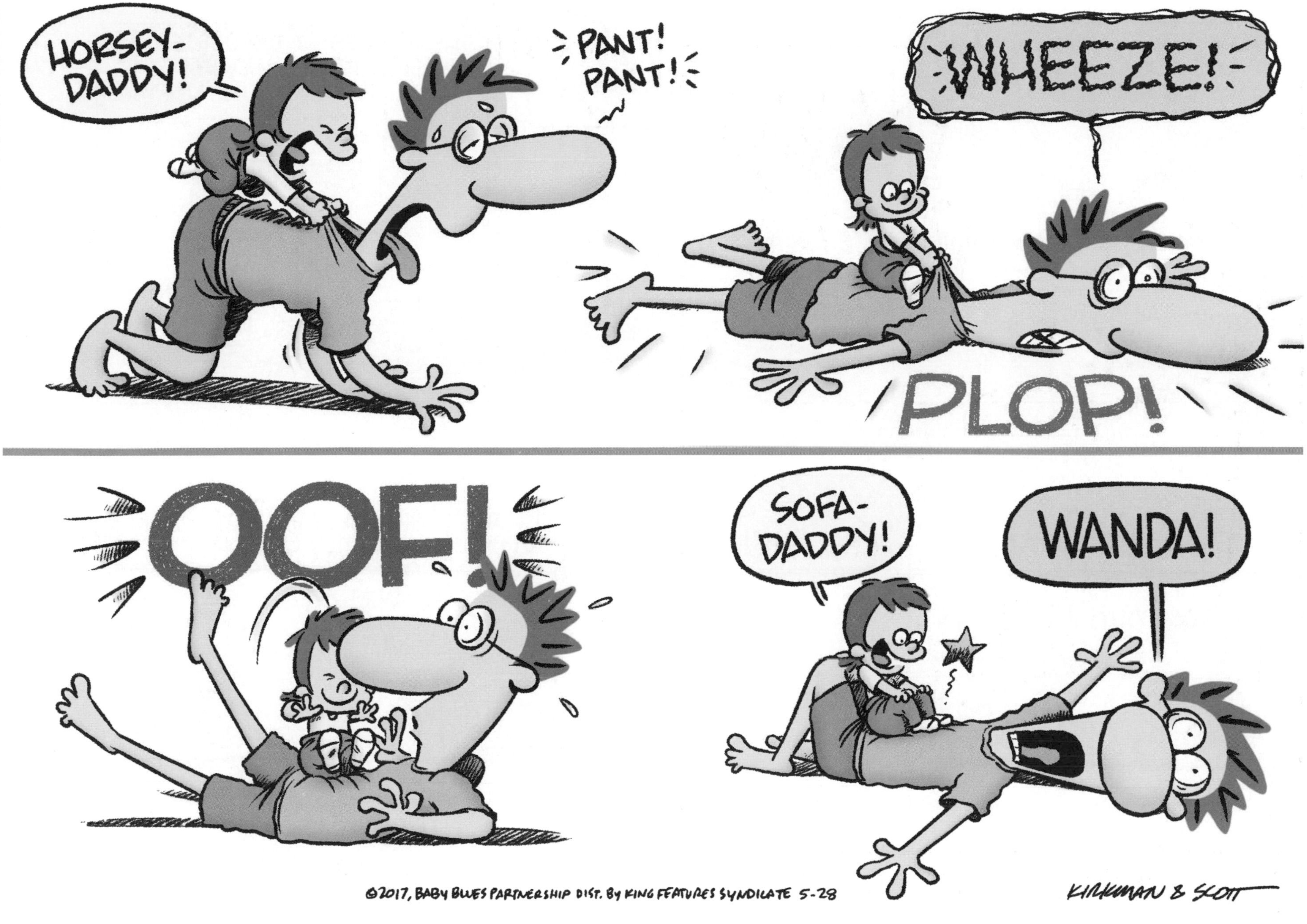
HORSEY-DADDY!
PANT! PANT!
WHEEZE!
PLOP!
OOF!
SOFA-DADDY!
WANDA!
©2017, BABY BLUES PARTNERSHIP DIST. BY KING FEATURES SYNDICATE 5-28
KIRKMAN & SCOTT

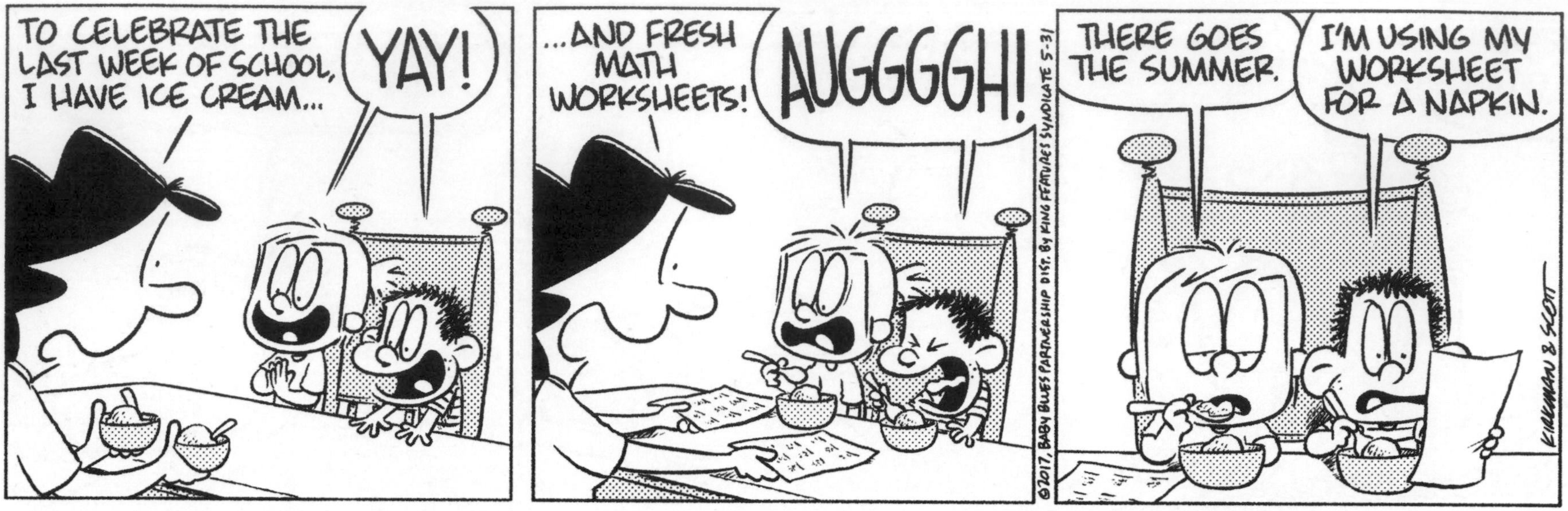
TO CELEBRATE THE LAST WEEK OF SCHOOL, I HAVE ICE CREAM...
YAY!
...AND FRESH MATH WORKSHEETS!
AUGGGGH!
©2017, BABY BLUES PARTNERSHIP DIST. BY KING FEATURES SYNDICATE 5-31
THERE GOES THE SUMMER.
I'M USING MY WORKSHEET FOR A NAPKIN.
KIRKMAN & SCOTT

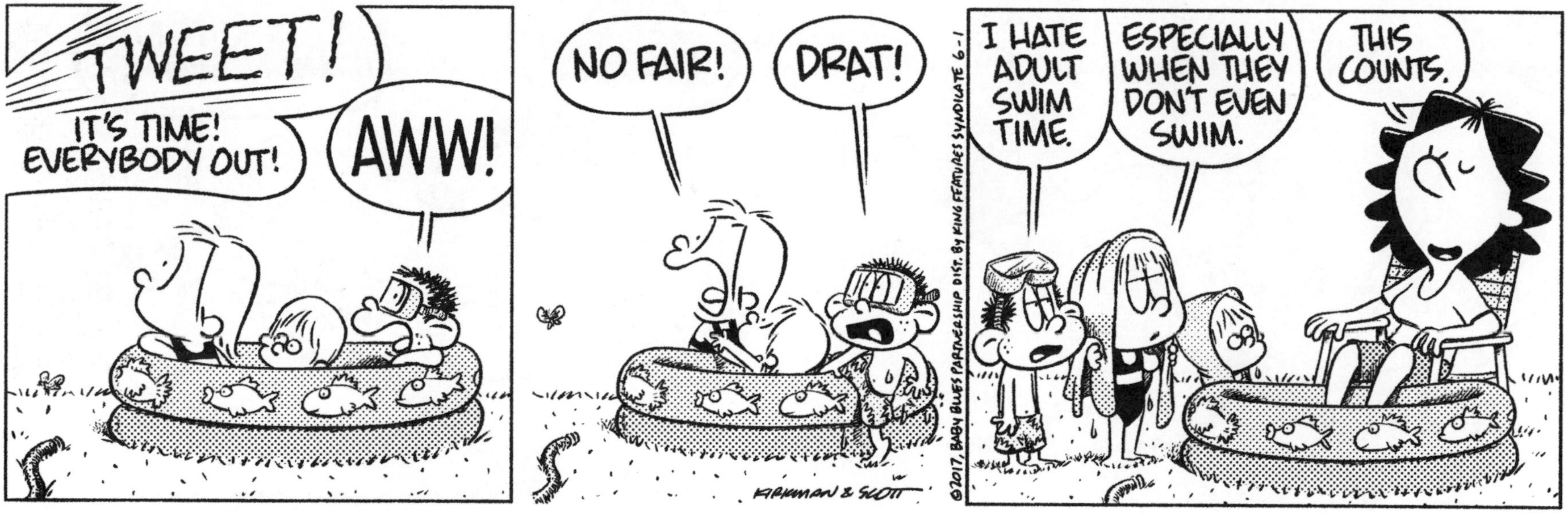
TWEET!
IT'S TIME! EVERYBODY OUT!
AWW!
NO FAIR!
DRAT!
KIRKMAN & SCOTT
©2017, BABY BLUES PARTNERSHIP DIST. BY KING FEATURES SYNDICATE 6-1
I HATE ADULT SWIM TIME.
ESPECIALLY WHEN THEY DON'T EVEN SWIM.
THIS COUNTS.

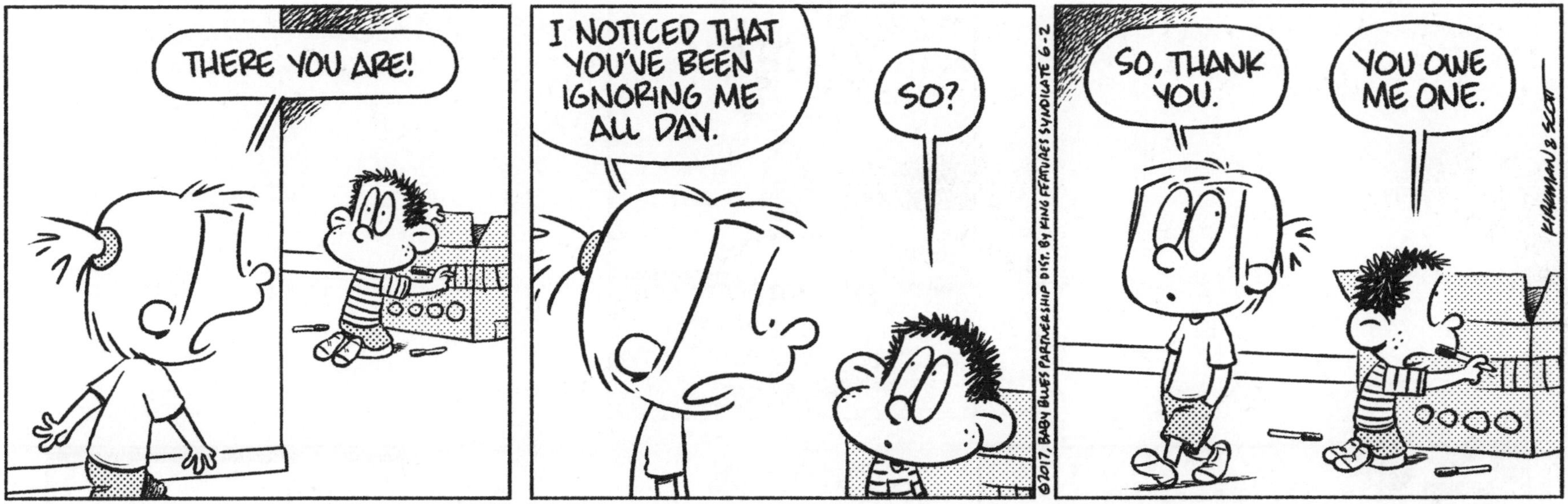

THERE YOU ARE!
I NOTICED THAT YOU'VE BEEN IGNORING ME ALL DAY.
SO?
SO, THANK YOU.
YOU OWE ME ONE.
©2017, BABY BLUES PARTNERSHIP DIST. BY KING FEATURES SYNDICATE 6-2
KIRKMAN & SCOTT

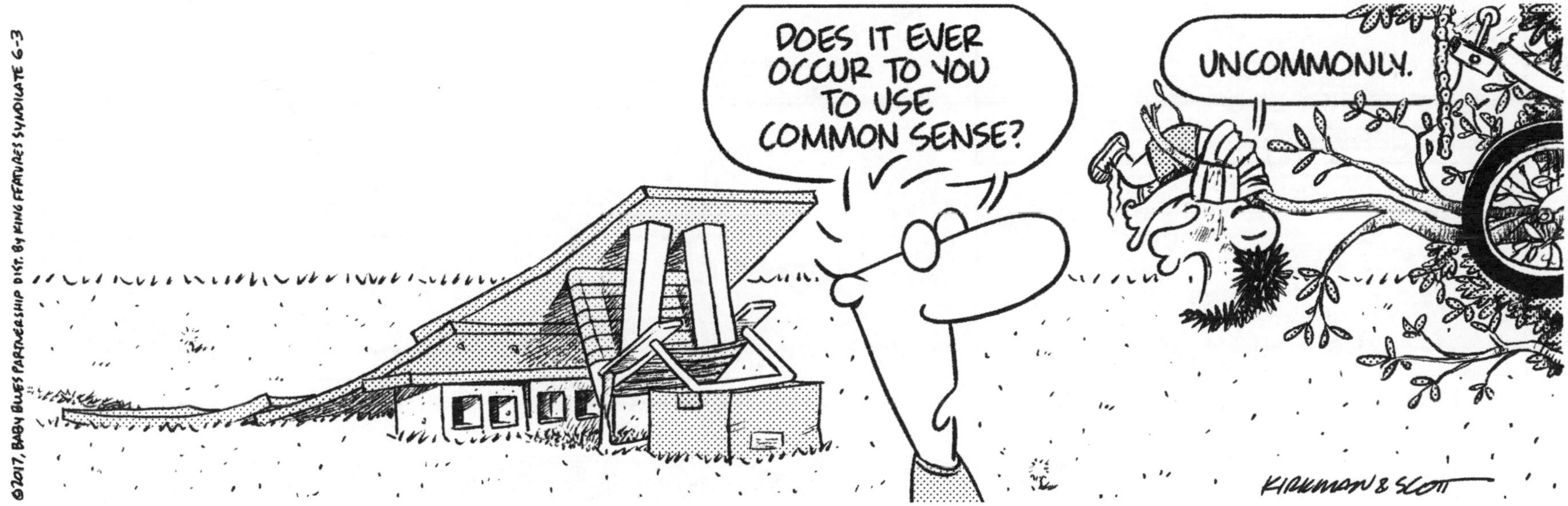

DOES IT EVER OCCUR TO YOU TO USE COMMON SENSE?
UNCOMMONLY.
©2017, BABY BLUES PARTNERSHIP DIST. BY KING FEATURES SYNDICATE 6-3
KIRKMAN & SCOTT

Rick: I think Hammie has a future as an engineer, if he lives long enough.

Jerry: If this ramp was based on Rick's experience, I'm surprised he survived his own childhood.

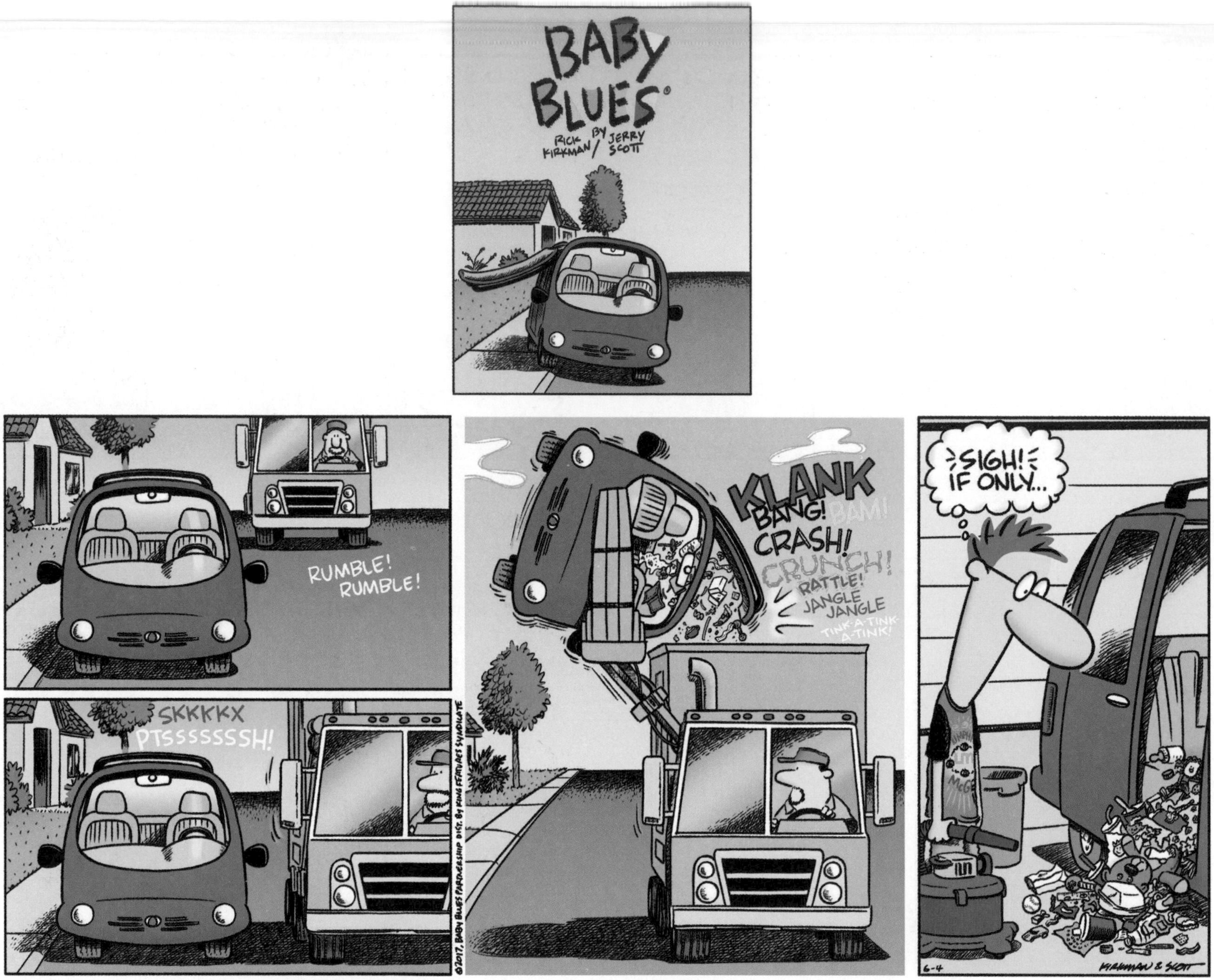
BABY BLUES®
BY RICK KIRKMAN / JERRY SCOTT
RUMBLE! RUMBLE!
SKKKKX
PTSSSSSSSH!
©2017, BABY BLUES PARTNERSHIP DIST. BY KING FEATURES SYNDICATE
KLANK
BANG! BAM!
CRASH!
CRUNCH!
RATTLE!
JANGLE JANGLE
TINK-A-TINK-A-TINK!
SIGH! IF ONLY...
6-4
KIRKMAN & SCOTT

Rick: If I remember correctly, the big middle panel was a drawing I did as a title panel for a different Sunday. We liked it too much to waste it on a title panel, so Jerry wrote a gag for it.

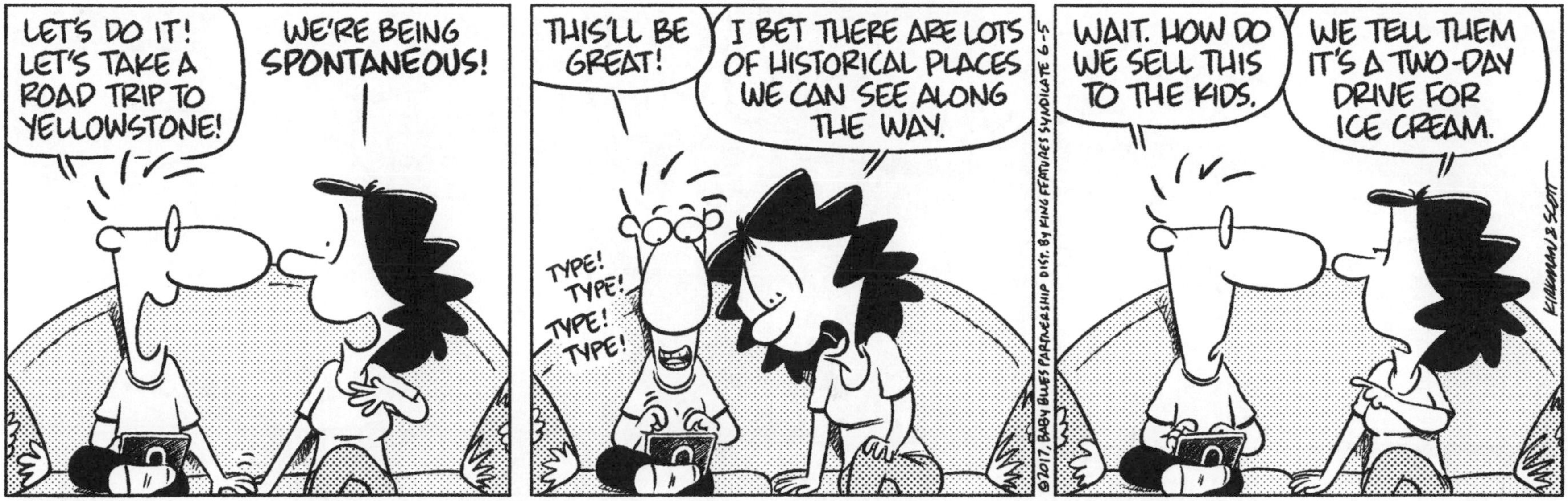
LET'S DO IT! LET'S TAKE A ROAD TRIP TO YELLOWSTONE!
WE'RE BEING SPONTANEOUS!
THIS'LL BE GREAT!
I BET THERE ARE LOTS OF HISTORICAL PLACES WE CAN SEE ALONG THE WAY.
TYPE! TYPE! TYPE! TYPE!
©2017, BABY BLUES PARTNERSHIP DIST. BY KING FEATURES SYNDICATE 6-5
WAIT. HOW DO WE SELL THIS TO THE KIDS.
WE TELL THEM IT'S A TWO-DAY DRIVE FOR ICE CREAM.
KIRKMAN & SCOTT

Rick: Let's just say, when I saw the word "Yellowstone" in Jerry's gag, I saw a whole sleepless week flash before me. Luckily, there were only two gags set in the park. Whew! Thanks, Jerry!

Jerry: My wife and daughters went to Yellowstone. Listening to their stories and making strips out of them is as close as I get to a vacation.

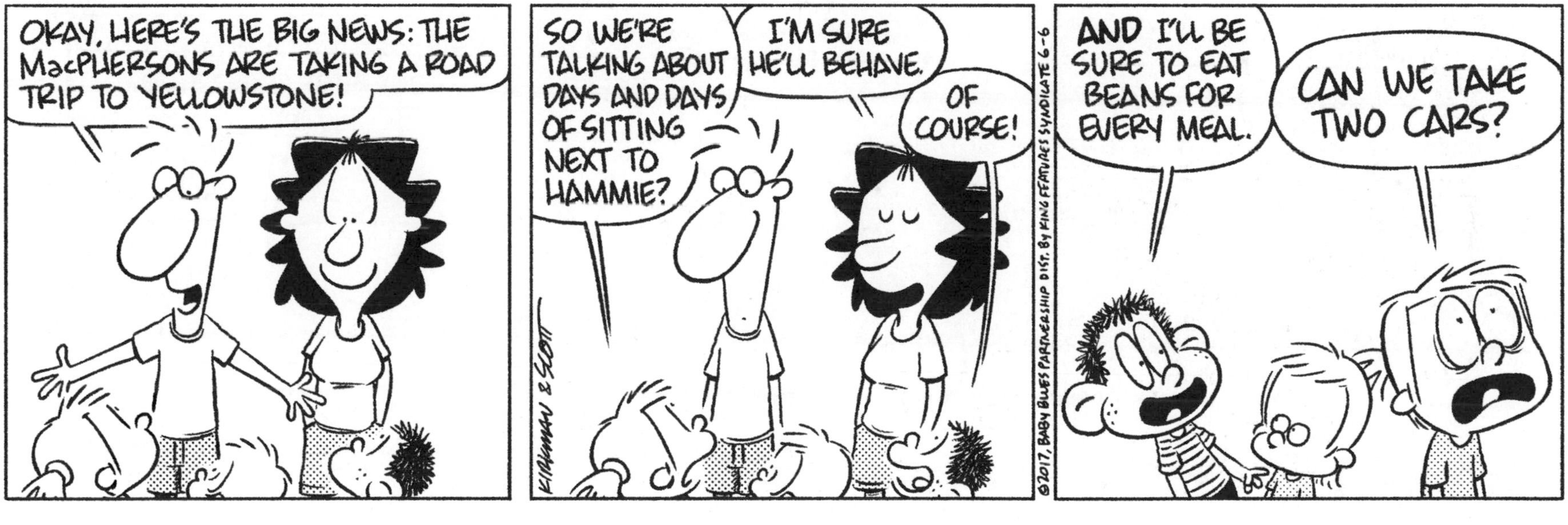
OKAY, HERE'S THE BIG NEWS: THE MacPHERSONS ARE TAKING A ROAD TRIP TO YELLOWSTONE!
KIRKMAN & SCOTT
SO WE'RE TALKING ABOUT DAYS AND DAYS OF SITTING NEXT TO HAMMIE?
I'M SURE HE'LL BEHAVE.
OF COURSE!
©2017, BABY BLUES PARTNERSHIP DIST. BY KING FEATURES SYNDICATE 6-6
AND I'LL BE SURE TO EAT BEANS FOR EVERY MEAL.
CAN WE TAKE TWO CARS?

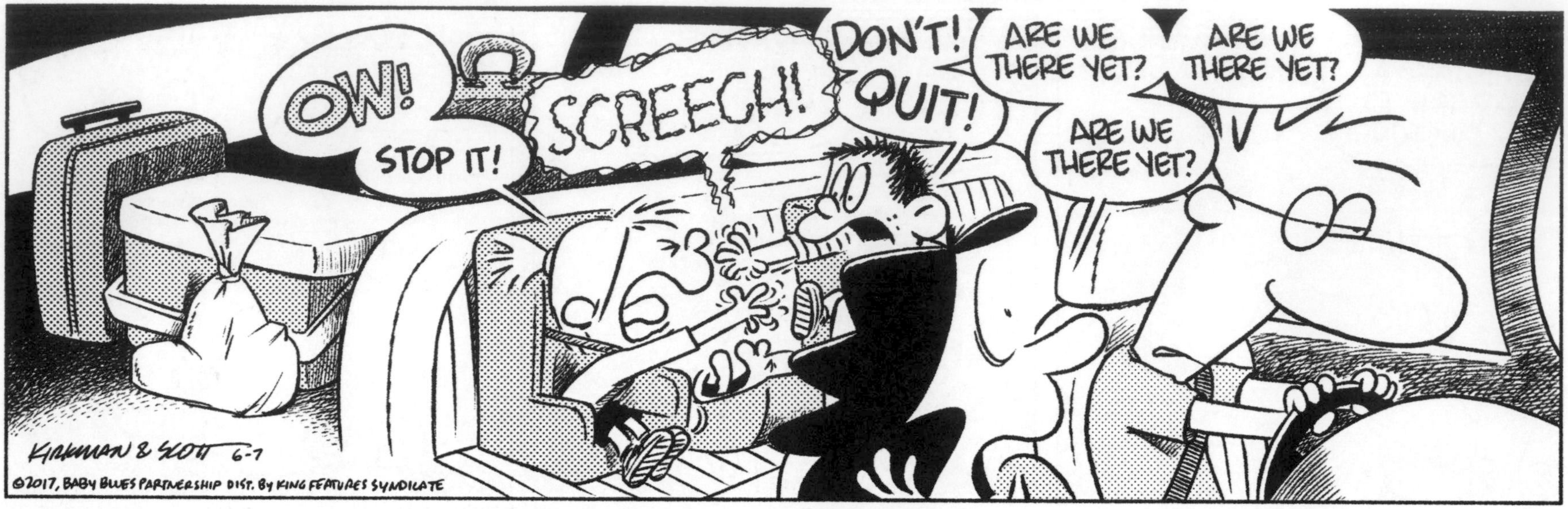
OW!
STOP IT!
SCREECH!
DON'T! QUIT!
ARE WE THERE YET?
ARE WE THERE YET?
ARE WE THERE YET?
KIRKMAN & SCOTT 6-7
©2017, BABY BLUES PARTNERSHIP DIST. BY KING FEATURES SYNDICATE

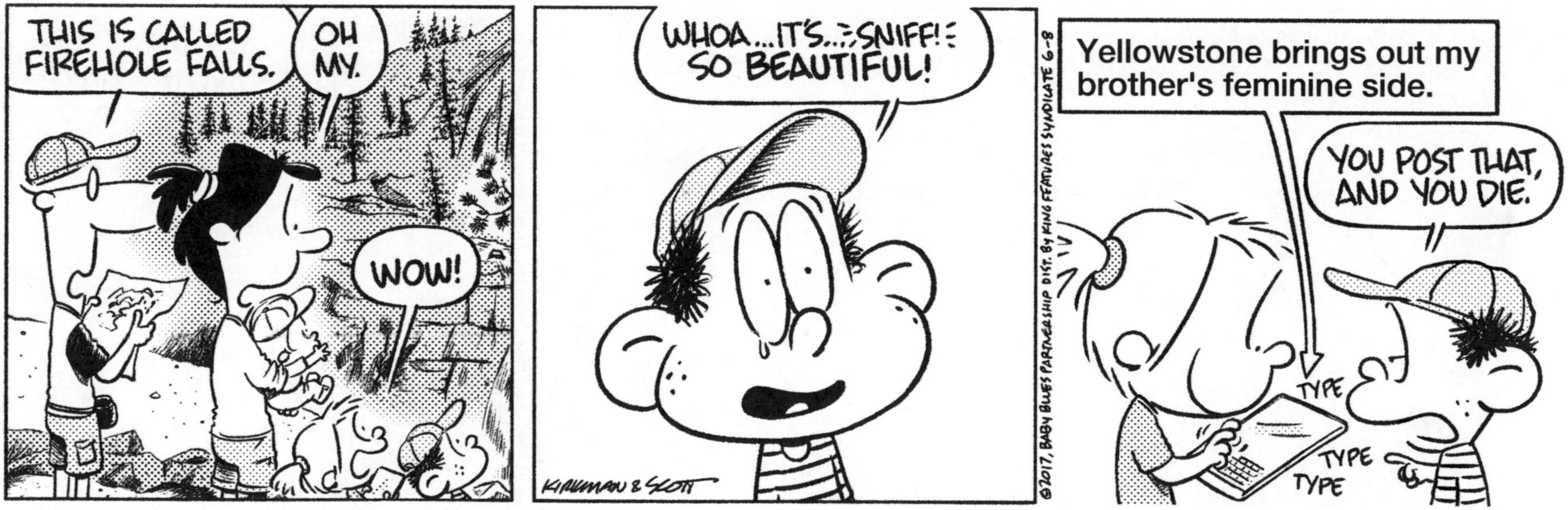
THIS IS CALLED FIREHOLE FALLS.
OH MY.
WOW!
WHOA...IT'S...SNIFF! SO BEAUTIFUL!
KIRKMAN & SCOTT
©2017, BABY BLUES PARTNERSHIP DIST. BY KING FEATURES SYNDICATE 6-8
Yellowstone brings out my brother's feminine side.
YOU POST THAT, AND YOU DIE.
TYPE
TYPE
TYPE

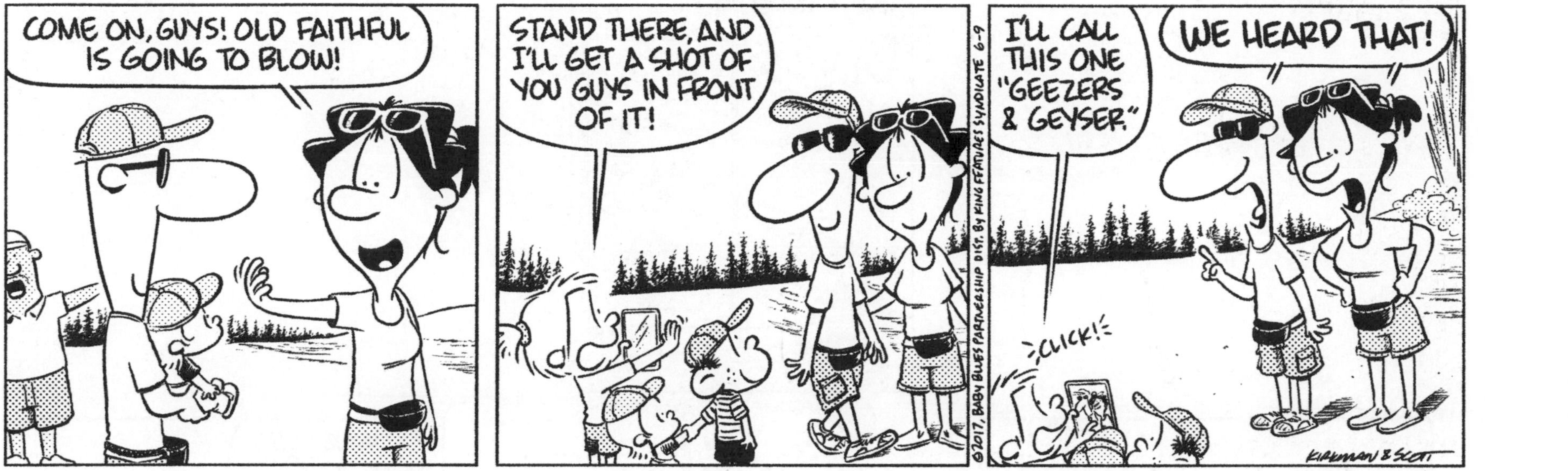
COME ON, GUYS! OLD FAITHFUL IS GOING TO BLOW!
STAND THERE, AND I'LL GET A SHOT OF YOU GUYS IN FRONT OF IT!
©2017, BABY BLUES PARTNERSHIP DIST. BY KING FEATURES SYNDICATE 6-9
I'LL CALL THIS ONE "GEEZERS & GEYSER."
CLICK!
WE HEARD THAT!
KIRKMAN & SCOTT

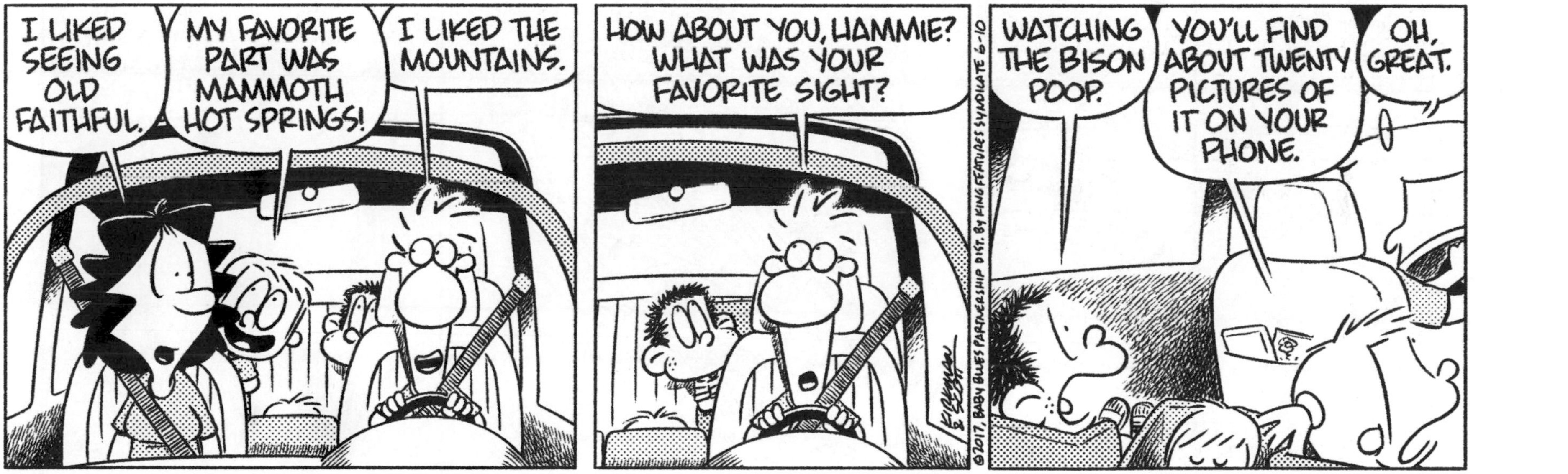
I LIKED SEEING OLD FAITHFUL.
MY FAVORITE PART WAS MAMMOTH HOT SPRINGS!
I LIKED THE MOUNTAINS.
KIRKMAN & SCOTT
HOW ABOUT YOU, HAMMIE? WHAT WAS YOUR FAVORITE SIGHT?
©2017, BABY BLUES PARTNERSHIP DIST. BY KING FEATURES SYNDICATE 6-10
WATCHING THE BISON POOP.
YOU'LL FIND ABOUT TWENTY PICTURES OF IT ON YOUR PHONE.
OH, GREAT.

Jerry: Yeah, my kids got pictures of that, too.

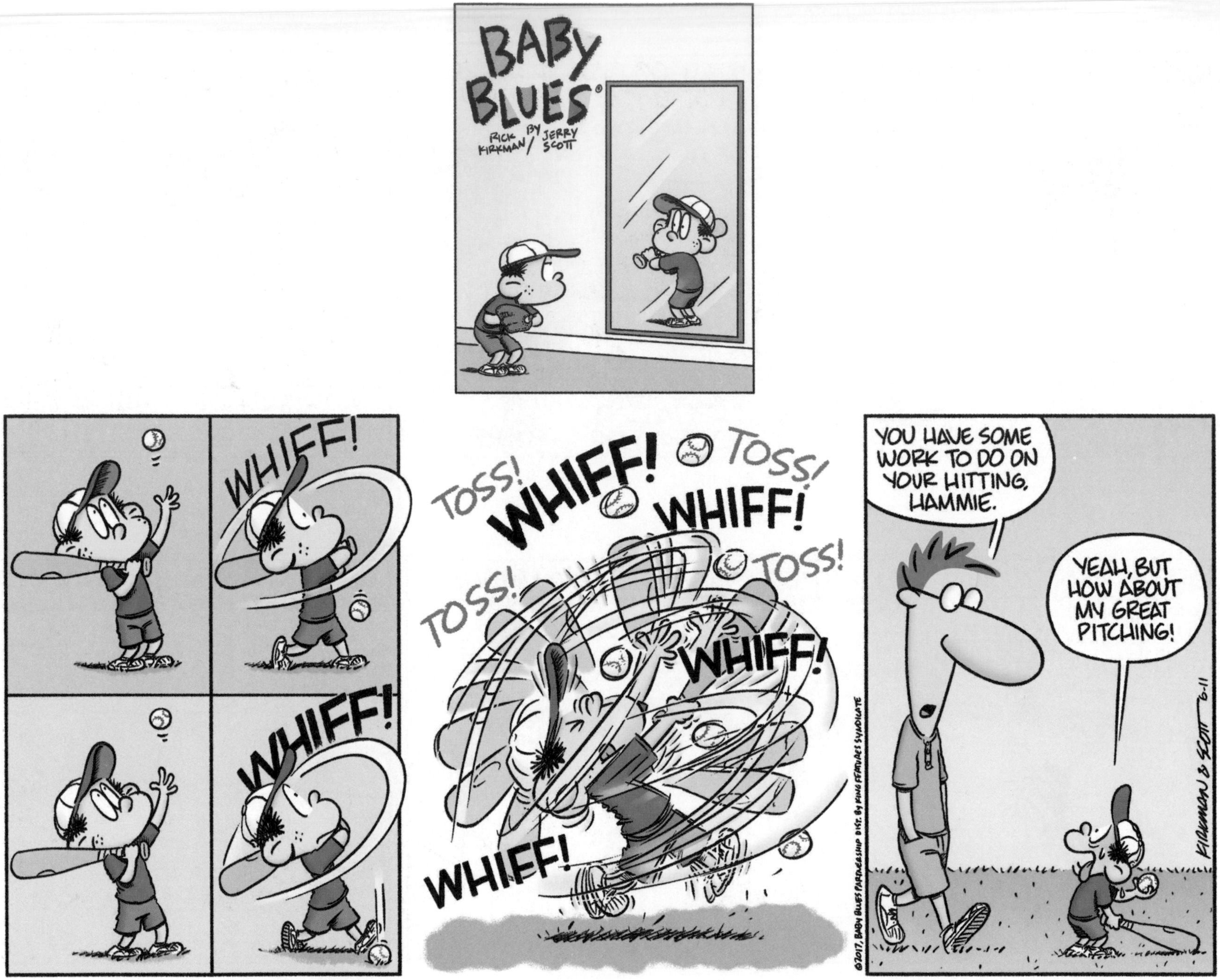
BABY BLUES®
RICK KIRKMAN / BY JERRY SCOTT
WHIFF!
WHIFF!
TOSS!
WHIFF!
TOSS!
WHIFF!
TOSS!
TOSS!
WHIFF!
WHIFF!
YOU HAVE SOME WORK TO DO ON YOUR HITTING, HAMMIE.
YEAH, BUT HOW ABOUT MY GREAT PITCHING!
©2017, BABY BLUES PARTNERSHIP DIST. BY KING FEATURES SYNDICATE
KIRKMAN & SCOTT 6-11

Rick: I do a lot of practice swings in the studio when I have to draw batting. I can never draw it properly from memory.

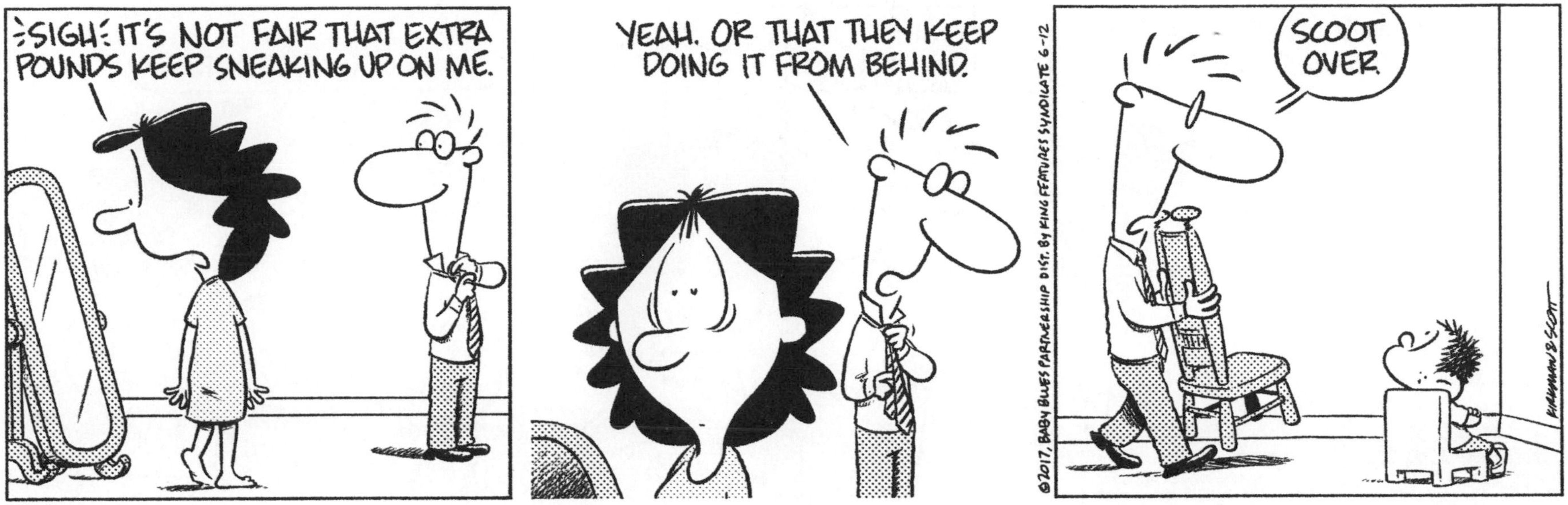

:SIGH: IT'S NOT FAIR THAT EXTRA POUNDS KEEP SNEAKING UP ON ME.
YEAH. OR THAT THEY KEEP DOING IT FROM BEHIND.
©2017, BABY BLUES PARTNERSHIP DIST. BY KING FEATURES SYNDICATE 6-12
SCOOT OVER.
KIRKMAN & SCOTT

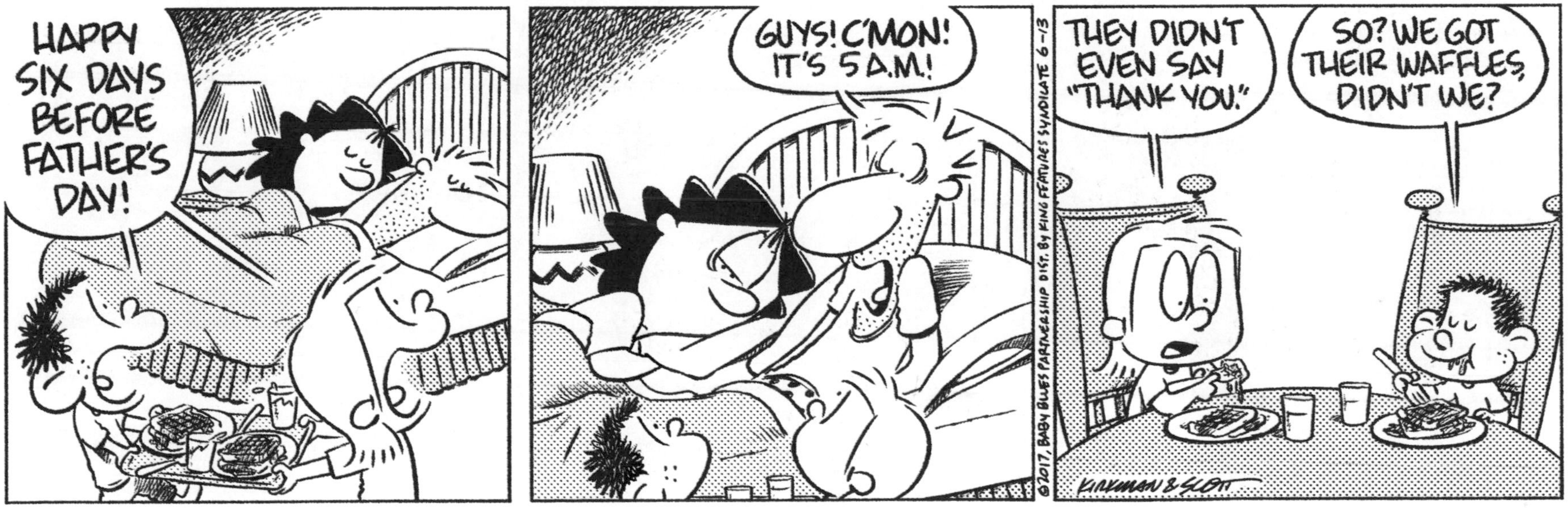

HAPPY SIX DAYS BEFORE FATHER'S DAY!
GUYS! C'MON! IT'S 5 A.M.!
©2017, BABY BLUES PARTNERSHIP DIST. BY KING FEATURES SYNDICATE 6-13
THEY DIDN'T EVEN SAY "THANK YOU."
SO? WE GOT THEIR WAFFLES, DIDN'T WE?
KIRKMAN & SCOTT

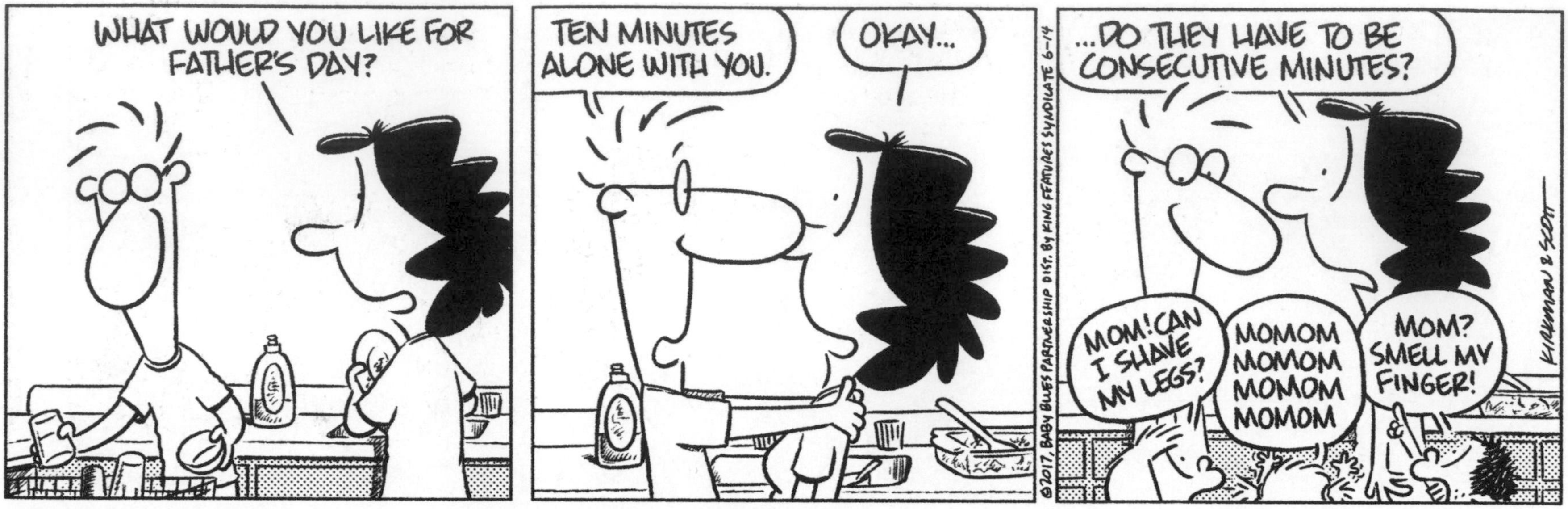
WHAT WOULD YOU LIKE FOR FATHER'S DAY?
TEN MINUTES ALONE WITH YOU.
OKAY...
©2017, BABY BLUES PARTNERSHIP DIST. BY KING FEATURES SYNDICATE 6-14
...DO THEY HAVE TO BE CONSECUTIVE MINUTES?
KIRKMAN & SCOTT
MOM! CAN I SHAVE MY LEGS?
MOMOM MOMOM MOMOM MOMOM
MOM? SMELL MY FINGER!

Rick: Favorite line: "Smell my finger!" **Jerry:** It's always a logistical problem having Darryl and Wanda directly facing each other. Somebody's nose always has to overlap.

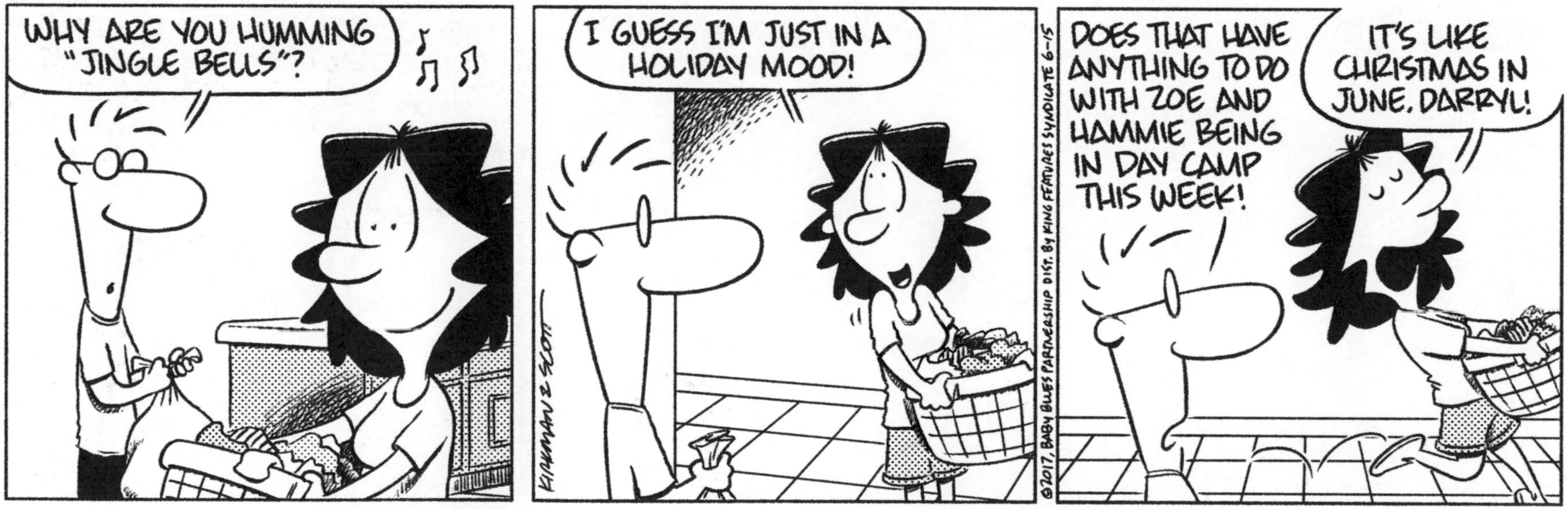
WHY ARE YOU HUMMING "JINGLE BELLS"?
KIRKMAN & SCOTT
I GUESS I'M JUST IN A HOLIDAY MOOD!
©2017, BABY BLUES PARTNERSHIP DIST. BY KING FEATURES SYNDICATE 6-15
DOES THAT HAVE ANYTHING TO DO WITH ZOE AND HAMMIE BEING IN DAY CAMP THIS WEEK!
IT'S LIKE CHRISTMAS IN JUNE, DARRYL!

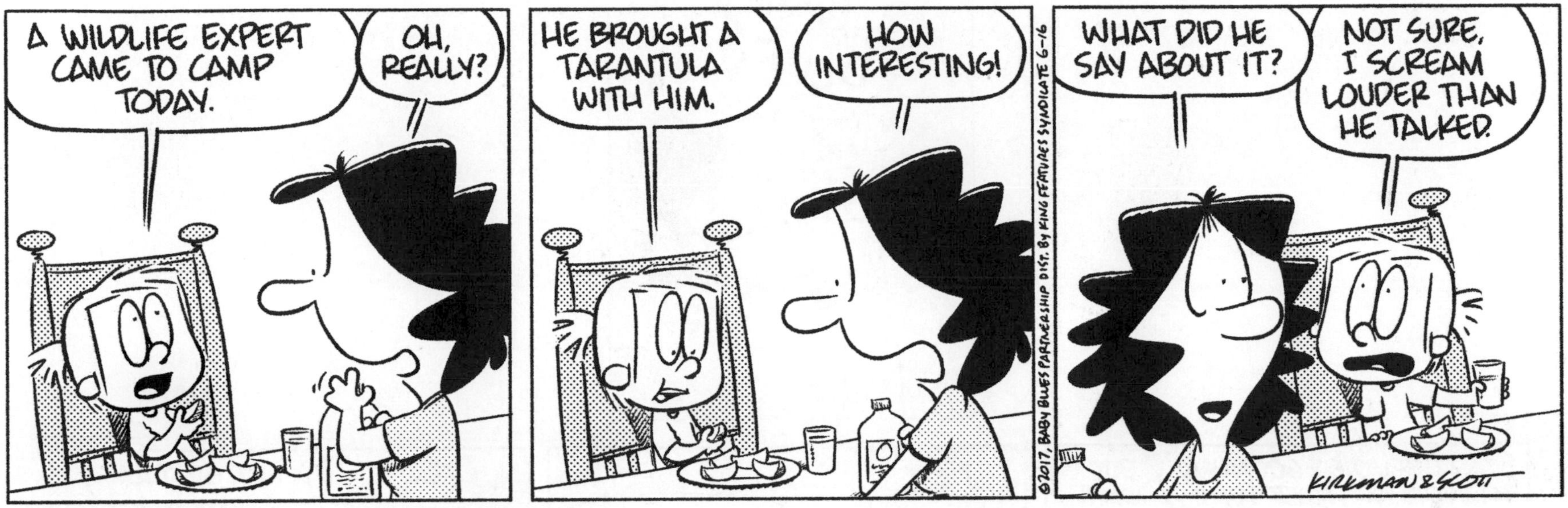
A WILDLIFE EXPERT CAME TO CAMP TODAY.
OH, REALLY?
HE BROUGHT A TARANTULA WITH HIM.
HOW INTERESTING!
©2017, BABY BLUES PARTNERSHIP DIST. BY KING FEATURES SYNDICATE 6-16
WHAT DID HE SAY ABOUT IT?
NOT SURE, I SCREAM LOUDER THAN HE TALKED.
KIRKMAN & SCOTT

Jerry: We used to live in an area that had an annual tarantula migration, and it wasn't unusual to see one walking across the yard or, say, your shoe. My older daughter was not a fan.

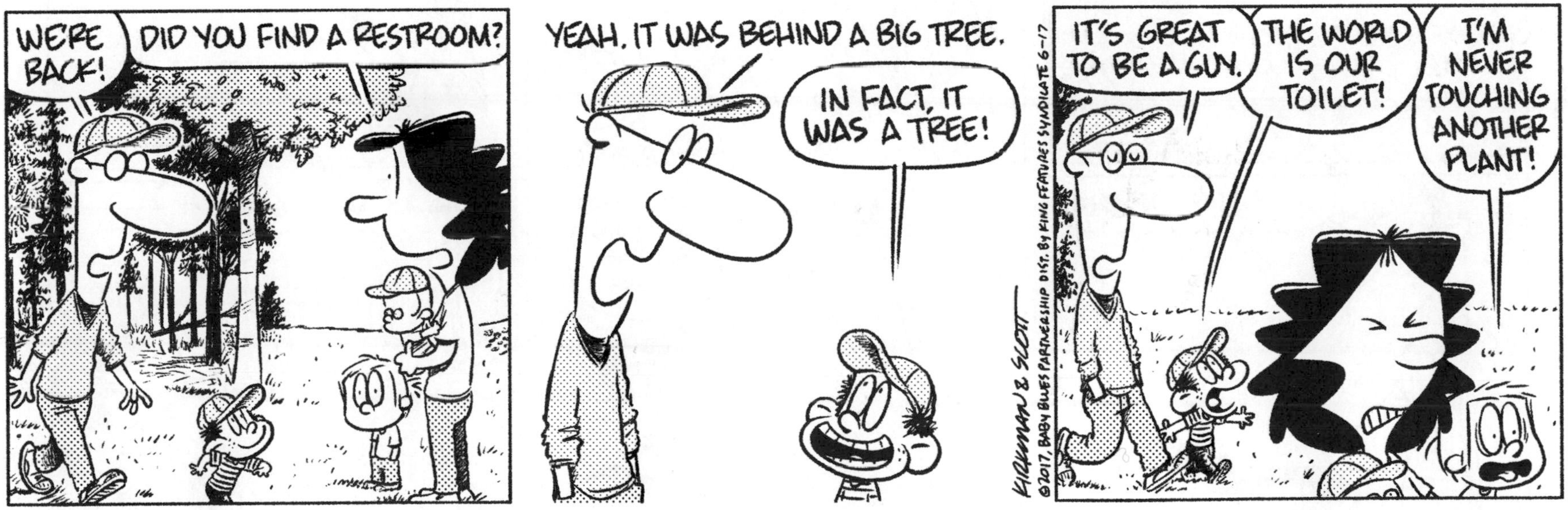
WE'RE BACK!
DID YOU FIND A RESTROOM?
YEAH. IT WAS BEHIND A BIG TREE.
IN FACT, IT WAS A TREE!
KIRKMAN & SCOTT
©2017, BABY BLUES PARTNERSHIP DIST. BY KING FEATURES SYNDICATE 6-17
IT'S GREAT TO BE A GUY.
THE WORLD IS OUR TOILET!
I'M NEVER TOUCHING ANOTHER PLANT!

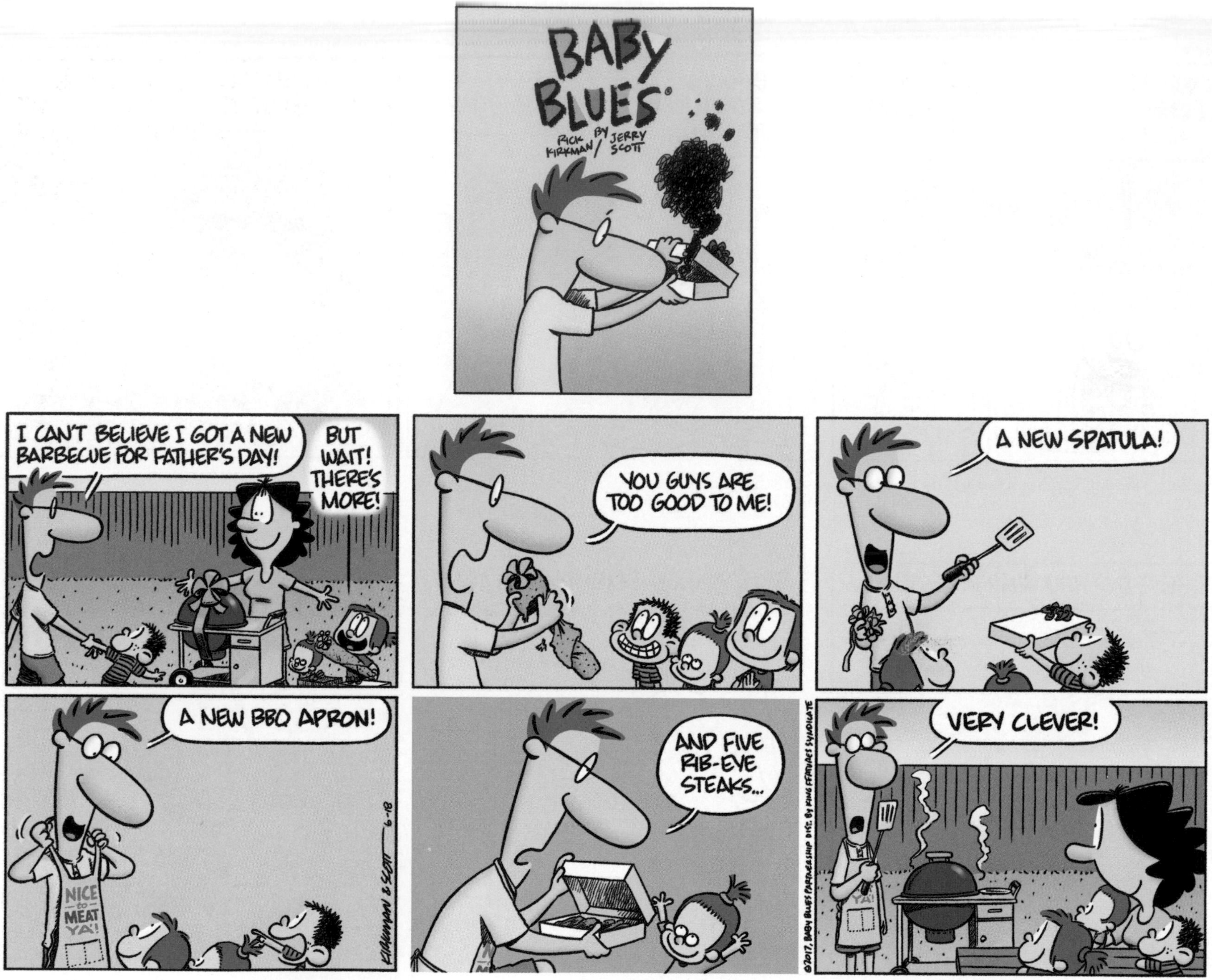
BABY BLUES®
BY RICK KIRKMAN / JERRY SCOTT
I CAN'T BELIEVE I GOT A NEW BARBECUE FOR FATHER'S DAY!
BUT WAIT! THERE'S MORE!
YOU GUYS ARE TOO GOOD TO ME!
A NEW SPATULA!
A NEW BBQ APRON!
NICE to MEAT YA!
KIRKMAN & SCOTT 6-18
AND FIVE RIB-EYE STEAKS...
©2017, BABY BLUES PARTNERSHIP DIST. BY KING FEATURES SYNDICATE
VERY CLEVER!
YA!

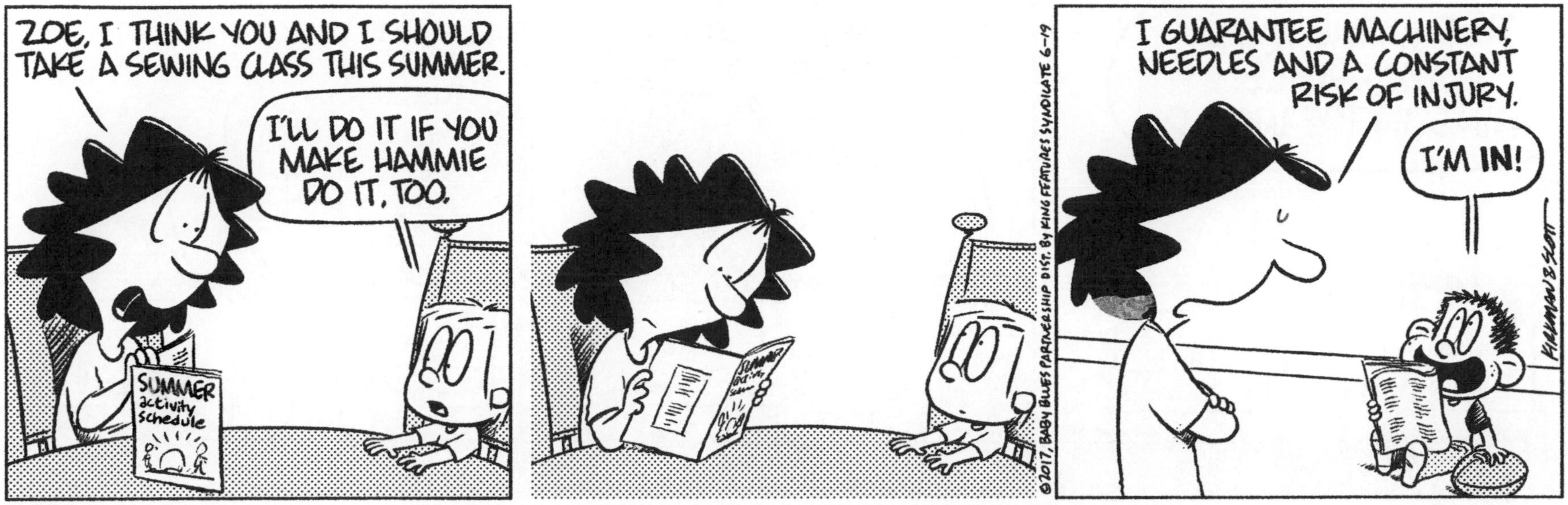
ZOE, I THINK YOU AND I SHOULD TAKE A SEWING CLASS THIS SUMMER.
I'LL DO IT IF YOU MAKE HAMMIE DO IT, TOO.
SUMMER activity schedule
©2017, BABY BLUES PARTNERSHIP DIST. BY KING FEATURES SYNDICATE 6-19
I GUARANTEE MACHINERY, NEEDLES AND A CONSTANT RISK OF INJURY.
I'M IN!
KIRKMAN & SCOTT

Rick: This may be one of the weirdest story lines we've done.

Jerry: Full disclosure: I tried sewing once when I was a kid. Results were mixed (and hilarious).

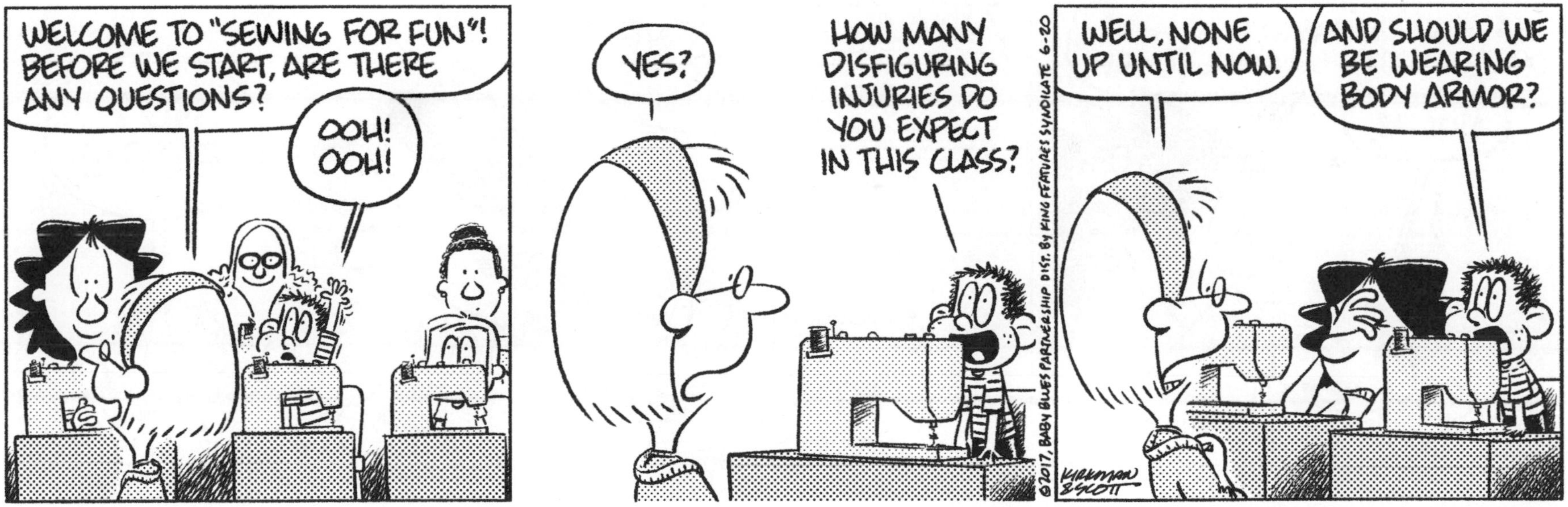
WELCOME TO "SEWING FOR FUN"! BEFORE WE START, ARE THERE ANY QUESTIONS?
OOH! OOH!
YES?
HOW MANY DISFIGURING INJURIES DO YOU EXPECT IN THIS CLASS?
©2017, BABY BLUES PARTNERSHIP DIST. BY KING FEATURES SYNDICATE 6-20
KIRKMAN & SCOTT
WELL, NONE UP UNTIL NOW.
AND SHOULD WE BE WEARING BODY ARMOR?

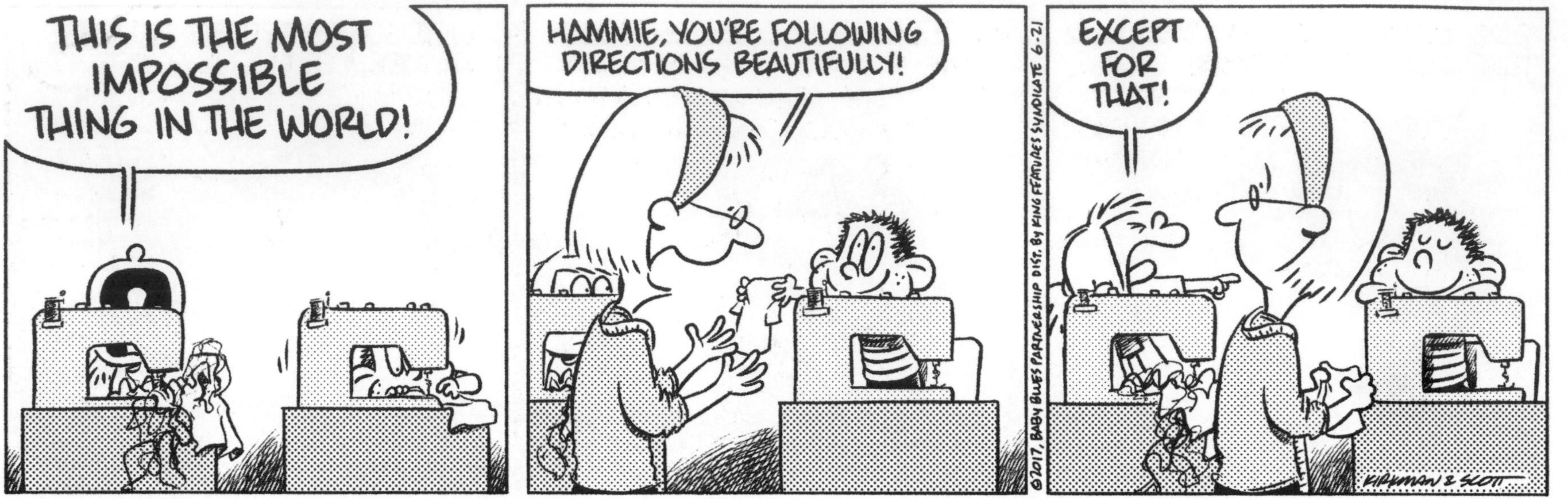
THIS IS THE MOST IMPOSSIBLE THING IN THE WORLD!
HAMMIE, YOU'RE FOLLOWING DIRECTIONS BEAUTIFULLY!
©2017, BABY BLUES PARTNERSHIP DIST. BY KING FEATURES SYNDICATE 6-21
EXCEPT FOR THAT!
KIRKMAN & SCOTT

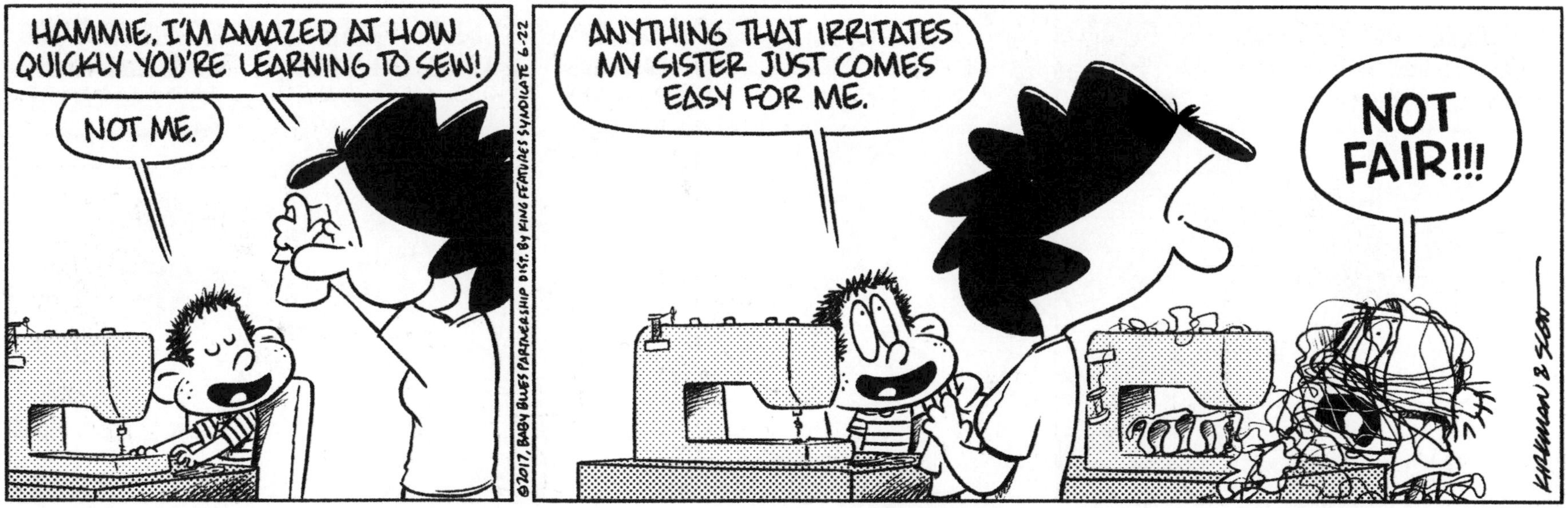
HAMMIE, I'M AMAZED AT HOW QUICKLY YOU'RE LEARNING TO SEW!
NOT ME.
©2017, BABY BLUES PARTNERSHIP DIST. BY KING FEATURES SYNDICATE 6-22
ANYTHING THAT IRRITATES MY SISTER JUST COMES EASY FOR ME.
NOT FAIR!!!
KIRKMAN & SCOTT

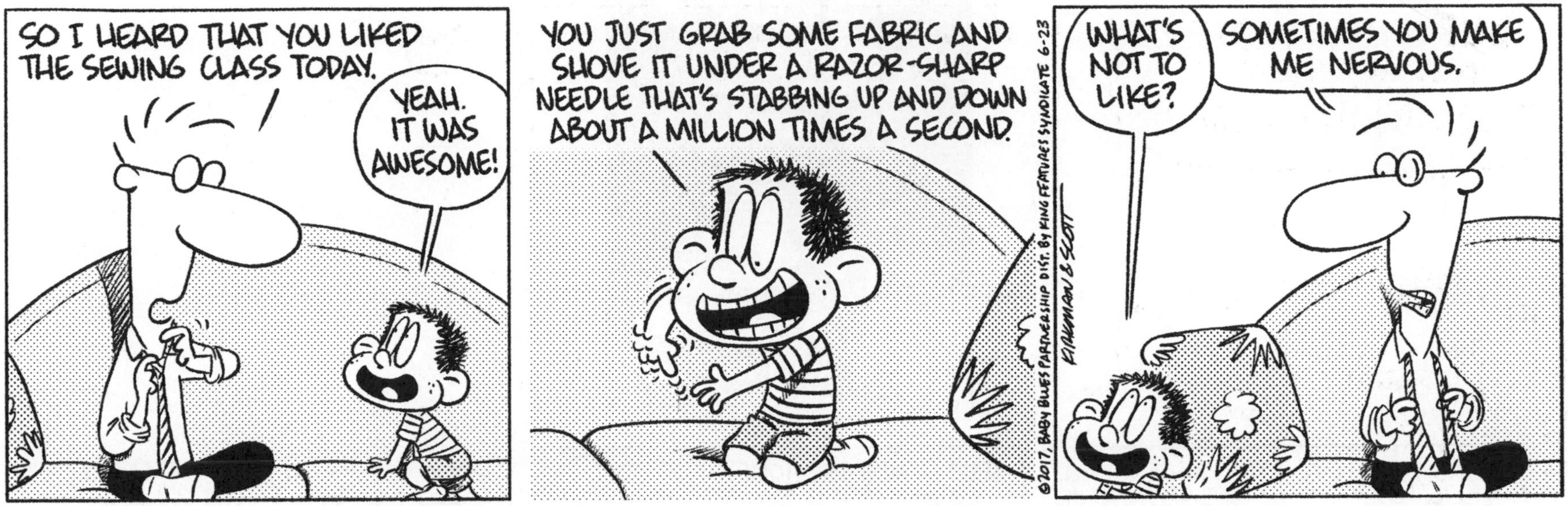
SO I HEARD THAT YOU LIKED THE SEWING CLASS TODAY.
YEAH. IT WAS AWESOME!
YOU JUST GRAB SOME FABRIC AND SHOVE IT UNDER A RAZOR-SHARP NEEDLE THAT'S STABBING UP AND DOWN ABOUT A MILLION TIMES A SECOND.
©2017, BABY BLUES PARTNERSHIP DIST. BY KING FEATURES SYNDICATE 6-23
KIRKMAN & SCOTT
WHAT'S NOT TO LIKE?
SOMETIMES YOU MAKE ME NERVOUS.

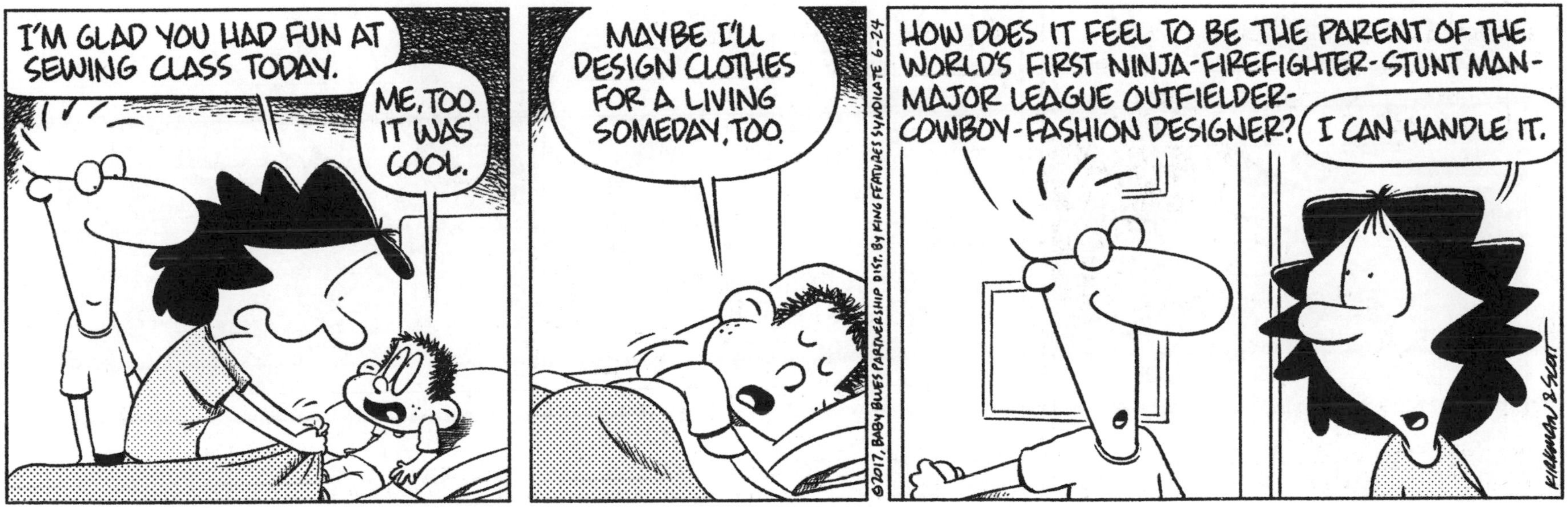
I'M GLAD YOU HAD FUN AT SEWING CLASS TODAY.
ME, TOO. IT WAS COOL.
MAYBE I'LL DESIGN CLOTHES FOR A LIVING SOMEDAY, TOO.
©2017, BABY BLUES PARTNERSHIP DIST. BY KING FEATURES SYNDICATE 6-24
HOW DOES IT FEEL TO BE THE PARENT OF THE WORLD'S FIRST NINJA-FIREFIGHTER-STUNT MAN-MAJOR LEAGUE OUTFIELDER-COWBOY-FASHION DESIGNER?
I CAN HANDLE IT.
KIRKMAN & SCOTT

Baby Blues
Rick Kirkman & Jerry Scott
ZZZZZ

...AND WAIT 'TIL I TELL YOU WHAT THEY DID TO TH-
WANDA, CAN I PUT YOU ON HOLD FOR A SECOND?
FLOUR
TED! HOW'S THE TONER IN THE COPIER?
JUST CHANGED IT.
WANT ME TO LOOK OVER THOSE NUMBERS, SAL?
NO, I HAD STACY DO IT.
ISN'T THERE A RETIREMENT PARTY FOR JEAN IN THE STAFF ROOM?
NOT 'TIL 4:30.
©2017, BABY BLUES PARTNERSHIP DIST. BY KING FEATURES SYNDICATE 6-25
SORRY. ARE YOU IN THE MIDDLE OF SOMETHING?
I'M AFRAID NOT. GO AHEAD.
KIRKMAN & SCOTT

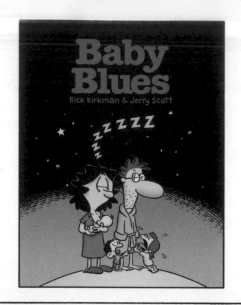

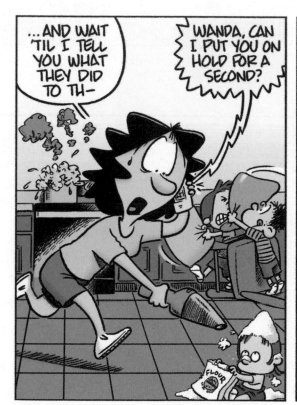

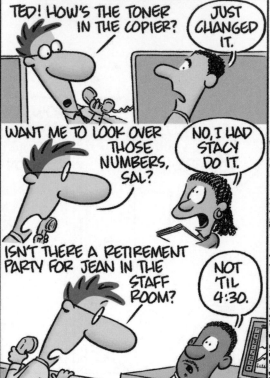

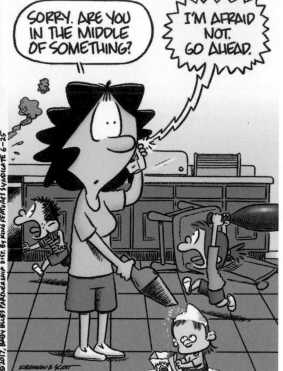

Rick: Nice try, Darryl.

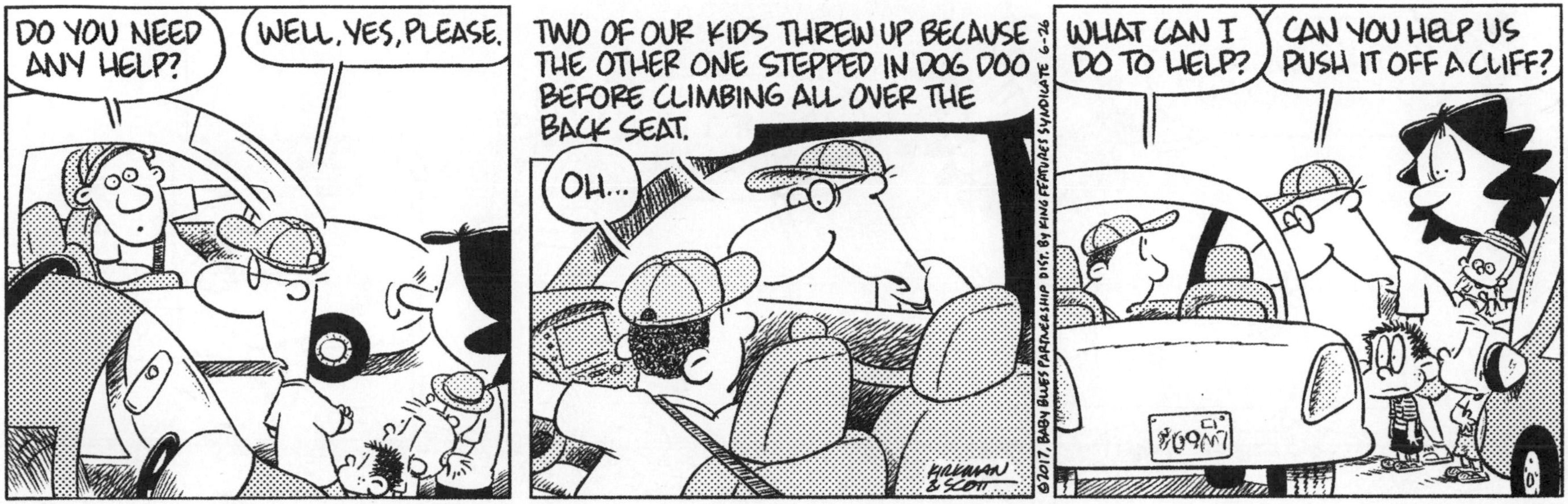
DO YOU NEED ANY HELP?
WELL, YES, PLEASE.
TWO OF OUR KIDS THREW UP BECAUSE THE OTHER ONE STEPPED IN DOG DOO BEFORE CLIMBING ALL OVER THE BACK SEAT.
OH...
KIRKMAN & SCOTT
©2017, BABY BLUES PARTNERSHIP DIST. BY KING FEATURES SYNDICATE 6-26
WHAT CAN I DO TO HELP?
CAN YOU HELP US PUSH IT OFF A CLIFF?

Rick: Could be a tie for my favorite gag of the year.

Jerry: I imagine that most people have a horrifying story like this. I just happen to be able to publish mine in a comic strip.

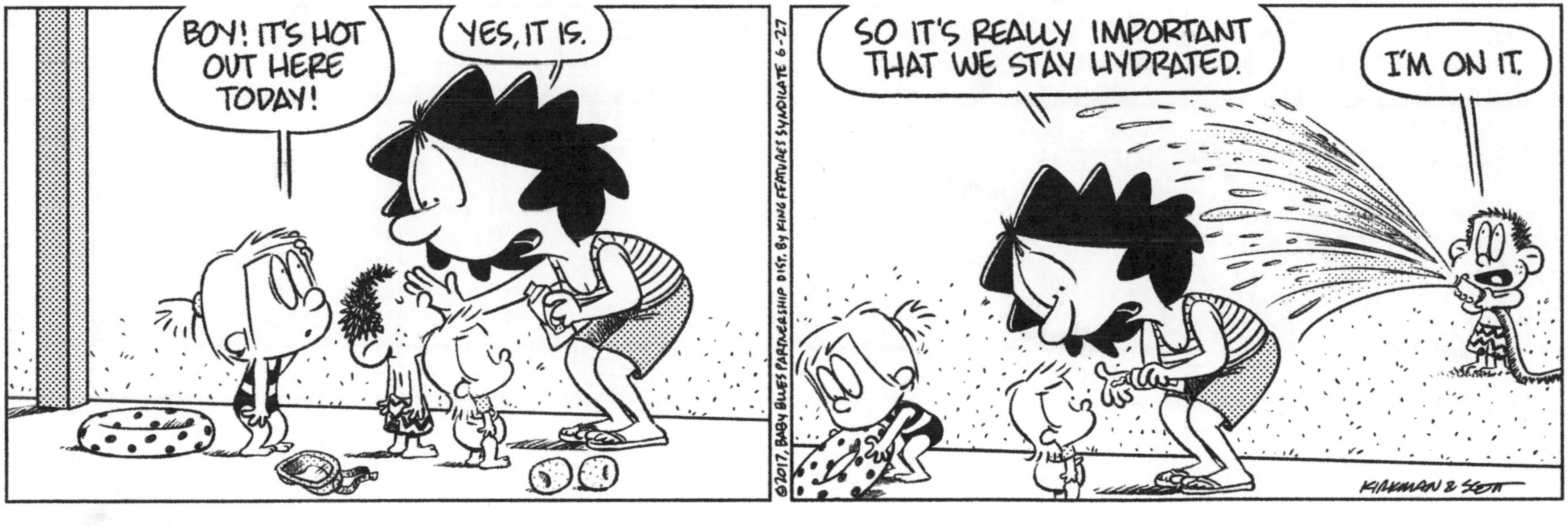
BOY! IT'S HOT OUT HERE TODAY!
YES, IT IS.
©2017, BABY BLUES PARTNERSHIP DIST. BY KING FEATURES SYNDICATE 6-27
SO IT'S REALLY IMPORTANT THAT WE STAY HYDRATED.
I'M ON IT.
KIRKMAN & SCOTT

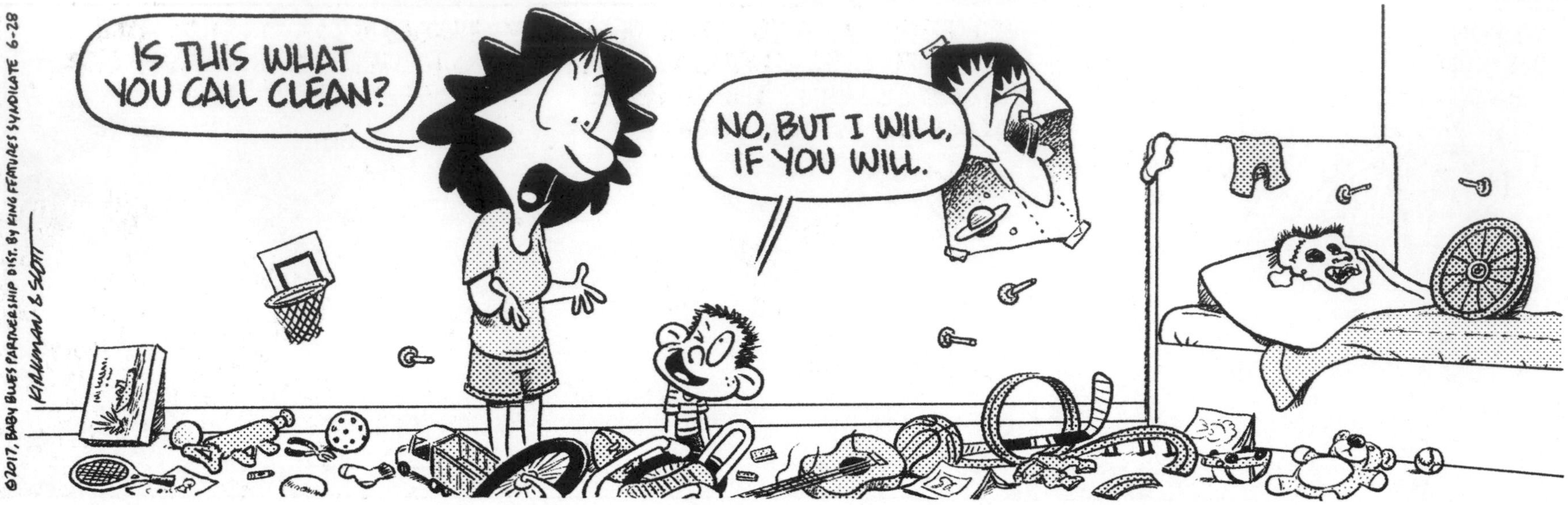
©2017, BABY BLUES PARTNERSHIP DIST. BY KING FEATURES SYNDICATE 6-28
KIRKMAN & SCOTT
IS THIS WHAT YOU CALL CLEAN?
NO, BUT I WILL, IF YOU WILL.

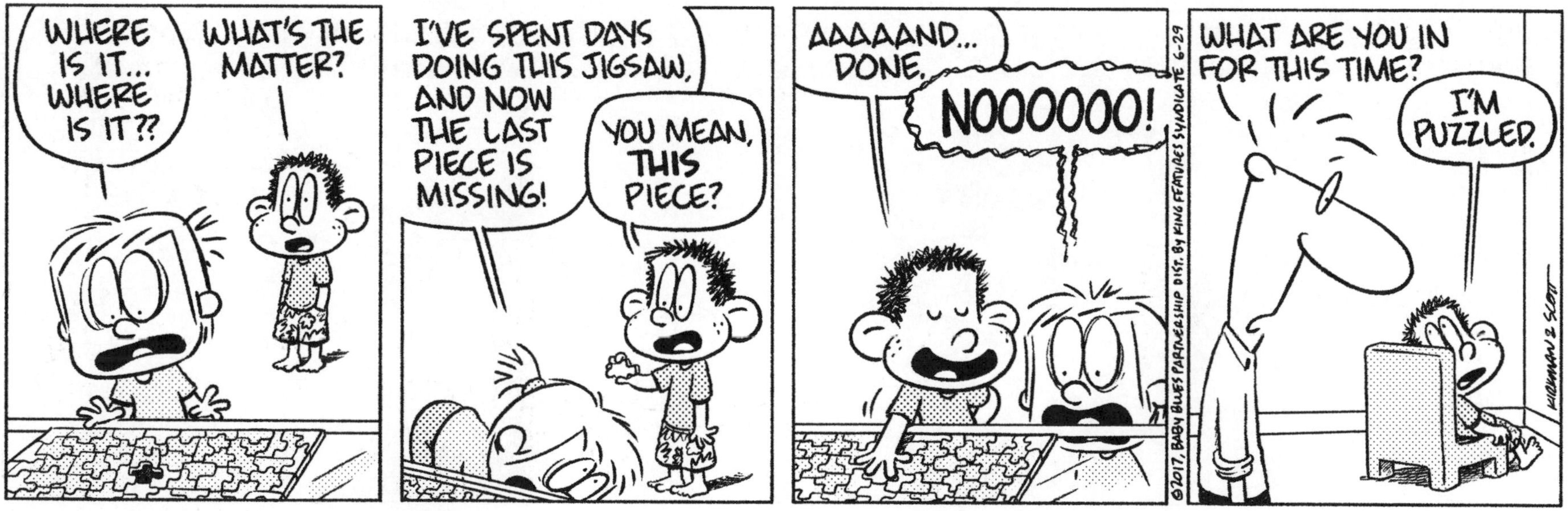
WHERE IS IT... WHERE IS IT??
WHAT'S THE MATTER?
I'VE SPENT DAYS DOING THIS JIGSAW, AND NOW THE LAST PIECE IS MISSING!
YOU MEAN, THIS PIECE?
AAAAAND... DONE.
NOOOOOO!
©2017, BABY BLUES PARTNERSHIP DIST. BY KING FEATURES SYNDICATE 6-29
WHAT ARE YOU IN FOR THIS TIME?
I'M PUZZLED.
KIRKMAN & SCOTT

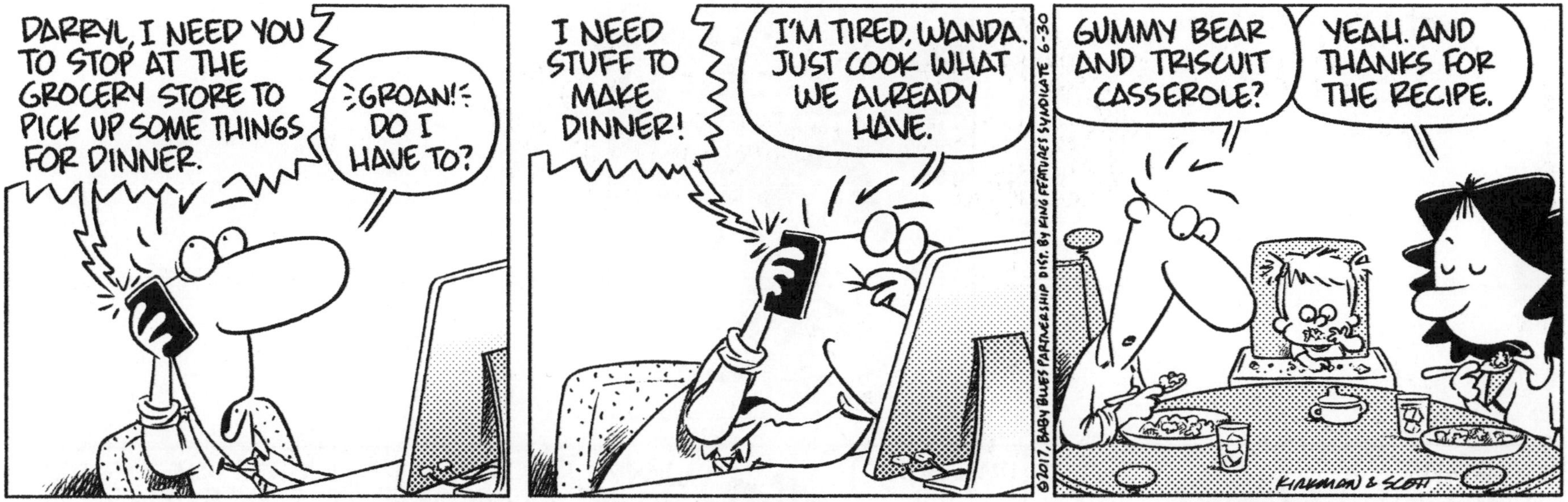
DARRYL, I NEED YOU TO STOP AT THE GROCERY STORE TO PICK UP SOME THINGS FOR DINNER.
GROAN! DO I HAVE TO?
I NEED STUFF TO MAKE DINNER!
I'M TIRED, WANDA. JUST COOK WHAT WE ALREADY HAVE.
©2017, BABY BLUES PARTNERSHIP DIST. BY KING FEATURES SYNDICATE 6-30
GUMMY BEAR AND TRISCUIT CASSEROLE?
YEAH. AND THANKS FOR THE RECIPE.
KIRKMAN & SCOTT

Rick: I certainly wouldn't spread the rumor that their meal came from my sister-in-law.

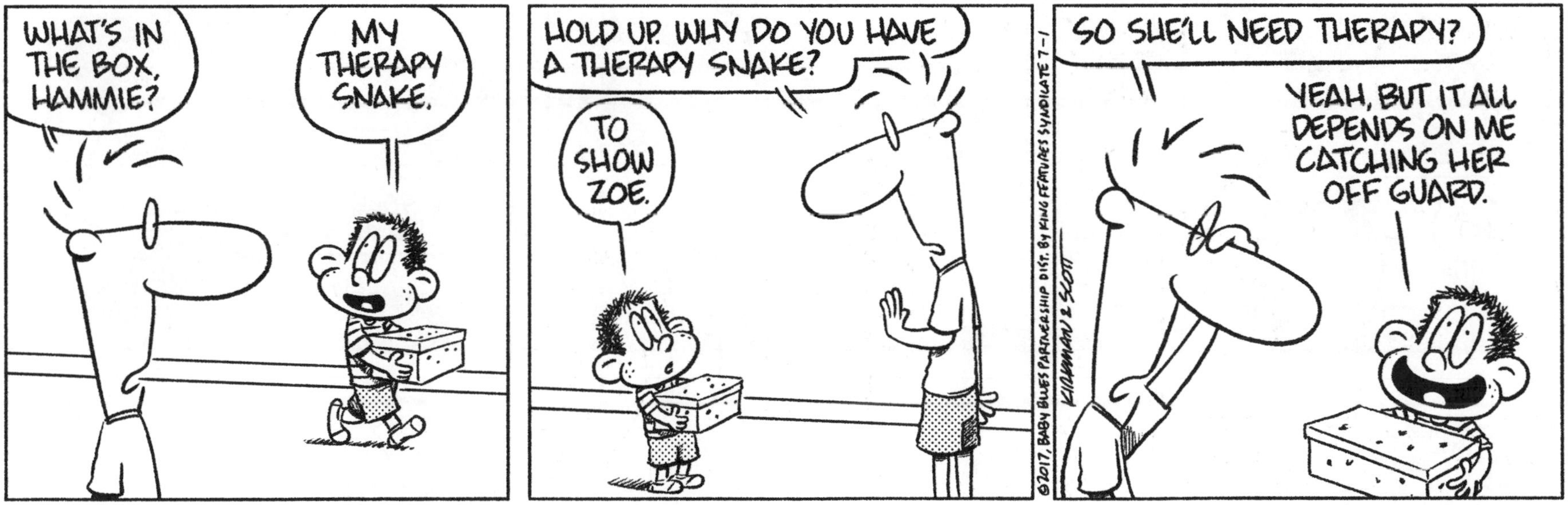
WHAT'S IN THE BOX, HAMMIE?
MY THERAPY SNAKE.
HOLD UP. WHY DO YOU HAVE A THERAPY SNAKE?
TO SHOW ZOE.
©2017, BABY BLUES PARTNERSHIP DIST. BY KING FEATURES SYNDICATE 7-1
KIRKMAN & SCOTT
SO SHE'LL NEED THERAPY?
YEAH, BUT IT ALL DEPENDS ON ME CATCHING HER OFF GUARD.

BABY BLUES®
RICK KIRKMAN / BY JERRY SCOTT

WHO PUT THIS EMPTY MILK CARTON BACK IN THE FRIDGE?
UM, I GUESS I DID.
WHY??
TO REMIND YOU THAT WE'RE OUT OF MILK SO YOU'D PUT IT ON THE GROCERY LIST.
DO I HAVE TO DO EVERYTHING AROUND HERE?
NO.
THEN WHY DIDN'T YOU JUST WRITE IT DOWN YOURSELF, AND THROW THE CARTON IN THE TRASH?
THE TRASH WAS FULL.
EVEN ROCK-SOLID REASONING DOESN'T WORK ON HER ANYMORE.
©2017, BABY BLUES PARTNERSHIP DIST. BY KING FEATURES SYNDICATE
KIRKMAN & SCOTT 7-2

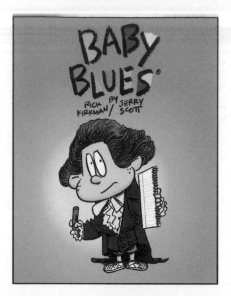

Rick: This was a deep dive for a title panel: Hammie is Thomas Paine, author of *The Age of Reason*. Never read it. Not even the CliffsNotes.

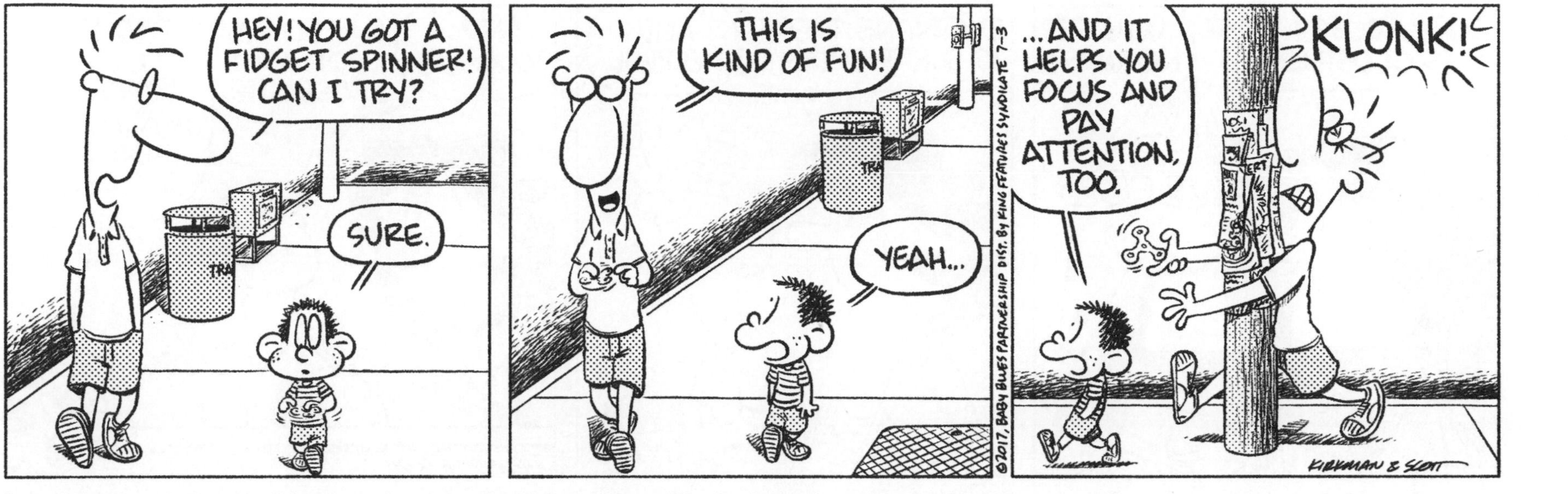
HEY! YOU GOT A FIDGET SPINNER! CAN I TRY?
SURE.
THIS IS KIND OF FUN!
YEAH...
©2017, BABY BLUES PARTNERSHIP DIST. BY KING FEATURES SYNDICATE 7-3
...AND IT HELPS YOU FOCUS AND PAY ATTENTION, TOO.
KLONK!
KIRKMAN & SCOTT

Jerry: Like Darryl, the only thing I can focus on when I play with my fidget spinner is my fidget spinner.

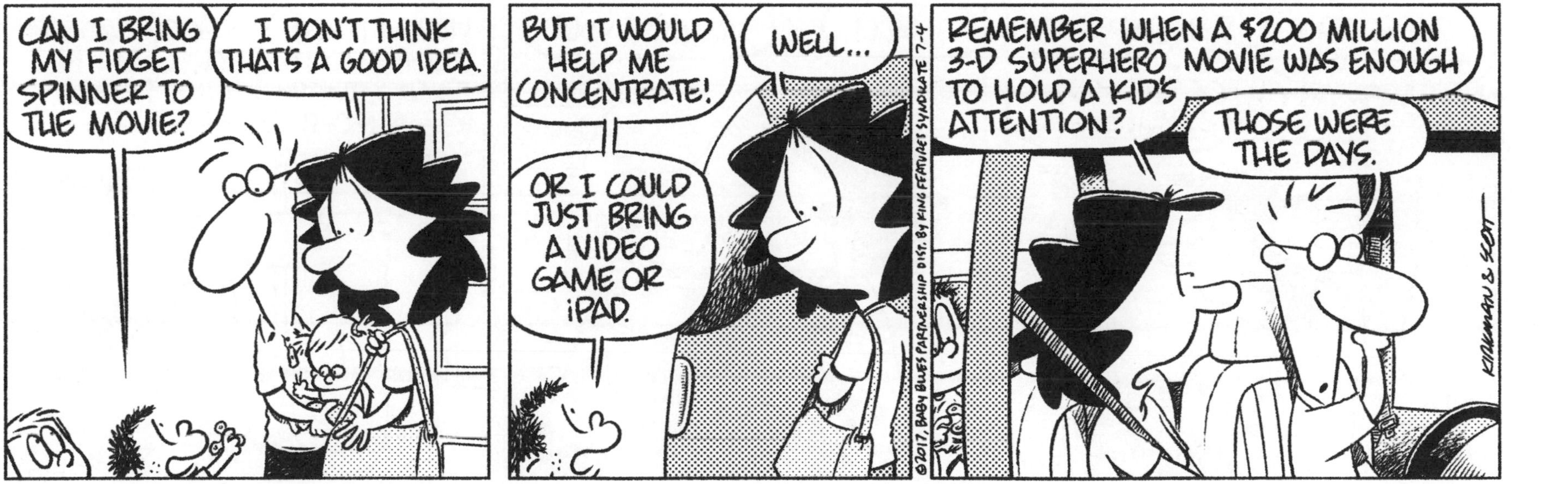
CAN I BRING MY FIDGET SPINNER TO THE MOVIE?
I DON'T THINK THAT'S A GOOD IDEA.
BUT IT WOULD HELP ME CONCENTRATE!
WELL...
OR I COULD JUST BRING A VIDEO GAME OR iPAD.
©2017, BABY BLUES PARTNERSHIP DIST. BY KING FEATURES SYNDICATE 7-4
REMEMBER WHEN A $200 MILLION 3-D SUPERHERO MOVIE WAS ENOUGH TO HOLD A KID'S ATTENTION?
THOSE WERE THE DAYS.
KIRKMAN & SCOTT

Rick: In my day, we had to fidget with a bolt and a nut.

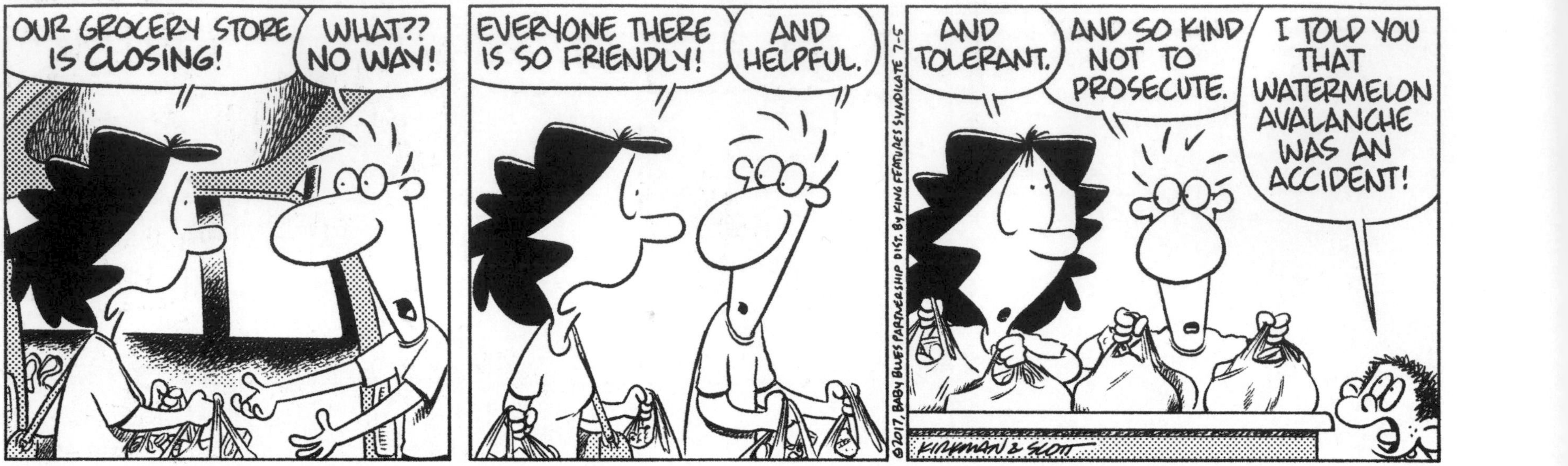
OUR GROCERY STORE IS CLOSING!
WHAT?? NO WAY!
EVERYONE THERE IS SO FRIENDLY!
AND HELPFUL.
©2017, BABY BLUES PARTNERSHIP DIST. BY KING FEATURES SYNDICATE 7-5
AND TOLERANT.
AND SO KIND NOT TO PROSECUTE.
I TOLD YOU THAT WATERMELON AVALANCHE WAS AN ACCIDENT!
KIRKMAN & SCOTT

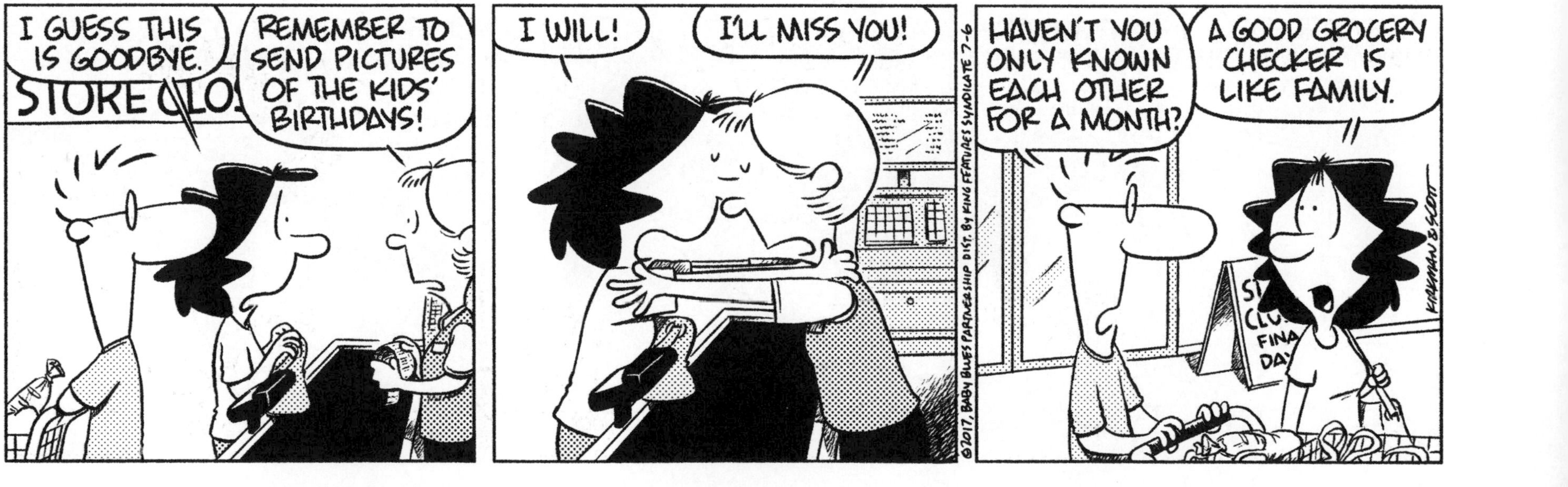
I GUESS THIS IS GOODBYE.
REMEMBER TO SEND PICTURES OF THE KIDS' BIRTHDAYS!
I WILL!
I'LL MISS YOU!
©2017, BABY BLUES PARTNERSHIP DIST. BY KING FEATURES SYNDICATE 7-6
HAVEN'T YOU ONLY KNOWN EACH OTHER FOR A MONTH?
A GOOD GROCERY CHECKER IS LIKE FAMILY.
KIRKMAN & SCOTT

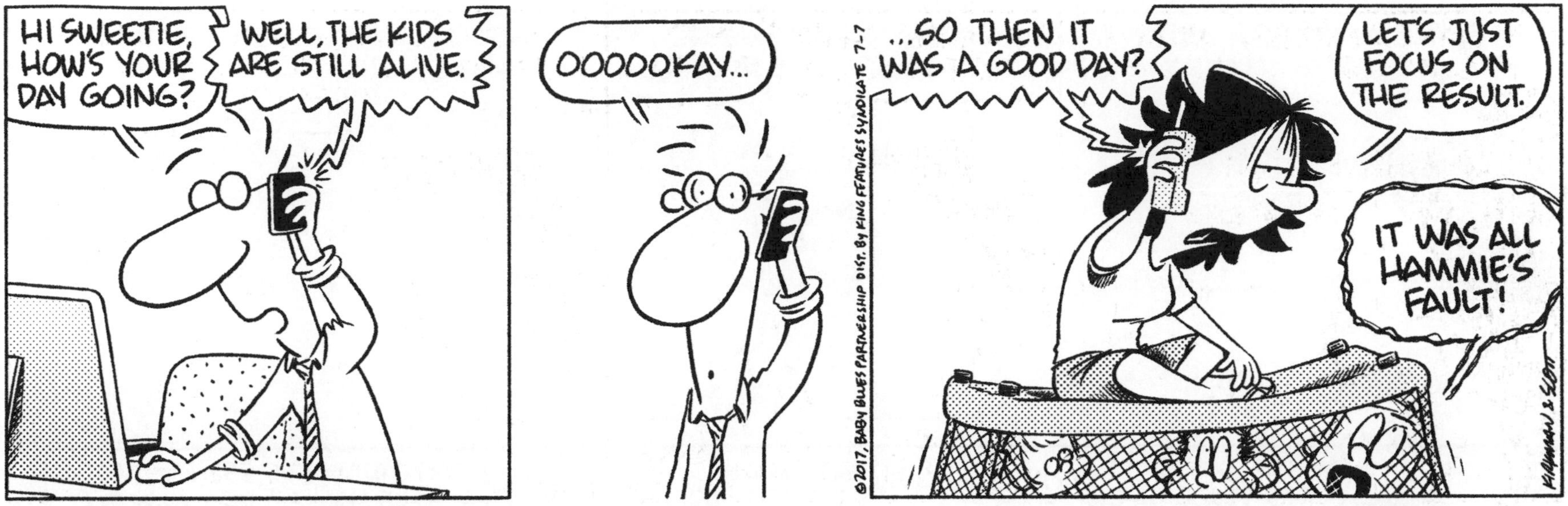
HI SWEETIE, HOW'S YOUR DAY GOING?
WELL, THE KIDS ARE STILL ALIVE.
OOOOOKAY...
...SO THEN IT WAS A GOOD DAY?
LET'S JUST FOCUS ON THE RESULT.
IT WAS ALL HAMMIE'S FAULT!
©2017, BABY BLUES PARTNERSHIP DIST. BY KING FEATURES SYNDICATE 7-7
KIRKMAN & SCOTT

Jerry: Sometimes you gotta look on the bright side.

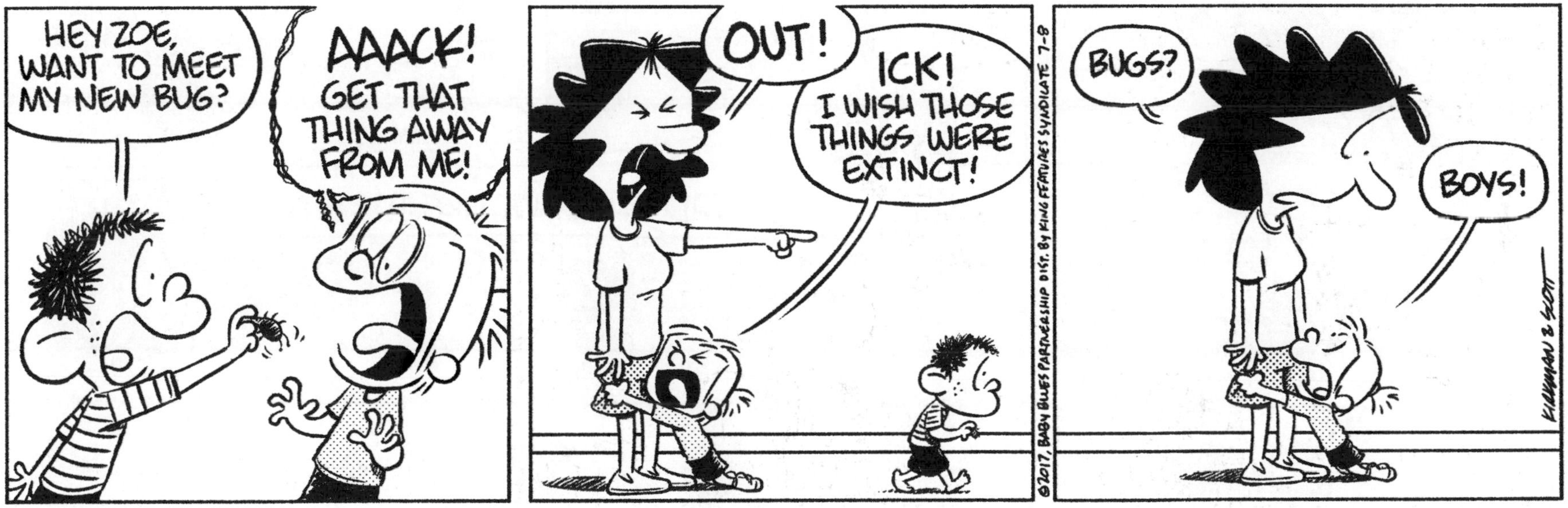
HEY ZOE, WANT TO MEET MY NEW BUG?
AAACK! GET THAT THING AWAY FROM ME!
OUT!
ICK! I WISH THOSE THINGS WERE EXTINCT!
©2017, BABY BLUES PARTNERSHIP DIST. BY KING FEATURES SYNDICATE 7-8
BUGS?
BOYS!
KIRKMAN & SCOTT

BABY BLUES®
Rick Kirkman & Jerry Scott
ZZZZZ

YOU'RE GOING TO LOVE THIS PLACE, WREN!
SWINGS!
SEE? WHAT DID I TELL YOU?
PARK HOURS
I DON'T THINK I'VE BEEN TO THIS PARK SINCE HAMMIE WAS YOUR AGE.
©2017, BABY BLUES PARTNERSHIP DIST. BY KING FEATURES SYNDICATE
KIRKMAN & SCOTT
7-9
THIS ONE'S NOT LIKE THE BOY!

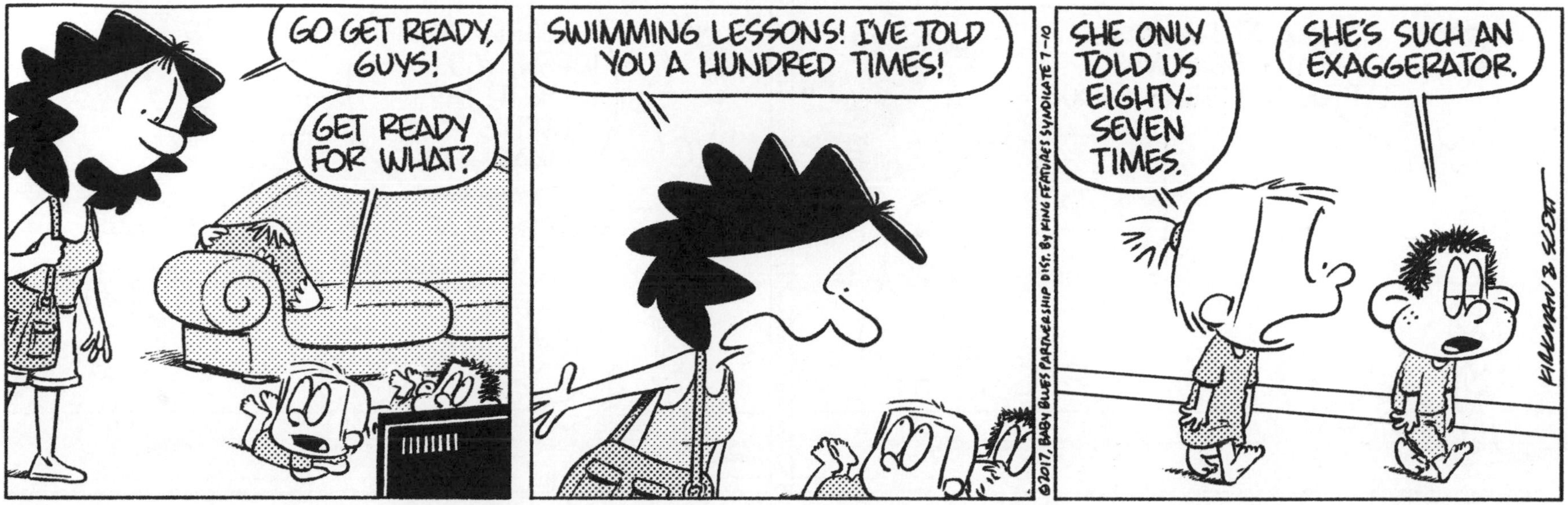
GO GET READY, GUYS!
GET READY FOR WHAT?
SWIMMING LESSONS! I'VE TOLD YOU A HUNDRED TIMES!
©2017, BABY BLUES PARTNERSHIP DIST. BY KING FEATURES SYNDICATE 7-10
SHE ONLY TOLD US EIGHTY-SEVEN TIMES.
SHE'S SUCH AN EXAGGERATOR.
KIRKMAN & SCOTT

Jerry: Yeah. How are you supposed to remember anything after only eighty-seven reminders?

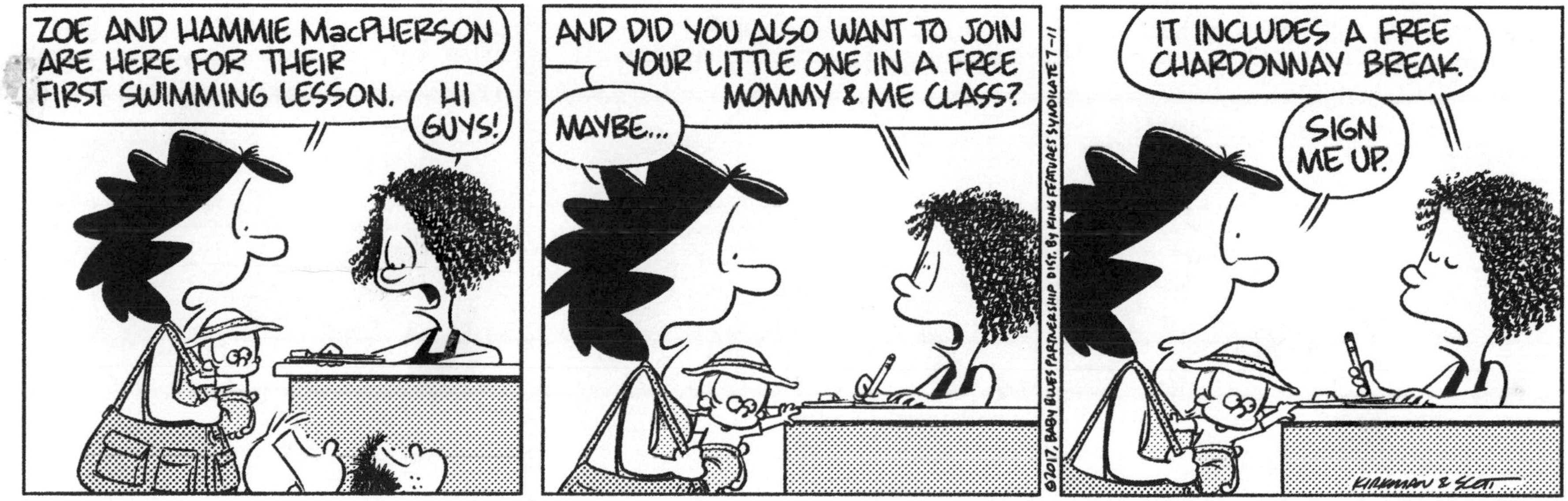
ZOE AND HAMMIE MacPHERSON ARE HERE FOR THEIR FIRST SWIMMING LESSON.
HI GUYS!
AND DID YOU ALSO WANT TO JOIN YOUR LITTLE ONE IN A FREE MOMMY & ME CLASS?
MAYBE...
©2017, BABY BLUES PARTNERSHIP DIST. BY KING FEATURES SYNDICATE 7-11
IT INCLUDES A FREE CHARDONNAY BREAK.
SIGN ME UP.
KIRKMAN & SCOTT

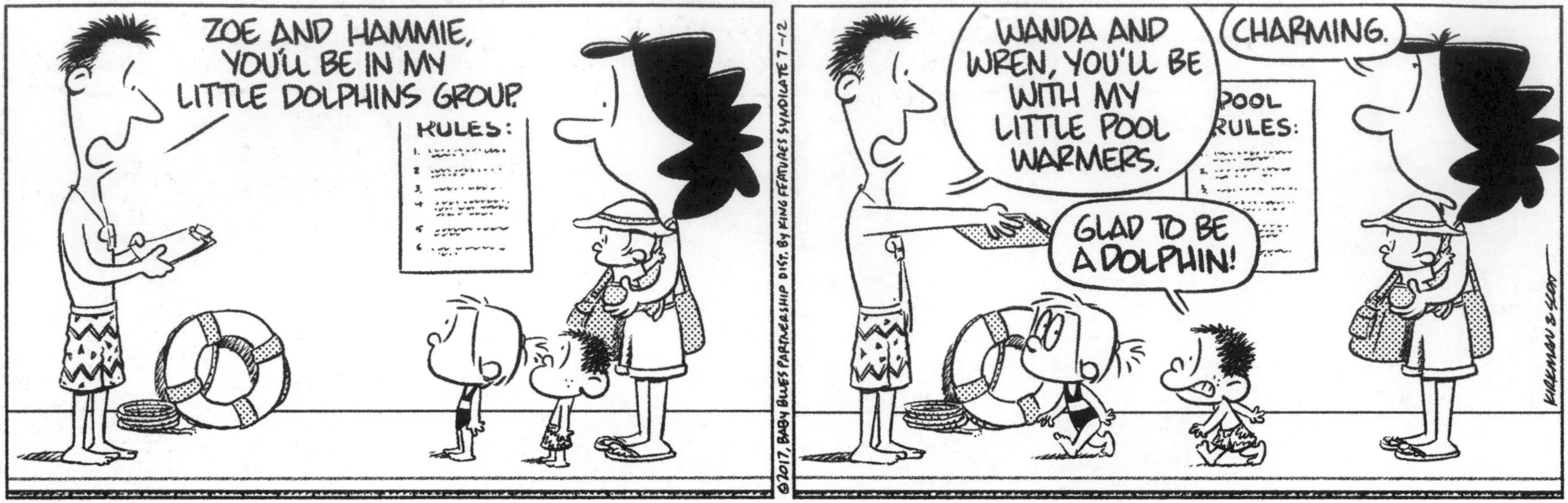

ZOE AND HAMMIE, YOU'LL BE IN MY LITTLE DOLPHINS GROUP.
RULES:
WANDA AND WREN, YOU'LL BE WITH MY LITTLE POOL WARMERS.
CHARMING.
POOL RULES:
GLAD TO BE A DOLPHIN!
©2017, BABY BLUES PARTNERSHIP DIST. BY KING FEATURES SYNDICATE 7-12
KIRKMAN & SCOTT

Rick: Eww.

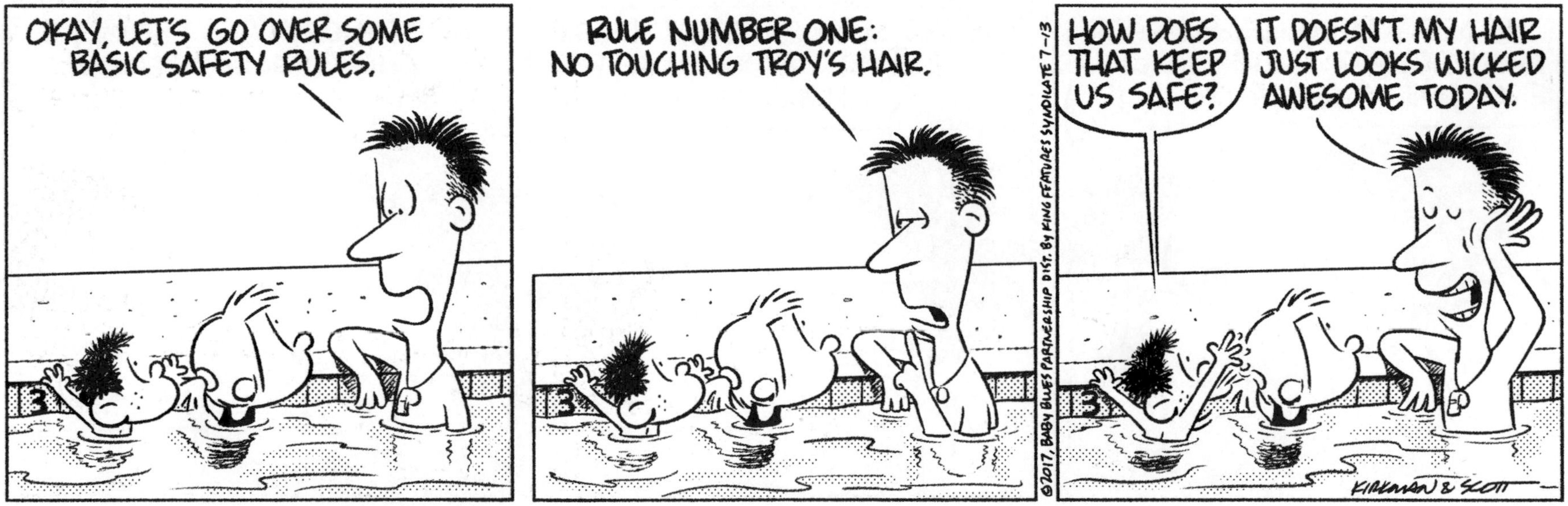

OKAY, LET'S GO OVER SOME BASIC SAFETY RULES.
RULE NUMBER ONE: NO TOUCHING TROY'S HAIR.
HOW DOES THAT KEEP US SAFE?
IT DOESN'T. MY HAIR JUST LOOKS WICKED AWESOME TODAY.
©2017, BABY BLUES PARTNERSHIP DIST. BY KING FEATURES SYNDICATE 7-13
KIRKMAN & SCOTT

Rick: Never trust a teacher who refers to himself in the third person.

NICE JOB, ZOE!
YOU SWAM ALL THE WAY TO THE ROPE AND BACK!
NEXT TIME TRY IT WITHOUT STOPPING TO DUNK YOUR BROTHER.
SORRY. INSTINCT KICKED IN.
KAF! SPUTTER!
©2017, BABY BLUES PARTNERSHIP DIST. BY KING FEATURES SYNDICATE 7-14
KIRKMAN & SCOTT

THE FIRST THING WE WANT TO DO IS GET WREN COMFORTABLE FLOATING ON HER BACK.
THAT'S IT. NOW, LET HER GO.
NO FAIR HOLDING HER UP WITH YOUR TOE.
BACK OFF, TROY!
©2017, BABY BLUES PARTNERSHIP DIST. BY KING FEATURES SYNDICATE 7-15
KIRKMAN & SCOTT

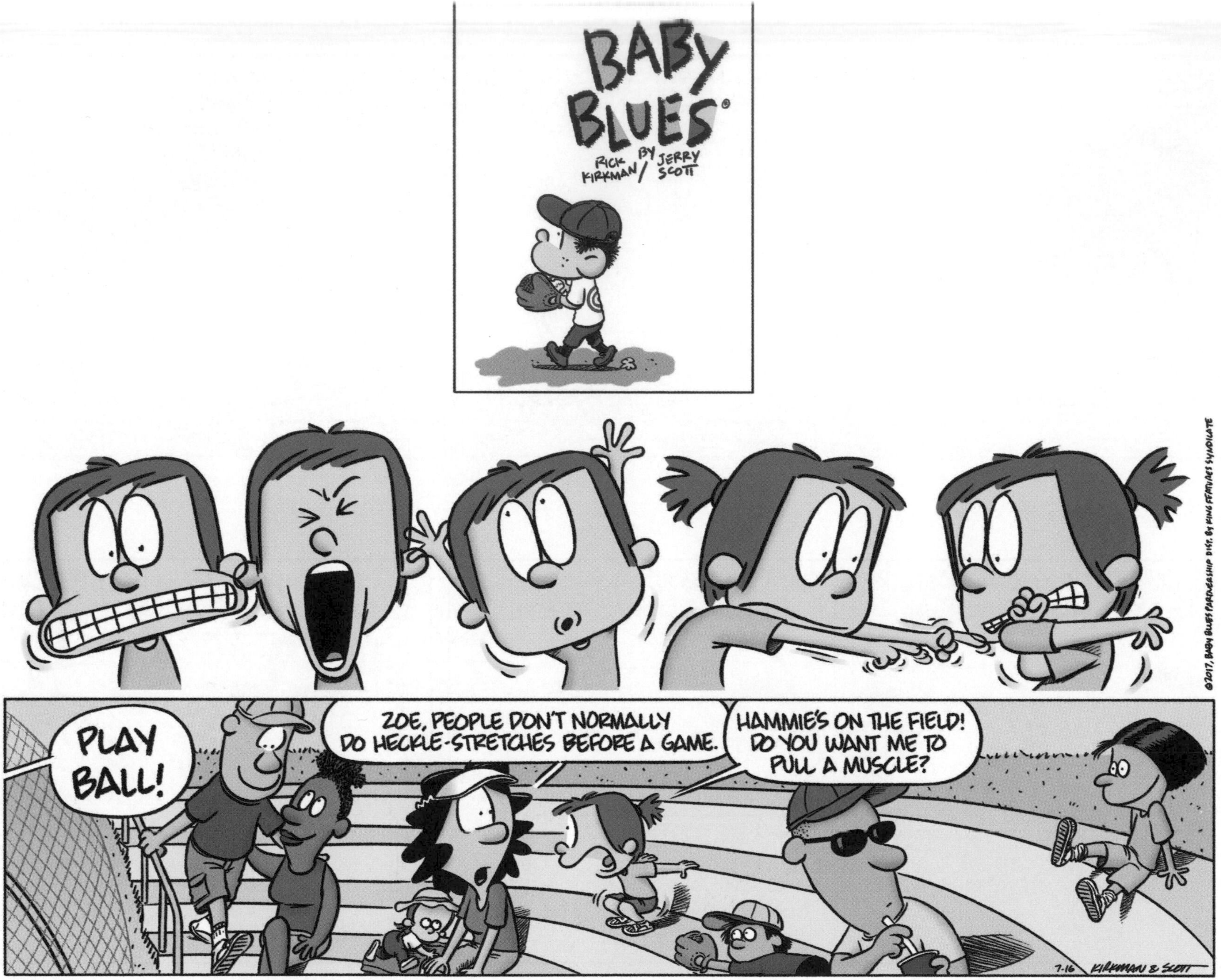
BABY BLUES®
BY RICK KIRKMAN / JERRY SCOTT
©2017, BABY BLUES PARTNERSHIP DIST. BY KING FEATURES SYNDICATE
PLAY BALL!
ZOE, PEOPLE DON'T NORMALLY DO HECKLE-STRETCHES BEFORE A GAME.
HAMMIE'S ON THE FIELD! DO YOU WANT ME TO PULL A MUSCLE?
7-16 KIRKMAN & SCOTT

Rick: It's definitely an unusual job when you spend part of your day trying to figure out what constitutes "heckle-stretches."

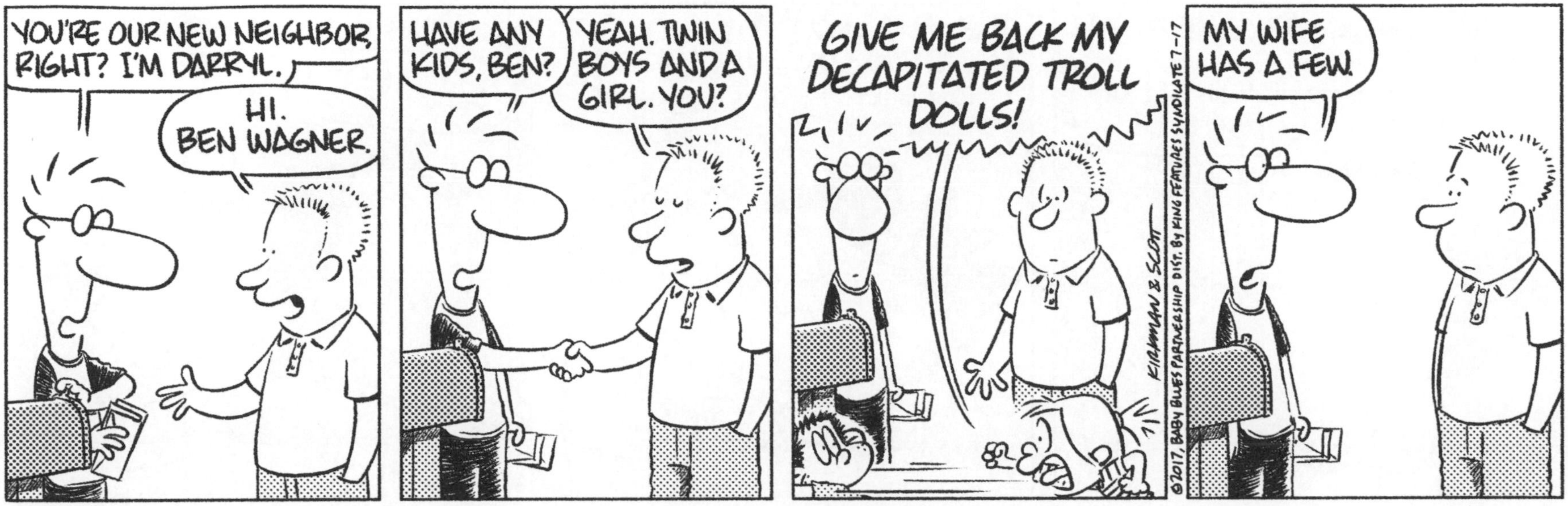
YOU'RE OUR NEW NEIGHBOR, RIGHT? I'M DARRYL.
HI. BEN WAGNER.
HAVE ANY KIDS, BEN?
YEAH. TWIN BOYS AND A GIRL. YOU?
GIVE ME BACK MY DECAPITATED TROLL DOLLS!
KIRKMAN & SCOTT
©2017, BABY BLUES PARTNERSHIP DIST. BY KING FEATURES SYNDICATE 7-17
MY WIFE HAS A FEW.

Rick: This character is notable in that my daughter sat on his head when they were both little.

Jerry: That's true. He's my nephew, and it didn't hurt him too much.

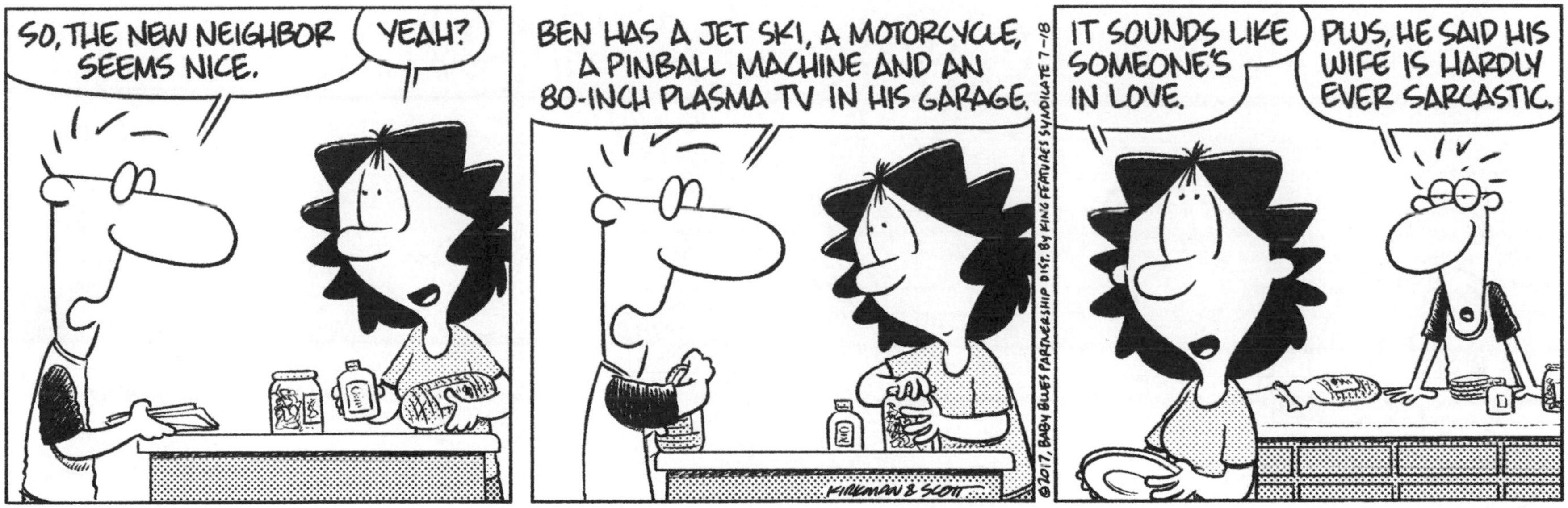
SO, THE NEW NEIGHBOR SEEMS NICE.
YEAH?
BEN HAS A JET SKI, A MOTORCYCLE, A PINBALL MACHINE AND AN 80-INCH PLASMA TV IN HIS GARAGE.
KIRKMAN & SCOTT
©2017, BABY BLUES PARTNERSHIP DIST. BY KING FEATURES SYNDICATE 7-18
IT SOUNDS LIKE SOMEONE'S IN LOVE.
PLUS, HE SAID HIS WIFE IS HARDLY EVER SARCASTIC.

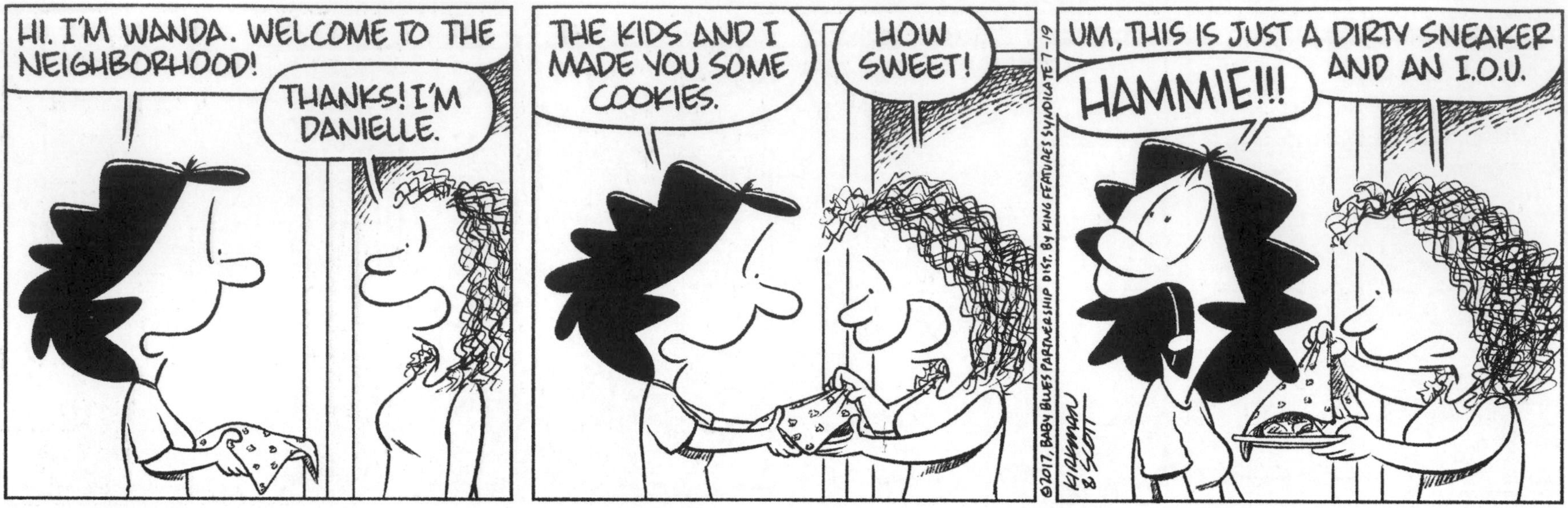

HI. I'M WANDA. WELCOME TO THE NEIGHBORHOOD!
THANKS! I'M DANIELLE.
THE KIDS AND I MADE YOU SOME COOKIES.
HOW SWEET!
©2017, BABY BLUES PARTNERSHIP DIST. BY KING FEATURES SYNDICATE 7-19
KIRKMAN & SCOTT
UM, THIS IS JUST A DIRTY SNEAKER AND AN I.O.U.
HAMMIE!!!

Jerry: I couldn't leave Ben's wife, Danielle, out of the series, now could I?

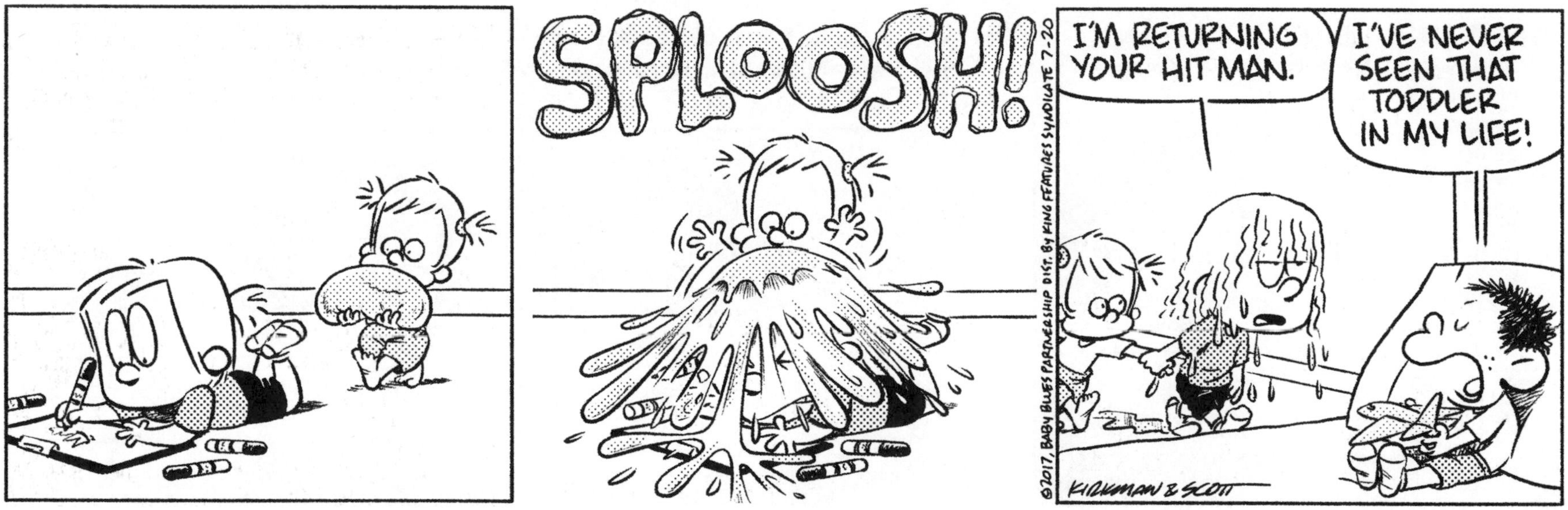

SPLOOSH!
©2017, BABY BLUES PARTNERSHIP DIST. BY KING FEATURES SYNDICATE 7-20
I'M RETURNING YOUR HIT MAN.
I'VE NEVER SEEN THAT TODDLER IN MY LIFE!
KIRKMAN & SCOTT

Jerry: I wonder if you can check a water balloon for fingerprints?

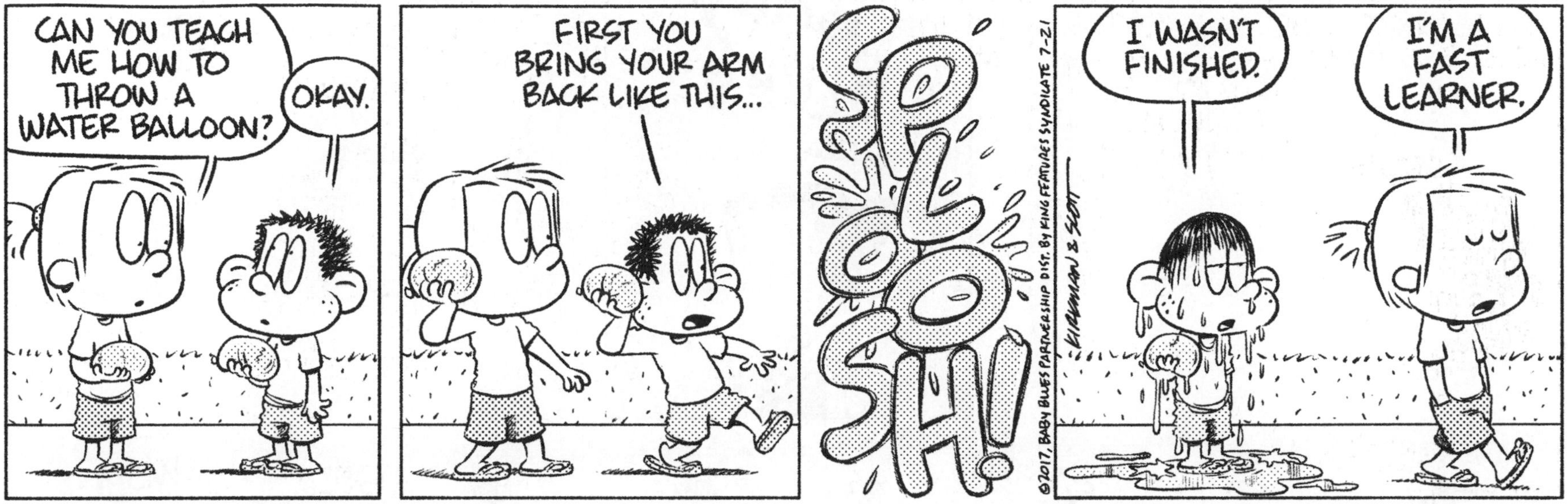
CAN YOU TEACH ME HOW TO THROW A WATER BALLOON?
OKAY.
FIRST YOU BRING YOUR ARM BACK LIKE THIS...
SPLOOSH!
©2017, BABY BLUES PARTNERSHIP DIST. BY KING FEATURES SYNDICATE 7-21
KIRKMAN & SCOTT
I WASN'T FINISHED.
I'M A FAST LEARNER.

Rick: Well played, Zoe.

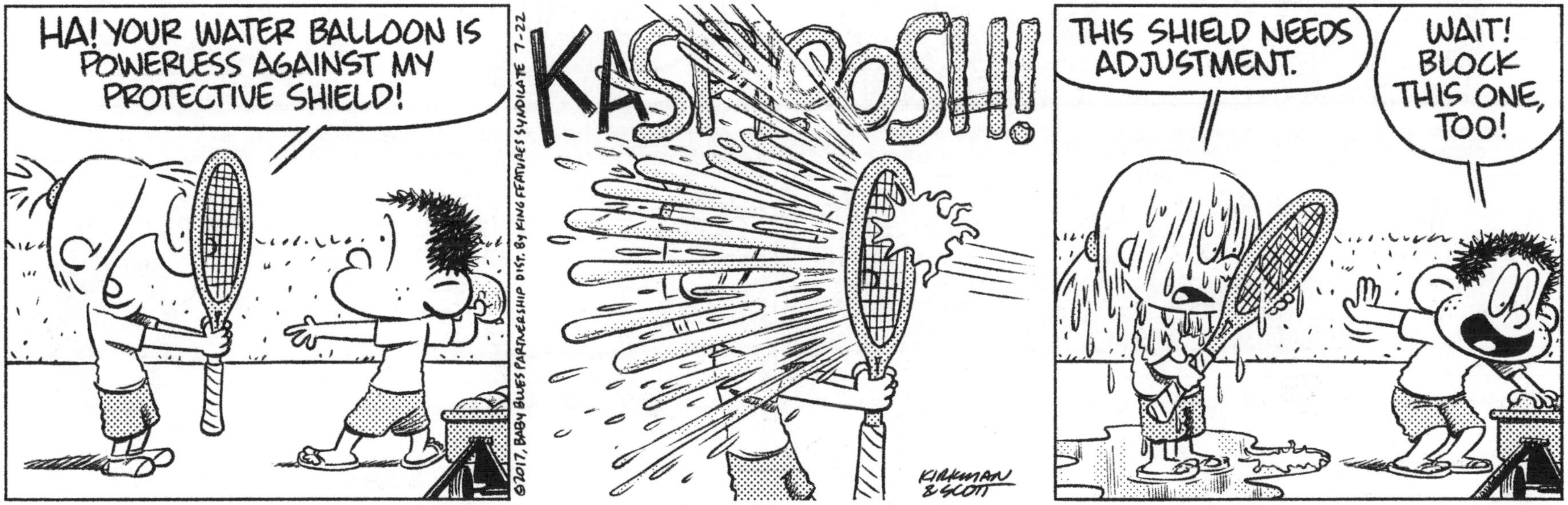
HA! YOUR WATER BALLOON IS POWERLESS AGAINST MY PROTECTIVE SHIELD!
©2017, BABY BLUES PARTNERSHIP DIST. BY KING FEATURES SYNDICATE 7-22
KIRKMAN & SCOTT
THIS SHIELD NEEDS ADJUSTMENT.
WAIT! BLOCK THIS ONE, TOO!

Rick: Never mind. (See previous strip.)

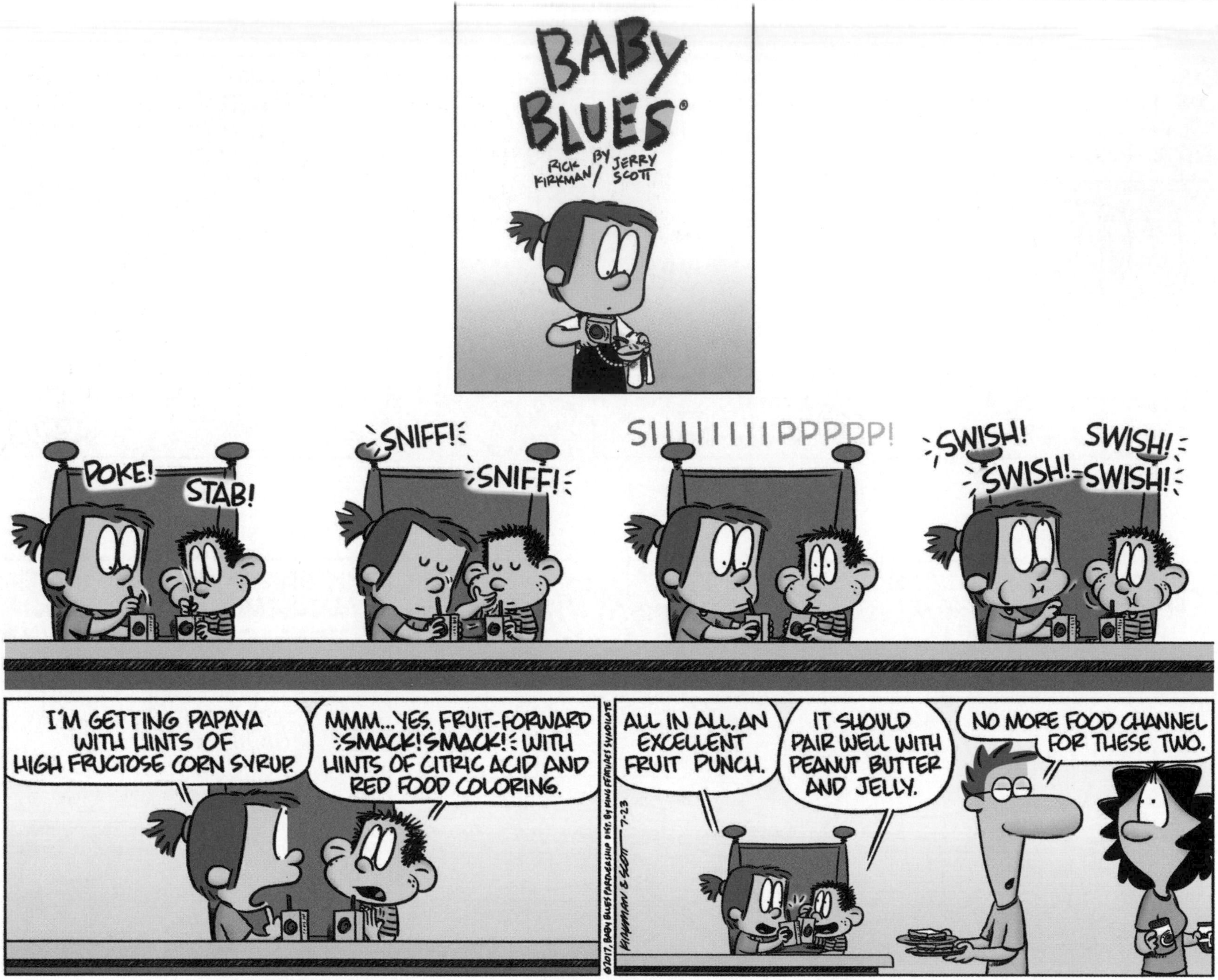
BABY BLUES®
BY RICK KIRKMAN / JERRY SCOTT
POKE!
STAB!
SNIFF!
SNIFF!
SIIIIIIIIPPPPPP!
SWISH!
SWISH!
SWISH!
SWISH!
I'M GETTING PAPAYA WITH HINTS OF HIGH FRUCTOSE CORN SYRUP.
MMM...YES. FRUIT-FORWARD SMACK! SMACK! WITH HINTS OF CITRIC ACID AND RED FOOD COLORING.
©2017, BABY BLUES PARTNERSHIP DIST. BY KING FEATURES SYNDICATE
KIRKMAN & SCOTT 7-23
ALL IN ALL, AN EXCELLENT FRUIT PUNCH.
IT SHOULD PAIR WELL WITH PEANUT BUTTER AND JELLY.
NO MORE FOOD CHANNEL FOR THESE TWO.

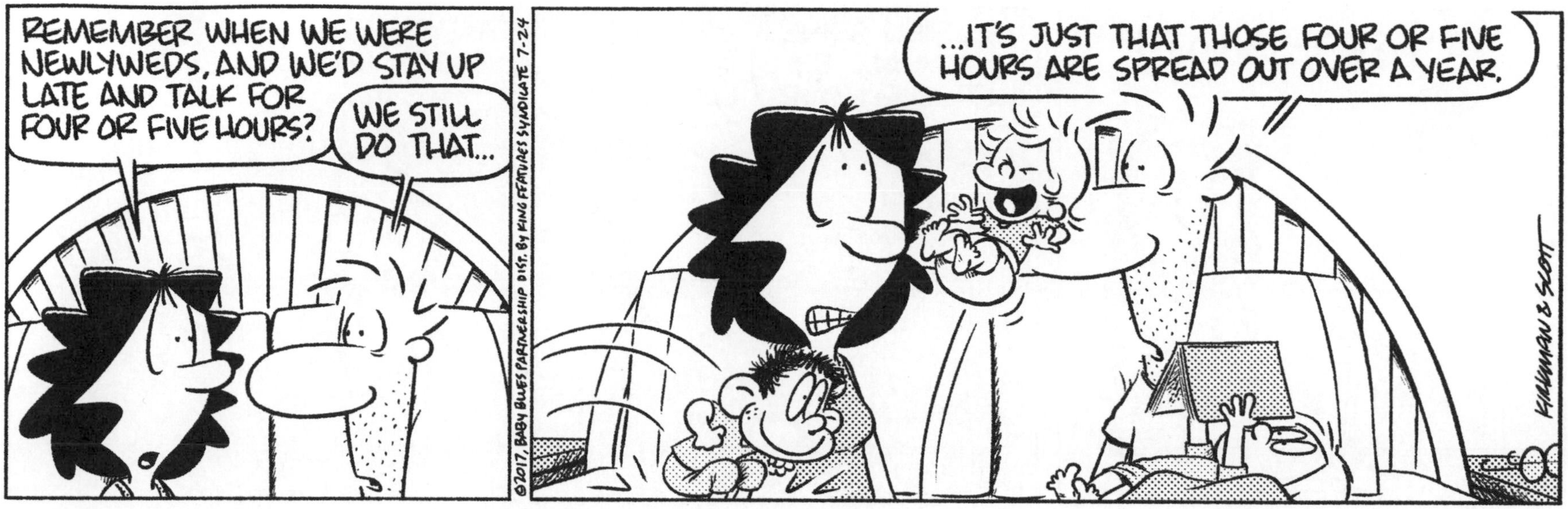
REMEMBER WHEN WE WERE NEWLYWEDS, AND WE'D STAY UP LATE AND TALK FOR FOUR OR FIVE HOURS?
WE STILL DO THAT...
...IT'S JUST THAT THOSE FOUR OR FIVE HOURS ARE SPREAD OUT OVER A YEAR.
©2017, BABY BLUES PARTNERSHIP DIST. BY KING FEATURES SYNDICATE 7-24
KIRKMAN & SCOTT

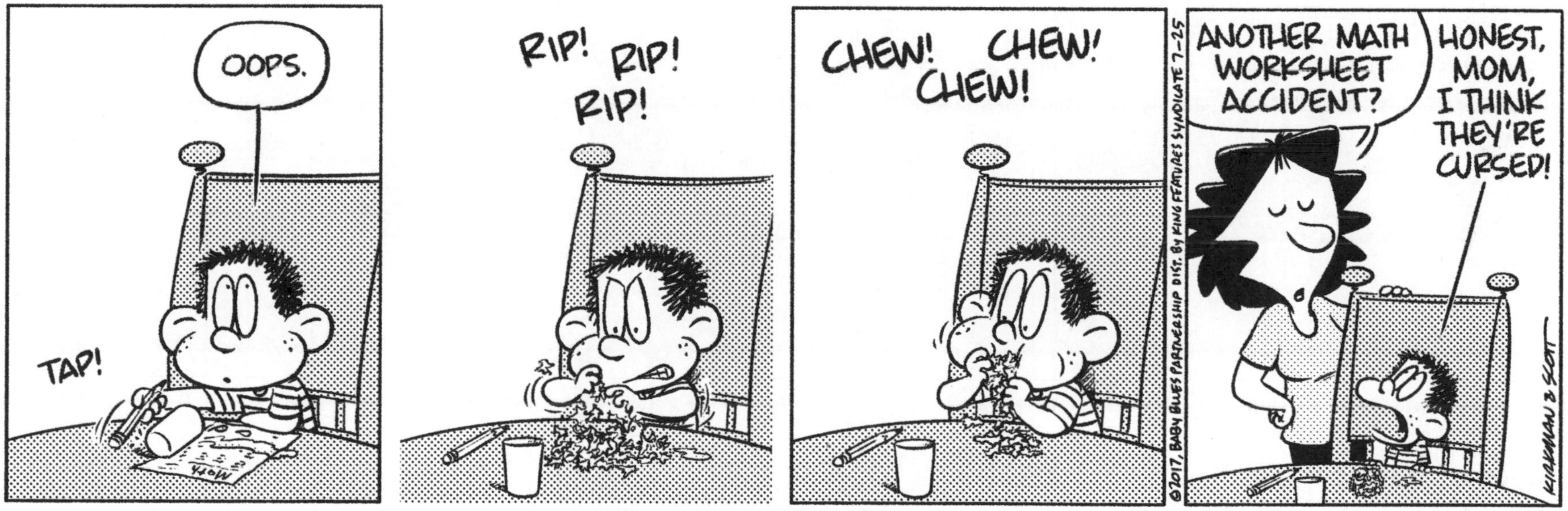
OOPS.
TAP!
Math
RIP! RIP! RIP!
CHEW! CHEW! CHEW!
©2017, BABY BLUES PARTNERSHIP DIST. BY KING FEATURES SYNDICATE 7-25
ANOTHER MATH WORKSHEET ACCIDENT?
HONEST, MOM, I THINK THEY'RE CURSED!
KIRKMAN & SCOTT

Jerry: A variation on the "dog ate my homework" scheme (necessary when you don't actually have a dog).

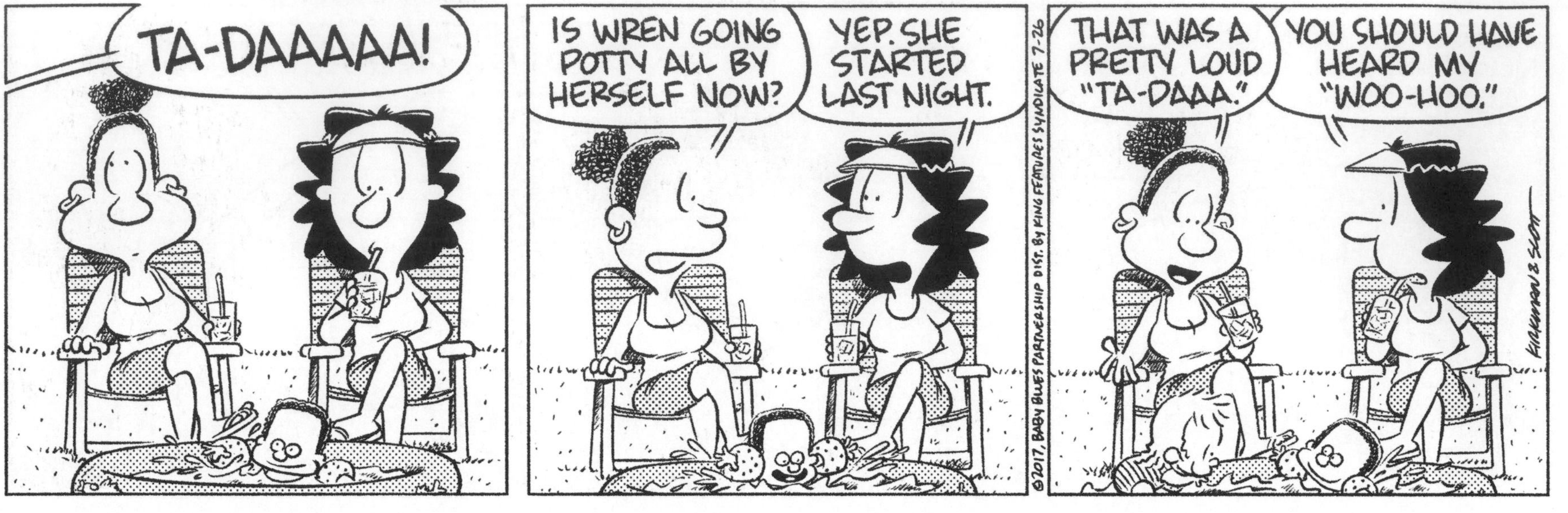
TA-DAAAAA!
IS WREN GOING POTTY ALL BY HERSELF NOW?
YEP. SHE STARTED LAST NIGHT.
©2017, BABY BLUES PARTNERSHIP DIST. BY KING FEATURES SYNDICATE 7-26
THAT WAS A PRETTY LOUD "TA-DAAA."
YOU SHOULD HAVE HEARD MY "WOO-HOO."
KIRKMAN & SCOTT

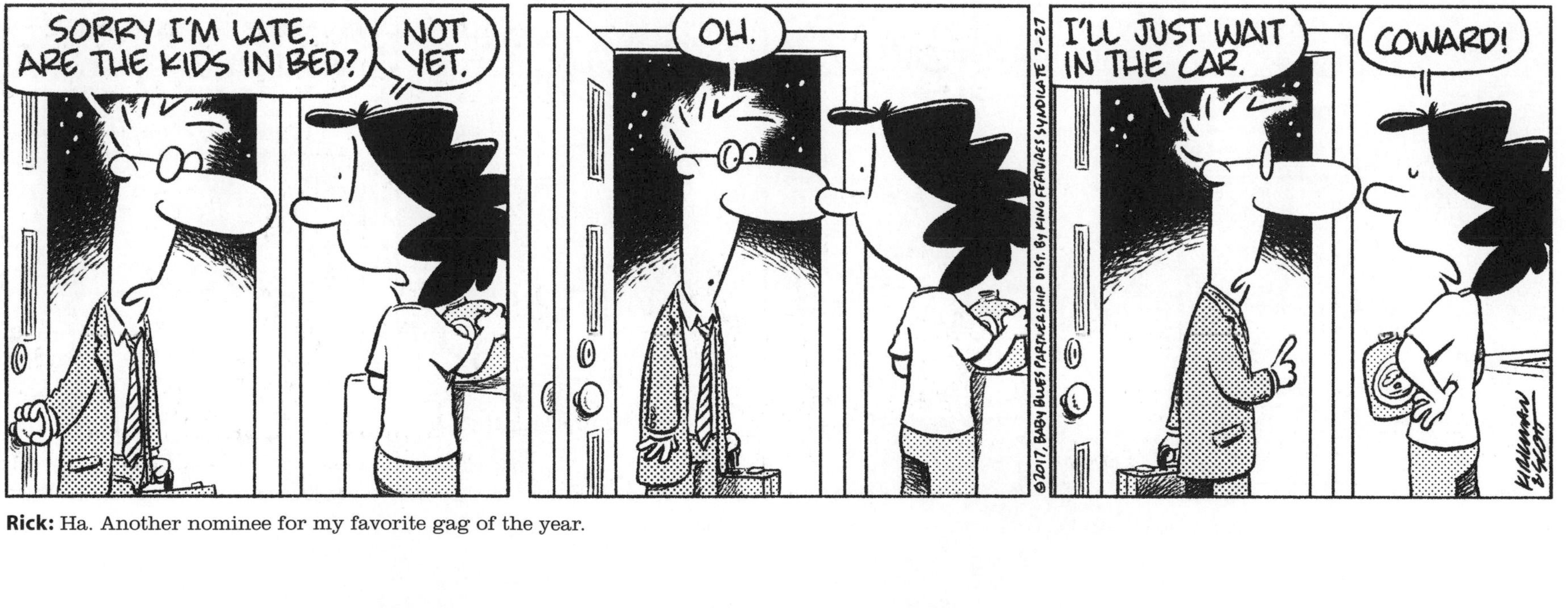
SORRY I'M LATE. ARE THE KIDS IN BED?
NOT YET.
OH.
©2017, BABY BLUES PARTNERSHIP DIST. BY KING FEATURES SYNDICATE 7-27
I'LL JUST WAIT IN THE CAR.
COWARD!

Rick: Ha. Another nominee for my favorite gag of the year.

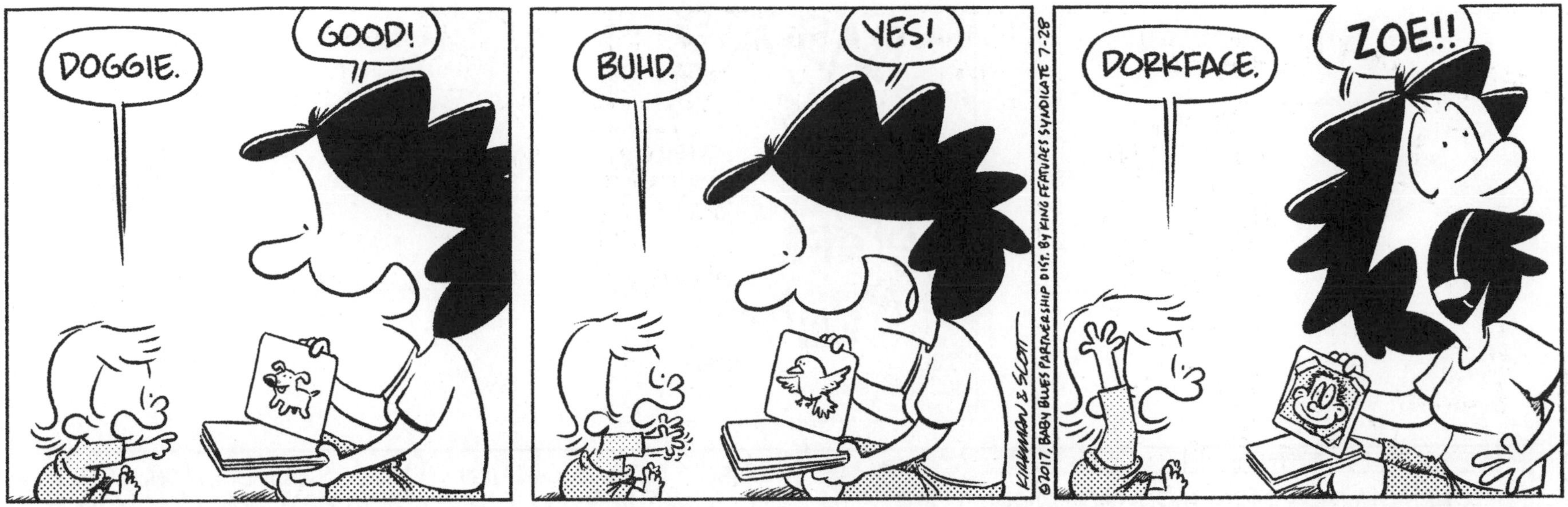
DOGGIE.
GOOD!
BUHD.
YES!
©2017, BABY BLUES PARTNERSHIP DIST. BY KING FEATURES SYNDICATE 7-28
KIRKMAN & SCOTT
DORKFACE.
ZOE!!

Jerry: Toddlers are fast learners.

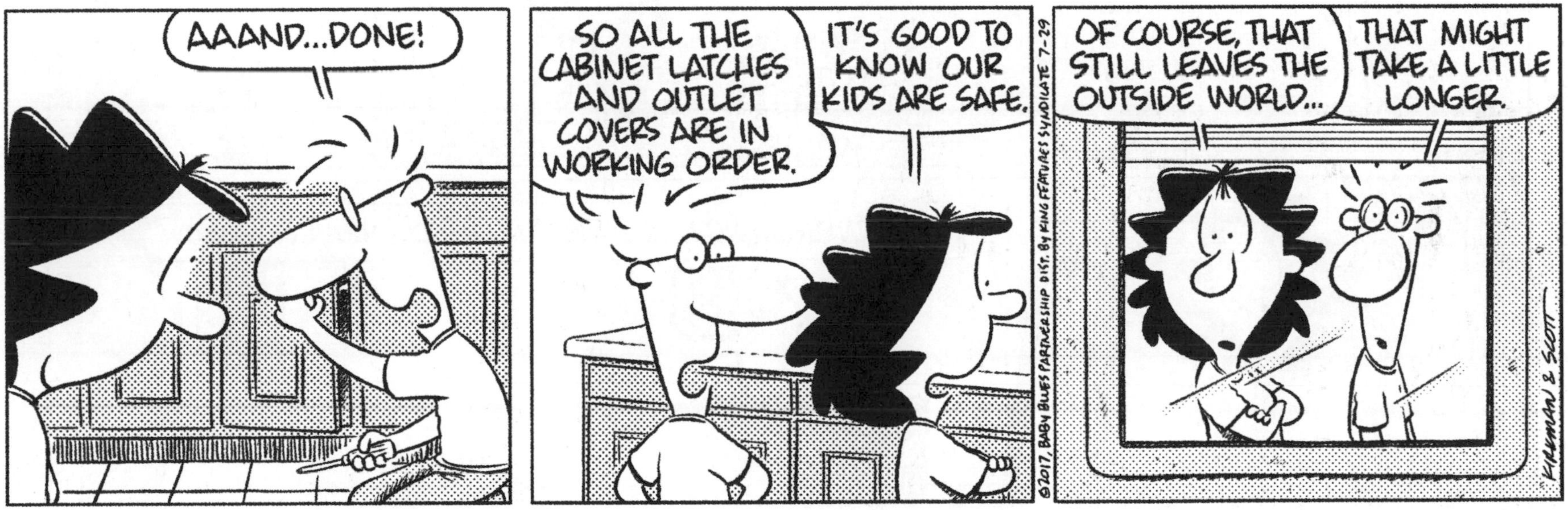
AAAND...DONE!
SO ALL THE CABINET LATCHES AND OUTLET COVERS ARE IN WORKING ORDER.
IT'S GOOD TO KNOW OUR KIDS ARE SAFE.
©2017, BABY BLUES PARTNERSHIP DIST. BY KING FEATURES SYNDICATE 7-29
OF COURSE, THAT STILL LEAVES THE OUTSIDE WORLD...
THAT MIGHT TAKE A LITTLE LONGER.
KIRKMAN & SCOTT

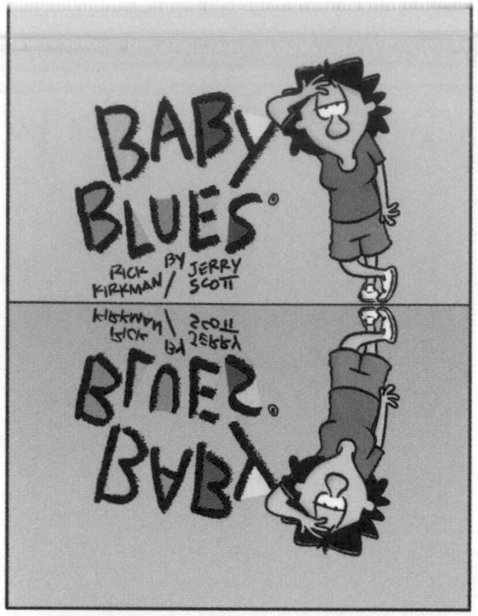
BABY BLUES®
BY RICK KIRKMAN / JERRY SCOTT

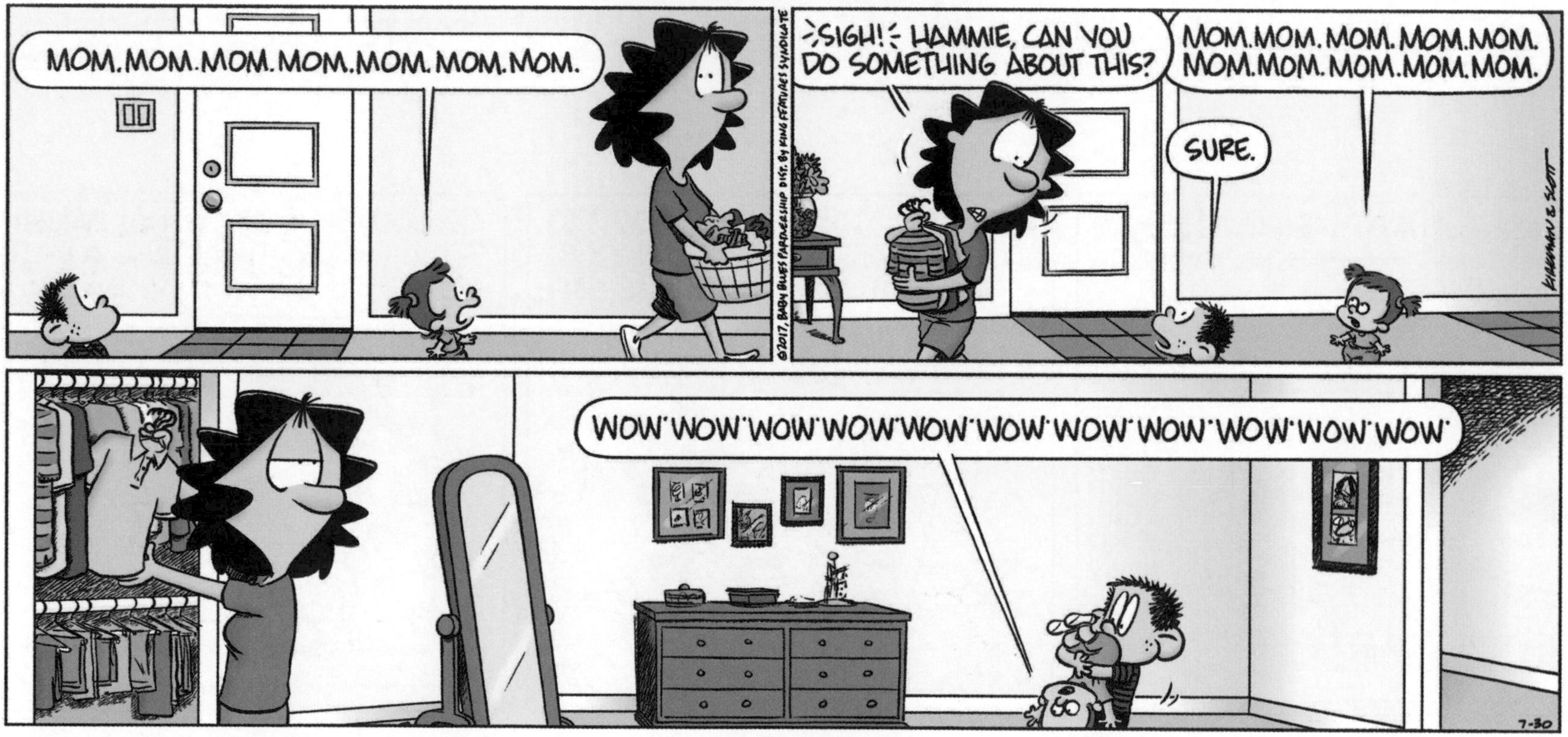
MOM.MOM.MOM.MOM.MOM.MOM.MOM.
©2017, BABY BLUES PARTNERSHIP DIST. BY KING FEATURES SYNDICATE
-SIGH!- HAMMIE, CAN YOU DO SOMETHING ABOUT THIS?
MOM.MOM.MOM.MOM.MOM. MOM.MOM.MOM.MOM.MOM.
SURE.
KIRKMAN & SCOTT
WOW·WOW·WOW·WOW·WOW·WOW·WOW·WOW·WOW·WOW·WOW·
7-30

Rick: We debated over the wording in the last panel. Even our editor got in on it.

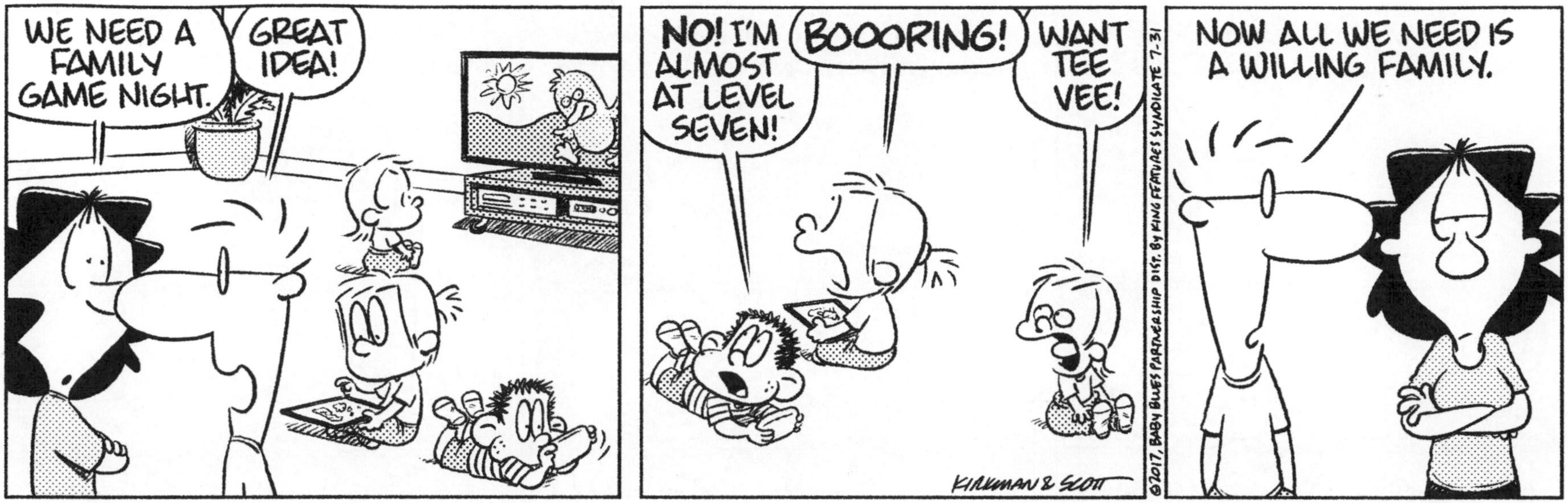
WE NEED A FAMILY GAME NIGHT.
GREAT IDEA!
NO! I'M ALMOST AT LEVEL SEVEN!
BOOORING!
WANT TEE VEE!
©2017, BABY BLUES PARTNERSHIP DIST. BY KING FEATURES SYNDICATE 7-31
KIRKMAN & SCOTT
NOW ALL WE NEED IS A WILLING FAMILY.

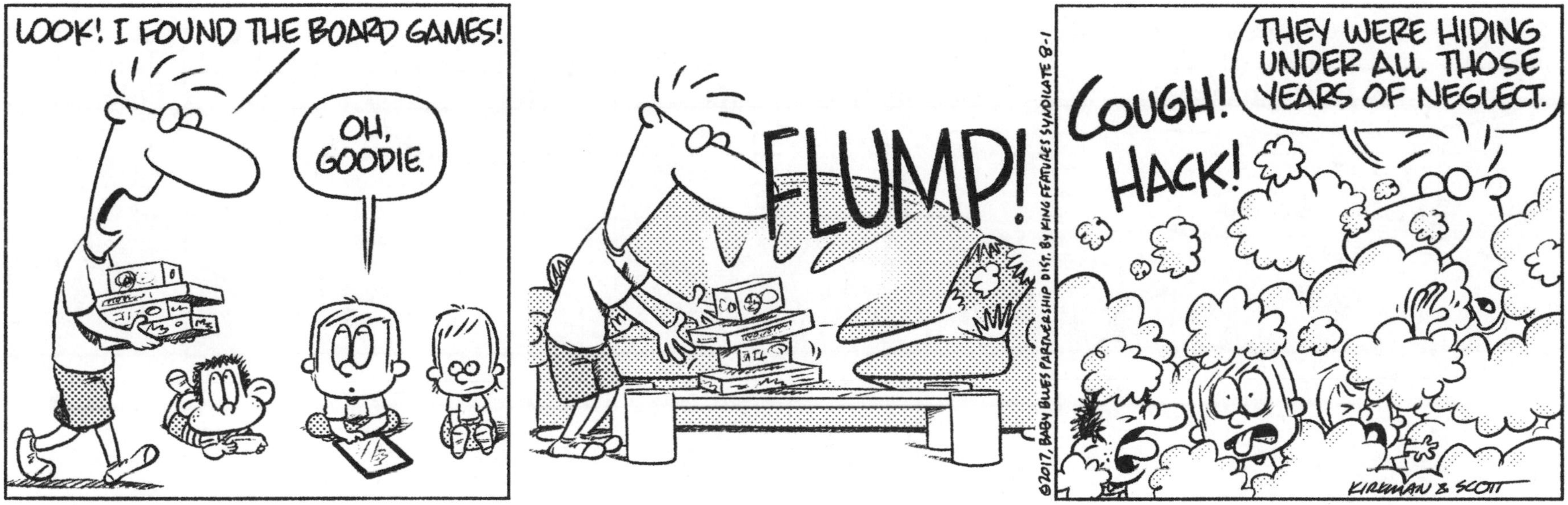
LOOK! I FOUND THE BOARD GAMES!
OH, GOODIE.
FLUMP!
©2017, BABY BLUES PARTNERSHIP DIST. BY KING FEATURES SYNDICATE 8-1
COUGH!
HACK!
THEY WERE HIDING UNDER ALL THOSE YEARS OF NEGLECT.
KIRKMAN & SCOTT

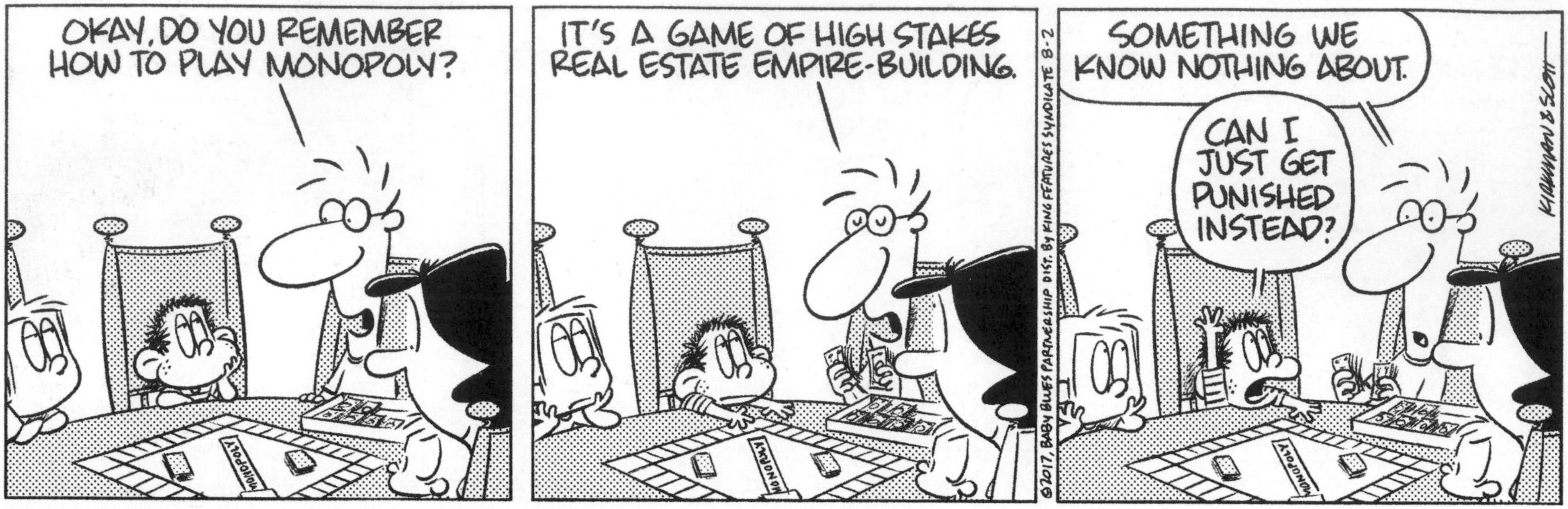

OKAY, DO YOU REMEMBER HOW TO PLAY MONOPOLY?
IT'S A GAME OF HIGH STAKES REAL ESTATE EMPIRE-BUILDING.
SOMETHING WE KNOW NOTHING ABOUT.
CAN I JUST GET PUNISHED INSTEAD?

Rick: Where did I leave off on my list of Things I Hate to Draw? Oh, yeah. Board games.

Jerry: I never really cared about winning at Monopoly, as long as I got the little race car game piece.

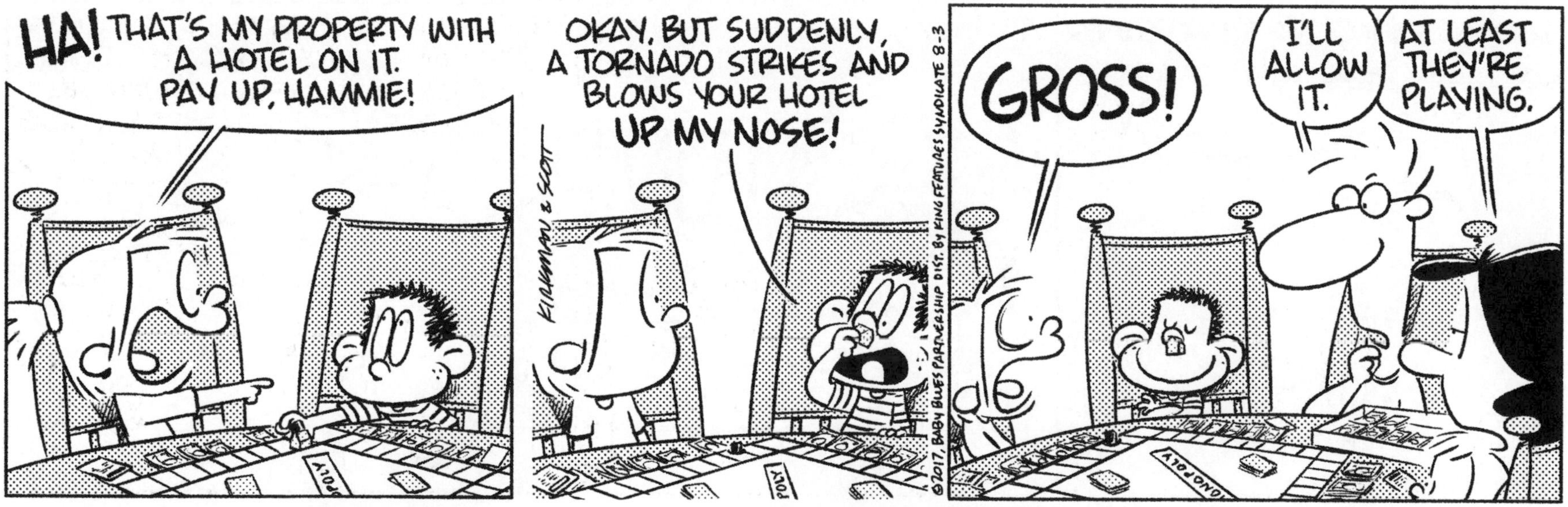

HA! THAT'S MY PROPERTY WITH A HOTEL ON IT. PAY UP, HAMMIE!
OKAY, BUT SUDDENLY, A TORNADO STRIKES AND BLOWS YOUR HOTEL UP MY NOSE!
GROSS!
I'LL ALLOW IT.
AT LEAST THEY'RE PLAYING.

Jerry: This is a good way to acquire a hotel, by the way. Sisters won't touch them once they've been up your nose.

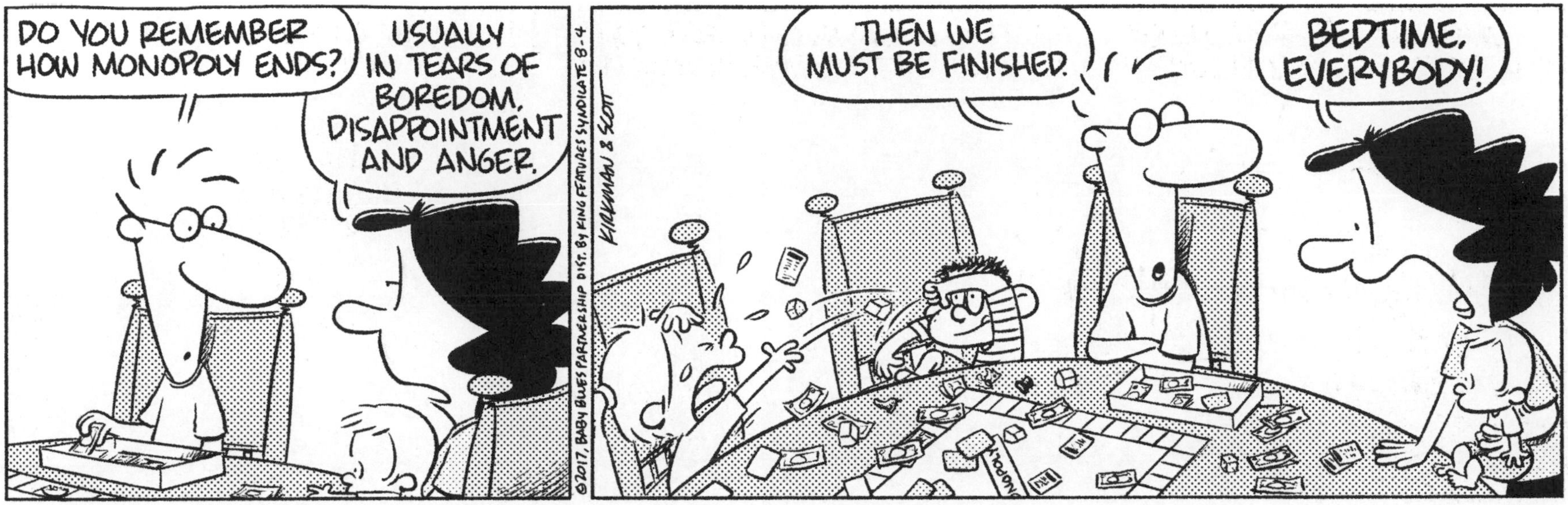
DO YOU REMEMBER HOW MONOPOLY ENDS?
USUALLY IN TEARS OF BOREDOM, DISAPPOINTMENT AND ANGER.
©2017, BABY BLUES PARTNERSHIP DIST. BY KING FEATURES SYNDICATE 8-4
KIRKMAN & SCOTT
THEN WE MUST BE FINISHED.
BEDTIME, EVERYBODY!

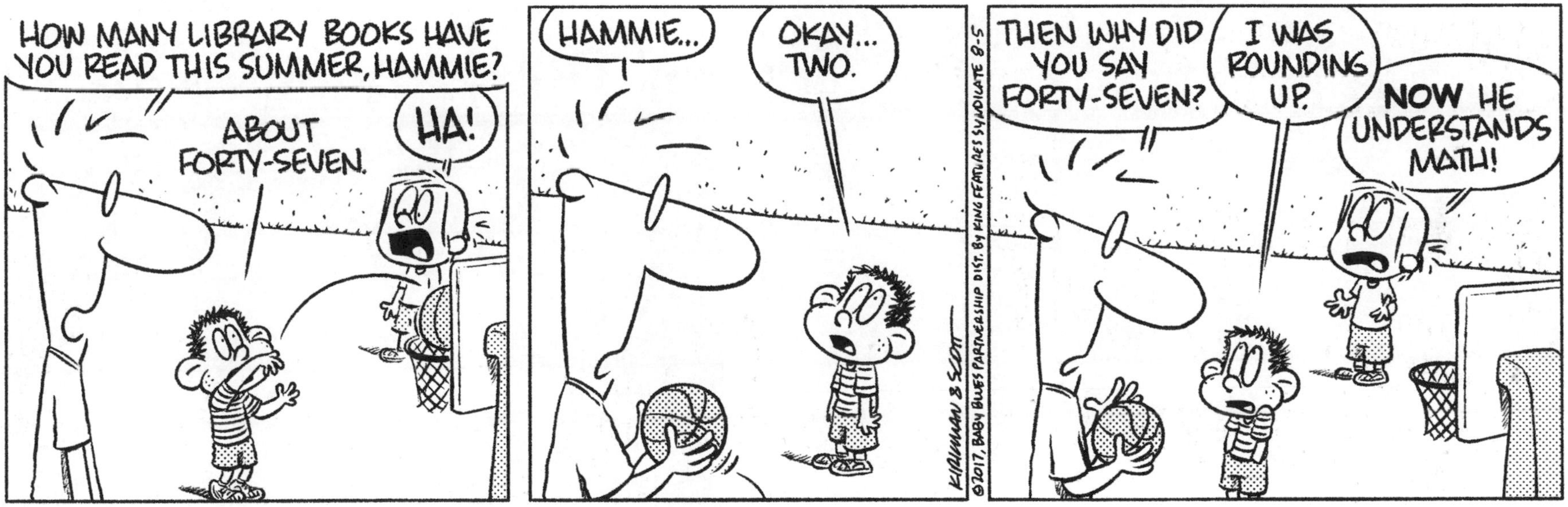
HOW MANY LIBRARY BOOKS HAVE YOU READ THIS SUMMER, HAMMIE?
ABOUT FORTY-SEVEN.
HA!
HAMMIE...
OKAY... TWO.
KIRKMAN & SCOTT
©2017, BABY BLUES PARTNERSHIP DIST. BY KING FEATURES SYNDICATE 8-5
THEN WHY DID YOU SAY FORTY-SEVEN?
I WAS ROUNDING UP.
NOW HE UNDERSTANDS MATH!

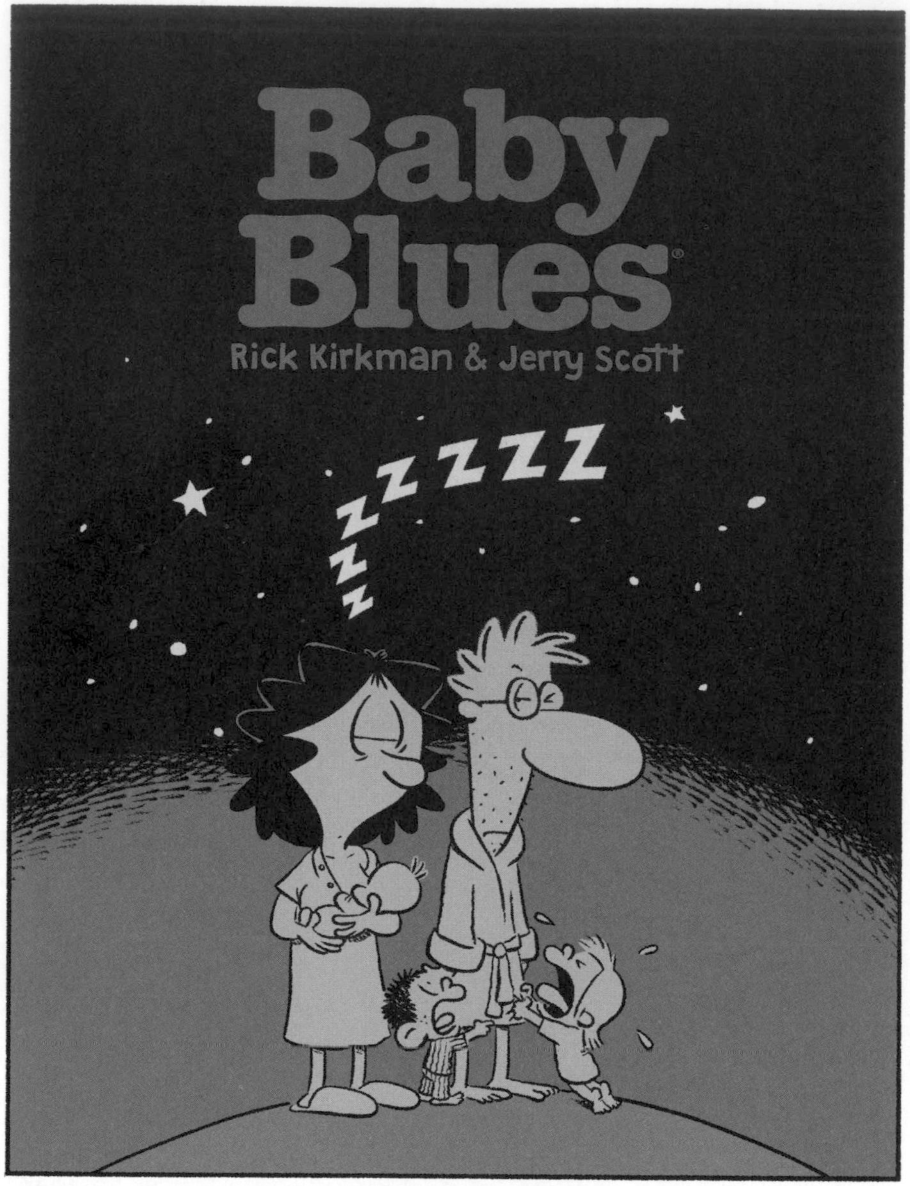
Baby Blues
Rick Kirkman & Jerry Scott
ZZZZZZZZZ

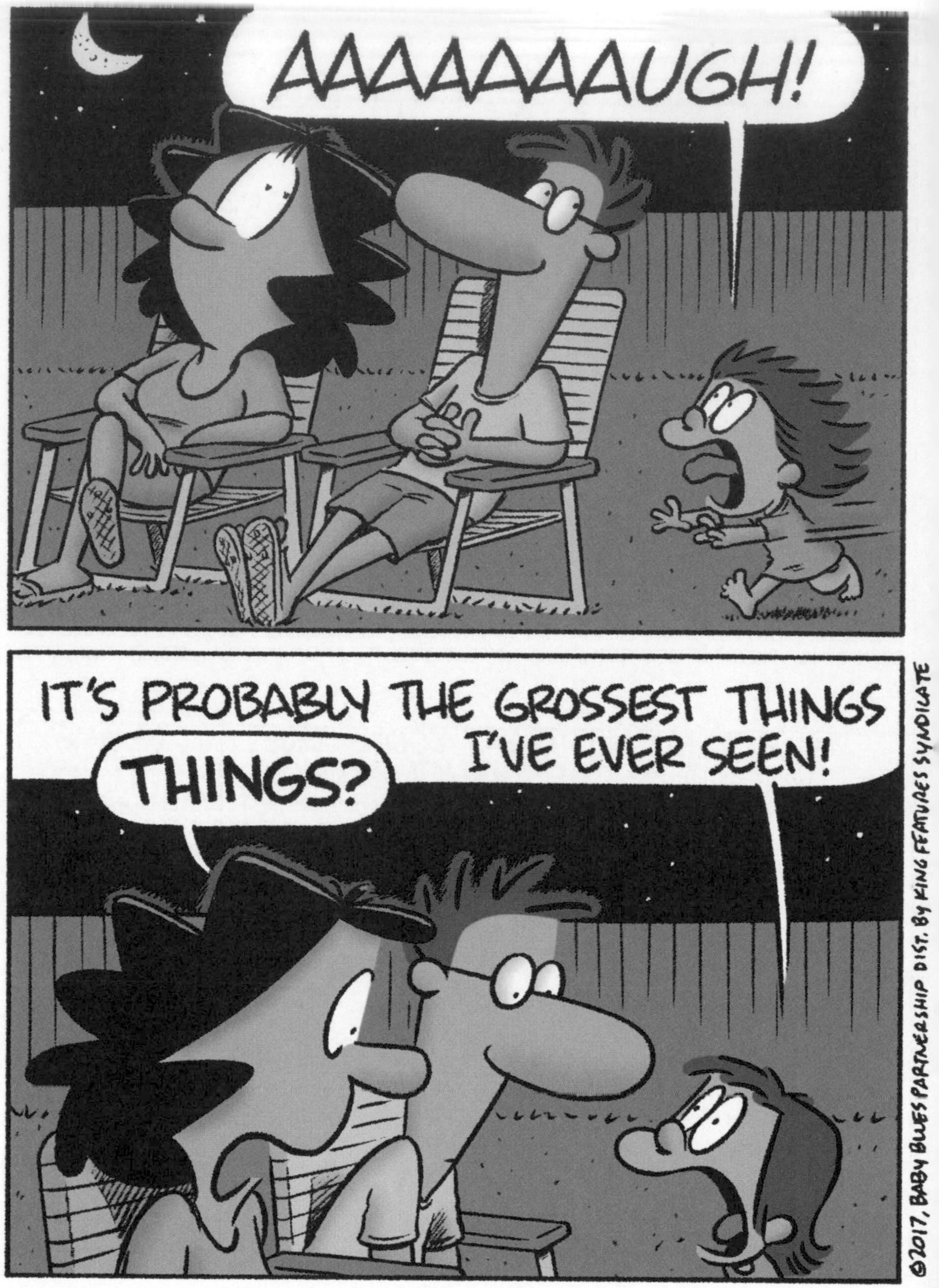
AAAAAAAUGH!
IT'S PROBABLY THE GROSSEST THINGS I'VE EVER SEEN!
THINGS?
©2017, BABY BLUES PARTNERSHIP DIST. BY KING FEATURES SYNDICATE

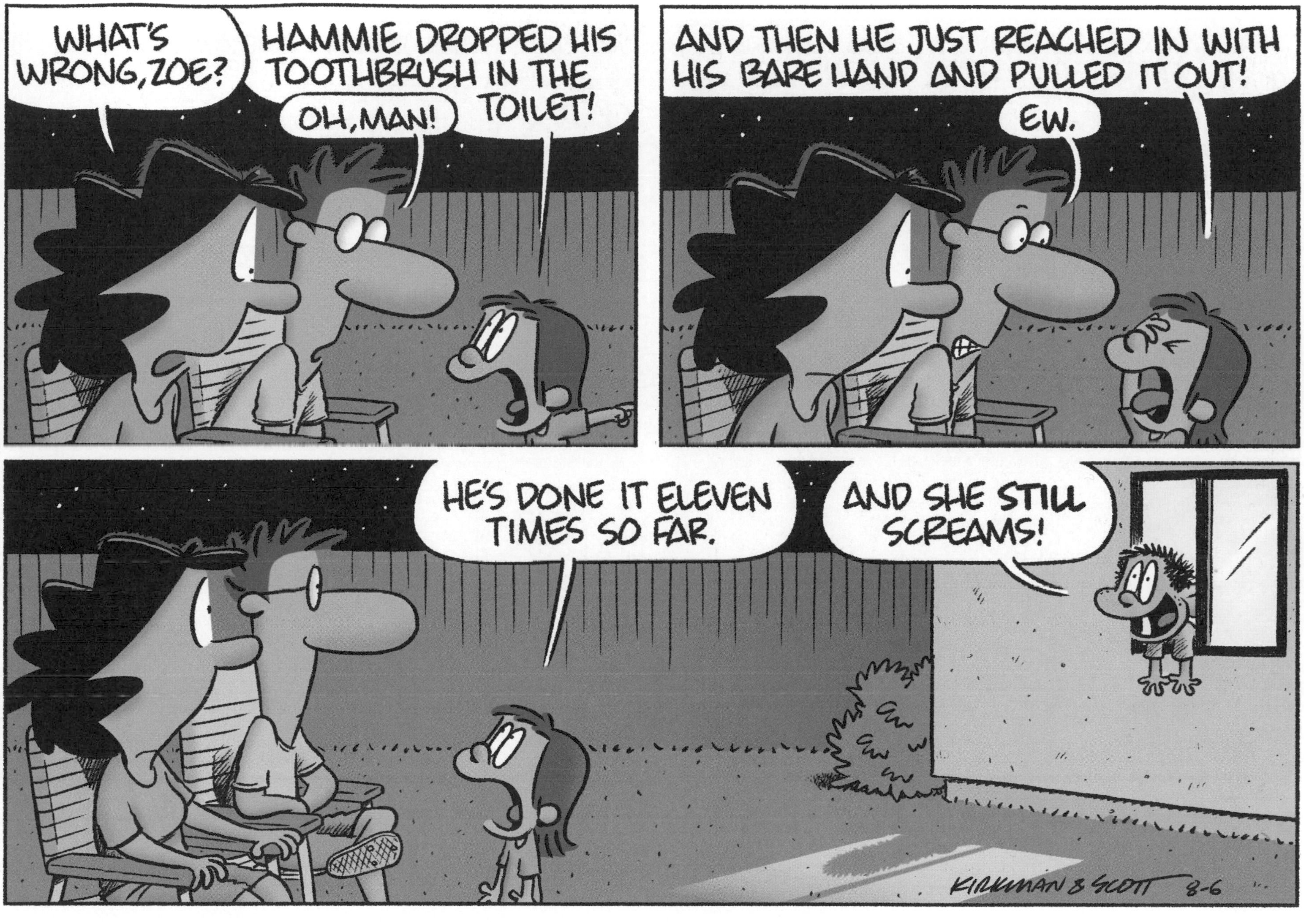
WHAT'S WRONG, ZOE?
HAMMIE DROPPED HIS TOOTHBRUSH IN THE TOILET!
OH, MAN!
AND THEN HE JUST REACHED IN WITH HIS BARE HAND AND PULLED IT OUT!
EW.
HE'S DONE IT ELEVEN TIMES SO FAR.
AND SHE STILL SCREAMS!
KIRKMAN & SCOTT 8-6

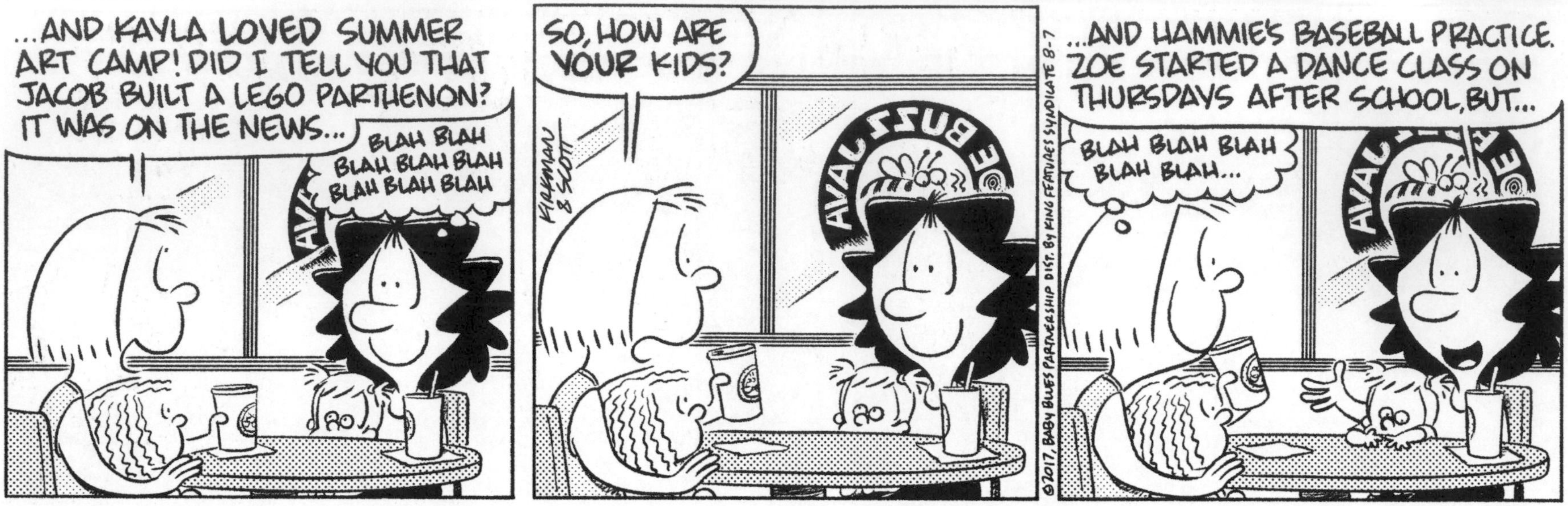
...AND KAYLA LOVED SUMMER ART CAMP! DID I TELL YOU THAT JACOB BUILT A LEGO PARTHENON? IT WAS ON THE NEWS...
BLAH BLAH BLAH BLAH BLAH BLAH BLAH BLAH
SO, HOW ARE YOUR KIDS?
KIRKMAN & SCOTT
©2017, BABY BLUES PARTNERSHIP DIST. BY KING FEATURES SYNDICATE 8-7
...AND HAMMIE'S BASEBALL PRACTICE. ZOE STARTED A DANCE CLASS ON THURSDAYS AFTER SCHOOL, BUT...
BLAH BLAH BLAH BLAH BLAH...

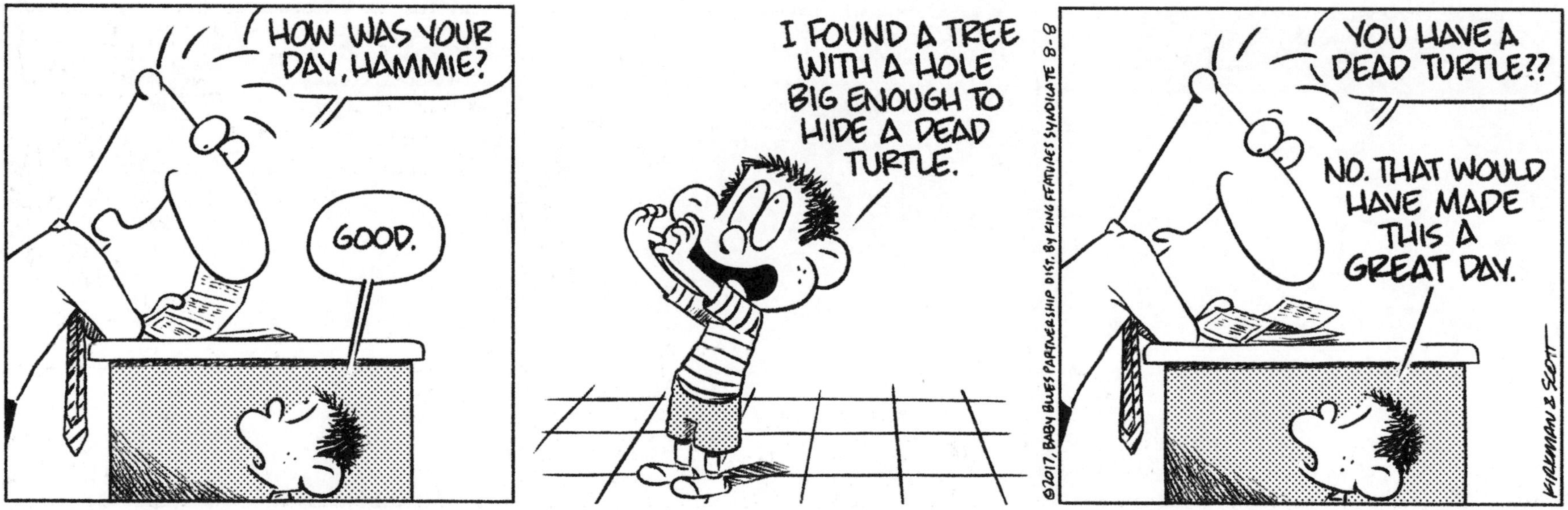
HOW WAS YOUR DAY, HAMMIE?
GOOD.
I FOUND A TREE WITH A HOLE BIG ENOUGH TO HIDE A DEAD TURTLE.
©2017, BABY BLUES PARTNERSHIP DIST. BY KING FEATURES SYNDICATE 8-8
YOU HAVE A DEAD TURTLE??
NO. THAT WOULD HAVE MADE THIS A GREAT DAY.
KIRKMAN & SCOTT

Jerry: Goals.

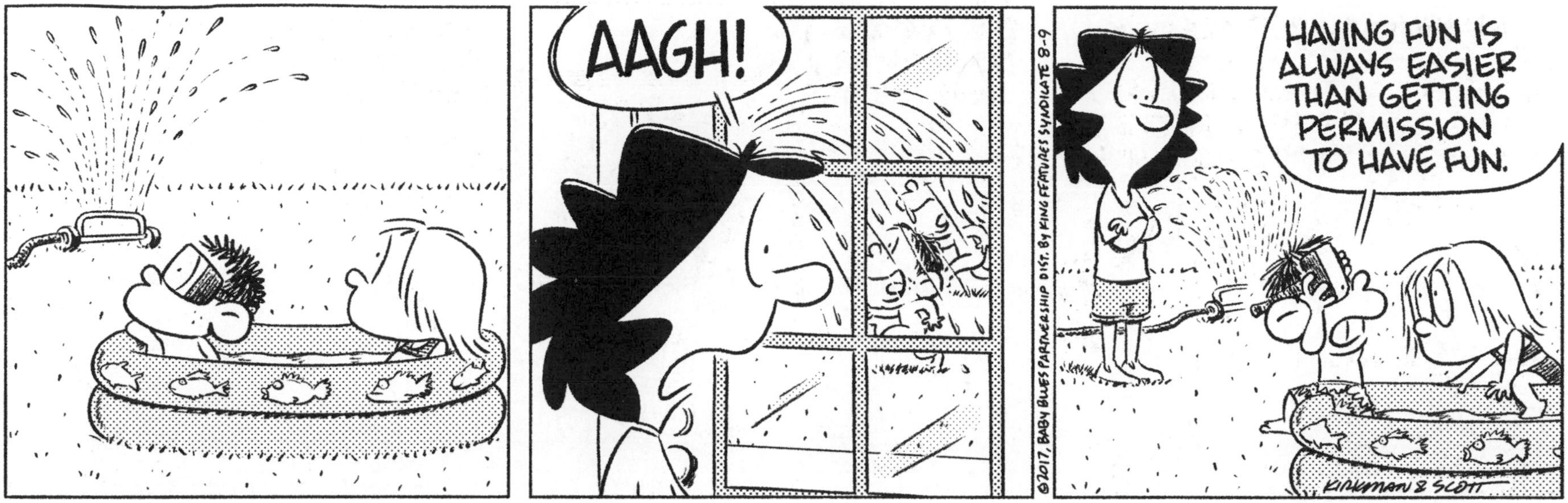
AAGH!
©2017, BABY BLUES PARTNERSHIP DIST. BY KING FEATURES SYNDICATE 8-9
HAVING FUN IS ALWAYS EASIER THAN GETTING PERMISSION TO HAVE FUN.
KIRKMAN & SCOTT

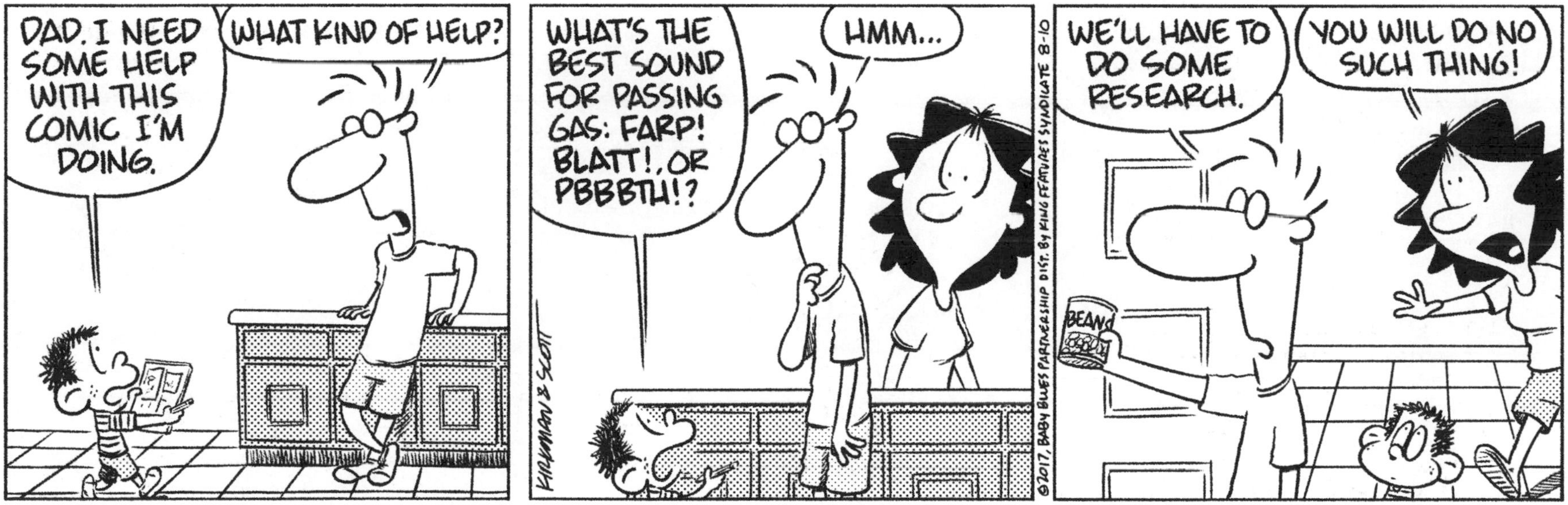
DAD. I NEED SOME HELP WITH THIS COMIC I'M DOING.
WHAT KIND OF HELP?
KIRKMAN & SCOTT
WHAT'S THE BEST SOUND FOR PASSING GAS: FARP! BLATT!, OR PBBBTH!?
HMM...
©2017, BABY BLUES PARTNERSHIP DIST. BY KING FEATURES SYNDICATE 8-10
WE'LL HAVE TO DO SOME RESEARCH.
BEANS
YOU WILL DO NO SUCH THING!

Rick: Scientifically speaking, those are all good sounds, as farts come in many varieties.

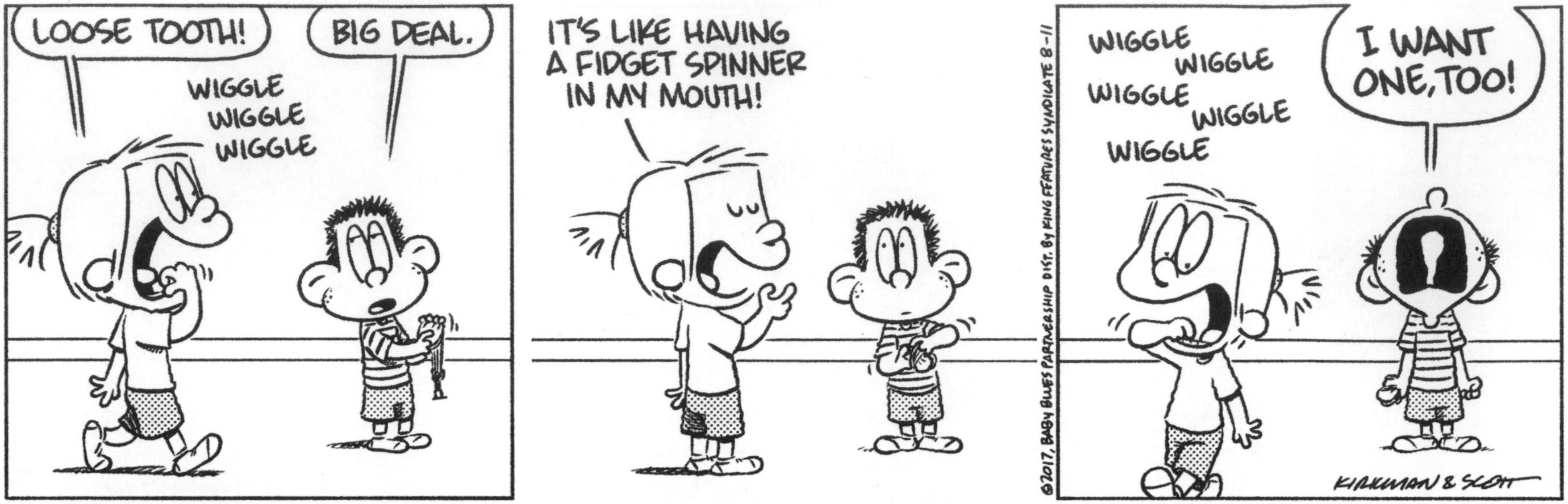

LOOSE TOOTH!
BIG DEAL.
WIGGLE WIGGLE WIGGLE
IT'S LIKE HAVING A FIDGET SPINNER IN MY MOUTH!
WIGGLE WIGGLE WIGGLE WIGGLE WIGGLE
I WANT ONE, TOO!
©2017, BABY BLUES PARTNERSHIP DIST. BY KING FEATURES SYNDICATE 8-11
KIRKMAN & SCOTT

Jerry: It's all in the selling.

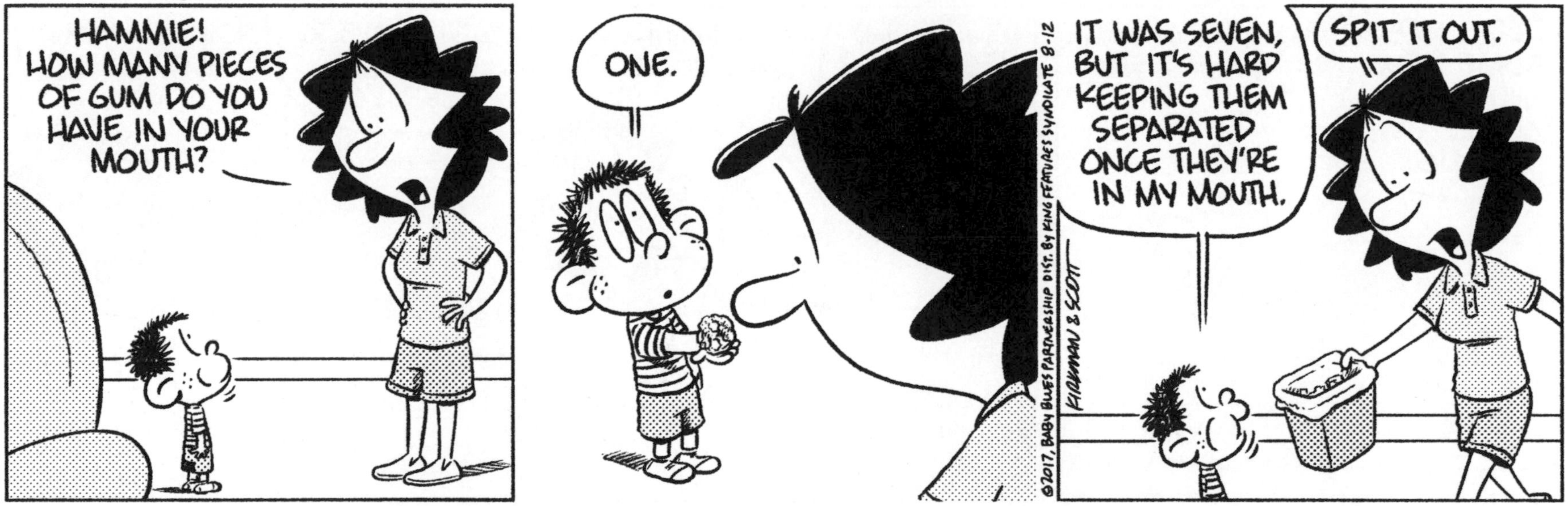

HAMMIE! HOW MANY PIECES OF GUM DO YOU HAVE IN YOUR MOUTH?
ONE.
IT WAS SEVEN, BUT IT'S HARD KEEPING THEM SEPARATED ONCE THEY'RE IN MY MOUTH.
SPIT IT OUT.
©2017, BABY BLUES PARTNERSHIP DIST. BY KING FEATURES SYNDICATE 8-12
KIRKMAN & SCOTT

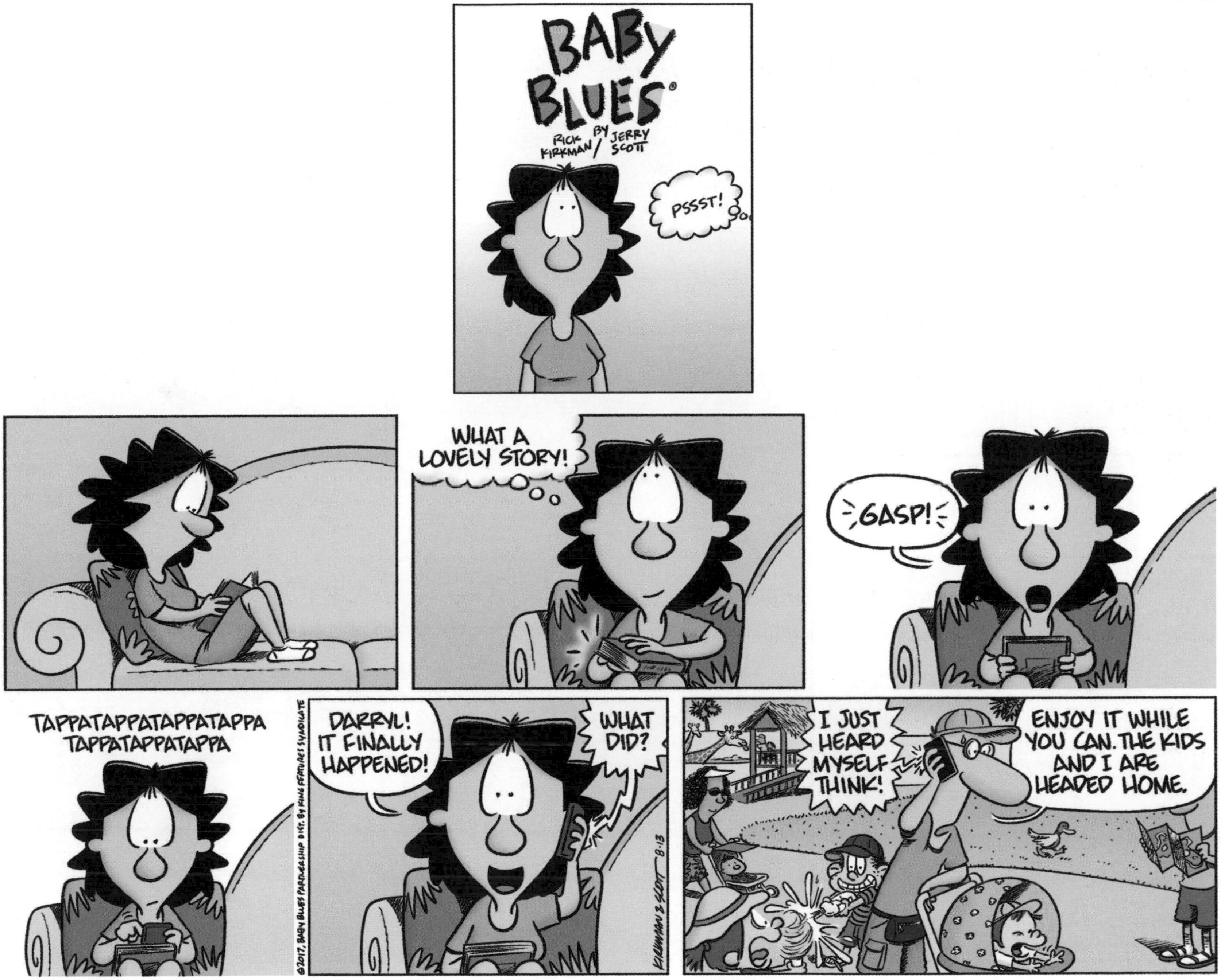
BABY BLUES®
BY RICK KIRKMAN / JERRY SCOTT
PSSST!
WHAT A LOVELY STORY!
GASP!
TAPPATAPPATAPPATAPPA TAPPATAPPATAPPA
DARRYL! IT FINALLY HAPPENED!
WHAT DID?
I JUST HEARD MYSELF THINK!
ENJOY IT WHILE YOU CAN. THE KIDS AND I ARE HEADED HOME.
©2017, BABY BLUES PARTNERSHIP DIST. BY KING FEATURES SYNDICATE
KIRKMAN & SCOTT 8·13

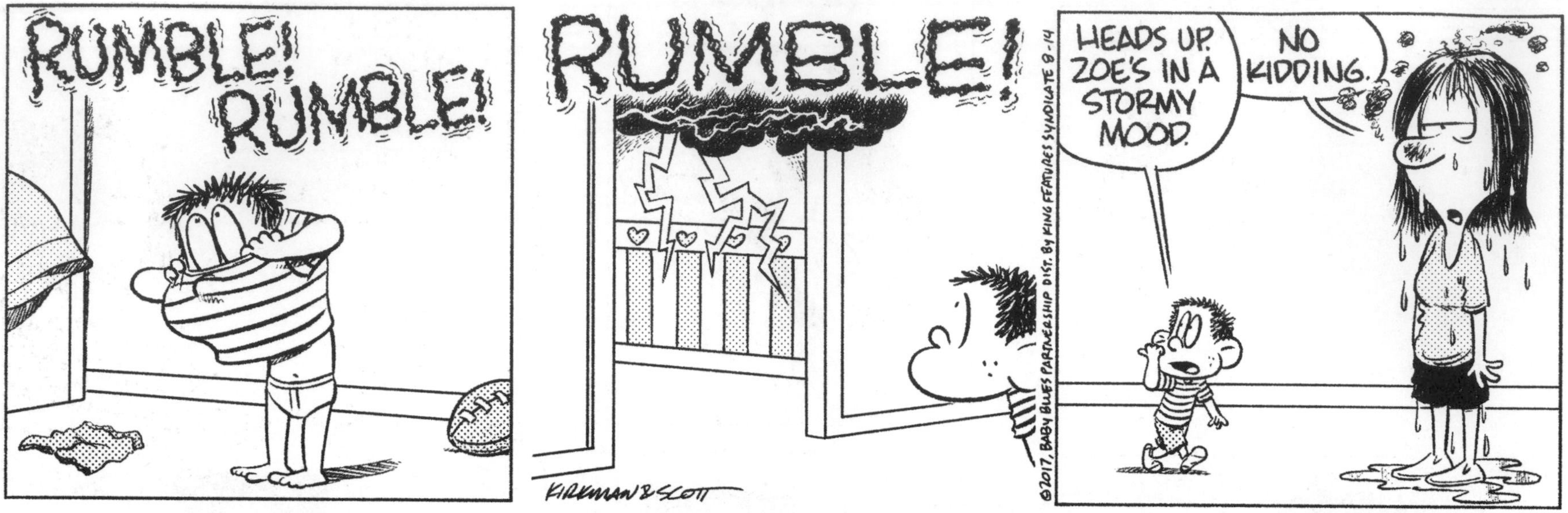
RUMBLE! RUMBLE!
RUMBLE!
KIRKMAN & SCOTT
©2017, BABY BLUES PARTNERSHIP DIST. BY KING FEATURES SYNDICATE 8-14
HEADS UP. ZOE'S IN A STORMY MOOD.
NO KIDDING.

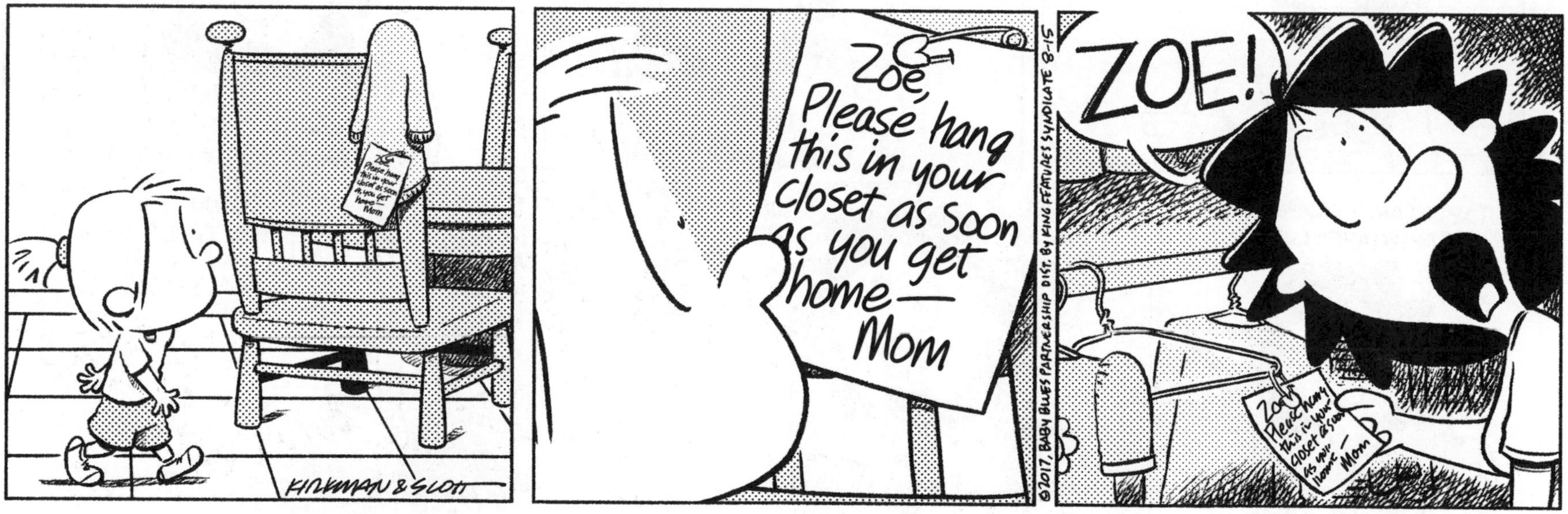
KIRKMAN & SCOTT
Zoe, Please hang this in your closet as soon as you get home— Mom
©2017, BABY BLUES PARTNERSHIP DIST. BY KING FEATURES SYNDICATE 8-15
ZOE!

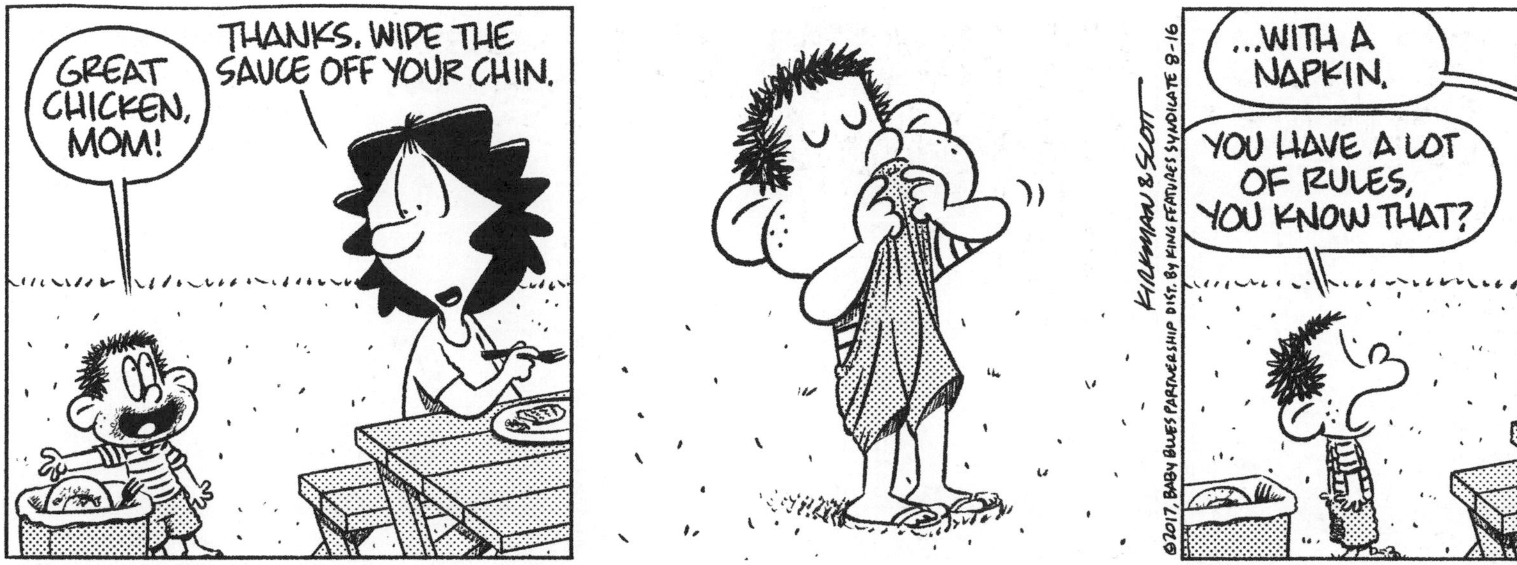
GREAT CHICKEN, MOM!
THANKS. WIPE THE SAUCE OFF YOUR CHIN.
KIRKMAN & SCOTT
©2017, BABY BLUES PARTNERSHIP DIST. BY KING FEATURES SYNDICATE 8-16
...WITH A NAPKIN.
YOU HAVE A LOT OF RULES, YOU KNOW THAT?

Jerry: Those baggy basketball shorts are so versatile.

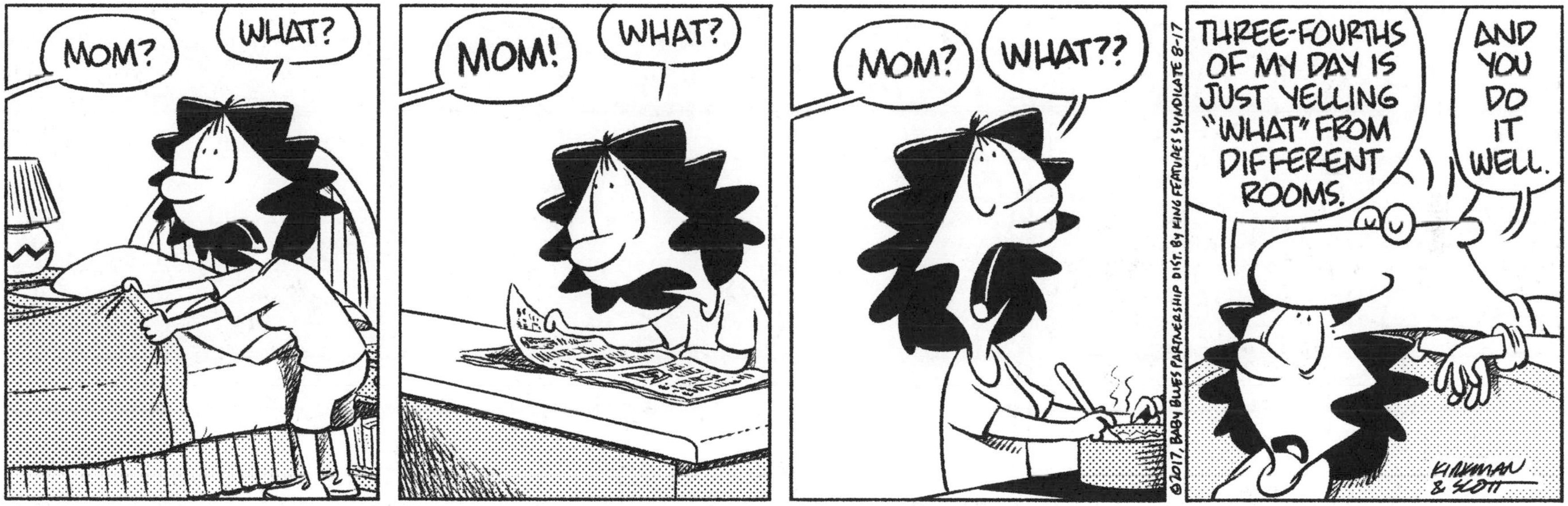
MOM?
WHAT?
MOM!
WHAT?
MOM?
WHAT??
©2017, BABY BLUES PARTNERSHIP DIST. BY KING FEATURES SYNDICATE 8-17
THREE-FOURTHS OF MY DAY IS JUST YELLING "WHAT" FROM DIFFERENT ROOMS.
AND YOU DO IT WELL.
KIRKMAN & SCOTT

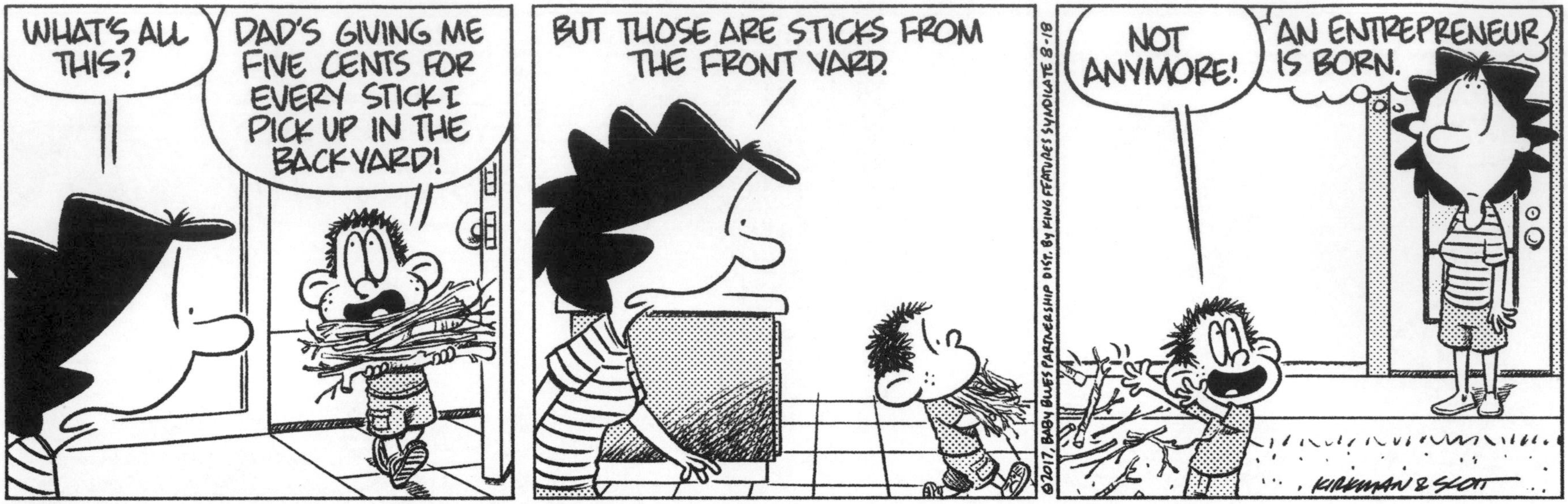
WHAT'S ALL THIS?
DAD'S GIVING ME FIVE CENTS FOR EVERY STICK I PICK UP IN THE BACKYARD!
BUT THOSE ARE STICKS FROM THE FRONT YARD.
NOT ANYMORE!
AN ENTREPRENEUR IS BORN.
©2017, BABY BLUES PARTNERSHIP DIST. BY KING FEATURES SYNDICATE 8-18
KIRKMAN & SCOTT

Rick: I might alter my speculation about Hammie's possible career—make that government contractor.

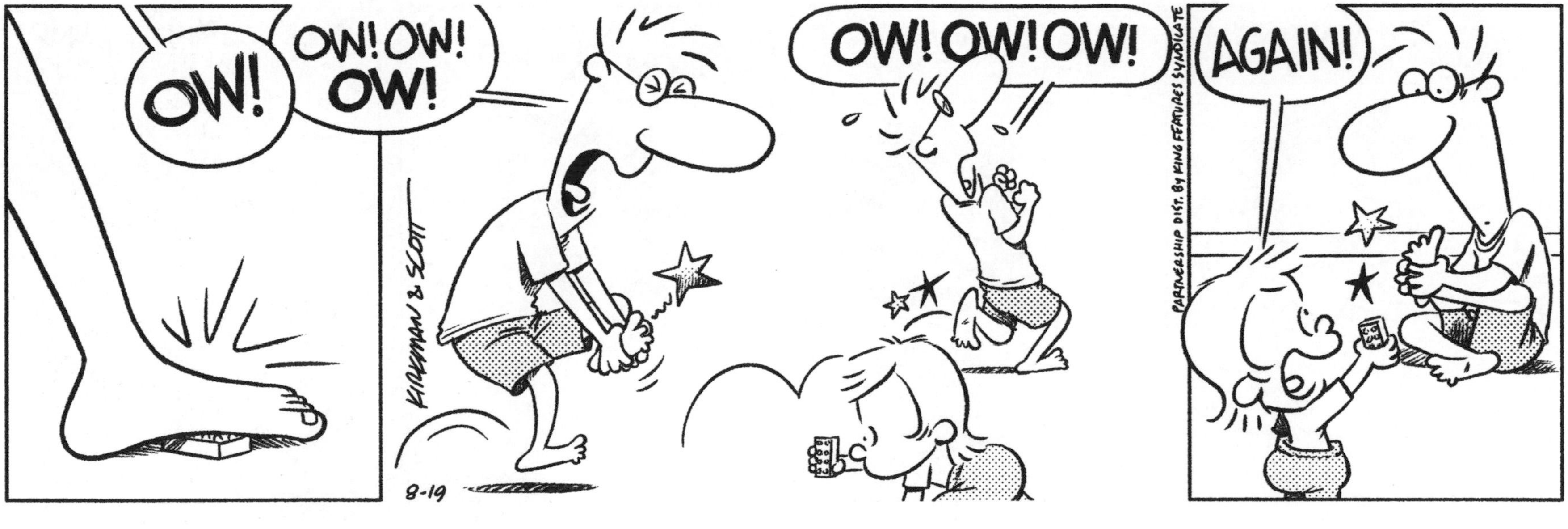
OW!
OW! OW! OW!
OW! OW! OW!
AGAIN!
KIRKMAN & SCOTT
8-19
PARTNERSHIP DIST. BY KING FEATURES SYNDICATE

BABY BLUES
Rick Kirkman & Jerry Scott

GO BRUSH YOUR TEETH AND PUT YOUR PAJAMAS ON. I'LL BE IN IN A COUPLE OF MINUTES.
Z
YAWN
WAIT, DARRYL! DON'T WAKE WREN!
WHAT?
Z
SHE'S SLEEPING SO SOUNDLY.
I KNOW, BUT...
Z
IF SHE OPENS HER EYES, SHE WON'T GET BACK TO SLEEP FOR TWO HOURS!
WELL, WE CAN'T LEAVE HER ALONE IN THE VAN!
I KNOW THAT!
SO WHAT DO YOU WANT TO DO?
KIRKMAN & SCOTT
©2017, BABY BLUES PARTNERSHIP DIST. BY KING FEATURES SYNDICATE
Z
FIRST OFF, I SHOULDN'T HAVE CALLED "TAILS"...

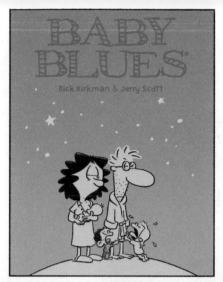

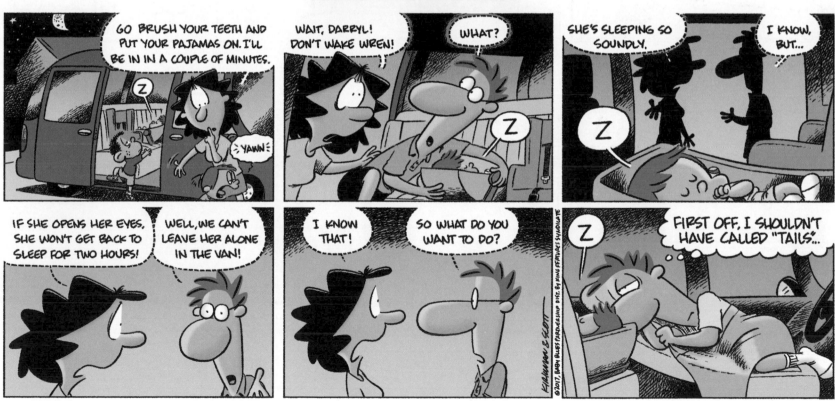

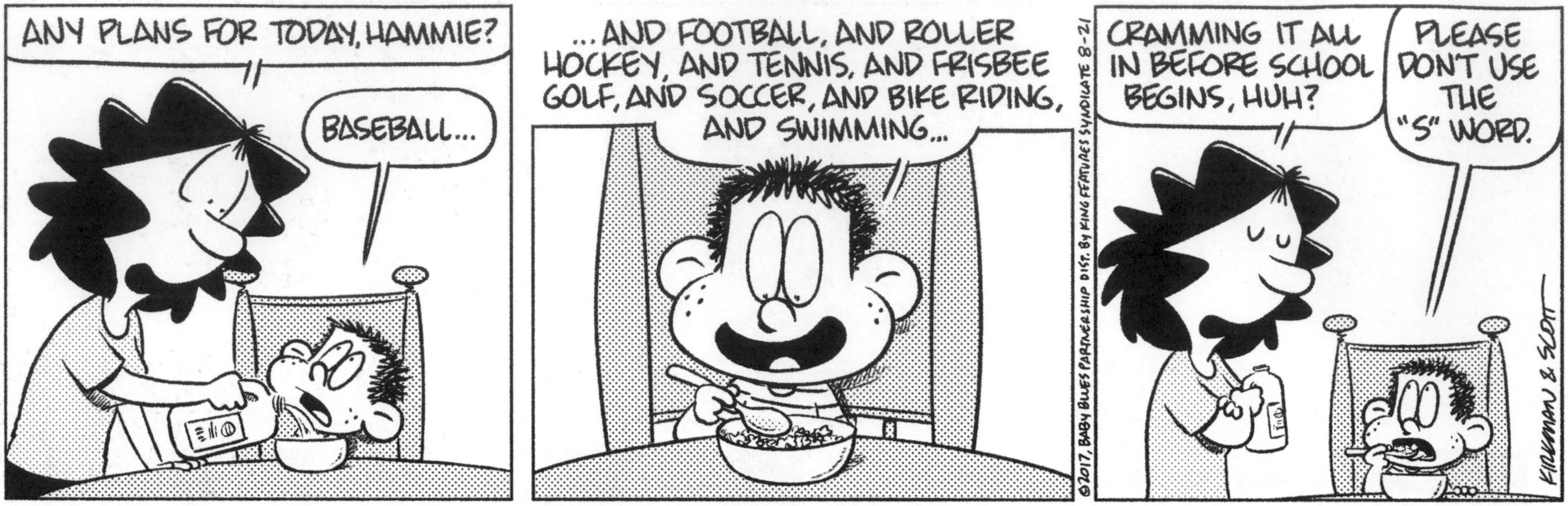
ANY PLANS FOR TODAY, HAMMIE?
BASEBALL...
...AND FOOTBALL, AND ROLLER HOCKEY, AND TENNIS, AND FRISBEE GOLF, AND SOCCER, AND BIKE RIDING, AND SWIMMING...
©2017, BABY BLUES PARTNERSHIP DIST. BY KING FEATURES SYNDICATE 8-21
CRAMMING IT ALL IN BEFORE SCHOOL BEGINS, HUH?
PLEASE DON'T USE THE "S" WORD.
KIRKMAN & SCOTT

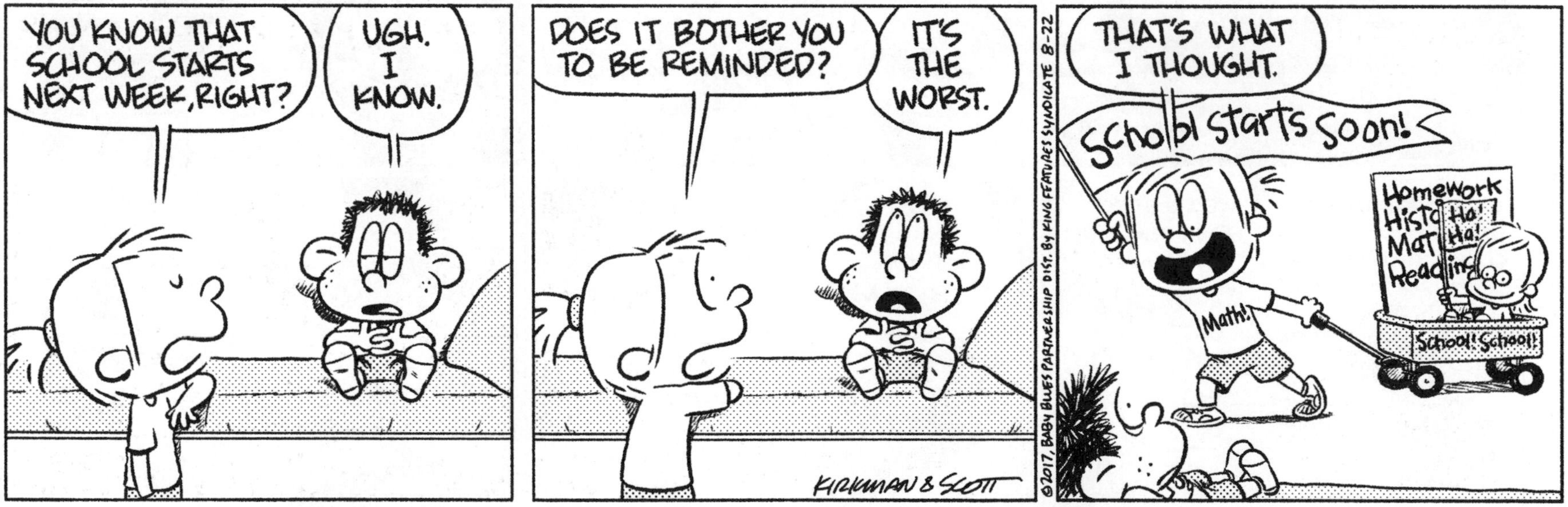
YOU KNOW THAT SCHOOL STARTS NEXT WEEK, RIGHT?
UGH. I KNOW.
DOES IT BOTHER YOU TO BE REMINDED?
IT'S THE WORST.
KIRKMAN & SCOTT
©2017, BABY BLUES PARTNERSHIP DIST. BY KING FEATURES SYNDICATE 8-22
THAT'S WHAT I THOUGHT.
School Starts Soon!
Homework
Ha! Ha!
Math!
School! School!

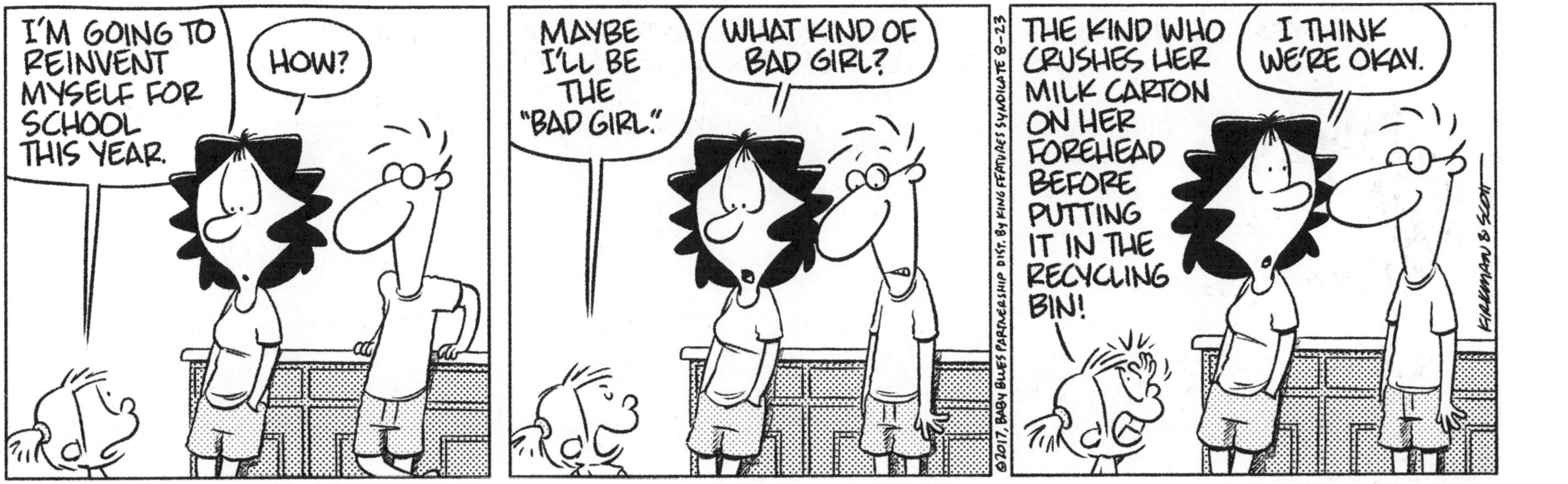
I'M GOING TO REINVENT MYSELF FOR SCHOOL THIS YEAR.
HOW?
MAYBE I'LL BE THE "BAD GIRL."
WHAT KIND OF BAD GIRL?
©2017, BABY BLUES PARTNERSHIP DIST. BY KING FEATURES SYNDICATE 8-23
THE KIND WHO CRUSHES HER MILK CARTON ON HER FOREHEAD BEFORE PUTTING IT IN THE RECYCLING BIN!
I THINK WE'RE OKAY.
KIRKMAN & SCOTT

Jerry: Whew.

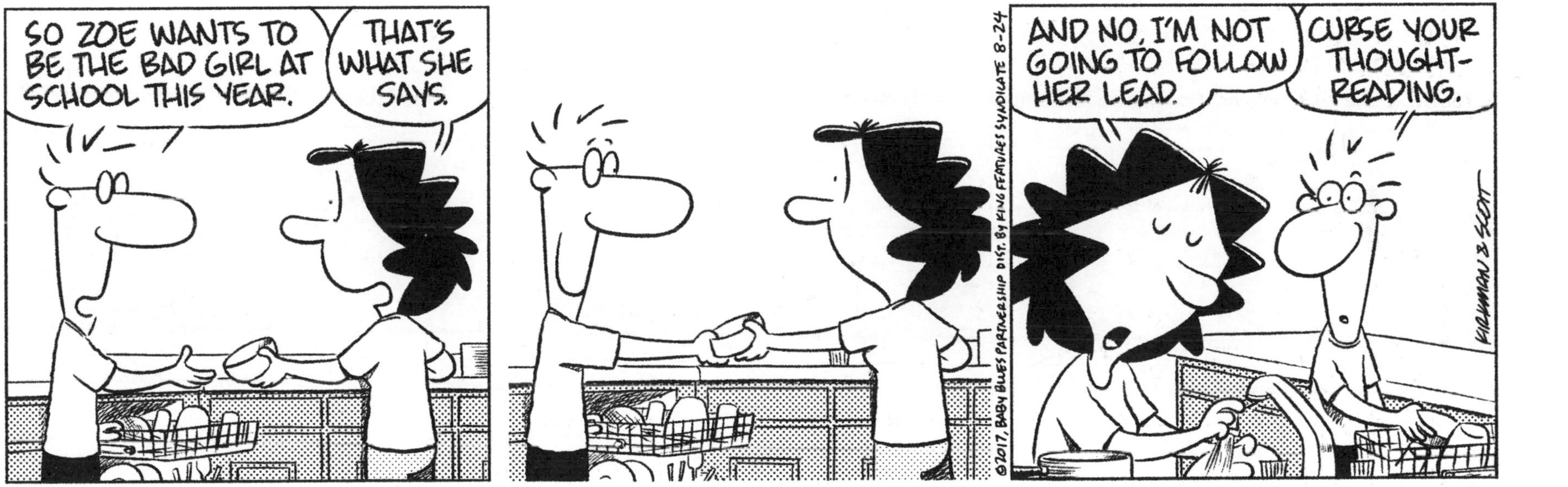
SO ZOE WANTS TO BE THE BAD GIRL AT SCHOOL THIS YEAR.
THAT'S WHAT SHE SAYS.
©2017, BABY BLUES PARTNERSHIP DIST. BY KING FEATURES SYNDICATE 8-24
AND NO, I'M NOT GOING TO FOLLOW HER LEAD.
CURSE YOUR THOUGHT-READING.
KIRKMAN & SCOTT

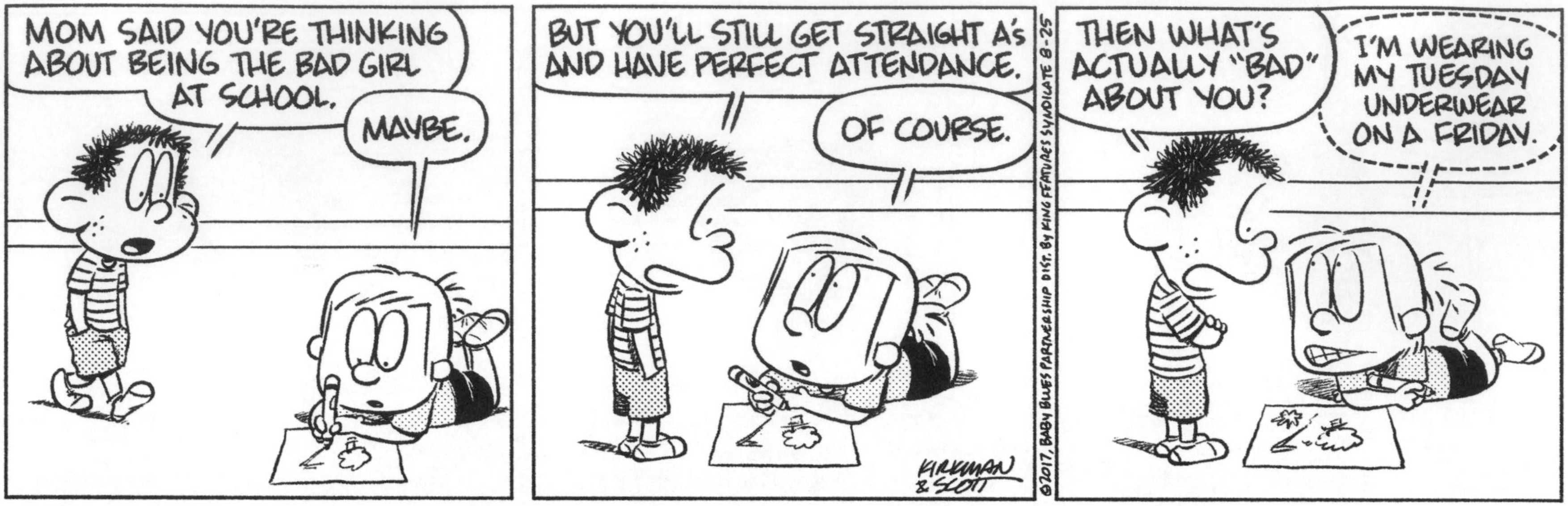
MOM SAID YOU'RE THINKING ABOUT BEING THE BAD GIRL AT SCHOOL.
MAYBE.
BUT YOU'LL STILL GET STRAIGHT A's AND HAVE PERFECT ATTENDANCE.
OF COURSE.
THEN WHAT'S ACTUALLY "BAD" ABOUT YOU?
I'M WEARING MY TUESDAY UNDERWEAR ON A FRIDAY.
KIRKMAN & SCOTT
©2017, BABY BLUES PARTNERSHIP DIST. BY KING FEATURES SYNDICATE 8-25

Jerry: Being bad takes some doing, and some folks are better at it than others.

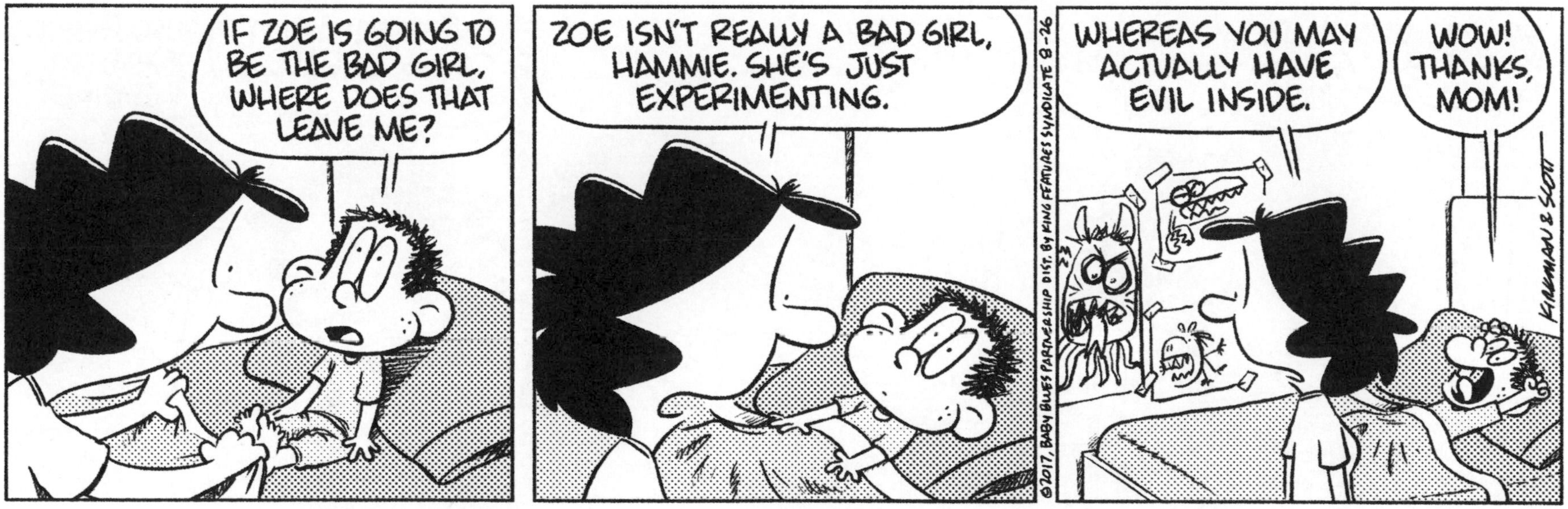
IF ZOE IS GOING TO BE THE BAD GIRL, WHERE DOES THAT LEAVE ME?
ZOE ISN'T REALLY A BAD GIRL, HAMMIE. SHE'S JUST EXPERIMENTING.
WHEREAS YOU MAY ACTUALLY HAVE EVIL INSIDE.
WOW! THANKS, MOM!
KIRKMAN & SCOTT
©2017, BABY BLUES PARTNERSHIP DIST. BY KING FEATURES SYNDICATE 8-26

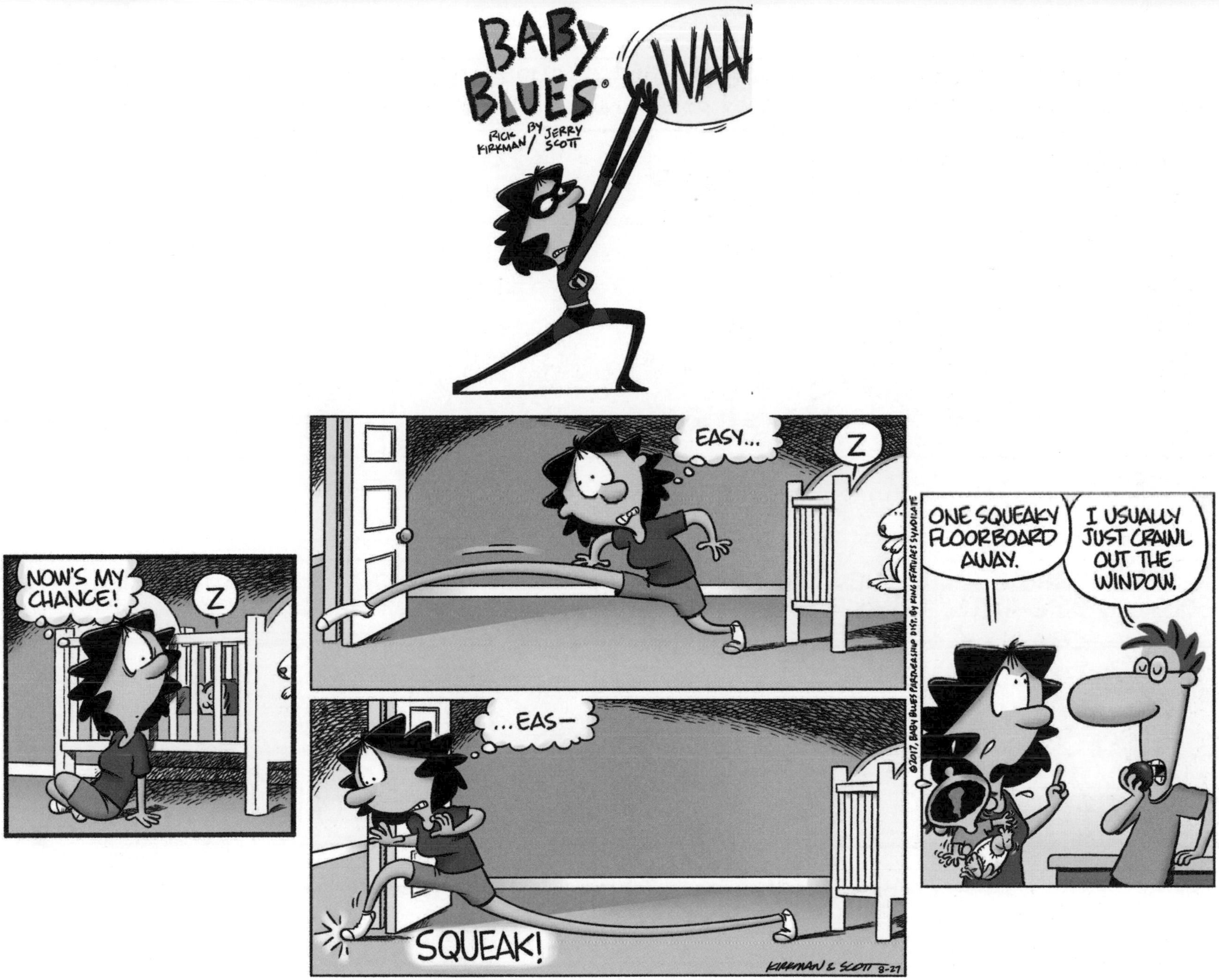
BABY BLUES®
BY RICK KIRKMAN / JERRY SCOTT
WAA
NOW'S MY CHANCE!
Z
EASY...
Z
...EAS—
SQUEAK!
©2017, BABY BLUES PARTNERSHIP DIST. BY KING FEATURES SYNDICATE
KIRKMAN & SCOTT 8-27
ONE SQUEAKY FLOORBOARD AWAY.
I USUALLY JUST CRAWL OUT THE WINDOW.

Rick: It sure feels like that's the way it happens. I really like how Wanda as Mrs. Incredible (a.k.a. Elastigirl) came out.

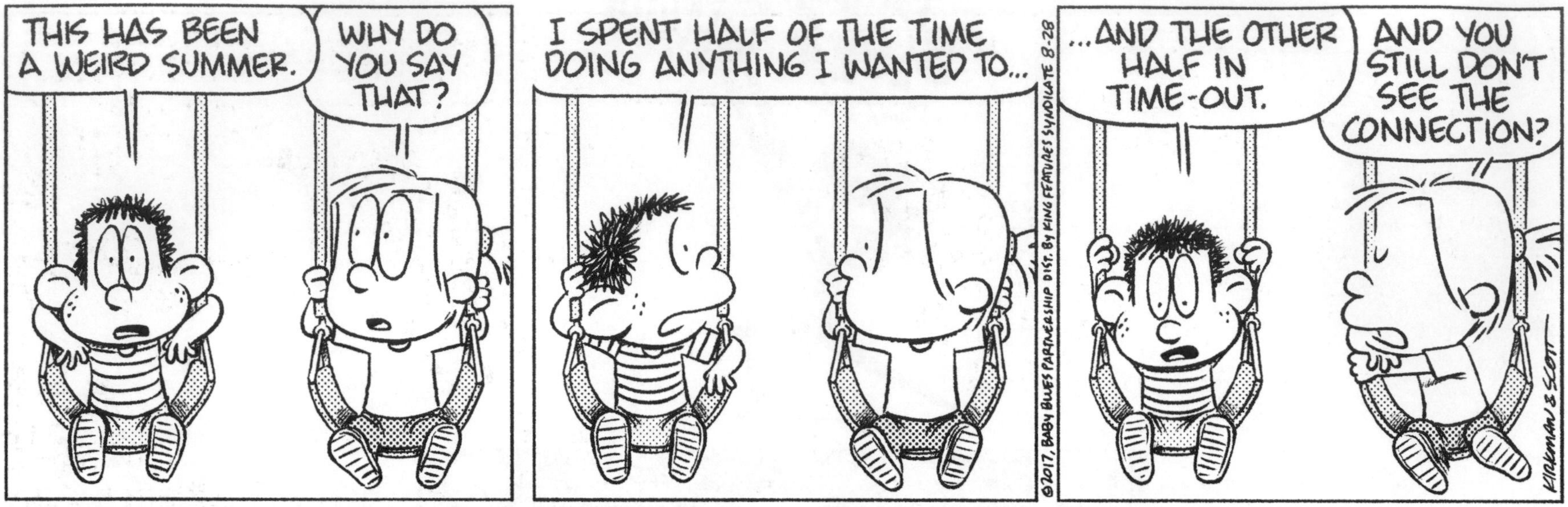
THIS HAS BEEN A WEIRD SUMMER.
WHY DO YOU SAY THAT?
I SPENT HALF OF THE TIME DOING ANYTHING I WANTED TO...
...AND THE OTHER HALF IN TIME-OUT.
AND YOU STILL DON'T SEE THE CONNECTION?
©2017, BABY BLUES PARTNERSHIP DIST. BY KING FEATURES SYNDICATE 8-28
KIRKMAN & SCOTT

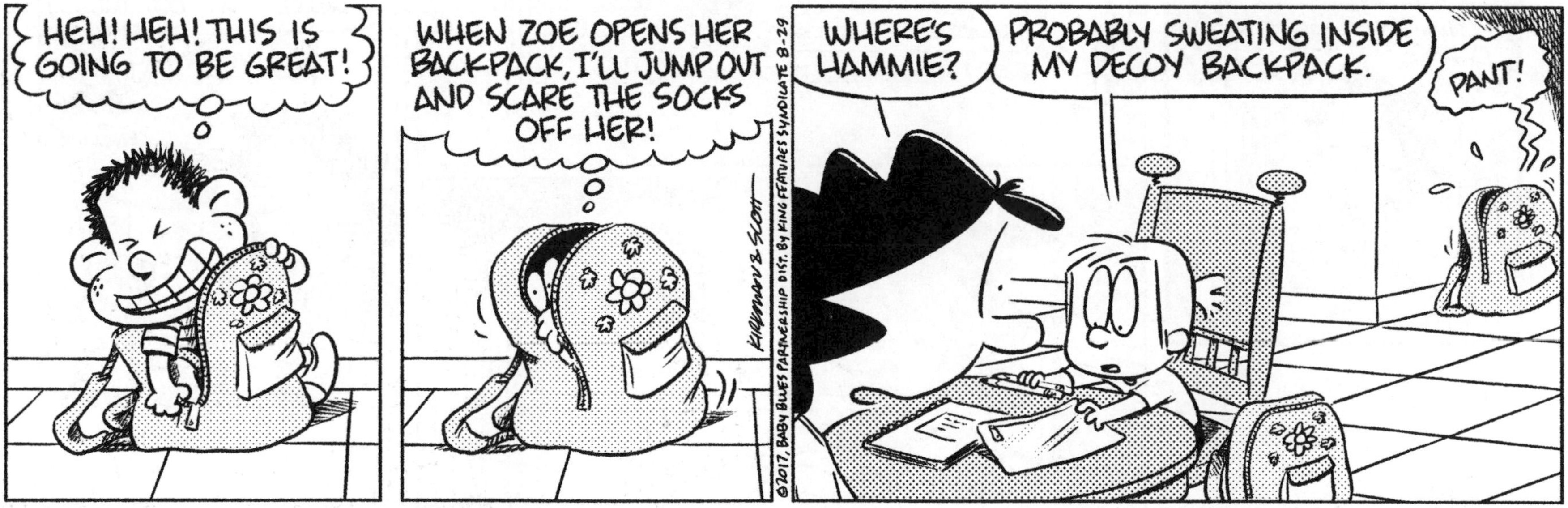
HEH! HEH! THIS IS GOING TO BE GREAT!
WHEN ZOE OPENS HER BACKPACK, I'LL JUMP OUT AND SCARE THE SOCKS OFF HER!
KIRKMAN & SCOTT
©2017, BABY BLUES PARTNERSHIP DIST. BY KING FEATURES SYNDICATE 8-29
WHERE'S HAMMIE?
PROBABLY SWEATING INSIDE MY DECOY BACKPACK.
PANT!

EXCUSE ME, I'M LOOKING FOR CRAYONS.
DIGITAL? 3-D? TWISTABLES?
PRINTERS
THE WAX KIND, WRAPPED IN PAPER.
©2017, BABY BLUES PARTNERSHIP DIST. BY KING FEATURES SYNDICATE 8-30
WHERE CAN I FIND THOSE?
I THINK MY GRANDMA STILL HAS SOME.
KIRKMAN & SCOTT

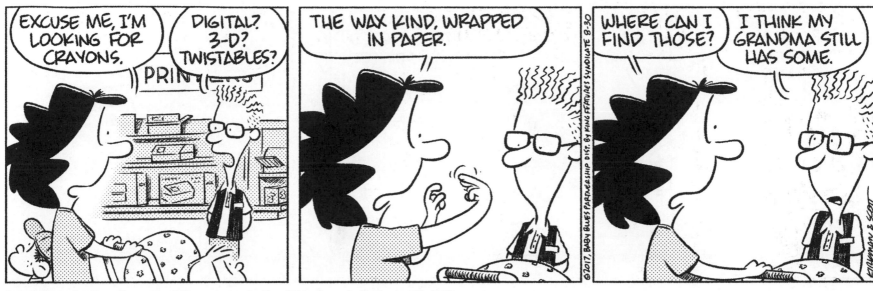

Jerry: They don't really make 3-D crayons, do they? I just made that up, didn't I?

HERE'S YOUR NEW BACKPACK, HAMMIE.
COOL.
JUST TO BE SAFE, LET'S WRITE YOUR NAME ON IT SO YOU WON'T LOSE THIS ONE.
KIRKMAN & SCOTT
©2017, BABY BLUES PARTNERSHIP DIST. BY KING FEATURES SYNDICATE 8-31
LOSE WHAT?
THAT'S A NEW RECORD.

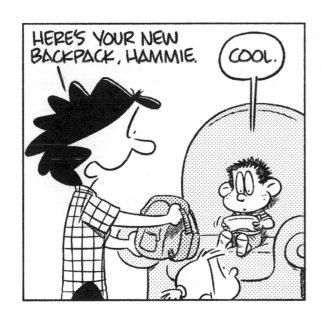

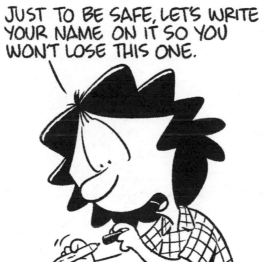

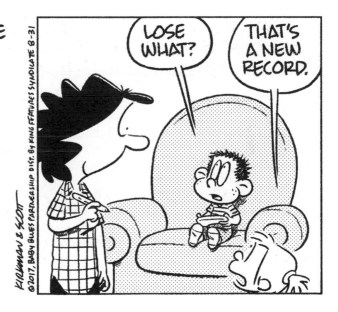

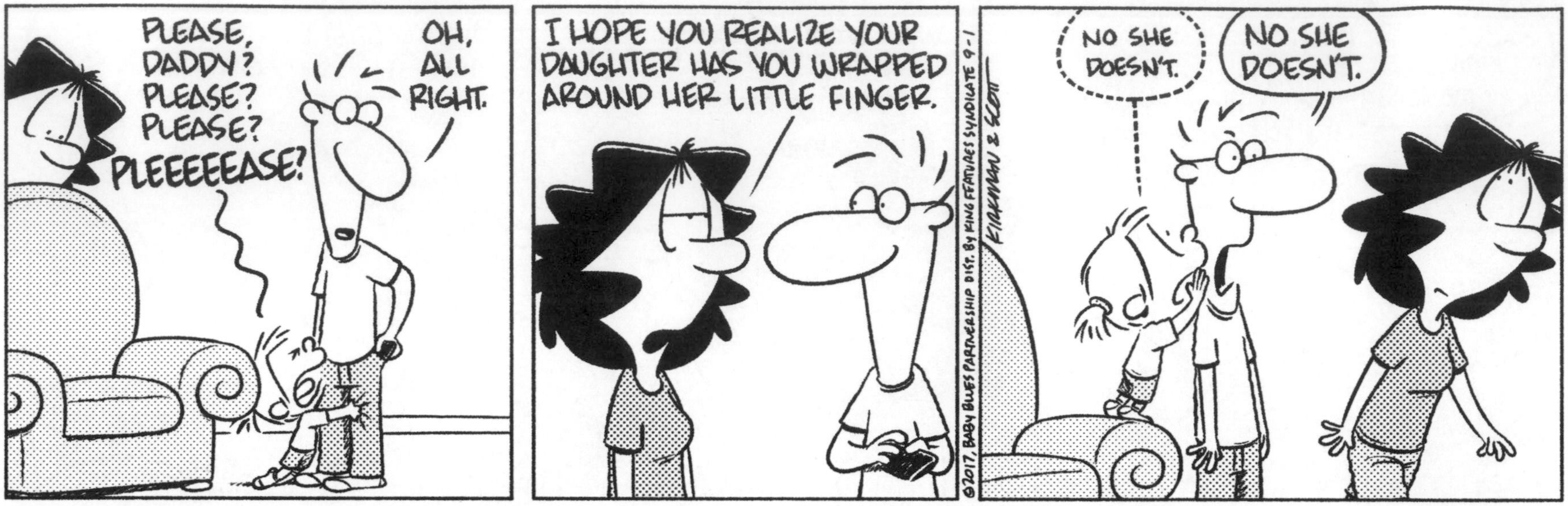
PLEASE, DADDY? PLEASE? PLEASE? PLEASE? PLEEEEEEASE?
OH, ALL RIGHT.
I HOPE YOU REALIZE YOUR DAUGHTER HAS YOU WRAPPED AROUND HER LITTLE FINGER.
©2017, BABY BLUES PARTNERSHIP DIST. BY KING FEATURES SYNDICATE 9-1
KIRKMAN & SCOTT
NO SHE DOESN'T.
NO SHE DOESN'T.

Jerry: Sometimes I just need to look at myself to get ideas.

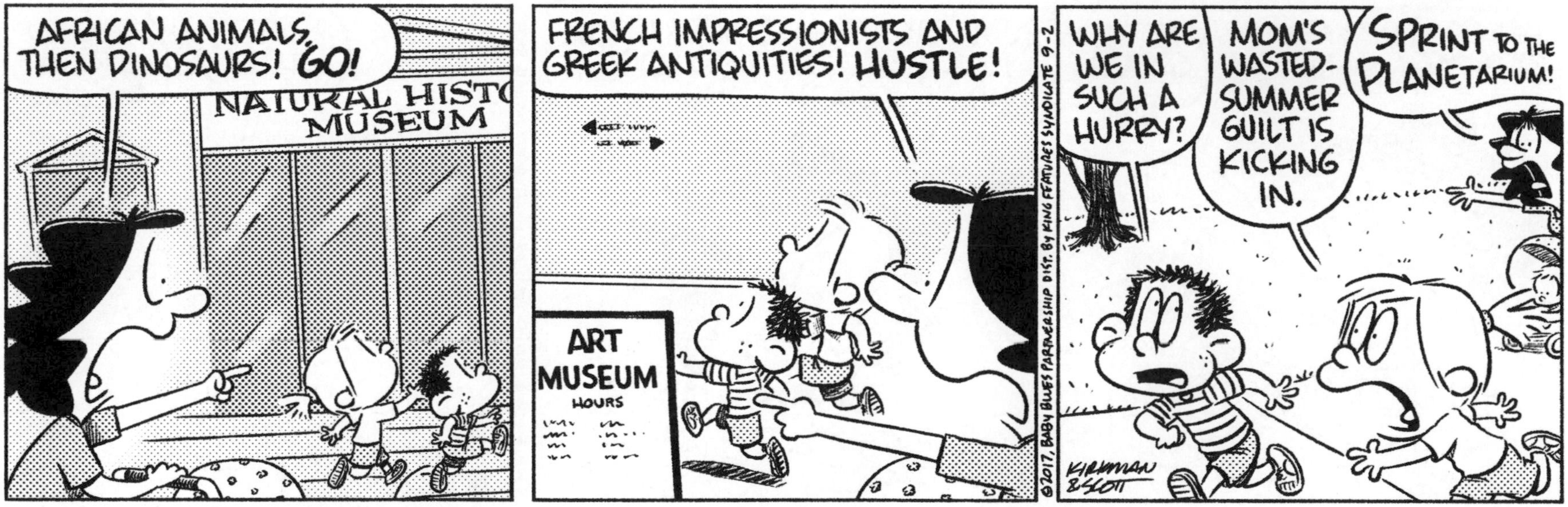
AFRICAN ANIMALS, THEN DINOSAURS! GO!
NATURAL HISTO MUSEUM
FRENCH IMPRESSIONISTS AND GREEK ANTIQUITIES! HUSTLE!
ART MUSEUM HOURS
©2017, BABY BLUES PARTNERSHIP DIST. BY KING FEATURES SYNDICATE 9-2
WHY ARE WE IN SUCH A HURRY?
MOM'S WASTED-SUMMER GUILT IS KICKING IN.
SPRINT TO THE PLANETARIUM!
KIRKMAN & SCOTT

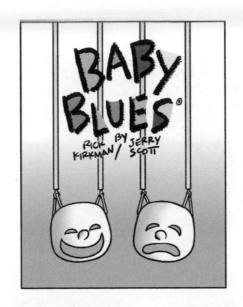

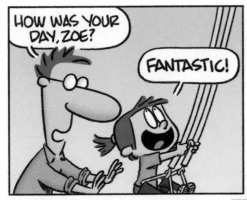

BABY BLUES®
BY RICK KIRKMAN/ JERRY SCOTT
HOW WAS YOUR DAY, ZOE?
FANTASTIC!
UNLESS YOU COUNT THE PART WHERE MOM CAUGHT ME SNEAKING ICE CREAM BARS OUT OF THE FREEZER.
WHICH WAS MY STUPID BROTHER'S IDEA, ANYWAY!
MOM PUT ME IN MY ROOM FOR A WHOLE HOUR!
BUT WHILE I WAS IN THERE, I GOT SOME HILARIOUS TEXTS!
AND THEN YOU CAME HOME.
WHERE HAVE YOU BEEN?
OUT AT THE MOOD SWINGS.
©2017, BABY BLUES PARTNERSHIP DIST. BY KING FEATURES SYNDICATE
9-3
KIRKMAN & SCOTT

Rick: I love the "mood swings" idea. It lent itself to a layout where the day's story is focused on Zoe and bookended by similar frames.

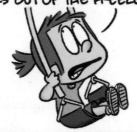

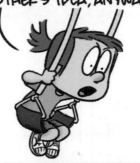

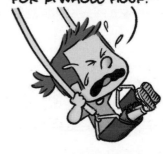

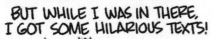

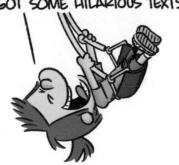

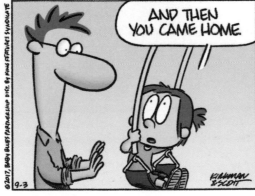

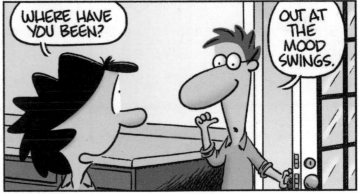

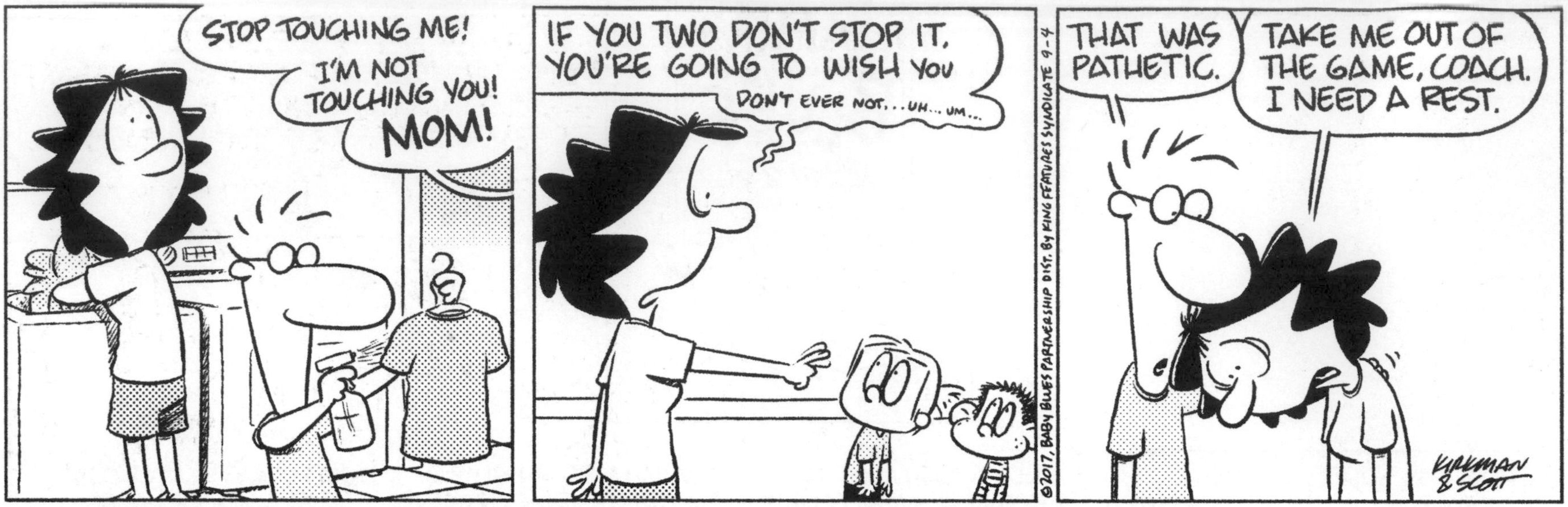
STOP TOUCHING ME!
I'M NOT TOUCHING YOU!
MOM!
IF YOU TWO DON'T STOP IT, YOU'RE GOING TO WISH YOU
DON'T EVER NOT... UH... UM...
©2017, BABY BLUES PARTNERSHIP DIST. BY KING FEATURES SYNDICATE 9-4
THAT WAS PATHETIC.
TAKE ME OUT OF THE GAME, COACH. I NEED A REST.
KIRKMAN & SCOTT

Rick: Great idea of Jerry's to have Wanda's line wind down visually.

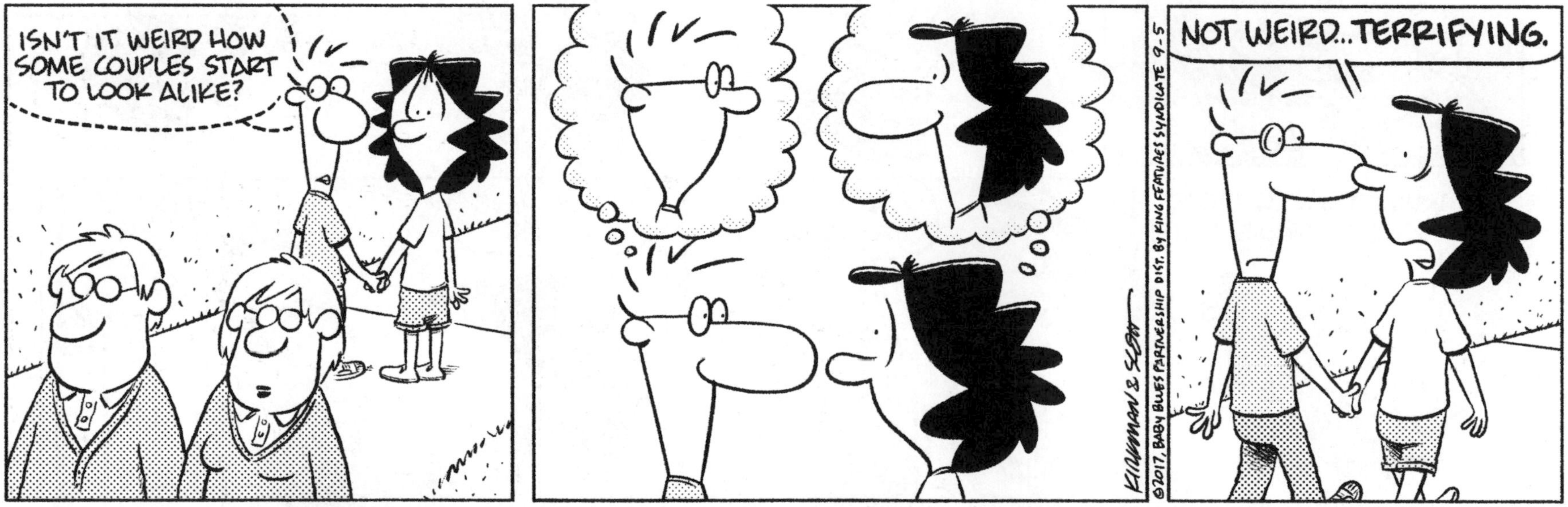
ISN'T IT WEIRD HOW SOME COUPLES START TO LOOK ALIKE?
KIRKMAN & SCOTT
©2017, BABY BLUES PARTNERSHIP DIST. BY KING FEATURES SYNDICATE 9-5
NOT WEIRD...TERRIFYING.

Rick: Sometimes I creep myself out—see panel 2.

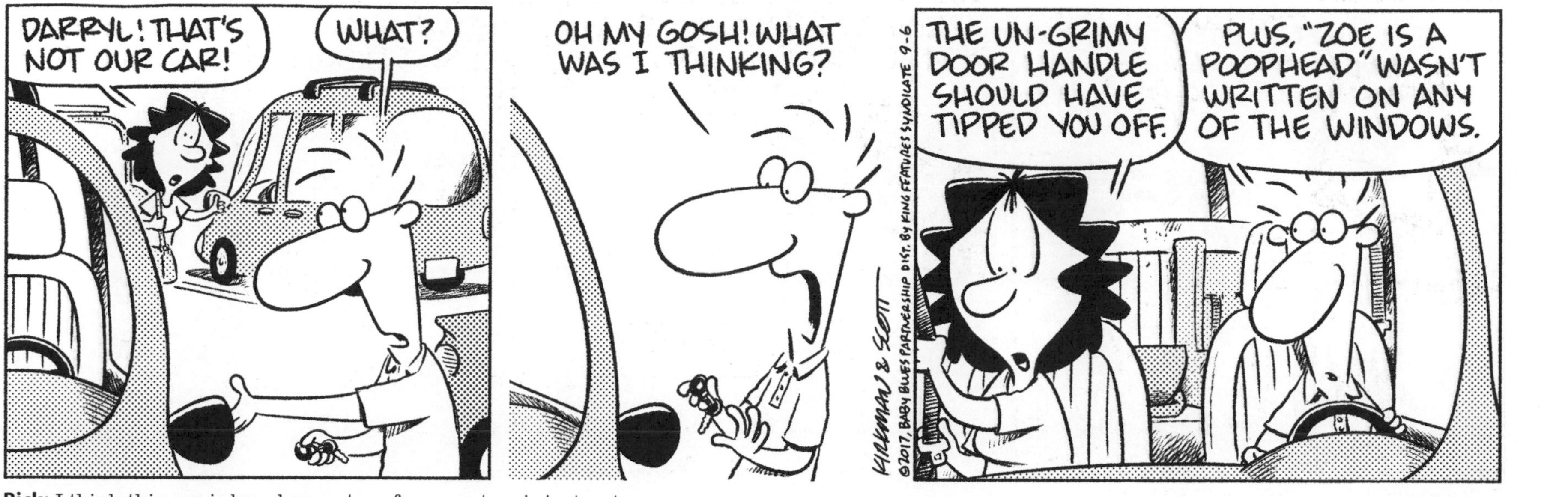
DARRYL! THAT'S NOT OUR CAR!
WHAT?
OH MY GOSH! WHAT WAS I THINKING?
KIRKMAN & SCOTT
©2017, BABY BLUES PARTNERSHIP DIST. BY KING FEATURES SYNDICATE 9-6
THE UN-GRIMY DOOR HANDLE SHOULD HAVE TIPPED YOU OFF.
PLUS, "ZOE IS A POOPHEAD" WASN'T WRITTEN ON ANY OF THE WINDOWS.

Rick: I think this one is based on a story from my tennis instructor.

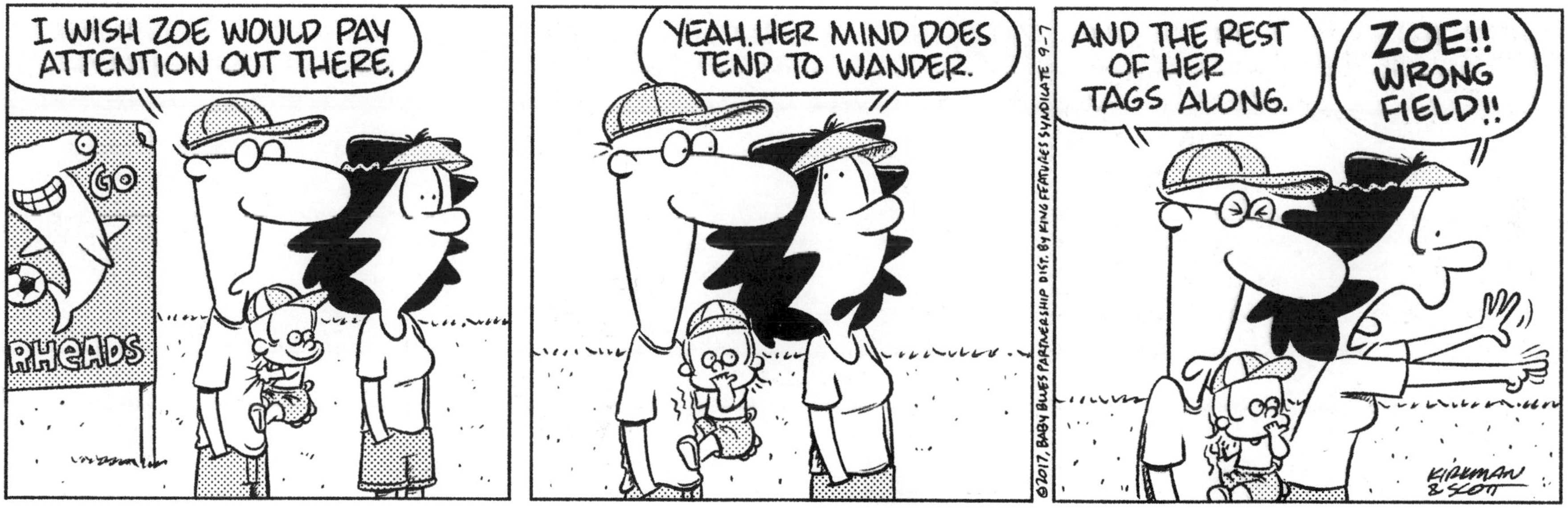
I WISH ZOE WOULD PAY ATTENTION OUT THERE.
GO
RHEADS
YEAH. HER MIND DOES TEND TO WANDER.
©2017, BABY BLUES PARTNERSHIP DIST. BY KING FEATURES SYNDICATE 9-7
AND THE REST OF HER TAGS ALONG.
ZOE!! WRONG FIELD!!
KIRKMAN & SCOTT

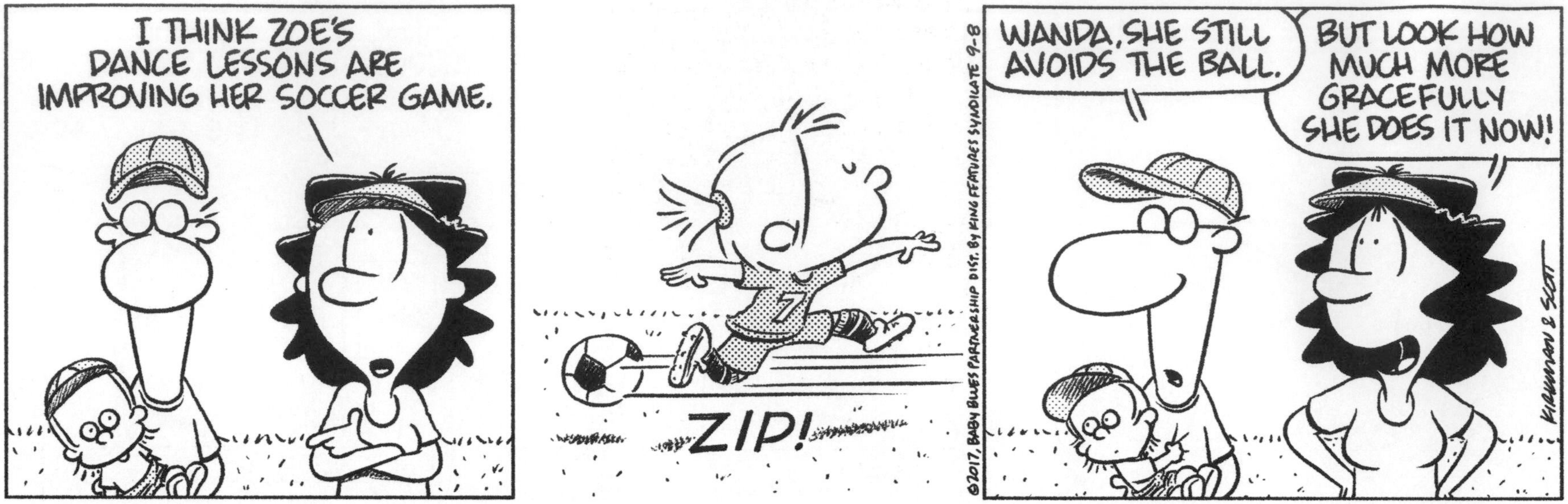
I THINK ZOE'S DANCE LESSONS ARE IMPROVING HER SOCCER GAME.
ZIP!
©2017, BABY BLUES PARTNERSHIP DIST. BY KING FEATURES SYNDICATE 9-8
WANDA, SHE STILL AVOIDS THE BALL.
BUT LOOK HOW MUCH MORE GRACEFULLY SHE DOES IT NOW!
KIRKMAN & SCOTT

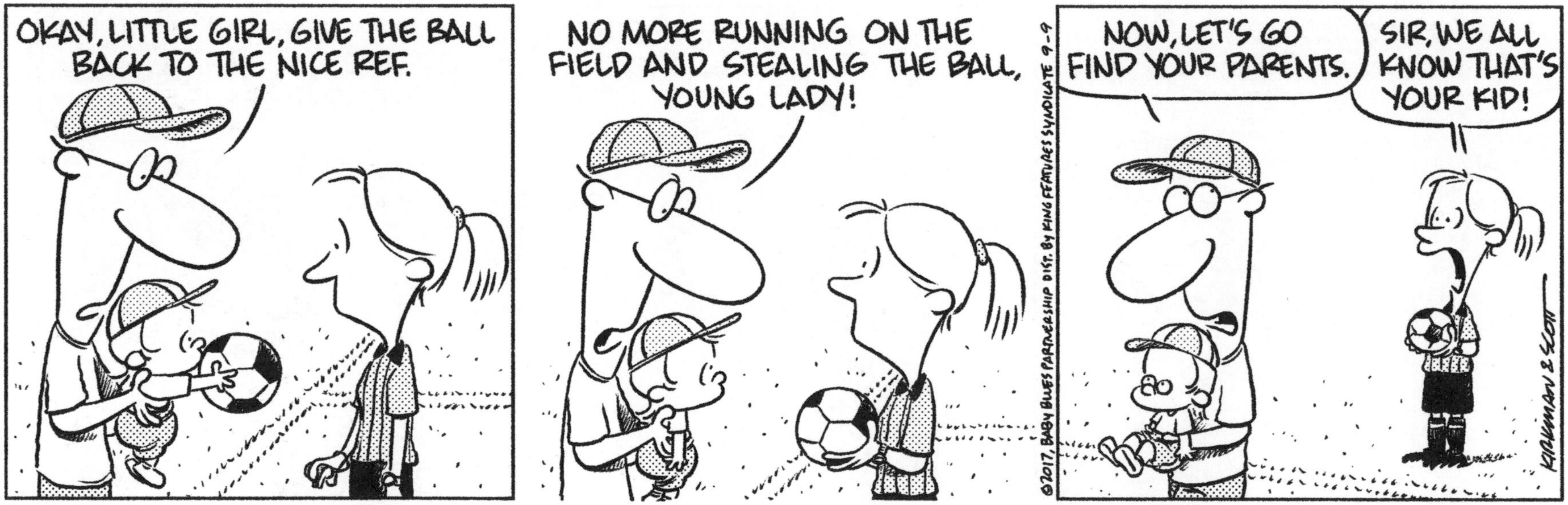
OKAY, LITTLE GIRL, GIVE THE BALL BACK TO THE NICE REF.
NO MORE RUNNING ON THE FIELD AND STEALING THE BALL, YOUNG LADY!
©2017, BABY BLUES PARTNERSHIP DIST. BY KING FEATURES SYNDICATE 9-9
NOW, LET'S GO FIND YOUR PARENTS.
SIR, WE ALL KNOW THAT'S YOUR KID!
KIRKMAN & SCOTT

Rick: Busted.

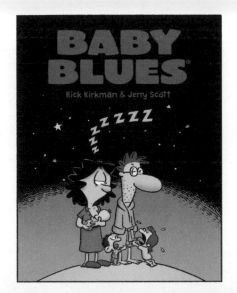

BABY BLUES®
Rick Kirkman & Jerry Scott
ZZZZZZZ

NO WAY!
C'MON, WREN!
ZOE, GET UP!!
MOM! MOM! MOM!
WHAT?
YEAH. WHAT'S GOING ON?
DAD'S MAKING PANCAKES!
©2017, BABY BLUES PARTNERSHIP DIST. BY KING FEATURES SYNDICATE
KIRKMAN & SCOTT
THESE??
THEY'RE ODOR LINERS FROM SOME OLD SHOES I'M CLEANING.
WELL, THEY LOOKED LIKE HIS PANCAKES.

HEY DARRYL, DID YOU TALK TO WANDA?
ABOUT SKIPPING THE SCHOOL PUPPET SHOW AND GOING WITH YOU TO THE HOCKEY GAME INSTEAD?
YEAH. WHAT DID SHE SAY?
EXACTLY WHAT I THOUGHT SHE'D SAY:
©2017, BABY BLUES PARTNERSHIP DIST. BY KING FEATURES SYNDICATE 9-11
KIRKMAN & SCOTT
"DO WHATEVER YOU WANT."
OKAY. I'LL ASK LARRY IF HE CAN GO.

Jerry: Every guy knows that line should never be taken literally.

IT'S TOTALLY CLOGGED WITH GREASE AND GRIME. I'LL HAVE TO GO OUT TO MY TRUCK AND GET MY SNAKE.
GREASE? GRIME? TRUCK? SNAKE?
KIRKMAN & SCOTT
©2017, BABY BLUES PARTNERSHIP DIST. BY KING FEATURES SYNDICATE 9-12
I HAVE JUST DISCOVERED THE COOLEST JOB IN THE WORLD!

Rick: Okay, forget government contractor.

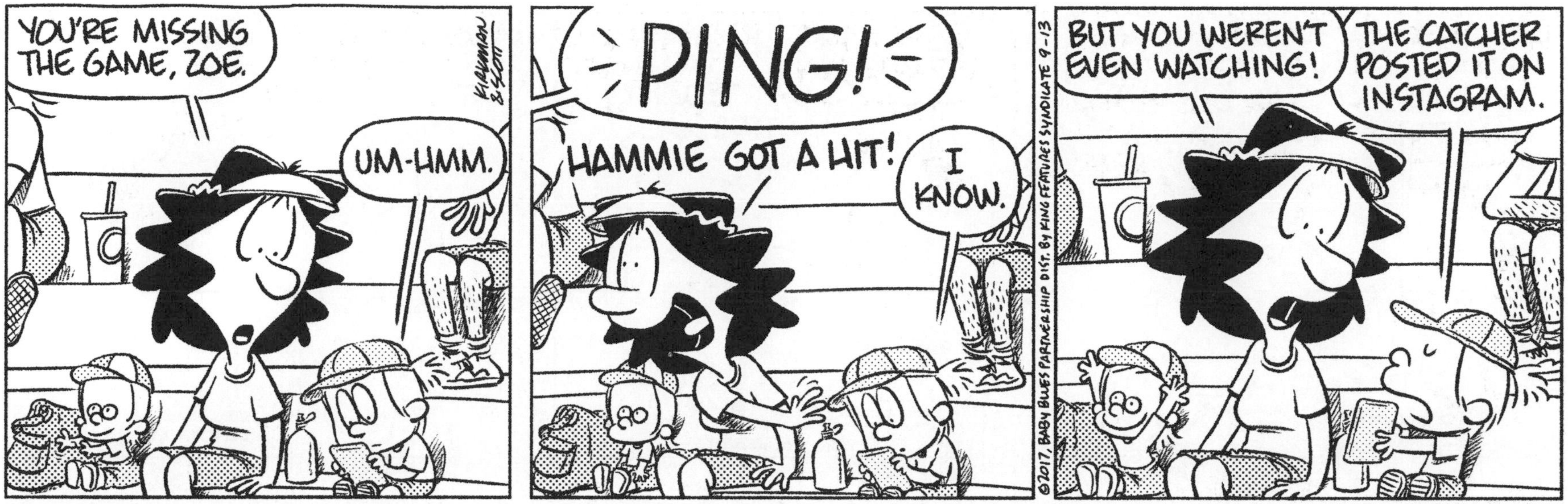
YOU'RE MISSING THE GAME, ZOE.
UM-HMM.
KIRKMAN & SCOTT
PING!
HAMMIE GOT A HIT!
I KNOW.
©2017, BABY BLUES PARTNERSHIP DIST. BY KING FEATURES SYNDICATE 9-13
BUT YOU WEREN'T EVEN WATCHING!
THE CATCHER POSTED IT ON INSTAGRAM.

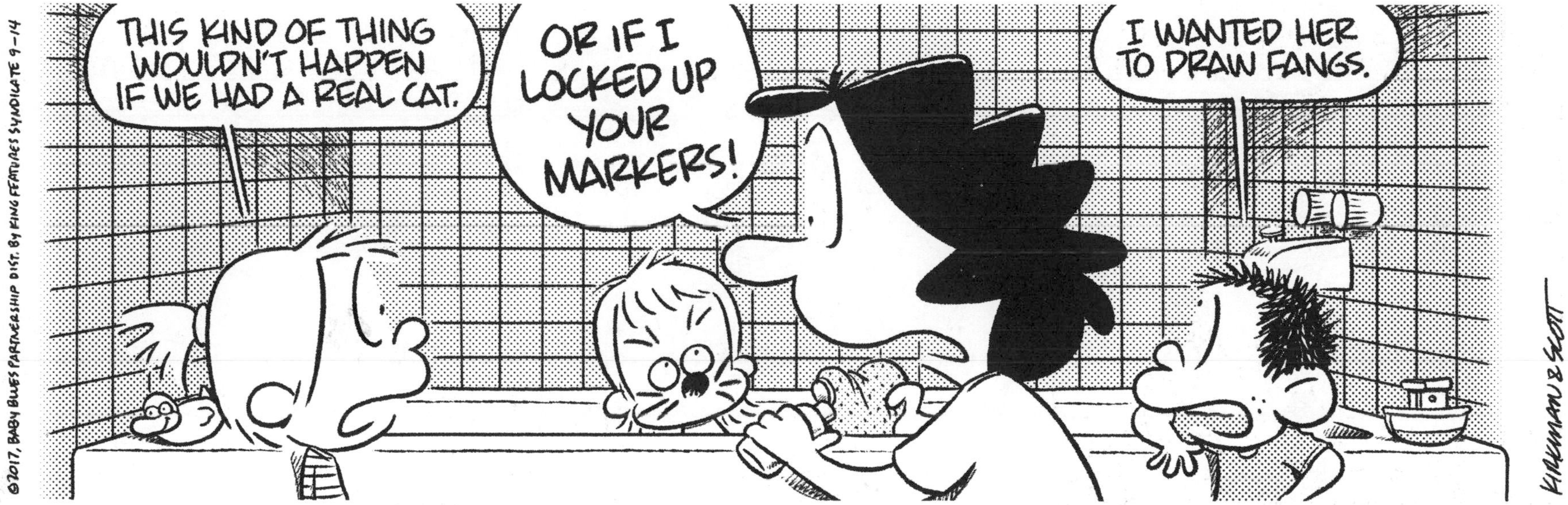
©2017, BABY BLUES PARTNERSHIP DIST. BY KING FEATURES SYNDICATE 9-14
THIS KIND OF THING WOULDN'T HAPPEN IF WE HAD A REAL CAT.
OR IF I LOCKED UP YOUR MARKERS!
I WANTED HER TO DRAW FANGS.
KIRKMAN & SCOTT

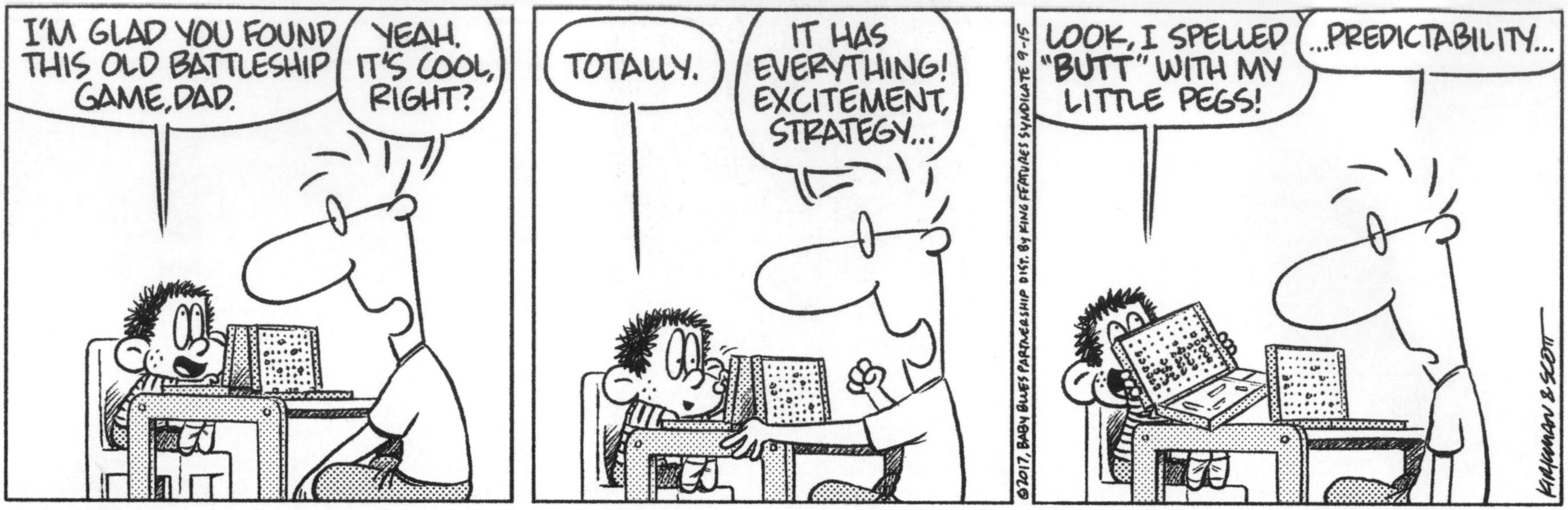
I'M GLAD YOU FOUND THIS OLD BATTLESHIP GAME, DAD.
YEAH. IT'S COOL, RIGHT?
TOTALLY.
IT HAS EVERYTHING! EXCITEMENT, STRATEGY...
©2017, BABY BLUES PARTNERSHIP DIST. BY KING FEATURES SYNDICATE 9-15
LOOK, I SPELLED "BUTT" WITH MY LITTLE PEGS!
...PREDICTABILITY...
KIRKMAN & SCOTT

Rick: I hate to admit I played Battleship in class before Milton Bradley's board game. We just used paper and pencil and drew our own grid.

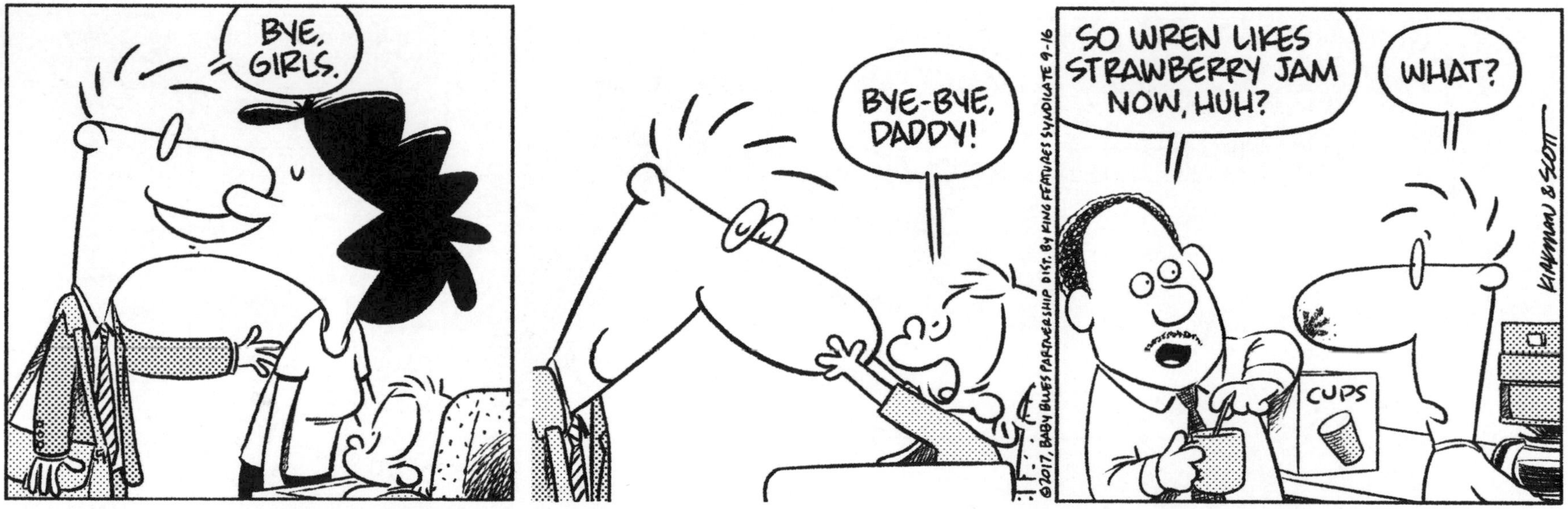
BYE, GIRLS.
BYE-BYE, DADDY!
©2017, BABY BLUES PARTNERSHIP DIST. BY KING FEATURES SYNDICATE 9-16
SO WREN LIKES STRAWBERRY JAM NOW, HUH?
WHAT?
CUPS
KIRKMAN & SCOTT

Jerry: My kids aren't little anymore, so any jam on my face is self-inflicted.

BABY BLUES
Rick Kirkman & Jerry Scott
ZZZZZZZ

MOM, CAN I BORROW YOUR PHONE FOR A SECOND?
UM, OKAY.
HERE. PLAY WITH THIS WHILE ZOE TRIES ON A FEW OUTFITS.
NO WAY!
I'LL PROVE IT! LET'S LOOK IT UP ON MOM'S PHONE!
HA! HA! HA! HAA!
©2017, BABY BLUES PARTNERSHIP DIST. BY KING FEATURES SYNDICATE
OUR CELL PHONE BILL WOULDN'T BE SO HIGH IF YOU DIDN'T USE SO MUCH DATA.
KIRKMAN & SCOTT 9-17

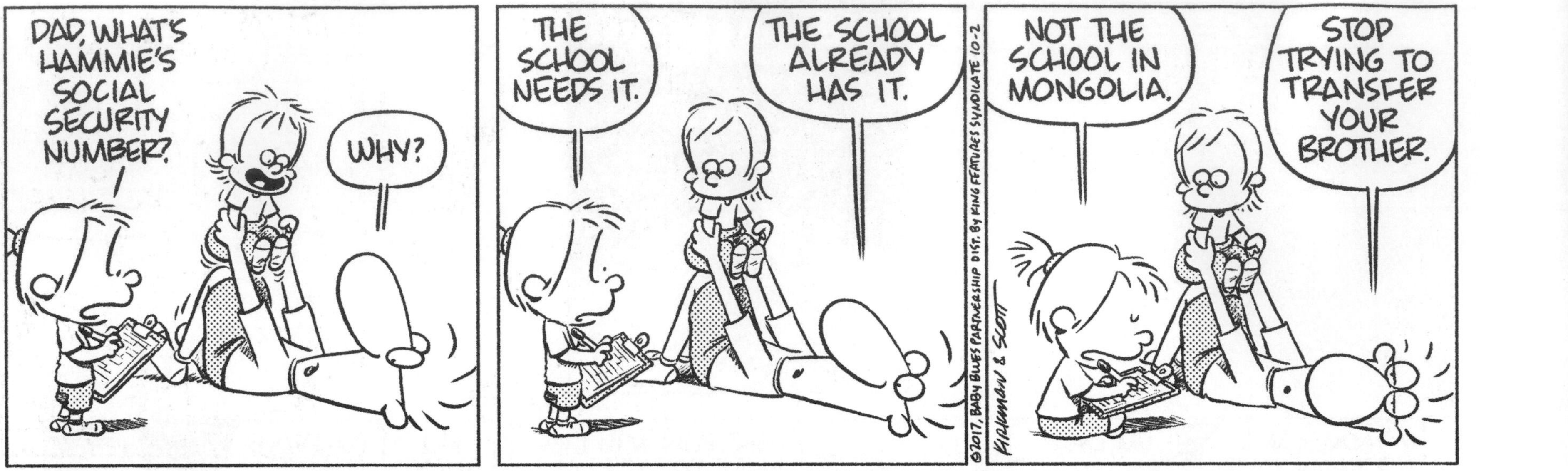
DAD, WHAT'S HAMMIE'S SOCIAL SECURITY NUMBER?
WHY?
THE SCHOOL NEEDS IT.
THE SCHOOL ALREADY HAS IT.
©2017, BABY BLUES PARTNERSHIP DIST. BY KING FEATURES SYNDICATE 10-2
NOT THE SCHOOL IN MONGOLIA.
STOP TRYING TO TRANSFER YOUR BROTHER.
KIRKMAN & SCOTT

Jerry: I like this gag, but I REALLY like Rick's drawings of Darryl and Wren playing.

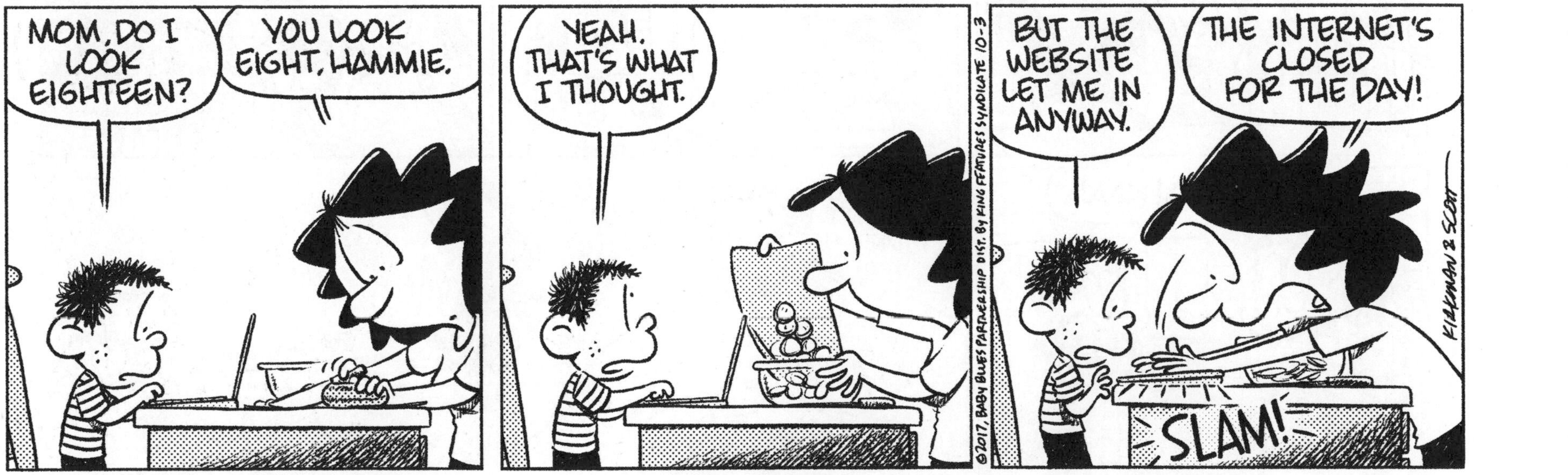
MOM, DO I LOOK EIGHTEEN?
YOU LOOK EIGHT, HAMMIE.
YEAH. THAT'S WHAT I THOUGHT.
©2017, BABY BLUES PARTNERSHIP DIST. BY KING FEATURES SYNDICATE 10-3
BUT THE WEBSITE LET ME IN ANYWAY.
THE INTERNET'S CLOSED FOR THE DAY!
SLAM!
KIRKMAN & SCOTT

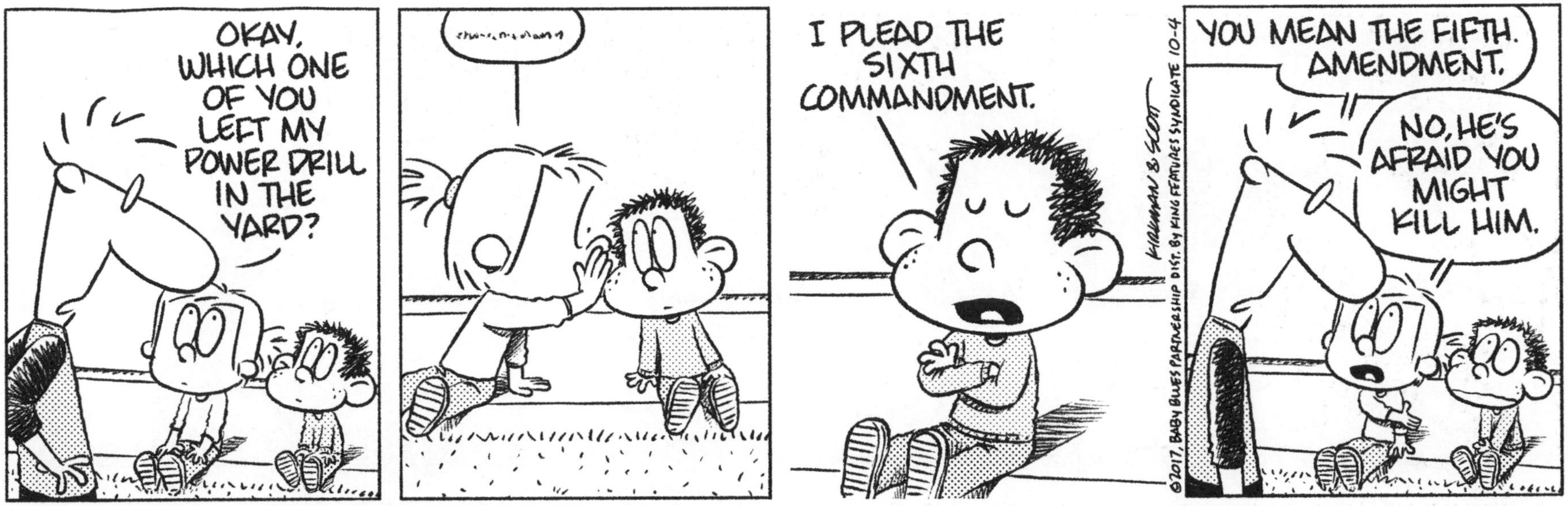
OKAY, WHICH ONE OF YOU LEFT MY POWER DRILL IN THE YARD?
I PLEAD THE SIXTH COMMANDMENT.
KIRKMAN & SCOTT
©2017, BABY BLUES PARTNERSHIP DIST. BY KING FEATURES SYNDICATE 10-4
YOU MEAN THE FIFTH AMENDMENT.
NO, HE'S AFRAID YOU MIGHT KILL HIM.

Jerry: Using the Old Testament for cartoon ideas is probably a sin.
I won't do it again. Probably.

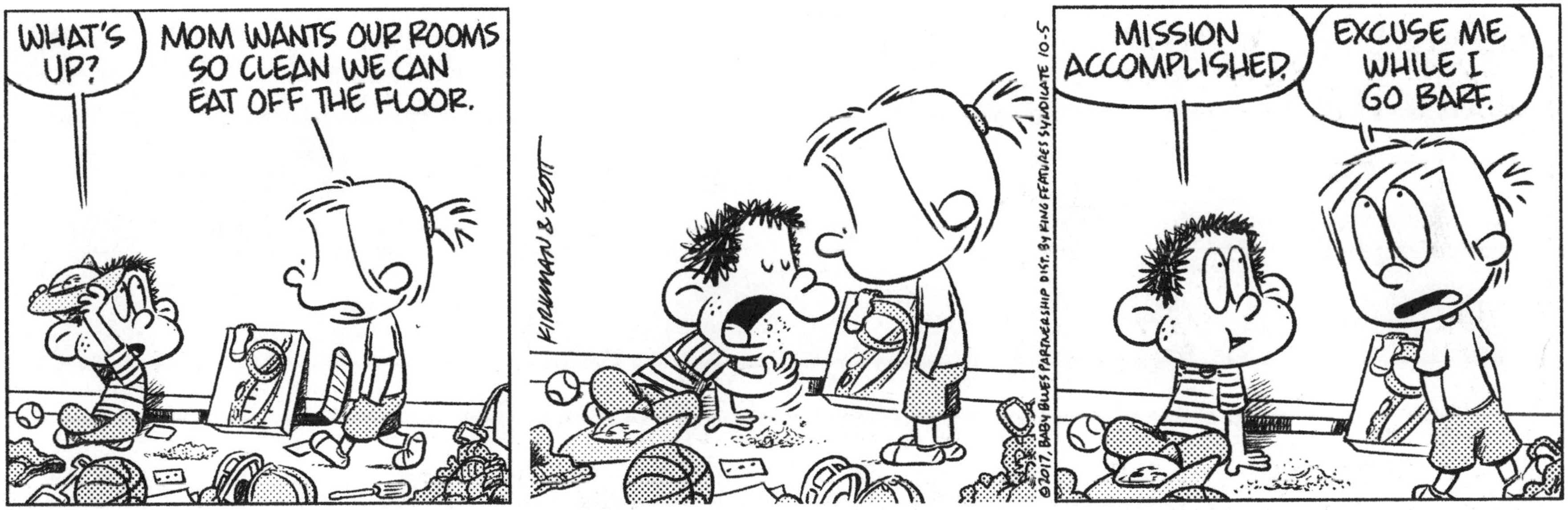
WHAT'S UP?
MOM WANTS OUR ROOMS SO CLEAN WE CAN EAT OFF THE FLOOR.
KIRKMAN & SCOTT
©2017, BABY BLUES PARTNERSHIP DIST. BY KING FEATURES SYNDICATE 10-5
MISSION ACCOMPLISHED.
EXCUSE ME WHILE I GO BARF.

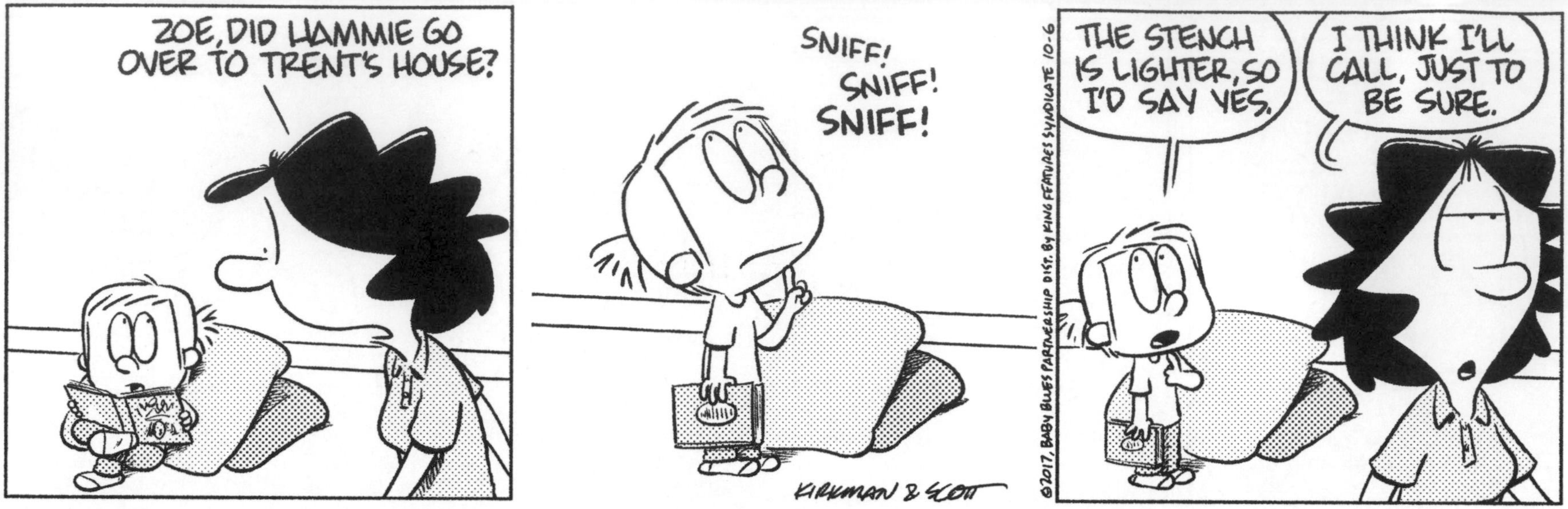
ZOE, DID HAMMIE GO OVER TO TRENT'S HOUSE?
SNIFF! SNIFF! SNIFF!
KIRKMAN & SCOTT
©2017, BABY BLUES PARTNERSHIP DIST. BY KING FEATURES SYNDICATE 10-6
THE STENCH IS LIGHTER, SO I'D SAY YES.
I THINK I'LL CALL, JUST TO BE SURE.

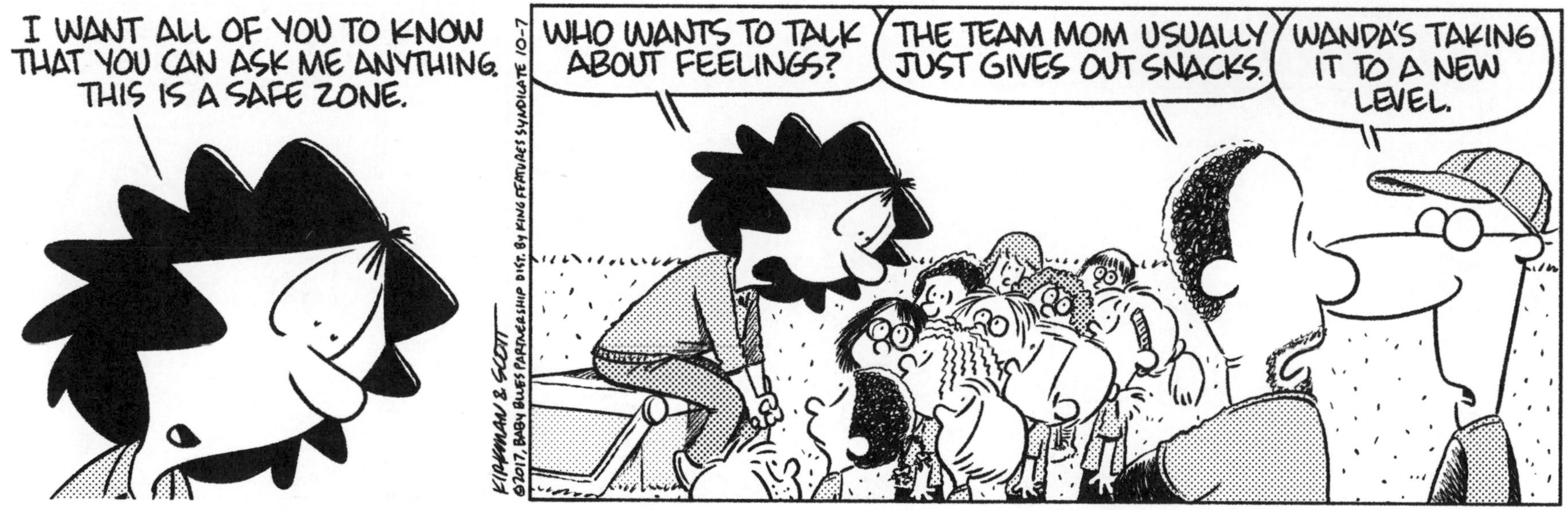
I WANT ALL OF YOU TO KNOW THAT YOU CAN ASK ME ANYTHING. THIS IS A SAFE ZONE.
KIRKMAN & SCOTT
©2017, BABY BLUES PARTNERSHIP DIST. BY KING FEATURES SYNDICATE 10-7
WHO WANTS TO TALK ABOUT FEELINGS?
THE TEAM MOM USUALLY JUST GIVES OUT SNACKS.
WANDA'S TAKING IT TO A NEW LEVEL.

Jerry: When I coached my daughter's soccer team, I was 10 percent coach and 90 percent therapist.

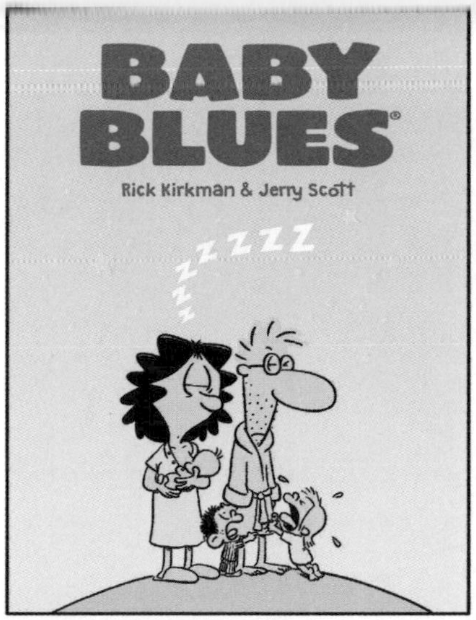
BABY BLUES®
Rick Kirkman & Jerry Scott
ZZZZZZ

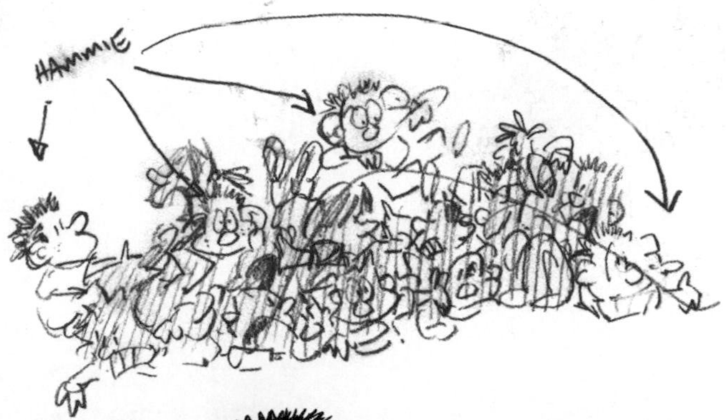
HAMMIE

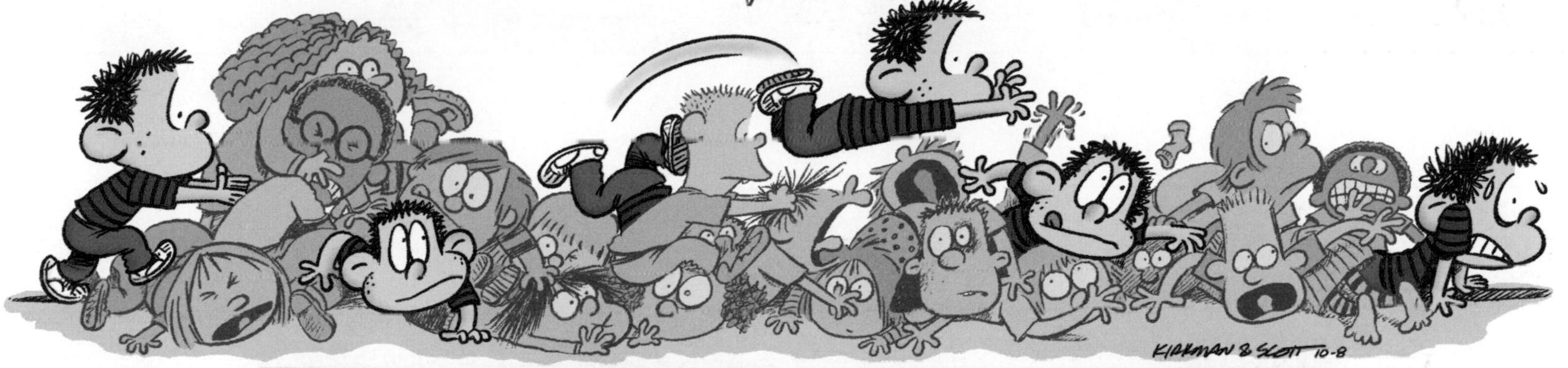
KIRKMAN & SCOTT 10-8

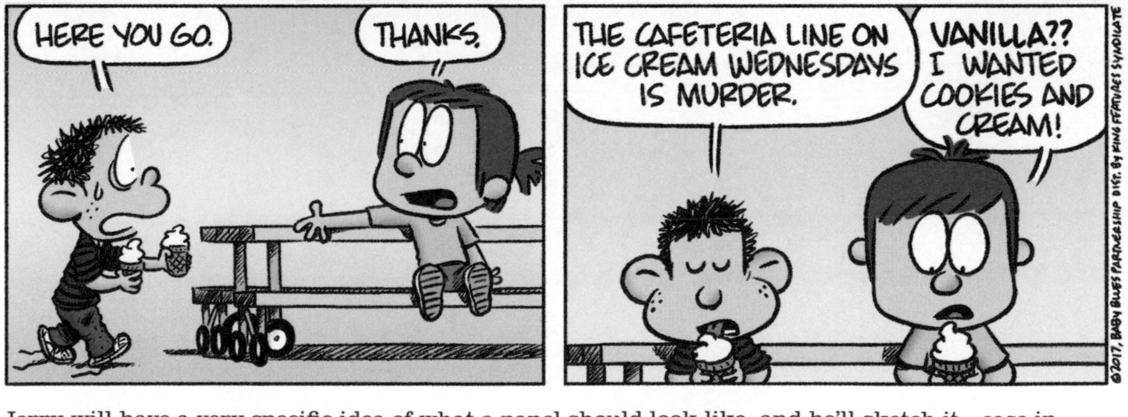
HERE YOU GO.
THANKS.
THE CAFETERIA LINE ON ICE CREAM WEDNESDAYS IS MURDER.
VANILLA?? I WANTED COOKIES AND CREAM!
©2017, BABY BLUES PARTNERSHIP DIST. BY KING FEATURES SYNDICATE

Rick: On rare occasions, Jerry will have a very specific idea of what a panel should look like, and he'll sketch it—case in point here. To make the best use of the space, I stretched it out. Then, instead of a fully monochromatic jumble of kids, I made them a muted faux monochromatic jumble and put Hammie in red so he'd stand out. It was a fun drawing idea.

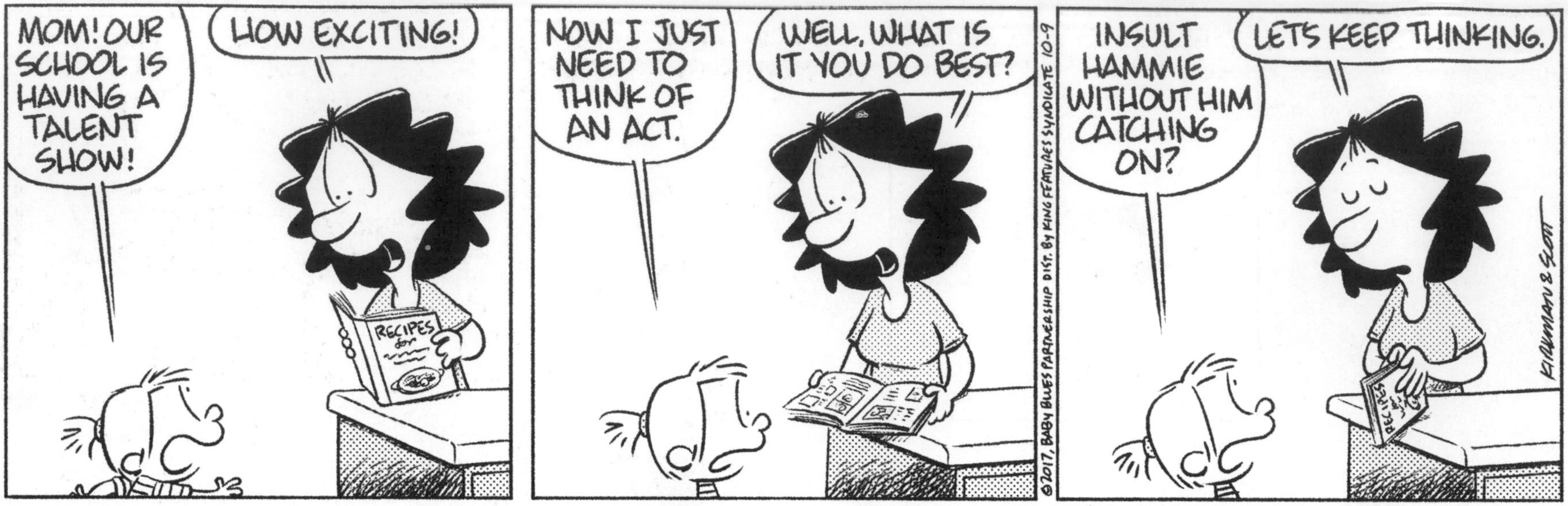
MOM! OUR SCHOOL IS HAVING A TALENT SHOW!
HOW EXCITING!
RECIPES for
NOW I JUST NEED TO THINK OF AN ACT.
WELL, WHAT IS IT YOU DO BEST?
©2017, BABY BLUES PARTNERSHIP DIST. BY KING FEATURES SYNDICATE 10-9
INSULT HAMMIE WITHOUT HIM CATCHING ON?
LET'S KEEP THINKING.
KIRKMAN & SCOTT

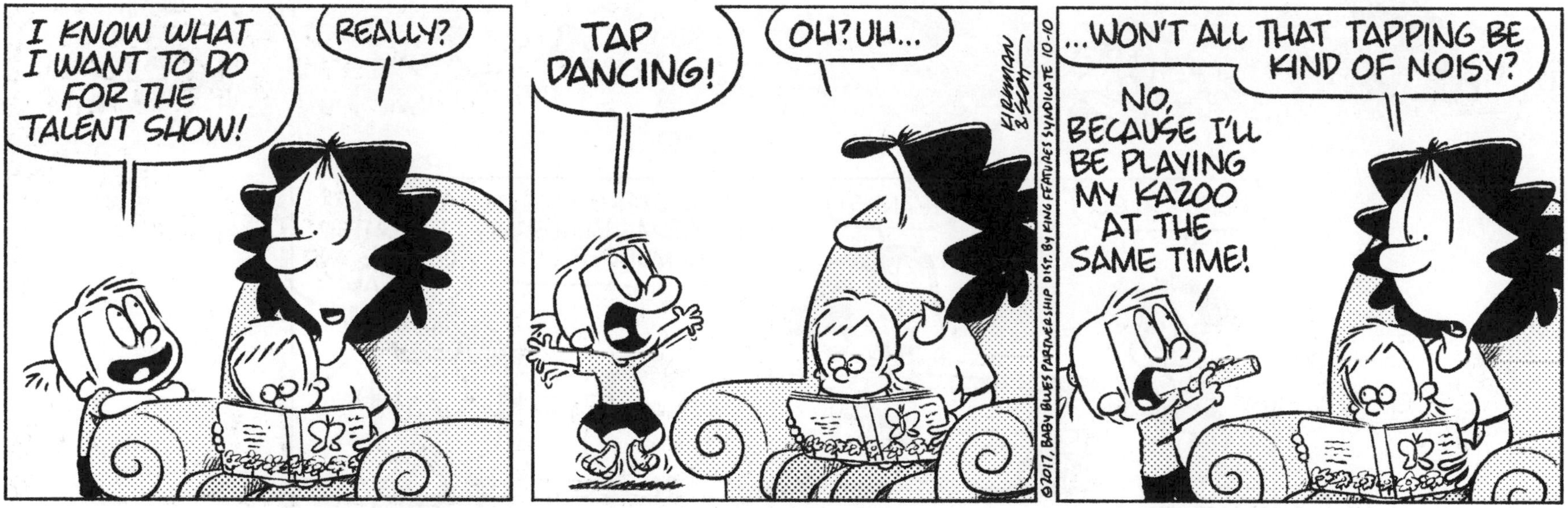
I KNOW WHAT I WANT TO DO FOR THE TALENT SHOW!
REALLY?
TAP DANCING!
OH? UH...
KIRKMAN & SCOTT
©2017, BABY BLUES PARTNERSHIP DIST. BY KING FEATURES SYNDICATE 10-10
...WON'T ALL THAT TAPPING BE KIND OF NOISY?
NO, BECAUSE I'LL BE PLAYING MY KAZOO AT THE SAME TIME!

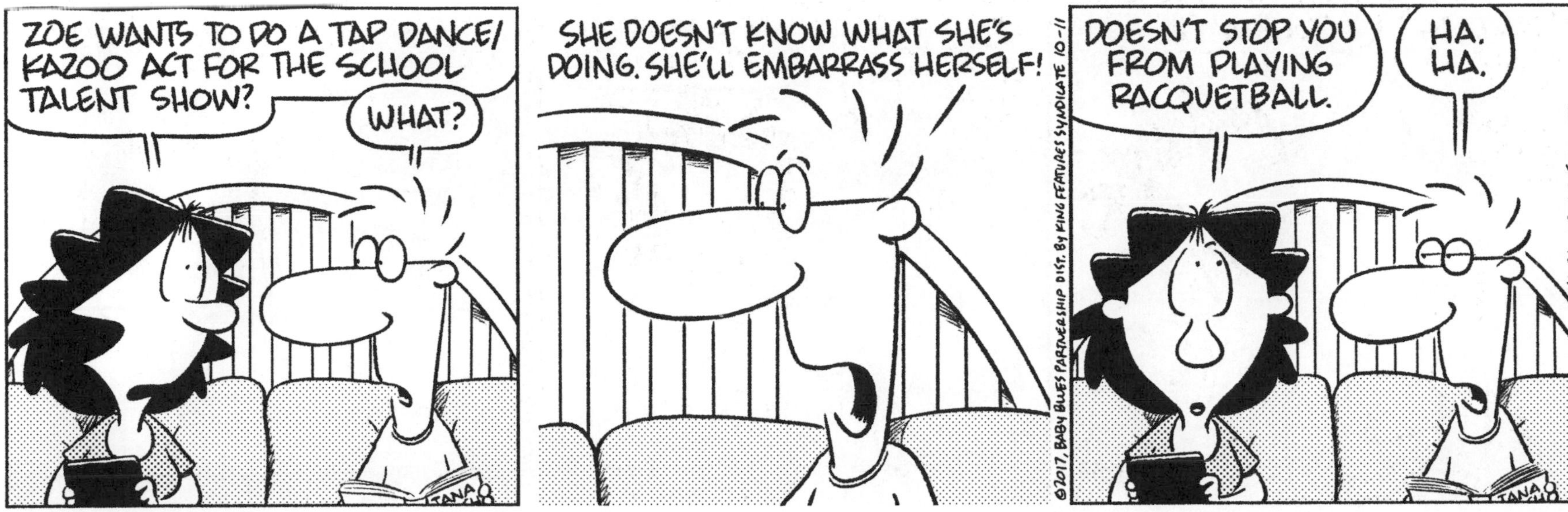
ZOE WANTS TO DO A TAP DANCE/KAZOO ACT FOR THE SCHOOL TALENT SHOW?
WHAT?
SHE DOESN'T KNOW WHAT SHE'S DOING. SHE'LL EMBARRASS HERSELF!
©2017, BABY BLUES PARTNERSHIP DIST. BY KING FEATURES SYNDICATE 10-11
DOESN'T STOP YOU FROM PLAYING RACQUETBALL.
HA. HA.
KIRKMAN & SCOTT

Rick: Ooh. Zing!

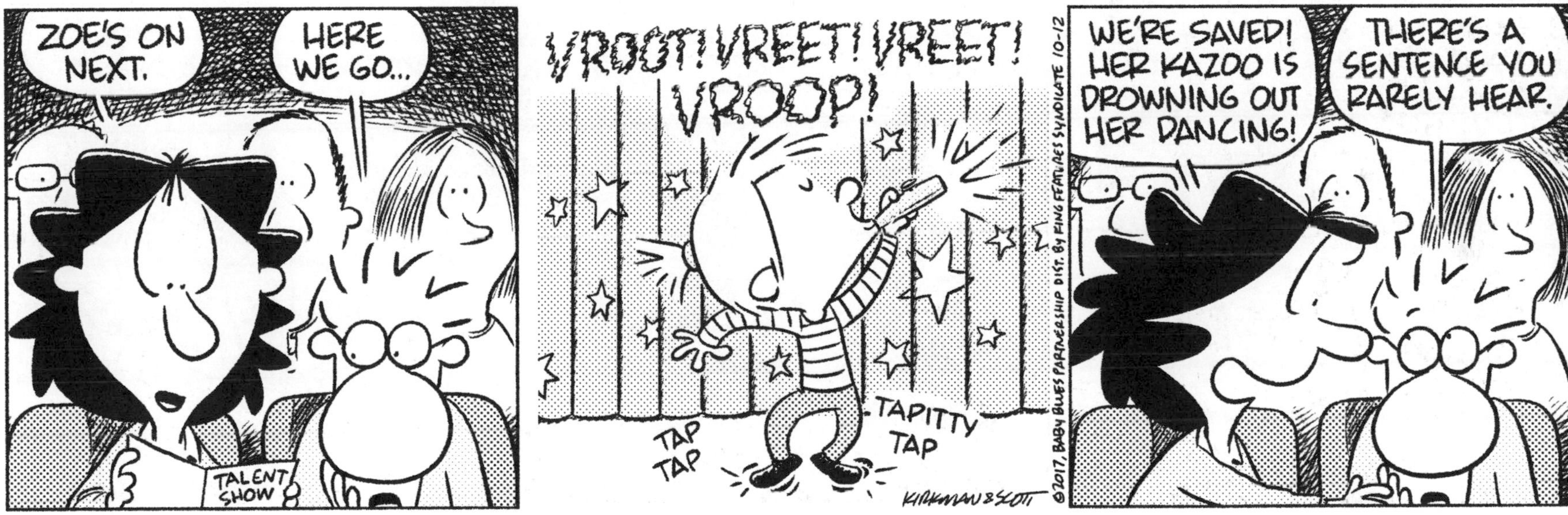
ZOE'S ON NEXT.
HERE WE GO...
TALENT SHOW
VROOT! VREET! VREET! VROOP!
TAP TAP
TAPITTY TAP
KIRKMAN & SCOTT
©2017, BABY BLUES PARTNERSHIP DIST. BY KING FEATURES SYNDICATE 10-12
WE'RE SAVED! HER KAZOO IS DROWNING OUT HER DANCING!
THERE'S A SENTENCE YOU RARELY HEAR.

WHERE'S HAMMIE?
LOOK UP.
WHY IS HE ON STAGE?
THIS SAYS HE'S PART OF THE ARMPIT VIRTUOSOS.
FWEEP! FAAP! FORP!
GROAN! TELL ME WHEN IT'S OVER.
HEY! THAT'S MY BOY ON LEAD PIT!
©2017, BABY BLUES PARTNERSHIP DIST. BY KING FEATURES SYNDICATE 10-13
KIRKMAN & SCOTT

MOM? WHAT ARE YOU DOING?
MEDITATING.
IT CLEARS THE MIND AND RELIEVES STRESS.
OKAY. I'LL JUST SLIDE YOU TOWARD THE KITCHEN SO YOU CAN MAKE ME A SNACK WHEN YOU'RE DONE.
THE STRESS IS MAKING A COMEBACK.
©2017, BABY BLUES PARTNERSHIP DIST. BY KING FEATURES SYNDICATE 10-14
KIRKMAN & SCOTT

Rick: Is there such a thing as multitasking meditation?

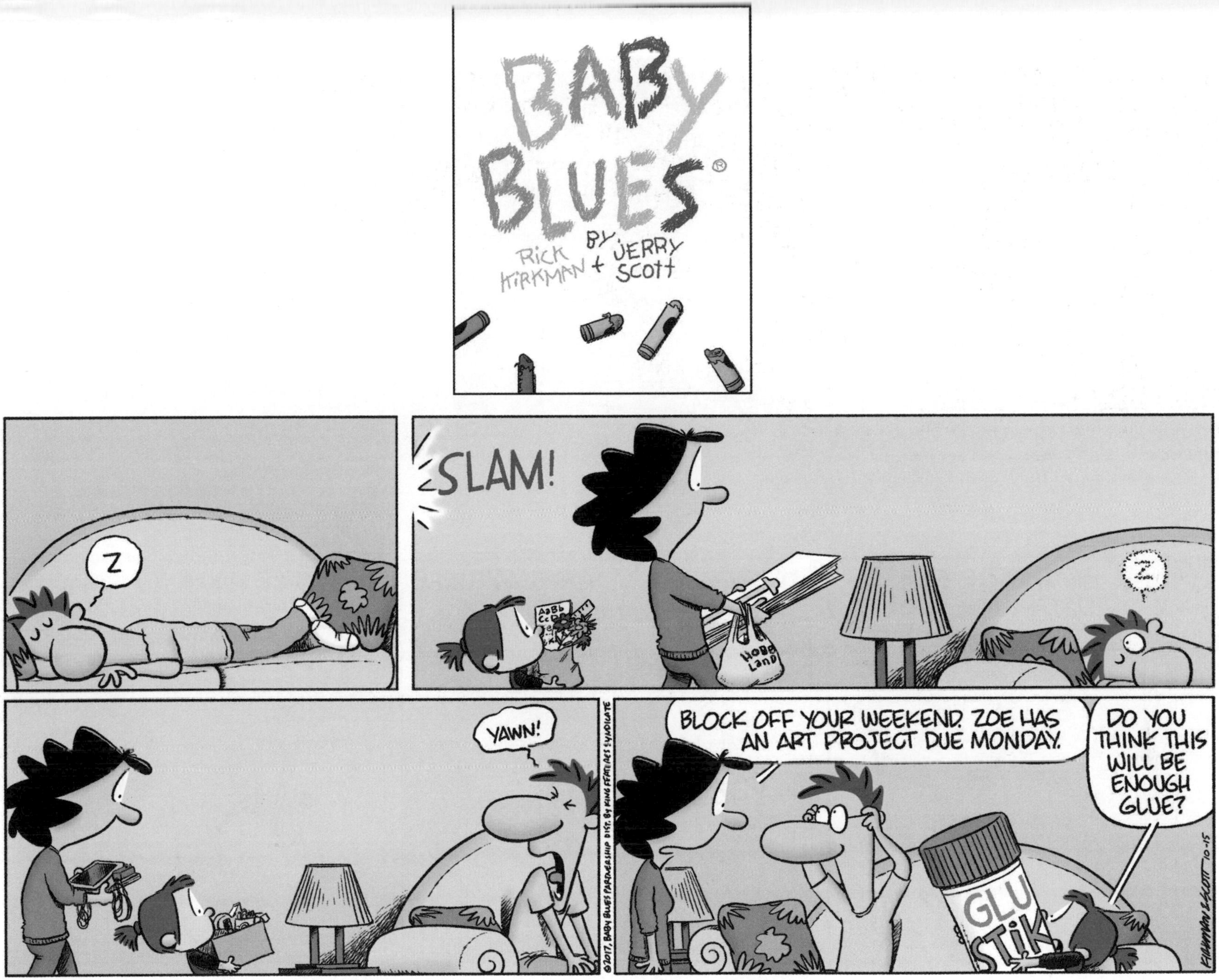
BABY BLUES®
BY RICK KIRKMAN + JERRY SCOTT
Z
SLAM!
Z
YAWN!
©2017, BABY BLUES PARTNERSHIP DIST. BY KING FEATURES SYNDICATE
BLOCK OFF YOUR WEEKEND. ZOE HAS AN ART PROJECT DUE MONDAY.
DO YOU THINK THIS WILL BE ENOUGH GLUE?
GLU STIK
KIRKMAN & SCOTT
10-15

Jerry: My kids were able to trick me into doing most of their school art projects. I'm a poster nerd.

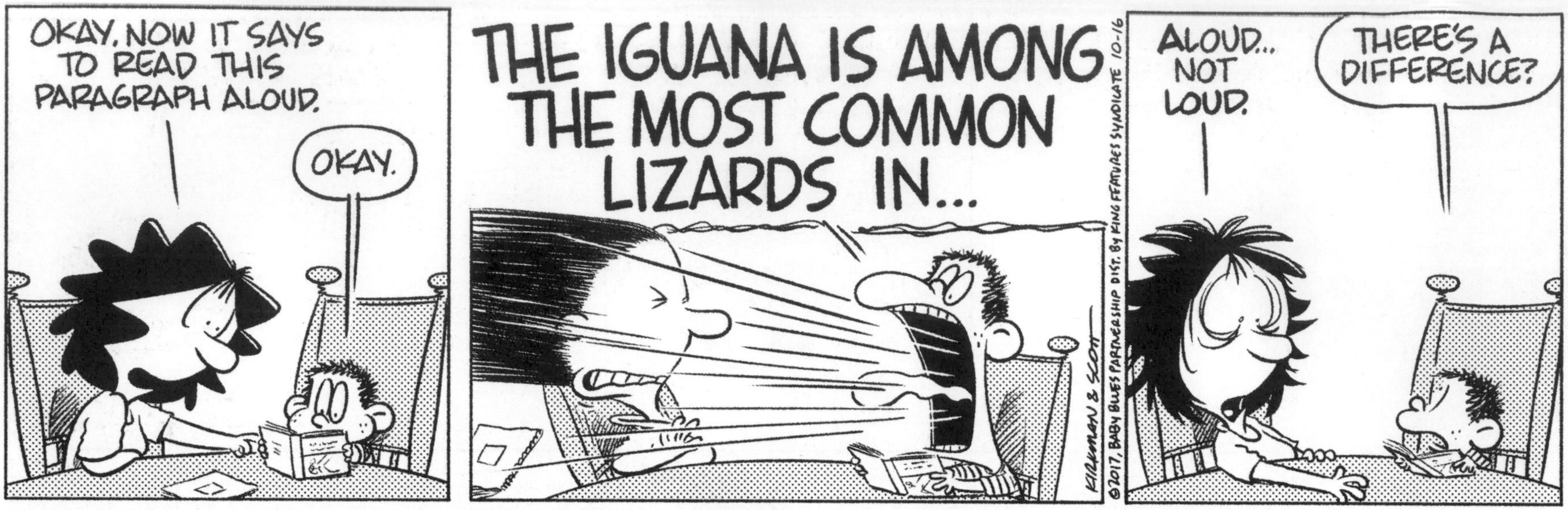
OKAY, NOW IT SAYS TO READ THIS PARAGRAPH ALOUD.
OKAY.
THE IGUANA IS AMONG THE MOST COMMON LIZARDS IN...
ALOUD... NOT LOUD.
THERE'S A DIFFERENCE?
©2017, BABY BLUES PARTNERSHIP DIST. BY KING FEATURES SYNDICATE 10-16
KIRKMAN & SCOTT

Rick: I got a kick out of Hammie's grotesquely unhinged jaw.

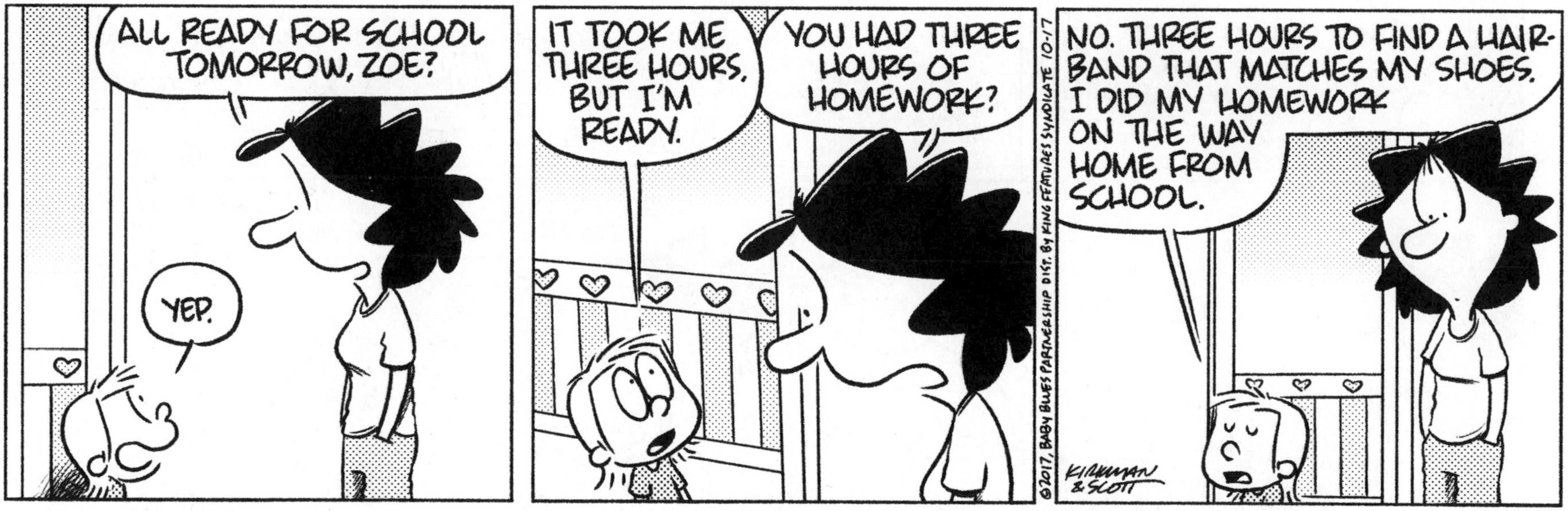
ALL READY FOR SCHOOL TOMORROW, ZOE?
YEP.
IT TOOK ME THREE HOURS, BUT I'M READY.
YOU HAD THREE HOURS OF HOMEWORK?
NO. THREE HOURS TO FIND A HAIR-BAND THAT MATCHES MY SHOES. I DID MY HOMEWORK ON THE WAY HOME FROM SCHOOL.
©2017, BABY BLUES PARTNERSHIP DIST. BY KING FEATURES SYNDICATE 10-17
KIRKMAN & SCOTT

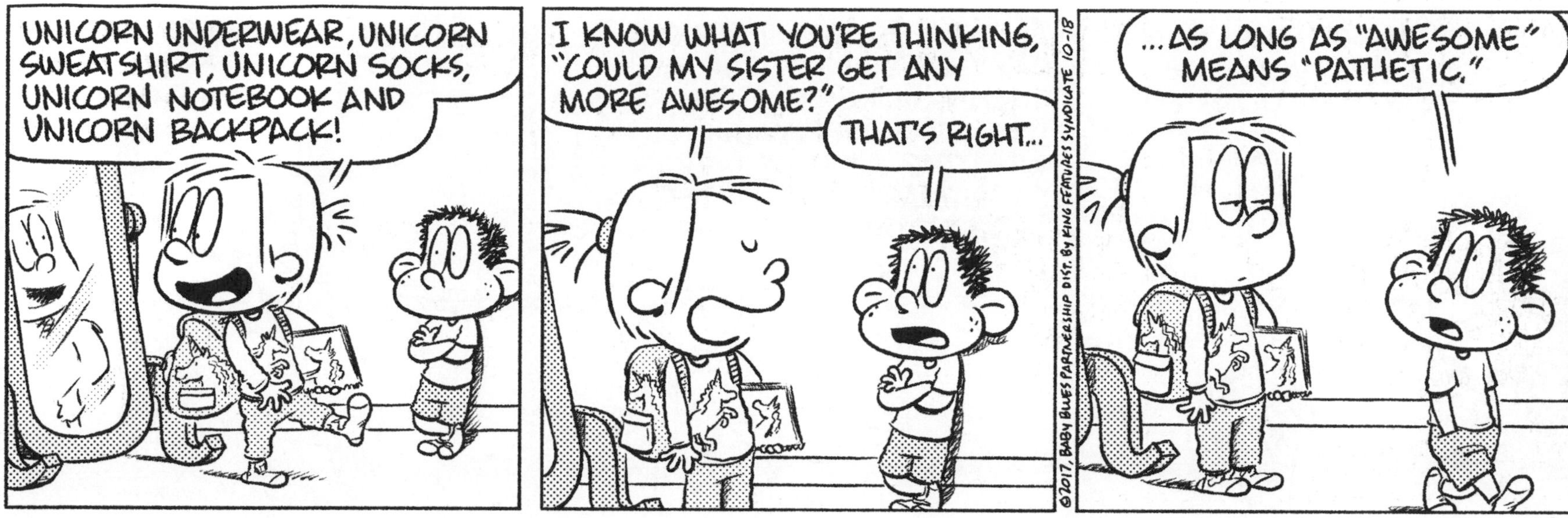
UNICORN UNDERWEAR, UNICORN SWEATSHIRT, UNICORN SOCKS, UNICORN NOTEBOOK AND UNICORN BACKPACK!
I KNOW WHAT YOU'RE THINKING, "COULD MY SISTER GET ANY MORE AWESOME?"
THAT'S RIGHT...
©2017, BABY BLUES PARTNERSHIP DIST. BY KING FEATURES SYNDICATE 10-18
...AS LONG AS "AWESOME" MEANS "PATHETIC."
KIRKMAN & SCOTT

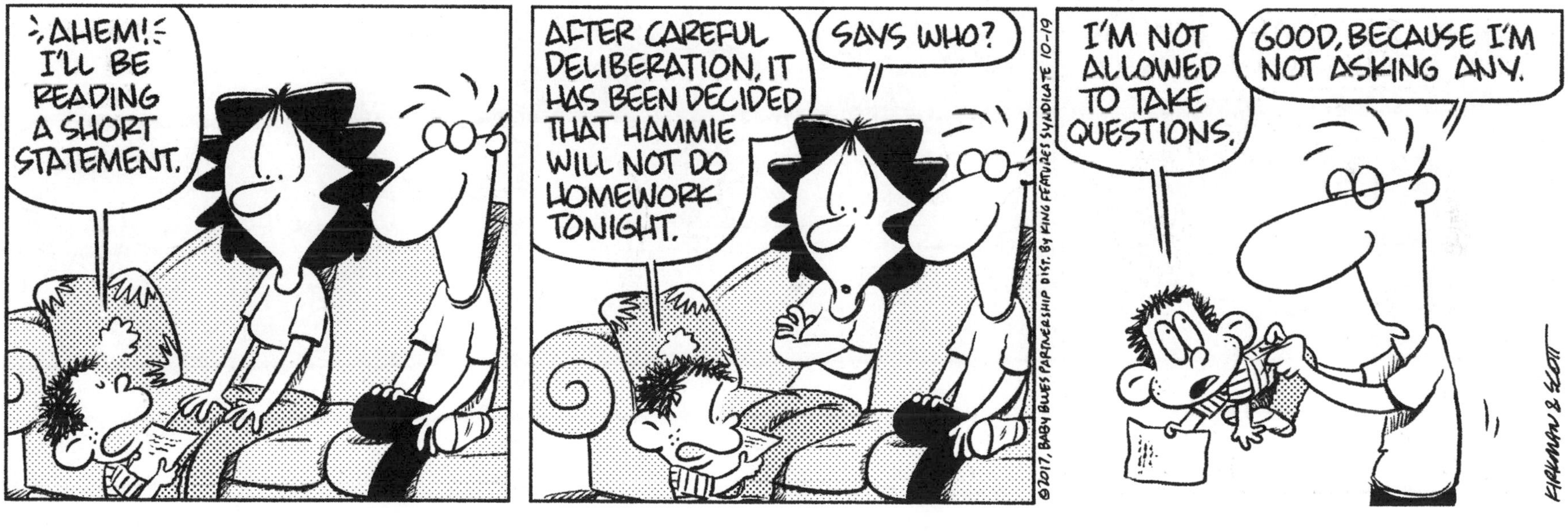
AHEM! I'LL BE READING A SHORT STATEMENT.
AFTER CAREFUL DELIBERATION, IT HAS BEEN DECIDED THAT HAMMIE WILL NOT DO HOMEWORK TONIGHT.
SAYS WHO?
©2017, BABY BLUES PARTNERSHIP DIST. BY KING FEATURES SYNDICATE 10-19
I'M NOT ALLOWED TO TAKE QUESTIONS.
GOOD, BECAUSE I'M NOT ASKING ANY.
KIRKMAN & SCOTT

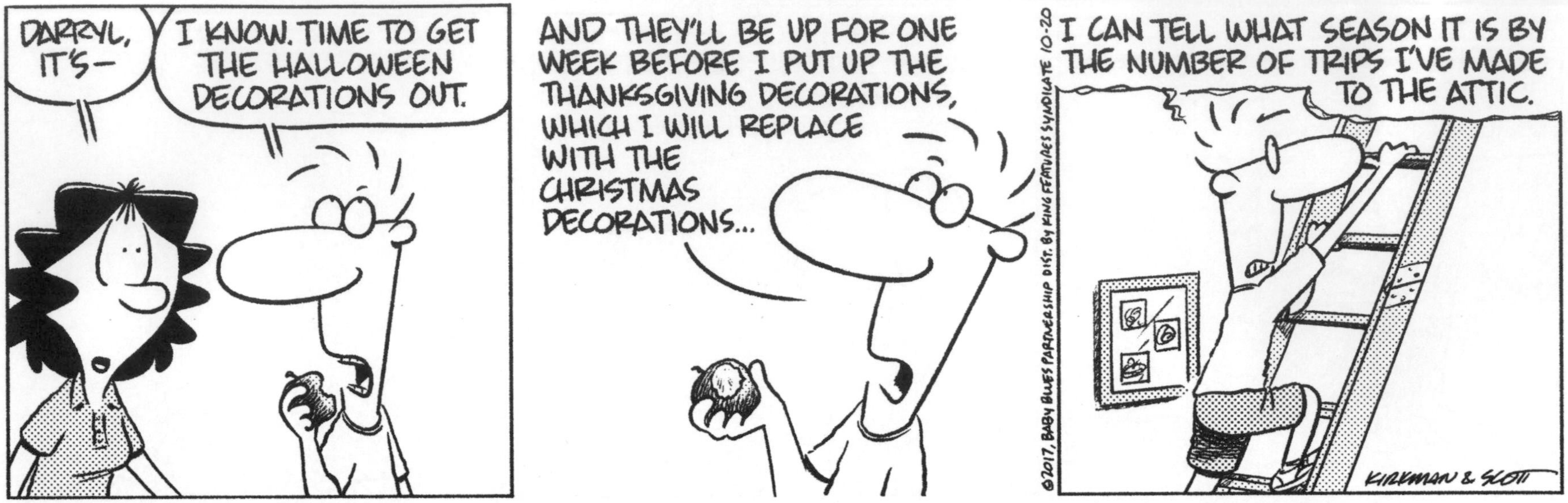
DARRYL, IT'S—
I KNOW. TIME TO GET THE HALLOWEEN DECORATIONS OUT.
AND THEY'LL BE UP FOR ONE WEEK BEFORE I PUT UP THE THANKSGIVING DECORATIONS, WHICH I WILL REPLACE WITH THE CHRISTMAS DECORATIONS...
I CAN TELL WHAT SEASON IT IS BY THE NUMBER OF TRIPS I'VE MADE TO THE ATTIC.
KIRKMAN & SCOTT

Rick: I suggest creating a lawn decoration of a Frankenstein Santa wearing a pilgrim hat and bunny ears, holding cupid's bow and flaming arrow, aiming to light a menorah. You could leave it out all year.

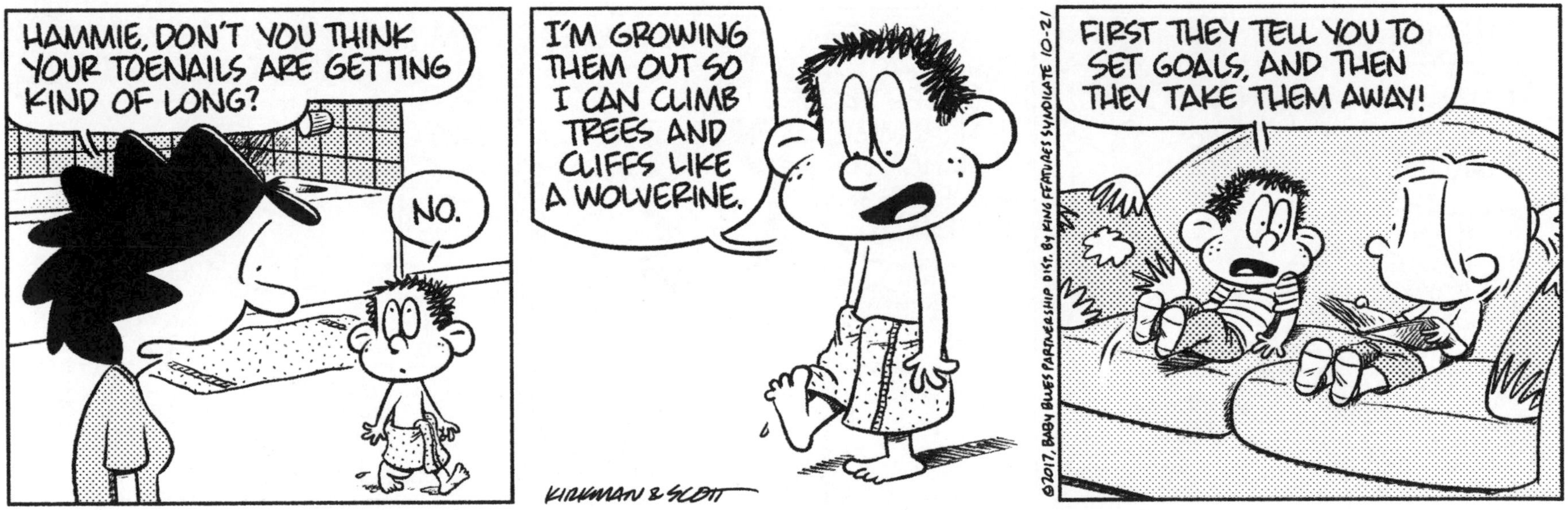
HAMMIE, DON'T YOU THINK YOUR TOENAILS ARE GETTING KIND OF LONG?
NO.
I'M GROWING THEM OUT SO I CAN CLIMB TREES AND CLIFFS LIKE A WOLVERINE.
KIRKMAN & SCOTT
FIRST THEY TELL YOU TO SET GOALS, AND THEN THEY TAKE THEM AWAY!

Jerry: There's not enough wolverine humor in the funnies, if you ask me.

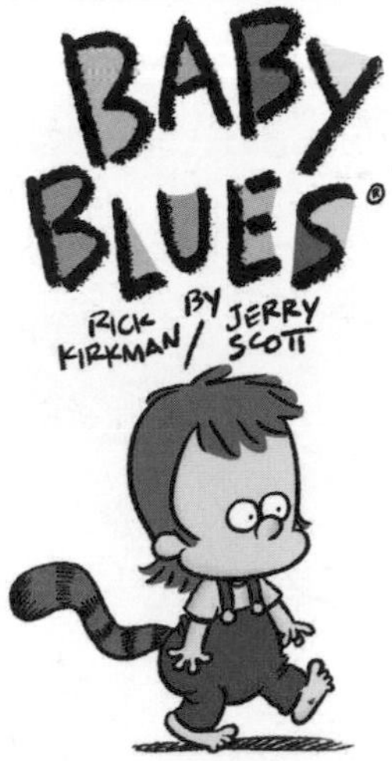
BABY BLUES®
RICK KIRKMAN / BY JERRY SCOTT

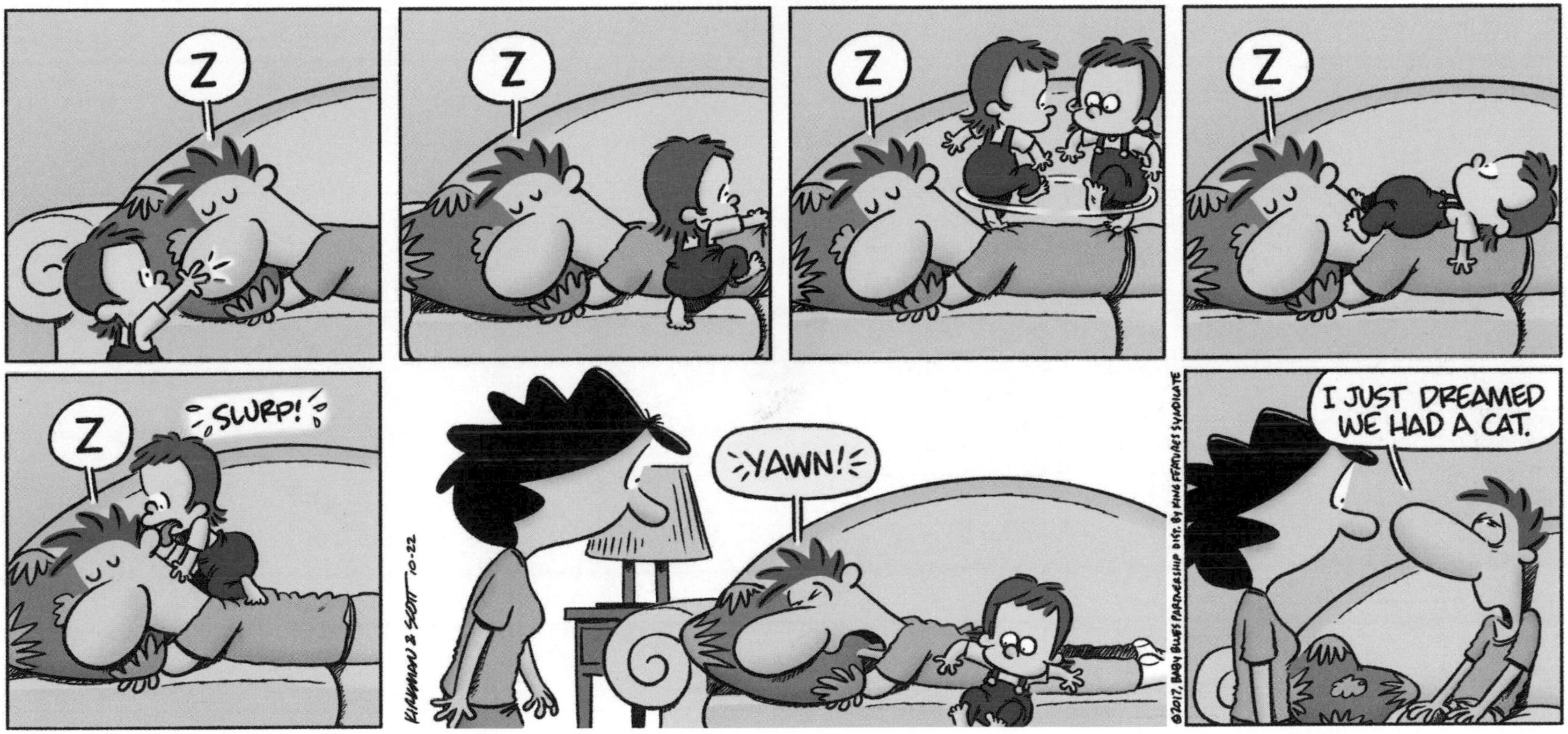
Z
Z
Z
Z
Z
SLURP!
KIRKMAN & SCOTT 10-22
YAWN!
©2017, BABY BLUES PARTNERSHIP DIST. BY KING FEATURES SYNDICATE
I JUST DREAMED WE HAD A CAT.

Rick: I really loved the simple action in this one.

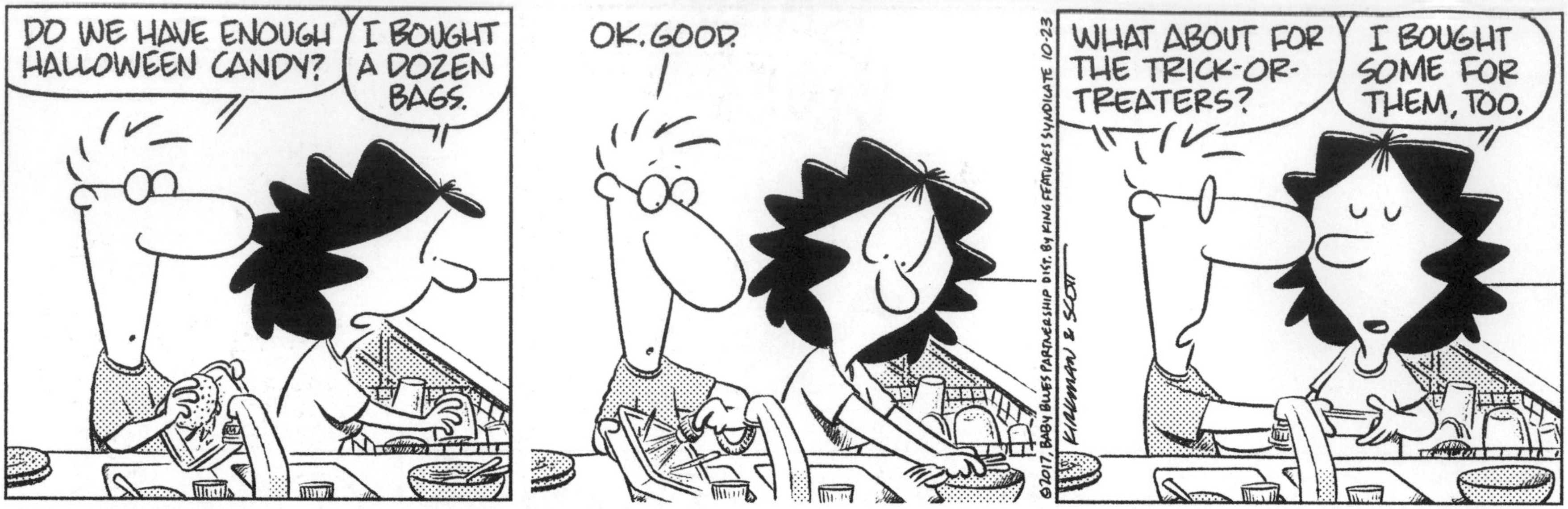
DO WE HAVE ENOUGH HALLOWEEN CANDY?
I BOUGHT A DOZEN BAGS.
OK. GOOD.
WHAT ABOUT FOR THE TRICK-OR-TREATERS?
I BOUGHT SOME FOR THEM, TOO.
©2017, BABY BLUES PARTNERSHIP DIST. BY KING FEATURES SYNDICATE 10-23
KIRKMAN & SCOTT

Rick: The annual excuse to binge on candy.

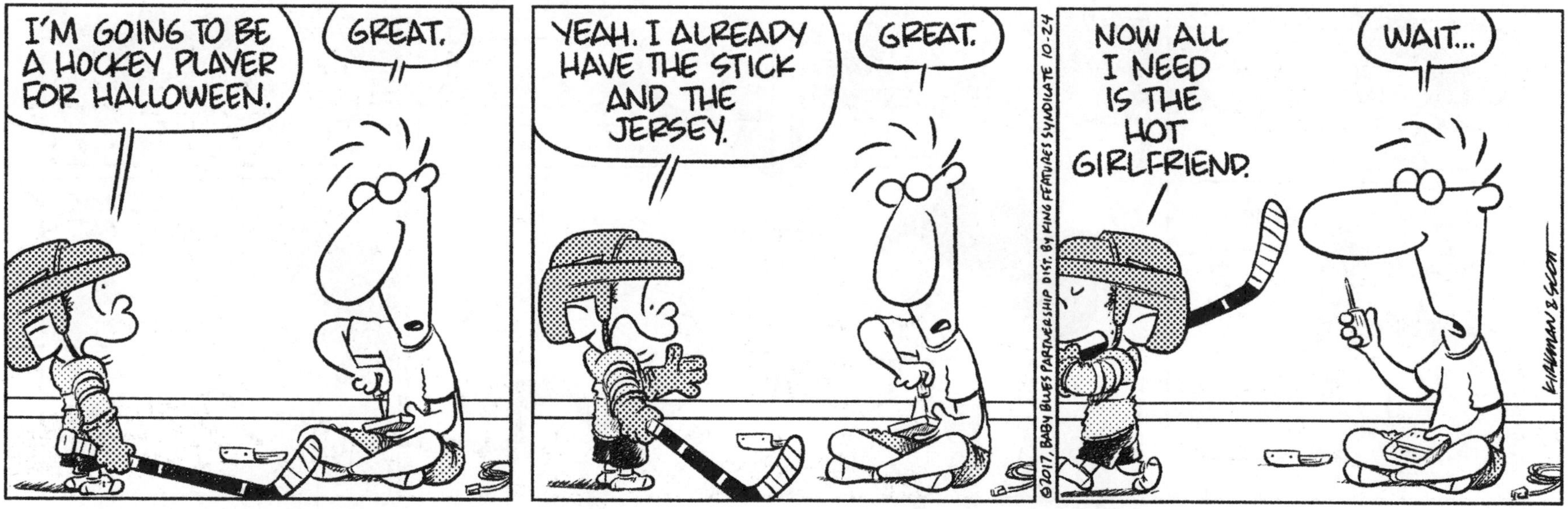
I'M GOING TO BE A HOCKEY PLAYER FOR HALLOWEEN.
GREAT.
YEAH. I ALREADY HAVE THE STICK AND THE JERSEY.
GREAT.
NOW ALL I NEED IS THE HOT GIRLFRIEND.
WAIT...
©2017, BABY BLUES PARTNERSHIP DIST. BY KING FEATURES SYNDICATE 10-24
KIRKMAN & SCOTT

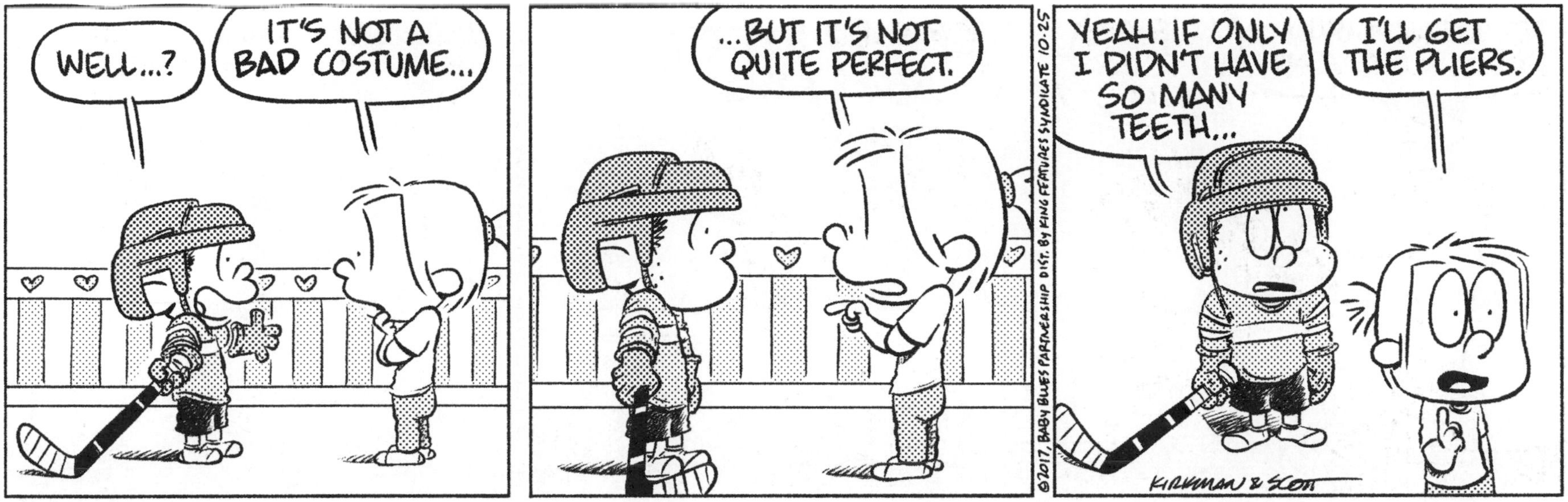
WELL...?
IT'S NOT A BAD COSTUME...
...BUT IT'S NOT QUITE PERFECT.
©2017, BABY BLUES PARTNERSHIP DIST. BY KING FEATURES SYNDICATE 10-25
YEAH. IF ONLY I DIDN'T HAVE SO MANY TEETH...
I'LL GET THE PLIERS.
KIRKMAN & SCOTT

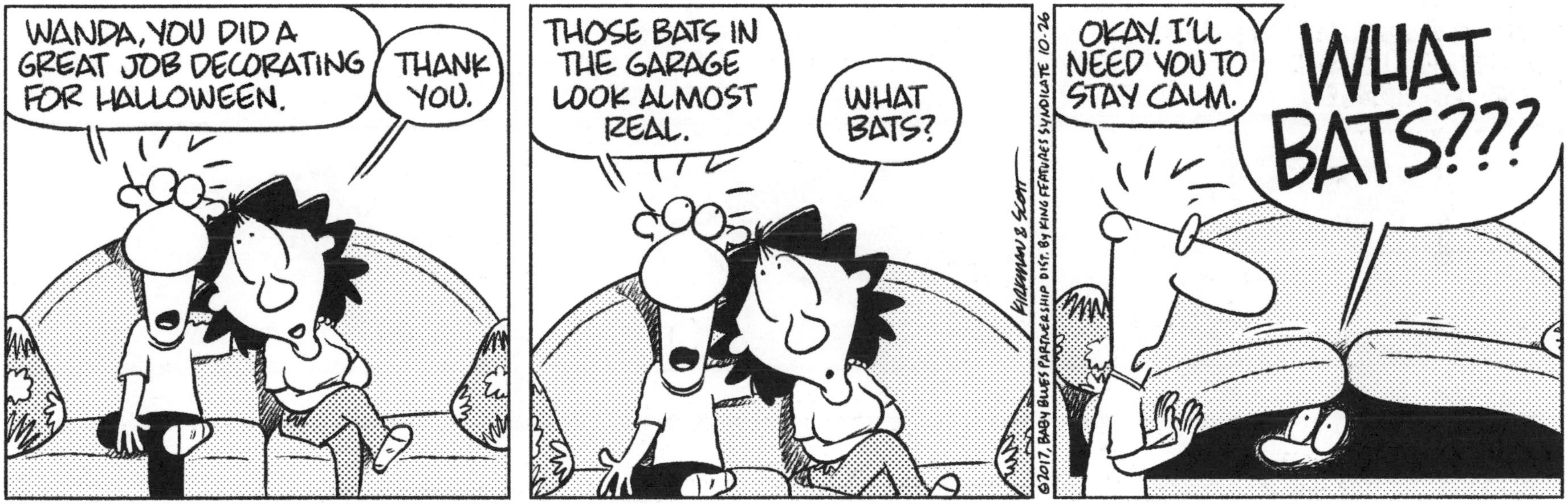
WANDA, YOU DID A GREAT JOB DECORATING FOR HALLOWEEN.
THANK YOU.
THOSE BATS IN THE GARAGE LOOK ALMOST REAL.
WHAT BATS?
KIRKMAN & SCOTT
©2017, BABY BLUES PARTNERSHIP DIST. BY KING FEATURES SYNDICATE 10-26
OKAY. I'LL NEED YOU TO STAY CALM.
WHAT BATS???

ALL CLEAR, GIRLS! THE BATS ARE GONE!
WHERE DID THEY GO?
THE GIANT SPIDERS ATE THEM!
AIEEEEE!
©2017, BABY BLUES PARTNERSHIP DIST. BY KING FEATURES SYNDICATE 10-27
KIRKMAN & SCOTT
YOU'RE NOT HELPING.
WAS I SUPPOSED TO?
BREATHE, ZOE! BREATHE!

WHY WOULD YOU EVEN DO SOMETHING LIKE THIS, HAMMIE?
TO SCARE ZOE.
DOES IT HURT?
NOT REALLY. IT'S JUST KIND OF HEAVY AND SLIMY.
©2017, BABY BLUES PARTNERSHIP DIST. BY KING FEATURES SYNDICATE 10-28
THEN I GUESS YOU WON'T TRY IT AGAIN.
WELL, NOT UNTIL NEXT HALLOWEEN SEASON.
KIRKMAN & SCOTT

BABY BLUES
Rick Kirkman & Jerry Scott
ZZZZZ

BZZZ! BZZZ!
HI SWEETIE.
I JUST REMEMBERED THAT WE NEED BANANAS, TOO.
BZZZ! BZZZ!
AND SOME OLIVE OIL. I FORGOT ABOUT THAT.
OKAY.
NEWS STUFF
BZZZ! BZZZ!
SIGH!
BZZZ! BZZZ!
GAH!
MONSTER PACK TP
MONSTER PACK TP
KIRKMAN & SCOTT 10-29
BZZZ! BZZZ!
GROAN!!
©2017, BABY BLUES PARTNERSHIP DIST. BY KING FEATURES SYNDICATE
LOOK, MOM! DAD WENT GROCERY SHOPPING!
WHAT A SURPRISE!
VERY CLEVER, WANDA. VERRRY CLEVER.

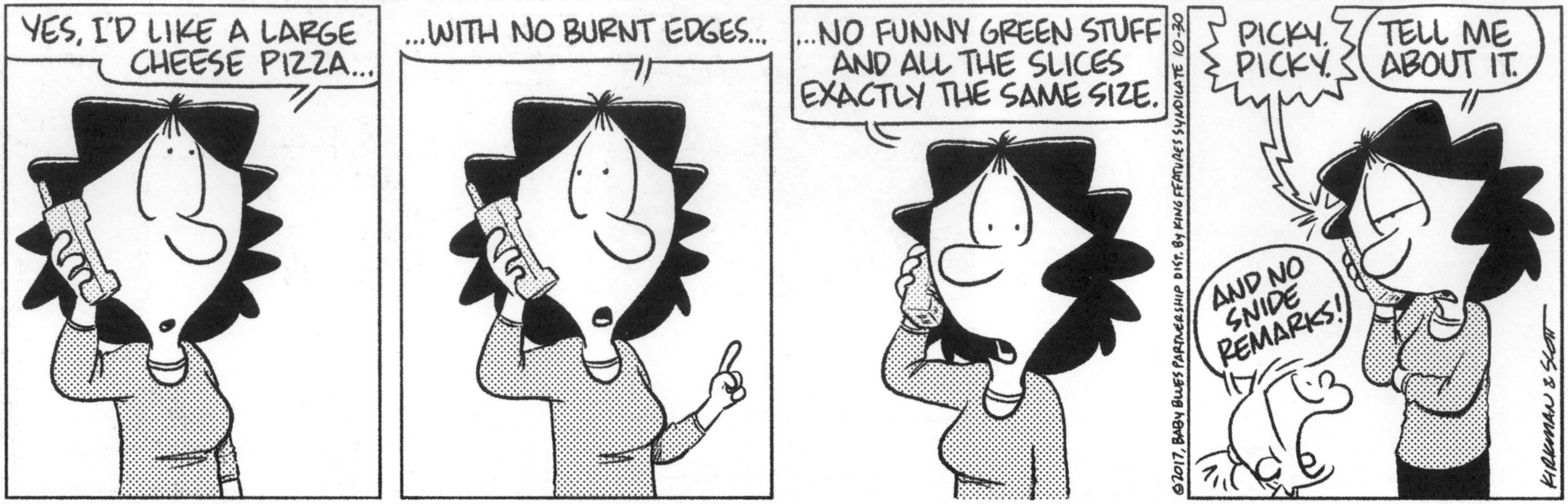
YES, I'D LIKE A LARGE CHEESE PIZZA...
...WITH NO BURNT EDGES...
...NO FUNNY GREEN STUFF AND ALL THE SLICES EXACTLY THE SAME SIZE.
PICKY, PICKY.
TELL ME ABOUT IT.
AND NO SNIDE REMARKS!
©2017, BABY BLUES PARTNERSHIP DIST. BY KING FEATURES SYNDICATE 10-30
KIRKMAN & SCOTT

Jerry: I wonder if pizza places get orders this specific.

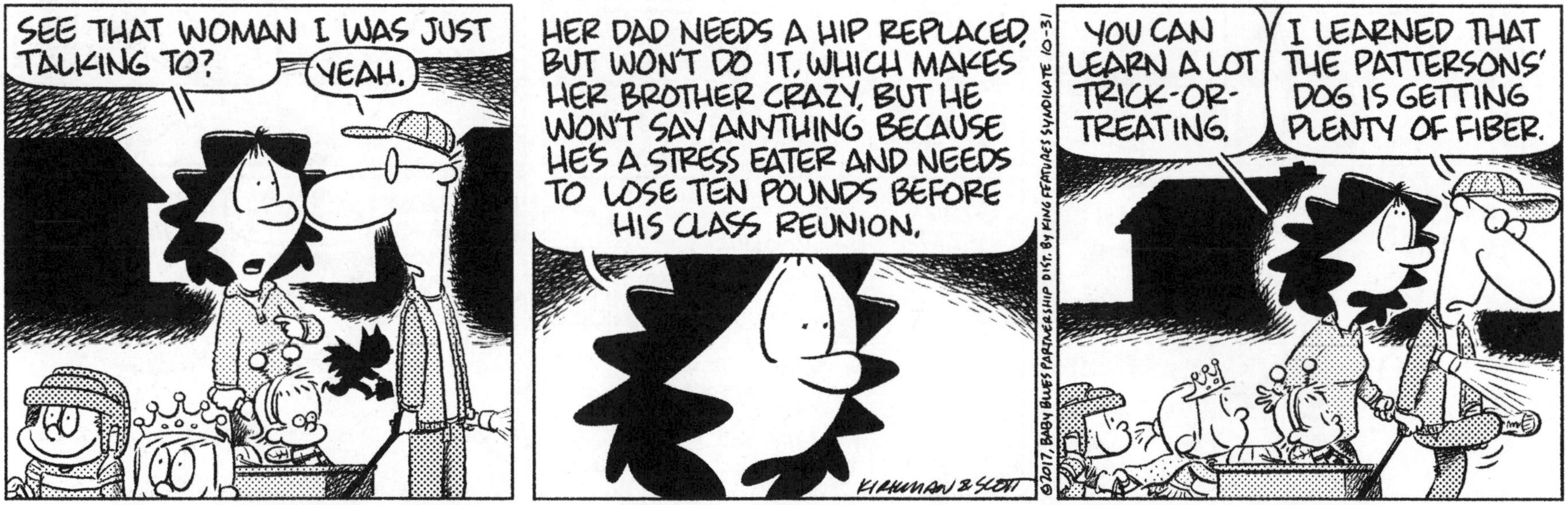
SEE THAT WOMAN I WAS JUST TALKING TO?
YEAH.
HER DAD NEEDS A HIP REPLACED, BUT WON'T DO IT, WHICH MAKES HER BROTHER CRAZY, BUT HE WON'T SAY ANYTHING BECAUSE HE'S A STRESS EATER AND NEEDS TO LOSE TEN POUNDS BEFORE HIS CLASS REUNION.
KIRKMAN & SCOTT
©2017, BABY BLUES PARTNERSHIP DIST. BY KING FEATURES SYNDICATE 10-31
YOU CAN LEARN A LOT TRICK-OR-TREATING.
I LEARNED THAT THE PATTERSONS' DOG IS GETTING PLENTY OF FIBER.

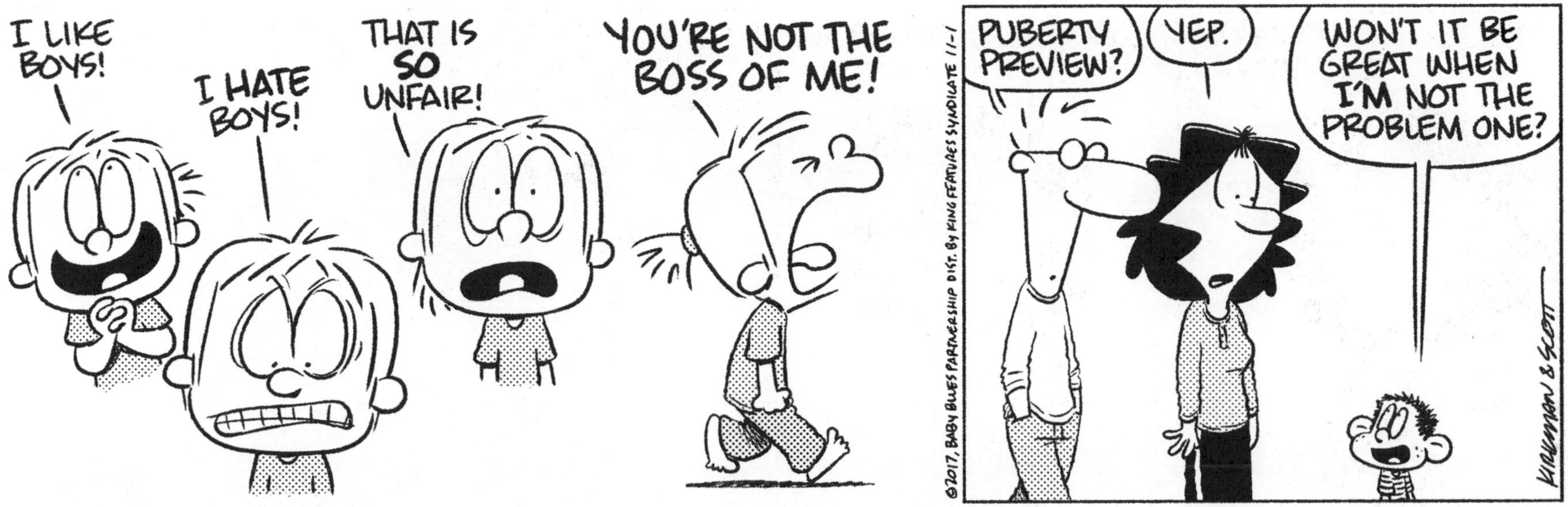
I LIKE BOYS!
I HATE BOYS!
THAT IS SO UNFAIR!
YOU'RE NOT THE BOSS OF ME!
PUBERTY PREVIEW?
YEP.
WON'T IT BE GREAT WHEN I'M NOT THE PROBLEM ONE?
©2017, BABY BLUES PARTNERSHIP DIST. BY KING FEATURES SYNDICATE 11-1
KIRKMAN & SCOTT

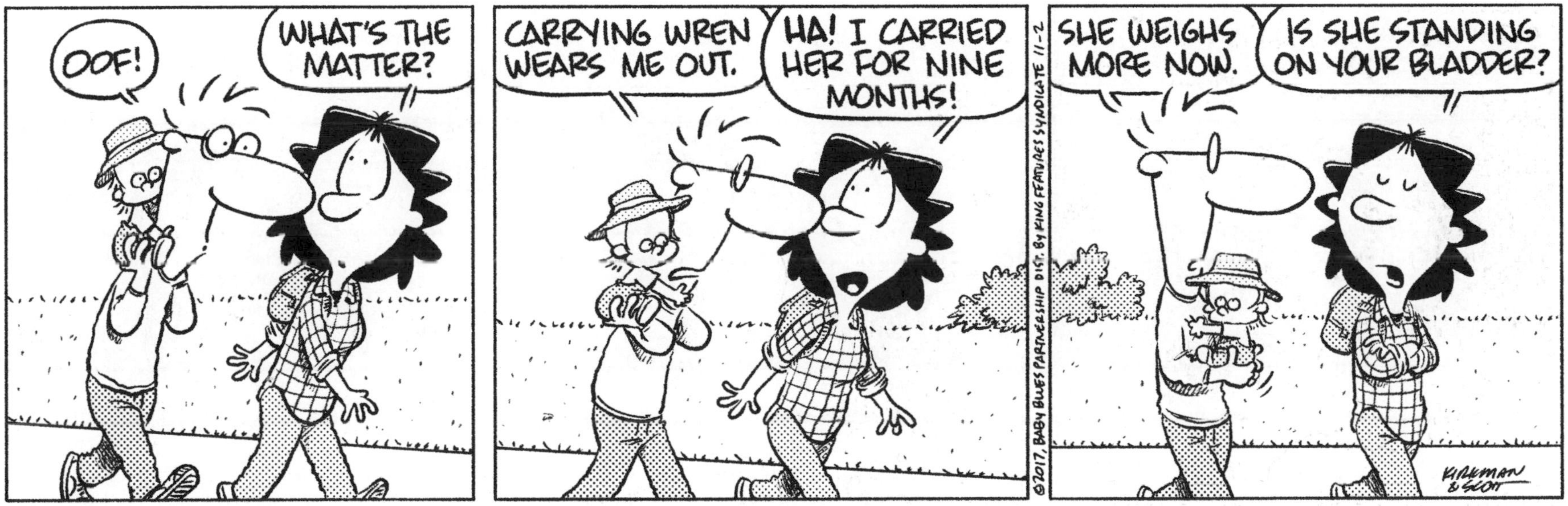
OOF!
WHAT'S THE MATTER?
CARRYING WREN WEARS ME OUT.
HA! I CARRIED HER FOR NINE MONTHS!
SHE WEIGHS MORE NOW.
IS SHE STANDING ON YOUR BLADDER?
©2017, BABY BLUES PARTNERSHIP DIST. BY KING FEATURES SYNDICATE 11-2
KIRKMAN & SCOTT

Rick: Darryl should know better.

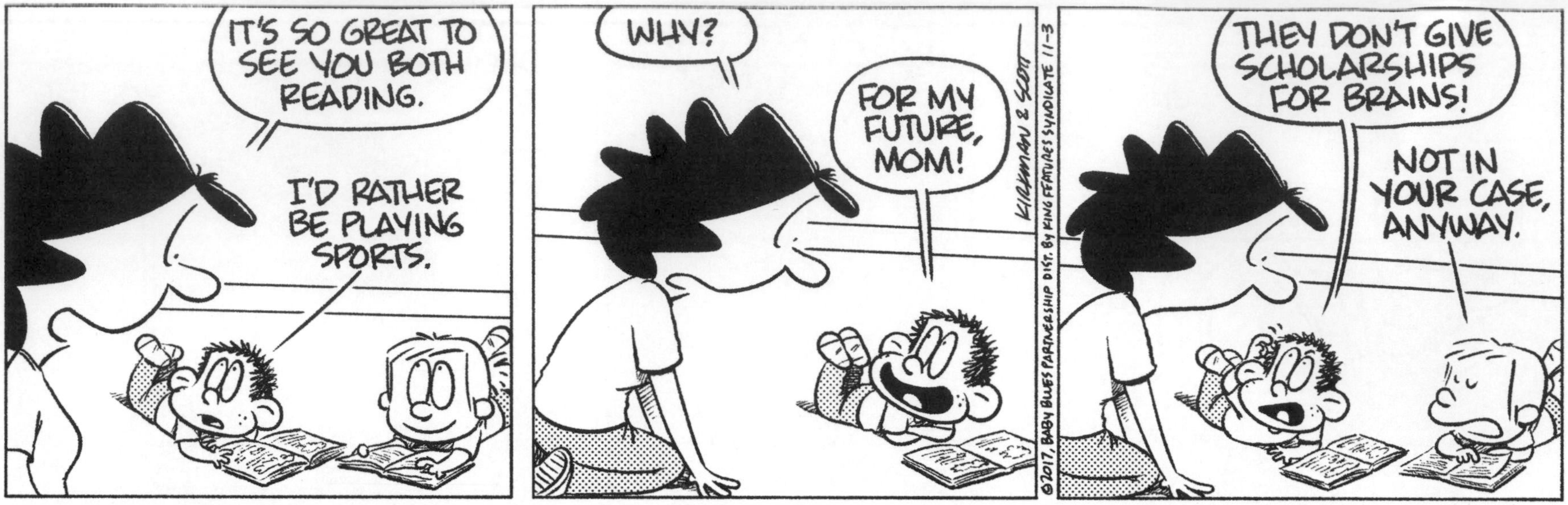
IT'S SO GREAT TO SEE YOU BOTH READING.
I'D RATHER BE PLAYING SPORTS.
WHY?
FOR MY FUTURE, MOM!
KIRKMAN & SCOTT
©2017, BABY BLUES PARTNERSHIP DIST. BY KING FEATURES SYNDICATE 11-3
THEY DON'T GIVE SCHOLARSHIPS FOR BRAINS!
NOT IN YOUR CASE, ANYWAY.

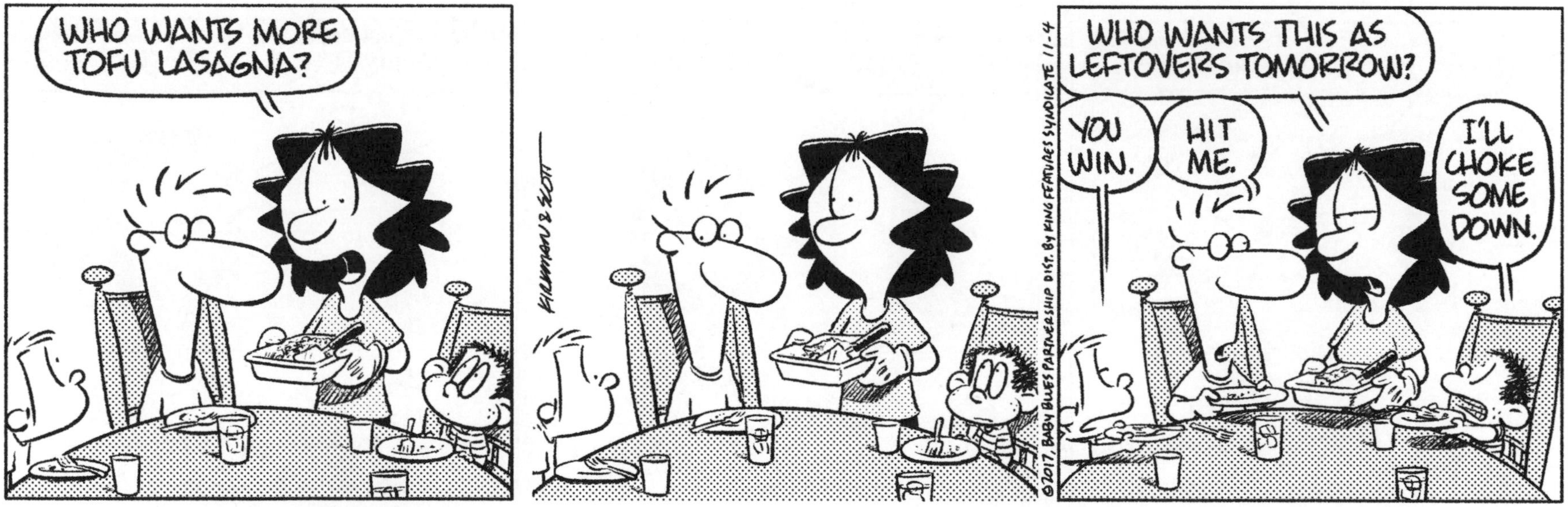
WHO WANTS MORE TOFU LASAGNA?
KIRKMAN & SCOTT
©2017, BABY BLUES PARTNERSHIP DIST. BY KING FEATURES SYNDICATE 11-4
WHO WANTS THIS AS LEFTOVERS TOMORROW?
YOU WIN.
HIT ME.
I'LL CHOKE SOME DOWN.

Jerry: Lasagna should never be weaponized.

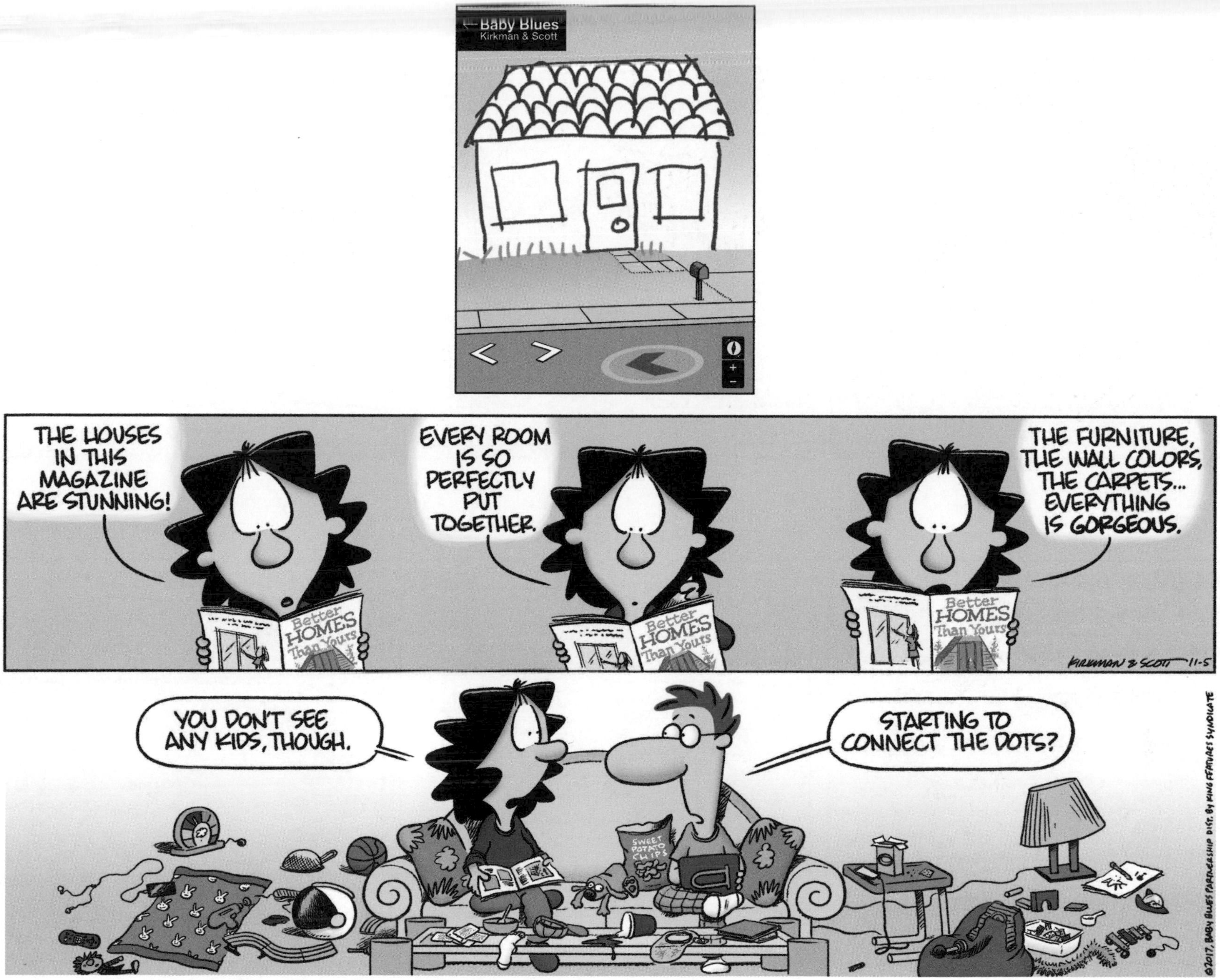

Baby Blues
Kirkman & Scott
THE HOUSES IN THIS MAGAZINE ARE STUNNING!
Better HOMES Than Yours
EVERY ROOM IS SO PERFECTLY PUT TOGETHER.
THE FURNITURE, THE WALL COLORS, THE CARPETS... EVERYTHING IS GORGEOUS.
KIRKMAN & SCOTT 11-5
YOU DON'T SEE ANY KIDS, THOUGH.
STARTING TO CONNECT THE DOTS?
SWEET POTATO CHIPS
©2017, BABY BLUES PARTNERSHIP DIST. BY KING FEATURES SYNDICATE

Rick: A bunch of time wasted here simulating Google Maps Street View. My favorite part, though, is Jerry's magazine name, *Better Homes Than Yours*. I can think of a few magazines that should change their names to that.

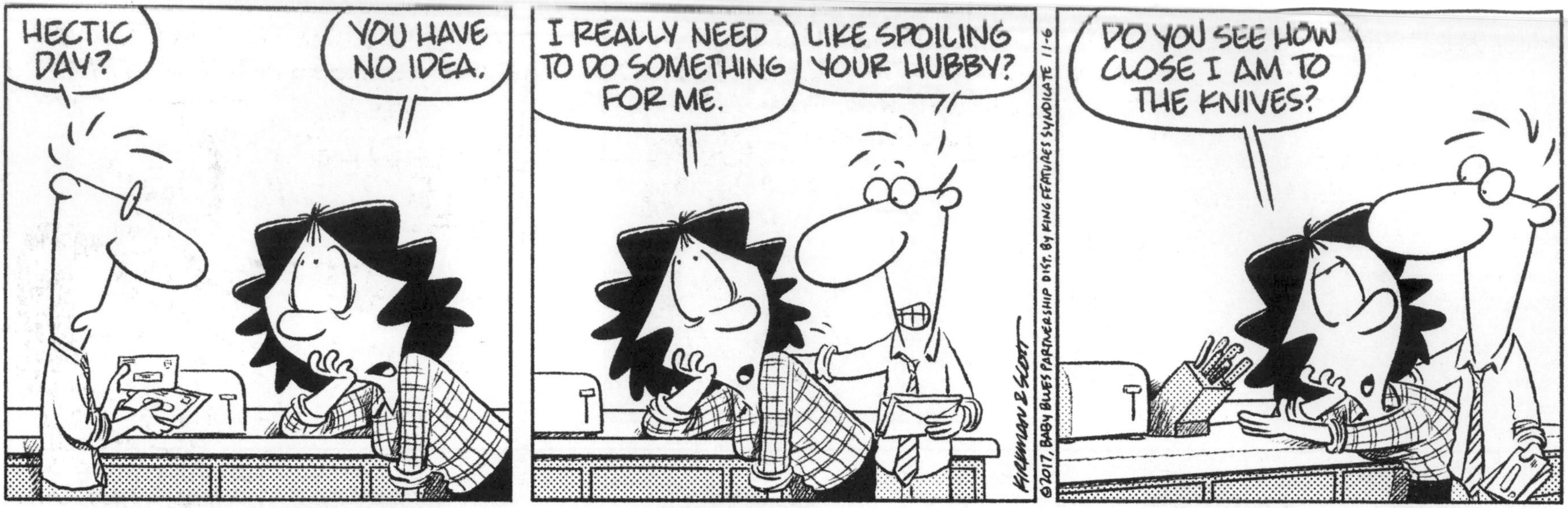
HECTIC DAY?
YOU HAVE NO IDEA.
I REALLY NEED TO DO SOMETHING FOR ME.
LIKE SPOILING YOUR HUBBY?
©2017, BABY BLUES PARTNERSHIP DIST. BY KING FEATURES SYNDICATE 11-6
KIRKMAN & SCOTT
DO YOU SEE HOW CLOSE I AM TO THE KNIVES?

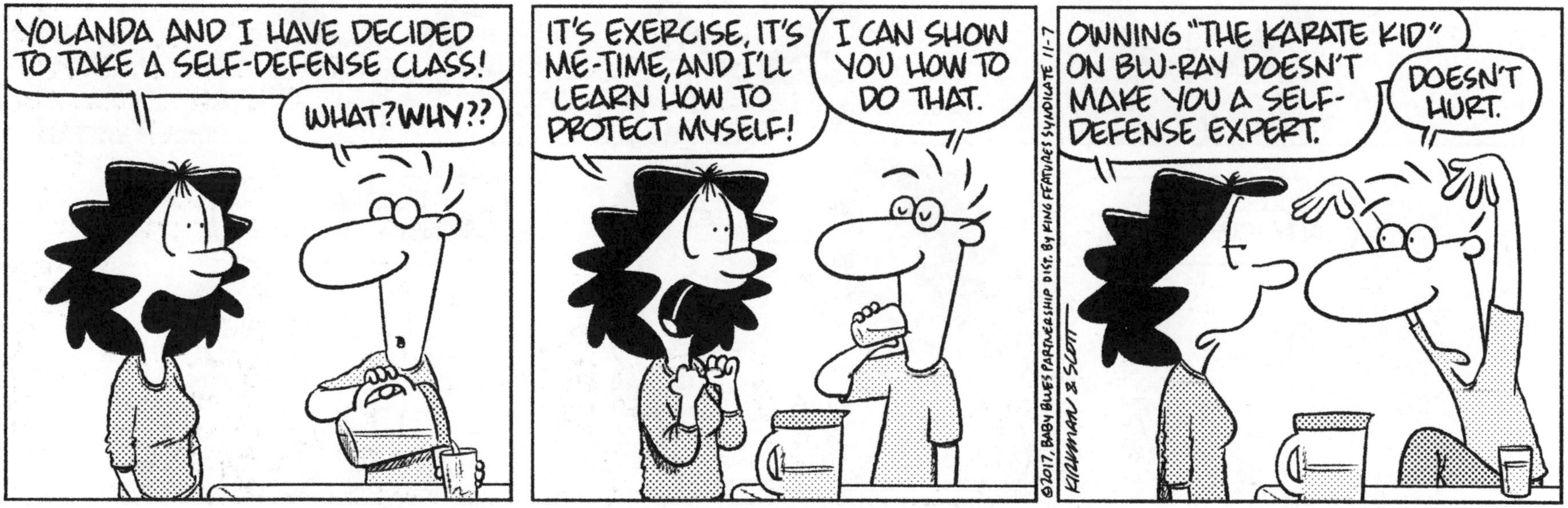
YOLANDA AND I HAVE DECIDED TO TAKE A SELF-DEFENSE CLASS!
WHAT? WHY??
IT'S EXERCISE, IT'S ME-TIME, AND I'LL LEARN HOW TO PROTECT MYSELF!
I CAN SHOW YOU HOW TO DO THAT.
©2017, BABY BLUES PARTNERSHIP DIST. BY KING FEATURES SYNDICATE 11-7
KIRKMAN & SCOTT
OWNING "THE KARATE KID" ON BLU-RAY DOESN'T MAKE YOU A SELF-DEFENSE EXPERT.
DOESN'T HURT.

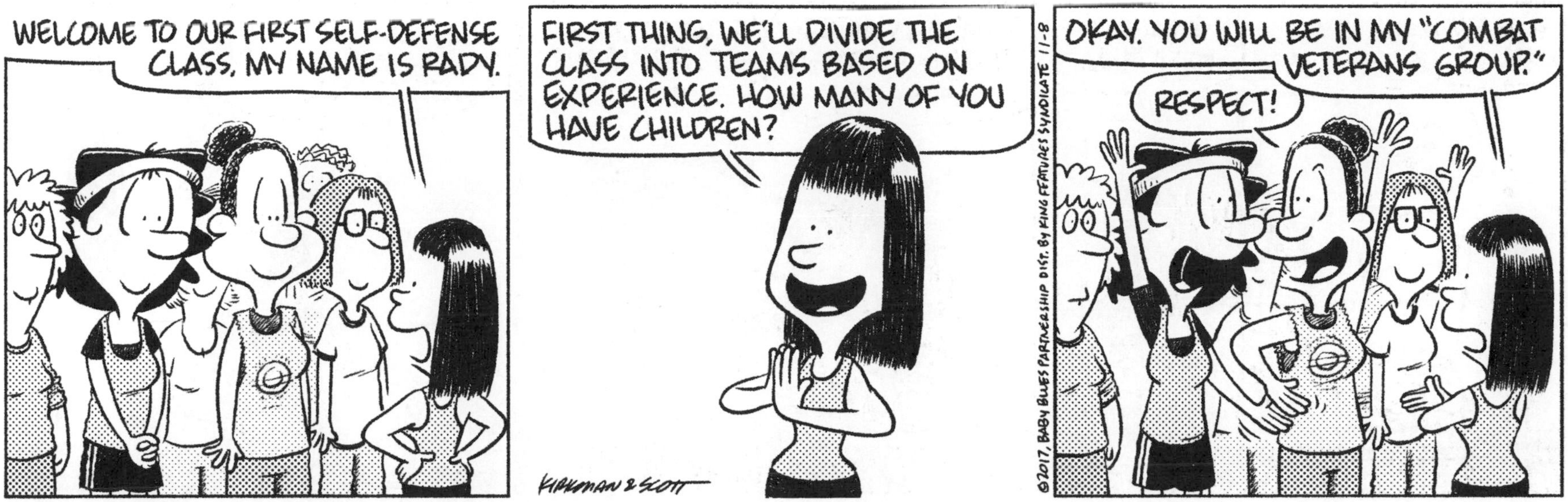
WELCOME TO OUR FIRST SELF-DEFENSE CLASS. MY NAME IS RADY.
FIRST THING, WE'LL DIVIDE THE CLASS INTO TEAMS BASED ON EXPERIENCE. HOW MANY OF YOU HAVE CHILDREN?
KIRKMAN & SCOTT
©2017, BABY BLUES PARTNERSHIP DIST. BY KING FEATURES SYNDICATE 11-8
OKAY. YOU WILL BE IN MY "COMBAT VETERANS GROUP."
RESPECT!

Jerry: Anybody who can get kids fed, bathed, and off to school five days a week is no wimp.

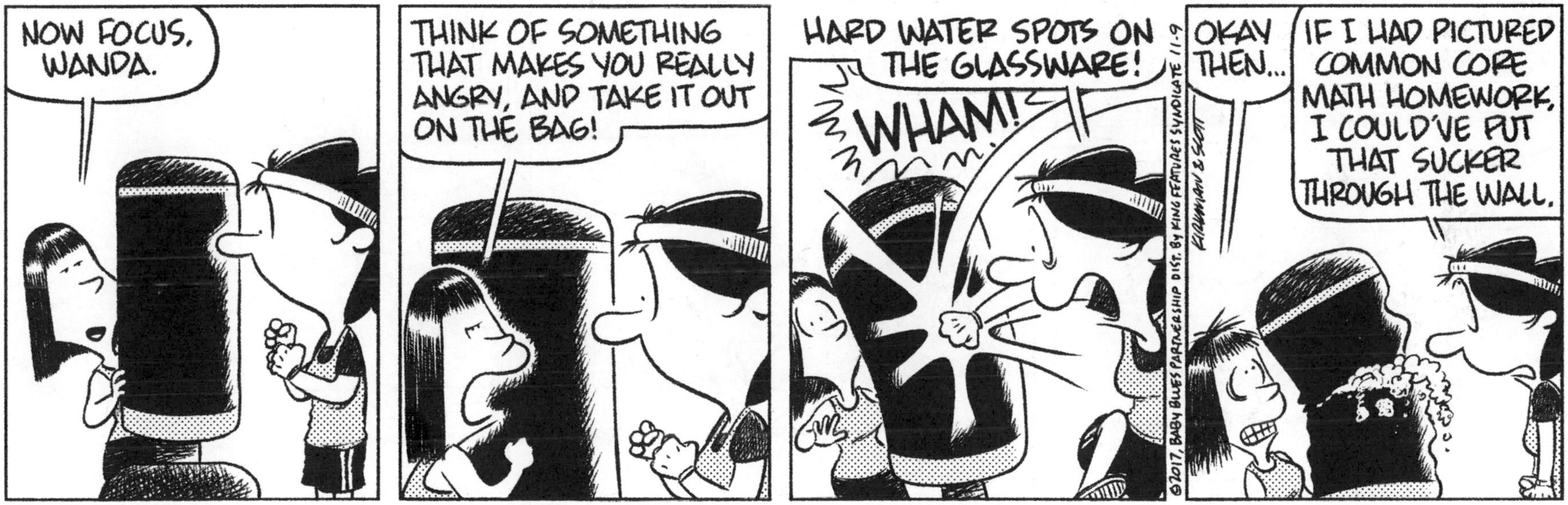
NOW FOCUS, WANDA.
THINK OF SOMETHING THAT MAKES YOU REALLY ANGRY, AND TAKE IT OUT ON THE BAG!
HARD WATER SPOTS ON THE GLASSWARE!
WHAM!
©2017, BABY BLUES PARTNERSHIP DIST. BY KING FEATURES SYNDICATE 11-9
KIRKMAN & SCOTT
OKAY THEN...
IF I HAD PICTURED COMMON CORE MATH HOMEWORK, I COULD'VE PUT THAT SUCKER THROUGH THE WALL.

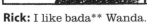

Rick: I like bada** Wanda.

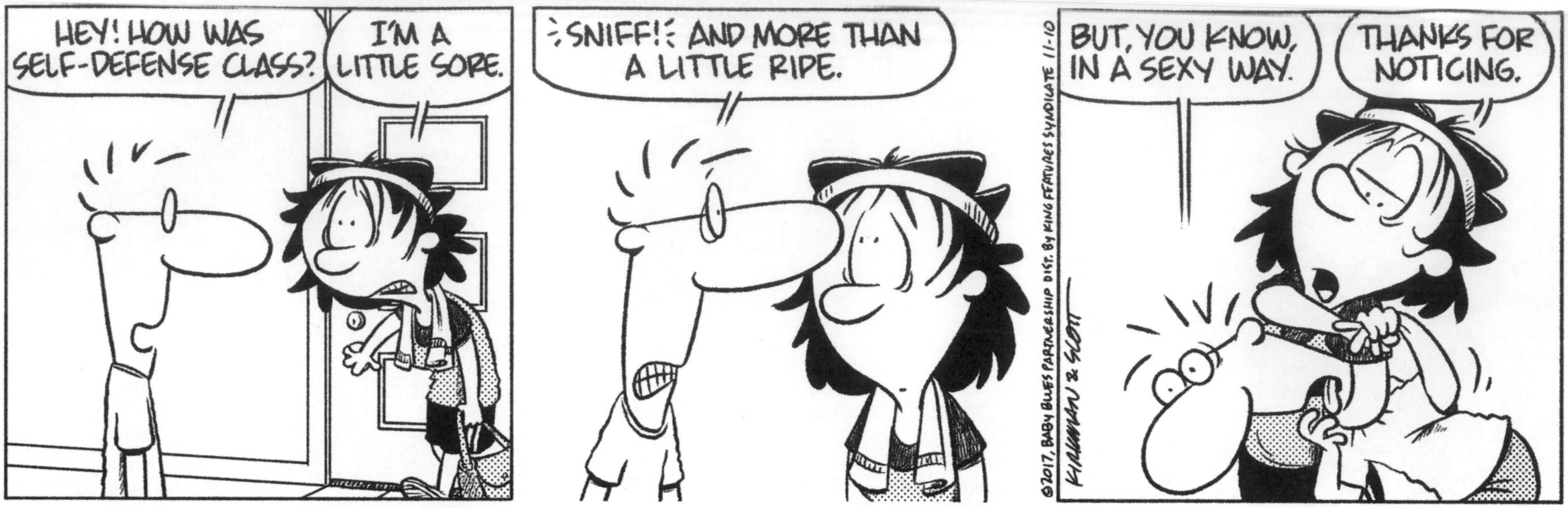
HEY! HOW WAS SELF-DEFENSE CLASS?
I'M A LITTLE SORE.
SNIFF! AND MORE THAN A LITTLE RIPE.
©2017, BABY BLUES PARTNERSHIP DIST. BY KING FEATURES SYNDICATE 11-10
KIRKMAN & SCOTT
BUT, YOU KNOW, IN A SEXY WAY.
THANKS FOR NOTICING.

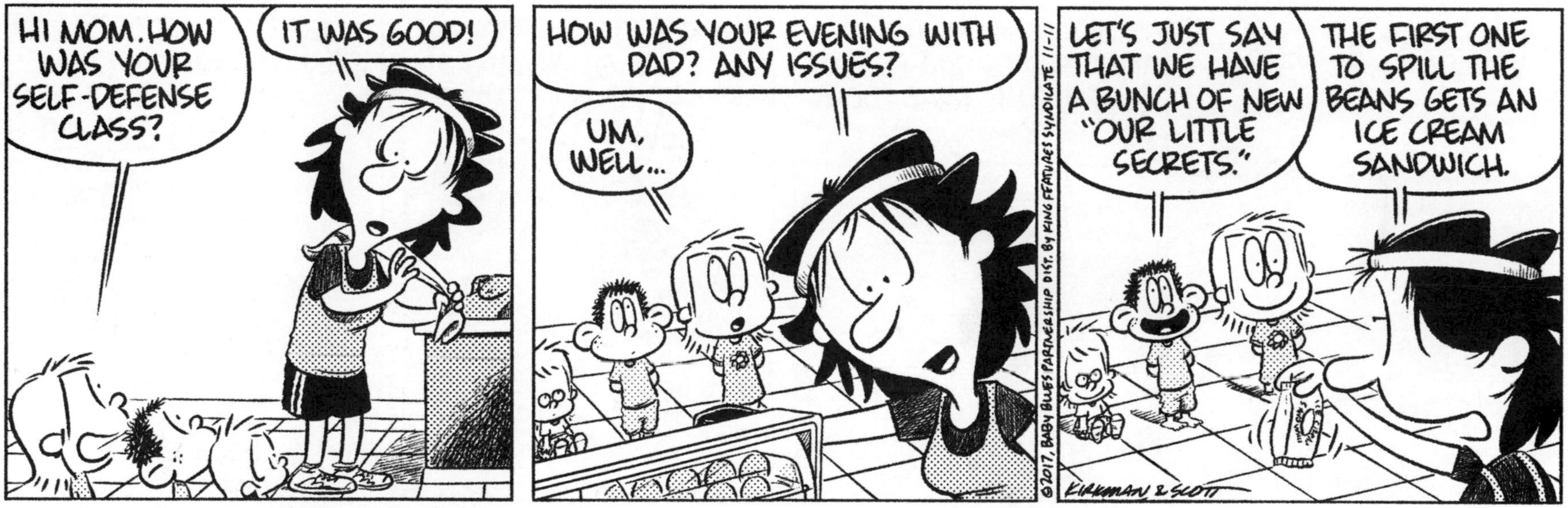
HI MOM. HOW WAS YOUR SELF-DEFENSE CLASS?
IT WAS GOOD!
HOW WAS YOUR EVENING WITH DAD? ANY ISSUES?
UM, WELL...
©2017, BABY BLUES PARTNERSHIP DIST. BY KING FEATURES SYNDICATE 11-11
LET'S JUST SAY THAT WE HAVE A BUNCH OF NEW "OUR LITTLE SECRETS."
THE FIRST ONE TO SPILL THE BEANS GETS AN ICE CREAM SANDWICH.
KIRKMAN & SCOTT

Jerry: Ice cream: the ultimate truth serum.

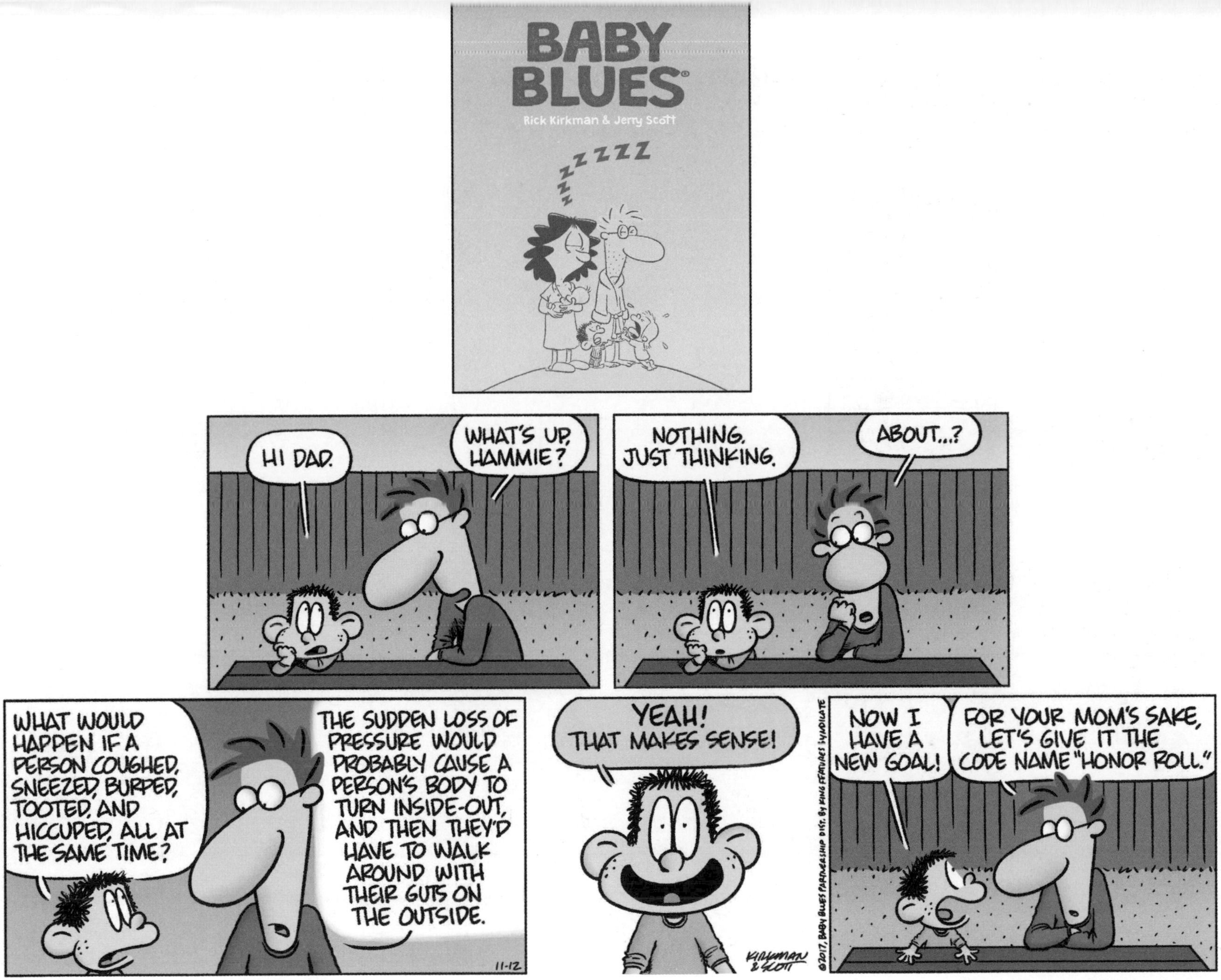

BABY BLUES®
Rick Kirkman & Jerry Scott
ZZZZZZZ
HI DAD.
WHAT'S UP, HAMMIE?
NOTHING. JUST THINKING.
ABOUT...?
WHAT WOULD HAPPEN IF A PERSON COUGHED, SNEEZED, BURPED, TOOTED, AND HICCUPED, ALL AT THE SAME TIME?
THE SUDDEN LOSS OF PRESSURE WOULD PROBABLY CAUSE A PERSON'S BODY TO TURN INSIDE-OUT, AND THEN THEY'D HAVE TO WALK AROUND WITH THEIR GUTS ON THE OUTSIDE.
11-12
YEAH! THAT MAKES SENSE!
KIRKMAN & SCOTT
©2017, BABY BLUES PARTNERSHIP DIST. BY KING FEATURES SYNDICATE
NOW I HAVE A NEW GOAL!
FOR YOUR MOM'S SAKE, LET'S GIVE IT THE CODE NAME "HONOR ROLL."

Rick: Great dad explanation.

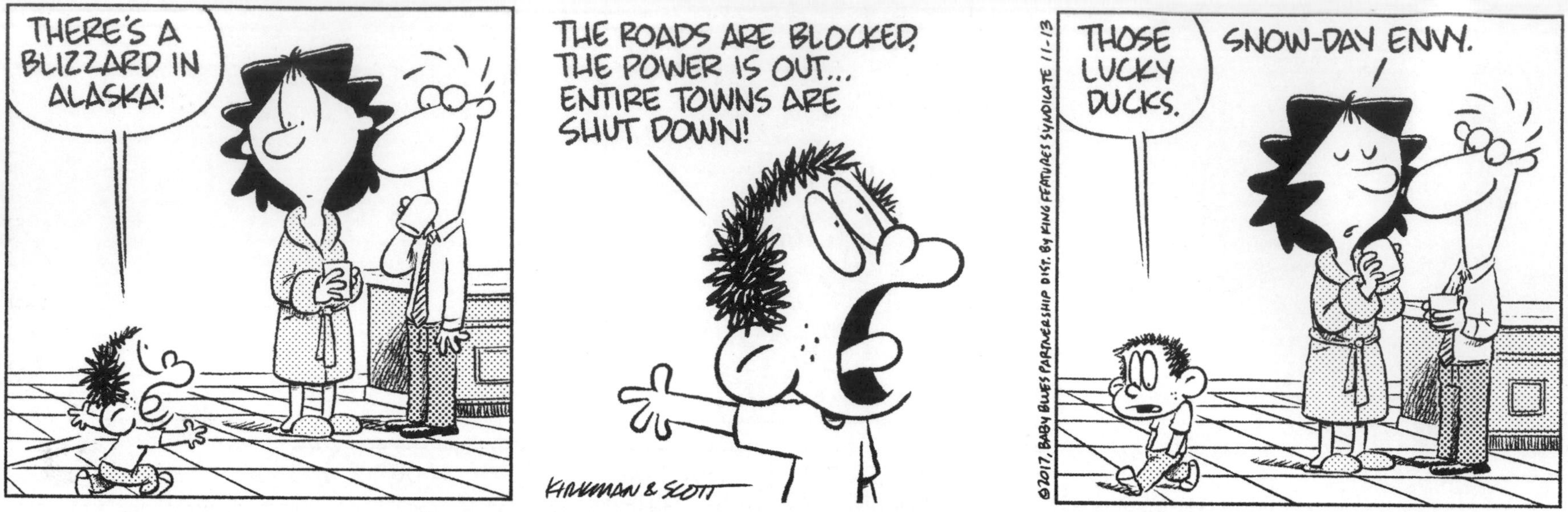
THERE'S A BLIZZARD IN ALASKA!
THE ROADS ARE BLOCKED, THE POWER IS OUT... ENTIRE TOWNS ARE SHUT DOWN!
KIRKMAN & SCOTT
©2017, BABY BLUES PARTNERSHIP DIST. BY KING FEATURES SYNDICATE 11-13
THOSE LUCKY DUCKS.
SNOW-DAY ENVY.

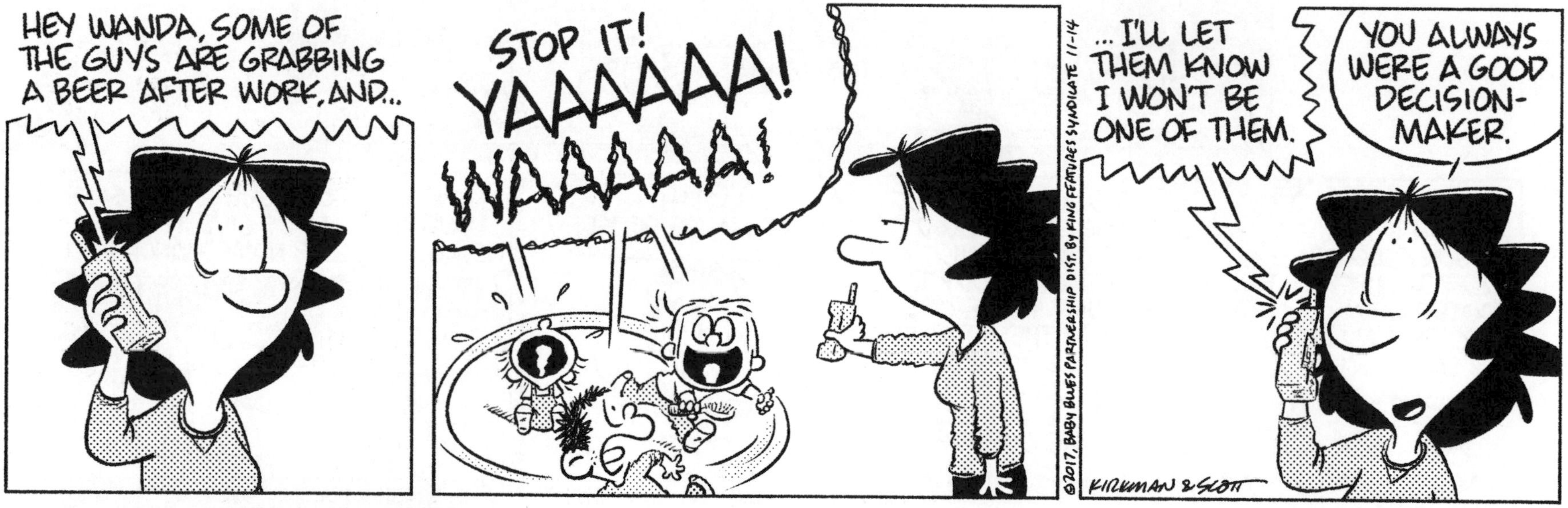
HEY WANDA, SOME OF THE GUYS ARE GRABBING A BEER AFTER WORK, AND...
STOP IT!
YAAAAAA!
WAAAAAA!
©2017, BABY BLUES PARTNERSHIP DIST. BY KING FEATURES SYNDICATE 11-14
... I'LL LET THEM KNOW I WON'T BE ONE OF THEM.
YOU ALWAYS WERE A GOOD DECISION-MAKER.
KIRKMAN & SCOTT

Rick: Darryl has an excellent turning radius.

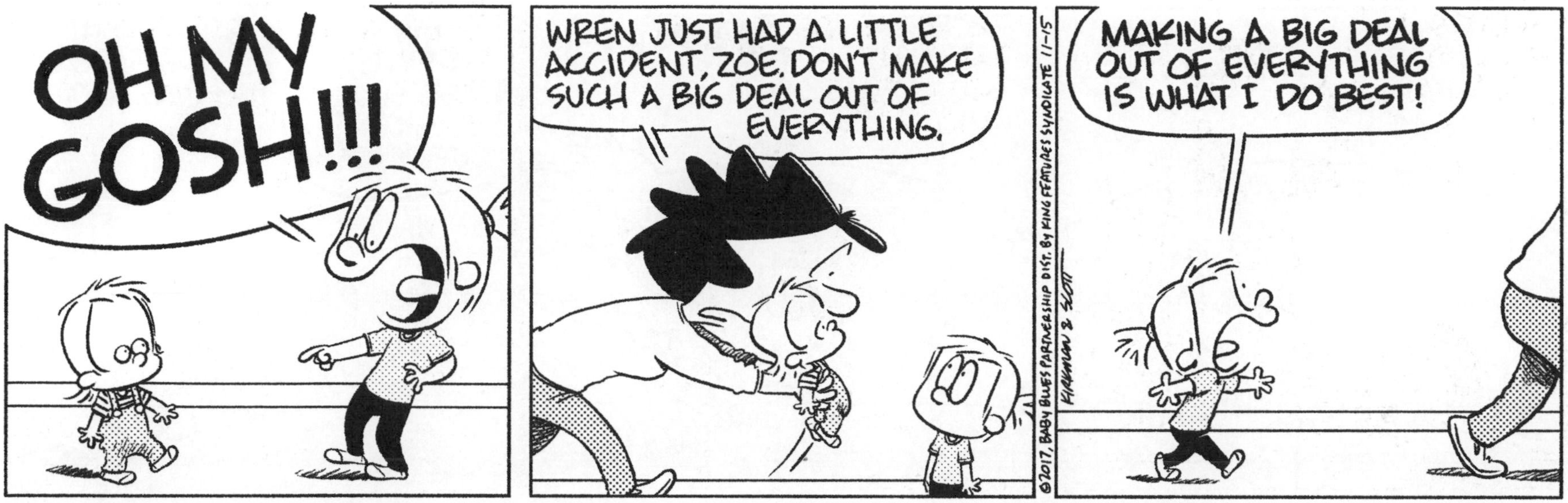
OH MY GOSH!!!
WREN JUST HAD A LITTLE ACCIDENT, ZOE. DON'T MAKE SUCH A BIG DEAL OUT OF EVERYTHING.
EVERYTHING.
MAKING A BIG DEAL OUT OF EVERYTHING IS WHAT I DO BEST!
©2017, BABY BLUES PARTNERSHIP DIST. BY KING FEATURES SYNDICATE 11-15
KIRKMAN & SCOTT

Jerry: Right. Go with your strengths.

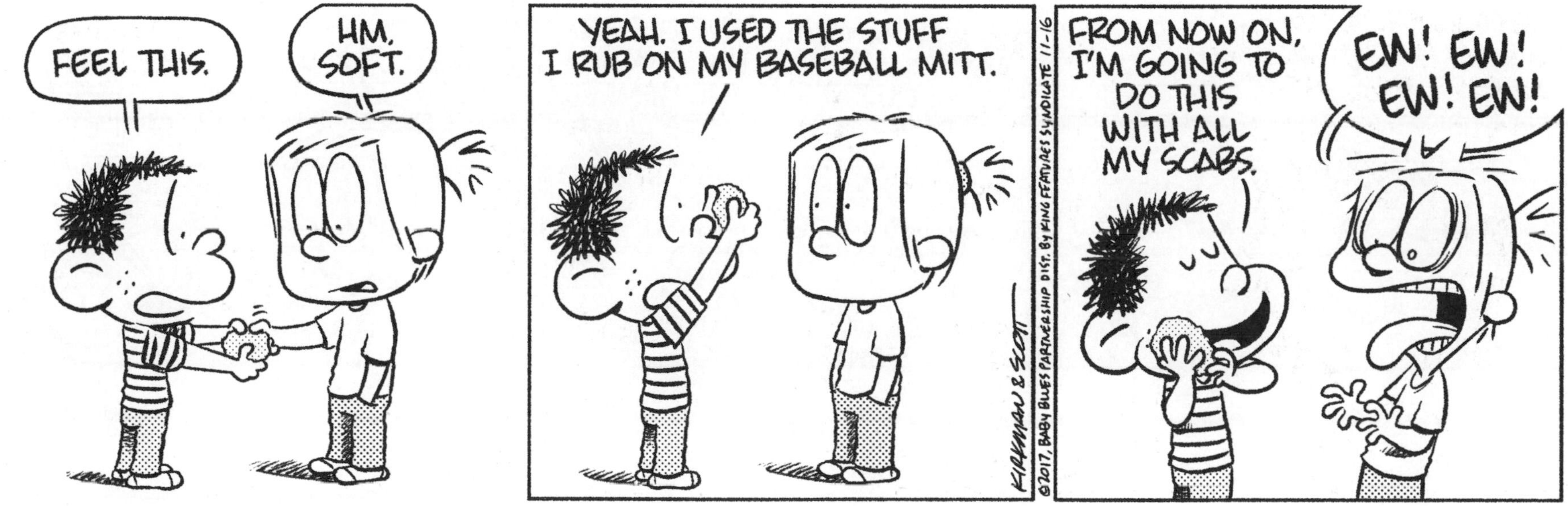
FEEL THIS.
HM. SOFT.
YEAH. I USED THE STUFF I RUB ON MY BASEBALL MITT.
FROM NOW ON, I'M GOING TO DO THIS WITH ALL MY SCABS.
EW! EW! EW! EW!
©2017, BABY BLUES PARTNERSHIP DIST. BY KING FEATURES SYNDICATE 11-16
KIRKMAN & SCOTT

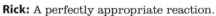

Rick: A perfectly appropriate reaction.

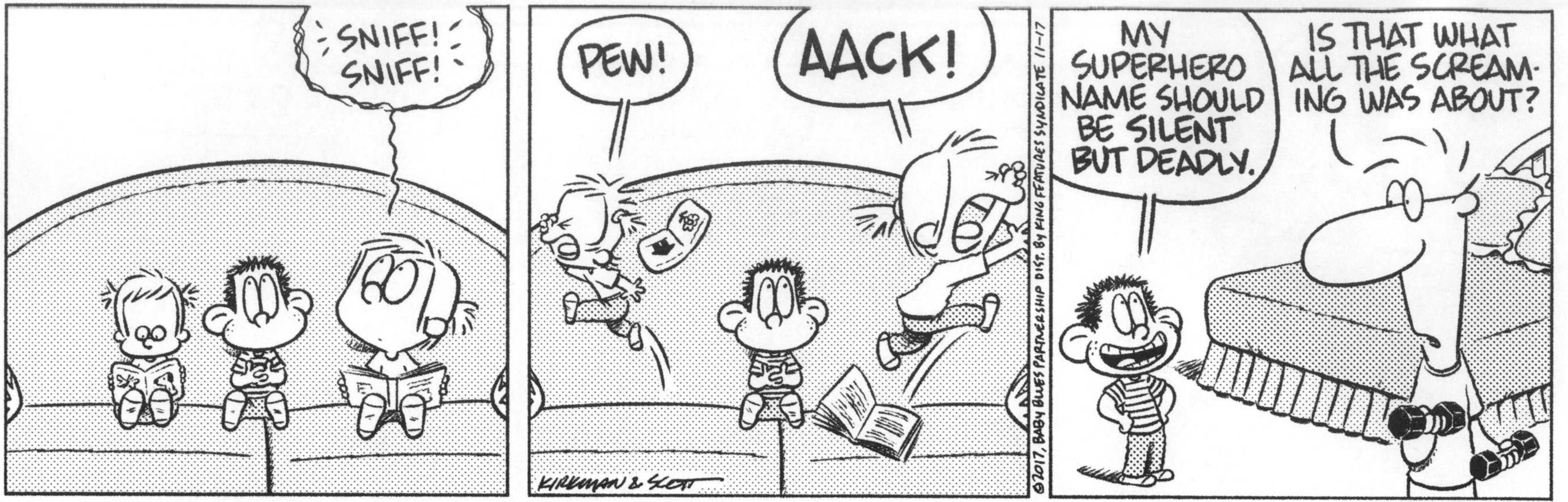

SNIFF! SNIFF!
PEW!
AACK!
KIRKMAN & SCOTT
©2017, BABY BLUES PARTNERSHIP DIST. BY KING FEATURES SYNDICATE 11-17
MY SUPERHERO NAME SHOULD BE SILENT BUT DEADLY.
IS THAT WHAT ALL THE SCREAMING WAS ABOUT?

Rick: That's one superhero costume I don't need to see.

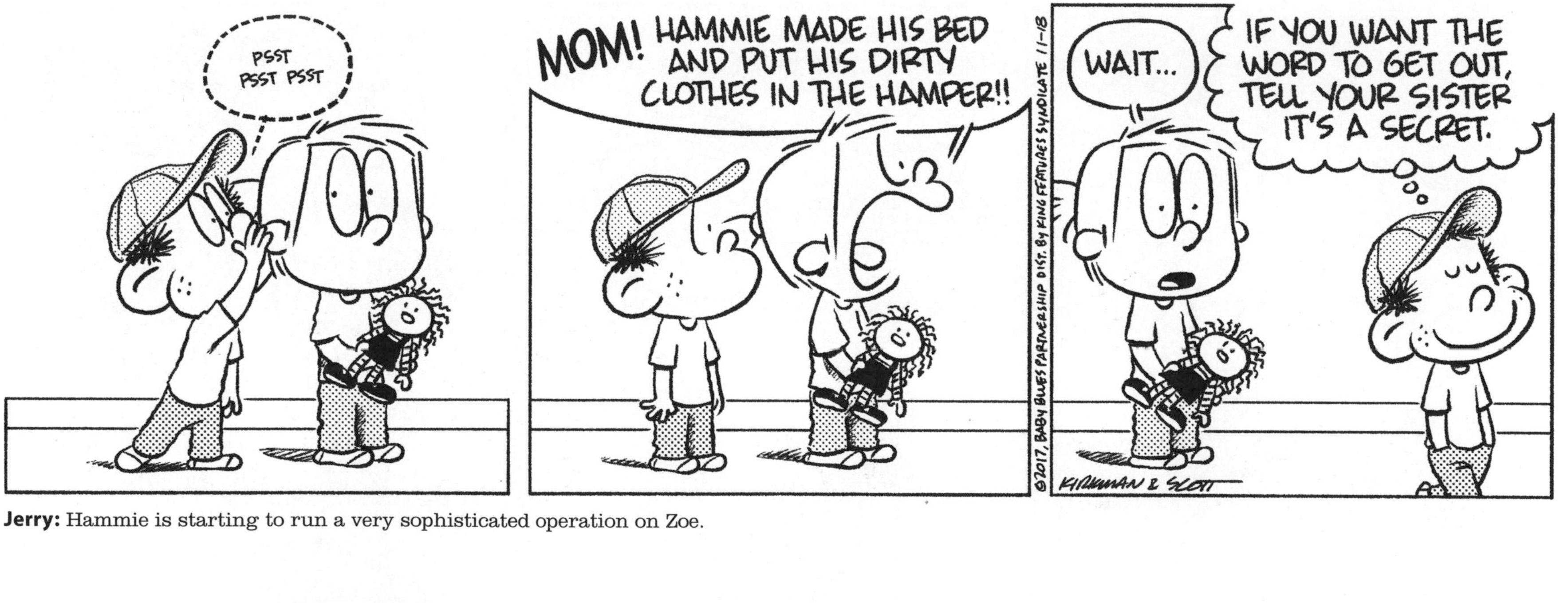

PSST PSST PSST
MOM! HAMMIE MADE HIS BED AND PUT HIS DIRTY CLOTHES IN THE HAMPER!!
©2017, BABY BLUES PARTNERSHIP DIST. BY KING FEATURES SYNDICATE 11-18
WAIT...
IF YOU WANT THE WORD TO GET OUT, TELL YOUR SISTER IT'S A SECRET.
KIRKMAN & SCOTT

Jerry: Hammie is starting to run a very sophisticated operation on Zoe.

BABY BLUES
Rick Kirkman & Jerry Scott
ZZZZZZZZ

SLURP!
YOU STILL DON'T REMEMBER WHERE YOU LEFT MY PHONE??
I EVEN RETRACED MY STEPS, LIKE YOU SAID!
©2017, BABY BLUES PARTNERSHIP DIST. BY KING FEATURES SYNDICATE
KIRKMAN & SCOTT

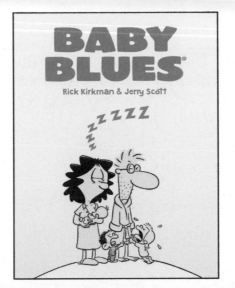

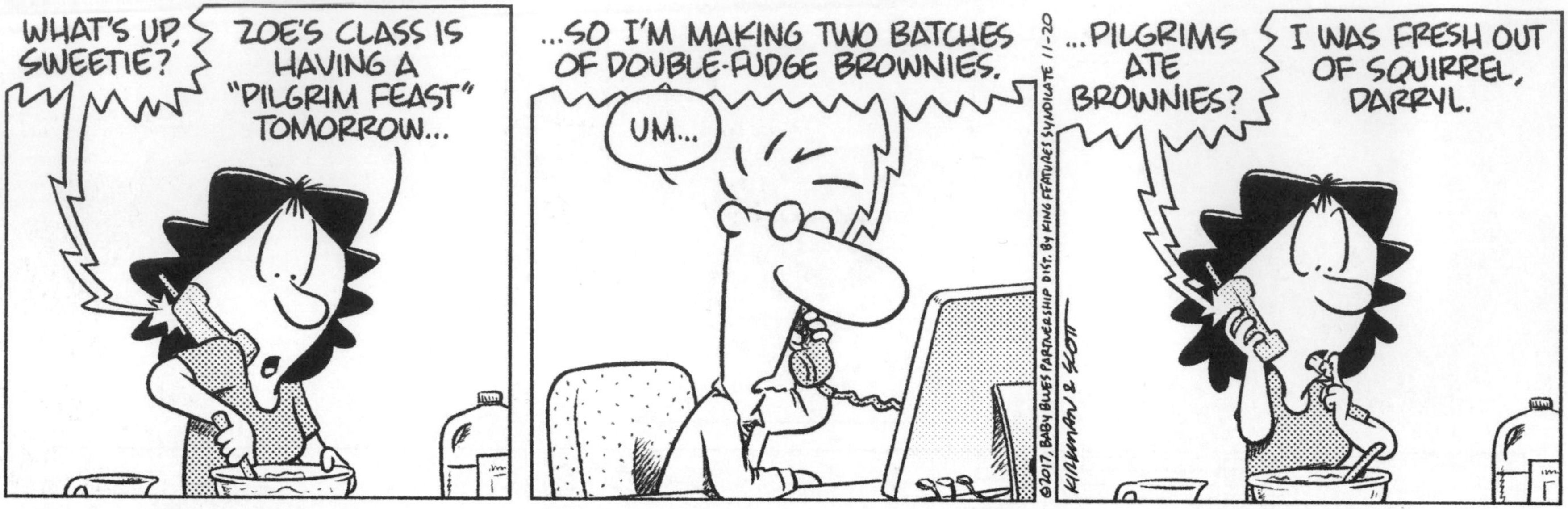
WHAT'S UP, SWEETIE?
ZOE'S CLASS IS HAVING A "PILGRIM FEAST" TOMORROW...
...SO I'M MAKING TWO BATCHES OF DOUBLE-FUDGE BROWNIES.
UM...
©2017, BABY BLUES PARTNERSHIP DIST. BY KING FEATURES SYNDICATE 11-20
KIRKMAN & SCOTT
...PILGRIMS ATE BROWNIES?
I WAS FRESH OUT OF SQUIRREL, DARRYL.

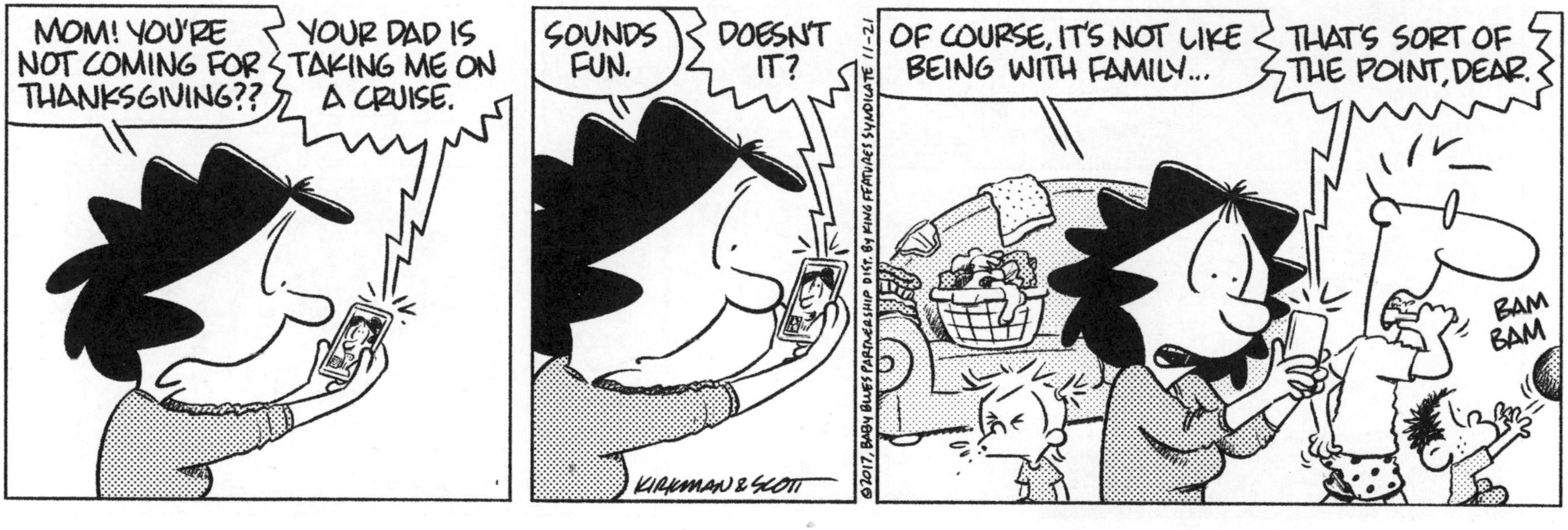
MOM! YOU'RE NOT COMING FOR THANKSGIVING??
YOUR DAD IS TAKING ME ON A CRUISE.
SOUNDS FUN.
DOESN'T IT?
KIRKMAN & SCOTT
©2017, BABY BLUES PARTNERSHIP DIST. BY KING FEATURES SYNDICATE 11-21
OF COURSE, IT'S NOT LIKE BEING WITH FAMILY...
THAT'S SORT OF THE POINT, DEAR.
BAM BAM

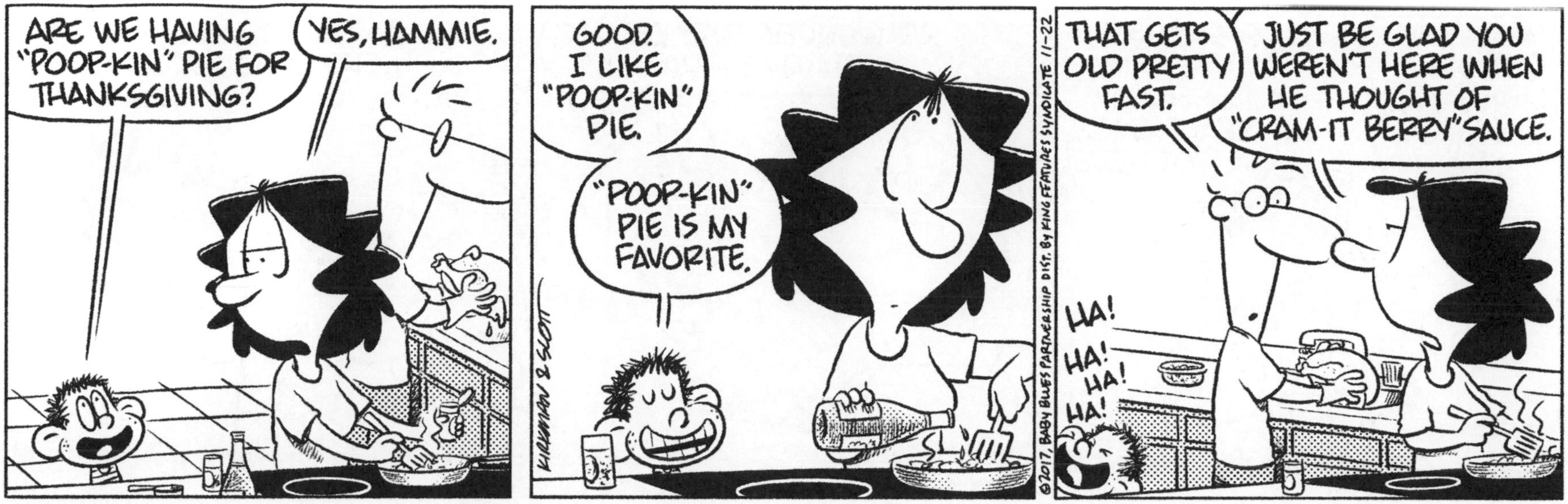
ARE WE HAVING "POOP-KIN" PIE FOR THANKSGIVING?
YES, HAMMIE.
KIRKMAN & SCOTT
GOOD. I LIKE "POOP-KIN" PIE.
"POOP-KIN" PIE IS MY FAVORITE.
©2017, BABY BLUES PARTNERSHIP DIST. BY KING FEATURES SYNDICATE 11-22
THAT GETS OLD PRETTY FAST.
JUST BE GLAD YOU WEREN'T HERE WHEN HE THOUGHT OF "CRAM-IT BERRY" SAUCE.
HA! HA! HA! HA!

Jerry: Reminiscent of my early joke-writing days.

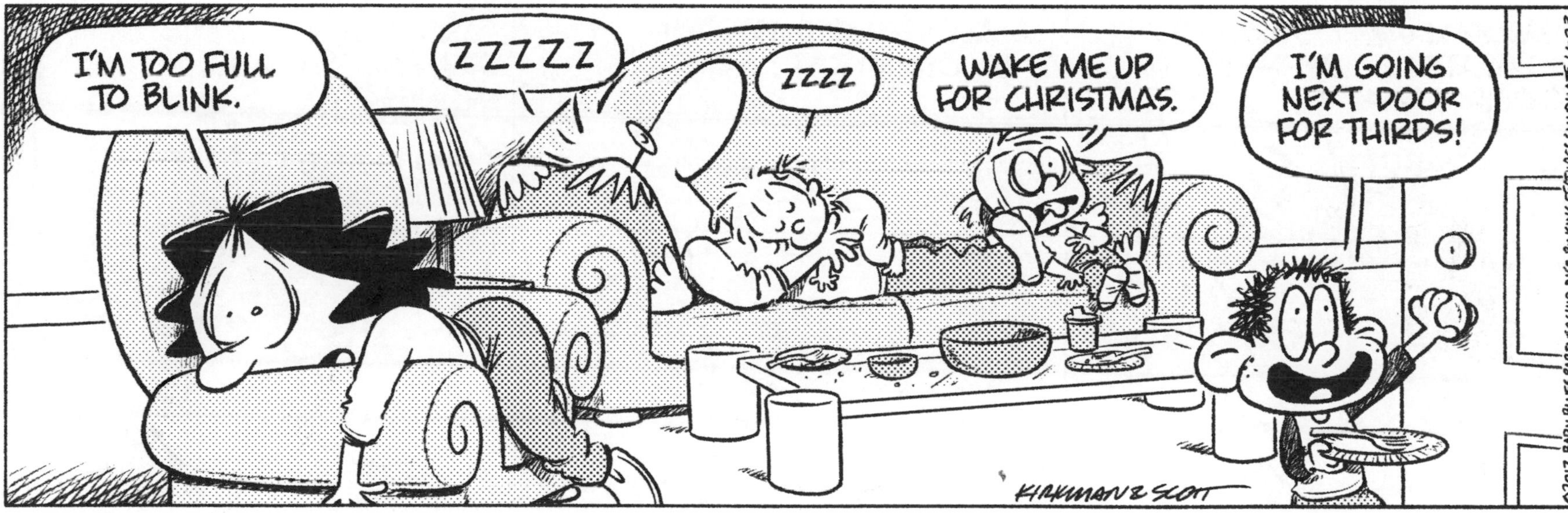
I'M TOO FULL TO BLINK.
ZZZZZ
ZZZZ
WAKE ME UP FOR CHRISTMAS.
I'M GOING NEXT DOOR FOR THIRDS!
KIRKMAN & SCOTT
©2017, BABY BLUES PARTNERSHIP DIST. BY KING FEATURES SYNDICATE 11-23

Rick: Another nominee for favorite gag of the year.

HOW'S IT GOING, DARRYL?
SHOVING, SCREAMING, GREED... IT'S PRACTICALLY A RIOT HERE!
©2017, BABY BLUES PARTNERSHIP DIST. BY KING FEATURES SYNDICATE 11-24
NO WONDER THEY CALL IT BLACK FRIDAY.
I'LL BE DONE SHOPPING SOON.
YAAAGH!
EEEEEEEK! AIAIAIAI!
KIRKMAN & SCOTT

DAD, CAN WE BUILD A HOCKEY RINK IN THE BACK YARD?
SURE!
ALL WE NEED IS SOME WOOD, A HOSE, A TARP...
KIRKMAN & SCOTT
©2017, BABY BLUES PARTNERSHIP DIST. BY KING FEATURES SYNDICATE 11-25
...AND A WAY TO MOVE OUR BACKYARD TO MINNESOTA.
YOU FIGURE THAT OUT. I'LL GET THE HOSE.

BABY BLUES®
Rick Kirkman & Jerry Scott
ZZZZZZ

WHATCHA' WATCHIN'?
FOOTBALL. DON'T TALK.
WHO'S PLAYING?
OUR FAVORITE TEAMS. SHHH.
IF THEY'RE BOTH YOUR FAVORITE TEAMS, WHO DO YOU WANT TO WIN?
DOESN'T MATTER.
QUIET.
WELL, IF IT DOESN'T MATTER WHO WINS, WHY BOTHER WATCHING IT?
©2017, BABY BLUES PARTNERSHIP DIST. BY KING FEATURES SYNDICATE
MEN AND SPORTS. PLEASE EXPLAIN.
TORTILLA CHIPS
SHH! IT'S THIRD AND GOAL...
KIRKMAN & SCOTT 11-26

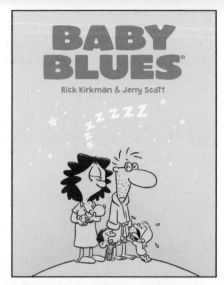

Rick: This originally had a less feministic last panel, but we made a course correction. In its revised version, it struck a chord with a lot of women.

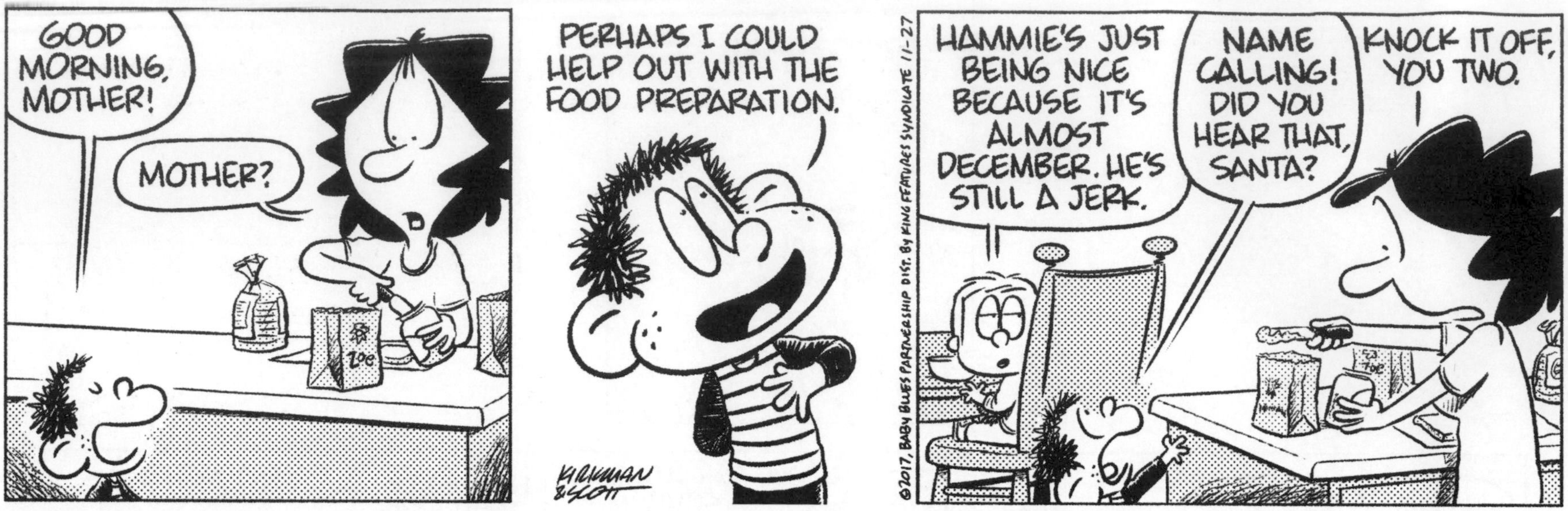
GOOD MORNING, MOTHER!
MOTHER?
PERHAPS I COULD HELP OUT WITH THE FOOD PREPARATION.
KIRKMAN & SCOTT
©2017, BABY BLUES PARTNERSHIP DIST. BY KING FEATURES SYNDICATE 11-27
HAMMIE'S JUST BEING NICE BECAUSE IT'S ALMOST DECEMBER. HE'S STILL A JERK.
NAME CALLING! DID YOU HEAR THAT, SANTA?
KNOCK IT OFF, YOU TWO.

Jerry: It's never too early to start sucking up to Santa.

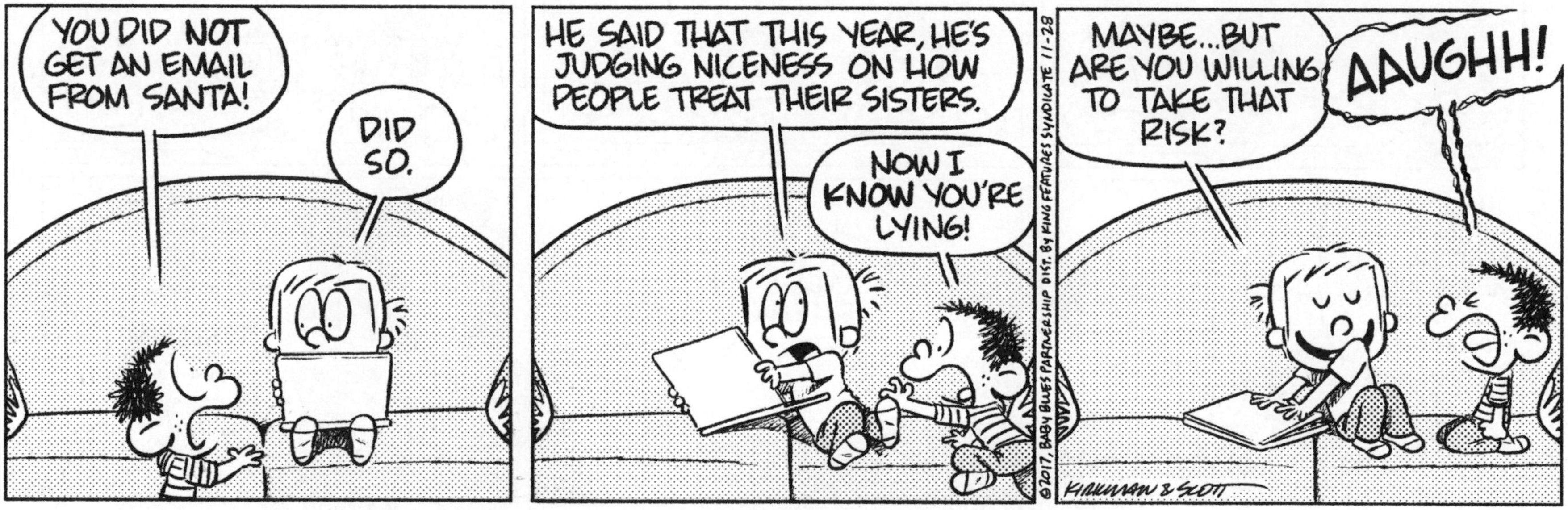
YOU DID NOT GET AN EMAIL FROM SANTA!
DID SO.
HE SAID THAT THIS YEAR, HE'S JUDGING NICENESS ON HOW PEOPLE TREAT THEIR SISTERS.
NOW I KNOW YOU'RE LYING!
©2017, BABY BLUES PARTNERSHIP DIST. BY KING FEATURES SYNDICATE 11-28
MAYBE...BUT ARE YOU WILLING TO TAKE THAT RISK?
AAUGHH!
KIRKMAN & SCOTT

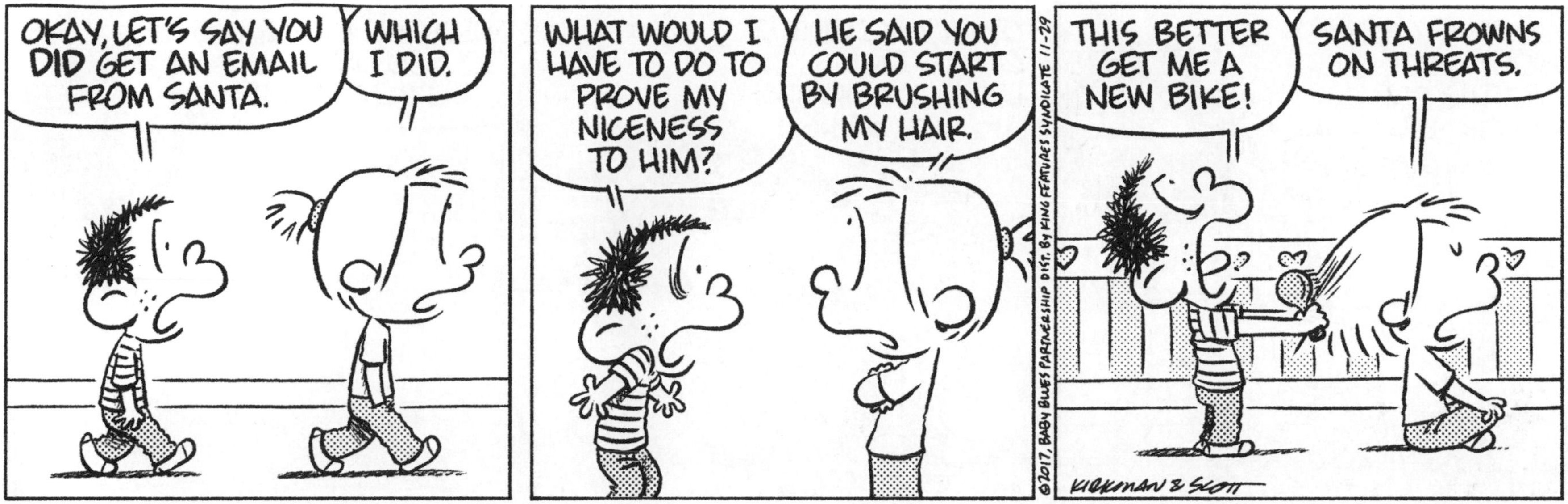
OKAY, LET'S SAY YOU DID GET AN EMAIL FROM SANTA.
WHICH I DID.
WHAT WOULD I HAVE TO DO TO PROVE MY NICENESS TO HIM?
HE SAID YOU COULD START BY BRUSHING MY HAIR.
©2017, BABY BLUES PARTNERSHIP DIST. BY KING FEATURES SYNDICATE 11-29
THIS BETTER GET ME A NEW BIKE!
SANTA FROWNS ON THREATS.
KIRKMAN & SCOTT

Rick: Zoe can run a pretty sophisticated scam herself.

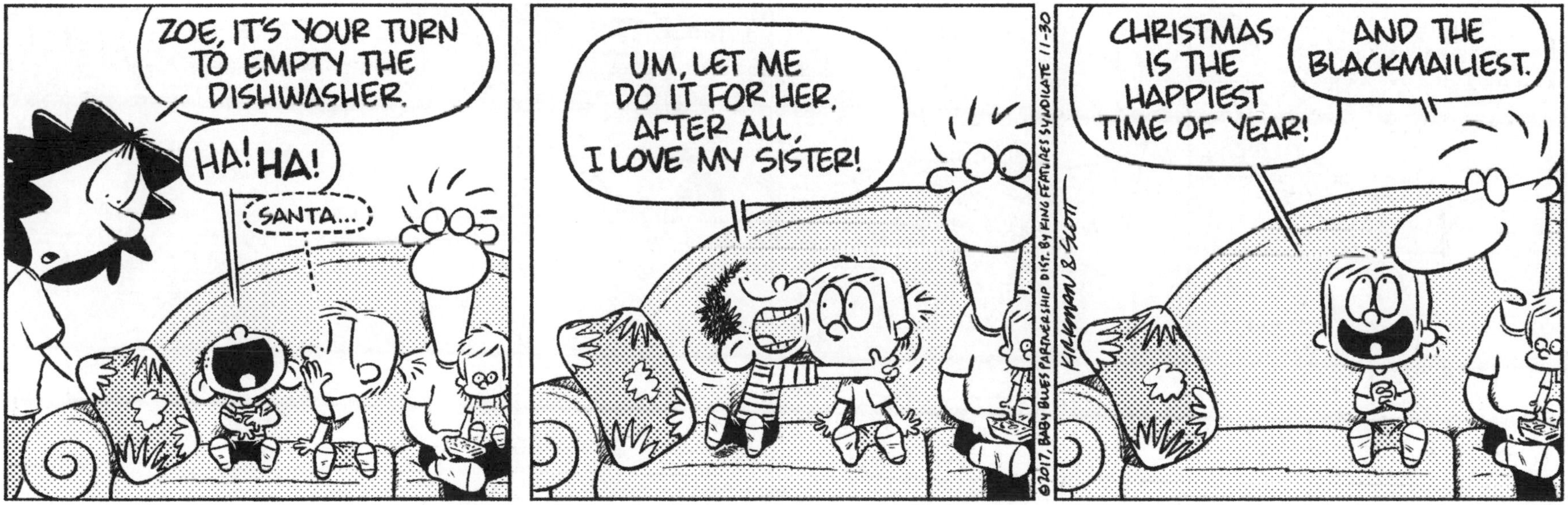
ZOE, IT'S YOUR TURN TO EMPTY THE DISHWASHER.
HA! HA!
SANTA....
UM, LET ME DO IT FOR HER. AFTER ALL, I LOVE MY SISTER!
©2017, BABY BLUES PARTNERSHIP DIST. BY KING FEATURES SYNDICATE 11-30
KIRKMAN & SCOTT
CHRISTMAS IS THE HAPPIEST TIME OF YEAR!
AND THE BLACKMAILIEST.

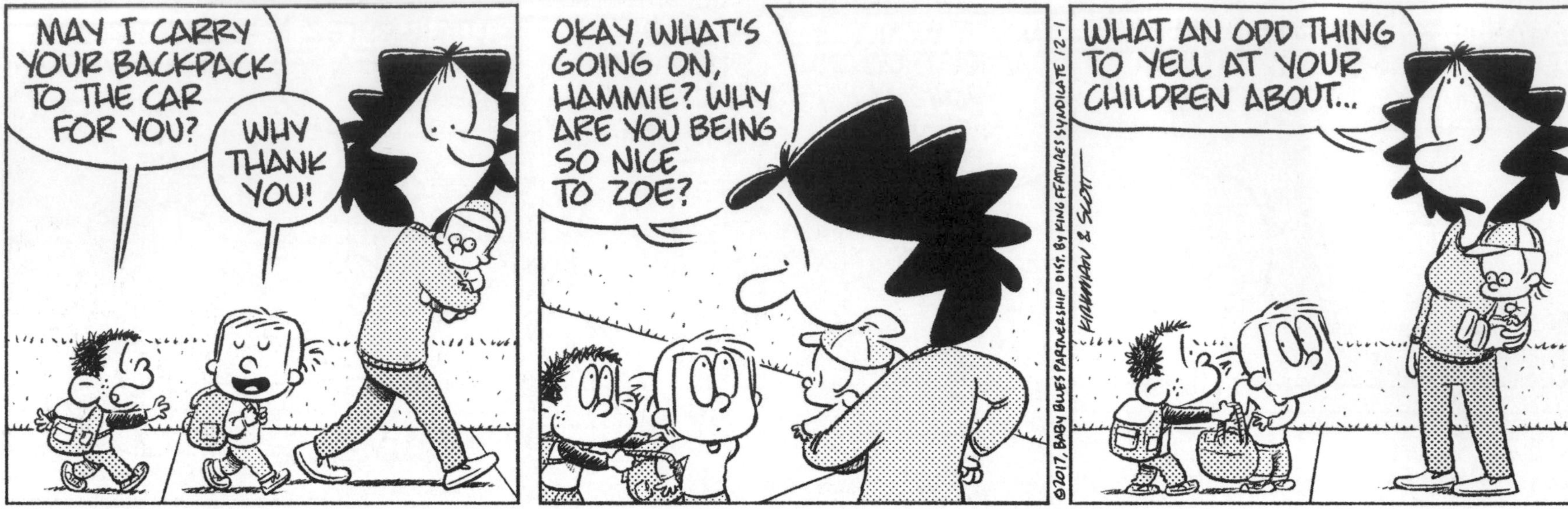
MAY I CARRY YOUR BACKPACK TO THE CAR FOR YOU?
WHY THANK YOU!
OKAY, WHAT'S GOING ON, HAMMIE? WHY ARE YOU BEING SO NICE TO ZOE?
©2017, BABY BLUES PARTNERSHIP DIST. BY KING FEATURES SYNDICATE 12-1
KIRKMAN & SCOTT
WHAT AN ODD THING TO YELL AT YOUR CHILDREN ABOUT...

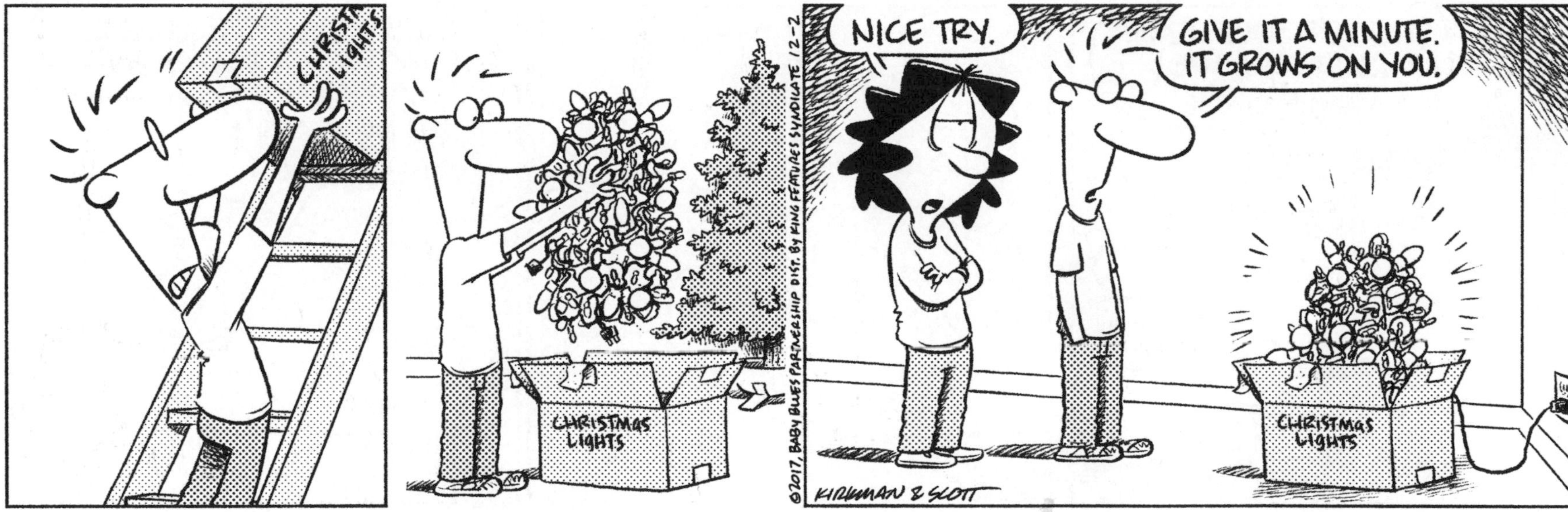
CHRISTMAS LIGHTS
©2017, BABY BLUES PARTNERSHIP DIST. BY KING FEATURES SYNDICATE 12-2
NICE TRY.
GIVE IT A MINUTE. IT GROWS ON YOU.
CHRISTMAS LIGHTS
KIRKMAN & SCOTT

Rick: I can see it now in an infomercial.

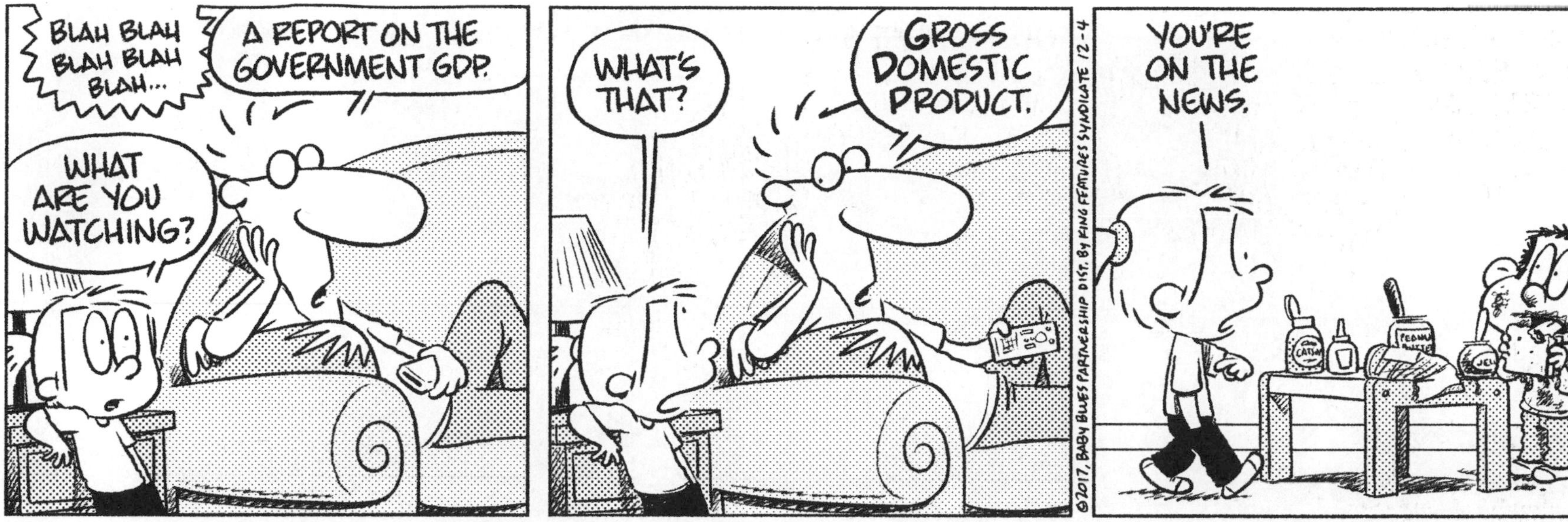
BLAH BLAH BLAH BLAH BLAH...
WHAT ARE YOU WATCHING?
A REPORT ON THE GOVERNMENT GDP.
WHAT'S THAT?
GROSS DOMESTIC PRODUCT.
©2017, BABY BLUES PARTNERSHIP DIST. BY KING FEATURES SYNDICATE 12-4
YOU'RE ON THE NEWS.
KIRKMAN & SCOTT

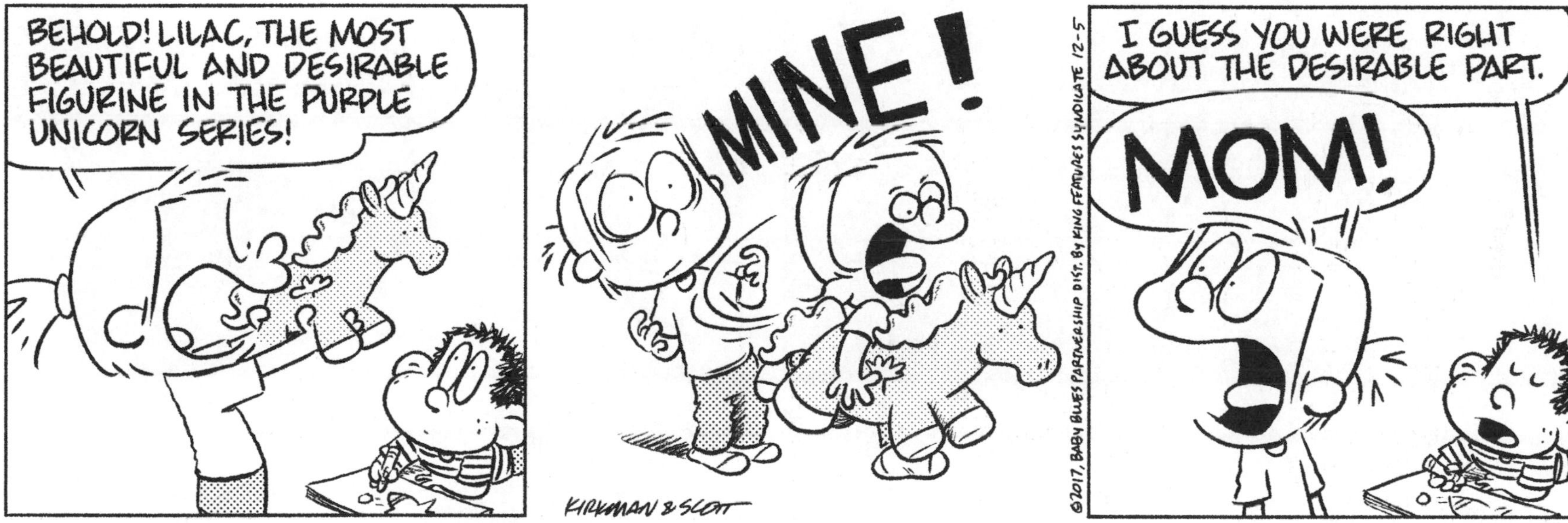
BEHOLD! LILAC, THE MOST BEAUTIFUL AND DESIRABLE FIGURINE IN THE PURPLE UNICORN SERIES!
MINE!
KIRKMAN & SCOTT
©2017, BABY BLUES PARTNERSHIP DIST. BY KING FEATURES SYNDICATE 12-5
I GUESS YOU WERE RIGHT ABOUT THE DESIRABLE PART.
MOM!

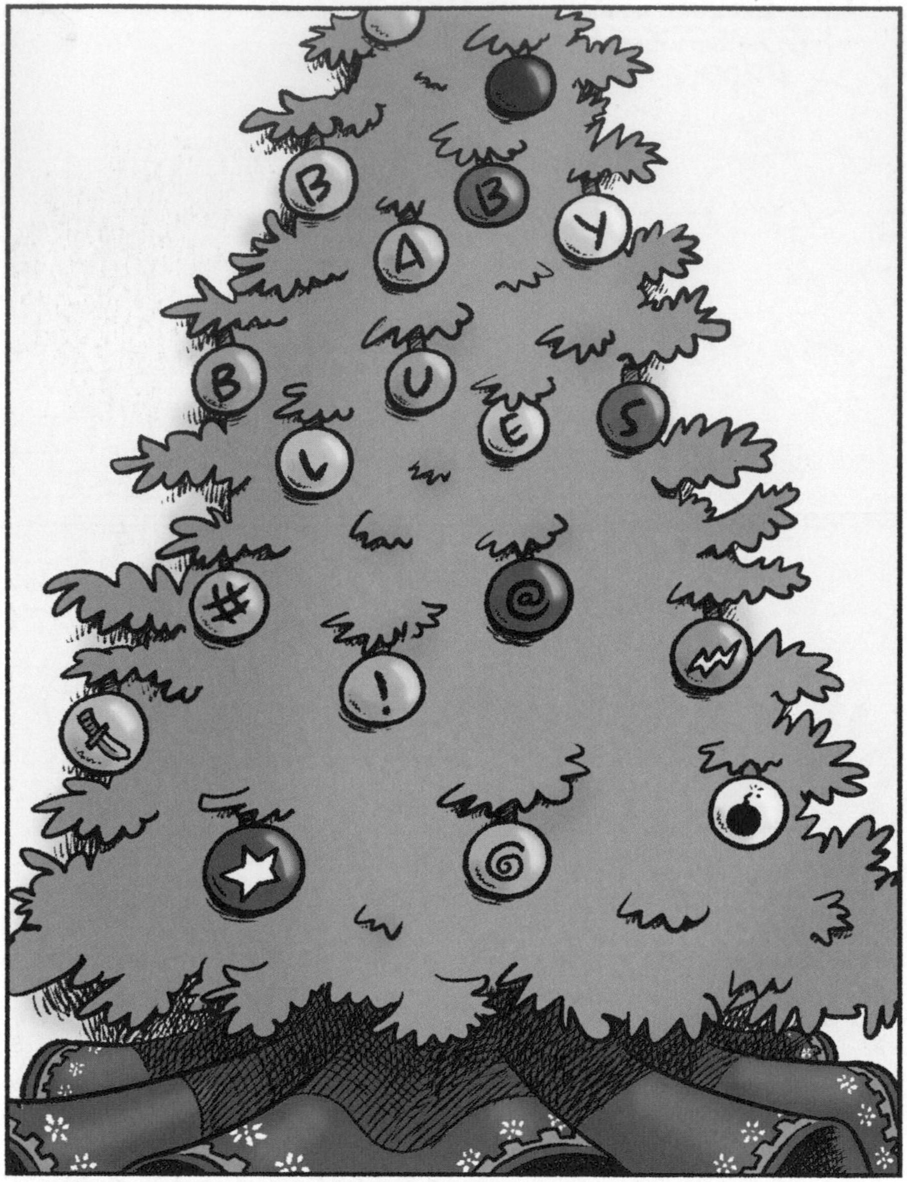
B A B Y
B L U E S

Jerry: "Cussing Around the Christmas Tree" was one of Bing Crosby's lesser-known songs.

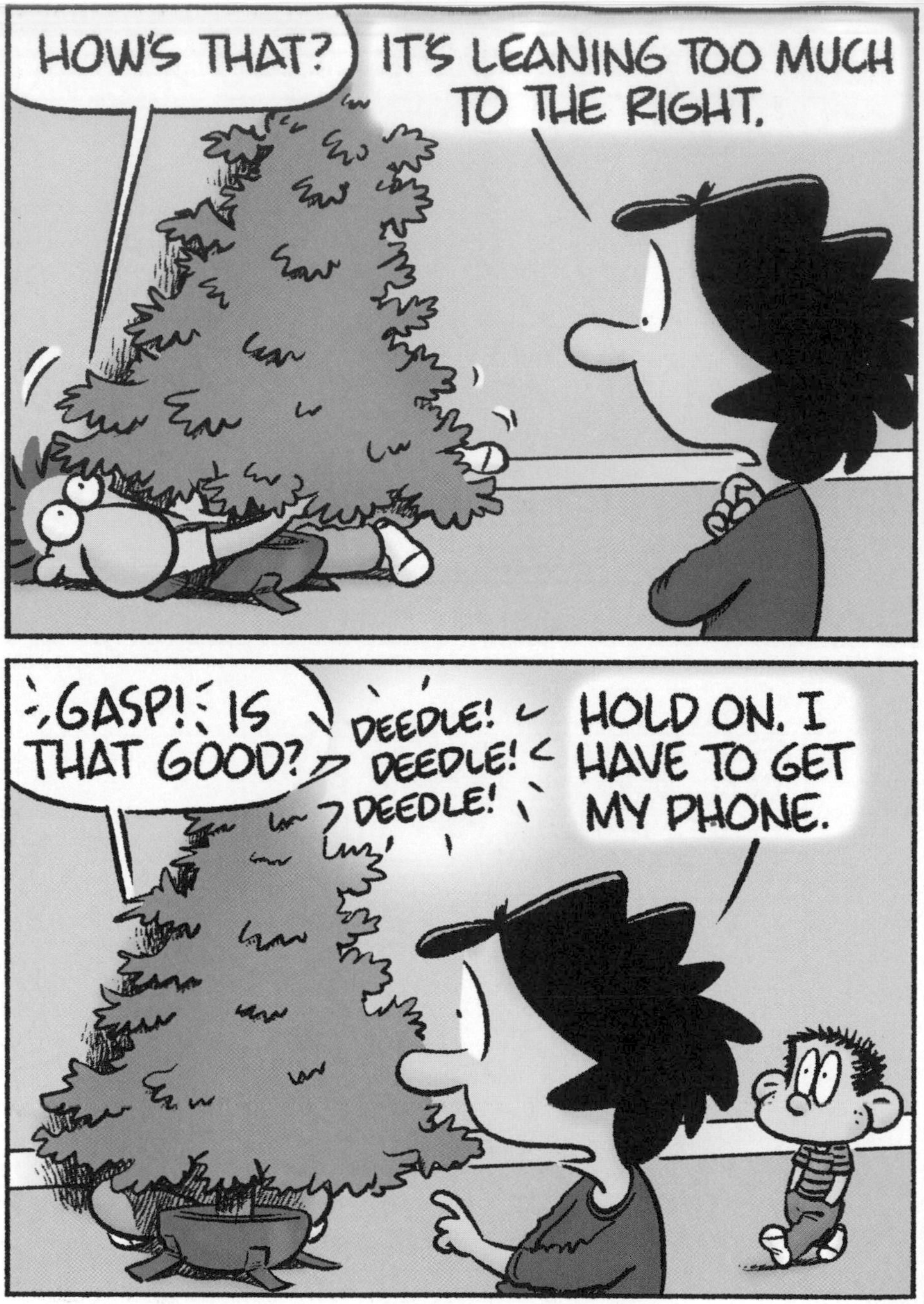
HOW'S THAT?
IT'S LEANING TOO MUCH TO THE RIGHT.
GASP! IS THAT GOOD?
DEEDLE! DEEDLE! DEEDLE!
HOLD ON. I HAVE TO GET MY PHONE.

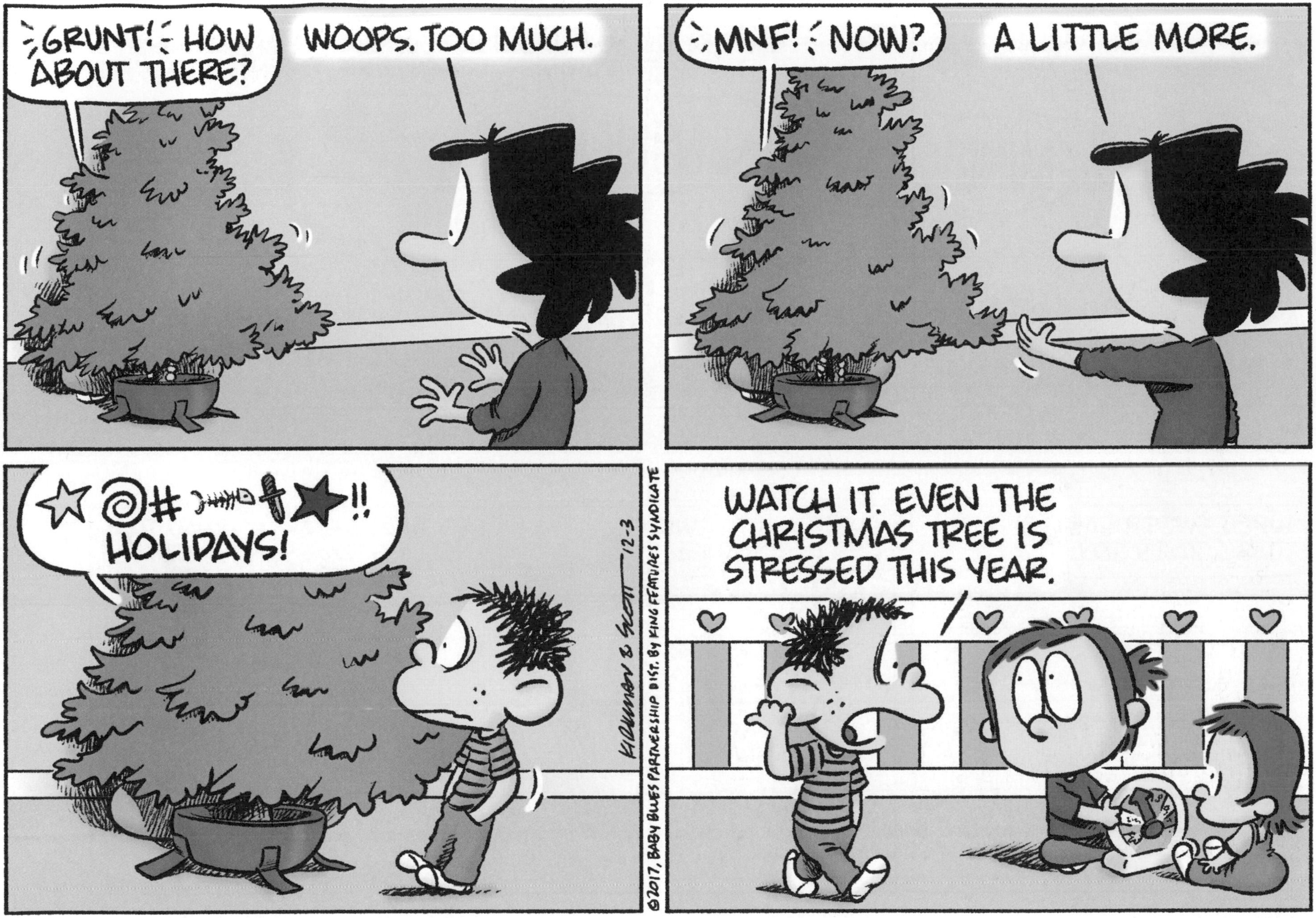
GRUNT! HOW ABOUT THERE?
WOOPS. TOO MUCH.
MNF! NOW?
A LITTLE MORE.
HOLIDAYS!
KIRKMAN & SCOTT 12-3
©2017, BABY BLUES PARTNERSHIP DIST. BY KING FEATURES SYNDICATE
WATCH IT. EVEN THE CHRISTMAS TREE IS STRESSED THIS YEAR.

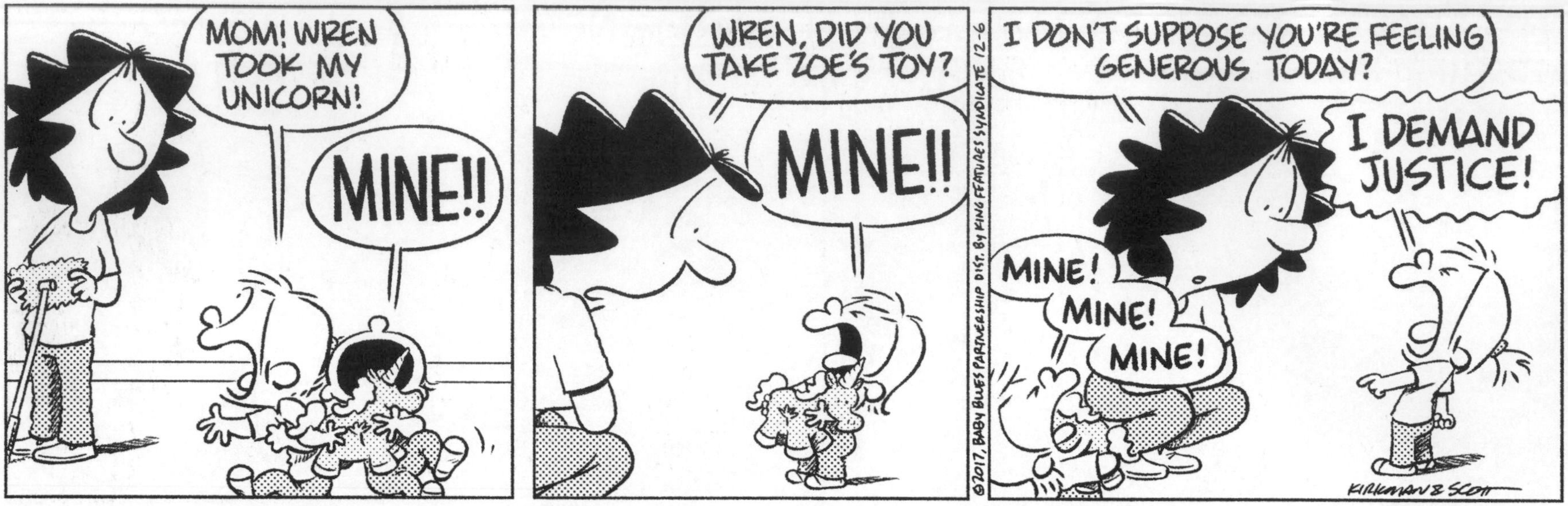

MOM! WREN TOOK MY UNICORN!
MINE!!
WREN, DID YOU TAKE ZOE'S TOY?
MINE!!
©2017, BABY BLUES PARTNERSHIP DIST. BY KING FEATURES SYNDICATE 12-6
I DON'T SUPPOSE YOU'RE FEELING GENEROUS TODAY?
I DEMAND JUSTICE!
MINE!
MINE!
MINE!
KIRKMAN & SCOTT

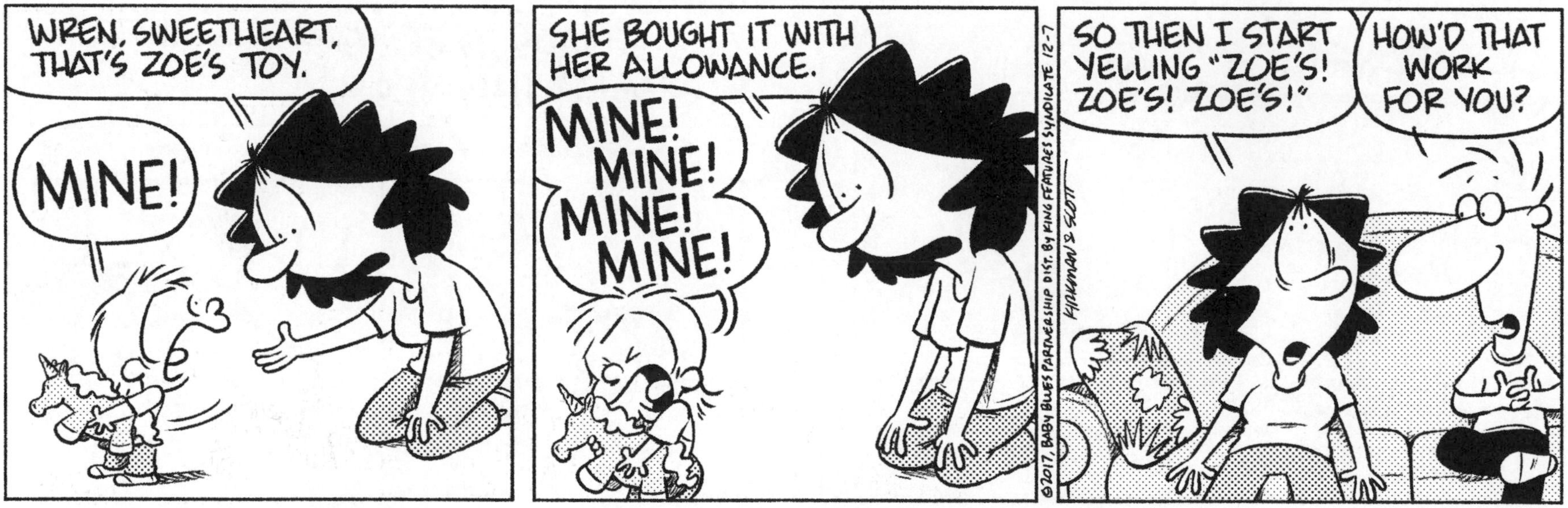

WREN, SWEETHEART, THAT'S ZOE'S TOY.
MINE!
SHE BOUGHT IT WITH HER ALLOWANCE.
MINE! MINE! MINE! MINE!
©2017, BABY BLUES PARTNERSHIP DIST. BY KING FEATURES SYNDICATE 12-7
KIRKMAN & SCOTT
SO THEN I START YELLING "ZOE'S! ZOE'S! ZOE'S!"
HOW'D THAT WORK FOR YOU?

Jerry: That's probably not a technique you'll learn in most conflict-resolution seminars.

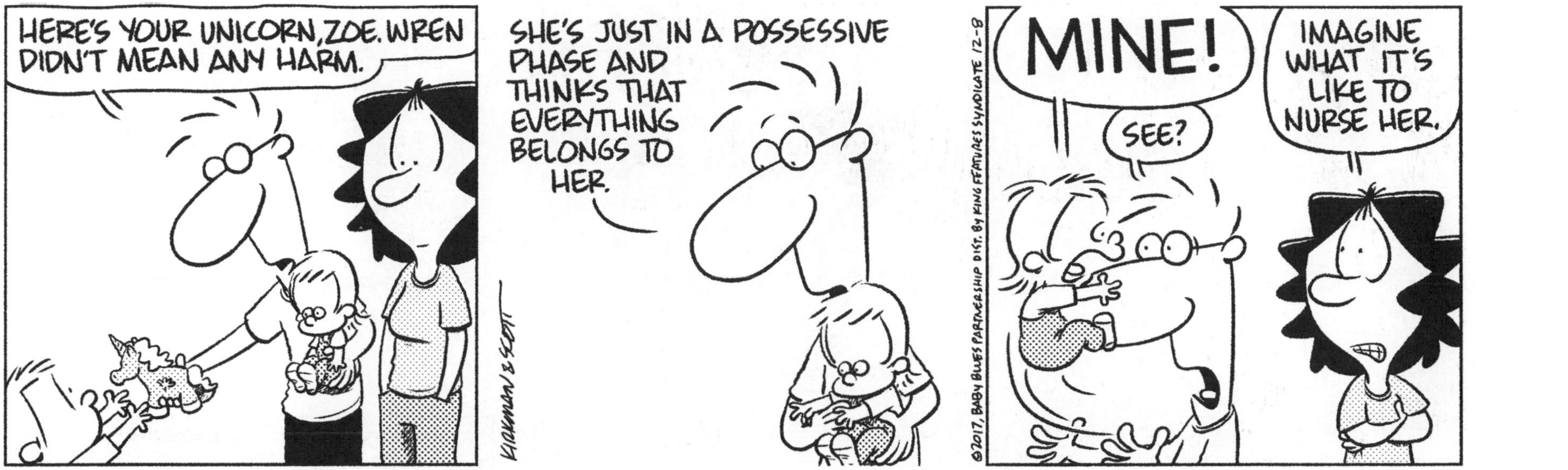
HERE'S YOUR UNICORN, ZOE. WREN DIDN'T MEAN ANY HARM.
KIRKMAN & SCOTT
SHE'S JUST IN A POSSESSIVE PHASE AND THINKS THAT EVERYTHING BELONGS TO HER.
©2017, BABY BLUES PARTNERSHIP DIST. BY KING FEATURES SYNDICATE 12-8
MINE!
SEE?
IMAGINE WHAT IT'S LIKE TO NURSE HER.

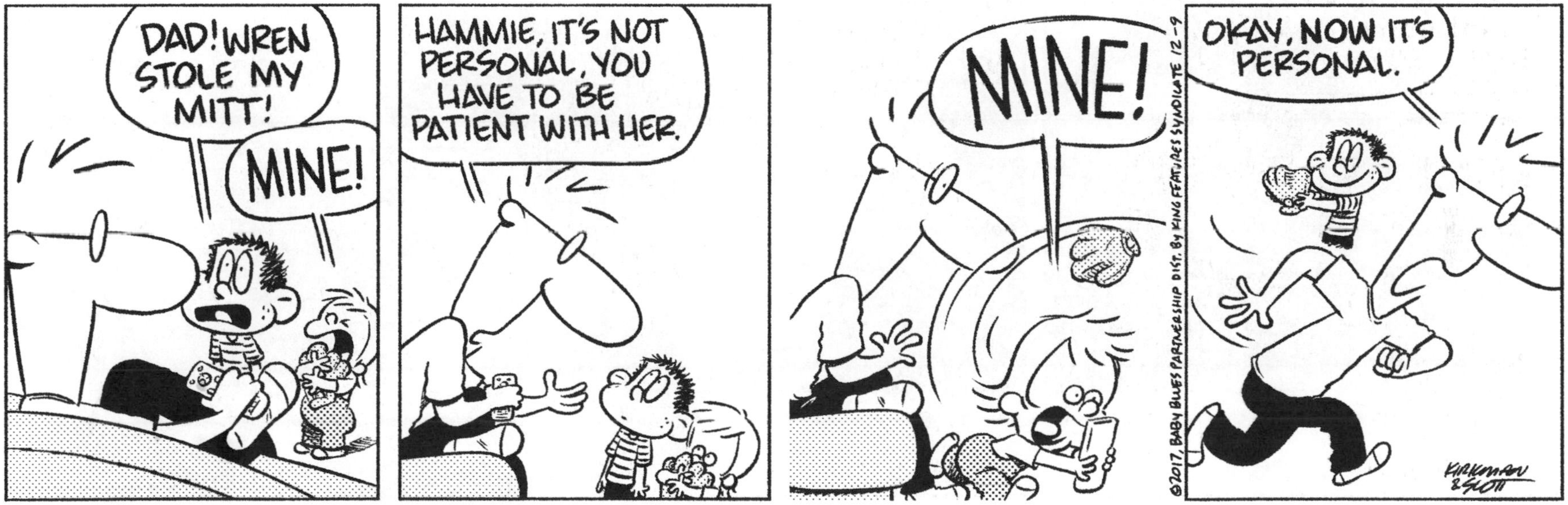
DAD! WREN STOLE MY MITT!
MINE!
HAMMIE, IT'S NOT PERSONAL, YOU HAVE TO BE PATIENT WITH HER.
MINE!
©2017, BABY BLUES PARTNERSHIP DIST. BY KING FEATURES SYNDICATE 12-9
OKAY, NOW IT'S PERSONAL.
KIRKMAN & SCOTT

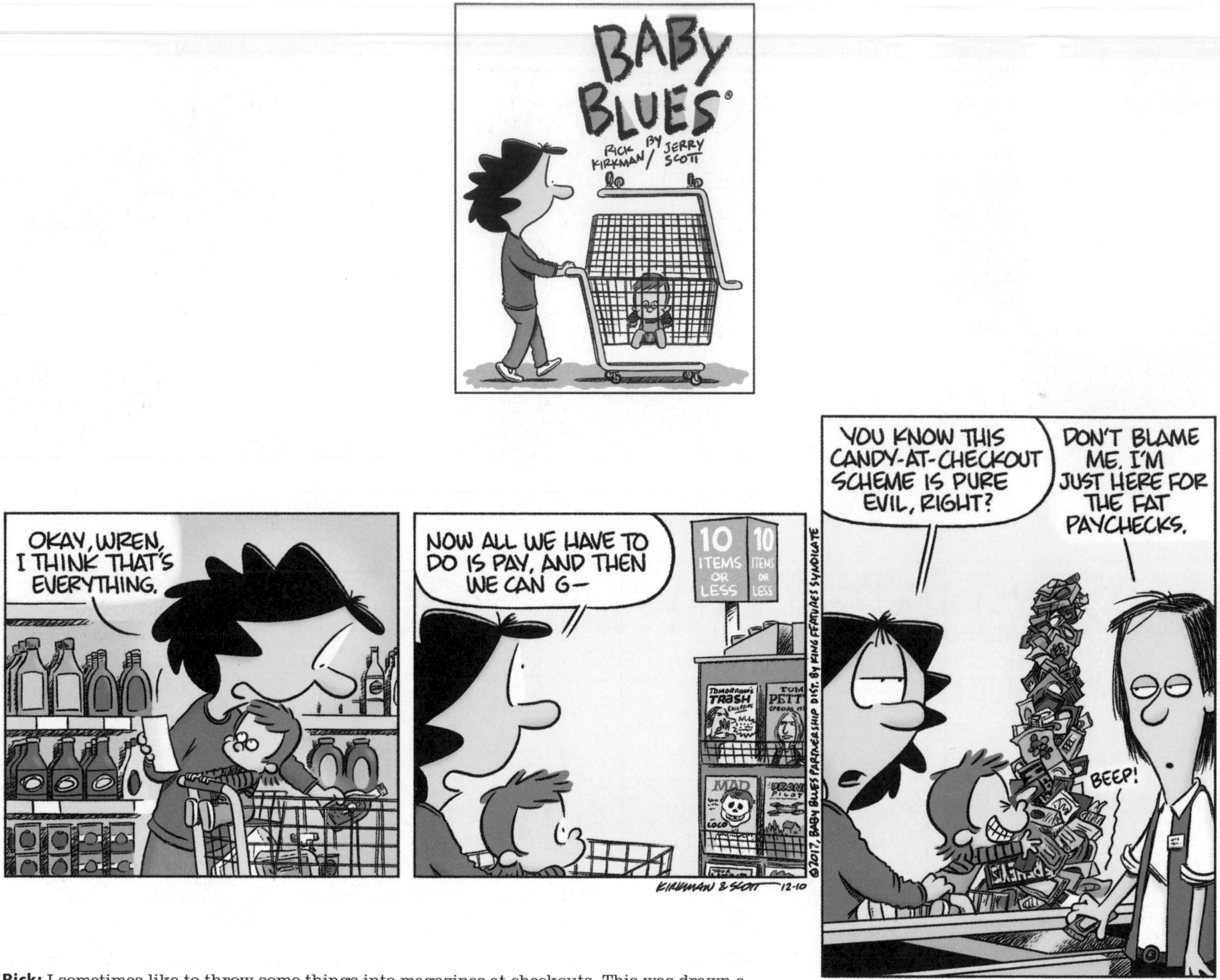
BABY BLUES®
BY RICK KIRKMAN / JERRY SCOTT
OKAY, WREN, I THINK THAT'S EVERYTHING.
NOW ALL WE HAVE TO DO IS PAY, AND THEN WE CAN G—
10 ITEMS OR LESS
TOMORROW'S TRASH
TOM PETTY
MAD
©2017, BABY BLUES PARTNERSHIP DIST. BY KING FEATURES SYNDICATE
KIRKMAN & SCOTT 12-10
YOU KNOW THIS CANDY-AT-CHECKOUT SCHEME IS PURE EVIL, RIGHT?
DON'T BLAME ME. I'M JUST HERE FOR THE FAT PAYCHECKS.
BEEP!

Rick: I sometimes like to throw some things into magazines at checkouts. This was drawn a week after Tom Petty died, so I put a special issue Tom Petty magazine on the stand.

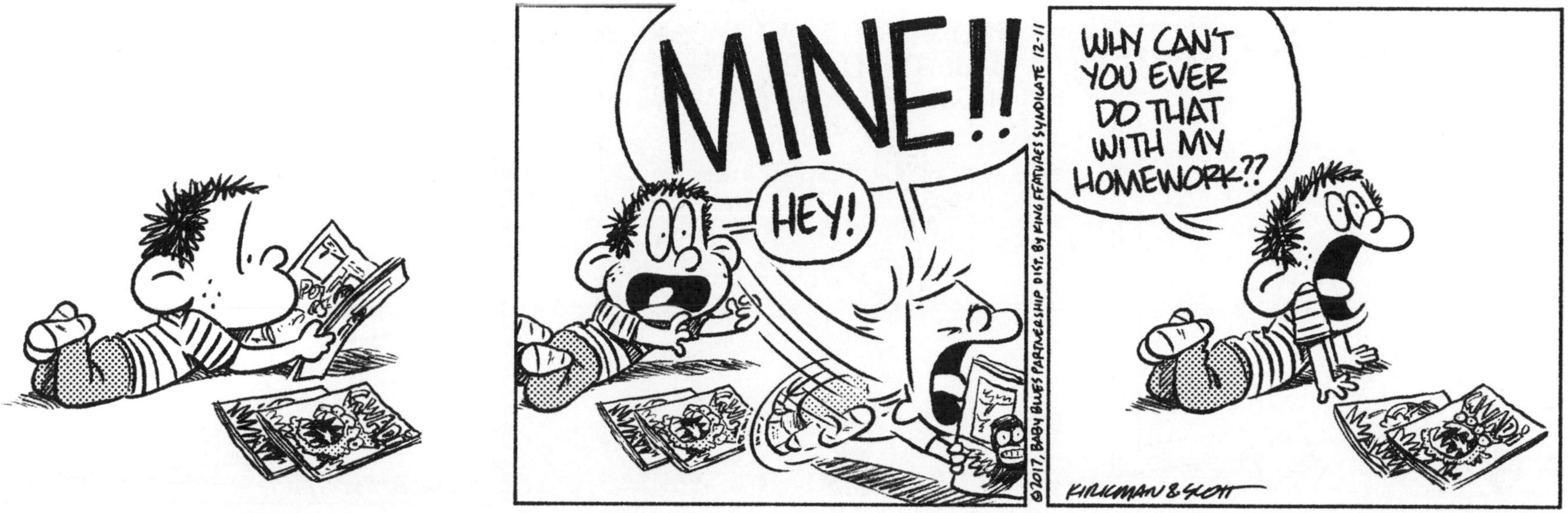
MINE!!
HEY!
©2017, BABY BLUES PARTNERSHIP DIST. BY KING FEATURES SYNDICATE 12-11
WHY CAN'T YOU EVER DO THAT WITH MY HOMEWORK??
KIRKMAN & SCOTT

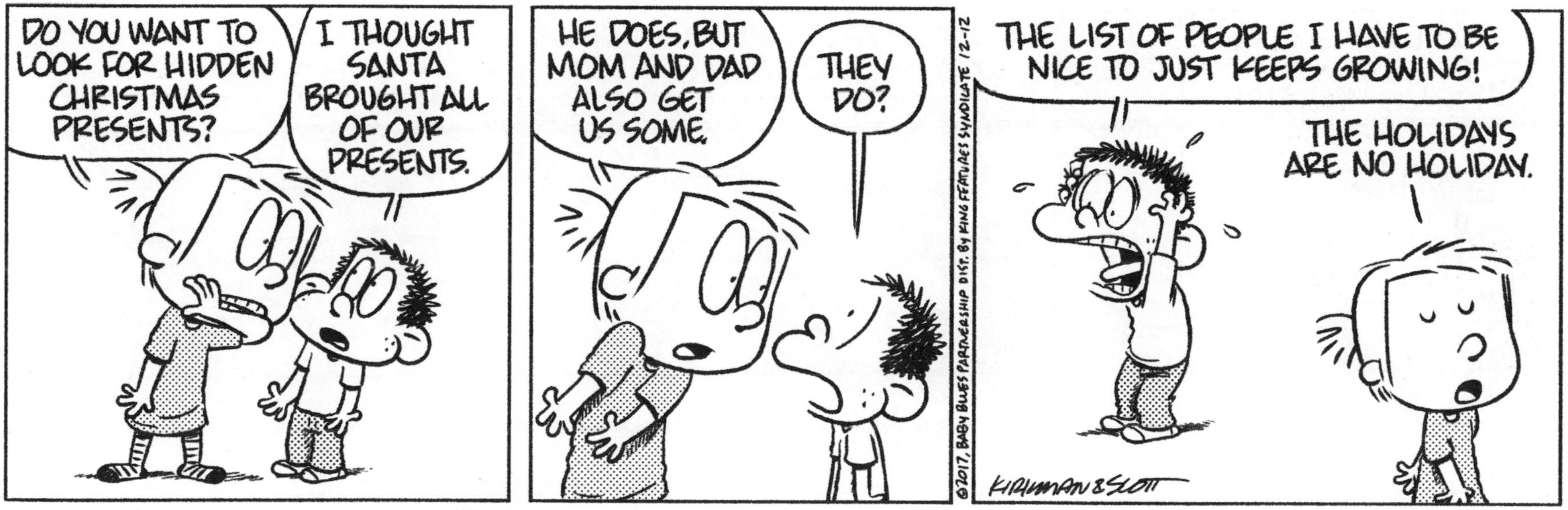
DO YOU WANT TO LOOK FOR HIDDEN CHRISTMAS PRESENTS?
I THOUGHT SANTA BROUGHT ALL OF OUR PRESENTS.
HE DOES, BUT MOM AND DAD ALSO GET US SOME.
THEY DO?
©2017, BABY BLUES PARTNERSHIP DIST. BY KING FEATURES SYNDICATE 12-12
THE LIST OF PEOPLE I HAVE TO BE NICE TO JUST KEEPS GROWING!
THE HOLIDAYS ARE NO HOLIDAY.
KIRKMAN & SCOTT

Rick: The abject terror of that realization was fun to draw.

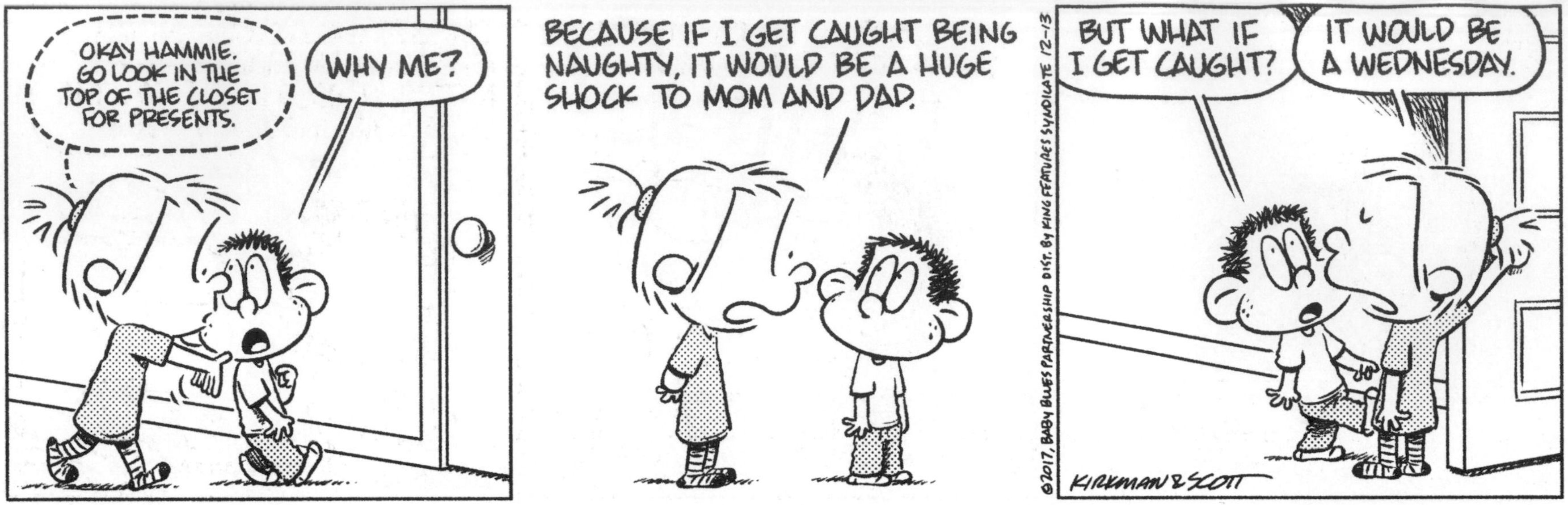
OKAY HAMMIE. GO LOOK IN THE TOP OF THE CLOSET FOR PRESENTS.
WHY ME?
BECAUSE IF I GET CAUGHT BEING NAUGHTY, IT WOULD BE A HUGE SHOCK TO MOM AND DAD.
BUT WHAT IF I GET CAUGHT?
IT WOULD BE A WEDNESDAY.
©2017, BABY BLUES PARTNERSHIP DIST. BY KING FEATURES SYNDICATE 12-13
KIRKMAN & SCOTT

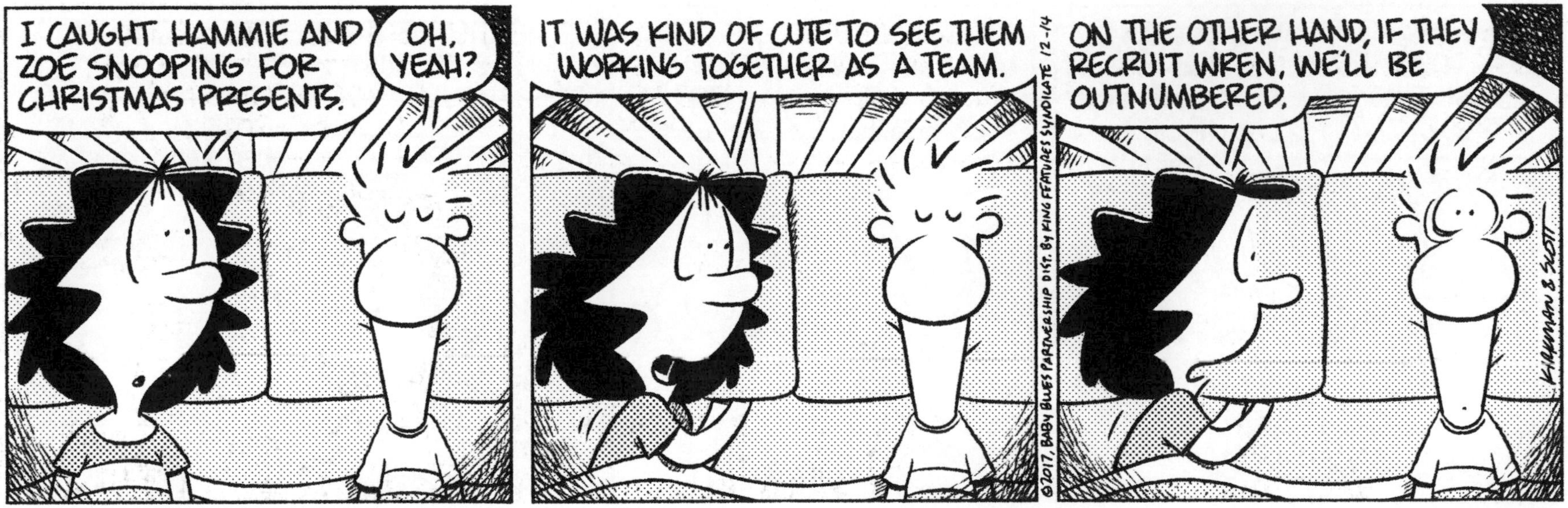
I CAUGHT HAMMIE AND ZOE SNOOPING FOR CHRISTMAS PRESENTS.
OH, YEAH?
IT WAS KIND OF CUTE TO SEE THEM WORKING TOGETHER AS A TEAM.
ON THE OTHER HAND, IF THEY RECRUIT WREN, WE'LL BE OUTNUMBERED.
©2017, BABY BLUES PARTNERSHIP DIST. BY KING FEATURES SYNDICATE 12-14
KIRKMAN & SCOTT

Jerry: Be very afraid . . .

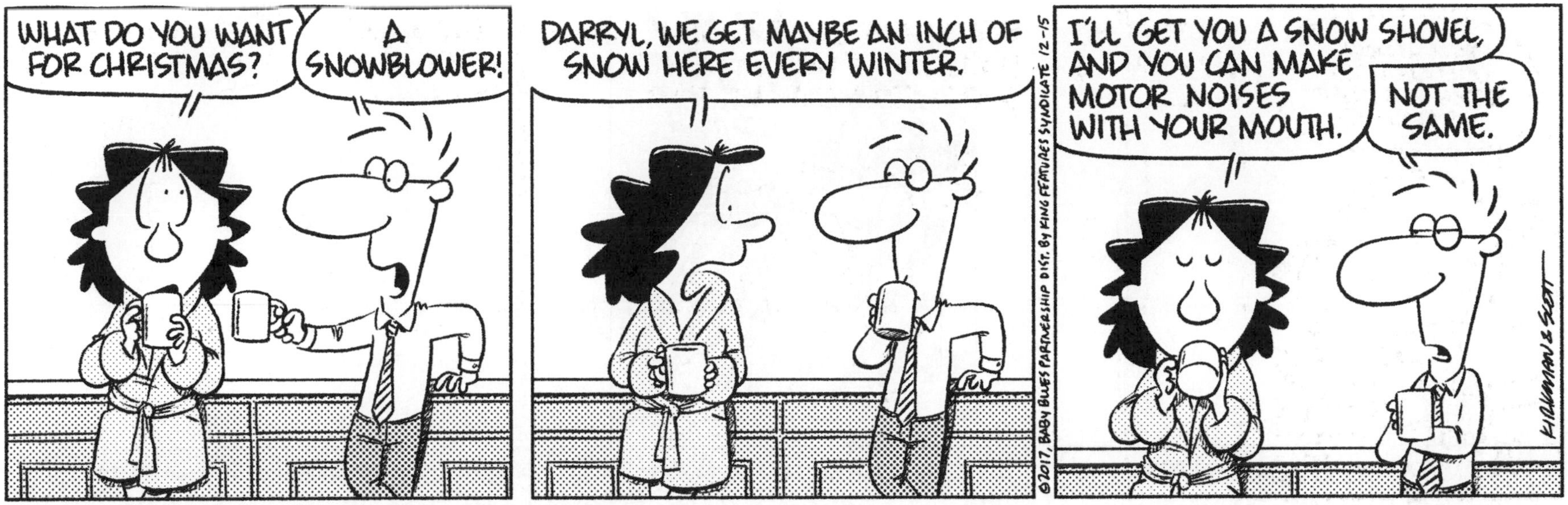
WHAT DO YOU WANT FOR CHRISTMAS?
A SNOWBLOWER!
DARRYL, WE GET MAYBE AN INCH OF SNOW HERE EVERY WINTER.
©2017, BABY BLUES PARTNERSHIP DIST. BY KING FEATURES SYNDICATE 12-15
I'LL GET YOU A SNOW SHOVEL, AND YOU CAN MAKE MOTOR NOISES WITH YOUR MOUTH.
NOT THE SAME.
KIRKMAN & SCOTT

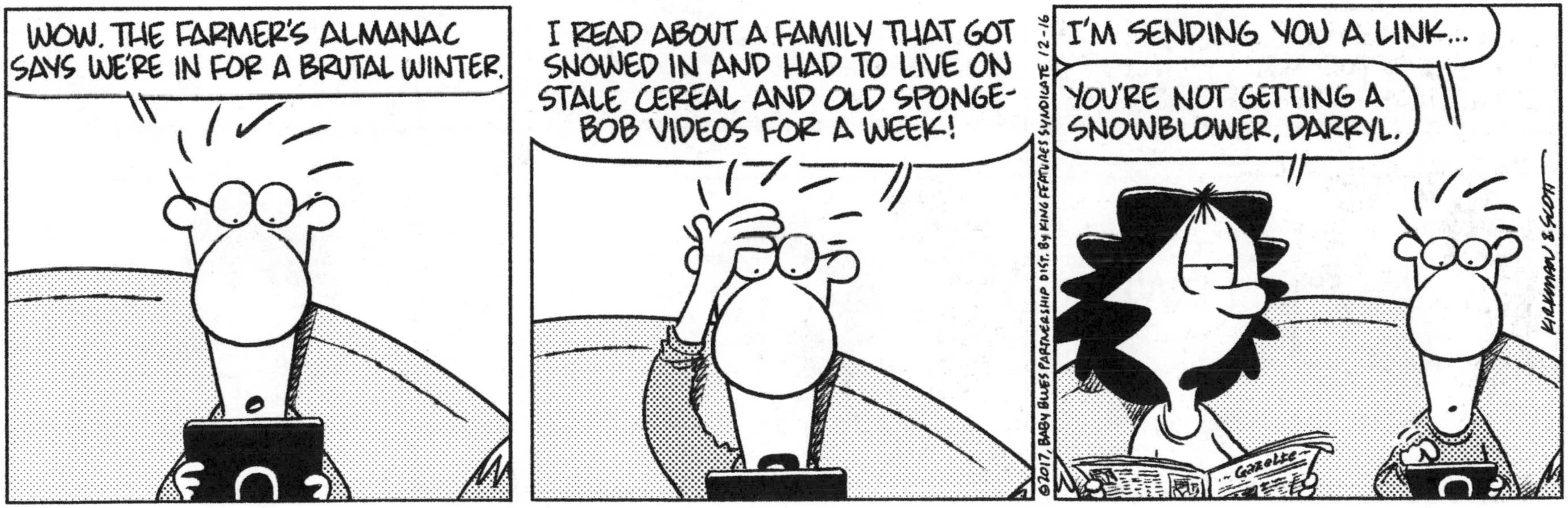
WOW. THE FARMER'S ALMANAC SAYS WE'RE IN FOR A BRUTAL WINTER.
I READ ABOUT A FAMILY THAT GOT SNOWED IN AND HAD TO LIVE ON STALE CEREAL AND OLD SPONGE-BOB VIDEOS FOR A WEEK!
©2017, BABY BLUES PARTNERSHIP DIST. BY KING FEATURES SYNDICATE 12-16
I'M SENDING YOU A LINK...
YOU'RE NOT GETTING A SNOWBLOWER, DARRYL.
KIRKMAN & SCOTT

BABY BLUES®
BY RICK KIRKMAN / JERRY SCOTT
HAMMIE, HAVE YOU CHOSEN A GIFT TO GIVE ZOE FOR CHRISTMAS?
YEAH. I HAD ONE IDEA.
A RADIO-CONTROLLED MONSTER TRUCK THAT DOES FLIPS AND BLOWS REAL SMOKE OUT OF THE EXHAUST PIPES!
THAT SOUNDS AWESOME! LET'S SEE IF WE—
UH-OH.
WHAT?
KIRKMAN & SCOTT 12-17
THEY'RE ON BACKORDER.
AW!
HOW ABOUT A CHAPTER BOOK INSTEAD?
FINE. WHATEVER.
©2017, BABY BLUES PARTNERSHIP DIST. BY KING FEATURES SYNDICATE
OKAY. HE'S GONE.
THANK YOU THANK YOU THANK YOU!

Jerry: It's another Christmas miracle.

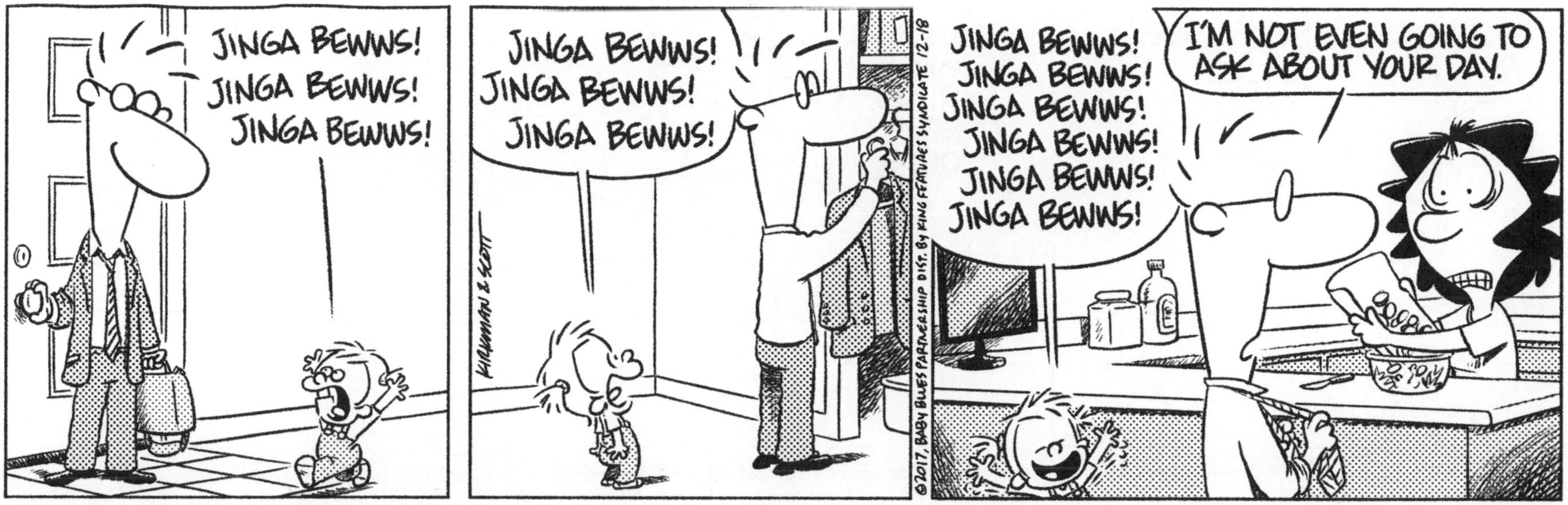
JINGA BEWWS! JINGA BEWWS! JINGA BEWWS!
JINGA BEWWS! JINGA BEWWS! JINGA BEWWS!
JINGA BEWWS! JINGA BEWWS! JINGA BEWWS! JINGA BEWWS! JINGA BEWWS! JINGA BEWWS!
I'M NOT EVEN GOING TO ASK ABOUT YOUR DAY.
KIRKMAN & SCOTT
©2017, BABY BLUES PARTNERSHIP DIST. BY KING FEATURES SYNDICATE 12-18

Rick: I need some ibuprofen from just reading it.

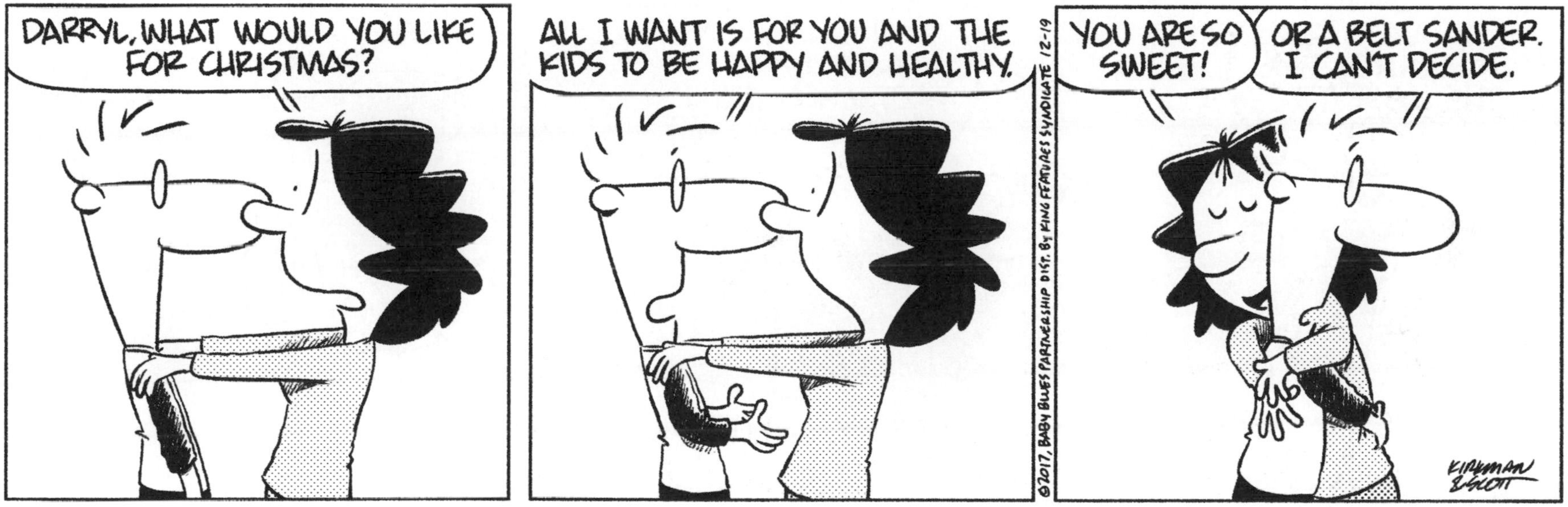
DARRYL, WHAT WOULD YOU LIKE FOR CHRISTMAS?
ALL I WANT IS FOR YOU AND THE KIDS TO BE HAPPY AND HEALTHY.
YOU ARE SO SWEET!
OR A BELT SANDER. I CAN'T DECIDE.
©2017, BABY BLUES PARTNERSHIP DIST. BY KING FEATURES SYNDICATE 12-19
KIRKMAN & SCOTT

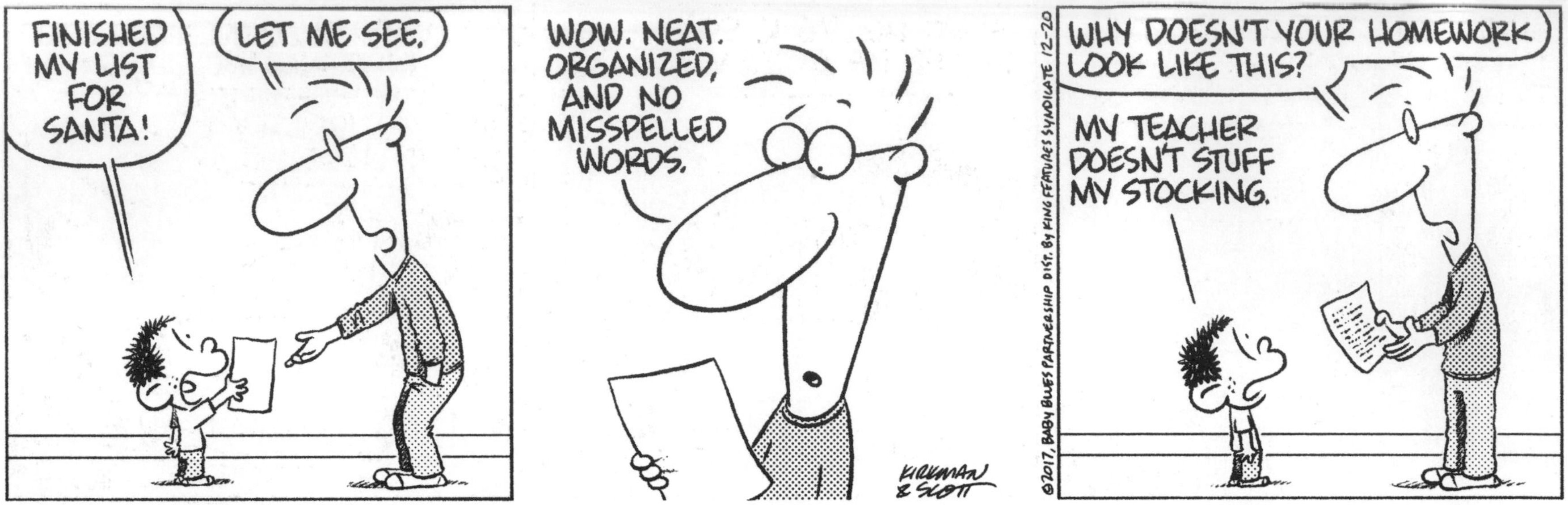

FINISHED MY LIST FOR SANTA!
LET ME SEE.
WOW. NEAT. ORGANIZED, AND NO MISSPELLED WORDS.
KIRKMAN & SCOTT
WHY DOESN'T YOUR HOMEWORK LOOK LIKE THIS?
MY TEACHER DOESN'T STUFF MY STOCKING.
©2017, BABY BLUES PARTNERSHIP DIST. BY KING FEATURES SYNDICATE 12-20

Jerry: Reward-based handwriting: It could be a thing.

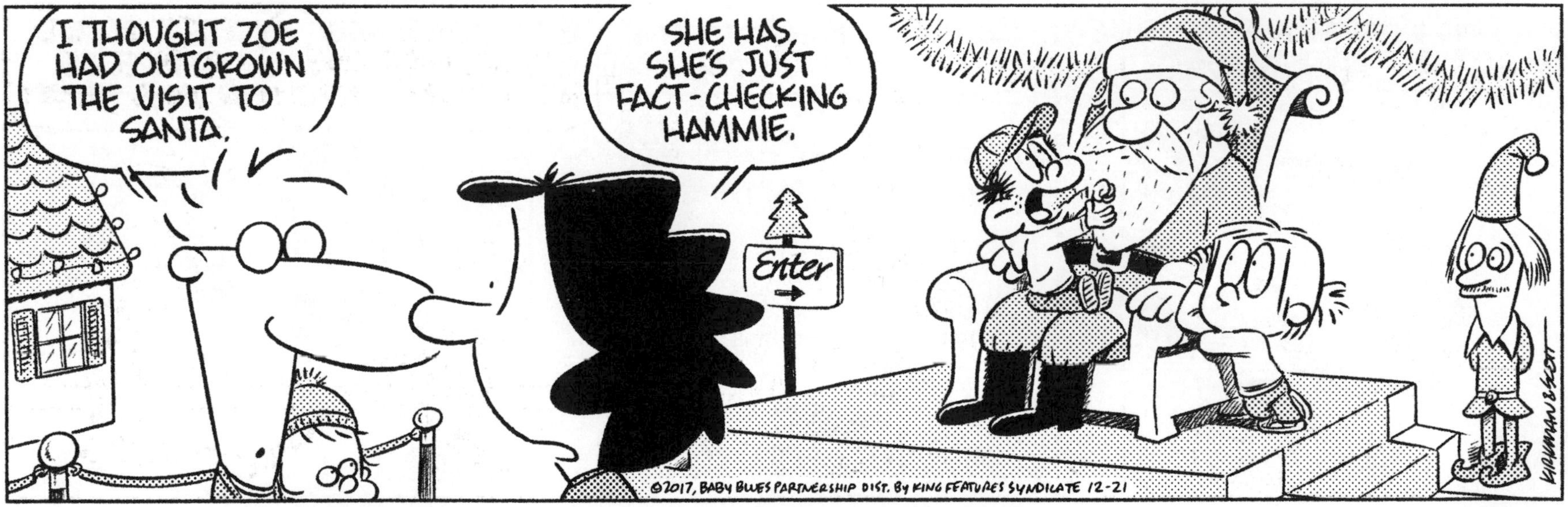

I THOUGHT ZOE HAD OUTGROWN THE VISIT TO SANTA.
SHE HAS, SHE'S JUST FACT-CHECKING HAMMIE.
Enter
KIRKMAN & SCOTT
©2017, BABY BLUES PARTNERSHIP DIST. BY KING FEATURES SYNDICATE 12-21

Rick: After I finished drawing this strip, it dawned on me that the elf looked suspiciously like David Sedaris . . . or how I imagined him looking dressed as an elf in "SantaLand Diaries."

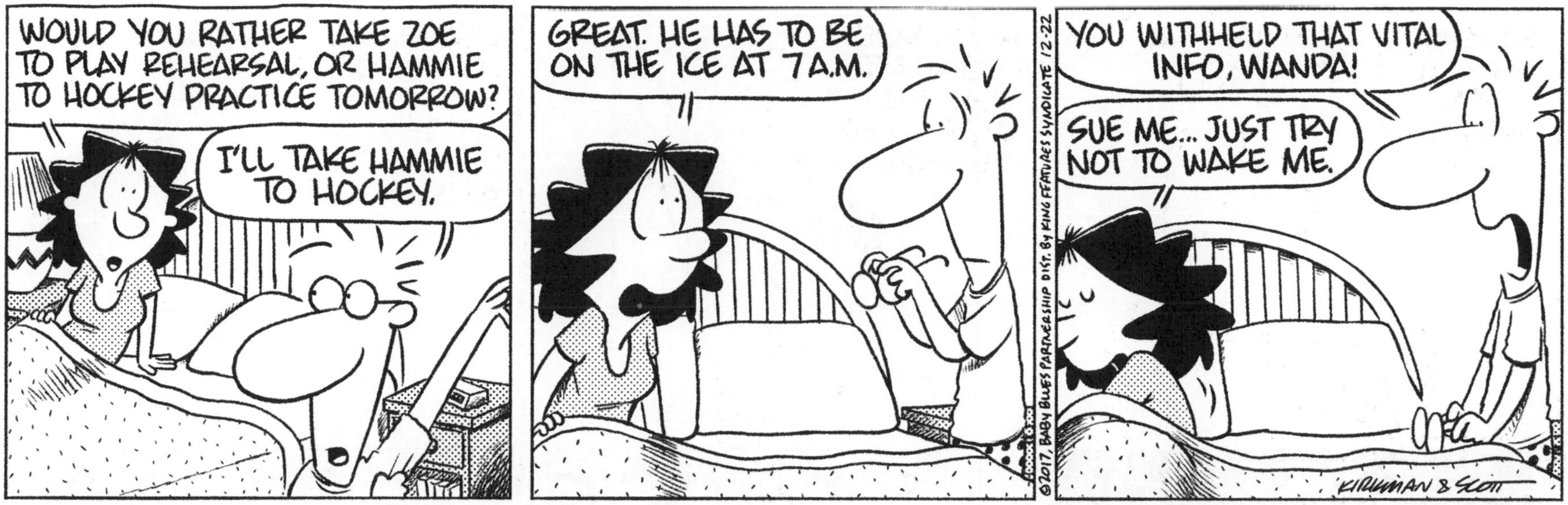
WOULD YOU RATHER TAKE ZOE TO PLAY REHEARSAL, OR HAMMIE TO HOCKEY PRACTICE TOMORROW?
I'LL TAKE HAMMIE TO HOCKEY.
GREAT. HE HAS TO BE ON THE ICE AT 7 A.M.
©2017, BABY BLUES PARTNERSHIP DIST. BY KING FEATURES SYNDICATE 12-22
YOU WITHHELD THAT VITAL INFO, WANDA!
SUE ME... JUST TRY NOT TO WAKE ME.
KIRKMAN & SCOTT

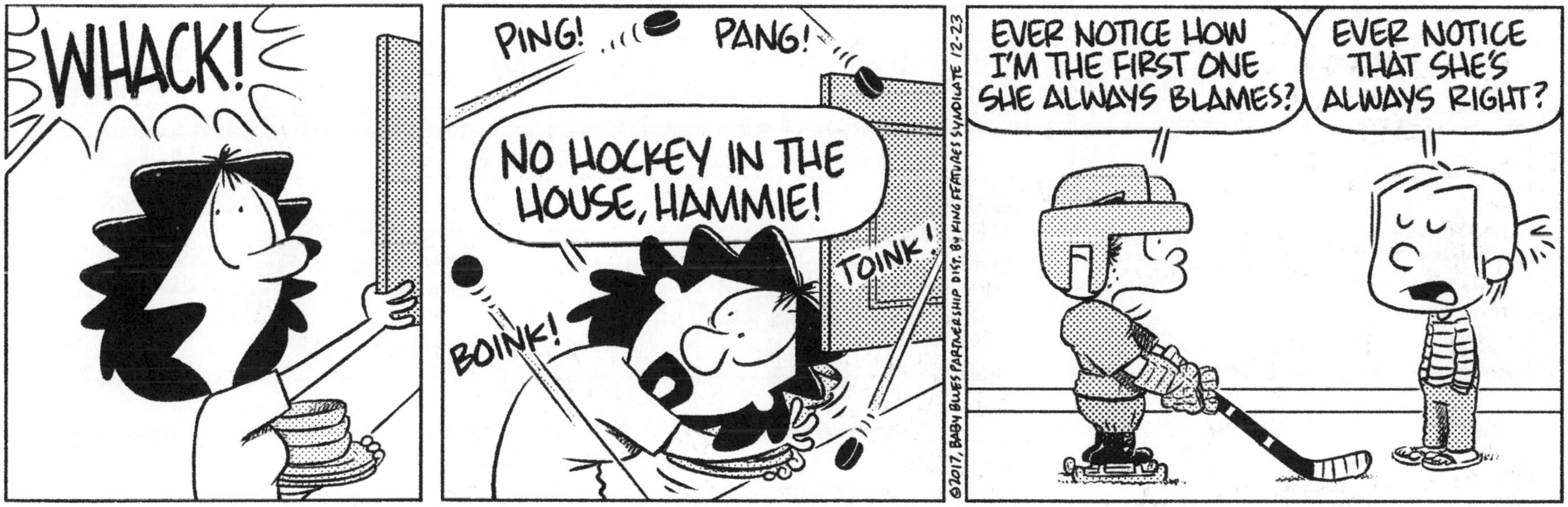
WHACK!
PING!
PANG!
NO HOCKEY IN THE HOUSE, HAMMIE!
TOINK!
BOINK!
©2017, BABY BLUES PARTNERSHIP DIST. BY KING FEATURES SYNDICATE 12-23
EVER NOTICE HOW I'M THE FIRST ONE SHE ALWAYS BLAMES?
EVER NOTICE THAT SHE'S ALWAYS RIGHT?

Jerry: It's profiling, plain and simple.

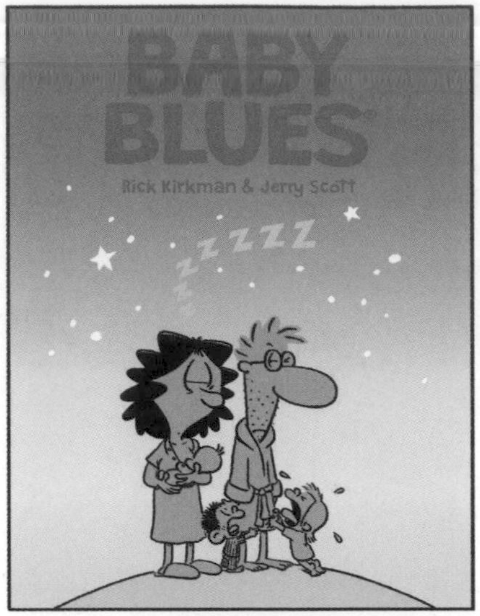
BABY BLUES
Rick Kirkman & Jerry Scott
ZZZZZ

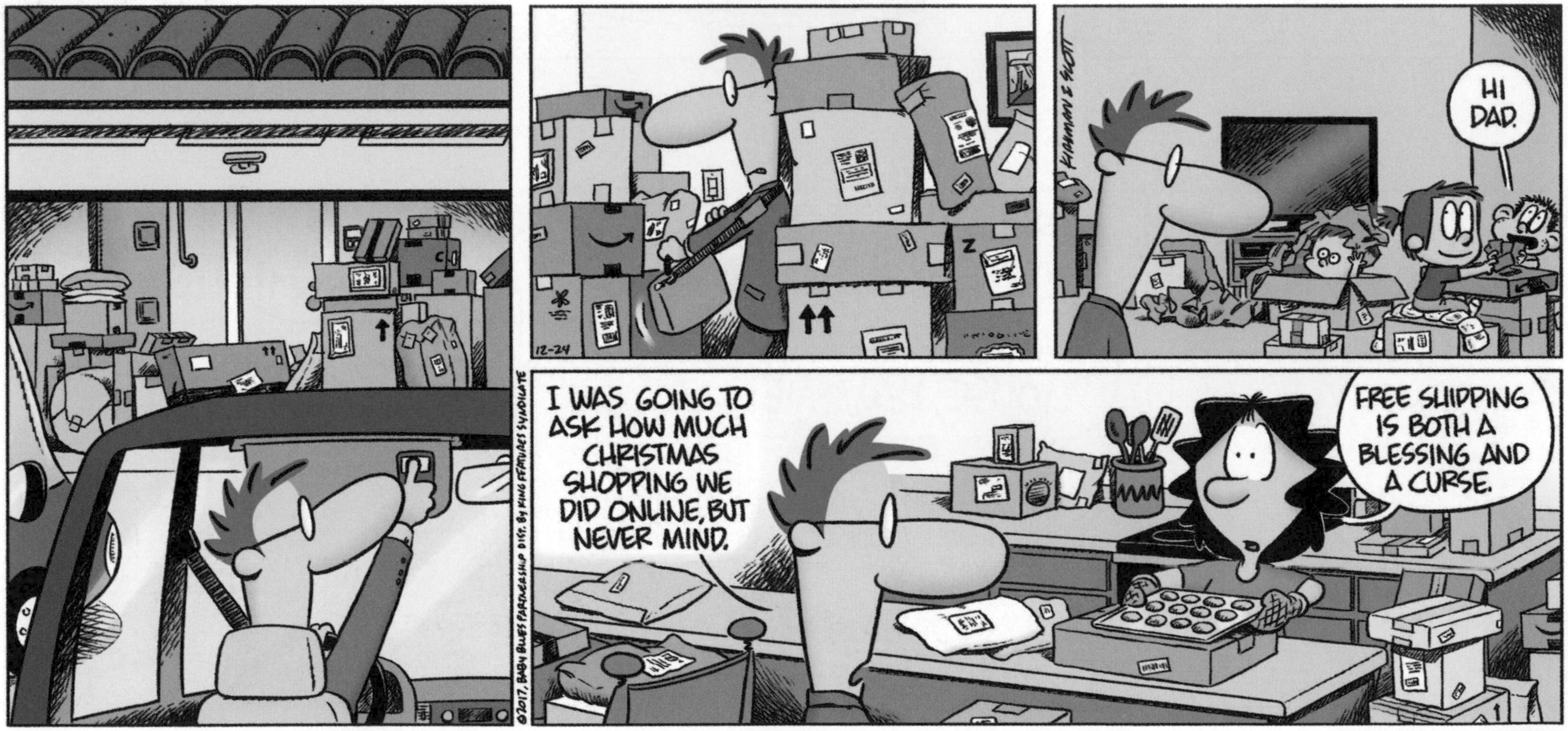
12-24
KIRKMAN & SCOTT
HI DAD.
©2017, BABY BLUES PARTNERSHIP DIST. BY KING FEATURES SYNDICATE
I WAS GOING TO ASK HOW MUCH CHRISTMAS SHOPPING WE DID ONLINE, BUT NEVER MIND.
FREE SHIPPING IS BOTH A BLESSING AND A CURSE.

Rick: Confession: This is my house.

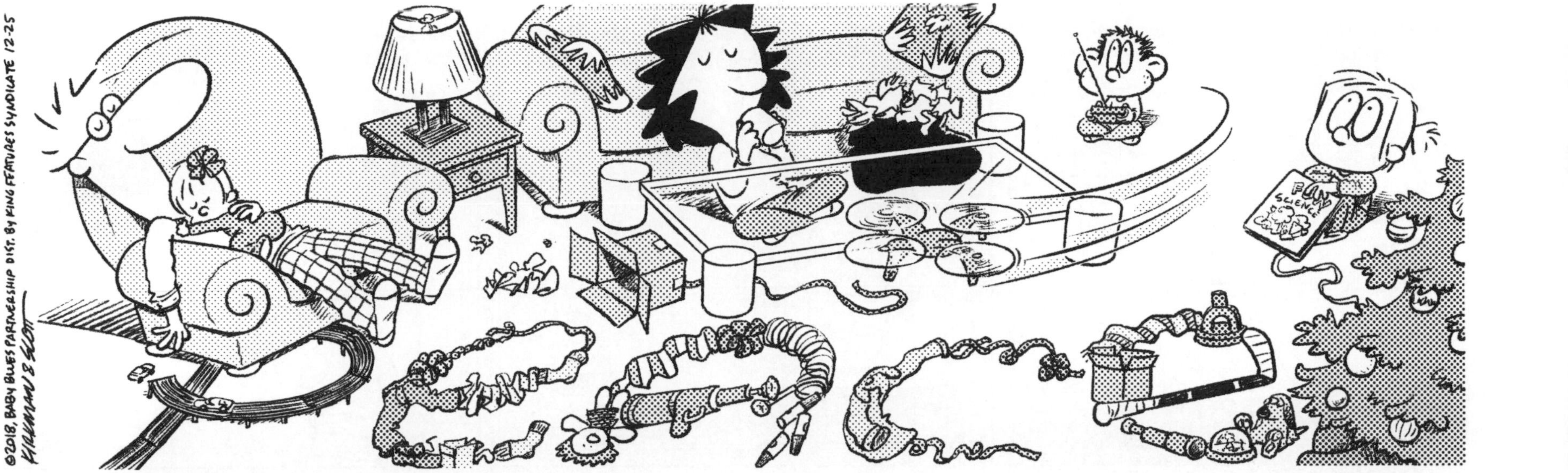
©2018, BABY BLUES PARTNERSHIP DIST. BY KING FEATURES SYNDICATE 12-25
KIRKMAN & SCOTT
FUN SCIENCE

Rick: This was a very tough one to pull off. Hope it succeeded.

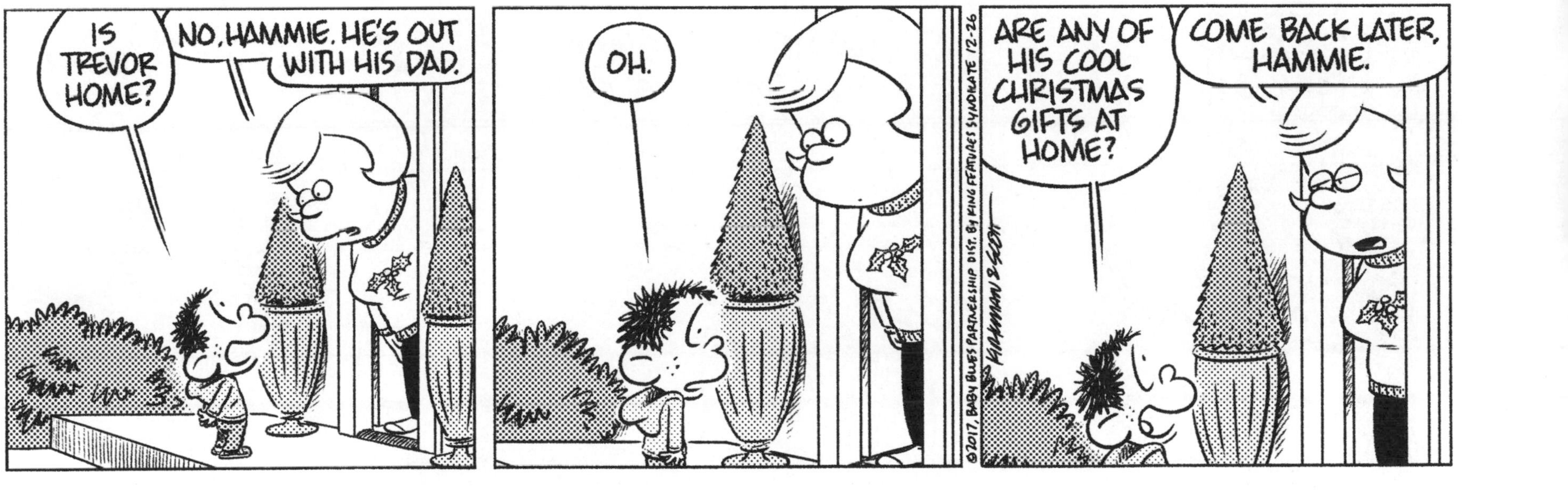
IS TREVOR HOME?
NO, HAMMIE. HE'S OUT WITH HIS DAD.
OH.
ARE ANY OF HIS COOL CHRISTMAS GIFTS AT HOME?
COME BACK LATER, HAMMIE.
©2017, BABY BLUES PARTNERSHIP DIST. BY KING FEATURES SYNDICATE 12-26
KIRKMAN & SCOTT

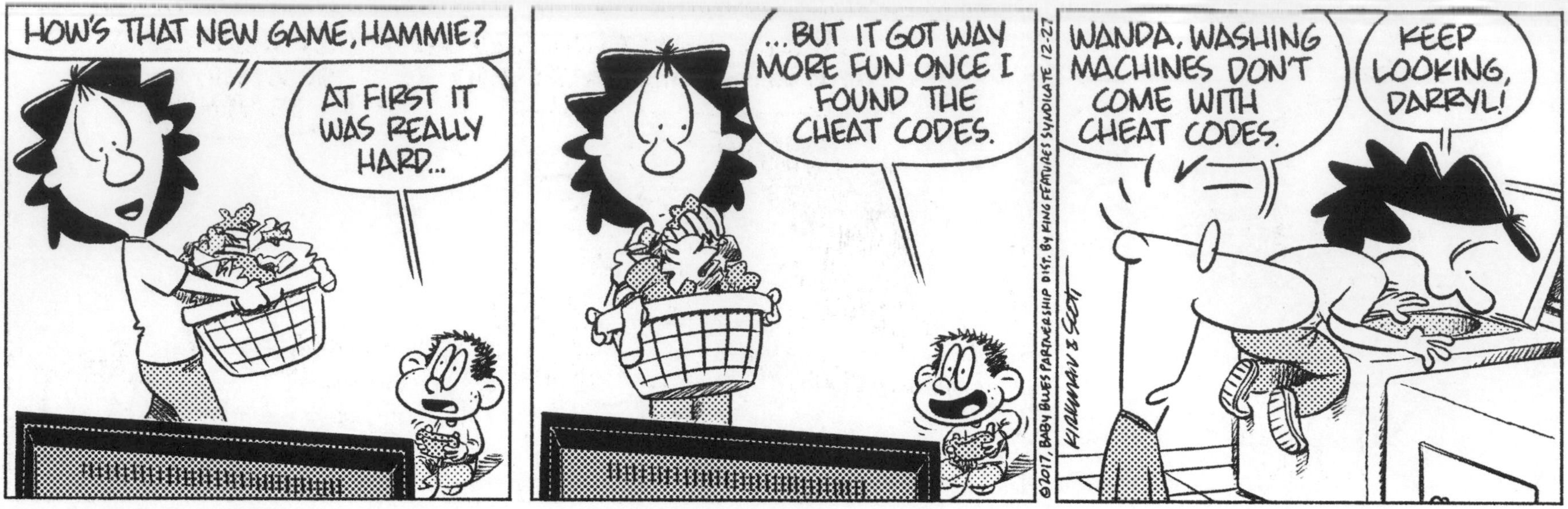
HOW'S THAT NEW GAME, HAMMIE?
AT FIRST IT WAS REALLY HARD...
...BUT IT GOT WAY MORE FUN ONCE I FOUND THE CHEAT CODES.
©2017, BABY BLUES PARTNERSHIP DIST. BY KING FEATURES SYNDICATE 12-27
KIRKMAN & SCOTT
WANDA, WASHING MACHINES DON'T COME WITH CHEAT CODES.
KEEP LOOKING, DARRYL!

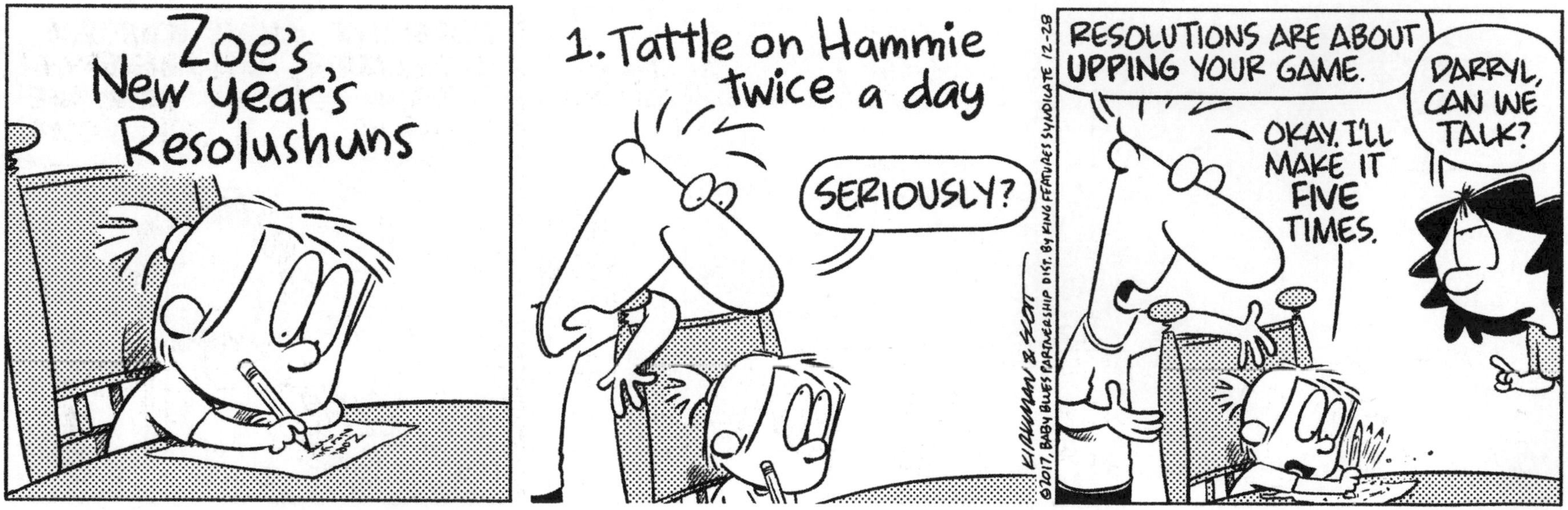
Zoe's New year's Resolushuns
1. Tattle on Hammie twice a day
SERIOUSLY?
©2017, BABY BLUES PARTNERSHIP DIST. BY KING FEATURES SYNDICATE 12-28
KIRKMAN & SCOTT
RESOLUTIONS ARE ABOUT UPPING YOUR GAME.
OKAY. I'LL MAKE IT FIVE TIMES.
DARRYL, CAN WE TALK?

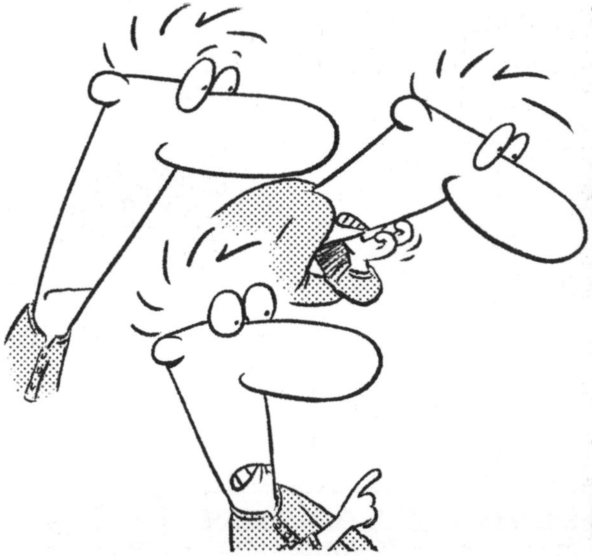

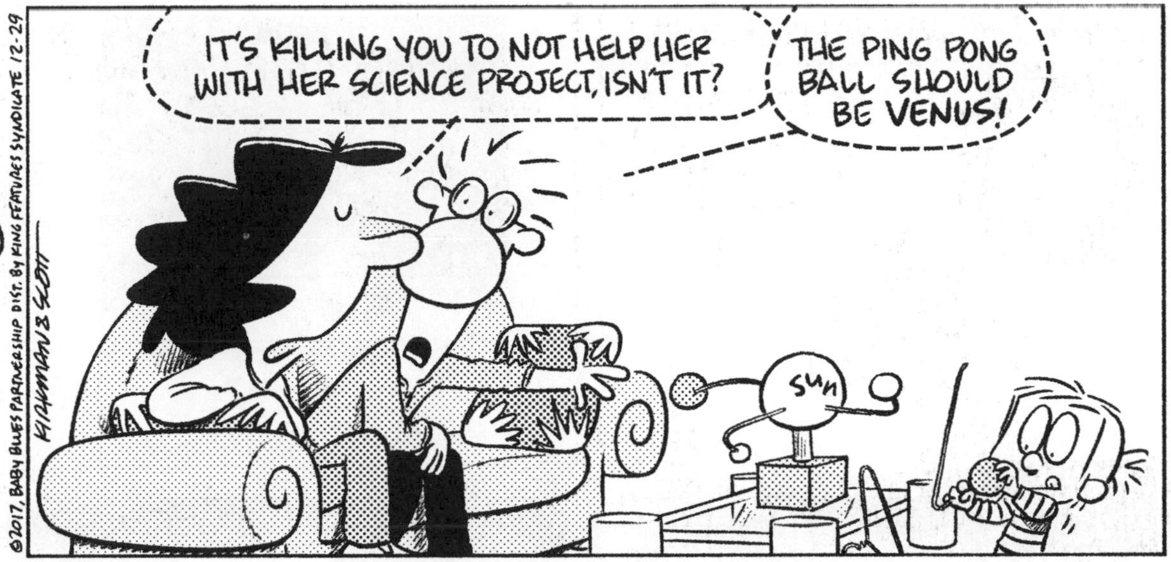

IT'S KILLING YOU TO NOT HELP HER WITH HER SCIENCE PROJECT, ISN'T IT?
THE PING PONG BALL SHOULD BE VENUS!
SUN
©2017, BABY BLUES PARTNERSHIP DIST. BY KING FEATURES SYNDICATE 12-29
KIRKMAN & SCOTT

Rick: I expected to hear from Neil deGrasse Tyson about this one.

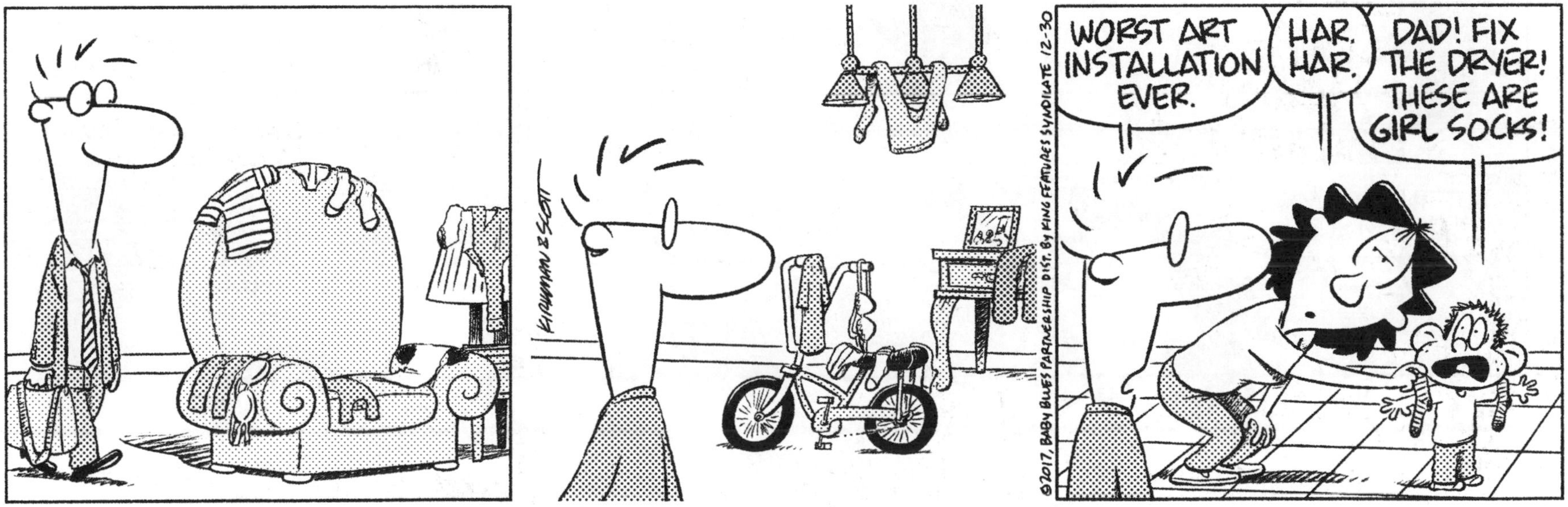

KIRKMAN & SCOTT
©2017, BABY BLUES PARTNERSHIP DIST. BY KING FEATURES SYNDICATE 12-30
WORST ART INSTALLATION EVER.
HAR. HAR.
DAD! FIX THE DRYER! THESE ARE GIRL SOCKS!

Jerry: It looks a lot like my first college dorm room, except they weren't clean clothes.

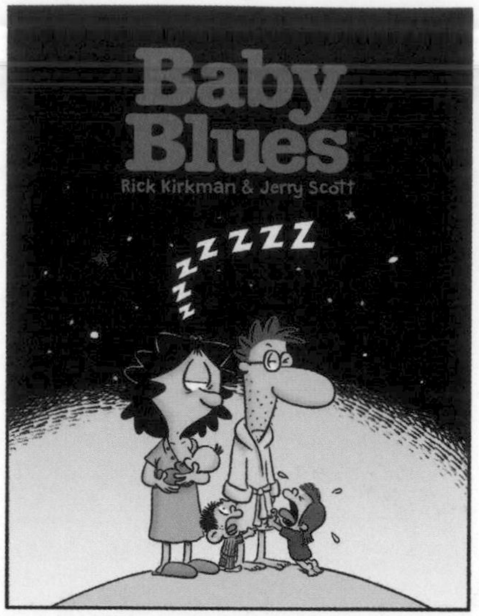
Baby Blues
Rick Kirkman & Jerry Scott
ZZZZZZ

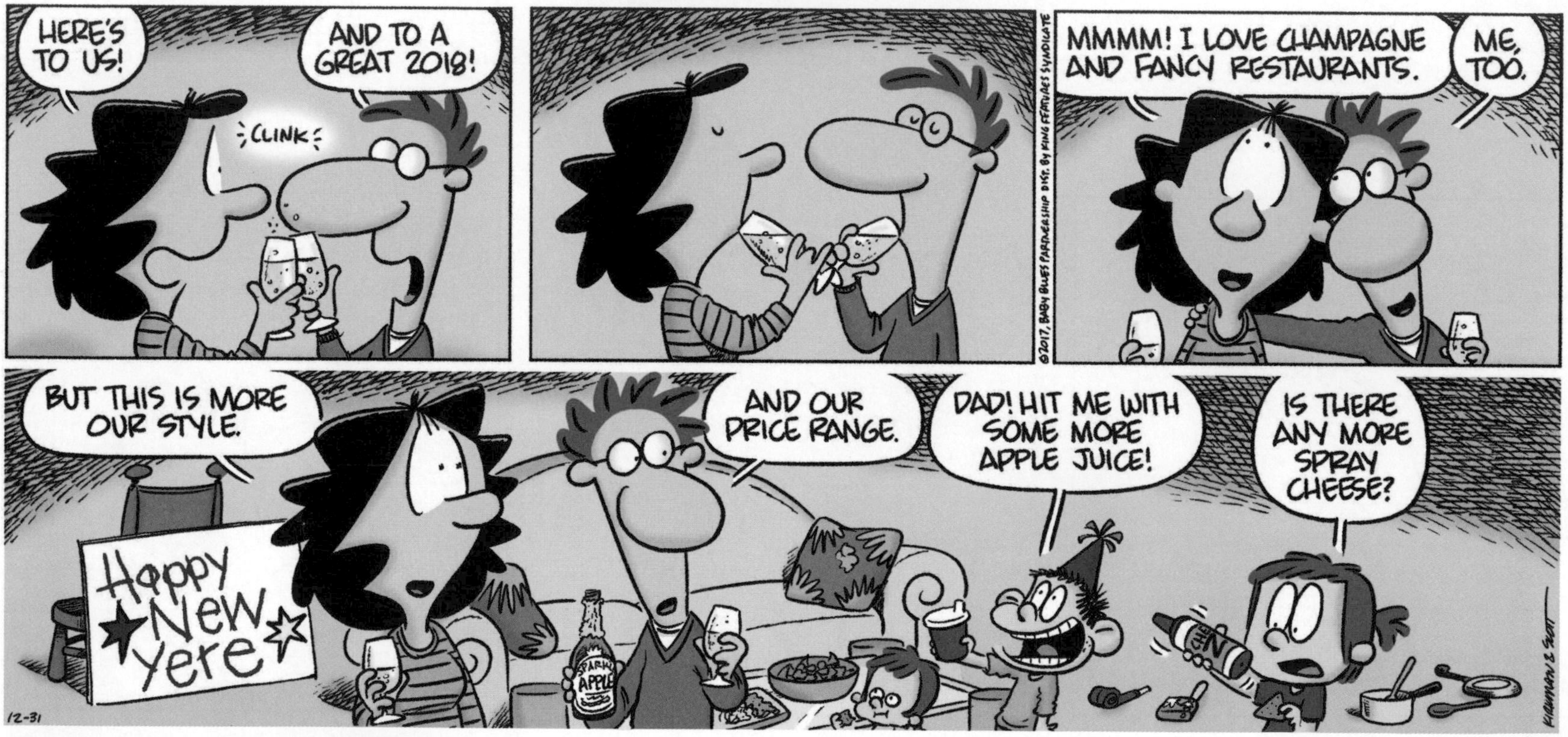
HERE'S TO US!
AND TO A GREAT 2018!
CLINK
©2017, BABY BLUES PARTNERSHIP DIST. BY KING FEATURES SYNDICATE
MMMM! I LOVE CHAMPAGNE AND FANCY RESTAURANTS.
ME, TOO.
BUT THIS IS MORE OUR STYLE.
AND OUR PRICE RANGE.
DAD! HIT ME WITH SOME MORE APPLE JUICE!
IS THERE ANY MORE SPRAY CHEESE?
Happy New yere
APPLE
12-31
KIRKMAN & SCOTT

Rick: Right there with ya, MacPhersons.

Baby Blues® is syndicated internationally by King Features Syndicate, Inc.
For information, write King Features Syndicate, Inc.,
300 West Fifty-Seventh Street, New York, New York 10019.

Andrews McMeel Publishing
a division of Andrews McMeel Universal
1130 Walnut Street, Kansas City, Missouri 64106
www.andrewsmcmeel.com

18 19 20 21 22 SDB 10 9 8 7 6 5 4 3 2 1

ISBN: 978-1-4494-8512-2

Library of Congress Control Number: 2018931852

Editor: Lucas Wetzel
Designer/Art Director: Julie Barnes
Production Manager: Chuck Harper
Production Editor: Amy Strassner
Demand Planner: Sue Eikos

Find *Baby Blues®* on the Web at www.babyblues.com.